Essentials of Retailing

Essentials of Retailing

Michael Levy, Ph.D.
University of Miami

Barton A. Weitz, Ph.D.
University of Florida

IRWIN

Chicago • Bogotà • Boston • Buenos Aires • Caracas
London • Madrid • Mexico City • Sydney • Toronto

Irwin Book Team

Senior sponsoring editor:	Stephen M. Patterson
Senior marketing manager:	Jim Lewis
Project editor:	Jane Lightell
Assistant manager, desktop services:	Jon Christopher
Production supervisor:	Laurie Kersch
Designer:	Laurie J. Entringer
Graphics supervisor:	Heather D. Burbridge
Assistant manager, graphics:	Charlene R. Breeden
Coordinator, graphics & desktop services:	Keri Kunst
Art studio:	ElectraGraphics, Inc.
Photo insert illustrator:	H&S Graphics
Interior photo illustrator:	Wm. C. Brown Publishers
Compositor:	Wm. C. Brown Publishers
Typeface:	9.5/11.5 Helvetica
Printer:	Von Hoffman Press, Inc.

Times Mirror
Higher Education Group

Library of Congress Cataloging-in-Publication Data

Levy, Michael.
    Essentials of retailing/Michael Levy, Barton A. Weitz.
        p.   cm.—(Irwin series in marketing)
    Includes bibliographical references and index.
    ISBN 0-256-16348-0
    1. Retail trade.   2. Retail trade—Management.   I. Weitz, Barton
A.   II Title.   III. Series.
    HF5429.L4826   1996
    658.8'7—dc20   95–33130

Printed in the United States of America
1 2 3 4 5 6 7 8 9 0 VH 21 0 9 8 7 6 5

To our Mothers,

Jacquie and Helen,

with love and appreciation

About the Authors

MICHAEL LEVY received his Ph.D. from The Ohio State University. He taught at Southern Methodist University before joining the Faculty as Professor and Chair of the Marketing Department at the University of Miami. He has taught retailing management for 17 years.

Professor Levy has developed a strong stream of research in retailing, business logistics, financial retailing strategy, pricing, and sales management that has been published in over 30 articles in leading marketing and logistics journals including *The Journal of Retailing, The Journal of Marketing,* and *The Journal of Marketing Research.* He currently serves on the editorial review board of several journals including *Journal of Retailing* and *Journal of the Academy of Marketing Science.* Professor Levy has made presentations at the national meeting of the National Retail Federation.

Professor Levy has worked in retailing and related disciplines throughout his professional life. Prior to his academic career, he worked for several retailers and a housewares distributor in Colorado. He has performed research projects with many retailers including Burdines Department Stores, Mervyn's, Neiman Marcus, and Zale Corporation.

BARTON A. WEITZ received an undergraduate degree in Electrical Engineering from MIT and MBA and Ph.D. from Stanford University. He has been on the faculty of the UCLA Graduate School of Management and the Wharton School at the University of Pennsylvania. He is presently the J.C. Penney Eminent Scholar Chair in Retail Management in the College of Business Administration at the University of Florida.

Professor Weitz is the Executive Director of the Center for Retailing Education and Research at the University of Florida. The activities of the center are supported by 12 national and regional retailers including J.C. Penney, Kmart, Wal-Mart, Burdines, Richs, Parisian, Office Depot, and Electronics Boutique. Each year the center places over 100 undergraduates in paid summer internships with 25 or more retailers. Professor Weitz has won awards for teaching excellence at UCLA and the University of Florida and has made presentations at the national meetings of the National Retail Federation and the Direct Selling Association.

Professor Weitz is well known for his innovative research on the effectiveness of salespeople, sales force and human resource management issues, and retail buyer-vendor relationships. He has published over 30 articles in marketing and management journals and served on the editorial review boards of numerous academic journals including the *Journal of Retailing, Journal of Marketing, Journal of Marketing Research,* and the *Journal of Consumer Research.* He is a former editor of the *Journal of Marketing Research* and his wife was born to shop.

Preface

E SSENTIALS OF RETAILING focuses on the exciting and dynamic nature of retailing. The retail industry, as it approaches the new millennium, is confronting some interesting challenges—changing customer demographics, needs, and shopping behaviors; the development of new retail formats and location opportunities to satisfy these changing needs; and the emergence of new technologies that dramatically affect retail operations.

Some of these changes in the retail environment and industry discussed in the text are:

- *New retail formats*. The fastest growing retailers are category specialists like Home Depot, Office Depot, and PetsMart; supercenters combining a discount store and supermarket; and nonstore retailing like TV home shopping, catalog retailing, and interactive home shopping. What is the appeal of these formats and how do traditional department and discount stores compete against them? (See Chapters 2, 3, 4, and 5.)

- *Changing customer needs.* The demographic profile of the U.S. consumer is changing. Generation X (18- to 34-year-olds) are becoming a major customer segment for retailers; the baby boomers are aging and changing their spending patterns; more families have two wage earners with limited time to shop; and minority markets are growing. How do retailers adjust their offering to meet these changing customer needs? (See Chapters 3 and 4.)

- *Service retailing.* Traditionally, retailers sold merchandise. Now many firms and organizations such as health care providers, entertainment and recreation firms, and financial institutions sell only services to consumers. What are the special issues facing these service retailers? (See Chapter 17.)

- *New Technologies Provide More Information.* The effective collection and analysis of data and the creation of information to use in decision making plays a critical role in retailing. Even small retailers are using personal computers to help manage their businesses. Chapter 6 provides an overview of retail information systems. Then we show how such information is used to manage inventory (Chapters 8 and 9), make pricing decisions (Chapter 10), evaluate sales associates (Chapter 12), and provide better customer service (Chapter 14).

In response to these changes in the environment, the importance of various retail activities is changing. Store management and providing better customer service is becoming more important than buying merchandise. The industry is consolidating to lower the cost to its customers, but significant entrepreneurial opportunities still exist.

STORE MANAGEMENT

Traditionally, retailers have emphasized the activities performed by buyers—merchandise planning, management, and promotions. Over the last 10 years, the emphasis has shifted from merchandise management to store management. Retailers are focusing more on developing a competitive advantage by providing high-quality customer service in an attractive environment. Due to this shift, career opportunities in store management are increasing, while the opportunities in the buying offices are actually shrinking.

In response to this increased attention to store management, chapters in Section 4 of ESSENTIALS OF RETAILING are devoted to recruiting, training, managing, compensating, and evaluating store employees (Chapter 12); creating a store environment that stimulates retail sales (Chapter 13); providing good customer service (Chapter 14); and selling merchandise (Chapter 15).

CUSTOMER SERVICE

All retailers, even traditional self-service discount stores, are emphasizing the need to provide better customer service. Chapter 14 reviews the approaches used by retailers to provide the service customers are demanding.

ENTREPRENEURSHIP

Even though the retailing industry is consolidating through acquisitions and mergers, retailing continues to provide some of the best opportunities for people to own their own businesses. This text provides information to help people with entrepreneurial interests to start a business and manage it effectively. The plans and strategies of highly successful entrepreneurs like Sam Walton (Wal-Mart) and Donald Fisher (The Gap) and entrepreneurs beginning to build their business are presented. The text illustrates how small, independent retailers organize their business, develop a merchandise budget plan, prepare advertisements, and sell merchandise.

ECONOMICS OF RETAILING

In response to intensifying competition, the business side of retailing is becoming increasingly important. The financial problems of large firms like Macy's and Kmart and many owner-operated small retailers highlight the need for a good understanding of the financial implications of retail decisions.

In this text, we provide the background needed to appreciate the economic aspects of retail decisions such as designing an organizational structure (Chapter 6), developing merchandise assortments (Chapter 8), buying merchandise (Chapter 9), setting prices (Chapter 10), determining advertising budgets and planning promotions (Chapter 11), and staffing stores and compensating sales associates (Chapter 12).

 ## BALANCED, DESCRIPTIVE HOW-TO APPROACH

ESSENTIALS OF RETAILING offers a balanced descriptive, how-to, and conceptual approach for understanding the retailing industry and the decisions made by retailers.

Throughout the text we have provided descriptive information so that students can learn about the retail institutions and the vocabulary used by retailers. The first section reviews the nature and types of decisions made by retailers (Chapter 1), the different types of retailers (Chapter 2), the trends in the retail environment (Chapter 3), and the needs of retail customers and the factors affecting the customer's decision to go to a particular store and buy merchandise in the store (Chapter 4). Chapter 16 provides an expanded discussion of the fashion industry and fashion retailing.

 ## DESCRIPTIVE INFORMATION

This descriptive information appears in all chapters, including the types of retail locations (Chapter 7), the typical organization of retail firms (Chapter 6), the flow of information and merchandise in a retail firm (Chapter 6), the branding strategies used by retailers (Chapter 8), methods for compensating employees (Chapter 12), types of store layouts and methods for displaying merchandise (Chapter 13), and career opportunities (Appendix A).

HOW-TO INFORMATION

ESSENTIALS OF RETAILING goes beyond this descriptive information to explain the tradeoffs retailers face when making decisions such as:

- The selection of strategic opportunities. (Chapter 5)
- Advantages and disadvantages of various retail locations. (Chapter 7)
- Tradeoffs associated with the amount and type of merchandise carried in stores. (Chapters 8 and 9)
- Benefits offered by different approaches for communicating with customers. (Chapter 11)
- Techniques for selecting and motivating employees. (Chapter 12)
- Evaluating approaches for laying out a store. (Chapter 13)
- Methods used to sell customers. (Chapter 15)

☼ CONCEPTUAL INFORMATION

ESSENTIALS OF RETAILING also includes conceptual information so that students will understand why decisions should be made as outlined in the text. To quote Mark Twain, "There is nothing as practical as a good theory." Students need to know these basic concepts so they can approach new situations that will arise in a rapidly changing environment. Examples of this conceptual material are:

- Customer decision-making process. (Chapter 4)
- Market attractiveness-competitive position matrix. (Chapter 5)
- Strategic planning process. (Chapter 6)
- Fashion diffusion theory. (Chapter 16)

☼ EMPHASIS ON EMERGING ISSUES

Relationship Marketing. Retailers are placing more emphasis on building long-term relationships with customers and vendors. We include information on marketing programs to build customer loyalty (Chapters 4 and 12) and to develop long-term, strategic relationships with vendors (Chapter 9).

Information and Distribution Systems. Chapter 6 is devoted to these important retail systems.

International, Ethical, and Legal Issues. Rather than concentrating the discussion in one or two chapters, we have incorporated this material throughout the text.

☼ SMOOTH AND ENGAGING READING

Examples and Illustrations. To make it easier for students to understand the material and make the textbook more interesting reading, we have included a large number of illustrations and examples. Examples are used extensively to illustrate the information presented in the text. Each chapter has several Re-Tales—short vignettes that amplify the text material by describing how a specific retailer confronts an issue discussed in the chapter. Five inserts of color photographs are provided to highlight the material.

The examples in the text involve a wide variety of retailers ranging from an African-American entrepreneur who started a successful direct-selling cosmetics business to the large national retailers like Wal-Mart, Safeway, McDonalds, Kmart, J.C. Penney, Lands' End, and The Limited. Most of these firms actively recruit students on college campuses and have management training programs for recent college graduates. Thus, ESSENTIALS OF RETAILING teaches students about retailing in general and about the firms for which they might like to work after graduation. Appendix A offers additional information about career opportunities and how to get a job in retailing.

Refacts. In each chapter, we have included Refacts (Retailing Facts) in the margins. These refacts are interesting pieces of information about the retailing issues and companies discussed in the chapter.

Cases. The cases range from short descriptions of a problem situation confronting a retailer to profiles of actual retailers. For example, The Tardy Trainee by Laura Bliss at Stephens College provides a vehicle for students to decide how to handle an underperforming employee. Where America Shops: Trouble in Sears Auto Centers by Douglas Hoffman and Judy Siguaw at the University of North Carolina at Wilmington illustrates the ethical and legal problems that arose when Sears adopted a commission plan for its service workers. Other cases describe new retailing formats issues including a southern California mall designed for the Generation X market, the made-to-fit jeans offered in the new Levi stores, and Peapod, a company offering electronic shopping for groceries.

Supplements. To expand the learning experience, ESSENTIALS OF RETAILING is complemented by a video package with 21 segments and an *Instructor's Manual* with additional cases and teaching suggestions.

> **Videos.** The **video package** is designed to complement the material in the text. For example, the segment on Burdines department store illustrates the demographics of its target market and positioning strategy adopted by the firm. This strategy is highlighted in the ads shown in the video segment. Many video segments are edited versions of high-quality training materials developed by retailers. For example, the segment on visual merchandising was prepared by Eckerds, a major drugstore chain, and illustrates the principles of store layout and merchandise display presented in Chapter 13.
>
> **Instructor's Manual.** We have endeavored to make the *Instructor's Manual* the most comprehensive available for a retailing text. It contains extensive materials to assist instructors in a clear, organized, and concise way. For each chapter, we have included:
>
> - Conversion notes.
> - Annotated listing of related cases and ancillary cases.
> - Annotated outline and instructor notes.
> - Discussion questions and problems with answers.
> - Ancillary lectures and exercises.
>
> In addition, the *Instructor's Manual* includes:
>
> - Sample syllabus format and schedules.
> - Cross listing of cases with appropriate chapters.
> - Information on coordinating videos, the test bank, and cases.

We have devoted considerable time to writing and revising ESSENTIALS OF RETAILING, and are very interested in improving it in future editions. We welcome any comments or suggestions you might have.

Acknowledgments

Throughout the development of this text, several outstanding individuals were integrally involved and made substantial contributions. The support, expertise, and occasional coercion from our editors at Irwin, Steve Patterson and Andy Winston, are greatly appreciated. The book would also never have come together without the editorial and production staff at Irwin: Jane Lightell, Kim Meriwether, Laurie Entringer, Laurie Kersch, Bruce Sylvester, Charlotte Goldman, and Harriet Stockanes. We wish to also express our sincere appreciation to Gina Morello, Marcia Levy, John F. Konarski III, Leda M. Perez, and Elliot B. Gant for their assistance in developing a superior *Instructor's Manual,* and to Thomas K. Pritchett of Kennesaw College and Betty M. Pritchett for their comprehensive *Manual of Tests.* Finally, Nancy Rodriguez (Marketing Department, University of Miami) and Kathy Brown and Margaret Jones (Center for Retailing Education and Research, University of Florida) provided invaluable assistance in preparing the manuscript.

ESSENTIALS OF RETAILING has also benefited significantly from contributions by several leading executives in retailing and related fields. We would like to thank:

Cole Peterson
Wal-Mart Stores, Inc.

Tom Amerman
Younkers

Richard C. Bartlett
Mary Kay Cosmetics

Robert Beall
Beall's Department Store

Harvey Braun
Deloitte & Touche TRADE

Vicki Carmichael
Spec's Music Stores

David Doub
Dillard's Department Store

Joseph Firestone
The Electronics Boutique, Inc.

David Fuente
Office Depot

Brenda Grindstaff
Florida Retail Federation

Peter Hisey
Discount Store News

Howard Kreitzman
Duty Free Stores

Donna Magee
Burdines

Kathleen McManus
Rich's/Goldsmith's

Carole Nelson
The Ben Tobin Companies

Frank Newman
Eckerd Drug Company

James Oesterreicher
J.C. Penney

Ann Ruppert
Burdines

Ron Sacino
Sacino's

John Schneider
Urban Decision Systems, Inc.

David Schuvie
Kmart Corp.

Don Singletary
Home Depot

Herbert Tobin
The Ben Tobin Companies

Cynthia Cohen Turk
MARKETPLACE 2000

Robert Unger
Burdines

Jeff Wells
Toys 'R' Us

ESSENTIALS OF RETAILING has benefited greatly from the reviews of several leading scholars and teachers of retailing and related disciplines. Together, these reviewers spent hundreds of hours reading and critiquing the manuscript. We gratefully acknowledge:

Joseph Hecht
Montclair State College

Cindy Istook
Texas Women's University

Patricia Manninen
North Shore Community College

Kabir C. Sen
Lamar University

Marsha Stein
Teikyo Post University

Joan Weiss
Bucks County Community College

Terrell Williams
Western Washington University

We received cases from professors from all over the country. Although we would like to have used more cases in the text and the *Instructor's Manual,* space was limited. We would like to thank all who contributed, but are especially appreciative to the following scholars whose cases were used in ESSENTIALS OF RETAILING or the *Instructor's Manual.*

Ronald Adams
University of North Florida

Laura Bliss
Stephens College

James Camerius
Northern Michigan University

David Ehrlich
Marymount University

Ann Fairhurst
Indiana University

Linda A. Felicetti
Clarion University of Pennsylvania

Joseph P. Grunewald
Clarion University of Pennsylvania

K. Douglas Hoffman
University of North Carolina at Wilmington

Dilip Karer
University of North Florida

Jan Owens
University of Wisconsin–Madison

Catherine Porter
University of Massachusetts

Richard Rausch
Hofstra University

Judy Siguaw
University of North Carolina at Wilmington

William R. Swinyard
Brigham Young University

Irvin A. Zaenglein
Northern Michigan University

Michael Levy
Marketing Department
University of Miami
Coral Gables, FL 33124

Barton A. Weitz
Marketing Department
University of Florida
Gainesville, FL 32611

Brief Contents

Contents

SECTION II   The Retail Firm   **84**

Essentials of Retailing

Retail Customers and Competitors: The Core of the World of Retailing

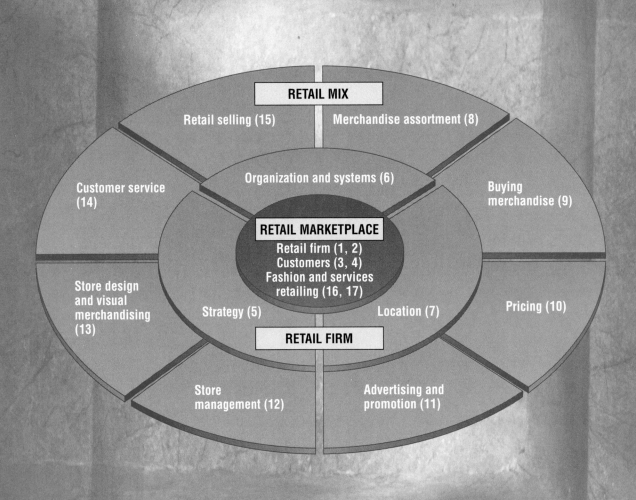

The chapters in this section focus on the core of the world of retailing—retail customers and competitors and the environment in which they interact. Chapter 1 defines retailing and describes the functions retailers perform. Chapter 2 covers different types of retailers and the nature of competition. Chapter 3 details changing elements of the retail environment, including shifting customer needs, the emergence of new types of retailers to satisfy those needs, and the development of new retail technologies. Chapter 4 describes what customers consider when they choose a store or purchase merchandise during a visit.

Section II focuses on the nature of retail companies. It discusses the strategies retailers use, how they organize their business, and where they locate their stores. Sections III and IV review the elements in the retail mix: merchandise planning, buying merchandise, pricing, advertising and promotion, visual merchandising, store management, customer service, and personal selling. Section V includes special topics: the retailing of fashion merchandise and services.

Introduction to the World of Retailing

Retail firm (1)

Questions that this chapter answers include

- **What is retailing?**
- **Why is retailing important in our society?**
- **What do retailers do?**
- **What career and entrepreneurial opportunities does retailing offer?**

Retailing is the set of business activities that adds value to the products and services sold to consumers for their personal or family use. Often people think of retailing only as the sale of products in stores. But retailing also involves the sale of services: overnight lodging in a motel, a doctor's exam, a haircut, a videotape rental, or a home-delivered pizza.

Not all retailing is done in stores. Examples of nonstore retailing are the direct sales of cosmetics by Avon, catalog sales by L.L. Bean and Spiegel, and the Home Shopping Network on cable TV.

Retailing is one of the most important industries in our society. The 1.4 million retailers in the United States generate over $2 trillion in sales annually. Approximately 20 million people are employed in retailing, about the same number employed in manufacturing. However, over the past 10 years, retail employment increased by 24 percent in the United States, while manufacturing employment decreased by 1 percent.[1]

The retail sector of the U.S. economy is going through dramatic, exciting changes. The Sears catalog has vanished. Wal-Mart, started only 30 years ago, is now the world's largest retailer. Toys "R" Us is one of the fastest growing retailers in Japan.

In response to changing consumer needs and increased competition, new retailing approaches have emerged such as category specialist (Circuit City, Best Buy, Home Depot, Blockbuster) and TV home shopping (Home Shopping Network and QVC). Twenty-five years ago, these major retail firms and formats were at most simply ideas in an entrepreneur's head. Re-Tale 1–1 describes how Wal-Mart became the largest retailer in the world.

Retailers now use state-of-the-art computer and communications technologies to respond quickly to changing customer needs.[2] Each time you buy something at many supermarkets, you trigger a sequence of electronic communications and decisions that determines what products will be delivered from the warehouse to the store tomorrow.

RE-TALE 1–1   Wal-Mart: How It Started

Wal-Mart was founded by Sam Walton. Walton majored in economics at the University of Missouri, graduating in 1940. He considered selling insurance, but an interview with J.C. Penney attracted him to retailing. He began working as a management trainee in the Des Moines store for $85 a month. In 1942, he left to join the military.

At the end of World War II, Walton sought a retail business to buy with money he had saved in the army. He bought a Ben Franklin variety store franchise in Newport, Arkansas. When his landlord declined to renew his lease in 1950, Walton relocated to Bentonville, Arkansas (which remains Wal-Mart's corporate headquarters) and opened a Walton 5 & 10. By 1962, his business had grown to 15 stores (mostly Ben Franklin franchises).

Sam Walton's understanding of his customers and employees was instrumental in building Wal-Mart into the world's largest retailer.

In the 1960s, the pioneers of modern discounting were building their businesses, primarily in the Northeast. Walton visited these stores, observed their merchandising techniques, and became convinced that discounting would revolutionize retailing. After failing to get Ben Franklin's upper management to join him in opening discount stores, he opened his first Wal-Mart discount store in Rogers, Arkansas, in 1962. "Old Number One" has now been joined by 1,800 additional Wal-Mart Discount City stores and 200 Sam's Warehouse Clubs in all 50 states and 5 countries.

Wal-Mart's initial strategy was to offer name-brand merchandise at discount prices to small communities. Walton felt that the key to his success was people: his customers and his employees (called *associates,* a term adopted from his initial job at Penney). He said, "Our goal has always been in our business to be the very best. We believe completely that in order to be the very best you've got to make a good situation and put the interests of your associates first. If we really do that consistently, they will in turn cause our business to be successful."

Sam Walton died in 1992, but his spirit and ideas remain a driving force at Wal-Mart. With annual sales over $100 billion, Wal-Mart is the largest retail merchant in the world.

SOURCE: David Hatch, "Sam Walton: Master Change Agent," *Executive Excellence,* June 1992, p. 19; and Bill Saporito, "What Sam Walton Taught America," *Fortune,* May 4, 1992, pp. 104–5.

Retailing is such a part of our everyday life that we often take it for granted. As customers, we aren't aware of the difficult business decisions managers make and the technologies they use to provide goods and services. Retail managers must make complex decisions in developing strategies, locating stores, determining what merchandise and services to offer, and deciding how to price, promote, and display merchandise. Making these decisions in the highly competitive, rapidly changing retail environment is challenging and exciting, with opportunities for big financial rewards.

This book describes the world of retailing and the activities retailers undertake. Learning more about retailing will help you develop management skills that you can use in many different business situations. For example, Dell Computer (America's fourth-largest computer designer and manufacturer) views direct-mail retailing skills as the key to its success. "We're more like Mary Kay Cosmetics than we are like General Motors."[3]

Many firms ultimately sell their products and services to retailers. Thus, if you are interested in professional selling, advertising, or many other careers connected with retailing, you will find this book useful.

WHAT IS A RETAILER?

A **retailer** is a business that sells products and services to consumers for their personal use. A retailer is the final business in a distribution channel that links manufacturers with consumers.[4] Exhibit 1–1 shows the role of retailers in a distribution channel. Manufacturers make products and sell them to retailers or wholesalers. Wholesalers buy products from manufacturers and resell these products to retailers, while retailers resell products to consumers.

Exhibit 1–2's list of the 25 largest U.S. retailers demonstrates the economic importance of retailing. The annual sales of Wal-Mart, Kmart, and Sears are much greater than the annual sales of Procter & Gamble, PepsiCo, and RJR Nabisco—the three largest consumer product manufacturers.

The list also shows the diverse and dynamic nature of the industry. The list includes companies that sell a few categories of merchandise (Toys "R" Us and Home Depot) as well as companies that sell a wide variety of merchandise through different retail formats, such as J.C. Penney (department stores and catalog) and Dayton Hudson (department and discount stores). Five firms on the list (The Limited, Toys "R" Us, Costco/Price, Food Lion, and Wal-Mart) have developed into major retailers during the past 30 years, while other firms have completely changed their

Distribution Channel

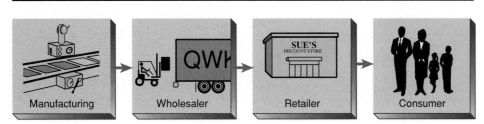

Manufacturing Wholesaler Retailer Consumer

EXHIBIT 1-2

The Largest U.S. Retailers, 1993

	Sales ($ millions)	*Profits ($ millions)*
1. Wal-Mart (Bentonville, AR)	$67,345	$2,333
2. Kmart (Troy, MI)	34,156	(1)
3. Sears, Roebuck (Chicago)	29,565	752
4. Kroger (Cincinnati)	22,384	(12)
5. J.C. Penney (Dallas)	19,578	940
6. Dayton Hudson (Minneapolis)	19,233	375
7. American Stores (Salt Lake City)	18,763	247
8. Safeway (Oakland, CA)	15,215	123
9. Price/Costco (San Diego)	15,155	233
10. May Department Stores (St. Louis)	11,529	771
11. Albertson's (Boise, ID)	11,284	340
12. Winn-Dixie Stores (Jacksonville, FL)	10,832	236
13. Melville (Rye, NY)	10,435	332
14. A&P (Montvale, NJ)	10,384	4
15. Woolworth (New York)	9,626	(485)
16. The Home Depot (Atlanta)	9,239	457
17. Walgreen (Deerfield, IL)	8,295	222
18. Toys "R" Us (Parmus, NJ)	7,946	483
19. Army & Air Force Exchange (Dallas)	7,700	315
20. Food Lion (Salisbury, NC)	7,610	4
21. The Limited	7,245	391
22. Federated Department Stores (Cincinnati)	7,229	190
23. Publix Super Markets (Lakeland, FL)	6,850	NA
24. Southland (Dallas)	6,744	71
25. Abold USA (Parsipanny, NJ)	6,620	343

SOURCE: "The State of the Industry" *Chain Store Age Executive,* August 1994, p. 4a. 21.

retailing approach over this period. For example, Kmart (Kresge) began as variety stores but became a leading discount chain.[5] Sears began as a catalog retailer, expanded to a national chain of retail stores, diversified into financial services and insurance, and is now refocusing on in-store retailing.

WHAT DO RETAILERS DO?

Retailers perform business activities that increase the value of the products and services they sell to consumers. These activities are

1.   Providing an assortment of products and services.
2.   Breaking bulk.
3.   Holding inventory.
4.   Providing services.

These activities typically account for between 20 and 50 percent of the final cost of merchandise bought from retailers. This high percentage emphasizes the importance of understanding what retailers do and why they play such an important role in our society.

Dell Computer views itself primarily as a retailer even though it is a major computer designer and manufacturer.

Providing an Assortment of Products. Supermarkets typically carry 15,000 different items made by over 500 companies. Offering this broad assortment enables customers to buy a wide selection of brands, designs, sizes, colors, and prices in one location.

Manufacturers, on the other hand, specialize in producing specific types of products. For example, Campbell makes soup, Kraft makes dairy products, and Kellogg makes breakfast cereals. If each of these manufacturers had its own stores that only sold its own products, consumers would have to go to many different stores to buy groceries to prepare a single meal.

All retailers offer assortments of products, but they specialize in the assortments they offer. Supermarkets provide assortments of food, health and beauty aids (HBA), and household products, while The Gap provides assortments of clothing and accessories. Most consumers are well aware of the product assortments retailers offer. Even small children know where to buy different types of products. But new types of retailers offering unique assortments appear each year, such as Rand McNally (with merchandise for the traveler) and The Body Shop (an environmentally and socially responsible company that develops, manufacturers, and sells hair, skin, and color cosmetic products).[6]

Breaking Bulk. To reduce transportation costs, manufacturers typically ship whole cases or cartons of their products to retailers. Retailers then offer the products in smaller quantities tailored to individual consumers' and households' usage patterns. Breaking the large shipments into smaller consumer quantities is called breaking bulk.

Holding Inventory. A major function of retailers is to keep inventory so that products will be available when consumers want them. Thus, as consumers we can keep only a small inventory of products at home because we know retailers will have the products available when we need more.

By maintaining an inventory, retailers provide a benefit to consumers: They reduce the consumer's cost of storing products.[7] Storing products would tie up consumers' money—money that could be put in an interest-earning bank account or used in some other way.

Providing Services. Retailers provide services that make it easier for customers to buy and use products. They offer credit so consumers can have a product now and pay for it later. They display products so that consumers can see and test them before making a purchase. Retailers may have salespeople on hand to answer questions and provide additional information about products.

Increasing the Value of Products and Services. In summary, by providing assortments, breaking bulk, holding inventory, and providing services, retailers increase the value consumers receive from their products and services. To illustrate, consider a side of beef in an Iowa meat-packing plant. This side of beef won't satisfy a family's need for steaks to barbecue for dinner tonight. The family wants to buy a few steaks from a convenient location before dinnertime. To satisfy the family's needs, a supermarket cuts the side of beef into small portions. It sells the steaks in a conveniently located store that is open when customers can shop. The supermarket helps

Grocery stores, like Albertson's, add value to the merchandise they sell by tailoring the portions to customer needs and providing useful information.

customers select the steaks by displaying them so they can be examined before they're purchased. An employee is available to explain which steaks are best for barbecuing. The supermarket may even have a butcher to provide special cuts of beef. Finally, the supermarket provides an assortment of other groceries—potatoes, ears of corn, and ice cream—so the family can buy ingredients for an entire meal along with the steaks.

CAREERS IN RETAILING

Management Opportunities

Students often view retailing as a part of marketing because management of distribution channels is part of a manufacturer's marketing function.[8] But retailers undertake most of the traditional business activities. Retailers raise capital from financial institutions; purchase goods and services; develop accounting and management information systems to control operations; manage warehouses and distribution systems; design and develop new products; and undertake marketing activities such as advertising, promotion, sales force management, and market research. Thus, retail firms offer management opportunities for people with a wide range of skills and interests. They employ people with expertise and interest in finance, accounting, human resource management, logistics, computer systems, and marketing.

RE-TALE 1-2   Managing a Business in a Retail Corporation

After graduating from Santa Clara University in 1983 with a B.S. in marketing, Del Hernandez went to work for Macy's. Hernandez's initial assignment was department manager for children's and infants' apparel in the Oakridge Mall store. A month after college, he was responsible for managing a department with $3 million in annual sales. In this position, he worked with buyers to make sure his department had the merchandise customers wanted. He developed and implemented plans for presenting merchandise, and he supervised 20 salespeople.

After 10 months, Hernandez was promoted to assistant buyer for junior separates at the division headquarters in San Francisco. In 18 months, he was promoted again to group sales manager in the Oakridge Mall store. The three departments he managed employed over 100 salespeople; their annual sales totaled $15 million.

In December 1986, a little over three years after he had graduated, Hernandez was promoted again. He became buyer for the $12 million of advanced consumer electronics and video games sold annually in all 25 Macy-California stores. He was responsible for selecting merchandise, negotiating with vendors, pricing merchandise, and providing guidelines for its presentation in stores.

Macy's consumer electronics department has an unusual assortment of merchandise that appeals to an upscale market. To locate unique items, Hernandez went to toy fairs, sporting goods shows, and gift shows. In June 1989, he saw some dancing flowers in an East Coast store and decided to make a major commitment to this novelty item. He placed a large order with the manufacturer and designed a 100-square-foot "flower garden" with 50 to 60 dancing flowers in each Macy store.

Hernandez's investment in inventory, selling space, and promotion of the dancing flowers was risky, but it paid off. Macy's was the first West Coast store to sell dancing flowers. Early commitment and significant investment resulted in sales of 50,000 pieces during 1989.

In 1993, Hernandez was promoted again to manage the Bullock's store (a division of Federated Department Stores) in Palm Desert. Annual sales for his store total $30 million, and it employs 200 people.

Due to Hernandez's performance as a department manager, assistant buyer, group sales manager, buyer, and store manager, his 1995 salary was more than six times his starting salary when he graduated from college in 1983.

SOURCE: Personal communication.

Retail managers are often given considerable responsibility early in their careers. Re-Tale 1–2 describes one college graduate's career path and responsibilities.

Retail management is also financially rewarding. After completing a management trainee program in retailing, managers can double their starting salary in three to five years if they perform well. The typical buyer in a department store earns $50,000 to $60,000 per year. Store managers working for department or discount store chains often make over $100,000. At the end of this book, Appendix A describes retail career opportunities in detail.

Starting Your Own Business

Retailing also provides opportunities for people who want to start their own business. Many retail entrepreneurs are among the wealthiest people in the United States.[9] Highly successful retail entrepreneurs include Leslie Wexner (The Limited), Donald Fisher (The Gap), Gary Comer (Lands' End), and Thomas Monaghan (Domino's Pizza).

Leslie Wexner's parents owned a retail clothing store, working 70 hours a week and never earning more than $10,000 in a year. Wexner dropped out of law school and went to work in the family store. When he disagreed with its buying and marketing techniques, he borrowed $5,000 from an aunt and, in 1963, opened his first sportswear store for young women, Leslie's. Leslie's was changed to The Limited. Over the past 30 years, it has grown to 5,100 stores with over $6.3 billion in annual sales. The firm acquired Henri Bendel, Victoria's Secret, Abercrombie & Fitch, Lane Bryant, and Lerner Shops and started Limited Express, Structure, Limited Two, Bath & Body Works, Victoria's Secret Bath, and Cacique. Wexner's stock in The Limited and his personal assets are valued at over $1.8 billion.[10]

Donald Fisher was a finance major and star swimmer at the University of California at Berkeley. After graduating in 1950, he entered his family's real estate development business. He cofounded The Gap with his wife in 1969, out of his frustration at not being able to find blue jeans that would fit his normally proportioned 6′1″, 34″-waist frame. The Gap stores were unique in offering every size and style of Levi's, arranged by size for convenience. When the teen-jean craze slowed in the mid-1970s, stores were repositioned for a more mature customer. Levi jeans were phased out in 1991. Now The Gap sells only its own brand of merchandise.

In 1983, The Gap acquired Banana Republic. GapKids was started in 1986, and Baby Gap began in 1989. Reminiscent of the founding of The Gap, GapKids was started when Mickey Drexler, the chief operating officer, couldn't find comfortable clothing for his children.[11]

Gary Comer was an award-winning copywriter for the Young & Rubicam advertising agency. Then he went to work as a salesperson for a sail-making company and competed in the sailing trials for the 1968 Olympics. Comer started the Lands' End mail order catalog, offering sailing supplies and accessories, with a small clothing section. More apparel items were added to the catalog, and by 1977, the sailing items were eliminated. Lands' End features entertaining catalogs and polite telephone operators. As Comer says, "I treat customers the way I want to be treated. What is best for our customers is best for all of us at Lands' End."[12]

Thomas Monaghan was fatherless at four and raised in orphanages. After being thrown out of a seminary for misconduct, he joined the Marines. In 1960, he bought his first pizza parlor in Ypsilanti, Michigan, with a $500 loan from his brother. One year later he swapped his Volkswagen for his brother's interest in the business. Domino's now has over 5,500 stores worldwide and annual sales over $3 billion.[13]

Re-Tale 1–3 concerns Joe Dudley, Sr., who started a highly successful direct selling business.

RE-TALE 1-3   Success Means Helping Others to Succeed

Joe Dudley, Sr., one of 11 children, grew up in a three-room farmhouse in a small North Carolina town. He was held back in first grade, labeled mentally retarded. Today he is the owner and founder of a multimillion dollar hair care and cosmetics company based in Greensboro, North Carolina.

Joe Dudley, founder and CEO of Dudley Products.

Dudley Products is one of the largest minority-owned businesses in the Southeast. Dudley got his start in retailing by selling Fuller Brush products door-to-door while he was a student at North Carolina A&T. Since 1967, when he and his wife began making their own line of hair products, Dudley Products has used direct selling to distribute its products to consumers and beauty salons throughout the United States.

Dudley realized his personal goal of making a million dollars by his 40th birthday. Since that time, he has devoted much of his effort to helping others reach their goals. Dudley Products instituted a high school mentor program. Students in the program meet bimonthly with Dudley executives and get a firsthand view of what it takes to succeed. Dudley and his company were honored with the North Carolina Governor's Business Award in Education, a designation as one of the 1,000 points of light by former President Bush, and a Horatio Alger award in 1995 for distinguished Americans who demonstrated that honesty, hard work, and determination can triumph over all obstacles.

SOURCE: Company documents.

THE WORLD OF RETAILING

The success of a small store owner or a major retail corporation depends largely on how well it understands the world of retailing. This book is organized around the basic elements in the world of retailing as shown in Exhibit 1–3.

At the core of the world of retailing are customers and competitors and their environment. Successful retailers must understand what their customers want and then provide merchandise and services to satisfy those needs. But successful retailers must be strong competitors. They can't achieve high performance by simply satisfying customers' needs. They must also keep a close watch to ensure that competitors don't attract their customers. Finally, retailers need to be aware of new customer needs, emerging competitors, and new technologies. The first section of this book provides a general overview of the retailing industry, its customers, and the changes occurring in the retail environment.

Three critical core factors in the world of retailing are (1) competition, (2) environmental trends including changing consumer demographics, lifestyles, and technological developments, and (3) the needs, wants, and buying processes of retail consumers. Ethical and legal issues are also important.

Core Elements: Competitors, Customers, and Environment

EXHIBIT 1-3

The World of Retailing

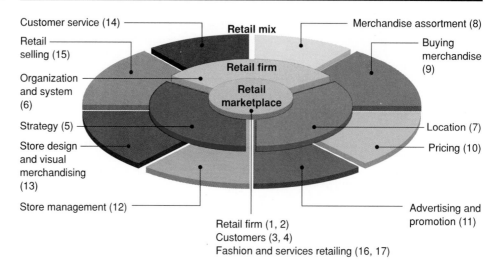

Customer service (14)

Retail selling (15)

Organization and system (6)

Strategy (5)

Store design and visual merchandising (13)

Store management (12)

Retail mix

Retail firm

Retail marketplace

Merchandise assortment (8)

Buying merchandise (9)

Location (7)

Pricing (10)

Advertising and promotion (11)

Retail firm (1, 2)
Customers (3, 4)
Fashion and services retailing (16, 17)

Competition. At first glance, identifying competitors appears easy. A retailer's primary competitors are those with the same format. Thus, department stores compete against other department stores, and supermarkets compete with other supermarkets. This competition between retailers with the same format is called **intratype competition.**

To appeal to a broader group of consumers and provide one-stop shopping, many retailers are offering a greater variety of merchandise. For example, clothing and food are now available in grocery stores, department stores, discount stores, and drugstores. The offering of merchandise not typically associated with the store type, such as clothing and sporting goods in a drugstore, is called **scrambled merchandising.**

Competition between retailers that sell similar merchandise using different formats, such as discount and department stores, is called **intertype competition.** Increasing intertype competition has made it harder for retailers to identify and monitor their competition. Most retailers now have scrambled merchandise to tailor their merchandise to the needs of a target segment. In one sense, all retailers compete against each other for the dollars consumers spend buying goods and services. But the intensity of competition among firms is greatest when customers view the retail mixes as very similar.

Because convenience of location is important in store choice, a store's proximity to competitors is a critical factor in identifying competition. Consider two video-tape rental stores, Blockbuster and Harry's Video, in two suburbs 10 miles apart. The stores are the only specialty videotape rental retailers within 50 miles, but a grocery store also rents videotapes in the same strip center as Blockbuster. Due to the distance between Blockbuster and Harry's Video, they probably don't compete against each other intensely. Customers who live near Harry's Video will rent tapes there, while customers close to Blockbuster will rent tapes at Blockbuster or the grocery store. In this case, Harry's major competitor may be movie theaters and cable TV because it's too inconvenient for customers close to Harry's to rent video-tapes elsewhere. On the other hand, Blockbuster competes most intensely with the grocery store.

Understanding the different types of retailers and how they compete with each other is critical for developing a successful retail strategy. Chapter 2 discusses various types of retailers and retail strategies.

Environmental Trends. The second core element of retailing is environmental trends. Today's retailers are confronting a particularly challenging business environment. Customer needs are continually changing at an increasing rate.[14] Retailers need to respond to the growth in the elderly and minority segments of the U.S. population, the importance of shopping convenience to the rising number of two-income families, and the shrinking number of people interested in retail sales positions.[15]

New technologies enable retailers to satisfy customer needs more effectively and to operate their businesses more efficiently. Retailers must be aware of these technologies and exploit the opportunities they present. For example, J.C. Penney started its catalog sales division in 1963, 78 years after Sears issued its first catalog. Even with a late start, Penney is now America's largest catalog retailer, while Sears has closed its catalog operation.

Penney's success in catalog sales is largely due to its initial investment in sophisticated telecommunications, data-processing, and distribution technologies. Each year over 100 million toll-free calls are automatically routed to an available operator in one of 22 answering centers. When a customer provides his or her phone number, the operator can access the customer's entire purchase history, address, and credit card numbers. The order entry system indicates whether the merchandise is in stock and then lists alternatives the service agent can suggest if the item is unavailable. On the operator's CRT screen, prompts (such as "You have ordered a blue shirt with a button-down collar in size 16–34") appear to ensure that the customer gets the merchandise he or she wants. Orders are automatically routed to the closest of Penney's seven distribution centers that has the merchandise in stock. Orders are then shipped. They arrive at the customer's door in two to three days.

Chapter 3 reviews the important changes in the environment confronting today's retailers.

Customers. Customers are the third core element. To be successful, retailers need to know the information in Chapter 4 about why customers shop, how they select a store, and how they select among that store's merchandise.

Ethical and Legal Issues. Ethical standards and legal and public policy are important considerations. Corporate values, legal opinions, and public policies must guide the actions of retailers. Federal, state, and local laws are enacted to ensure that business activities are consistent with society's interests. Some laws define unfair competitive practices related to suppliers and customers. They regulate advertising, promotion, and pricing practices and restrict store locations.

Retailers often use ethical standards to guide their decision making when confronting questionable situations not covered by laws. For example, retail salespeople may wonder if they should use high-pressure, manipulative sales techniques to sell merchandise that seems inappropriate for a customer. Buyers may have to decide whether to accept a supplier's offer of free tickets to a football game. Some retailers have policies for employees that outline correct behavior in these situations, but in many situations people must rely on their own code of ethics.

Due to the importance of these issues, we discuss ethical and legal considerations throughout this book and relate them to each retail management decision area.

The Retail Firm

The middle circle in Exhibit 1–3 ("The World of Retailing") is the retail firm—its strategy, location, and organization. This second section of the book describes the objectives and organization of retail companies.

Retail Strategy. The **retail strategy** indicates how the firm plans to focus its resources to accomplish its objectives. It identifies which customers the retailer will focus on, what merchandise and services it will offer, and how the retailer will build a long-term advantage over competitors.

The nature of a retail strategy can be illustrated by comparing strategies of Wal-Mart and Toys "R" Us.[16] Initially Wal-Mart identified its target market as small towns (under 35,000 in population) in Arkansas, Texas, and Oklahoma. It offered name-brand merchandise at low prices in a broad array of categories, ranging from laundry detergent to girls' dresses. While Wal-Mart stores have many different categories of merchandise, selection in each category is limited. A store might have only three brands of detergent in two sizes, while a supermarket carries eight brands in five sizes.

In contrast to Wal-Mart, Toys "R" Us identified its target as consumers living in suburban areas of large cities. Rather than carrying a broad array of merchandise categories, Toys "R" Us stores specialize in toys, games, bicycles, and furniture, primarily for children. While Toys "R" Us has few categories of merchandise, it has almost all the different types of toys and games currently on the market.

Both Wal-Mart and Toys "R" Us emphasize self-service. Customers select their merchandise, bring it to the checkout line, and then carry it to their cars. Frequently customers must assemble the merchandise at home. Since Wal-Mart and Toys "R" Us emphasize low price, they've made strategic decisions to develop a cost advantage over competitors. Both firms have sophisticated distribution and management information systems to handle inventory. Their strong relationships with suppliers enable them to buy merchandise at low prices.

The different strategies undertaken by retailers are reviewed in Chapter 5.

Organization and Systems. Retailers design their organization and use information systems to meet their customers' needs. For example, retailers that attempt to serve national or regional markets must make trade-offs between the efficiency of centralized buying and the need to tailor merchandise and services to local needs. Retailers use sophisticated computer and distribution systems to monitor the flow of information and merchandise from vendors to retail distribution centers to retail stores. Point of sale (POS) terminals read price and product information that's coded into Universal Product Codes (UPC) affixed to the merchandise. This information is then transmitted to distribution centers or transmitted directly to vendors electronically, computer-to-computer. These technologies are part of an overall inventory management system that enables retailers to (1) give customers a more complete selection of merchandise and (2) decrease their inventory investment.

The organization of a retail firm and the systems used to manage the flow of information and merchandise are discussed in Chapter 6.

Location. Retailers can put their stores in a wide variety of locations, ranging from enclosed malls to stand-alone stores on busy streets. These location opportunities (reviewed in Chapter 7) can play a major role in the retailer's performance. Locations are important to both consumers and retailers.

First, location is typically consumers' top consideration when selecting a store. Generally consumers buy gas at the closest service station and patronize the shopping mall that's most convenient to their home or office. Second, location offers retailers an opportunity to gain long-term advantage over their competition. When a retailer has the best location, a competing retailer has to settle for the second-best location.

J.C. Penney Moves from Main Street to the Mall. The interrelationships between the retailer's strategy, its location, and organization are illustrated by a major change J.C. Penney made in the early 1960s.[17]

In the late 1950s, Penney was one of the most profitable national retailers. Its target market was small towns. In its Main Street locations, Penney sold staple soft goods—underwear, socks, basic clothing, sheets, tablecloths, and so forth—at low prices, with minimal service. All sales were cash; the company didn't offer credit to its customers. Penney had considerable expertise in the design and purchase of soft goods with **private labels**—brands developed by the retailer and sold exclusively at its stores.

Organizational structure was decentralized. Each store manager controlled the type of merchandise sold, the pricing of merchandise, and the management of store employees. Promotional efforts were limited and also controlled by store managers. Penney store managers were active participants in their community's social and political activities.

Although Penney was a highly successful retailer, there was a growing awareness among company executives that environmental trends would have a negative impact on the firm. First, as the nation's levels of education and disposable income rose, consumers grew more interested in fashionable rather than staple merchandise. Second, with the development of a national highway system, the growth of suburbs, and the rise of regional malls, small-town residents were attracted to conveniently located, large, regional shopping malls. Third, Sears (the nation's largest retailer at the time) was beginning to locate stores and auto centers in regional malls. These trends suggested a decline in small-town markets for staple soft goods.

In the early 1960s, Penney undertook a new strategic direction that was consistent with changes it saw in the environment. All new Penney stores were located in regional malls across the United States. Penney opened several mall locations in each metropolitan area to create significant presence in each market. The firm began to offer credit to its customers and added new merchandise lines: appliances,

Penney's has undertaken a dramatic strategic change in its move from Main Street USA to becoming the largest U.S. department store in regional malls.

auto supplies, paint, hardware, sporting goods, consumer electronics, and moderately priced fashionable clothing.

Besides altering its merchandise and locations, Penney made its organizational structure more centralized. Store managers continued to have considerable responsibility for selecting merchandise and managing store operations, but advertising was done centrally, using national print and TV media. Penney emphasized a consistent presentation and similar merchandise in all locations. Buyers at corporate headquarters had more responsibility for providing the general merchandise direction the firm would pursue.

To effectively control its 1,500 stores, Penney installed a sophisticated communication network. Each store manager can monitor daily sales of each type of merchandise in his or her store and every other store in the chain. Buyers at corporate headquarters in Dallas communicate daily with merchandise managers in each store over a satellite TV link.

This illustrates how retailers must respond to a changing environment. These changes often result in new directions that must be supported by new locations, new organizational design, and new information and communication systems.

The Retail Mix

The elements in the outer circle of Exhibit 1–3's "World of Retailing" are the day-to-day activities undertaken by retail firms. These activities are referred to as the *retail mix*. The **retail mix** is the combination of activities retailers use to satisfy customer needs and influence their purchase decisions. Elements in the retail mix (Exhibit 1–4) include the types of merchandise assortments offered, merchandise pricing, advertising and promotional programs, store design and visual merchandise, and customer services provided by the retailer and its salespeople. Section III examines elements in the retail mix undertaken by employees in the buying organization, while Section IV examines the elements undertaken by employees in the stores.

Buying elements. Managers in the buying organization must decide how much and what type of merchandise to buy (Chapter 8), which vendors and purchase terms to use (Chapter 9), what retail prices to set (Chapter 10), and how to advertise and promote merchandise (Chapter 11).

 EXHIBIT 1-4   **Elements in the Retail Mix**

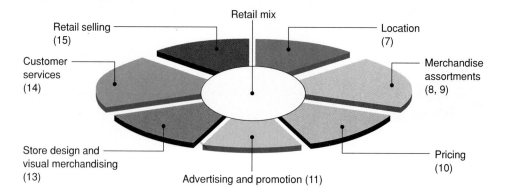

Retail mix

Retail selling (15)

Location (7)

Customer services (14)

Merchandise assortments (8, 9)

Store design and visual merchandising (13)

Pricing (10)

Advertising and promotion (11)

Store elements. Store managers must determine how to recruit, select, and motivate sales associates (Chapter 12), where and how to display merchandise (Chapter 13), what services to provide customers (Chapter 14), and which selling skills sales associates will need (Chapter 15).

Burdines: The Florida Store. Elements in the retail mix must be consistent with and reinforce the retailer's strategy. Burdines illustrates this interrelationship between retail strategy and mix.

In 1898, two years after the East Coast Railroad was completed, William M. Burdine opened the first Burdines store in Miami. It sold work clothes, notions, and piece goods. The first branch store opened in 1912, followed by additional outlets in South Florida. In 1973, Burdines began to expand to central Florida and the state's west coast. By 1993, Burdines' 30 stores had annual sales over $1 billion. The chain is now part of Federated Department Stores, Inc., a corporation composed of regional department store chains.

Burdines' long-term strategy considered the possibilities of expanding beyond Florida to other southeastern states either through acquisitions or by opening new stores. In 1988, department store competition in south Florida increased dramatically as two Macy's and two Bloomingdale's stores opened. These northern retailers' invasion of Burdines' Florida market led to a reevaluation of Burdines' long-term strategy. Burdines decided to focus exclusively on the Florida market, identify itself

The interior of a Burdines store illustrates how the firm implements the Florida store strategy through visual merchandising. The tropical colors and palm trees identify the store with its Florida target market.

as The Florida Store, and forsake expansion plans through the Southeast. It would defend its position in its Florida target market by (1) creating unique merchandise tailored to Florida's climate and (2) displaying this merchandise in a unique Florida style. This focused strategy would be difficult for out-of-state retailers to copy cost-effectively because those competitors wouldn't have enough Florida stores to justify developing unique buying plans and visual presentations.

To implement this strategy, Burdines' visual merchandise department redesigned stores to be tropical, colorful, and whimsical. One clearly identifiable Florida symbol used throughout the stores is the palm tree. In the newest stores, palms are used as column enclosures and as symbols to denote entrances and significant areas in the store. In addition, the palm frond often is used in the design of tables that display merchandise.

Lighting is another key element reinforcing the Florida theme. Daylight from atrium skylights, filtered by a unique shutter system, is introduced into the store to reinforce the tropical atmosphere and establish a focal point for customers. Burdines uses pastel colors extensively. White in the cosmetics and electronics departments is an exciting innovation. Traditionally electronics departments use dark colors, which results in a cavern-like atmosphere, while cosmetics are usually displayed with an odd assortment of colors selected by the manufacturer.

Burdines' unique visual merchandising isn't the only aspect of creating The Florida Store. Buyers have adapted their buying seasons to Florida's climate. For example, Florida customers continue to buy summer merchandise through autumn, so Burdines' buyers ask vendors to make extra cuttings of summer merchandise in new colors rather than buying merchandise made for autumn that's sold to northern department stores.

Special Topics. The final two chapters in the text review two important types of retailing: fashion retailing (Chapter 16) and services retailing (Chapter 17).

SUMMARY

An important institution in our society, retailing provides considerable value to consumers while giving people opportunities for rewarding and challenging careers. Due to significant shifts in consumers' needs and in technology, the retail industry too is changing. Retail formats and companies that were unknown 30 years ago are now major factors in the industry.

The key to profitable retailing is offering the right product, at the right price, in the right place, at the right time, in the right quantity. To accomplish all this, retailers must understand what customers want and what competitors are offering now and in the future. Retailers engage in a wide range of activities from setting the price of a brown wool sweater to determining whether a new multimillion-dollar store should be built in a mall. This book explains (1) the nature of retailing as an institution in our society and (2) activities undertaken by retailers.

KEY TERMS

breaking bulk, 9	intratype competition, 14	retail mix, 18	retailing, 5
intertype competition, 14	private label, 17	retail strategy, 16	scrambled merchandising, 14
		retailer, 7	

Retail Institutions

Retail firm (2)

Questions that this chapter answers include

• **What are the different types of retailers?**
• **How do their retail mixes differ?**
• **How do retailers differ in terms of ownership?**

A t the core of Figure 1–3's world of retailing are customers and retailers interacting in the marketplace. The retailers are competing against each other for a portion of the customer's disposal income. This chapter reviews the different types of firms competing in retail markets—the competitors at the core of the world of retailing.

TYPES OF RETAILERS

There are over 1 million retailers in the United States, ranging from street vendors selling hot dogs to large corporations such as Sears that have become an integral part of American culture. Each retailer survives and prospers by satisfying a group of consumers' needs more effectively than its competitors. Over time, different types of retail institutions also have emerged and prospered because they effectively satisfied a large group of consumers' needs. A **retail institution** is a group of retailers that provides a similar retail mix designed to satisfy the needs of a specific group of customers.

Retail Mix

The most basic characteristic of a retailer is its retail mix—the approach retailers use to satisfy their customers' needs. (See Exhibit 1–4.) As you read about the different types of retailers, notice how each type has a unique pattern of retail mix elements. For example, department stores typically have higher prices because they have higher costs due to their emphasis on stocking a lot of fashionable apparel, providing high levels of service with considerable personal selling, and using more convenient and expensive mall locations.

Four elements of the retail mix that are particularly useful for classifying retailers are the type of merchandise sold, the variety and assortment of merchandise sold, the level of service provided to customers, and the price of merchandise.

Merchandise

You might think that a retailer's principal competitors are other retailers selling the same type of merchandise. However, type of merchandise often does not determine which retailers compete against each other. For example, convenience stores (such as 7-Eleven and Circle K), traditional supermarkets, and warehouse grocery stores all sell the same type of merchandise, but they attract customers with different needs. The convenience store caters to customers who value convenience over low prices or a broad selection. The warehouse grocery store, on the other hand, caters to customers who want low prices and don't place much importance on service or store atmosphere.

The degree to which retailers compete against each other isn't simply based on the similarity of their merchandise. The variety and assortment of the merchandise they offer and the services they provide must also be considered.

REFACT

Over one-third of all U.S. retail sales are for food, automobiles, and gasoline. Department and discount stores only account for 10 percent of retail sales.

Variety and Assortment. Variety is the number of different merchandise categories a retailer offers. **Assortment** is the number of different items in a merchandise category. Each different item of merchandise is called an **SKU (stock keeping unit).** For example, a 32-ounce box of Tide laundry detergent or a white, long-sleeved, button-down collar Hathaway shirt, size 16–33, is an SKU.

Department stores and toy stores both sell toys. However, department stores offer greater variety because they sell many other categories of merchandise in addition to toys. Stores specializing in toys offer the greatest assortment; they stock the most types of toys (and more SKUs). For each type of toy, such as dolls, the toy specialist will offer more models, sizes, and brands than general merchants such as department stores.

Variety is often referred to as the **breadth of merchandise** carried by a retailer; assortment is referred to as the **depth of merchandise.** Exhibit 2–1 shows the breadth and depth of bicycles carried in a local bicycle shop (a specialty store), in Toys "R" Us (a category specialist), and in Wal-Mart (a general merchandise discount store). Toys "R" Us carries three types and has a narrower variety than the bicycle shop (four types) or Wal-Mart (four types). Toys "R" Us has the greatest depth of assortment in children's bicycles. Wal-Mart has the lowest number of SKUs (28) compared to 73 at Toys "R" Us and 169 at the bicycle shop. Note, however, that Wal-Mart and Toys "R" Us have many of the same brands, but the bicycle shop offers a completely different set of brands.

Customer Services

Retailers also differ in the services they offer customers. For example, the bicycle shop assists customers in selecting the appropriate bicycle, adjusts bicycles to fit the individual, and repairs bicycles. Toys "R" Us and Wal-Mart don't provide any of these services.

Variety and Assortment Offered by Three Retailers

EXHIBIT 2-1

	RETAILER		
Types of Bicycles	*Bicycle Shop*	*Toys "R" Us*	*Wal-Mart*
Adult road	Trek		Murray
	Ross		
	Mongoose		
	Bridgestone		
	Specially built		
	(27 SKUs)		(2 SKUs)
	$195–$4,000		$93
Adult hybrid	Trek	Murray	Murray
	Ross	Huffy	Huffy
	Mongoose	Roadmaster	
	Bridgestone	Nice	
	Specially built		
	(29 SKUs)	(9 SKUs)	(10 SKUs)
	$190–$1,079	$88–$130	$96–$130
Mountain	Trek	Murray	Murray
	Ross	Huffy	Huffy
	Mongoose	Roadmaster	Roadmaster
	Bridgestone	Pacific	
	Specially built	Rand	
		Trendy	
		Dynacraft	
		Range Union	
	(77 SKUs)	(26 SKUs)	(9 SKUs)
	$130–$3,080	$88–$200	$96–$150
Child	Ross	Murray	Murray
	Mongoose	Huffy	Huffy
	Jazz	Roadmaster	Roadmaster
	Specially built	Pacific	
		Rand	
		Trendz	
		Dynacraft	
		Range Union	
		Rallye	
		Paragon	
		Kent	
	(36 SKUs)	(38 SKUs)	(7 SKUs)
	$57–$320	$53–$160	$90–$100

Customers expect retailers to provide some services: accepting personal checks, providing parking, and displaying merchandise. Some retailers charge customers for other services, such as home delivery and gift wrapping. Retailers that cater to service-oriented consumers offer customers most of these services at no charge. Nordstrom (discussed in Re-Tale 2–1) is considered one of America's most outstanding service-oriented retailers.

Price and the Cost of Offering Breadth and Depth of Merchandise and Services

Stocking a broad variety and deep assortment like the Toys "R" Us selection of bicycles is appealing to customers but costly for retailers. When a retailer offers customers many SKUs, inventory investment increases because the retailer must have back-up stock for each SKU.

Similarly, services attract customers to the retailer, but they're also costly. More salespeople are needed to provide information and assist customers, to alter merchandise to meet customers' needs, and to demonstrate merchandise. Child care facilities, rest rooms, dressing rooms, and check rooms take up valuable store space that could be used to stock and display merchandise. Offering delayed billing, credit, and installment payments requires a financial investment that could be used to buy more merchandise. So retailers that offer many SKUs and/or outstanding service usually have to charge higher prices.

RETAIL INSTITUTIONS

While there are over a million retailers in the United States, there's a limited number of retail institutions. The following sections discuss the most common retail institutions: traditional food and general merchandise retailers, newer retail institutions (such as category specialists), and nonstore retailers.

RE-TALE 2-1 Nordstrom Does It with Service

Nordstrom, a Seattle-based department store chain, has 59 stores in Washington, Oregon, Utah, California, Alaska, Virginia, and Illinois. Largely due to its reputation for outstanding service, the chain has become one of the nation's most respected fashion retailers. Its no-questions-asked return policy and highly motivated, service-oriented salespeople have developed strong customer loyalty as well as an image for quality service and merchandise. Due to Nordstrom's success, many department store chains now follow its lead, realizing the customer comes first.

When new salespeople start working at Nordstrom, they learn one rule: Use your best judgment to satisfy the needs of our customers. To implement this service policy, salespeople carry merchandise to the customer's car, pick up and deliver merchandise to customers' homes, and even buy and resell merchandise that a customer wants from a competitive store. Customers are allowed to return any item (including items that aren't sold by Nordstrom) for any reason and get a complete refund or replacement. Although some customers abuse this policy, it reinforces Nordstrom's service image.

Here's an example of Nordstrom's service. Don Johnson, vice president of American Health Group, accidentally laundered the pants from a suit purchased at Nordstrom. He visited his local store to buy a replacement pair. The salesman searched through all the stores

in the chain and even called the manufacturer to locate a replacement pair, without success. When the salesman called Johnson with the bad news, he said he was crediting the price of the suit to Johnson's Nordstrom account. Johnson protested because he had made the mistake. The salesman agreed but responded that Johnson had a worthless half suit and that wouldn't do. He looked forward to taking care of Johnson when he came to use the credit.

Nordstrom rewards its salespeople for meeting these high service standards. Salespeople are compensated with sales commissions, profit sharing, and some of the highest salaries in the industry. Typically, Nordstrom salespeople make 20 to 50 percent more than salespeople working for competitors. Nordstrom also provides many opportunities for advancement in the company because it only promotes from within. All Nordstrom executives have started their careers on the sales floor.

SOURCE: Joan Bergman, "Nordstrom Gets the Gold," *Stores,* January 1990, pp. 44–63; "Why Nordstrom Got There," *Stores,* January 1990, pp. 75–85; "Why Rivals Are Quaking as Nordstrom Heads East," *Business Week,* June 15, 1987, pp. 99–100; and Ron Zemke and Dick Schaaf, *The Service Edge* (New York: Plume, 1989), p. 66.

Exhibit 2–2 shows the number of stores, sales revenues, and retail mixes for different types of food retailers.

Conventional Supermarkets. A **conventional supermarket** is a self-service food store offering groceries, meat, and produce with annual sales of over $2 million and size of under 20,000 square feet. In conventional supermarkets, the sale of nonfood items, such as health and beauty aids and general merchandise, is limited.

Superstores and Supercenters. Over the past 20 years, supermarkets have increased in size and have begun to sell a broader variety of merchandise. **Superstores** are large supermarkets (20,000 to 50,000 square feet). **Supercenters** are a combination of a supermarket and a general merchandise discount store under one roof. They are typically 150,000 square feet. Supercenters offer customers one-stop shopping. Customers will typically drive farther to shop at these stores than they would to shop at conventional supermarkets (which offer a smaller selection of merchandise).

REFACT

8.2 percent of disposable income is spent on food consumed at home; 4.0 percent is spent on food consumed away from home.[1]

Warehouse Supermarkets. Warehouse supermarkets are discount food retailers that offer merchandise in a no-frills environment. There are different types of warehouse stores. **Limited-line warehouse supermarkets** (also called **box stores**) typically carry 1,500 items (one size and brand per item), with no refrigerated or perishable merchandise. Merchandise is displayed in cut boxes on shipping pallets. These stores provide no services. Customers bag their purchases and pay with cash.

The largest and fastest-growing type of warehouse supermarket is the full-line warehouse. These stores range in size from 50,000 to 70,000 square feet and generate from $30 to $50 million in sales per store. Re-Tale 2–2 describes a super-warehouse store.

Full-line warehouse supermarkets typically sell national brands of packaged goods at low prices and make low profits as a percentage of sales. Like conventional supermarkets, superstores, and supercenter stores, warehouse stores are increasing their emphasis on perishables and freshly prepared foods because these merchandise categories are especially profitable.

Convenience Stores. Convenience stores provide a limited variety and assortment of merchandise at a convenient location in a 3,000-to-8,000–square-foot store with speedy checkout. They are the modern version of the neighborhood mom-and-pop grocery store.

A convenience store's principal benefit (as the name implies) is convenience, so they only have to offer a limited assortment and variety and can charge higher prices than supermarkets. They carry merchandise in a number of different categories, but usually have only one or two national brands and sizes in each category.

While the growth of convenience stores has been substantial over the past 30 years, industry sales by this type of food retailer have matured and are beginning to level off. The major merchandise categories are gasoline, tobacco products, beer and wine, soft drinks, and prepared foods.

Convenience stores enable consumers to make purchases quickly, without having to search through a large store and wait in long checkout lines. Over half the items bought are consumed within 30 minutes of purchase. Due to their small size and high sales, convenience stores typically receive deliveries every day.[2]

Types of Food Retailers

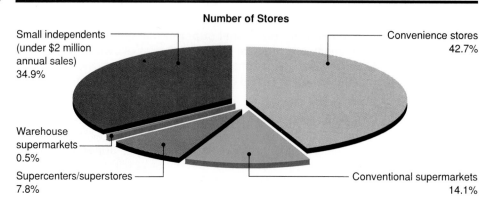

Number of Stores

Small independents
(under $2 million
annual sales)
34.9%

Convenience stores
42.7%

Warehouse
supermarkets
0.5%

Supercenters/superstores
7.8%

Conventional supermarkets
14.1%

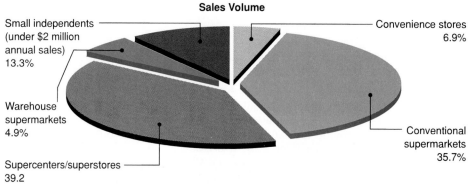

Sales Volume

Small independents
(under $2 million
annual sales)
13.3%

Convenience stores
6.9%

Warehouse
supermarkets
4.9%

Conventional
supermarkets
35.7%

Supercenters/superstores
39.2

	Convenience Store	Conventional Supermarket Superstore	Supercenter	Warehouse Supermarket/ Wholesale Club
Sales ($ millions)	$27,000[a]	$141,300	$103,400	$58,100[a]
Number of stores	58,200	19,920	6,700	4,280
Variety	narrow	average	broad	broad
Assortment	shallow	average	deep	average
Service	average	average	low	low
Prices	high	average	low	low
Size (sq. ft.)	2,000–4,000	8,000–75,000	100,000–150,000	50,000–70,000
SKUs	2,000	15,000	30,000	30,000
Largest U.S. chains	7-Eleven Circle K	A&P Winn-Dixie Kroger American Stores Safeway	Meirer Kmart Wal-Mart	Cub Food Sun Food Market Food 4 Less

[a]Only supermarket items.

SOURCE: Data on sales and number of stores from "1993 Grocery Sales" in "62nd Annual Report of the Grocery Industry," *Progressive Grocer,* April 1994, p. 49.

RE-TALE 2-2   An Xtraordinary Shopping Experience

The low-price emphasis is apparent when you enter one of Xtra's 10 super-warehouse grocery stores in south Florida. At the entrance, customers see full shopping carts on a platform with the total cost based on Xtra's prices and prices at competing stores. But not only low prices attract consumers to Xtra. When asked what she liked about Xtra, one said, "Everything. There's so much going on here. Shopping is fun."

The store buzzes with activity. Employees are stocking shelves, handing out samples, and keeping the store immaculately clean. Some employees are moving around the store on roller skates. Alfalfa and bean sprouts are growing in hydroponic chambers in the produce department. Peanuts are roasting in the bulk food department. The juice factory is producing hundreds of gallons of fresh-squeezed orange juice each day.

The store has a colorful decor and exciting visual appeal. For instance, the produce department displays mounds of fruits and vegetables in color-coordinated patterns. Neon signs are mounted over refrigerated cases.

The store is laid out so that a customer enters the produce department and then walks along the outer circle of the store past the juice factory and fresh fish, meat, and dairy departments followed by bakery, deli, and wine cellar before entering the center of the store, where packaged goods are sold. Cases on pallets in warehouse racks are stacked on top of 6-foot-high displays of Tide boxes and Campbell soup cans.

Xtra is a division of Pueblo International, the largest food retailer in Puerto Rico and the Virgin Islands.

Xtra's super warehouse grocery stores combine colorful decor, low prices, and a broad assortment of high-quality produce.

SOURCE: Priscilla Donegan, "An Xtraordinary Experience," *Progressive Grocer,* March 1989, pp. 87–89. Reprinted by permission from PROGRESSIVE GROCER, March 1989, copyright 1989 by Progressive Grocer Magazine.

The traditional **general merchandise retail stores** are department stores, discount stores, and specialty stores. During the past 30 years, however, a number of new types of general merchandise retailers have emerged and are becoming increasingly important to consumers. These include category specialists, home-improvement centers, off-price retailers, catalog showrooms, and warehouse clubs. Exhibit 2–3 summarizes characteristics of general merchandise retailers that sell through stores, and of nonstore general merchandise retailers. Nonstore retailers are discussed later in this chapter.

Traditional General Merchandise Retail Stores

Exhibit 2–4 shows the proportion of retail sales for different formats. In this exhibit, specialty stores include traditional soft goods specialty stores, such as The Gap, and new specialty retailers using a discount format, such as PetsMart. Since the mid-1980s, the shares of retail sales for general merchandise discount stores and hard goods specialty stores have been increasing, while department stores' and soft goods specialty retailers' shares have been decreasing.[3]

Department Stores. Department stores are retailers that carry a broad variety and deep assortment, offer considerable customer services, and are organized into separate departments for displaying merchandise. The largest U.S. department store

EXHIBIT 2-3 **Characteristics of General Merchandise Retailers**

Type	Variety	Assortment	Service	Prices	Size (sq. ft.)	SKUs	Location
Department stores	Broad	Deep to average	Average to high	Average to high	100,000– 200,000	100,000	Regional malls
Traditional discount stores	Broad	Average to shallow	Low	Low	60,000– 80,000	25,000– 30,000	Stand-alone, power strip centers
Traditional specialty stores	Narrow	Deep	High	High	4,000– 12,000	5,000	Regional malls
Category specialists	Narrow	Very deep	Low	Low	50,000– 120,000	25,000– 40,000	Stand-alone, power strip centers
Warehouse clubs	Average	Shallow	Low	Very low	80,000– 100,000	4,000– 5,000	Stand-alone
Hypermarkets	Broad	Average	Low	Low	200,000	50,000	Stand-alone
Off-price stores	Average	Deep, but varying	Low	Low	25,000– 40,000	100,000	Stand-alone, power strip centers Outlet malls
Catalog showrooms	Narrow	Average	Low	Average to low	5,000– 40,000	10,000– 15,000	Strip centers
Direct-mail catalogs	Average to narrow	Average to shallow	Average	Average	—	10,000– 100,000	—
TV home shopping	Average	Shallow	Average	Average	—	75,000	—
Interactive electronic retailing	Narrow	Shallow	Average	Average	—	N/A	—
Direct selling	Narrow	Shallow	High	High	—	1,000	—

EXHIBIT 2-4 **Store Sales for Publicly Held General Merchandise Retailers**

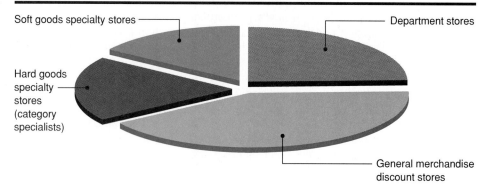

SOURCE: Jill Lettich, "Discounters Up Share in '92 Sales," *Discount Store News,* July 5, 1993, pp. 3, 118.

corporations are J.C. Penney, May Company, and Federated Department Stores. Most department store corporations own several regional department store chains. Ownership of retail stores is covered later in this chapter.

A department store is organized into departments selling men's, women's, and children's clothing and accessories; home furnishings and furniture; toys and games; consumer electronics such as TVs, VCRs, and stereos; and kitchenware and small appliances. Women's wear typically accounts for over half the sales volume, so women's merchandise is subdivided into departments based on size (petite, full-figure), use (sportswear, business attire, evening wear), lifestyle (conservative, traditional, update), or age (juniors, misses).

A buyer is responsible for the merchandise concept conveyed by this Donna Karan boutique in a May Company department store.

Home Depot sells home improvement merchandise at discount prices in a warehouse atmosphere, but still offers personalized service to help customers select and use the merchandise.

Each department within the store is typically allocated a specific selling space, a point-of-sales (POS) electronic terminal to transact and record sales, and salespeople to assist customers. The department store often resembles a collection of specialty shops.

Department stores are unique in terms of the services they provide to customers. Their labor costs are higher than other types of general merchandise retailers because they employ more sales associates to assist customers. Most department stores offer the full range of customer services.

To make the shopping experience exciting, department stores also emphasize promotions, such as elaborate displays during the Christmas season. Some department stores hold special promotions throughout the year, such as back-to-school or white sales.

Traditional department stores have changed considerably over the years. With few exceptions, traditional department stores have eliminated many departments.[4] No longer can a customer buy a new outfit and then walk to the next aisle for a record album, refrigerator, best-selling book, or toy. Traditional department stores are concentrating more on apparel and soft home furnishings (sheets, bedspreads, pillows). They are cutting back or eliminating toys and games, furniture, and consumer electronics.

Department stores' overall sales have stagnated in recent years due to increased competition from discount stores and specialty stores. Discount stores offer lower prices and are beginning to sell some of the same brand-name clothing as department stores. In addition, many customers now feel that specialty stores provide better service and merchandise assortments than department stores.[5]

In response to this increased competition, department stores are improving their customer service and altering their merchandise mix and presentation of merchandise. Besides focusing more on apparel, department stores are developing unique merchandise that consumers can buy only at their stores. This merchandise has a brand name such as Stafford (J.C. Penney) or Outback Red (The Limited) that is developed by the retailer and only available in the retailer's stores. These brands are referred to as store brands or private labels.

They're also creating "merchandise concepts" directed toward specific consumer groups. For example, buyers are responsible for a merchandise concept rather than a specific category of merchandise. Rather than buying just men's trousers or women's blouses, buyers are responsible for a specific designer or a specific shop, such as young men's sportswear. This type of organization focuses buyers on the needs of a group of customers and makes them more market-oriented than merchandise-oriented.

Discount Stores. A **discount store** is a general merchandise retailer that offers a broad variety of merchandise, shallow assortments, limited service, and low prices. Discount stores tend to concentrate on lower- to middle-income consumers. They offer national brands, but these brands are typically less fashion-oriented than brands in department stores.

Discount stores can charge lower prices than department stores because they provide less service at low-cost locations in a more Spartan atmosphere. Discount stores emphasize self-service. Customers pick out their merchandise, put it in their cart, and take it to the checkout counter at the front of the store. Salespeople are available only in departments where they're absolutely needed, such as photography, consumer electronics, and jewelry.

Discount and department stores provide similar numbers of SKUs, but discount stores tend to offer more variety and less depth of merchandise. They typically carry fewer brands and sizes in each category than department stores. Merchandise categories that are typically available in discount stores but not department stores include hardware, auto supplies, athletic equipment, and gardening supplies.

The three largest general merchandise discount store chains are Wal-Mart, Kmart, and Target (a division of Dayton Hudson).[6]

Sears' unique retail format incorporates aspects of both department and discount stores. Its broad assortment, which ranges from home appliances to dresses, resembles discount stores. However, Sears has mall locations, apparel offerings, and a service level that are similar to those of department stores. Sears' financial problems are due to inability to (1) compete with department stores on fashionable apparel and (2) compete with discount stores on price.[7]

Just as department stores face intense competition from specialty stores that focus on a single category of merchandise, the category specialists compete intensely with traditional discount stores. (Category specialists are described in a subsequent section.) To respond to category specialists' domination of hard goods (appliances, consumer electronics, automotive, sporting goods), many general merchandise discount retailers are upgrading their apparel offerings.[8]

Specialty Stores. A traditional **specialty store** concentrates on a limited number of complementary merchandise categories and provides a high level of service in an area under 8,000 square feet. In contrast to department and discount stores, specialty stores focus on a narrow market segment. By carrying a narrow variety but deep assortment, they offer customers a better selection and sales expertise in that category than department or discount stores provide. Consumers are attracted to specialty stores by deep assortments, personal attention, and intimate store atmosphere.

Some of the largest specialty store chains are The Gap and The Limited (apparel), Barnes & Noble (books), Pier 1 (furniture), Zale (jewelry), Payless (shoes), and Electronic Boutique (computer software). While most specialty stores concentrate on one merchandise category, Re-Tale 2–3 describes a specialty retailer that focuses on customers desiring a European lifestyle.

A group of new general merchandise retailers has emerged on the retailing scene during the past 20 years. These new retailers include category specialists, home-improvement centers, warehouse clubs, and off-price retailers.

New Types of General Merchandise Retailers

Category Specialists. A **category specialist** is a discount store that offers a narrow variety but deep assortment of merchandise in stores over 8,000 square feet. These retailers are basically discount specialty stores. Their stores are about the same size as traditional discount stores and located similarly in stand-alone sites or strip shopping centers. But their merchandise assortment is the exact opposite of a traditional discount store, where you find broad variety but shallow assortment.

Most category specialists use a self-service approach, but some specialists in consumer durables offer significant service to customers. For example, Circuit City stores have a warehouse atmosphere, with TVs, VCRs, and stereos in shipping containers on pallets stacked to the ceiling. However, some models are displayed in the middle of the store, and salespeople in the display area are available to answer questions and make suggestions.[9]

By offering a complete assortment in a category at low prices, category specialists can "kill" a category of merchandise for other retailers; thus, they are frequently called *category killers.* For example, Toys "R" Us accounts for over 40 percent of all toys and games sold in the United States. Because category

RE-TALE 2-3   **Capturing the Romance of Italy**

The inspiration for Starbucks Coffee came to Howard Schultz (founder and CEO) as he wandered through the ancient piazzas of Milan in 1983. Passing the cheerful espresso bars, he realized that Americans lacked the opportunity to savor a good cup of coffee in a pleasant environment. "I saw what Italy had captured was the romance of the beverage. That same romance has been

captured in the shopping experience at all Starbucks stores. It's romance, theatrics, community—the totality of the coffee experience."

In 1988, Schultz opened the first Starbucks in Seattle, a city called *Latteland* for its coffee connoisseurs. ("Even Skid Row derelicts line up for their $1.85 caffe lattes," says Schultz.) The chain has grown to over 250 outlets as it expands eastward.

To offer the highest-quality coffee, Starbucks buyers scour the globe for premium Arabica coffee beans. But coffee is just one part of the retail offering. Stores are physically attractive, spacious, and well lit, with wood paneling, artwork, gleaming espresso machines, and jazz playing in the background. Customers wander around the store, drinking their coffee and considering the purchase of coffee paraphernalia ranging from coffee beans and brushes for cleaning coffee grinders to $1,000 home espresso machines. Schultz envisions a nation of coffee connoisseurs patronizing Starbucks in their local neighborhoods.

SOURCE: Charles McCoy, "Entrepreneur Smells Aroma of Success in Coffee Bars," *The Wall Street Journal,* January 8, 1993, p. B2; and Ingrid Abramovitch, "Miracles of Marketing: How to Reinvent Your Product," *Success,* April 1993, pp. 23–27.

specialists dominate a category of merchandise, they can use their buying power to negotiate lower prices, excellent terms, and be assured of supply when items are scarce. Department stores and traditional discount stores located near a Toys "R" Us store typically have to reduce their offering of toys and games because local consumers are drawn to the deep assortment and low prices at Toys "R" Us. Re-Tale 2–4 describes Blockbuster Video, a category specialist in videotape rentals that has significantly affected mom-and-pop video rental stores.

The largest category specialist chains in the United States are Toys "R" Us in toys and games, Circuit City in consumer electronics, Sports Authority in sporting goods, Office Depot in office supplies, Pep Boys in auto supplies, and CompUSA in computer products.[10]

Home-Improvement Centers. A **home-improvement center** is a category specialist that combines the traditional hardware store and lumber yard. It focuses on providing material and information that enable do-it-yourselfers to maintain and improve their homes. Merchandise includes an extensive assortment of building materials, paints and painting equipment, plumbing materials, electrical supplies, hardware, power tools, and garden and yard equipment.

While merchandise in home-improvement centers is displayed in a warehouse atmosphere, salespeople are available to assist customers in selecting merchandise and to tell them how to use it. For example, Home Depot has a licensed

---

RE-TALE 2-4   Blockbuster Video Bursts into the Videotape Category

When people walk into a Blockbuster Video for the first time, the first word that comes out may be "Wow!" This "wow" factor is a key to Blockbuster's success. The typical video rental store has 1,500 square feet and 2,500 tapes. In comparison, Blockbuster stores are more than four times larger (6,500 square feet) with four times more tapes (10,000). Each Blockbuster usually has 50 copies of new releases, while the typical video store only has 5.

Blockbuster, a division of Viacom, doesn't just offer selection; it also provides better service than the typical video rental store. Most Blockbusters are open until midnight. They all have outside return boxes to accommodate customers who return tapes when the store's closed. Salespeople are trained to know the selection of tapes and to be polite in responding to customers.

A companywide computer and communication system enables Blockbuster to monitor inventory and sales transactions at each of its 1,000 stores. By combining demographic data about the store's trade area and buying patterns, Blockbuster can refine its selection of tapes and tailor the selection to local markets. For example, research indicated that the typical Blockbuster customer rents two tapes at a time. To accommodate this customer, Blockbuster adopted a unique rental fee of $3 for three nights and two days.

Blockbuster emphasizes that it's a family-oriented store by refusing to stock soft-core pornographic videos and X-rated films. Stores are careful to rent R-rated videos only to people over 17 years old.

In 1995, Blockbuster's annual sales, rental fees, and videotape sales exceeded $2 billion. Blockbuster went international by opening outlets in Great Britain in 1989 and Australia in 1990.

SOURCE: "Blockbuster Video and the 'Wow' Factor," *Chain Store Age Executive*, May 1988; and Gail DeGeorge, "The Video King Who Won't Hit 'Pause'," *Business Week*, January 22, 1990, pp. 47–48.

---

electrician in most stores. Experts in specific areas lead workshops to show customers how to do things themselves. All Home Depot salespeople are required to attend "product knowledge" classes and are paid for the time they spend learning about water heaters and power tools.[11]

The largest U.S. home-improvement chains are Home Depot, Lowe's Companies, and Payless Cashways.[12]

Warehouse Clubs. A **warehouse club** is a general merchandise retailer that offers a limited merchandise assortment with little service at low prices to consumers and small businesses.[13] Stores are large (about 100,000 square feet) and located in low-rent districts. They have simple interiors and concrete floors. Aisles are wide so forklifts can pick up pallets of merchandise and arrange them on the selling floor. Little service is offered. Customers pick merchandise off shipping pallets and take it to checkout lines in the front of the store.

Along with low-cost locations and store designs, warehouse clubs reduce inventory holding costs by carrying a limited assortment of fast-selling items. Merchandise usually is sold before the clubs need to pay for it.

Merchandise in warehouse clubs is about half food and half general merchandise. Specific brands and items may differ from time to time because the stores buy merchandise available on special promotions from manufacturers.

Most warehouse clubs have two types of members. Wholesale members are small-business people, and individual members purchase for their own use. Some clubs require individual members to have an affiliation with a government agency, utility, or credit union.

The largest warehouse club chains are Sam's Warehouse (a division of Wal-Mart) and Price/Costco.[14]

Off-Price Retailers. Off-price retailers offer an inconsistent assortment of brand-name, fashion-oriented soft goods at low prices.[15] America's largest off-price retail chains are Marshall's, T.J. Maxx, Burlington Coat Factory, and Ross Stores.[16]

Off-price retailers can sell brand-name and even designer-label merchandise at low prices due to their unique buying and merchandising practices. Most merchandise is bought opportunistically from manufacturers or other retailers with excess inventory at the end of the season. This merchandise might be in odd sizes or unpopular colors and styles, or there may be minor mistakes in garments' construction (irregulars). Typically, merchandise is purchased at one-fifth to one-fourth of the original wholesale price. Off-price retailers can buy at low prices because they don't ask suppliers for money to support advertising their merchandise, return privileges, refunds for marking merchandise down, or delayed payments.

Due to this pattern of opportunistic buying, customers can't be confident that the same type of merchandise will be in stock each time they visit the store. Different bargains will be available on each visit. To improve their offerings' consistency, some off-price retailers complement opportunistically bought merchandise with merchandise bought at regular wholesale prices.

Three special types of off-price retailers are outlet, closeout, and single-price stores. **Outlet stores** are off-price retailers owned by manufacturers or department or specialty store chains.[17] Outlet stores owned by manufacturers are frequently referred to as **factory outlets.** Many manufacturers have one or two outlet stores.

Manufacturers view outlet stores as an opportunity to improve their revenues from irregulars, production overruns, and merchandise returned by retailers. Outlet stores also allow manufacturers some control over where their branded merchandise is sold at discount prices.

Retailers with strong brand names such as Saks and Brooks Brothers operate outlet stores too. By selling excess merchandise in outlet stores rather than selling it at markdown prices in their primary stores, department and specialty store chains can maintain an image of offering desirable merchandise at full price.

To prevent conflicts with their department and specialty store customers, manufacturers and retailers typically locate their outlets in malls exclusively devoted to outlet stores. These malls are usually in out-of-the-way locations far from regional malls where their brands are sold.

Closeout retailers are off-price retailers that sell a broad but inconsistent assortment of general merchandise as well as apparel and soft home goods. Some closeout stores sell both merchandise purchased opportunistically and excess merchandise from other retail chains owned by the parent corporation. The largest closeout chains are Consolidated Stores, MacFrugal's, and Bud's Warehouse Outlets, a division of Wal-Mart.[18]

Single-price retailers are closeout stores that sell all their merchandise at a single price, typically $1. The largest single-price retailer is Everything's A $1.[19]

Catalog Showrooms. A catalog showroom is a retailer whose showroom is adjacent to its warehouse.[20] These retailers typically specialize in hard goods such as housewares, jewelry, sporting equipment, garden equipment, and consumer electronics. Catalog showrooms can offer low prices because they minimize the cost of displaying merchandise, focus on a narrow range of merchandise, provide minimal service, and are located in lower-cost areas than regional malls.

In most showrooms, the customer writes up an order for merchandise using the number on the display item or in a catalog. Then the order is handed to a clerk, who gets the merchandise from a warehouse. In some catalog showrooms, customers can order merchandise using a computer terminal in the store.

The largest catalog showroom chains in the United States are Service Merchandise and Best Products.[21] This retailing format's attractiveness has been declining. Category specialists can offer the same low prices and let customers browse through their "warehouse," selecting merchandise they want to buy. In addition, some customers find it inconvenient to wait for merchandise to be retrieved from the warehouse.

More than 90 percent of all retail sales are made in stores. However, nonstore sales now are growing faster than sales in retail stores. The three types of **nonstore retailing** are direct retailing, direct selling, and vending machines.[22]   **Nonstore Retailing**

Direct Retailing. In **direct retailing,** customers first are exposed to merchandise through an impersonal medium and then purchase the merchandise by telephone or mail. The different types of direct retailing are based on the medium they use. The mail is used for direct-mail catalog retailing; television is used for TV home shopping; and computers and cable TV are used for interactive electronic retailing.

A wide variety of products and services are sold directly to customers through impersonal methods. About two-thirds of the direct-mail sales are for merchandise, and one-third are for services. The fastest-growing areas for direct-mail sales are apparel, drugs and vitamins, and sporting goods. Sales of low-cost jewelry and gifts, insurance, food, books, and photo processing are growing more slowly.

While direct retailing involves impersonal contact with consumers, the consumer contact is personal in direct selling. With direct selling, salespeople contact consumers directly or by telephone at home or at work.

Finally, with vending machine retailing, sellers have no direct contact with customers. Here customers purchase and receive merchandise from a machine.

Nonstore retailing offers consumers the convenience of selecting and purchasing merchandise in a location of their choosing. Usually, merchandise is delivered to a location specified by the customer—typically the customer's home. But nonstore retailing transactions often take place at work or at a neighbor's house.[23] These benefits of nonstore retailing appeal to time-conscious consumers and consumers who can't easily go to stores, such as the handicapped, the elderly, mothers with young children, and rural residents.[24]

Nonstore retailing can involve highly personalized services provided by direct selling, in which a salesperson has one-on-one contact with the customer; or it may involve the very impersonal interactions associated with TV home shopping.

While nonstore retailing provides some unique benefits over traditional in-store retailing, it often lacks some important services. For example, direct retailing customers can't see a broad assortment of merchandise, feel the merchandise, try it on, attend sessions on how to use it, or have it altered prior to purchase. The next two sections discuss the types of nonstore retailing in more detail.

Direct catalog retailing. Historically, mail-order retailing was most successful with rural consumers, who lacked ready access to retail stores. With the rise of dual-income families and other people with limited time for shopping in stores, **direct catalog retailing** has grown in popularity with a broad cross section of consumers. About 5 percent of all retail sales are through direct catalog retailing.[25]

Successful direct-mail catalog retailers have sophisticated information, communication, and distribution systems. For example, Lands' End maintains a mailing list of 9 million people, 45 percent of whom have purchased merchandise from the firm in the previous 36 months. In 1995, it mailed out 150 million catalogs, which generated sales of over $1 billion. When customers call the toll-free number to place orders, Lands' End operators can access information about their past purchases and address, making it easier for customers to order. Operators can also access information about merchandise and provide detailed information about measurements for a garment and its fabrication. Ninety percent of all orders are mailed to the customer in 24 hours. If customers don't like their merchandise, they can return it for a cash refund, and Lands' End will pay the return mail costs.[26]

Many store-based retailers use direct mail to complement their in-store retailing efforts. More than half of the top 50 department stores also sell through direct-mail catalogs. For example, in 1995, Bloomingdale's mailed 25 different catalogs to 40 million potential customers. To make a clear and consistent statement, these retailers prefer to offer the same merchandise in their catalogs as in their stores. But they must make some adjustments because direct-mail customers, compared to in-store customers, tend to be younger, have lower income, and buy merchandise at lower price points.[27]

Direct-mail retailers confront some challenging problems.[28] First, costs of paper and third-class mail have been rising 20 to 25 percent per year. Second, it's increasingly hard to capture consumers' attention as they receive more catalogs in their mail each year. Each American household receives an estimated 140 catalogs and newspaper inserts annually.[29] Some direct-mail retailers' misleading and deceptive practices have led to government regulations concerning return policies and notification of delays in delivery. Finally, the length of time required to design, develop, and distribute catalogs makes it difficult for direct-mail retailers to respond quickly to new trends and fashions.

TV home shopping. More than 60 million American consumers now have access to a **TV home shopping** network.[30] The largest are Home Shopping Network and QVC.

In what amounts to a 24-hour commercial, hosts of these cable TV networks demonstrate such items as computers, fur coats, diamond and cubic zirconium jewelry, and porcelain coiled snake ashtrays. Viewers order merchandise by telephone, paying by credit card. Merchandise is delivered to their home within 24 hours.

TV home shopping networks' major problem is that only 20 percent of the potential viewing audience even watches. To enlarge audiences, networks are incorporating entertainment into their programming and are scheduling categories of merchandise for specific times so customers looking for specific merchandise can plan their viewing time.

Interactive electronic retailing. **Interactive electronic retailing** is an electronic system in which customers can engage in two-way communications over cable or telephone lines with a retailer using a TV or computer terminal. The key feature in this retailing format is that systems are interactive. In the Prodigy system, customers use a personal computer and modem to communicate with the database managed by the retailer. Typically, consumers pay a monthly fee to use the system.

Interactive electronic retailing resembles catalog shopping. Unlike with TV home shopping networks, customers determine what they want to see. They don't have to wait for merchandise to be presented on a TV show. While interactive electronic retailing is an exciting new approach, most test systems have been delayed due to technological problems, including poor visual quality of the merchandise presentations.[31] However, these technological problems will eventually be solved. Thus, many major retailers and cable TV and telecommunication companies are forming joint ventures to explore this exciting opportunity.

Direct Selling. In 1995, **direct selling** sales totaled $15.0 billion.[32] The largest categories of merchandise sold through direct selling are cosmetics and fragrances, decorative accessories, vacuum cleaners and other home appliances, cooking and kitchenware, jewelry, food and nutritional products, and encyclopedias and educational materials. About three-quarters of all direct sales are made in the home, with 12 percent made in the workplace, and 8 percent completed over the phone.

Almost all of the 5.5 million salespeople who work in direct sales are independent agents. They aren't employed by the direct sales firm but act as distributors, buying merchandise from the firms and then reselling it to consumers. Eighty percent of the salespeople work part-time (fewer than 30 hours per week). In most cases, direct salespeople may sell their merchandise to anyone. But some companies (such as Avon) assign territories to salespeople who regularly contact each household in their territory.

About 20 percent of all direct sales are made using a party plan system. In a **party plan system,** salespeople encourage people to act as hosts and invite friends or coworkers to a "party" at which the merchandise is demonstrated. The host or hostess receives a gift or commission for arranging the meeting.

Almost two-thirds of all direct sales are made through **multilevel sales networks.** In a multilevel network, people serve as master distributors, recruiting other people to become distributors in their network. The master distributors either buy merchandise from the firm and resell it to their distributors or receive a commission on all merchandise purchased by their distributors.

Vending Machines. Vending machines are machines from which a customer can get food or merchandise after making a payment by cash or credit card. While over $20 billion in goods is sold annually through vending machines in the United States, almost all products sold are hot and cold beverages, food, candy, and cigarettes.[33] Vending machines are used extensively to sell more expensive merchandise in Europe and Japan. For example, it's fashionable for French retailers to have vending machines outside their stores to accommodate their customers 24 hours a day.

Services Retailing

Most retail firms discussed in this section sell tangible products to consumers. There's also considerable growth in **services retailing.** Many organizations that offer services to consumers—such as banks, hospitals, health spas, doctors, legal clinics, entertainment firms, and universities—traditionally haven't considered themselves retailers. Due to increased competition, these organizations are adopting retailing principles to attract customers and satisfy their needs.

Other retailers that offer services for consumers include auto rental companies (Hertz, Avis), auto repair and service stations (Jiffy Lube, Midas), fitness centers (Jazzercise), child care centers (Kindercare, Gymboree), hotels and motels (Holiday Inn, Marriott, Days Inn), home maintenance companies (Chemlawn, Mini Maid, Roto-Rooter), and income tax preparers (H & R Block). Most traditional service retailers offer a limited variety, like a specialty store. Some provide services in the customer's home, while others provide services in shopping centers. Many service retailers are national franchise chains.

Chapter 17 discusses services retailing in more detail.

Small independent retailers compete effectively against large national chains by offering merchandise and service tailored to the needs of their local customers.

TYPES OF OWNERSHIP

The first part of this chapter examined how retailers can be classified in terms of their retail mix (the variety and depth of merchandise and services offered to customers). Another important difference between retailers is ownership. The major types of retail ownership are (1) independent, single-store establishments, (2) corporate chains, and (3) franchises.

Independent, Single-Store Establishments

Over 90 percent of all U.S. retailers own and operate a single store. Yet single-store retailers account for less than 50 percent of all retail store sales.[34] Nevertheless, retailing is one of the few sectors in our economy where entrepreneurship thrives.

In 1992, over 60,000 new retail businesses were started in the United States.[35] Many of these businesses are owner-managed. Thus, management has direct contact with customers and can respond quickly to their needs. Small retailers are also very flexible. They aren't bound by bureaucratic rules that restrict store location or types of merchandise sold.

While single-store retailers can tailor their offering to their customers' needs, corporate chains can more effectively negotiate lower prices for merchandise and advertising due to their larger size. In addition, corporate chains have a broader management base, with people who specialize in specific retail activities. Single-store retailers typically have to rely on owner-managers' capabilities to make the broad range of retail decisions.

Corporate Retail Chains

A **retail chain** consists of multiple retail units under common ownership. It usually has some centralization of decision making in defining and implementing its strategy. Retail chains can range in size from a drugstore with two stores to retailers

Retail Corporations Operating Multiple Chains

Dayton Hudson	**May Department Store**	**Mercantile Stores**
Department store chains	**Company**	**Company**
Dayton's	*Department store chains*	*Department store chains*
Hudson's	L. S. Ayres	Bacons/Root
Marshall Field	Famous-Barr	de Lendrecie's
Mervyn's	Filene's	Hennessey's
Discount store chains	Foley's	Gayfers
Target	Hecht's	Glass Block
	Kaufmann's	The Jones Stores
The Limited	Lord & Taylor	Joslins
Specialty store chains	May California	Lion
Abercrombie & Fitch	May Co. Ohio	Maison Blanche
Bath & Body Works	Meier and Frank	McAlpin
Cacique	Robinson's	J. B. White
Henri Bendel	*Specialty store chain*	
Lane Bryant	Payless Shoe	**TJX Corporation**
Lerner Shops		*Off-price chain*
The Limited	**Melville Corporation**	T.J. Maxx
Limited Express	*Off-price chain*	Winner's Family
Limited Too	Marshall's	Apparel
Structure	*Specialty store chains*	*Specialty store chain*
Victoria's Secret	Accessory Lady	Hit or Miss
Direct mail	Bob's Stores	*Direct mail*
Lane Bryant Direct	Foot Action	Chadwick's
Lerner Direct	Kay-Bee	
Victoria's Secret Catalog	Linens 'N' Things	
	Prints Plus	
	This End Up	
	Thom McAn	
	Wilson's Suede and	
	Leather	

SOURCE: Company annual reports.

with over 1,000 stores such as Safeway, Wal-Mart, Kmart, and J.C. Penney. Fewer than 500 retail chains have over 100 stores, but these chains account for more than 30 percent of the retail store sales in the United States.[36]

While chain stores may have cost advantages over single-store retailers, large retail chains can be very bureaucratic, stifling managers' creativity with excessive rules and procedures. Often, all stores have the same merchandise and services, and individual stores' offerings may be incompatible with local market needs.

Many retail chains are divisions of larger corporations or holding companies. Frequently, these corporations have grown by acquiring retail chains. Exhibit 2–5 lists some chains owned by large retail corporations. Many corporations permit individual chains to operate independently. Other corporations fully integrate acquired chains into the corporation, which includes changing their names.

There has been considerable concern that corporate retail chains will eventually drive independent retailers out of business. For example, Wal-Mart and other discount store chains have pursued a strategy of opening stores on the outskirts of small rural towns with populations between 25,000 and 50,000. These stores offer a broader selection of merchandise at much lower prices than previously available from local retailers. The stores also employ 200 to 300 people from the local community. Due to scale economies and an efficient distribution system, corporate chains can sell at lower prices. This forces some competing local retailers out of business, while altering the community fabric.

But local retailers offering merchandise and services that aren't available at corporate chains can still prosper. When the large discount stores open, more consumers are attracted to the community from surrounding areas.

Franchises

Franchising is a contractual agreement between a franchisor and a franchisee that allows the franchisee to operate a retail outlet using a name and format developed and supported by the franchisor. Approximately one-third of all U.S. retail sales are made by franchisees.[37] Some franchise retail chains are Budget Rent A Car, Ace Hardware, Holiday Inn, 7-Eleven, and Midas.

In a franchise contract, the franchisee pays an annual fee plus a royalty on all sales for the right to operate a store in a specific location. The franchisee also agrees to operate the outlet in accordance with procedures prescribed by the franchisor. The franchisor provides assistance in locating and building the store, developing the products and/or services sold, training managers, and advertising. To maintain the franchise's reputation, the franchisor also makes sure that all outlets provide the same quality of services and products.

The franchising ownership format attempts to combine the advantages of intense manager involvement in owner-managed businesses with the efficiencies of centralized decision making used by chain store operations. Franchisees are motivated to make their store successful because they receive the profits (after paying the royalty). The franchisor is motivated to develop new products and systems and to promote the franchise because the franchisor receives a royalty on all sales. Advertising, product development, and system development are efficiently done by the franchisor, with costs shared by all franchisees.

☼ SUMMARY

This chapter explained different types of retailers and how they compete with different retail mixes to sell merchandise and services to customers. The most useful approach for understanding the retail marketplace is classifying retailers based on their retail mix: the merchandise variety and assortment, services, location, pricing, and promotion decisions made to attract customers.

Over the past 30 years, U.S. retail markets have seen the emergence of many new retail institutions. Traditional institutions (supermarkets, department, discount, and specialty stores) have been joined by category specialists, superstores, convenience stores, home-improvement centers, warehouse clubs, off-price retailers, and catalog showrooms. In addition, nonstore retailing—retailing to customers through direct-mail catalogs, personal selling, TV, interactive electronic retailing, and vending machines—has grown considerably.

Traditional retail institutions have changed in response to these new retailers. For example, department stores have increased their emphasis on fashion-oriented apparel and improved the services they offer. Constantly devising new ways to meet customers' needs is how all retail institutions survive in the competitive world of retailing.

KEY TERMS

assortment, 22
breadth of
  merchandise, 22
catalog showrooms,
  34
category specialists,
  31
closeout retailer, 34
convenience store,
  25
conventional
  supermarket, 25
department store, 27
depth of
  merchandise, 22

direct catalog
  retailing, 35
direct retailing, 35
direct selling, 37
discount store, 30
factory outlet, 34
franchising, 40
general merchandise
  retail store, 27
home-improvement
  center, 32
interactive electronic
  retailing, 36

limited-line
  warehouse
  supermarkets (box
  store), 25
multilevel sales
  networks, 37
nonstore retailing, 35
off-price retailer, 34
outlet store, 34
party plan system, 37
retail chain, 38
retail institution, 21
services retailing, 37
single-price retailer,
  34

SKU (stock keeping
  unit), 22
specialty store, 31
superstore, 25
supercenters, 25
TV home shopping,
  36
variety, 22
vending machine, 37
warehouse club, 33
warehouse
  supermarket, 25

DISCUSSION QUESTIONS AND PROBLEMS

1. What is the difference between retail mixes at traditional discount stores and those at off-price retailers?
2. Give examples of retailers involved in intratype and intertype competition.
3. Why would a retailer such as Bloomingdale's, a fashion-forward upscale department store, want to expand its direct-marketing catalog business?
4. What is the difference between variety and assortment?
5. How can a small independent retailer compete against a corporate chain?
6. Compare and contrast the retail mixes of convenience stores, traditional supermarkets, superstores, and warehouse stores. Can all of these food retail institutions survive over the long run? Why?
7. Some department and specialty store retailers argue that factory outlet stores, such as Ralph Lauren/Polo, compete with their businesses to the point that sales are lost. Others argue that factory outlets don't affect their store sales. Explain the reasons for each position.
8. A chef wants to open an Italian restaurant and plans to do an analysis of the competition. Besides other Italian restaurants in town, what type of retailers might be considered competition for her restaurant?
9. The same brand and model personal computer is sold in specialty computer stores, discount stores, category specialists, and warehouse stores. Each type of retailer offers a different retailing mix for selling the personal computer. Why?
10. Since the 1970s, U.S. department store sales haven't kept pace with overall retail sales growth. Specialty stores, category specialists, and mail-order firms have captured American consumers' interest, reducing traditional department stores' market shares and profits. Will this trend continue and eventually cause the department store as we now know it to become extinct? Why? How might department stores reverse this trend?

The Changing Retail Environment

Customers (3)

Questions that this chapter answers include

- **How are retailers responding to demographic trends like the maturing baby boomers and the emerging baby busters?**
- **How are retailers meeting the needs of time-starved consumers?**
- **How is the green movement affecting retailing?**

Consider the near future, the year 2001. The place: the new Walgreens drugstore in the shopping center next to Blockbuster Video and the Winn-Dixie supermarket. The parking lot is jammed with shoppers hurrying to do some errands and one-stop shopping before they get dinner on the table for their families.

Walgreens' part-time pharmacist is a man in his seventies who retired from his own drugstore a few years ago. He's filling a prescription for a tourist from New Jersey, getting the tourist's prescription information from a Walgreens in the tourist's hometown via satellite. His assistant scans the bar code on the prescription label at the point-of-sale terminal. Walgreens uses this information to update the inventory management system that automatically reorders merchandise and produces a sales receipt.

Some products as well as the store's music are geared to its primarily His-panic-American clientele. Most employees are bilingual; announcements are made in both English and Spanish. The store is readily accessible to the handicapped. Signs use large, easy-to-read lettering; employees are trained to cater to the special needs of the elderly. Walgreens employees are encouraged to participate in civic events and charities. Recycling bins are found in the parking lot.

This Walgreens store has succeeded by anticipating and accommodating the profound demographic trends of today's population. Walgreens understands the ethnic mix, ages, busy lifestyles, and environmental awareness of its customers. The store meets customers' needs using the latest technology.

This chapter (the third of the four in Section I on the world of retailing) describes important recent changes in consumer demographics and values, how they affect demand for retail goods and services, and how retailers have responded to these changes in their customer base.

DEMOGRAPHIC CHANGES THAT AFFECT RETAILING

To be successful, retailers must recognize that their customers are constantly changing. Consider the following:

The number of Americans age 65 and older is expected to more than double in the next 50 years.[1]

In Los Angeles and Miami, Hispanics represent nearly one-third of the population.[2]

Twelve percent of American households are headed by single mothers.[3]

What do these changing **demographics** mean to retailers? All retailers must purchase merchandise, design stores, and train employees with the special needs of older consumers in mind. Recognizing the growing importance and special needs of certain ethnic groups is also imperative in many markets. Finally, due to the rise of both dual-income couples and single mothers, people have less leisure time than in previous decades. As a result, they're spending more time at home, creating demand for new types of products and services. This section examines these and other demographic changes that affect demand for retailers' merchandise and services.

Changes in Age Distribution

As America ages, retailers are devising new strategies to meet the needs of value-conscious consumers in every age bracket—from market-savvy twenty-somethings to their baby boomer parents to mature customers interested in travel and luxury items.

The Youth Population. Due to falling birth rates during the 1960s and 1970s, there are fewer young people in the United States today than 10 years ago, and this trend will continue. Although the youth market is becoming relatively small, retailers consider its purchasing potential to be strong. Today's children have baby boomer parents. They're members of families with a smaller number of children than in the past, and probably live in a two-income or single-parent household. Children often have a relatively large disposable income, have influence over their parents' purchases, and, possibly most important, are a future market for all goods and services.[4]

Specialty retailers have realized the gigantic opportunity to sell goods to children and their baby boomer parents. Probably the most successful retailer to target this group is Toys "R" Us, the supermarket for toys.

The Baby Busters. The next-oldest group is the **baby busters,** also known as twentysomethings and Generation X.[5] They are children of the baby boomers discussed

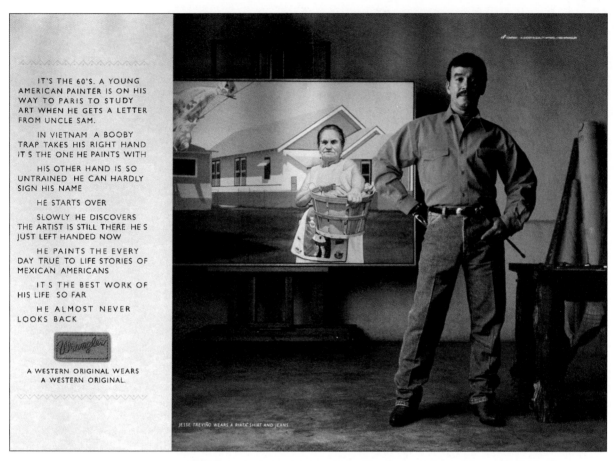

IT'S THE 60'S. A YOUNG AMERICAN PAINTER IS ON HIS WAY TO PARIS TO STUDY ART WHEN HE GETS A LETTER FROM UNCLE SAM.

IN VIETNAM A BOOBY TRAP TAKES HIS RIGHT HAND IT S THE ONE HE PAINTS WITH

HIS OTHER HAND IS SO UNTRAINED HE CAN HARDLY SIGN HIS NAME

HE STARTS OVER

SLOWLY HE DISCOVERS THE ARTIST IS STILL THERE HE S JUST LEFT HANDED NOW

HE PAINTS THE EVERY DAY TRUE TO LIFE STORIES OF MEXICAN AMERICANS

IT S THE BEST WORK OF HIS LIFE SO FAR

HE ALMOST NEVER LOOKS BACK

A WESTERN ORIGINAL WEARS A WESTERN ORIGINAL.

This ad for Wrangler supports several consumer trends: relaxed fit jeans are popular with middle-aged Americans (baby boomers) who are less trim than they once were; Americans with physical handicaps and minorities are popularly featured in mainstream advertising; "old-fashioned" values of back-to-basics are the trend.

in the next section. Baby busters were born between 1965 and 1976 and represent some 41 million Americans. This group is very different from their baby boomer parents. For instance, they're the first generation that has had so many **latchkey children** (those who grew up in homes where both parents worked) and over 50 percent of their parents' marriages ended in divorce. Baby busters are more likely than their parents were to be unemployed. They live at home longer and stay single longer than their parents did, which leads to frustration among many busters. Furthermore, busters have different values, shopping habits, and income levels than their parents.

Although the busters are a group in disarray, they possess considerable spending power. However, they're much less interested in shopping than their parents. Busters tend to spend their disposable income on items such as CDs, stereos, sneakers, clothing, beer, and cosmetics. Busters are also considered to be astute consumers, more cynical than baby boomers. They're more likely to disbelieve advertising claims and what salespeople tell them. Busters developed shopping savvy at an early age because many grew up in dual-career households where their parents didn't have much time for shopping. As a result, many baby busters learned at

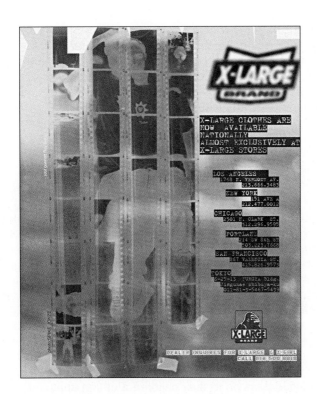

X-Large Stores project a streetwise image that will appeal to baby busters.

an early age how to make shopping decisions, so they grew more knowledgeable about products and more risk-averse than other shoppers.

To effectively target the valuable baby buster market, many companies have revised their ad campaigns to adapt to the more knowledgeable, cynical 18- to 29-year-old. Today's retailers of athletic shoes, cosmetics, fashion, and fast food (who flourish because of busters) are making their ads more candid, while not pushing the product too hard on the customer.

Many retailers have found success by focusing on **green marketing** to lure environmentally conscious busters. Measures such as recycling, discontinuing the use of Styrofoam boxes, and donating money to save the rain forests are examples of green marketing.

The Aging Baby Boomers. After World War II, the birth rate rose sharply, giving rise to a group known as the **baby boomers**—the 76 million Americans born between 1946 and 1964.[6] Today this group is relatively large, economically comfortable, and well educated.

Although significant in size and wealth, aging baby boomers pose significant challenges to retailers. First, unlike busters, they don't need to make those first-time purchases of furniture, appliances, or business attire. Further, as people reach middle age, they're thought to become less materialistic. For instance, The Sharper Image based its success in the 1980s on providing expensive toys to **yuppies** (*y*oung *u*rban *p*rofessionals). In the 1990s, it had to redefine its merchandising strategy to provide more practical products and lower price points.

Baby boomers are also hard to reach through advertising and promotion. Boomers will pay more attention to ads' images and text if they subtly portray the image that the retailer wishes to project. For example, Kmart's TV ad campaign doesn't simply outline the benefits of shopping at Kmart. Instead, the ad shows ordinary people discussing the good prices and selection. Rather than saying that Kmart stores are equipped to accommodate the disabled or that they welcome all types of people, the ad conveys this information indirectly with the actors it uses.

Boomers are going to be less likely than previous generations of older people to believe that they have to think or act a certain way. They'll also be more active and youth-oriented than older people in the past. Even though boomers have an orientation toward home (known as *cocooning,* which is described later in this chapter), they still get out to exercise and are interested in health, fitness, and proper nutrition. Retailers of sportswear, athletic equipment, and healthful foods all benefit from this trend.

Silver Streakers: The Older Population. Also referred to as *empty nesters, the gray market, prime-of-lifers, jitterbugs, pioneers of leisure,* and *WOOFS* (*well-off older folks*), the 50-and-over age group isn't ready to be put out to pasture yet.[7] The oldest group of baby boomers is already over 50, and their numbers are growing. But are they an important market segment for retailers to pursue? The American Association of Retired Persons (AARP) reports that compared to other age groups, older consumers are more likely to complain, to need special attention, to take time browsing before making a purchase, and to dislike changes. On the other hand, the 65-plus age group is the fastest-growing age category. They have time to shop and money to spend.

In the past, silver streakers were very conservative with their savings. They wanted something to pass on to their children. But that attitude is changing. Older people seem to be buying goods and services at the same pace as their boomer children. How do they spend this money? Travel, second homes, luxury cars, electronic equipment, investments, home furnishings, clothing, and gifts are frequent purchases.

Silver streakers like "made in the U.S." items, natural fibers, recognizable brand names (but generally not designer labels), value, quality, and classic styles. They're loyal and willing to spend, but are extremely quality conscious and demand hassle-free shopping. Most mature customers prefer to buy a few high-quality items rather than a larger number of low-quality items. Convenience is a major consideration. The majority agree that they would pay more for the same merchandise if it were offered closer to home. They also don't like long checkout lines—but who does?

Some retailers have created special programs for mature customers. Many Kmart stores, for example, offer an annual "seniors-only shopping spree" one day each December. On that day, the store opens for special shopping hours just for senior citizens and provides gift selection counseling, free gift wrapping, mailing services, and other specials.

REFACT

Silver streakers are an important market for retailers because twice as many of their household dollars are open for discretionary spending as for persons aged 25 to 35.[8]

Increasing Ethnic Diversity

America is becoming more ethnically diverse as immigration increases and minority birth rates rise.[9] Minorities now represent about a quarter of the population; by 2010 they will represent about a third. Some retailers are correctly focusing on the growing number of middle-class and affluent minority customers.

African-Americans. African-Americans represent about 12.3 percent of the U.S. population.[10] Although their household income is slightly lower than white consumers', they spend about 5 percent more than whites on an average trip to a mall. In fact, they're some retailers' best customers. For instance, African-Americans spend 75 percent more per capita than other groups on boys' clothing, but 1 percent less than whites on girls' clothing. They also spend almost twice as much as other groups for TV, appliance, and furniture rentals.

Retailers have seized the opportunity to directly target African-Americans. For instance, J.C. Penney has opened boutiques that sell authentic African clothing, housewares, and art. Kmart and Toys "R" Us have used minority advertising agencies to develop campaigns designed specifically for African-American customers. In Atlanta, the South DeKalb Mall has repositioned itself as an "Afrocentric retail center." Several retailers in the mall have tried to orient their goods to African-Americans. Camelot Music more than doubled its selection of gospel, jazz, and rhythm and blues. Foot Locker stocks styles that do well in African-American markets, such as suede and black athletic shoes and baseball shirts from the Negro League of the 1930s. Re-Tale 3–1 examines how Z-Mart has targeted the African-American consumer.

Hispanic-Americans. There is a lot of interest in the Hispanic market. Hispanic-Americans make up over 9 percent of the U.S. population and will grow another third over the next 10 years. Hispanic households tend to be larger than other households. Forty-one percent of Hispanic households have annual incomes of at least $25,000. Importantly, there's little difference in education, employment, and income between whites and Hispanics who were born in the United States or have lived here at least five years. The Hispanic market is particularly large in certain states

REFACT

One out of seven Californians speaks a language other than English at home.[11]

RE-TALE 3-1   Z-Mart Succeeds in an Ethnic Niche

One successful retailer in ethnic markets is Z-Mart, a Miami-based, African-American–owned discount store that caters predominantly to African-Americans. The store was established by three former Ames/Zayre executives who reopened a Zayre store in an area where the customer base is 95 percent African- and Hispanic-American, and where 65 percent of the clientele are on welfare. To most, this may not seem like a great opportunity, but it proved successful for Z-Mart.

The store attempts to keep prices low, while targeting fashions toward African-American customers. Z-Mart offers a great deal of clothing for church-going African-American women who prefer more dressy dresses with accessories than white customers do. By carrying fine jewelry and dress shoes at reasonable prices, Z-Mart has developed a merchandising niche.

During holidays such as Easter and Christmas, Z-Mart operates differently than other retailers. At Easter-time, the store increases its selection of boys' suits and women's dresses and hats. Furthermore, it brings these items into inventory about a week later during these periods because African-American customers tend to purchase closer to the actual holiday. This also leads to a shorter selling season for Christmas toys due to financial concerns of Z-Mart's lower-income customers.

Posters and pictures (such as one of Dr. Martin Luther King, Jr.) convey Z-Mart's ethnic theme. Musically, Z-Mart emphasizes gospel and dance more than other stores.

Overall, African-Americans tend to spend about 30 percent more on hair care products than whites. Thus, Z-Mart carries ethnic brands of hair products and stocks cosmetics in dark shades to accommodate African- and Hispanic-American women.

To reach its target market, Z-Mart advertises on radio as well as in the African-American–owned *Miami Times* newspaper. Furthermore, Z-Mart maintains a presence in the community by taking part in festivals, functions, and holiday celebrations. By realizing ethnic markets' vast potential, Z-Mart has flourished simply by adjusting to the needs of its customer base. Minorities and ethnic groups represent a powerful market that shouldn't be ignored. Through minority marketing, need recognition, and demographic understanding, other companies too can succeed in this market.

SOURCE: "Z-Mart Taps Ethnic Offerings," *Discount Store News.* Reprinted by permission from DISCOUNT STORE NEWS (May 18, 1992). Copyright Lebhar-Friedman, Inc., 425 Park Avenue, New York, NY 10022.

and cities, such as California, Arizona, New Mexico, Texas, Miami, New York City, and Chicago.

Asian-Americans. Although Asian-Americans comprise only about 3 percent of the U.S. population, they're the fastest-growing minority population. They also earn more, have more schooling, and are more likely to be professionally employed or to own a business than whites.

The Aberdeen Centre near Vancouver, British Columbia, Canada, has targeted the large Asian market in its area. Nearly 80 percent of the merchants and customers are Chinese-Canadians. The mall has shops with Hong Kong-made clothing and traditional Chinese medicines. Chinese movies, kung fu martial arts demonstrations, and Chinese folk dances help make this mall an important destination for its customers.

Changes in Income Distribution

Income distribution in the United States is becoming more polarized; the highest-income groups are growing, while some middle- and lower-income groups' real purchasing power is declining. Polarization of income has helped to polarize retail institutions. Many retailers have targeted upscale customers, while others have found success with middle- and lower-income groups.

Targeting the Upscale Customer. In 1980, only about 10 percent of U.S. families earned over $50,000, but the number, in constant dollars, is projected to be about 20 percent by 1995. This represents nearly 15 million families.[11] The increase in high-income families is due to the maturing of the population, the increase in dual-income households, and higher levels of education.

Retailers have adjusted their market strategies to meet the needs of the better-educated, high-income customer. Some middle-market retailers—particularly specialty stores—have upgraded their stores and merchandise. The Williams Sonoma chain of cooking utensil stores, for instance, caters specifically to upscale customers. Re-Tale 3–2 describes one of the most upscale retailers in the world, Hermès.

Targeting the Mass Middle and Lower-Income Markets. The 1980s were the heyday for upscale retailers. Many department stores, including J.C. Penney, upgraded their stores and merchandise. But the 1990s are different. Notably, Penney has scaled back its fashion image by searching for products offering customers better **value**— more quality for less money. The mass middle and lower-income markets are more appealing today than ever before. The lower-income market represents consumers with household incomes below $25,000, whereas the mass middle market includes households with incomes between $25,000 and $50,000.

Why are customers searching for value more today than in recent decades? For the first three decades after World War II, most American families experienced real income growth. But in the late 1970s and 1980s, that growth began to stagnate. Family incomes have stayed slightly ahead of inflation, while health care costs, property taxes, and tuition bills have risen much faster than inflation. To compound the problem of income stagnation, the recession and resulting increased unemployment of the late 1980s have lasted into the 1990s, profoundly affecting both consumers and retailers.

For example, where does a customer go if she's unable or unwilling to spend $100 for a skirt and blouse by Liz Claiborne in a department store—especially if she wants better service and a nicer shopping environment than she would find in most

RE-TALE 3-2   Hermès Prospers with Upscale Customer Niche

In this era of outlet malls and warehouse stores, one company that has thrived by targeting the upscale customer is Hermès-Paris. Hermès is a unique corporation, one that has differentiated from others by turning away from automation and mass production, using "old-world" techniques of craftsmanship to manufacture its products. This concept has stood the test of time.

Hermès-Paris has flourished since 1837 due to the generations of artisans who create by hand every product Hermès sells. Hermès has over 250 stores around the world, and its products can be found in 10 boutiques in the United States. Along with Neiman Marcus, which carries its scarves and ties, there are 12 Boutique du Monde d'Hermès (stores within a store) throughout the United States.

Hermès' target market is the classic-minded, affluent, upscale consumer concerned with quality, durability, and elegance. Although its target market is minuscule compared to the likes of Wal-Mart, Hermès still generates worldwide sales of over $400 million a year—a number always on the rise.

Hermès products are some of the most expensive of their kind in the world, with handbags selling for $3,000 to $10,000, saddles for over $3,000, and silk shirts for over $1,500. There are waiting lists for its $115 scarf-print ties and $245 scarves. But these prices don't seem to stop a loyal clientele. At times during the Christmas season in Paris, a scarf is sold every 20 seconds.

Why are its products so expensive? The scarves, for instance, begin with raw silk from China. It may take up to two and one-half years from design conception until the actual finished scarf is in the store. Scarves are silk-screened with up to 35 screens used to produce one design, as each color is printed separately. Once the scarf is nearly finished, the edges are hand rolled and hemmed by a group of only 80 *abeilles* who take an average of 30 minutes on each scarf.

Hermès operates differently than nearly all other retailers in the world. It has proven that success is possible without succumbing to automation or mass production. Positive word of mouth, fine workmanship, and reputation account for this success.

SOURCE: Corporate sources.

Hermès-Paris has flourished by catering to a minuscule but affluent market of upscale customers that is drawn to fine craftsmanship regardless of price. The Hermès scarf, priced at $250, sells like hotcakes at Christmastime.

discount stores? Leaders servicing the mass middle market include J.C. Penney, Mervyn's, Kohl's, and Charming Shoppes. Clearly, in the discount store arena, Wal-Mart, Kmart, and Target are the stores of choice.

Decline of Household Managers

When baby boomers were growing up in the 1950s and 1960s, it was common for women to be at home raising a family. That scenario has changed! More women are working, and more households are headed by single women. Teenagers and men have taken on more household responsibilities, including purchasing groceries. Unfortunately, women's changing role in the family coupled with the career pressures of all adults have resulted in a society that's short on time. These changes have created significant opportunities for retailers, however. Let's look at the changing women's market and the implications for our time-poor society.

The Changing Women's Market. From cars to copiers, from sweaters to sweeteners, women make the majority of purchasing decisions and influence most of the rest.[12] For instance, they purchase about 80 percent of men's merchandise in department stores and over 50 percent of merchandise bought at Home Depot. Further, women now head almost 30 percent of American households. Clearly, the working women's segment is a large, complex, and lucrative market for retailers.

Many working women now have more disposable income than women in earlier generations, and they're spending it in new ways. Charles Lazarus, founder and CEO of Toys "R" Us, feels one reason for his business's success is that working mothers now buy toys throughout the year because they feel guilty about not being home with their children. Women are also spending more money on themselves for luxury items like jewelry and watches.

The Time-Poor Society. When both husband and wife work while raising a family, leisure time is in short supply. In the past, shopping provided an opportunity for social interaction and entertainment. Today, shopping takes time away from other activities that many customers either must do or would prefer to do. To succeed in this environment, retailers may adopt some of the following strategies.

Be available when the customer needs you. Specifically, retailers should stay open longer and provide higher levels of service. For instance, Safeway advertises that it restocks its produce twice a day—morning and afternoon—so workers can shop after work and still buy fresh produce.

Provide alternatives to store visits. Nonstore retailing has expanded in many directions, as described in Chapter 2. Major retailers such as J.C. Penney and Neiman Marcus have expanded their use of catalogs. Although some are struggling, TV home shopping stations and interactive electronic retailing networks such as Prodigy provide time-saving alternatives to shopping in stores.

Improve customer service. Many retailers recognize the opportunity to serve the short-on-time customer by providing strong customer service. For instance, many department stores are again attempting to provide the benefits that originally attracted customers to their stores. Department stores such as Nordstrom and Neiman Marcus have lately refocused their attention on customer service by using more full-time salespeople and offering higher compensation to attract better staff. Some discount and off-price retailers now provide services formerly reserved for their more upscale competition. Most now accept credit cards, have salespeople in some departments such as consumer electronics and jewelry, and offer **layaway** (a method of deferred payment in which a store holds merchandise for a customer until it's completely paid for). Wal-Mart employs a **greeter** (a person who greets customers when they enter the store and provides information and/or assistance).

Another strategy for improving customer service is to empower salespeople to make decisions. Customers don't like to wait for authorization for check approval

---

ℛ ℰ ℱ ℛ ℂ Ⴀ

In 1995, 80 percent of women age 25 to 44 will be working—80 percent of them full-time.

ℛ ℰ ℱ ℛ ℂ Ⴀ

In 1988, the average consumer spent 90 minutes on a mall shopping trip, compared to 68 minutes by 1991.[12]

or merchandise returns. Retailers from Montgomery Ward to Neiman Marcus authorize sales associates to make these decisions without managerial approval.

Give information. Providing customers with important information can reduce their shopping time. Many specialty stores keep track of their good customers' sizes and preferences so that they can call customers when appropriate merchandise arrives. Some fashion stores, like Saks Fifth Avenue, offer personal shoppers who can help speed the decision process. These fashion consultants may even meet with customers in their home or office.

Automate processes. Automated selling or service processes can help customers save time. For instance, A&P, Shop Rite, and Publix are experimenting with automated grocery checkout systems that reduce waiting time in checkout lines.

Offer opportunities for one-stop shopping. Finally, retailers should offer customers opportunities to make multiple purchases in one location. For instance, grocery stores are experimenting with videotape rentals and branches of traditional banks within their stores.[13]

CHANGES IN CONSUMER VALUES

The previous section examined retail customers' changing demographic makeup. As a result of these changes and other environmental factors, consumer values also are changing. For instance, certain demographic groups (notably baby boomers and their children, the baby busters) respond well to retailers with a strong social consciousness and commitment to the environment. Dual-income families and older Americans appear to be searching for convenience and value. This section examines changing consumer values and retailers' reactions to them.

Social Consciousness

Retailers and their employees play an important role in their communities. For example, Target contributes 5 percent of sales back to the community. Also, because nutrition is so vital in everyone's life, many fast-food retailers have added healthier items to their menus and make nutritional information readily available. Re-Tale 3–3 illustrates how one famous retailer has created a mutually beneficial relationship between itself and society.

Environmental Sensitivity. Green marketing is a strategic focus by retailers and their vendors on supplying customers with environmentally friendly merchandise.[14] Retailers are implementing green marketing in a variety of ways:

- Safeway has taken out full-page ads in local papers to promote "Environmental Options." The program includes specially designed shelf signs that identify environmentally safe products and explain their environmental benefits. Safeway sells (at cost) a durable reusable cloth shopping bag to carry heavy groceries. Safeway and other California supermarkets are also promoting recycling by offering five cents to customers who return any large bag to reuse in packaging their groceries.
- Wal-Mart has challenged its vendors to provide more environmentally safe products. For example, to cut down on waste, it had Procter & Gamble package merchandise like Sure deodorant without a box. Products that benefit the environment are promoted through shelf labels and store signage. Wal-Mart

RE-TALE 3-3   America's Hamburger Helper

As Ray Kroc, founder of McDonald's, said, "If you are going to take money out of a community, give something back. It's only good business."

When the smoke cleared after mobs burned through South Central Los Angeles in April 1992, hundreds of businesses (many owned by African-Americans) had been destroyed. Yet not a single McDonald's restaurant had been torched. Within hours after the curfew was lifted, every South Central McDonald's was open, feeding firefighters, police, and National Guard troops as well as burned-out citizens.

For Edward H. Rensi, president and CEO of McDonald's U.S.A., the explanation of what happened—or didn't happen—was simple: "Our businesses there are owned by African-American entrepreneurs, who hired African-American managers, who hired African-American employees, who served everybody in the community, whether they be Korean, African-American, or Caucasian."

SOURCE: Edwin M. Reingold, "America's Hamburger Helper," *Time*, June 29, 1992, pp. 66–67.

Patagonia and The Body Shop both appeal to consumers in part due to their environmental sensitivity.

also includes "green" information in its monthly flyers and has an extensive recycling program.

- To reduce the number of trees that are harvested for Christmas and then abandoned, Ikea rents live Christmas trees for $10 with a $10 deposit.

Return to Traditional Values

Value, home, family, back-to-the-basics—these are consequences of many demographic changes discussed earlier in this chapter. Stagnation in real household income growth coupled with a serious recession from the late 1980s into the 1990s has caused several value changes among customers. As discussed earlier, people are looking for better value—more for a lot less—in everything they purchase. For instance, basic clothing (made popular by The Gap, L.L. Bean, and others) is fashionable again. People are also spending more time in their homes with their families—a boon to retailers specializing in home entertainment and home furnishings.[15]

The Value-Oriented Customer. Offering better value has been an important tactic for a variety of companies in recessionary times. For example, during the 1980s, J.C. Penney became more fashion-forward and higher priced, as it pushed more national brands like Oshkosh B'Gosh and Levi's. But in the early 1990s, it returned to its moderately priced roots. The shift in strategy appears to be working.

In their search for bargains, value-oriented customers often sacrifice the perceived safety of purchasing national brands for merchandise offered on sale, through coupons, or by manufacturers' rebates. (See Chapter 10.) Special promotions (such as frequent shopper plans, Discover Card cumulative discounts, magazine subscriptions, gifts, and sweepstakes) are expected to become even more popular in the future.

When they're not out searching for bargains, today's consumers are increasingly turning to the nice, safe, familiar environment of their homes to spend their precious leisure time. This phenomenon, known as **cocooning,** is due to (1) a return to traditional values, (2) families having children later in life, and (3) individuals' time-consciousness. Cocooning means strong markets for VCRs, home computers, stereo systems, security systems, answering machines, and other products used in the home. Restaurants and supermarkets are offering home delivery and gourmet prepared foods.

During the 1980s and into the 1990s, America has seen much of its dominance in manufacturing move offshore. Products ranging from clothing and shoes to computers are made elsewhere, causing a loss of jobs and income for Americans. This has caused a "buy American" backlash. Some retailers (notably Penney and Wal-Mart) have seized the opportunity to promote this national furor. Approximately 65 percent of Penney merchandise is purchased from domestic manufacturers. Although every effort is made to buy American products, ultimately the firm buys merchandise that best meets customers' needs.

Some experts believe, however, that consumers have more important priorities in purchasing a product than its country of origin. In the apparel industry, at least, many believe that availability, appearance, style, color, fashion, fabric, fit, quality, brand, and especially cost are more important to consumers than where the garment was made.

The Made-in-America Controversy

REFACT

Forty percent of U.S. shoppers believe it's best to buy American-made products, regardless of product quality.[16]

 ## RETAILERS' RESPONSE TO THEIR CHANGING CUSTOMERS

Retailers are reacting to fundamental customer changes. In recent years, retailers have embraced new cost-effective technologies enabling them to offer better customer value.

One important innovation is the **quick-response (QR) inventory management system,** a cooperative effort between a retailer and a vendor to reduce the lead time for receiving merchandise. QR lowers inventory investment, improves customer service, and reduces distribution expenses. Here's how it works. Sales information is collected at the store and transmitted computer-to-computer to

Many consumers look for the "Made in America" label but make their purchase decision considering other factors, such as style, quality, and price.

buyers, distribution centers, and then to vendors, who in turn quickly ship replenishment merchandise. Many major retailers—including Wal-Mart, Dillard's, and J.C. Penney—use QR programs. QR is discussed in Chapter 6.

Another technological innovation is **satellite communication networks.** It's hard for corporate headquarters of large retail chains like Penney and Wal-Mart to communicate with hundreds of stores all over the country. Therefore, these and many other retailers have installed headquarters-to-store satellite communications networks. Buyers can present merchandise to store managers. Salespeople can participate in training and product knowledge seminars via satellite. Store management can have "face-to-face" meetings with the home office to resolve problems and answer questions on topics ranging from merchandise to personnel.

A third new technology is **video selling systems,** which are used in stores to present commercials, disseminate coupons, list items on sale, and provide customers with useful shopping information, such as how to get a refund or have film developed. Currently one of the most sophisticated video selling systems is the Innovis Design Center. This custom computer system sells merchandise at home centers by helping people design do-it-yourself projects like backyard patio decks. With the help of a salesperson, the customer answers a series of questions and sketches the project on a control pad with a button and ball. A three-dimensional image emerges, giving the user a view from all sides. Once the design is finished, the computer provides a list of needed materials and total cost based on the store's price structure. If the price seems too high, the user can go back into the system and scale down the project.

A second important response of retailers to their changing customer base is the continued growth of newer types of retailers. As we discussed in Chapter 2, the value-oriented customer will continue to seek out power retailers, warehouse stores, and off-price retailers.

Finally, due to shifting demographics, retailers' labor pool is changing. As we noted earlier in this chapter, there are fewer young people and more women in the workplace now than before. Many retail jobs traditionally have been staffed by young people. But to adjust to the smaller youth labor pool, retailers are having to do a better job of marketing positions to youth and are also pursuing the older population. Retailers are also accommodating the large number of working couples in the labor force by providing reasonably priced child care and flexible working hours (flextime).

☼ SUMMARY

Not many years ago, customers had relatively few choices. They could choose among department and specialty stores for clothing, appliances, and home furnishings; discount stores for housewares, tools, and bargain clothing; grocery stores for food; and convenience stores for a candy bar or pack of cigarettes. Successful retailers in the 1990s have adapted to changes in their customer base and have improved their previous offerings. Others have opened new retail formats.

Some retailers target the affluent but small youth market; others concentrate on older groups. Yet one of the hardest groups to reach is the baby busters—those born between 1965 and 1976. As the United States becomes more ethnically diverse, and assorted ethnic groups grow larger and more economically viable, many retailers are developing specific marketing programs aimed at minority consumers. The number of women in the work force and the fact that they make the majority of purchasing decisions provide interesting challenges to retailers. To meet upscale, dual-income, well-educated, time-poor customers' needs, department and specialty stores have rediscovered how to provide excellent service. Retailers that offer mail-order catalogs and those that specialize in products that can be used at home (like videocassettes and gourmet food) are prospering as customers spend their limited leisure time at home (cocooning).

Retailers are also responding to changes in consumer values. Many have found that displaying a strong social consciousness is good not only for society, but also for business. Many have had to adjust to customers with lower real incomes than previous generations enjoyed. A world recession from the late 1980s into the 1990s has exacerbated the situation. Retailers who've developed strategies to attract and maintain more price-sensitive, value-oriented customers have survived. Many people react positively to a "made in America" promotional theme, though some don't care where their merchandise is made. Successful retailers have stayed abreast of these consumer attitude trends and have found ways to benefit from them.

KEY TERMS

baby boomers, 45	latchkey children, 44	satellite communication network, 54	value, 48
baby busters, 43	layaway, 50		video selling system, 54
cocooning, 53	QR (quick-response) inventory management system, 53	silver streakers, 46	yuppies, 45
demographics, 43		time-poor society, 50	
green marketing, 45			
greeter, 50			

DISCUSSION QUESTIONS AND PROBLEMS

1. Explain the dramatic changes in the women's market over the past 25 years. Discuss various business strategies that could be useful for targeting this group.
2. In many ways, baby busters have changed the face of retailing. How do baby busters differ from baby boomers? How can retailers that once catered to boomers alter their marketing strategy to appeal to busters?
3. Retailers often go out of business in a recession. How could a retail manager keep the business in the black until times improve?
4. Cocooning is a direct result of America's time-poor society. Explain cocooning. What strategies can retailers use to cater to time-poor customers?
5. Retailers involved in home furnishings are expected to enjoy significant growth over the next 10 years. What demographic changes may account for increased sales of products such as refrigerators?
6. Companies such as Chem Lawn that provide lawn care services (e.g., planting, feeding, and general lawn care) experienced tremendous growth during the 1980s and are expected to grow more throughout the 1990s. How do such companies benefit consumers, and what markets are they targeting?
7. Assume that Kmart is opening three new locations in the New York City area. Location A's area is 75 percent African-American. Location B's trade area is 80 percent Hispanic; of those, half are Cuban and half are Mexican. Location C is in Chinatown. How can Kmart target each ethnic group in each area? Discuss potential marketing problems.
8. To remain competitive, retailers and their employees must play an important part in their communities at both local and national levels. Give examples of how various companies can give back to the community and respond to America's environmental concerns.

Customer Buying Behavior

Customers (4)

Questions that this chapter answers include

- **What steps do customers go through as they decide on a store and then buy merchandise?**
- **What factors influence the customer's buying process?**
- **How can retailers get customers to visit their store more frequently and buy more merchandise during each visit?**
- **How do retailers segment markets?**

T he two elements at the core of the world of retailing are competitors and customers. The various types of retail competitors were reviewed in Chapter 2. This chapter focuses on retail customers.

Retail management decisions are based on understanding customer needs and buying behavior. Chapter 3 outlined broad trends in consumer behavior, such as the aging population and the growth in two-income families, and showed how retailers are reacting to these trends. This chapter focuses on needs and buying behavior of individual customers and market segments. It describes the steps customers go through to purchase merchandise and the factors that influence the buying process. Then retailers' actions are related to aspects of the buying process.[1]

TYPES OF BUYING PROCESSES

Exhibit 4–1 describes how Tom Jackson, a typical retail customer, bought a new suit. Such purchases typically involve several steps. The **buying process** begins when customers recognize an unsatisfied need. Then they seek information about how to satisfy the need: what products might be useful and where they can be bought. Customers evaluate the various stores where the desired products are available and then choose one to visit. This visit provides more information and may alert customers to additional needs. After evaluating the store's merchandise, customers may make a purchase or go to another store to collect more information. Eventually, customers make a purchase, use the product, and then decide whether the product satisfies their needs.

The previous discussion focuses on stores, but customers also use catalogs and TV home shopping networks to shop. Even when customers purchase from nonstore retailers, they go through a similar buying process. The information search, product evaluation, and product selection steps occur while the customer is looking through a catalog or watching a TV program rather than shopping in a retail store. Re-Tale 4–1 describes a new technology that enables consumers to experience a shopping trip in their home.

In some situations customers like Tom spend time and effort selecting a store and evaluating the merchandise, while in other situations buying decisions are made

EXHIBIT 4–1   **Tom Jackson Buys a New Suit**

Tom Jackson, at Cal State–Long Beach in southern California, is beginning to interview for jobs. For the first interviews on campus, Tom plans to wear the blue suit his parents bought him three years ago.

But when he looks at his suit, he realizes that it's not very stylish and that the jacket is beginning to show signs of wear. Wanting to make a good first impression during his interview, he decides to buy a new suit. Tom likes to shop at Structures and The Gap, but neither sells business suits. He remembers an ad in the *Los Angeles Times* for men's suits at The Broadway, a regional department store chain. He decides to go to The Broadway store in the mall close to his apartment and asks his friend, Deion, to come along. Tom values Deion's opinion because Deion is a real clothes horse and has good taste.

Walking through the store, they see some Perry Ellis suits. Tom looks at them briefly and decides they're too expensive for his budget and too stylish. He wants to interview with banks and thinks he needs a more conservative suit.

Tom and Deion are approached by a salesperson in the men's department. After asking Tom what type of suit he wants and his size, the salesperson shows him three suits. Tom asks Deion what he thinks about the suits and then selects one to try on. When Tom comes out of the dressing room, he feels that the shoulders in the suit just don't look right, but Deion and the salesperson think the suit is attractive. Tom decides to buy the suit after another customer in the store tells him he looks very professional in it.

Tom doesn't have a Broadway charge card, so he asks if he can pay with a personal check. The salesperson says yes, but the store also takes Visa and MasterCard. Tom decides to pay with his Visa card.

As the salesperson walks with Tom and Deion to the cash register, they pass a display of shirts and ties. The salesperson stops, picks up a shirt and tie, and holds them against the suit to show Tom how good they look together. Tom decides to buy the shirt and tie also.

quickly, with little thought. Three types of customer decision making are extended problem solving, limited problem solving, and habitual decision making.

Customers spend considerably more time and effort when they feel their purchase decision involves a lot of risk and uncertainty.[2] There are many types of risks. Financial risks arise when customers purchase an expensive product. Physical risks

Extended Problem Solving

RE-TALE 4-1   Taking a Shopping Trip in Your Living Room

Imagine going shopping simply by turning on your computer or TV. The store—its aisles, display racks, and shelves—appear on your screen. As you "walk" down the aisle using a computer mouse, you scan the products on the shelves. You "reach" over, pick up a product, rotate it, and bring it closer to read the fine print on the package. Price, order, and delivery information appear on the screen so you can purchase the product without leaving your home. In mid-1995, Time Warner cable company and US West started a test market for a virtual reality home shopping system in Orlando, Florida, and Omaha, Nebraska.

SOURCE: Arthur Marches, "Virtual Shopping Virtually Here," *Discount Store News,* January 3, 1994, pp. 1, 46.

With the interactive home shopping system developed by Professor Ray Burke at the Harvard Business School, customers use a control box to "pick" a box of cereal off the shelf, bring it closer, rotate it to look at the label, and "put" it in a shopping cart if they want to buy it.

are important when customers feel a product may affect their health or safety. Social risks arise when customers believe a product will influence how others view them.

The buying process is more involved when customers are shopping to satisfy an important need, or when they have little knowledge about the product or service. Due to high risk and uncertainty in these situations, customers engage in extended problem solving. They devote considerable time and effort to searching for information and evaluating alternatives. Customers go beyond their personal knowledge to consult with friends, family members, or experts. They may visit several retail stores before making a purchase decision.

Customers in *extended problem-solving* situations often have limited information about the available alternatives and what factors to consider in evaluating them. Retailers, therefore, can influence such decisions by providing the necessary information in a manner that customers can understand and easily use. For example, retailers whose customers engage in extended problem solving may provide brochures describing their merchandise and its specifications, have informational displays in their stores (such as a sofa cut in half to show its construction), and use salespeople to present the merchandise and answer questions.

Limited Problem Solving

When customers have had some prior experience with the products or service and their risk is moderate, they engage in *limited problem solving.* These customers tend to rely more on personal knowledge than on external information. They don't engage in extensive evaluation of alternatives. They usually choose a store they've shopped at before and select merchandise they've bought in the past. The majority of customer decisions involve limited problem solving.

Retailers attempt to reinforce this buying pattern when customers are shopping at their stores. If customers are shopping elsewhere, however, retailers need to break these buying patterns by introducing new information or offering different merchandise or services.

Tom Jackson's buying process illustrates both limited and extended problem solving. He selected a store based on an ad in the *Los Angeles Times* and his prior knowledge of the merchandise available in various stores. He felt selecting the store wasn't very risky and engaged in limited problem solving when deciding to visit The Broadway. But his buying process for the suit was more extended. This decision was important to him, and he spent time acquiring information from his friend and the salesperson to evaluate his choices and select a suit.

One common type of limited problem solving is impulse buying. Customers make **impulse purchases** when they buy merchandise even though they had no intention of purchasing it before going to the store. Tom's decision to buy the shirt and tie was an impulse purchase.[3]

The display of merchandise can have a significant effect on impulse buying behavior. For example, sales of a grocery item are greatly increased when the item is featured in an end-aisle display, when a BEST BUY sign is placed on the shelf with the item, or when the item is placed at eye level (typically on the third shelf from the bottom). These display factors attract a customer's attention and stimulate a purchase decision based on little analysis. Due to the impact of these display factors, supermarkets use the prime locations for profitable items such as gourmet food rather than for commodities such as flour and sugar, which are usually planned purchases.

REFACT

More than half of all supermarket purchases are unplanned, impulse purchases.

Habitual Decision Making

As noted in Chapter 3, today's customers have many demands on their time. One way they cope with these time pressures is by simplifying their decision-making process. When a need arises, customers may automatically respond by thinking, I'll buy the same thing I bought last time from the same store. Typically, customers use this habitual decision-making process when decisions aren't very important to them. They spend no effort searching for information or evaluating alternatives.

Brand loyalty and store loyalty are examples of habitual decision making. Brand loyal customers like and consistently buy a specific brand in a product category. They won't switch to other brands if their favorite brand isn't available. Thus, retailers can only satisfy these customers' needs if they offer the specific brands desired.

Brand loyalty creates both opportunities and problems for retailers. Customers are attracted to stores carrying popular brands. But, since retailers must carry the high-loyalty brands, they may not be able to negotiate favorable terms with the supplier (the brand manufacturer).

Store loyalty means that customers like and habitually visit the same store to purchase a type of merchandise. All retailers would like to increase their customers' store loyalty. However, most consumers shop at two or three different stores for similar merchandise. Thus, maintaining inclusion in the customer's consideration set might become a more reasonable goal than developing absolute loyalty. Some approaches for maintaining a place in the consideration set are selecting a convenient location (see Chapter 7), offering complete assortments and reducing the number of stockouts (Chapter 8), rewarding customers for frequent purchases (Chapter 11), and providing good customer service (Chapter 14).

☼ THE BUYING PROCESS

Exhibit 4–2 outlines the steps in the store selection and merchandise-buying process. Each step in the buying process is addressed in the following sections.

As the steps in the buying process are discussed, you should recognize that customers may not go through the steps in the order shown in Exhibit 4–2. For example, a person might first decide that he wants to buy a pair of Air Jordan basketball shoes. He then visits a store that sells athletic shoes, discovers that it doesn't have Air Jordans in his size, leaves, and tries to find a store that stocks his size. Here the customer decides what he wants before committing to buying at a specific store.

The buying process is triggered when people recognize that they have an unsatisfied need. *Unsatisfied needs* arise when customers' desired level of satisfaction differs from their present level of satisfaction. For example, Tom Jackson recognized that he had a problem when he considered interviewing for jobs in his blue suit. He needed a suit that would make a good impression and realized that his worn, outdated blue suit wouldn't satisfy this need.

Need recognition can be as straightforward as discovering there's no milk in the refrigerator, or it can be as ambiguous as feeling the need for an uplifting experience after a final exam. Visiting stores and purchasing products is one approach to satisfying different needs.

Need Recognition

Types of Needs. The needs that motivate customers to go shopping and purchase merchandise can be classified as functional or psychological. **Functional needs** are directly related to the performance of the product. For example, people who need to style their hair might be motivated to purchase a hair dryer. This purchase is based on the expectation that the hair dryer will assist them in styling their hair.

EXHIBIT 4-2   **Stages in the Buying Process**

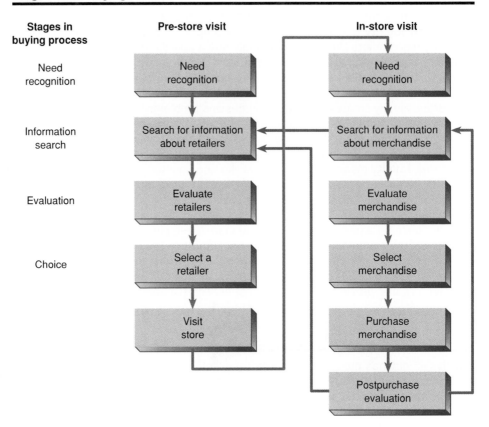

Psychological needs are associated with the personal gratification customers get from shopping or from purchasing and owning a product. For example, a Tommy Hilfiger shirt may not serve the function of clothing any better than a knit shirt from Kmart, but the Hilfiger shirt may also satisfy the customer's need to be perceived as a fashionable dresser. When products are purchased to satisfy psychological needs, the product's functional characteristics are of secondary importance.

Many products satisfy both functional and psychological needs. The principal reason for purchasing a Tommy Hilfiger shirt may be to enhance one's self-image, but the shirt also satisfies the functional need for clothing. Most Americans have more income than they require to satisfy their functional needs of hunger, thirst, clothing, and shelter. As disposable income rises, psychological needs become increasingly important.[4] Thus, store ambiance, service, and fashionable merchandise are more important to American retail customers than to customers in countries with less-developed economies.

Functional needs are often referred to as *rational needs,* and psychological needs are called *emotional needs.* These labels may suggest that visiting stores or buying products to satisfy psychological needs is irrational. But is it really irrational for people to buy designer clothing because it makes them feel more successful?

The Mall of America in Minnesota offers a wide range of entertainment plus shopping opportunities to attract customers.

Anything customers do to improve their satisfaction can be considered rational, whether the action satisfies a functional or psychological need.

Psychological needs that customers satisfy through shopping and purchasing merchandise include the following.[5]

Stimulation. Shopping is a stimulating experience for some customers. It provides a break in their daily environment. The background music, visual displays, scents, and demonstrations in stores and malls offer a carnivallike atmosphere.[6]

Self-reward. Customers frequently purchase merchandise to reward themselves when they've accomplished something or want to dispel depression.[7]

Social experience. Marketplaces have traditionally been centers of social activity—places where people could meet friends and develop new relationships. Regional shopping malls in many communities have replaced open markets as social meeting places, especially for teenagers.

Status and power. Some customers have a need for status and power that's satisfied through shopping. When shopping, a person can be waited on without having to pay for the service. For some people, a store is one of the few places where they get the attention and respect they need.

RE-TALE 4-2   Window Shopping

One of the oldest methods for attracting customers to stores is still one of the most effective. The Saks Fifth Avenue store in Manhattan has 310 feet of store frontage along 49th and 50th Streets and the famed Fifth Avenue. Each day at lunchtime, about 3,000 people walk by the 31 window displays. Saks has 1,200 different window displays each year, and the Fifth Avenue windows change each week. At Christmastime, elaborate displays, including toy-studded productions, draw crowds that are five deep.

Saks' window displays can dramatically impact sales. For example, when Donna Karan clothes were featured in window displays, they sold over five times better than comparable designer lines. One display in the middle of a July heat wave resulted in a dramatic increase in sales of fall wool and heavy velvet fashions.

A Saks divisional merchandise manager for gifts was concerned that sales in his area would decrease when the gift department was moved from the first to the ninth floor. He estimated that sales might drop as much as 15 percent. But an eye-catching window display during the first week of the move produced a 20 percent increase in sales.

SOURCE: Adapted from Lisa Gubernick, "Through a Glass, Brightly," *Forbes,* August 11, 1986, p. 34.

Learning new trends. By visiting stores, people learn about new trends and ideas. These visits satisfy customers' needs to be informed about their environment. For example, people interested in music may visit record stores just to see what new trends and artists are emerging.

Conflicting needs. Most customers attempt to satisfy multiple needs by shopping. These needs often conflict and can't be satisfied in one store or by one product. For example, the need to buy something conveniently may conflict with the need to spend little money; the need to wear the latest fashions may conflict with the need to be thrifty. For example, Tom Jackson would like to wear a Perry Ellis suit. Such a suit would enhance his self-image and may earn him the respect and admiration of his college friends. But this need conflicts with his budget and his need to get a job. Employers might feel that he's not responsible if he wears an expensive suit to an interview for an entry-level position. Typically customers make trade-offs between their conflicting needs.

Stimulating Need Recognition. As we've said, customers must recognize unsatisfied needs before they're motivated to visit a store and buy merchandise. Sometimes these needs are stimulated by an event in a person's life. For example, Tom's department store visit to buy a suit was stimulated by his impending interview and his examination of his blue suit. An ad motivated him to look for a new suit at The Broadway.

Retailers try to start the buying process by stimulating need recognition. For example, a salesperson showed Tom a tie to stimulate his need for an accessory to complement his new suit.

Retailers use a variety of approaches to stimulate problem recognition and motivate customers to visit their stores and buy merchandise. Advertising, direct mail, publicity, and special events communicate the availability of merchandise or special prices. Within the store, visual merchandising and salespeople can stimulate need recognition.[8] Re-Tale 4–2 describes how window displays can initiate the buying process.

Once customers identify a need, they may seek information about retail outlets and/ or products that might help them satisfy the need. Tom's **information search** was limited to the three suits shown him by the salesperson at The Broadway. He was satisfied with this limited information search because he and friend Deion had confidence in The Broadway's merchandise and pricing, and he was pleased with the selection of suits presented to him. More extended buying processes may involve collecting a lot of information and visiting several stores.

Amount of Information Searched. In general, the amount of information customers seek depends on the value customers feel they'll gain from searching versus the cost of searching. The value of the search is in how it improves the customer's purchase decision. Will the search help the customer find a lower-price product or one that will give superior performance? The search's cost includes both time and money. Traveling from store to store can cost money for gas and parking, but the major cost incurred is the customer's time.

Research reveals that specific factors influencing the amount of information sought are (1) the nature and use of the product being purchased, (2) characteristics of the individual customer, and (3) aspects of the market and buying situation in which the purchase is made.[9]

Some people search more than others. For example, customers who enjoy shopping search more than those who don't like to shop. Also, customers who are self-confident or have prior experience purchasing and using the product tend to search less than those who feel unsure of themselves or lack experience.

Sources of Information. Customers have two sources of information: internal and external. **Internal sources of information** include the customer's memory of the names and images of different stores. For example, Tom chose The Broadway because he remembered its ad for suits. **External sources of information** include advertisements, comments by friends, and signs.

Customers are exposed to an overload of information about stores and products. Each day an individual sees hundreds of ads in print and ads in electronic media. They notice signs for many retail outlets each day and get even more information about products and retailers from friends and family members.

A major source of information is the customer's past shopping experience. Even if they remember only a small fraction of the information they're exposed to, customers have an extensive information bank to draw on when deciding where to shop and what to buy.

If customers feel their internal information is inadequate or out of date, they may turn to external information sources. Suppose a customer needs to replace a TV purchased five years ago. She might feel that there will be a benefit to learning more about the new models and new stores selling TVs now. She may seek additional information by going to a library to read a *Consumer Reports* TV evaluation; by talking to friends; or by visiting a number of stores, looking at the sets displayed, and talking with salespeople. Friends and relatives are an important external information source. For example, Tom Jackson asked a respected friend to help him make the purchase decision.[10]

Reducing the information search. Each retailer wants to limit the customer's information search to its own store. Retailers can use each element of the retailing mix to achieve this objective.

First, retailers can provide a good selection of merchandise so customers will find something within the store to satisfy their needs. Services provided by retailers can also limit consumers' search. The availability of credit and delivery may attract consumers who want to purchase large durable goods such as furniture and appliances. And salespeople can provide enough information to customers so they won't feel the need to collect additional information by visiting other stores. For example, L.L. Bean (a mail-order retailer of sportswear and sports equipment) gives employees 40 hours of training before they interact with their first customer. Due to this extensive training, L.L. Bean's salespeople offer consumers across the United States advice on such subjects as what to wear for cross-country skiing and what to take on a trip to Alaska. If the employee answering the phone can't provide the information, he or she switches the customer to an expert within the company.[11] Thanks to L.L. Bean's reputation for expertise in sportswear and sporting goods, customers feel they can collect all the information they need to make a purchase decision from this one retailer.

To improve the chances that customers will rent a video at its stores, Blockbuster has terminals customers can use to easily identify alternative videos if their first choice is unavailable. By responding to a set of questions generated by a computer, the screen suggests videos starring the customer's favorite actors or videos of a particular genre.[12]

Everyday low pricing is another way retailers increase the chance that customers will buy in their store and not search for a better price elsewhere. Both Wal-Mart and Toys "R" Us have everyday low pricing policies so customers can feel confident that the store won't offer their merchandise at a lower price in the future. Many stores with everyday low pricing offer money-back guarantees if a competitor offers the same merchandise at a lower price. Chapter 10 talks about the benefits and limitations of various pricing strategies.

Evaluation of Alternatives

Customers collect and review information about alternative products or stores, evaluate the alternatives, and select one that best satisfies their needs.

In selecting a store, customers often must make trade-offs. For example, convenience stores typically are easier to shop at but have higher prices than supermarkets. The choice depends on the customer's needs at the time. When customers want to buy ice cream late at night, they are willing to pay a higher price at a conveniently located store. However, people with large families will drive some distance to a store offering lower prices.

Retailers can use the following techniques to increase the chances that consumers will shop in their store:

1. *Getting into the consideration set.* The retailer must make sure that its store is included in the customer's consideration set. The **consideration set** is the set of alternatives the customer evaluates when making a selection.[13] To be included in the consideration set, the retailer must develop programs to increase the likelihood that customers will remember the retailer's store when they're about to go shopping. The retailer can influence this consumer awareness through advertising and location strategies. Heavy advertising expenditures that stress the store's name increase consumer awareness. Another strategy retailers use is locating several stores in one geographic area, so customers are exposed more frequently to the store name as they drive through the area.

2. *Increasing customers' evaluation of the store performance on key characteristics.* For example, a supermarket could improve the customer's view of its assortment by stocking more gourmet and ethnic foods. It's costly for a retailer

The Retail Marketplace

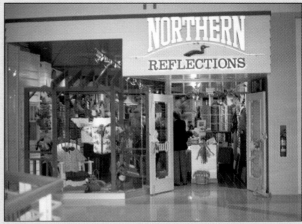

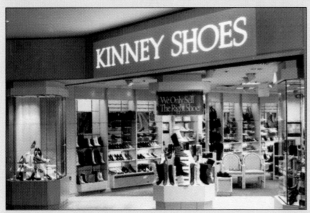

◎ Four of the mall-based specialty store chains owned by the Woolworth Corporation, a company that began as a chain of five and dime variety stores. (Chapter 1)

◎ Pier 1 imports is a home and apparel fashion-oriented chain, which targets middle-class baby boomers with exotic goods at reasonable prices. What type of retail institution is Pier 1? (Chapter 2)

© Blockbuster competes with independent video rental stores and a variety of other retailers that offer video rental as part of their mix of goods and services. (Chapter 1)

© Many product categories are now dominated by category specialists, such as Circuit City in electronics and HomeBase in home improvement and repair. (Chapter 2)

© Shoppers now have many more kinds of stores to choose from. Retailer outlet stores, such as this Brooks Brothers store in Maine (top), often located in malls exclusively devoted to outlets, allow shoppers to find brand name merchandise at bargain prices. Warehouse stores, such as BJ's Wholesale Club (left), often require shoppers to pay a membership fee in order to have access to the wide range of goods they sell—including everything from widescreen televisions to snow tires to gallon jugs of mustard. (Chapter 2)

Avon (top) is famous for its direct selling retail approach to reaching consumers, and has even expanded successfully into emerging markets in Asia, Europe, and South America. The direct marketing catalog retail approach used by L.L Bean (below) is increasingly popular with all consumers. (Chapters 2 and 5)

7-Eleven changed the design of its stores to attract more female customers.

to improve its performance on all characteristics. Thus, retailers focus on improving the characteristics that are important to customers in the target market. For example, 7-Eleven's market research found that women avoid convenience stores because they view them as dingy and unsafe. To attract more women, 7-Eleven improved the shopping environment in a number of its stores. To create a sense of space, they installed brighter lighting and wider aisles. Cigarette racks and other clutter were cleared off checkout counters, and colorful signage now designates merchandise areas.[14]

3. *Decreasing the evaluation of competitors.* Another approach is to try to worsen the customers' evaluation of a competing store. This approach may be illegal and usually isn't very effective because customers typically don't believe a firm's negative comments about its competitors.

Customers don't always purchase the brand or item of merchandise with the highest overall evaluation because this item may not be in the store they visit, or the store might not have the size and color they want. Even if the customer locates the desired item, the store might not be open when he or she wants to buy it, or the store might not accept the customer's credit card. Retailers must take steps to ensure that customers can easily convert their positive merchandise evaluation into purchases at the cash register. **Purchasing the Merchandise**

The buying process doesn't end when a customer purchases a product. Afterward, the customer consumes or uses the product and then evaluates it as satisfactory or unsatisfactory. **Satisfaction** is a postconsumption evaluation of how well a store or product meets, or exceeds, customer expectations.[15] **Postpurchase Evaluation**

     This **postpurchase evaluation** becomes part of the customer's internal information and it affects future store and product decisions. Unsatisfactory experiences can motivate customers to complain to the retailer and to patronize other stores.[16] Chapter 14 discusses ways to increase customer satisfaction such as offering quality merchandise, providing accurate information about merchandise, and contacting customers after a sale.

FACTORS AFFECTING THE DECISION-MAKING PROCESS

Factors that influence customers' decision-making process include family members and cultural environment.

Many hotel chains now offer services that appeal to families with small children to make the hotel stay a more pleasant experience.

Family Members

Family members frequently play various roles in the decision-making and consumption processes.[17] For example, the husband might buy the groceries, while the wife uses them to prepare their child's lunch, and the child consumes the lunch at school.

Retailers consider these different roles when selling to families. In the preceding example, the husband might choose the store, while the wife might choose the brand, with great input from the child.

Many baby boomers are in two-income families that have decided to have children late in life. They often have high disposable income and want to stay in luxury resorts, but they still want to take their children on vacations. Resort hotels now realize they must satisfy children's needs as well as adults'. For example, Hyatt hotels greet families by offering books and games tailored to the children's ages. Parents checking in with infants receive a first-day supply of baby food or formula and diapers at no charge. Baby-sitting and escort services to children's attractions are offered.[18]

Culture and Subculture

Culture is the meaning and values shared by most members of a society. For example, core values shared by most Americans include individualism, freedom, mastery and control, self-improvement, achievement and success, material comfort, and health and fitness.[19]

Retailers are sensitive to how these values translate into different needs and shopping behaviors. For example, gift giving plays a much more important role in Japanese culture than in American culture. Most Japanese feel a need to buy souvenirs for family and friends. In one study, about half of the Japanese tourists returning home from Los Angeles bought gifts for over 15 family members and friends. They spent as much on gifts for others as on merchandise for themselves. Gift packaging and wrapping offered by retailers is particularly important to these

---

RE-TALE 4-3   A Hidden Subculture

Although the gay subculture has significant buying power, many retailers are reluctant to target the estimated 20 million homosexuals in the United States. Gay consumers tend to be younger, wealthier, and better educated than the average American. One study reported that the average income of a gay household was $55,100 compared to $32,100 for the average U.S. household.

Despite these attractive demographics, some retailers are concerned that gay customers will offend homophobic customers. However, some manufacturers have successfully targeted the gay subculture. For example, Remy Martin advertises extensively in gay publications and is the number one cognac brand in the gay community, even though it only ranks fifth nationally.

SOURCE: Cyndee Miller, "Gays Are Affluent, But Often Overlooked," *Marketing News,* December 24, 1990, p. 2; and Joan Rigson, "Overcoming a Deep-Rooted Reluctance, More Firms Advertise to Gay Community," *The Wall Street Journal,* July 18, 1991, pp. B1, B8.

Japanese tourists because gifts aren't opened in front of the gift giver. Thus, the gift's appearance is particularly important to the giver.[20]

Subcultures are distinctive groups of people within a culture. Members of a subculture share some customs and norms with the overall society but also have some unique perspectives. Subcultures can be based on geography (Southerners), age (baby boomers), ethnicity (Asian-Americans), or life-style (punks). Re-Tale 4–3 describes a distinctive subculture with considerable buying power.

MARKET SEGMENTATION

The preceding discussion focused on (1) how individual customers evaluate and select stores and merchandise and (2) factors affecting this decision-making process. Retailers can't economically provide merchandise and services uniquely tailored to individual customers. They must identify groups of customers (a market segment) and target their offering to meet the needs of that segment. A **retail market segment** is a group of customers whose needs are satisfied by the same retail mix because they have similar needs and go through similar buying processes.

For example, Lane Bryant and Limited Express (two divisions of The Limited) have retail mixes that appeal to distinctly different market segments. Lane Bryant caters to women who wear large-size clothing, while Limited Express targets young, trendy women who wear smaller junior sizes. Lane Bryant's customers' needs wouldn't be satisfied by Limited Express's retail mix, and vice versa.

Approaches to Segmenting Markets

Exhibit 4–3 illustrates the wide variety of approaches for segmenting retail markets. No one approach is best for all retailers. Retailers segment markets based on important factors that affect customer store choice and buying decisions. Some common approaches for segmenting markets are geography, demographics, life-style, buying situations, and benefits sought.

Geographic Segmentation. Geographic segmentation groups customers by where they live. A retail market can be segmented by countries, states, counties, cities, or neighborhoods. Customers typically shop at stores convenient to where they live and work, so individual retail outlets usually focus on a customer segment reasonably close to the outlet.

Methods for Segmenting Retail Markets

Segmentation Bases/ Descriptors	Illustrative Categories
Geographic	
Region	Pacific, Mountain, West North Central, West South Central, East North Central, East South Central, South Atlantic, Middle Atlantic, New England
Size of city, country, or standard metropolitan statistical area (SMSA)	Under 5,000, 5,000–19,999, 20,000–49,999, 50,000–99,999, 100,000–249,999, 250,000–499,999, 500,000–999,999, 1,000,000–3,999,999, 4,000,000 or over
Population density	Urban, suburban, rural
Climate	Warm, cold
Demographic	
Age	Under 6, 6–12, 13–19, 20–29, 30–39, 40–49, 50–59, 60–70, 70+
Gender	Male, female
Family size	1–2, 3–4, 5+ persons
Family life cycle	Young, single; young, married, no children; young married, youngest child under 6; young, married, youngest child 6 or over; older, married, with children; older, married, no children under 18; older, single; other
Income	Under $10,000, $10,000–$14,999, $15,000–$24,999, $25,000–$34,999, $35,000–$49,999, $50,000–$74,999, over $75,000
Occupation	Professional and technical; manager, official, and proprietor; clerical, sales; craftsperson, foreperson; operative; farmer; retired; student; housewife or househusband; unemployed
Education	Grade school or less; some high school; graduated from high school; some college; graduated from college; some graduate work; graduate degree
Religion	Catholic, Protestant, Jewish, other
Race	White, Asian, African-American, Hispanic-American
Nationality	U.S., British, French, German, Italian, Japanese
Psychosocial	
Social class	Upper class, middle class, working class, lower class
Life-style	Traditionalist, sophisticate, swinger
Personality	Compliant, aggressive, detached
Feelings and behaviors	
Attitudes	Positive, neutral, negative
Benefits sought	Convenience, economy, prestige
Readiness stage	Unaware, aware, informed, interested, desirous, intention to purchase
Perceived risk	High, moderate, low
Innovativeness	Innovator, early adopter, early majority, late majority, laggard, nonadopter
Involvement	Low, high
Loyalty status	None, some, total
Usage rate	None, light, medium, heavy
User status	Nonuser, exuser, potential user, current user
Usage situation	Home, work, commuting, vacation

SOURCE: J. Paul Peter and Jerry C. Olson, *Consumer Behavior and Marketing Strategy,* 3d ed. (Burr Ridge, Ill.: Richard D. Irwin, 1993), pp. 554–55.

Geographic Segments Used by Retailers

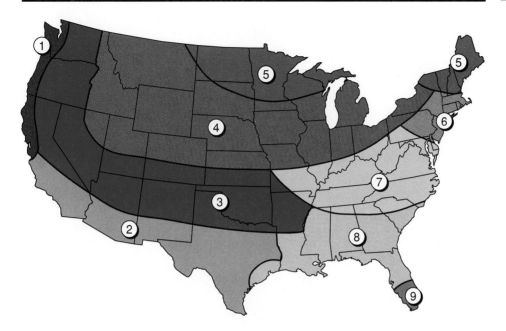

Many department store chains concentrate on regions of the country. For example, Rich's concentrates on Georgia and surrounding states, The Broadway on southern California, Strawbridge and Clothier on the Philadelphia area, and Bergstroms on Milwaukee. Other retailers, like Wal-Mart, initially focused on small rural markets and then opened in large urban markets.

Even though national retailers such as The Gap and J.C. Penney have no geographic focus, they do tailor their merchandise selections to different regions of the country. Snow sleds don't sell well in Florida, and surfboards don't sell well in Colorado. Even within a metropolitan area, stores in a chain must adjust to the unique needs of customers in different neighborhoods. For example, supermarkets in affluent neighborhoods typically have more gourmet foods than stores in less affluent neighborhoods. Exhibit 4–4 shows the geographic zones used by some retailers. Since the climate conditions are similar for the region in each zone, the retailer will send the same type of apparel to all of the stores in the zone.

Demographic Segmentation. Chapter 3 discussed special demographic segments retailers focus on, such as African-Americans, Hispanic-Americans, the elderly, and baby boomers. However, demographics aren't always related to customer needs and buying behavior. For example, demographics are poor predictors for users of active wear, such as jogging suits and running shoes. At one time, retailers assumed that only young people would purchase active wear, but the health and fitness trend has led people of all ages to buy this merchandise. Initially, retailers felt that VCRs would be a luxury product purchased mainly by wealthy customers. But retailers found that low-income customers and families with young children were strongly attracted to VCRs because they offered low-cost, convenient entertainment.

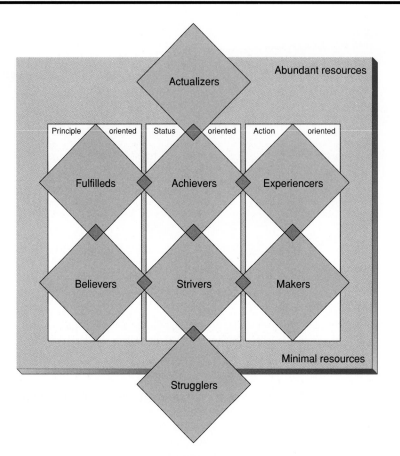

Lands' End's unconditional guarantee builds customer satisfaction during the postpurchase evaluation stage of the buying process.

(concluded)

Actualizers
Highest income. High self-esteem.
Indulge in self- oriented activities.
Image is important. Wide range of
interests. Open to change. Want the
finer things in life.

Fulfilleds
Mature responsible, well-educated
professionals. Leisure activities
center on the home. Well informed
about what is going on in the world.
Open to new ideas and social
change. High income but practical,
value-oriented consumers.

Achievers
Successful. Work-oriented. Life
centers around jobs and family.
Politically conservative. Respect
authority. Favor established products
that demonstrate their status to their
peers.

Experiencers
Youngest of all segments. Want to
affect the environment in meaningful
way. Have a lot of energy. Spend time
on physical and social activities. Avid
consumers. Spend heavily on
clothing, fast food, music, and
anything new.

Believers
Modest income. Conservative and
predictable consumers. Favor
American products and established
brands. Life centers around family,
church, and community.

Strivers
Similar values as Achievers but have
fewer resources. Style is very
important. Attempt to emulate people
who they wish they were.

Makers
Practical. Value self-sufficiency.
Focus activities on family, work, and
physical recreation. Have little
interest in events outside their
immediate surroundings. Not
impressed by material possessions.

Strugglers
Lowest income. Oldest segment.
Tend to be brand loyal.

SOURCE: Martha Farnsworth Riche, "Psychographics for the 1990s," *American Demographics,* July
1989, p. 26. Reprinted with permission. © *American Demographics,* July 1989, Ithaca, New York.

Life-Style Segmentation. *Life-style* refers to how people live, how they spend their
time and money, what activities they pursue, and what attitudes and opinions they
hold about the world around them. Retailers today are placing more emphasis on
life-styles (**psychographics**) than on demographics to define a target segment.

VALS2® is one of several commercially available segmentation approaches
based on consumer values and life-styles.[21] Segments are based on two national
surveys of 2,500 consumers conducted by SRI International. The surveys ask consumers to indicate whether they agree or disagree with statements like "My idea of
fun in a national park would be to stay in an expensive lodge and dress up for
dinner," or "I could not stand to skin a dead animal." Based on an analysis of responses to the survey, eight life-style segments were identified (Exhibit 4–5). Note
how consumers in each segment are described in terms of different attitudes, ambitions, and buying behaviors, not in terms of age or where they live.

The eight life-style segments are arranged in two dimensions. The vertical dimension indicates the amount of resources (money, education, health, self-confidence, and energy level) people in the segment have. Actualizers have a lot of resources; strugglers have limited resources.

The horizontal dimension describes the self-orientation of consumers in the segment. The behavior of people in principle-oriented segments (fulfilleds and believers) is based on their beliefs about how the world is or should be. People in status-oriented segments are guided by the actions and opinions of others. Those in action-oriented segments are guided by their need for social and physical activity, variety, and risk taking.

Many businesses use the VALS2® segments to better understand their customers and target markets. For example, a survey of air travelers found that 37 percent were actualizers compared to 8 percent of the general population. Because actualizers buy merchandise that reflects their high income and status, the research suggests that stores like The Nature Company and The Sharper Image would succeed in airport locations.[22]

SRI International provides information about the number of people in each segment living in different zip-code areas and buying different products. While it's harder to identify and access consumers in a life-style segment than in a demographic segment, life-styles are typically more closely related to consumer needs and buying behavior. Thus, it's easier to develop an effective retail mix for a life-style segment than for a demographic segment.

Buying Situation Segmentation. Customers' buying behavior can vary depending on their buying situation, even when demographics and life-style remain unchanged. For example, parents with four children may choose a convenience store for fill-in needs and go to a warehouse store for their weekly shopping trip.

Benefit Segmentation. Another approach for defining a target segment is to group customers seeking similar benefits. For example, customers who seek the most fashionable clothing form a fashion segment, while customers who primarily seek low price form a price segment.

Composite Segmentation Approaches. Most effective segmentation plans use multiple factors to identify customers in the target segment. They define target customers by benefits sought, life-styles, and demographics. An illustration of a **composite segmentation** scheme is J.C. Penney's segmentation of the women's apparel market.

The market for women's apparel is typically segmented into five categories: conservative, traditional, update, bridge, and designer or fashion-forward. The conservative segment is the most price-conscious and least fashion-oriented. The designer segment seeks just the opposite—fashion and style with little regard for price.

J.C. Penney customers are in the first three segments, but the firm decided to target its offering to customers in the traditional and update segments. Exhibit 4–6(A) shows characteristics of each apparel segment. Note how these descriptions include segment size, customers' values, benefits they seek, and demographic information. Penney has different departments within each store and different brands tailored to meet each segment's needs. Exhibit 4–6(B) lists which Penney's retail offerings are directed toward these segments.

J.C. Penney Segments for Women's Apparel

EXHIBIT 4-C

A. SEGMENT DESCRIPTION		
	Conservative	*Traditional*	*Update*
Size	23% of population 16% of total sales	38% of population 40% of total sales	16% of population 24% of total sales
Age	35–55 years old	25–49 years old	25–49 years old

Values	Conservative values
	Satisfied with present
	    status
		Traditional values
		Active, busy, independent,
		    self-confident
			Contemporary values
			Active, busy, independent,
			    very self-confident

Employment	Has job, not career	Family and job/career-
		    oriented
			Family and job/career-
			    oriented

Income	Limited disposable income	Considerable income	Considerable income

Benefits
  sought
	Price driven, reacts to
	    sales
	Wants easy care and
	    comfort
	Not interested in fashion
	Defines value as
	    price
	    quality
	    fashion
		Quality driven, will pay a little
		    more
		Wants traditional styling,
		    seeks clothes that last
		Interested in newness
		Defines value as
		    quality
		    fashion
		    price
			Fashion driven, expresses
			    self through apparel
			Wants newness in color and
			    style
			Shops often
			Defines value as
			    fashion
			    quality
			    price

B. RETAIL OFFERING		
Retail Mix	*Conservative*	*Traditional*	*Update*
Pricing	Budget	Moderate	Moderate to better

Merchandise	Basic styles, easy-care
	    fabrics, comfortable fit
		Traditional styling, good
		    quality, tailored look
			Fashion-forward, more
			    selection, newer colors

Brands	Alica Cobble Lane Motion Cabin Creek	Joneswear Worthington Halston Wyndham Russ Togs Hunt Club Dockers	Claude Mary McFadden Counterparts Jacqueline Ferrar

Merchandising
  approach
	Price signing, "save
	    stories," stack-out tables
		Well-coordinated
		    merchandise, collections,
		    uncluttered displays,
		    knowledgeable salespeople
			Color statements,
			    mannequins, theme areas

☀ SUMMARY

Retailers base their strategies on an understanding of how customers make store
choice and purchase decisions and what factors they consider when deciding. This
chapter described the six steps of the buying process (need recognition, information
search, evaluation of alternatives, choice of alternatives, purchase, and postpurchase evaluation) and how retailers can influence each step. A step's importance

depends on the nature of the customer's decision. When decisions are important and risky, the buying process is longer; here customers spend more time and effort on information search and evaluating alternatives. When buying decisions are less important to customers, they spend little time in the buying process, and their buying behavior may become habitual.

To develop cost-effective retail programs, retailers group customers into segments and target their retailing efforts toward one segment. Some approaches for segmenting markets are based on geography, demographics, life-styles, usage situations, and benefits sought. Each approach has its advantages and disadvantages, so retailers typically define their target segment by several characteristics.

KEY TERMS

benefit segmentation, 74
brand loyalty, 61
buying process, 58
buying situation segmentation, 74
composite segmentation, 74
consideration set, 66

culture, 68
demographic segmentation, 71
external sources of information, 65
functional needs, 61
geographic segmentation, 69
impulse purchase, 60

information search, 65
internal sources of information, 65
life-style segmentation, 73
postpurchase evaluation, 67

psychographics, 73
psychological needs, 62
retail market segment, 69
satisfaction, 67
store loyalty, 61
subculture, 69

DISCUSSION QUESTIONS AND PROBLEMS

1. Why doesn't the customer buying process end when a customer buys some merchandise?
2. Give reasons why a teenager might go shopping at a mall.
3. Why would a consumer switch from making a habitual store choice decision to making a limited or extended store choice decision?
4. Reflect on your decision process in selecting a college. (State universities are nonprofit service retailers.) Was your decision-making process extensive, limited, or habitual? Did you go through all of the steps listed in Figure 4–2?
5. Using the VALS2® categories, suggest retail strategies for a restaurant chain attempting to attract each category of consumer.
6. A family-owned bookstore across the street from a major university campus wants to identify its target market. What approaches might the store owner use to segment its market? List the potential target

market segments based on this segmentation approach. Then contrast the retail mix that would be most appropriate for two potential target segments.
7. When would a retailer want to increase the amount of information searched by consumers? When would it want to decrease the amount?
8. What are the advantages and disadvantages to consumers of purchasing from a mail-order catalog rather than from a store? What types of merchandise do consumers prefer to purchase in a store? From a catalog? Why?
9. What factors influence which airline consumers use? How does importance of these factors' differ for people taking a business trip versus a family vacation?
10. Any retailer's goal is to get a customer in the store to stop searching and buy a product. What can a department store retailer do to ensure that the customer buys a tie or scarf there?

Cases for Section 1

Some things don't need much explanation. When you see the Golden Arches, you think of McDonald's. When you see a swirling red, white, and blue sphere, you think "Pepsi." And when you see the curvy little swoosh, "Just do it" comes to mind.

With so many nontraditional shopping alternatives competing for the customer's attention, a key to survival in the 90s will depend on retailers' ability to maximize their in-store environments. Customers are bored with ordinary shopping experiences. Convenience and price aren't enough. They want to be entertained.

With this in mind, Nike Town was developed to create brand awareness about Nike as a company in an informative and fun way. It was established to promote a lifestyle as much as the product. "We wanted to engage the customer in both our products and the sport and fitness lifestyle that Nike represents," said Mary Burns, director of operations, Nike, Beaverton, Oregon.

There are five Nike Town stores in operation: Portland, Oregon; Chicago; Atlanta; Costa Mesa, California; and San Francisco's Union Square. The stores are tourist attractions and it's easy to see why. If you were to visit the Portland store (which is the original Nike Town), this is what you would see: Flying superhumanly above the square is a life-sized statue of Michael Jordan. Nearby are other statues, Bo Jackson lifting weights and Andre Agassi running to smash a tennis ball.

Nike Town's background design is Disney-like characters and the city of the future, featuring the cartoon show, "The Jetsons." Fourteen small, themed salesrooms, which Nike calls *pavilions,* feature an array of sports shoes and apparel for everything from tennis to hockey.

The majority of the pavilions feature the sounds associated with that sport. If you enter one basketball pavilion (The Flight Pavilion) you'll hear the distant sound of basketballs bouncing on hardwood floors. If you enter the tennis pavilion, you'll hear the sounds of the racket smashing against the little yellow ball.

In the Land of Barkley, named after basketball player Charles Barkley, basketball hoops hold up display shelves, and basketballs support benches. The sounds being played are shoes squeaking on hardwood. The actual floor is hardwood so "wanna-be" Barkleys can pull on a pair of shoes and squeak them on the floors like the big guys. The tennis pavilion features a sunken, miniature tennis court with its most popular piece—John McEnroe's broken racket. There's even a kid's pavilion, with bootie-sized Air Jordan look-a-likes, and a measure on a wall that shows the height of Jordan's leap. At 40 inches, it's higher than some of his small fans' heads.

Even with all of this, one of the biggest attractions is the swim and volleyball area. The seats are surfboards. There's an aquarium with tropical fish and the floor features a center section designed to simulate a glass-bottomed boat, with videos of sea life playing.

Nike cares more that customers carry away fond memories of the brand than a new pair of sneakers. "Nike Towns provide Nike the opportunity to present the full scope of Nike's sports and fitness lines to our customers and to educate them on the value, quality, and benefits of Nike products," said Bruce Fabel, vice president of Nike's Retail Division. "Our research indicates customers who do not make a purchase at Nike Town will be more likely to buy Nike in the future from one of our retail accounts in the area."

Nike is not the only company pushing their own stores. A growing number of big-name manufacturers are turning into mainstream merchants, opening flashy stores called flagship stores all over the nation. Swimsuit maker Speedo, children's clothing company OshKosh B'Gosh, and shoemaker Nine West are just a few that are opening stores similar to Nike Town showcasing their brands and enhancing their image.

Discussion Questions

1. Why are manufacturers like Nike opening their own retail outlets?

2. What will be the reaction of consumers and retailers who sell Nike merchandise to these new stores?

This case was prepared by Laura Hooks at the University of Florida.

CASE 1–2: THE GREAT CATALOG ITEM

Late one afternoon, just as Julie Brenner was getting ready to send a merchandise transfer to the main store from her branch, she received an urgent call from the assistant buyer there: "Julie, I hate to ask you this, but you've got to pull every piece you've got of style 2030 and send it to me today."

Julie was the manager of several sportswear departments, and the style she had been asked to return was her very best-selling blouse. It was a $75 silk, and since coming to the store ten days earlier, had sold 45 of 96 pieces. She had already called New York demanding a reorder, and been told it would take six weeks.

Needless to say, she was not pleased. "Why should I send you my best seller?"

Cindy, the assistant, replied in a harassed tone, "I know you're selling it like crazy, but it's sold in the hundreds through the catalog, and they're grabbing every piece they can get their hands on."

"Great," said Julie. "I don't get paid for making sales through the catalog. Why should I waste the store's money shipping these to you when I can sell them all out in another week?"

Cindy's reply was "The store considers these already sold. They're no longer in our stock."

Julie recognized that she had no choice, so she stopped what she was doing, and reluctantly went to the floor and pulled the remaining blouses and sent them off to New York as requested.

"I'm going to send somebody a note about this," she thought, as she was walking back from the transfer room. "It's got to cost the store at least a dollar a garment to take them back from me and then another couple of dollars in labor to repack them and send them to the catalog warehouse. I don't get credit for the sale here, and for that matter, I'll get precious little credit for doing what they want me to. It's not only unfair, but it wastes the store's money."

She decided to discuss it with Jeff Friedman, her store manager, who agreed that it was expensive for the store, but that the store had determined to become a major factor in the mail-order business. "It's what management wants, so we have to do it."

Julie pursued her point: "Why do they insist on carrying the same stuff in the stores and the catalog? The catalog customer won't come to the store to see the merchandise. Why don't they pick different styles?"

Friedman said, "Now, come on, Julie, look at it through the store's eyes. Suppose they lay an egg with a catalog item. Aren't you glad to get a nice markdown when something bombs in the catalog? You know that's the rule—if it doesn't sell through the catalog, they have to take the markdown there and ship it to the stores at a third off. You aren't stuck with taking that markdown, and the extra volume doesn't hurt, does it?"

Somewhat mollified, Julie went back to her department. But it still didn't feel right.

Discussion Questions

1. What are the benefits of a department store retailer having a catalog business?
2. What do you think is the best way to handle conflict like the one described in the case?

This case was prepared by Professor David Ehrlich, Marymount University.

CASE 1–3 THE "ANTI-MALL"

Imagine shopping at a "mall" with crumbling walls with graffiti, weeds creeping up through cracks in the pavement, broken signs, and people in cut-off shorts and hiking boots sipping coffee on thrift-shop furniture. A mall without The Gap, Waldenbooks, Victoria's Secret, or Sears.

This is The Lab, a shopping complex in Southern California. Its nickname is the "Anti-Mall." It prides itself on being the first mall in the United States to be conceived for the X generation. This mall is aimed at the 90s culture. It's for those who see sameness in every shopping center and would prefer a shopping experience scented with attitude, decay, and patchouli. Its appeal is to 18- to 29-year olds.

Instead of creating another lookalike mall, Shaheen Sadeghi, The Lab's developer, gutted a vacant plant that once manufactured goggles for the military and transformed it into The Lab. "Malls are all marble and buffed out," Sadeghi said. "This building is raw, soulful, and comfortable, a place where you can sip coffee, play chess, or read a book."

Sadeghi doesn't expect The Lab to rival other malls in California. He sees it as strong enough to support a smaller, alternative way of shopping. The age group targeted by The Lab represents huge success opportunity because it is, "the only group of people who actually want to spend more of their discretionary time shopping," said Watts Wacker, a futurist with Yankelovich and Partners in New York. Unfortunately for conventional retailers, these consumers are also, "a group of people who feel unbelievably mistreated by the mainstream," according to Wacker.

The Lab has exposed wooden ceilings, massive iron roof beams, and cement floors. It is anchored by Urban Outfitters, which sells hip clothing and home decoration items, and Tower Records, which operates a large alternative music store. It also houses more than a dozen shops, including a comicbook shop called Collector's Library and a florist called Weeds.

So far, The Lab's strategy seems to work. "It allows us to reach our target market," said Rodney Metoyer, manager of Tower Alternative. Tower Alternative is a subsidiary of the music store Tower Records. Tower Alternative was created specifically for the Lab, and stocks recordings of trendy bands such as The Cranberries, Green Day, and Nirvana, as well as unsigned local bands from the area. It carries some mainstream pop, but little in the way of classical or country.

Urban Outfitters is the biggest store in The Lab. This cool, funky, freethinking apparel and home furnishing chain is excelling in Generation X appeal. Its intention is to be a non–chain store. It is sure to win the hearts of those who hate pastels, orderly displays, and light wood interiors. Urban Outfitter stores are decorated in a style best described as a junk store. But behind the blown apart dry walls, Salvation Army props, and haphazard fixtures is a carefully calculated, well thought-out strategy that ropes in its audience.

The retailer embraces the tastes, peculiarities, and interests of its customers. The background music in the stores is 100 percent alternative and the salespeople, who are often indistinguishable from the customers, are trained to be laid back. To be sure Urban Outfitters doesn't remind customers of their parents' favorite department store, they are helped by employees with tattoos and pierced body parts. The stores are filled with funky candles, affordable cotton throws, inexpensive t-shirts, and wool sweaters.

Apart from Urban Outfitters and Tower Alternatives, The Lab has no large chain stores because Sadeghi believes Generation X opposes the homogenization of American culture. Instead of "food courts" (the cluster of restaurants in most malls), The Lab sells health foods and specialty coffees in an area furnished with lumpy sofas to lounge on.

The Lab also capitalizes on Generation X's desire for good causes. Instead of car expos and fashion shows, The Lab sponsors special charity events. For example, The Lab invited shoppers to buy broken tiles to decorate walls. Proceeds went to a charity for the homeless.

Discussion Questions

1. What characteristics of the X-generation are reflected in The Lab?
2. Do you think anti-malls like The Lab will be successful throughout the United States? Why or why not?

This case was prepared by Lora Hooks, University of Florida.

C A S E   1–4   ☼   GETTING PERSONALLY DESIGNED LEVI'S

Do you ever have problems finding the perfect pair of jeans? Are they too short? Too baggy? Too tight in the legs? Not big enough in the waist? If these problems seem familiar to you, Levi Strauss and Co. has a solution.

Their solution is "made-to-measure" jeans, a retail innovation which is the first of its type in the fashion industry. It's all done with a computer and a tape measure. The process begins with a salesperson in the Levi stores in California, Ohio, Washington, and Minnesota taking four measurements on the customer: waist, hips, rise (the distance from the front waistband between the legs up to the back waistband) and inseam. The measurements are entered into a computer, which spits out the number of a prototype pair of jeans with those measurements. The customer tries on the prototypes, and the salesperson notes any modifications, as minor as 1/2-inch in the fit.

Once the modifications are determined, the new measurements are entered into a computer that produces another try-on prototype for the customer. "On an average, it takes two or three prototypes before a customer is totally satisfied with the fit," a Levi spokesperson said.

The final fit numbers are sent by computer to a Levi factory in Mountain City, Tennessee, where the jeans are made. About three weeks later, they are sent to the Levi store, or they can be express-mailed directly to the customer. The Levi store is only offering this service for women. Traditionally, men have been able to get a better fit in pants because they can often choose waist and inseam measurements. Until now, women were limited to standard sizes. Levi's makes more than 170 fits and sizes in its woman's jeans lines. However, some 4,000 combinations are possible.

The service is aimed at two types of women. "We see these jeans to be targeted to the woman who is discriminating about how her jeans fit or who is just a denim connoisseur in search of the 'ultimate jean,'" said Annette Lim, retailing marketing services manager for Levi's.

Demands for the jeans are rising quickly. In Cincinnati, sales have risen 300 percent over the last year. "Women have been flying to Cincinnati to get their jeans fitted," said Sean Fitzgerald, senior manager of corporate communications for Levi's. "We've had thousands of calls. It's unbelievable."

What Levi's is doing is an industrial trend called "mass customization." The concept entails using computerized instruction to enable factories to tailor mass-market items to suit individual buyers. Levi's joins a limited number of mass-produced products—including windows and electronic pagers—that are being customized by the use of computers to suit the individual needs of the purchasers. For example, Anderson Windows places computers in retail stores, where customers can design factory-made windows in an almost infinite variety of shapes and sizes.

Discussion Questions

1. What are the advantages and disadvantages of mass customization for customers? For retailers?
2. To what extent will mass customization affect the way in-store retailing is done?

This case was prepared by Lora Hooks, University of Florida.

CASE 1–5 ☼ PEAPOD GROCERY SERVICE

Gone are the days of searching for a can of potato soup on aisle 10 of the grocery store and waiting in a long checkout line—electronic shopping is here. With decreasing amounts of spare time, customers can now dial Peapod from their personal computers to order groceries without ever leaving their homes. The concept is simple. Using special software and a modem, customers order groceries by computer, look to see what items are on special, and specify a time for delivery.

When customers dial up Peapod, they can gain access to 25,000 grocery items stocked at a nearby supermarket. The system is set up so customers can browse by department such as produce, dairy products, and cleaning supplies or can search by item or brand.

Type "pasta" on your computer for example, and Peapod lists everything in the store from fettucini to wheat lasagna noodles, including brand name, prices, and cost per ounce. By pushing a function key, all items are sorted by cost, so the customer can choose the most economical item. With another function key, customers are able to move federally mandated nutritional details from the back of the can to their computer screen.

To speed up the ordering process, the customer can start by selecting their "frequent shopping list" of items they buy every week—milk, eggs, bread, Butterball turkey, and Oreo cookies. They can request substitutions in case an item is out of stock, or leave other instructions such as "pack bread carefully" or "pick overripe bananas for a banana bread."

Peapod assembles orders by using its own employees, who are referred to as "shoppers." At a typical store, 40 Peapod shoppers work alongside store staff. Besides hourly wages, shoppers receive bonuses for accuracy. Deliveries are made Tuesday through Sunday, between the hours of 9:30 A.M. and 9 P.M. on weekdays, and until 2 P.M. on weekends. Customers pick a 90-minute window for delivery and pay electronically by credit card or through a prearranged account with the service.

Peapod takes the unusual step of guaranteeing satisfaction on every order. "If we make a mistake, we'll make it right," promises a Peapod advertisement. Perishable products are carefully selected. Refrigerated and frozen items are delivered in temperature-controlled coolers.

In 1995, Peapod has about 8,500 customers in Chicago and San Francisco, and plans to expand to Boston. In the past year, it has experienced a 300 percent growth rate and has secured high-profile investors like Ameritech and the Tribune Co. Peapod is making money on a market-by-market basis, but the company overall is not yet profitable because it's reinvesting funds into expansion.

One customer said the service is his salvation because it saves what little amount of free time he has. "Sure, we still go to the convenience store to pick up milk and soda pop when we run out and we would never abandon Kelly's Meats, but it's an incredible relief to download a mind-numbing task like grocery shopping."

Of course, this top quality convenience of shopping via computer doesn't come cheap. Chicagoans pay $4.95 a month, plus $5 per delivery and 5 percent of the final bill—about $35 monthly for somebody with an average $100 grocery bill who shops three times per month. San Franciscans pay a flat $29.95 monthly fee. In both cities, there's a $29.95 software set-up fee.

Peapod is not the first to attempt an on-line supermarket service. Prodigy, the largest consumer-oriented on-line network, tested the field in 1988 with grocers in nine cities, but withdrew after three years because it didn't attract a huge amount of subscribers.

To Andrew Parkinson, the founder and CEO of Peapod, "Prodigy's problem was the same as virtually every other company that has gone into the supermarket home delivery business." They focus on the telemarketing aspect of the business, but fail to adequately get involved with the fulfillment aspects. Once they transmit an order to the retailer, they wash their hands of it, leaving it to the retailer to assemble the order and employ a third-party courier to deliver it.

Discussion Questions

1. Taking the customer's perspective, compare grocery shopping from Peapod and the other types of food retailers described in this chapter. What are the advantages and disadvantages of shopping from Peapod?
2. What types of customers will be attracted to Peapod? What types of customers will continue to shop at grocery stores?

This case was prepared by Lora Hooks, University of Florida.

CASE 1-6 ☼ THE MCGEES BUY THREE BICYCLES

The McGees live in Riverside, California, west of Los Angeles. Terry is a physics professor at the University of California, Riverside. His wife Cheryl is a volunteer 10 hours a week at the Crisis Center. They have two children: Judy, age 10, and Mark, age 8.

In February, Cheryl's parents sent her $50 to buy a bicycle for Judy's birthday. They bought Judy her first bike when she was five. Now they wanted to buy her a full-size bike for her 11th birthday. Even though Cheryl's parents felt every child should have a bike, Cheryl didn't think Judy really wanted one. Judy and most of her friends didn't ride their bikes often and she was afraid to ride to school because of traffic. So Cheryl decided to buy her the cheapest full-sized bicycle she could find.

Since most of Judy's friends didn't have full-sized bikes, she didn't know much about them and had no preferences for a brand or type. To learn more about the types available and their prices, Cheryl and Judy checked the J.C. Penney catalog. After looking through the catalog, Judy said the only thing she cared about was the color. She wanted a blue bike, blue being her favorite color.

Using the Yellow Pages, Cheryl called several local retail outlets selling bikes. To her surprise, she found that a department store actually had the best price for a 26-inch bicycle, even lower than Toys "R" Us and Wal-Mart.

Cheryl drove to the department store, went straight to the toy department, and selected a blue bicycle before a salesperson approached her. She took the bike to the cash register and paid for it. Since making the purchase, the McGees found out that the bike was cheap in all senses. The chrome plating on the wheels was very thin and rusted away in six months. Both tires split and had to be replaced.

A year later, Cheryl's grandparents sent another $50 for a bike for Mark. Based on their experience with Judy's bike, the McGees by then realized that the lowest-priced bike might not be the least expensive option in the long run. Mark is very active and somewhat careless, so the McGee's wanted to buy a sturdy bike. Mark said he wanted a red, 10-speed, lightweight imported bike with lots of accessories: headlights, special foot pedals, and

so forth. The McGees were concerned that Mark wouldn't maintain an expensive bike with all these accessories.

When they saw an ad for a bicycle sale at Montgomery Ward, Cheryl and Terry went to the store with Mark. A salesperson approached them at an outdoor display of bikes and directed them to the sporting goods department inside the store. There they found row after row of red three-speed bikes with minimal accessories—the type of bike Cheryl and Terry felt was ideal for Mark.

A salesperson approached them and tried to interest them in a more expensive bike. Terry dislikes salespeople trying to push something on him and interrupted her in mid-sentence. He said he wanted to look at the bikes on his own. With a little suggestion, Mark decided he wanted one of these bikes. His desire for accessories was satisfied when they bought a wire basket for the bike.

After buying a bike for Mark, Terry decided he'd like a bike for himself to ride on weekends. Terry had ridden bikes since he was five. In graduate school, before he was married, he'd owned a 10-speed. He frequently took 50-mile rides with friends. But he hadn't owned a bike since moving to Riverside 15 years ago.

Terry really didn't know much about current types of touring bicycles. He bought a copy of *Touring* at the news stand to see what was available. He also went to the library to read *Consumer Reports'* evaluation of touring bikes. Based on this information, he decided he wanted a Serrato. It had all the features he wanted: light weight, durable construction, and flexible setup. When Terry called the discount stores and bicycle shops, he found they didn't carry Serrato. He then decided he might not really need a bike. After all, he'd done without one for 15 years.

One day, after lunch, he was walking back to his office and saw a small bicycle shop. The shop was run down with bicycle parts scattered across the floor. The owner, a young man in grease-covered shorts, was fixing a bike. As Terry was looking around, the owner approached him and asked him if he liked to bicycle. Terry said he used to but had given it up when he moved to

Riverside. The owner said that was a shame because there were a lot of nice places to tour around Riverside.

As their conversation continued, Terry mentioned his interest in a Serrato and his disappointment in not finding a store in Riverside that sold them. The owner said he could order a Serrato for Terry but that they weren't very reliable. He suggested a Ross and showed Terry one he had in stock. Terry thought the $400 price was too high, but the owner convinced him to try it next weekend. They would ride together in the country. The owner and some of his friends took a 60-mile tour with Terry. Terry really enjoyed the experience, recalling his college days. After the tour, Terry bought the Ross.

Discussion Questions

1. Outline the decision-making process for each of the McGees' bicycle purchases.
2. Compare the different purchase processes for the three purchases. What stimulated each of them? What factors were considered in making the store choice decisions and purchase decisions?

This case was prepared by Professor Barton A. Weitz, University of Florida.

The Retail Firm

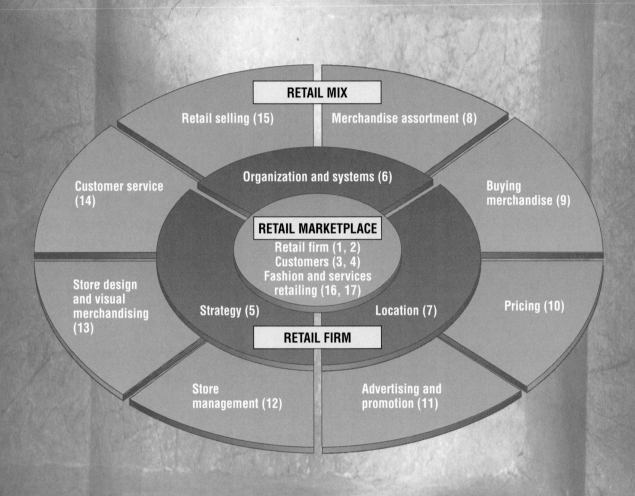

RETAIL MIX

Retail selling (15)

Merchandise assortment (8)

Customer service (14)

Organization and systems (6)

Buying merchandise (9)

RETAIL MARKETPLACE
Retail firm (1, 2)
Customers (3, 4)
Fashion and services retailing (16, 17)

Store design and visual merchandising (13)

Strategy (5)

Location (7)

Pricing (10)

RETAIL FIRM

Store management (12)

Advertising and promotion (11)

Section I described the core of the World of Retailing—retail customers and retailers who compete for their business. It reviewed the different types of retailers and retail competition, the changing nature of retail consumer needs, and factors that affect consumers' choice of stores and merchandise. This broad overview of retailing should help you understand the nature of retail firms and the activities they undertake.

This section describes retail firms, including the strategies retailers pursue (Chapter 5), the organization of retail firms and the systems they use (Chapter 6), and the various places where retailers locate their stores (Chapter 7). The characteristics of each retail firm vary according to its target customers.

The next two sections review tactical elements in the retail mix that retailers use to compete effectively for customers. These elements include the merchandise assortment, purchasing, pricing, advertising and promotion, store management, store layout and merchandise display, customer service, and personal selling.

Retail Strategy

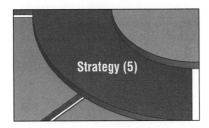

Strategy (5)

Questions that this chapter answers include

- **What is a retail strategy?**
- **How does a retailer build a sustainable competitive advantage?**
- **What growth opportunities do retailers pursue?**
- **What steps do retailers go through to develop a strategy?**
- **How are U.S. retailers participating in the global retail environment?**

Retail competition is increasingly intense due to the emergence of new formats and technology plus shifts in customer needs (outlined in Chapter 3). These changes are forcing retailers to devote more attention to long-term strategic thinking.[1] A retail strategy provides retailers with direction in dealing effectively with the core elements in the World of Retailing—its environment, customers, and competitors.

The first part of this chapter defines the term *retail strategy* and discusses its three important elements: the target market, retail format, and sustainable competitive advantage. Next it outlines approaches for building a sustainable competitive advantage. The chapter concludes with a discussion of the strategic retail planning process.

OBJECTIVES AND MISSION STATEMENT

Every publicly held firm's objective is to maximize its stockholders' wealth by increasing the value of its stock and paying dividends.[2] Owners of small, privately held firms frequently have other objectives such as providing a specific level of income while avoiding risks rather than maximizing profit.

Many retailers have an explicit mission statement. The **mission statement** is a broad description of a retailer's objectives and the scope of activities it plans to undertake.[3] It defines the target segments and retail formats that the firm will consider. For example, the mission statement for a small dry cleaning chain might read, "The mission of Dry Cleaner is to be the leading quality-oriented dry cleaner in Sacramento, provide a stable income of $100,000 per year for the owner, and develop a base of loyal customers by satisfying their needs."

This mission statement defines Dry Cleaner's objectives and the scope of its planned activities. Dry Cleaner's mission statement indicates its management won't consider retail opportunities outside the Sacramento area, opportunities for price-oriented dry cleaning, merchandise-based retailing opportunities (even if they're quality-oriented and in Sacramento), or opportunities that would jeopardize its ability to generate $100,000 in annual income for the owner.

Retail strategy, discussed in the next section, indicates the specific target markets and retail formats that a retailer will pursue.

WHAT IS RETAIL STRATEGY?

Why does a retailer need a retail market strategy? Isn't the key to success simply buying low and selling high? Don't retailers want to sell as much merchandise as possible to anyone who wants to buy it? Why does a retailer need to target specific markets and build competitive advantages in those markets?

A broad, unfocused approach to retailing is similar to generals telling their troops to charge ahead in any direction, capturing as much territory as they can. This undirected system doesn't succeed in either a military or business context. An unfocused approach may lead to short-term increases in sales or territory gains, but these gains are not sustainable over time. A retailer who focuses on specific targets can provide a superior offering to a specific group of customers, while the unfocused retailer may be a second or third choice for everyone.

REFACT

The word *strategy* comes from a Greek wording meaning the art of the general.

Definition of Retail Market Strategy

A **retail strategy** is a statement identifying (1) the retailer's target market, (2) the format the retailer plans to use to satisfy the target market's needs, and (3) how the retailer plans to build a sustainable competitive advantage.[4] The **target market** is the market segment(s) on which the retailer plans to focus its resources and retail mix. A **retail format** is the retailer's retail mix (nature of merchandise and services offered, pricing policy, advertising and promotion program, approach to store design and visual merchandising, and typical location). Here are examples of retail strategies.

Gymboree. Gymboree is a specialty retailer of children's apparel and accessories. It targets families with children under age six. Annual sales are about $200 million. Its retail format offers high-quality, private-label children's apparel in bright colors and bold, "fun" prints. Its traditional merchandise is sold in colorful, brightly lit 1,000-to-1,300–square-foot stores in regional malls. Gymboree developed an advantage over its principal specialty store competitor, GapKids, by creating a unique shopping environment for families seeking conventional apparel for their children. The stores display coordinated outfits on their store walls (1) to make it easy for customers to select wardrobes and (2) to provide floor space for them to maneuver strollers. While parents are shopping, children are encouraged to play with small toys and watch Gymboree videos.[5]

Spiegel. Spiegel, a catalog retailer, has annual sales of more than $2 billion. Its target market is working women age 21 to 59 with incomes in the upper 30 percent of American households. Its primary retail format directed toward this target market is a 600-page catalog, prepared twice a year, with attractive presentations of apparel and home furnishings. Spiegel strives for an advantage over its competition by offering unique, high-quality merchandise provided by its network of suppliers; presenting the merchandise in such an attractive format that customers keep the catalog for months; and operating an efficient order fulfillment system. Each year, its 900 telephone operators handle 18.7 million calls, answering almost all by the second ring. The warehouse system can process and ship 100,000 orders in one shift.[6]

Autozone. Autozone is a Memphis-based auto parts retailer started in 1979. Its annual sales now exceed $1 billion. Its target market is lower-income people who repair their cars themselves out of economic necessity. Autozone has built significant loyalty in this segment by providing exceptional convenience and service. Stores are located in neighborhoods near their customers and stay open until midnight. Almost all employees (called *Autozoners*) have prior automotive repair experience. They're encouraged to go out to the store parking lot with a customer to check on the exact part needed and even help the customer install simple items like headlights and hoses.[7]

Family Dollar. A unique discount chain, Family Dollar has over 1,500 stores generating $800 million in annual sales. Its target market is women age 25 to 49 with family income between $15,000 and $25,000. Family Dollar keeps prices low for people with limited disposable income by operating a no-frills discount retail format. The format is a cross between a discount store and a convenience store. Stores are small (6,000 to 8,000 square feet); have limited service, few employees, and cash-and-carry sales; and are conveniently located in neighborhood centers. Family Dollar has developed a cost advantage over its competition through its distribution system. Merchandise is shipped to stores weekly from a fully automated distribution center based on inventory reports reviewed by buyers and on orders placed directly by store managers using electronic hand-held calculators. Cases are routed across 6.2 miles of mechanized conveyer belts, past laser scanners that divert them to one of 14 shipping lanes. Each lane has a telescoping extension that enables merchandise to be directly loaded into a tractor trailer.[8]

Each of these retail strategies involves the identification of a target market and retail format and the development of capabilities that will enable the retailer to gain a long-term competitive advantage. Now let's examine these central concepts of a retail strategy.

TARGET MARKET AND COMPETITORS

The retailer's strategy needs to consider both elements in the World of Retailing core: customers and competitors. Successful retailers satisfy the needs of customers in their target market better than the competition does. By selecting a target market, retailers indicate which consumers they will attempt to satisfy. By choosing

Traditional retail markets are like this farmers' market where transactions between buyer and seller are made face-to-face.

a retail format, retailers determine the general nature of the retail mix they will use to satisfy needs of customers in the target market.

In some respects, all retailers compete with each other for consumer purchases because consumers have a limited amount of money to spend. Every dollar they spend at the grocery store reduces the amount of merchandise they can buy at a home-improvement center. But competition between home-improvement centers and grocery stores isn't very intense because their retail mixes satisfy different consumer needs. The most intense competition occurs among retailers in the same geographic area with similar retail mixes directed toward the same target market.

The Retailer's Target Market

Traditional markets, like a farmers' market, are places where buyers and sellers meet and make transactions: A consumer buys six ears of corn from a farmer. But in modern markets, potential buyers and sellers aren't located in one place; transactions can occur without face-to-face interactions. Customers can contact potential suppliers and place orders using a telephone or computer.

We define a **retail market** not as a specific place where buyers and sellers meet, but as a group of consumers with similar needs (a *segment*) and a group of retailers using a similar retail format to satisfy those consumer needs. Thus a retail market is defined in terms of consumers (a **target segment** or market) and competitors (other firms using the retail format).[9]

Exhibit 5–1 illustrates a set of retail markets for women's clothing. A number of retail formats are listed in the left-hand column. As described in Chapter 2, each format offers a different retail mix to its customers. Market segments toward which these retail formats are directed are listed in the exhibit's top row. This illustration uses the J.C. Penney fashion segments described in Chapter 4. Each square of the matrix describes a potential retail market where two or more retailers compete with

Retail Markets for Women's Apparel

 EXHIBIT 5-1

Fashion segments

Retail formats	Conservative		Traditional	Updated	Designer
	Ultra	Moderate			
Specialty stores		Charming Shops	Limited Express		
			The Gap		
Department stores			J.C. Penney A&S Burdines Richs	Bloomingdale's Neiman Marcus Sak's	
		Mervyn's			
Discount stores	Wal-Mart		Target		
	Kmart				
Off-price stores		Pic N Save	Marshall's Loehmann's	Steinmart	
Catalog		J.C. Penney	Lands' End	Spiegel	

each other. For example, Limited Express and The Gap stores in the same geographic area compete with each other in two squares: specialty store format catering to the needs of traditional and updated customers. Wal-Mart and Kmart compete with each other by providing a discount retail format directed toward a conservative fashion segment.

The women's clothing market shown in Exhibit 5–1 is just one of several representations that could have been used. Retail formats could be expanded to include outlet stores and TV home shopping. Rather than being segmented by fashion orientation, the market could have been segmented using the other approaches described in Chapter 4, such as demographics and life-style. While Exhibit 5–1 isn't the only way to describe the women's retail clothing market, it does illustrate how retail markets (the squares in the diagram) are defined in terms of retail format and market segment.

Basically, Exhibit 5–1's matrix describes the battlefield where women's clothing retailers compete. The position in this battlefield indicates the first two elements of a retailer's strategy: its target market and retail format. Consider Target's retail strategy. Target decided to focus on one retail market—traditional fashion segment with a discount store format—rather than compete in all 25 markets listed in Exhibit 5–1. Target's retail strategy indicates how it plans to focus its resources.[10]

EXHIBIT 5-2   **Approaches for Developing Competitive Advantage**

A. Advantages based on external relationships

Customer relations (Chapters 4, 14)
 More loyal customers

Legal
 Zoning laws to prohibit competitive entry
 Tax advantages

Location (Chapter 7)

Vendors
 Strong relationships (Chapter 12)

B. Advantages based on internal operations

Merchandise management (Chapters 10–13)
 Exclusive merchandise
 Lower costs for merchandise—scale economies
 More merchandise
 Better assortments
 Better terms
 Lower prices
 Better buyers
 Better advertising
 More sales

Store operations (Chapters 12–15)
 Better service
 Better visual presentation
 Better security, less theft
 Better sales associates
 Better store managers

Retail control systems (Chapter 6)
 Better management information systems
 More efficient distribution
 Better inventory control

Note: **color** type indicates sustainable advantages.

SUSTAINABLE COMPETITIVE ADVANTAGE

The final element in a retail strategy is the retailer's approach to building a sustainable competitive advantage. A **sustainable competitive advantage** is an advantage over competition that a retailer can maintain over a long time. Exhibit 5–2 shows some approaches a retailer can use to gain an advantage over competitors. The list isn't exhaustive. Any business activity that a retailer engages in can be a basis for a competitive advantage.

Some advantages are sustainable over a long period of time, while others can be duplicated by competitors almost immediately.[11] For example, it would be hard for Star Market to get a long-term advantage over Stop & Shop supermarkets in Boston by simply offering coffee at lower prices. Stop & Shop would probably realize quickly—within hours—that Star had lowered its prices and match Star the next day if it found the lower prices were attracting customers. Similarly, it's hard for retailers to develop a long-term advantage by offering broader or deeper assortments. If broader and deeper assortments attract a lot of customers, competitors can simply go out and buy the same merchandise for their stores.

Establishing a competitive advantage means that a retailer builds a wall around its position in the retail market. This wall makes it hard for competitors to contact customers in the retailer's market. If the retailer has built a wall around an attractive market, competitors will attempt to break down the wall. Over time, all advantages will be eroded by these competitive forces; but by building high walls, retailers can sustain their advantage, minimize competitive pressure, and boost profits for a longer time. Thus establishing a sustainable competitive advantage is the key to long-term financial performance.

Five important opportunities for retailers to develop sustainable competitive advantages are (1) customer loyalty, (2) location, (3) vendor relations, (4) management information and distribution systems, and (5) low-cost operations. Let's look at each of these approaches.

Customer loyalty means that customers are committed to shopping at a store. Loyalty is more than simply consumers liking one store more than another. For example, loyal customers may continue to shop at Home Depot home-improvement centers even if Builders Square opens a store nearby and provides a slightly superior assortment or slightly lower prices. Three approaches for developing customer loyalty are positioning, providing good customer service, and offering unique merchandise.

Customer Loyalty

Positioning. One way retailers can foster customer loyalty is by developing a clear and distinct image of their retail offering and consistently reinforcing that image through their merchandise and service. The process of creating and supporting this image is called *positioning*.

Positioning is the design and implementation of a retail mix to create an image in the customer's mind of the retailer, as compared to its competitors.[12] Positioning emphasizes that the image in the customer's mind (not the retail manager's mind) is critical. Thus the retailer needs to research what its image is and make sure that its image matches the needs of customers in its target market.[13] A *perceptual map* is frequently used to represent the customer's image and preference for retailers.

Exhibit 5–3 is a hypothetical perceptual map of retailers selling women's clothing in the Washington, D.C., area. The two dimensions in this map—degree of fashion and service—represent the two primary characteristics that consumers in this example might use in forming their impression of retail stores. On perceptual maps the distance between two retailers indicates how similar the stores appear to consumers. For example, Neiman Marcus and Bloomingdale's are very close to each other on the map because consumers see them as offering similar service and fashion. On the other hand, Nordstrom and Kmart are far apart, indicating consumers' belief that they're quite different. Note that stores close to each other compete vigorously with each other because consumers feel they provide similar benefits.

Based on this example, The Limited has an image of offering moderately fashionable women's clothing with good service. T.J. Maxx offers more fashionable clothing with less service. Sears is viewed as a retailer offering women's clothing that's more traditional in its styling and provides limited service.

Hypothetical Perceptual Map for Women's Apparel Retailers in Washington, D.C.

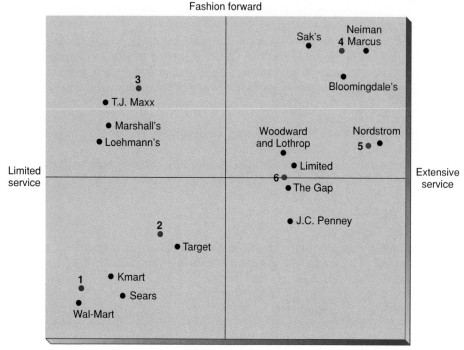

Numbers are ideal combinations of fashion and service for each of six target markets.

The ideal points (marked by green dots on the map) indicate the characteristics of an ideal retailer for consumers in different market segments. For example, consumers in segment 3 prefer a retailer that offers high-fashion merchandise with low service, while consumers in segment 1 want more traditional merchandise and aren't concerned about service. The distance between the retailer's position and the ideal point indicates how consumers in the segment evaluate the retailer. Retailers that are closer to an ideal point are evaluated more favorably by the consumers in the segment than retailers located farther away. Thus consumers in segment 6 prefer The Gap to J.C. Penney because The Gap is closer to their image of their ideal retailer. Re-Tale 5–1 describes Penney's efforts to reposition itself from a mass merchandise store targeting segment 1, to a national department store targeting segment 6.

Service. Through customer service, a retailer can differentiate its offering and build long-term competitive advantage. But offering good service consistently is difficult. Customer service is provided by retail employees, and humans are harder to train and less consistent than machines. Retailers that offer good customer service instill its importance in their employees over a long period of time. For example, Neiman Marcus's service tradition began on opening day in 1907, when Al Neiman met and greeted every customer who visited the store.[14]

It takes considerable time and effort to build a tradition and reputation for customer service, but good service is a valuable strategic asset. Once a retailer has

RE-TALE 5-1   J.C. Penney Develops a New Positioning Strategy

Until the late 1950s, J.C. Penney sold private-label, staple soft goods in small towns across the United States. (See Chapter 1.) When the company started to open stores in the developing regional malls in the 1960s, it emulated Sears, positioning itself to satisfy the needs of segment 1 in Exhibit 5–3, a segment attracted to the fashionable merchandise with high levels of service offered by department stores. Besides clothing, the Penney stores sold appliances, paint, lawn mowers, and car batteries. Many stores had auto repair centers.

In the early 1980s, sales and profits from regional mall stores stagnated. Market research revealed that consumers who shopped in malls were mostly in segments 4, 5, and 6 in Exhibit 5–3. They sought fashionable clothing, not car batteries and refrigerators. In addition, many customers were buying only staples (such as men's underwear and socks and children's clothing) from Penney. They would go across the mall to the other anchor department store for more fashionable clothing.

To rekindle growth in its mall locations, Penney decided to reposition itself as a department store selling fashionable clothing at good value to middle-class consumers. Penney closed the garden and lawn, appliances, paint, hardware, and automotive departments in 1983, and home electronics and sporting goods departments in 1988. These departments accounted for over $1.5 billion in annual sales. Between 1983 and 1987, Penney spent more than $1 billion modernizing its stores so the visual image was consistent with the more fashionable orientation.

To complete the transition from a mass merchant to a department store, Penney complemented its private-label merchandise with national brands that appeal to its target market. Penney is the largest retailer for Dockers by Levi.

Source: Karen Blumenthal, "Penney Moves Upscale in Merchandise but Still Has to Convince the Public," *The Wall Street Journal*, June 7, 1990, pp. A1, A8; and Francine Schwadel, "Fashion Statement, Its Earnings Sagging, Sears Upgrades Line of Women's Apparel," *The Wall Street Journal*, May 9, 1990, pp. A1, A6.

---

earned a service reputation, it can sustain this advantage for a long time because it's hard for a competitor to develop a comparable reputation. Chapter 14 discusses how retailers develop a service advantage.

Merchandise. It's difficult for retailers to develop customer loyalty through merchandise because competitors typically can purchase and sell the same items. But some retailers such as The Gap and The Limited achieve a sustainable competitive advantage by having the merchandise made exclusively for them (as a *private label*).[15]

Location

The classic response to the question "What are the three most important things in retailing?" is "Location, location, and location." Besides being a critical factor in consumers' selection of a store, location lets a retailer gain a sustainable advantage over its competition. For example, when McDonald's occupies a street's best location in terms of traffic patterns, competing fast food retailers are at a disadvantage. Burger King and Wendy's can only overcome this disadvantage if McDonald's abandons its location.[16] Chapter 7 discusses this approach to developing a sustainable competitive advantage.

Vendor Relations

By developing strong relations with vendors, retailers may gain exclusive rights (1) to sell merchandise in a region, (2) to buy merchandise at lower prices or with better terms than competitors, or (3) to receive merchandise in short supply. Relationships with vendors, like relationships with customers, are developed over a long time and may not be easily offset by a competitor.

Kmart has electronic links with 2,600 of its 3,000 vendors and provides 250 vendors with point-of-sale data. By developing computer links with its vendors, Kmart increases its opportunity to have the right merchandise at the right store when the customer wants it.[17] Chapter 9 discusses vendor relationships in detail.

Management Information and Distribution Systems

A key to Wal-Mart's success is its distribution system. It was very costly and took a long time for Wal-Mart to develop enough sales volume in different areas to justify an efficient distribution system. But now that Wal-Mart has developed this advantage, it may be even more costly and difficult for Kmart (which competes in the same retail market) to establish the same level of sales and same low-cost distribution system. In other words, Wal-Mart can maintain its advantage of low-cost distribution for a long time. Similarly, its management information systems enable Wal-Mart to respond quickly to customer needs.[18] Chapter 6 discusses various types of operating systems and shows how some retailers have developed sustainable competitive advantages through them.

Low-Cost Operations

All retailers are concerned about the costs of providing their retail offering. Costs are important even to retailers such as Neiman Marcus that offer excellent service and sell high-priced merchandise to customers who aren't very price-sensitive. If Neiman Marcus can offer the same merchandise quality and service as its competitor at a lower cost, then Neiman Marcus will either make a higher profit margin than its competitors or use the potential profits to attract more customers and increase sales. If Neiman Marcus feels that its customers aren't very price-sensitive, it may decide to attract more customers from its competitors by offering even better service, merchandise assortments, and visual presentation rather than lower prices.

Multiple Sources of Advantage

To build a sustainable advantage, retailers typically don't rely on a single approach such as low cost or excellent service. They need multiple approaches to build as high a wall around their position as possible. For example, Toys "R" Us's success is based on developing loyal customers, maintaining good vendor relations, having excellent information and distribution systems, and controlling costs.[19]

Toys "R" Us's target segment doesn't expect much customer service. Customers know they'll get little assistance in picking out the merchandise. But customers do expect that the store will have any toy they're looking for, that prices will be lower than at most other retail outlets, that any defective merchandise can be returned without question, and that the wait in the checkout line won't be long. Toys "R" Us has developed a loyal group of customers by meeting these expectations every time.

To consistently meet customer expectations, Toys "R" Us has developed capabilities in a number of areas. Its relationships with vendors ensure that it will always have the most popular toys in stock. Its distribution and inventory control systems enable it to carry the appropriate assortment of toys in each of its stores. By providing a number of checkout stands and extensive training for checkout clerks, Toys "R" Us reduces customers' wait in line. This training also means that customers are handled quickly and courteously if they want to return merchandise. By developing a number of unique capabilities, Toys "R" Us has built a high wall around its position as a category specialist serving families with young children.

Re-Tale 5–2 describes an entrepreneur who developed a successful mail-order retail flower business and maintains its performance by developing a unique distribution system and building strong vendor and customer relationships.

RE-TALE 5-2   Calyx & Corolla Builds Competitive Advantage through Distribution

In 1987, Ruth Owades formed a direct mail firm, Calyx & Corolla, retailing fresh-cut flowers. The company was based on an innovative distribution concept giving it a sustainable competitive advantage by directly linking customer and supplier.

Annual flower and plant retail sales are more than $9 billion in the United States. Most sales are made through retail florists (60 percent) and supermarkets (20 percent). Florists are very service-oriented, making special arrangements and providing home delivery. FTD, a worldwide cooperative owned by 25,000 retail florists, enables florists to make deliveries beyond their trading area.

Describing her retail concept, Owades says, "I envision a table with three legs, and Calyx & Corolla is only one of them. The second is the best flower growers available, and the third is Federal Express." Calyx & Corolla mails out more than 100,000 catalogs describing a variety of floral offerings each month. Orders are transmitted directly to growers, who ship directly to customers via Federal Express.

Because most growers are very small businesses, Calyx & Corolla educates them on how to perform their retail activities. Growers are provided with shipping boxes, labels, vases, and sales forecasts. Growers tell Calyx & Corolla when their stock of certain flowers is low so Calyx & Corolla can discuss substitutes with the customer. Federal Express delivery people are trained not to leave packages to freeze when no one is home to take delivery.

Customers can enjoy their flowers one to two weeks longer by ordering from Calyx & Corolla rather than a local florist. Due to its unique distribution system, customers receive flowers two days after they're cut; flowers ordered through FTD or bought at a retail florist are typically cut one to two weeks before purchase.

Source: David Wylie, "Calyx and Corolla," Harvard Business School (Boston), Case 9–592–035, revised October 28, 1992; Patti Hagan, "Hearts and Flowers: The Nose Gay Express," *The Wall Street Journal*, February 14, 1991, p. 36; and "Ruth Owades," *Working Woman Magazine*, February 1991, pp. 10–12.

Calyx & Corolla has developed a strategic advantage through its partnering relationship with Federal Express and flower growers.

GROWTH STRATEGIES

Four types of growth opportunities that retailers pursue (market penetration, market expansion, retail format development, and diversification) are shown in Exhibit 5–4. The vertical axis indicates the degree to which growth opportunities being considered are similar to the market segments the retailer is presently pursuing. A growth opportunity positioned at the lower end of the axis would involve the markets

EXHIBIT 5-4   **Growth Opportunities**

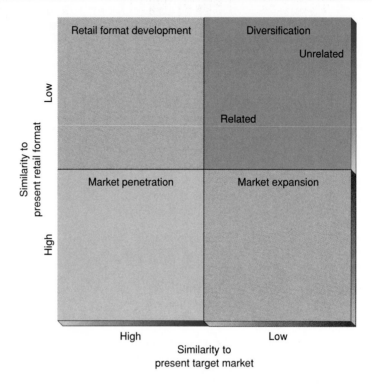

the retailer is targeting now. An opportunity at the upper end of the axis would involve markets that are new and very dissimilar to the retailer's present markets.

The horizontal axis indicates the degree to which the growth opportunities are similar to the retailer's present format. Opportunities positioned to the left involve the same formats being used by the retailer, while opportunities to the extreme right involve new and very dissimilar formats.

Market Penetration

A **market penetration opportunity** involves directing investments toward existing customers, using the present retailing format. An example is attempting to increase sales by inducing current customers to visit the store more often or by attracting consumers in the retailer's target market who don't shop at its stores.

One approach for accomplishing this objective would be to open more stores in the target market in locations convenient to more of the firm's customers. Another approach would be training salespeople to cross-sell. **Cross-selling** means that sales associates in one department attempt to sell customers complementary merchandise from other departments. For example, a sales associate who has just sold a dress takes the customer to the accessories department to sell her a handbag or scarf to go with the dress. More cross-selling will increase sales from existing customers.

A **market expansion opportunity** employs the existing retail format in new market segments. For example, The Gap's strategy is using a specialty store retail format to sell updated sportswear to upscale men and women between ages 20 and 45. GapKids was a market expansion opportunity in which the same specialty store format was directed toward a different segment—families with children aged 2 to 12. Another example—international expansion—is discussed in the following section. International growth involves entering a new geographic segment with a similar retail format.

Market Expansion

A **retail format development opportunity** involves offering present customers a new retail format. For example, Talbots, a catalog retailer, exploited a format development opportunity when it opened specialty stores to sell its present line of merchandise to the same target segment through a new retail format. Another example of a retail format development opportunity would be a retailer's adding additional merchandise categories or altering the breadth and depth of assortments in its stores. Adjusting the type of merchandise or services offered typically involves a small investment, while providing an entirely different format—such as a department store going into catalog retailing—means a much larger investment.

Retail Format Development

A **diversification opportunity** involves an entirely new retail format directed toward a market segment that's not presently served. Sears' entry into retail financial services (Dean Witter) and real estate services (Coldwell Banker) was a diversification investment—an unsuccessful growth strategy it is no longer pursuing.

Diversification

Vertical integration. Vertical integration is an example of diversification. Retailers vertically integrate when they make investments in wholesaling and/or manufacturing merchandise. Examples of vertical integration are The Limited's acquisition of Mast Industries (a trading company that contracts for private-label manufacturing) and Zales's manufacture of jewelry. Typically a backward integration into manufacturing represents diversification because manufacturing merchandise is a very different "format" than retailing merchandise; different operating skills are required. In addition, the immediate customers for a manufacturer's merchandise are retailers, while the retailer's customers are consumers. Thus a manufacturer's marketing activities are very different from a retailer's.

Typically retailers have the greatest competitive advantage in opportunities that are very similar to their present retail strategy. Thus retailers would be most successful engaging in market penetration opportunities that don't involve entering new, unfamiliar markets or operating new, unfamiliar retail formats.[20]

Strategic Opportunities and Competitive Advantage

When retailers pursue market expansion, they build on their strengths in operating a retail format and applying this competitive advantage in a new market. In a retail format extension opportunity, retailers build on their reputation and success with present customers. Even if a retailer doesn't have an advantage in operating the new format, it hopes to attract its loyal customers to a new format.

Retailers have less competitive advantage with opportunities that involve new markets or new retail formats. But retailers must often consider market expansion or retail format extension opportunities. For example, Kmart felt it had saturated its U.S. target market using a general merchandise discount format and decided to pursue a market expansion strategy by opening discount stores in Eastern Europe and Mexico. Kmart also pursued a retail format expansion strategy by opening category specialist stores (Sports Authority, Pace Warehouse, and Builders Square) in the United States, a division which it has now sold off.

Retailers have the least competitive advantage when they pursue diversification opportunities. Thus these opportunities are very risky. In part, Sears' financial problems resulted from its diversification into insurance, real estate, and stockbrokering.

INTERNATIONAL GROWTH OPPORTUNITIES

International expansion is one form of a market expansion growth strategy. Many U.S. retailers are expanding beyond the United States.[21] The most commonly targeted regions are Mexico, Europe, and Japan. Like foreign companies entering the United States, American companies entering these countries face specific government regulations, different cultural traditions, and language barriers. Many U.S. retailers have strong incentives to expand globally because U.S. markets are saturated in terms of the number of stores, available locations, and competition.

Experts believe that many American retailers have a natural advantage when competing globally. American culture is emulated throughout Europe and Japan, giving U.S. retailers an advantage. Also, many U.S. retailers and manufacturers are already accustomed to marketing to this country's culturally diverse population, making their adjustment to global markets easier.

Today's consumers in any developed country share the same important characteristics that high-performance American retailers already understand. Specifically, they enjoy a relatively high level of disposable income—due, in part, to having fewer children per household than in the past, dual-income families, generous benefits from employers and governments, and a strong work ethic. Consumers are also more knowledgeable than ever before about products, brands, and prices. The more consumers in Europe and Japan travel, the more they question why prices on some products in their home country seem artificially high. They don't want to waste time shopping, and they look for value, bargains, and sales. Finally, today's consumers appreciate the selection, convenience, and prices available from category killers like Toys "R" Us and Blockbuster.

Category specialists may be particularly suited to succeed internationally because of the expertise they've already developed at home. For instance, firms like Toys "R" Us provide consumers with an assortment of brand name merchandise procured from sources around the world. This advantage is particularly valuable if brand name merchandise is important to consumers. Second, retailers like Wal-Mart have become the low-price provider in every market they enter because of their buying power and efficient distribution systems. Such expertise can transcend national boundaries. Third, despite differences in the international environment, category specialists have developed unique systems and standardized formats that facilitate control over multiple stores, and these should operate well in any country. Finally, because of the category specialist's narrow assortment and focused strategy, management policies and procedures can be easily communicated to employees with different cultural backgrounds.

Next we'll look at specific issues and opportunities for U.S. retailers in Mexico, Europe, and Japan.

Mexico has become attractive to U.S. retailers for several reasons.[22] The *North*   **Mexico**
American Free Trade Agreement (NAFTA) provides complete access for U.S. retailers to invest in Mexico and Canada.

Mexico has the 14th largest economy in the world, and it's projected to be in
the top 10 in the first decade of the 21st century. Its demographics are also changing.
It's a relatively young nation, with more than one-third of the population under age
14 and 50 percent between ages 15 and 44. This suggests a large consumer
base. Traditionally Mexicans have high brand recognition for U.S. products and
are brand loyal.

A problem facing retailers in Mexico is targeting customers with disposable
income. Fifty-seven percent of the population earn roughly $5 to $10 per day, and
less than 5 percent earn more than $30 per day. Price/Costco, for instance, isn't
moving into Mexico currently because Mexico's small middle class limits the number
of membership warehouses that can do business there. Another formidable issue
is finding a good, yet affordable, location. In the country's population center, Mexico
City, rent can be twice as high as it is in the United States.

Wal-Mart, J.C. Penney, and Dillard are beginning to penetrate Mexican markets, as are Oshman's Sporting Goods, Radio Shack, Blockbuster Video, Pizza Inn,
and Woolworth. However, growth opportunities in Mexico have become less attractive with the devaluation of the peso. Devaluation can dramatically increase the cost
of imported merchandise.

Western Europe has been part of many U.S. retailers' expansion strategies for   **Europe**
some time. Toys "R" Us has been particularly successful. Entering Europe through
England in 1985, the category-killer toy store has spread to France, Germany,
Spain, and Austria. Food retailers such as McDonald's, TGI Friday's, Pizza Hut,
and Häagen-Dazs have also done well in Western Europe. With its purchase of
Cityvision PLC, Blockbuster Entertainment has more than 850 stores in Great Britain
in addition to stores in Germany and Spain. The United States has a fashion presence as well. The Gap and Polo by Ralph Lauren are in Great Britain and on the
Continent.

Although it's still too early to assess the total impact on the European Community (EC) in general and on retailing in particular, 1992 marked the removal of
many physical, fiscal, and technical trade barriers. U.S. retailers positioned in
Europe are experiencing lower costs, easier cross-border expansion, greater
access to advanced computer technology, and fewer restrictions on capital move-
ments and franchising.

A unified EC isn't a panacea for unrestricted Western European growth, how-   **REFACT**
ever. Even though many trade restrictions have been removed, retailers must realize
that European countries, and even regions within those countries, vary widely in   The average U.S.
habits, tastes, customs, and laws. For instance, national planning restrictions have   consumer purchases
prevented hypermarkets from expanding in many countries. Some European gov-   about 1.5 pairs of athletic
ernments have restricted advertising and sales to specific times—mainly end-of-   footwear per year,
summer and post-Christmas clearances. Unions, sometimes backed by religious   compared to about one
organizations, force retailers to close during the evening and on Sunday.   pair every five years for

A number of EC proposals, directives, and cultural trends influence the retail   the average European.[23]
industry. Consumer protection and environmental concerns have become hot
issues. For instance, rules on labeling refillable containers and the civil liability of
batteries and other waste products impact retailing within the EC. Retailers in Germany must recycle packaging materials sold in their stores.

What do successful U.S. firms operating in Europe have in common? First, many Europeans are enamored of retailers and products that embody the American life-style. In fact, Levi's 501 jeans are such a status symbol in Europe that they sell for up to $100 and are often counterfeit. Another important success factor that has crossed the Atlantic is good old American service with a smile. Euro-Disney had difficulty training its largely French staff to always offer courteous, friendly service. Finally, a retailing mix that was previously unavailable in Western Europe has spelled the key to success for American retailers like TGI Friday's in Great Britain. A big menu with simple American cuisine coupled with fast, friendly service at a modest price has filled an important niche in a market previously dominated by expensive white-tablecloth restaurants, pubs, and fish 'n' chips shops. Warehouse club Price/Costco expects to be successful in France and Spain because its membership concept is an improvement on the cash-and-carry stores already there. Price/Costco stores have a large assortment of fresh produce, bakery goods, and nonfood items plus services like pharmacies.

A few U.S.-based retailers are carefully moving into Eastern Europe, where many obstacles await them. Bureaucracies still prevail, and privatization of business has been slow. Laws about land and business ownership are still unclear. Workers are unfamiliar with market economies, and many aren't used to competitive working conditions. Production, distribution, technology, and, in some cases, electrical power are insufficient. Finally, unemployment is high.[24]

Japan

Like Europeans, the Japanese thrive on American culture and fashion. Twenty years ago, many people wore traditional dress like the kimono. Today streetwear is strictly Western. Brides typically wear the traditional bridal kimono only for pictures. Then they change into a white bridal gown that could be found at any American wedding.

Although the Japanese demand Western products, business practices in Japan are very different from those in the United States. In some respects, Japanese store design is way ahead of the United States and other Western countries. For instance, a children's department in a large store is scaled for child-size buyers. An enormous play area is filled with stuffed animals. The Japanese have two gift-giving seasons. Each season represents 20 to 25 percent of their annual business. Their department stores are three to four times the size of their U.S. counterparts. It's not uncommon for a million people to walk into a department store on a Saturday. Some retailers use armies of door-to-door salespeople, as many U.S. companies did 30 years ago.

The distribution system is also different. Unlike in the United States, wholesalers are very strong in Japan, and merchandise is often sold on consignment. Frequently, wholesalers negotiate with retailers for space and operate leased departments within a store. In effect, the retailer has less risk, but also has a lower profit margin than a similar American retailer. Japan offers great opportunity for efficient U.S. retailers with sophisticated distribution systems and a willingness to experiment with new promotional strategies.

Perhaps the most important factor for retail expansion into Japan is the repeal of the Large-Scale Retail Stores Law, which prohibits the opening of large stores (over 500 square meters) without the agreement of a majority of small independent stores in the market area. This law protects both small retailers and larger concerns that are already entrenched in the market. Due to the repeal of this law, Toys "R" Us has been very successful in opening many stores in Japan.[25]

In the next section, we describe how retailers develop strategic plans.

☼ THE STRATEGIC PLANNING PROCESS

The **strategic retail planning process** is the set of steps a retailer goes through to develop a strategic retail plan. (See Exhibit 5–5.) The process enables retailers to target markets, determine the appropriate retail format, and build sustainable competitive advantages.

An analysis of the business relative to its environment is needed to identify retail opportunities, to determine the needs of customers in various markets, and to assess the capabilities needed to satisfy these needs. This analysis, referred to as a **situation audit,** is composed of three elements: (1) assessment of the attractiveness of retail markets where the retailer is competing or might compete, (2) assessment of competitor's objectives and capabilities, and (3) assessment of the retailer's strengths and weaknesses relative to its competition (a self-analysis).[26]

Step 1: Conduct a Situation Audit

Market Attractiveness Analysis. Some factors used to determine the attractiveness of a retail market are the market size and growth; the level of competition in the market; and environmental factors such as technological, economic, regulatory, and social changes that might affect the market.

For example, retail markets for specialty stores are attractive because they are growing faster than those for department stores. Typically, margins and prices are higher in growing markets because competition is less intense than in mature markets.

Retail markets are more attractive when new competitors have little opportunity to enter. Retailers are reluctant to enter a market when a competitor has a cost advantage due to its size. For example, a small entrepreneor would avoid opening a videocassette rental business in a market dominated by Blockbuster Video. Blockbuster would have a considerable cost advantage over the entrepreneur because it buys and rents many more videocassettes. Re-Tale 5-3 discusses how some small retailers develop sustainable advantages over national chains with larger-scale economies.

EXHIBIT 5-5   **Steps in the Strategic Planning Process**

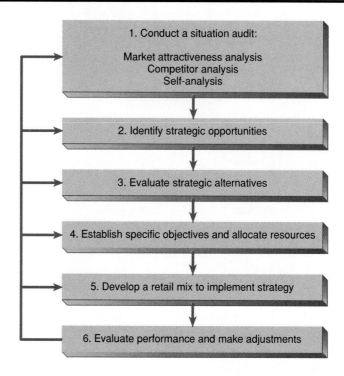

1. Conduct a situation audit:

Market attractiveness analysis
Competitor analysis
Self-analysis

2. Identify strategic opportunities

3. Evaluate strategic alternatives

4. Establish specific objectives and allocate resources

5. Develop a retail mix to implement strategy

6. Evaluate performance and make adjustments

RE-TALE 5-3   **Competing against the Giants**

To compete against national chains, small retailers provide unique merchandise and customer service, and they target market segments that value these benefits. Toys "R" Us and Wal-Mart are primarily interested in selling well-known toys and games at low prices and letting their manufacturers advertise how the toys work. But many toys are too complicated to explain in a 30-second commercial. For example, Playmobil construction toys are only sold through independent toy stores because these stores are interested in setting up Playmobil playpens on their floors so parents and children can have "an out-of-box experience."

Independent fishing tackle shops compete against discount giants (like Wal-Mart and Toys "R" Us) and sporting goods category specialists by offering special services. In Sarasota, Florida, Mr. CB's Bait & Tackle teams up with local charter boat captains to offer seminars and discounted trips. The captains get the fishing trips and Mr. CB's sells the fishing gear. K & K True Value Hardware in Bettendorf, Iowa, focuses on fishing experts who want to make their own lures. The store stocks the raw materials: spinner blades in 14 sizes, tinsel in 40 colors, chicken feathers, deer fur, weights, and hooks.

Source: Barbara Marsh, "Small Fish in the Tackle Business Are Trying New Lure," *The Wall Street Journal,* June 23, 1993, p. B2; and Joseph Pereira, "Toys 'R' Them: Mom-and-Pop Stores Put Playthings Like Thomas on a Fast Track," *The Wall Street Journal,* January 14, 1993, pp. B1, B8.

To evaluate the third aspect of market attractiveness, the impact of environmental factors, retailers need to answer three questions about each environmental factor:

1. What new developments or changes might occur, such as new technologies and regulations or different social factors and economic conditions?
2. What is the likelihood that these environmental changes will occur? What key factors affect whether these changes will occur?
3. How will these changes impact each retail market, the firm, and its competitors?

Competitor Analysis. The most critical aspect of the situation audit is for a retailer to determine its unique capabilities. With a thorough understanding of these capabilities, a retailer can invest in opportunities that exploit its strengths and avoid those that emphasize its weaknesses. Retailers use competitor analysis and self-analysis to assess their unique capabilities.

Competitor analysis focuses on the strategies that competitors are likely to pursue and on their ability to successfully implement these strategies.[27] By understanding its competitors in depth, a retailer can develop an effective strategy to compete against them now and to anticipate competitors' future actions.

Self-Analysis. The **self-analysis** is an internally focused examination of a retailer's strengths and weaknesses.[28] These strengths and weaknesses indicate how well the business can seize opportunities and avoid harm from threats in the environment. Competition is another consideration in self-analysis because a retailer's strengths and weaknesses are defined as its capabilities relative to the competition's.

The second step is to identify potential opportunities. For examples of these opportunities, review our previous discussion of retail markets (Exhibit 5–1) and growth opportunities (Exhibit 5–4).

Step 2: Identify Strategic Opportunities

The third step in the strategic planning process is to evaluate the opportunities identified in the second step. The retailer must analyze its potential to establish a sustainable competitive advantage and reap long-term profits from the opportunities under evaluation. Thus a retailer must focus on opportunities that utilize its strengths—its areas of competitive advantage. For example, expertise in distribution is one of Wal-Mart's sources of competitive advantage. Thus Wal-Mart would consider opportunities that require excellent distribution.

Step 3: Evaluate Strategic Opportunities

After evaluating the strategic opportunities, the next step in the strategic planning process is to establish a specific objective for each opportunity. The retailer's overall objective is included in the mission statement. The specific objectives are goals that measure progress toward the overall objective. Thus specific objectives have three components: (1) the performance sought, including a numerical index used to measure progress, (2) a time frame for achieving the goal, and (3) the level of investment needed to achieve the objective. Typically performance levels are financial criteria, such as return on investment, sales, or profits. Another commonly used objective, market share, is becoming more popular. It's easier to measure and often

Step 4: Establish Specific Objectives and Allocate Resources

more objectively assessed than financial measures based on accounting information (which can be dramatically affected by accounting rules).

Step 5: Develop a Retail Mix to Implement Strategy

The fifth step in the planning process is to develop a retail mix for each opportunity. The elements in the retail mix are discussed in Sections III and IV.

Step 6: Evaluate Performance and Make Adjustments

The final step in the planning process is evaluating the results of the strategy and implementation program. If the retailer is meeting or exceeding its objectives, changes aren't necessary. But if the retailer fails to meet its objectives, re-analysis is needed. Typically this re-analysis starts with reviewing the implementation programs; but it may indicate that the strategy (or even the mission statement) must be reconsidered. This conclusion would result in starting a new planning process including a new situation audit.

Strategic Planning in the Real World

The planning process in Exhibit 5–5 indicates that retailers make strategic decisions sequentially. They perform the situation audit, identify strategic opportunities, evaluate alternatives, set objectives, allocate resources, develop the implementation plan, and, finally, evaluate performance and make any necessary adjustments. But in actual planning processes, the steps interact. For example, the situation audit may uncover a logical alternative for the firm to consider, even though this alternative isn't included in the mission statement. Thus the firm may need to reformulate its mission statement. Development of the implementation plan might reveal that the firm must allocate more resources to achieve the objective. Therefore the firm needs to change its objective, increase its resources, or consider not investing in the opportunity.

Strategic planning is an ongoing process. Every day, retailers audit their situations, examine life-style trends, study new technologies, and monitor competitive activities. But they don't change the retail strategy statement every year or every six months. Retailers review and alter their strategy statement only when major changes occur in their environment or capabilities.

When a retailer undertakes a major reexamination of its strategy, developing a new strategy statement may take a year or two. Potential strategic directions are suggested by people at all levels of the organization. These ideas are evaluated by senior executives and operating people to ensure that the eventual strategic direction can be implemented and will be profitable in the long run.

☼ SUMMARY

A retailer's long-term performance is largely determined by its strategy. The strategy coordinates employees' activities and communicates the direction the retailer plans to take. Retail market strategy includes both the strategic direction and the process by which the strategy is developed.

The retail strategy statement includes the identification of a target market and the retail offering to be directed toward that market. In addition, the strategy needs to indicate the retailer's methods for building a sustainable competitive advantage.

Four growth opportunities that retailers pursue are market penetration, market expansion, format development, and diversification. International expansion is one market expansion strategy that many U.S. retailers are undertaking.

The strategic planning process consists of a sequence that includes a detailed analysis of (1) the environment in which the retailer operates and (2) the retailer's unique capabilities. Based on this analysis, the retailer can evaluate alternatives using financial theory and a market attractiveness/competitive position matrix.

KEY TERMS

competitor analysis, 105

cross-selling, 98

customer loyalty, 93

diversification opportunity, 99

market expansion opportunity, 99

market penetration opportunity, 98

mission statement, 88

positioning, 93

retail format, 88

retail format, development opportunity, 99

retail market, 90

retail strategy, 88

self-analysis, 105

situation audit, 104

strategic retail planning process, 104

sustainable competitive advantage, 92

target market, 88

target segment, 90

DISCUSSION QUESTIONS AND PROBLEMS

1. Why should a retailer have a written statement of its retail strategy?
2. Give an example of a market penetration opportunity, retail format extension, and market extension opportunity for Domino's Pizza.
3. Why should a retailer periodically review its retail strategy?
4. What are McDonald's' competitive advantages? What environmental threats might it face over the next 10 years? How could it prepare for these threats?
5. Give an example of a retailer using the retail format development growth strategy.
6. Disney decided to expand its retail operations by opening specialty stores in malls. What are the advantages and disadvantages of Disney's pursuing this opportunity?
7. Many retailing experts have suggested that improving customer service is the basis for capturing a sustainable competitive advantage in the 1990s. What practical changes can a food/grocery retailer make to improve customer service?
8. A competing ski and surf shop is located in a mall, while your larger store is in a strip shopping center with much less traffic. How can you use elements in the retail mix to overcome the disadvantage of your location?
9. The Limited has expanded its operations through the purchase of Lane Bryant, Structures, Lerner Shops, Victoria's Secret, Henri Bendel, and Limited Express. We might argue that it was good for The Limited to enter new markets and formats and thus improve its market share as well as its profit levels. On the other hand, we could argue that The Limited has lost its focus and is involved in too many businesses. How can The Limited continue to expand and grow while maintaining a clear mission for its businesses?
10. In 1992, the official inauguration of the European Economic Community marked the removal of many physical, fiscal, and technical trade barriers in Europe. What potential advantages and problems are presented to U.S. corporations that wish to enter the European Common Market?
11. Imagine you're a Baskin-Robbins franchisor seeking to open a store in Barcelona, Spain. Discuss this market's special difficulties and opportunities.

Retail Organization and Information Systems

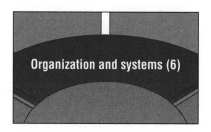

Organization and systems (6)

Questions that this chapter answers include

- **What activities do retail employees undertake, and how are these activities typically organized?**
- **How do retailers coordinate employees' activities?**
- **What systems do retailers use to control the flow of merchandise and information?**
- **How have technological changes of the 1990s like *POS*, *EDI*, and *QR* changed how retailers operate?**

T oday's retail environment is complex. Many retailers have expanded their markets and operate stores in multiple locations—often across the world. Organizing employees and controlling merchandising and store operations have become more difficult.

This chapter describes how retailers organize themselves, coordinate employees' activities, and design systems that control the flow of merchandise (from the vendor to the stores) and the flow of information (from the point of sale at the store, to distribution centers, and on to vendors). Chapter 12 discusses specific human resource activities related to managing store operations, including recruiting, selecting, training, supervising, evaluating, and compensating employees.

TASKS PERFORMED IN A RETAIL FIRM

The **organizational structure** identifies the tasks to be performed by specific employees and determines the lines of authority and responsibility in the retail firm. The first step in developing an organizational structure is to determine which tasks must be performed. Exhibit 6–1 shows tasks typically performed in a retail firm.

These tasks are divided into four major categories: strategic management, merchandise management, store management, and administrative management (operations). Different types of managers are responsible for each type of task. For example, retail strategy decisions (discussed in Chapter 5) are undertaken primarily by senior management: the CEO, president, vice presidents, and the board of directors representing shareholders in publicly held firms.

Tasks Performed in a Retail Firm

Strategic management

Develop a retail strategy
Identify the target market
Determine the retail format
Design organizational structure
Select locations

Merchandise management

Buy merchandise
   Locate vendors
   Evaluate vendors
   Negotiate with vendors
   Place orders
Control merchandise inventory
   Develop merchandise budget plans
   Allocate merchandise to stores
   Review open-to-buy and stock position
Price merchandise
   Set initial prices
   Adjust prices

Store management

Recruit, hire, train store personnel
Plan work schedules
Evaluate performance of store personnel
Maintain store facilities
Locate and display merchandise
Sell merchandise to customers
Repair and alter merchandise
Provide services such as gift wrapping
   and delivery
Handle customer complaints
Take physical inventory
Prevent inventory shrinkage

Administrative management (operations)

Promote the firm, its merchandise,
and services
   Plan communication programs
   Develop communication budget
   Select media
   Plan special promotions
   Design special displays
   Manage public relations
Manage human resources
   Develop policies for managing store
     personnel
   Recruit, hire, train managers
   Plan career paths
   Keep employee records
Distribute merchandise
   Locate warehouses
   Receive merchandise
   Mark and label merchandise
   Store merchandise
   Ship merchandise to stores
   Return merchandise to vendors
Establish financial control
   Provide timely information on
     financial performance
   Forecast sales, cash flow, profits
   Raise capital from investors
   Bill customers
   Provide credit

Operating managers, who are involved in buying merchandise and managing stores, implement the strategic plans. They make the day-to-day decisions that directly affect the retailer's performance.

Administrative management provides plans, procedures, and information to assist operating managers in implementing the firm's strategic plans. Administrative support is provided by employees with specialized skills in human resource management, finance, accounting, management information systems, advertising, and marketing research.

RETAIL ORGANIZATIONAL STRUCTURES

The organizational structure needs to match the firm's retail strategy. For example, retailers such as Circuit City and Costco/Price Club that target price-sensitive customers are very concerned about building a competitive cost advantage to keep their prices low. Thus they minimize the number of employees by having decisions made by a few people at corporate headquarters. These centralized organizational structures are very effective when there are limited regional or local differences in customer needs.

On the other hand, high-fashion clothing customers often aren't very price-sensitive, and tastes vary across the country. Retailers targeting these segments tend to have more managers and more decision making at the local store level. These decentralized organizations have higher human resource costs, but they increase sales by tailoring their merchandise and services to the specific needs of local markets.

Retail organizational structures also differ according to the type and size of the retailer. For example, a retailer with a single store will have an organizational structure quite different from a national department store chain.

Organization of Small Stores

Owner-managers of small stores may be the entire organization. When they go to lunch or go home, the store closes. As sales grow, the owner-manager will hire employees. Coordinating and controlling employees' activities are easier in a small store than in a large firm. The owner-manager simply assigns tasks to each employee and watches to see that these tasks are performed properly. Because the

EXHIBIT 6-2   **Organization of a Small Retailer**

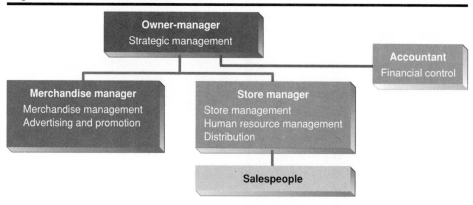

NOTE: The box color for the position on the organization chart matches the tasks shown in Exhibit 6–1 throughout the chapter.

number of employees is limited, small retailers have little specialization. Each employee must perform a wide range of activities, and the owner-manager is responsible for all management tasks.

When sales increase, management specialization may occur when the owner-manager hires management employees. Exhibit 6–2 illustrates the common division of management responsibilities into merchandise and store management. The owner-manager continues to perform strategic management tasks. Besides the store management tasks listed in Exhibit 6–1, the store manager also may be responsible for distribution tasks and human resource management. The merchandise manager may handle promotion tasks as well as the merchandise tasks. Often the owner-manager hires an accounting firm to perform financial control tasks.

Organization of Regional Department Store Chains

In contrast to the management of small retailers, retail chain management is complex. Managers must supervise units that are geographically distant from each other. In this section, we use Rich's (a regional department store chain headquartered in Atlanta, Georgia) to illustrate the organization of a large, multi-unit retailer.

Traditionally department stores were family-owned and -managed. Their organization was governed by family circumstances, with executive positions designed to accommodate family members involved in the business. In the 1930s, most department stores began to adopt a more rational organization plan grouping employees into strategic, merchandising, store operations, and staff activities.[1]

Exhibit 6–3 shows Rich's organization. Most regional department store chains—such as Strawbridge & Clothier in Philadelphia, Weinstock's in Sacramento, Parisian in Alabama, and The Broadway in Los Angeles—have similar structures. Vice presidents responsible for specific merchandise, store, and administrative tasks report to the chairperson and president.

Most managers and employees in the stores divisions work in stores located throughout the geographic region. The distribution center employees and managers

Abdul Qaiyum is the owner and manager of Merz Apothecary, a homeopathic and alternative pharmaceutical store in Chicago. He does not have a problem coordinating decisions because he makes all of them.

EXHIBIT 6-3 **Organization of a Rich's Department Store Chain**

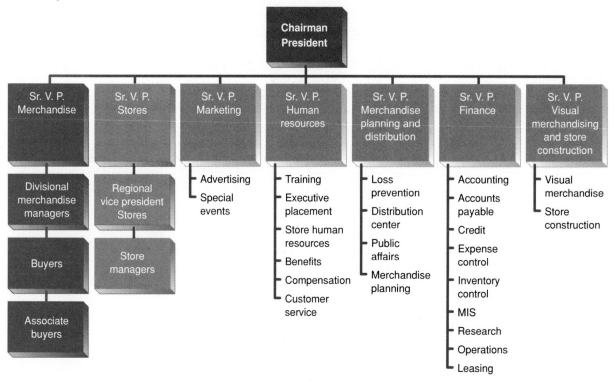

work in one or two distribution centers in the region. Senior executives and the merchandise, marketing, and human resource division employees work at corporate headquarters.

Merchandise Division. The merchandise division is responsible for procuring the merchandise sold in the stores and ensuring that the quality, fashionability, assortment, and pricing of merchandise is consistent with the firm's strategy. Chapters 8 through 10 discuss these elements of the retail mix that are controlled by the merchandise division.

Exhibit 6–4 shows in detail the organizational structure of Rich's merchandise division. Each vice president is responsible for specific categories of merchandise. Vice presidents report directly to the chairperson, the executive in charge of the merchandising activities.

The buyer is the key operating manager in the merchandise division. Each buyer is responsible for a specific category of merchandise, such as girls' sizes 7 to 14 or infants' clothing. Buyers may have one or two associate or assistant buyers reporting to them. The buyers actually select merchandise and price it. They determine what merchandise each store stocks and sells, and manage their "business" with profit-and-loss responsibility.

Merchandise Division Organization—Rich's

EXHIBIT 6-4

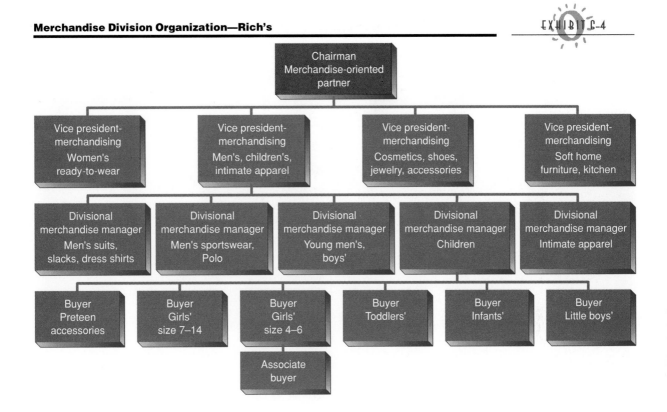

Stores Division. The stores division is responsible for the group of activities undertaken in stores, including merchandise sales and customer services. Each vice president is in charge of a set of stores. A general manager or store manager is responsible for each store.

Exhibit 6–5 shows the organizational chart of a Rich's store. The general manager has a director of selling services reporting to him or her. The director of selling services is responsible for presenting the store's merchandise, selling merchandise, and providing service to customers. Group sales managers, sales managers, and the salespeople who work for them are responsible for working with customers in a specific area of the store. For example, a sales manager might be responsible for the area in which kitchen appliances, gifts, china, silver, and tableware are sold, while a group sales manager might be responsible for an entire floor of the store.

Exhibit 6–5 shows that two administrative managers—personnel and operations—are assigned to each store. The personnel manager assists the selling services and merchandise managers as well as the general manager in recruiting, selecting, and evaluating store personnel. The director of administration is responsible for store maintenance; store security; receiving, shipping, and storage areas of the store; some customer service activities such as returns, complaints, and gift wrapping; and leased areas, such as a restaurant or hair styling salon.

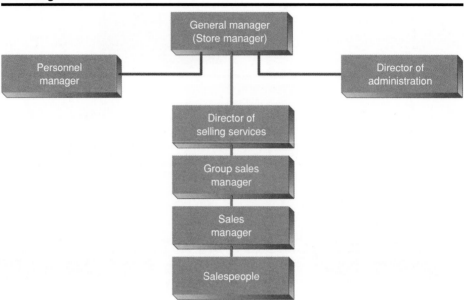

Administrative Divisions. Exhibit 6–6 summarizes responsibilities for the departments within administrative divisions at Rich's: marketing, human resources, operations, and finance.

ORGANIZATIONAL DESIGN ISSUES

Centralized versus Decentralized Decision Making

Federated Department Stores, Inc., is a retail corporation that owns a number of regional department store chains including Burdines, Rich's, The Bon Marche, Bloomingdale's, and Macy's. The corporation is an example of a decentralized organization because many retailing decisions are made by regional department store chains, not by corporate managers. **Centralization** is the degree to which authority for retailing decisions is delegated to corporate managers rather than to geographically dispersed regional, district, and store managers.

Most national and large regional specialty and discount store chains have a much more centralized organizational structure than Federated Department Stores. For example, The Gap, The Limited, and Wal-Mart make all merchandise decisions at corporate headquarters. None are made at regional or local levels.

However, store management is quite similar in centralized and decentralized retail organizations because the stores are decentralized geographically. One person is responsible for stores and operations at The Gap, in contrast to the seven regional executives for stores and operations in the decentralized Federated Stores organization. But The Gap, which has over 1,000 stores, needs more levels of store management (four zone vice presidents, 18 regional managers, 195 district managers) than Rich's, which has 40 stores.

Advantages and Disadvantages of Centralization. Retailers can reduce costs when decision making is centralized in corporate management. First, overhead falls

Responsibilities of Administrative Divisions

EXHIBIT 6-6

Marketing Division. Development of marketing strategy and management of advertising and special events.

Advertising Department. Design and placement of newspaper, radio, and TV ads; the design and distribution of catalogs sent through the mail; and customer research.

Special Events Department. Planning and implementation of special events such as Elizabeth Taylor's store visits to promote Passion perfume.

Visual Merchandising and Store Planning Department. Design and development of window and interior displays. Displays are sent to the stores and then are installed by store personnel.

Human Resources Division. Personnel planning and policies. Recruits, selects, and trains hourly management trainees and executives. Establishes and administers personnel policies and procedures. Determines employee benefit packages and negotiates with vendors that provide these benefits. Develops and administers employee compensation programs. Administers employee evaluation and career planning activities. Hiring, training, evaluating, and supervising hourly employees is done in the stores. Chapter 12 details these activities.

Operations Division. Loss prevention programs, the physical distribution of merchandise from vendors to the stores, and special services provided in some stores (such as restaurants and hair styling salons).

Loss Prevention. Minimizes inventory shrinkage by designing stores appropriately, installing procedures and systems to monitor and locate the cause of losses, and communicating the importance of loss prevention to employees.

Distribution Center. Moves merchandise from vendors to the stores.

Finance Division. Long-range financial planning, budgeting, and financial control activities. Maintains accounting records, prepares financial records. Assists other divisions in preparing budgets and monitors performance of these budgets. Manages the firm's credit program. Receives and disburses cash.

MIS Department. Collects data and provides reports that assist buyers in managing the inventory for which they're responsible.

because fewer managers are required to make the merchandise, human resource, marketing, and financial decisions. For example, Federated has eight women's blouse buyers (one in each regional department store chain) and a corporate buyer for private-label blouses. The Gap has one buyer for women's blouses at the corporate headquarters.

Second, by coordinating its efforts across geographically dispersed stores, the centralized organization achieves lower prices from suppliers. Finally, centralization provides an opportunity to have the best people make decisions for the entire corporation. For example, in a centralized organization, people with the greatest expertise in areas such as MIS, buying, store design, and visual merchandise can have all stores benefit from their skills.[2]

Most centralized retail organizations emphasize efficiency. Standard operating policies are used for store and personnel management; these policies limit the decisions of store managers. Often stores are similar physically and carry similar merchandise. Corporate merchandisers do considerable research to determine the best method for presenting merchandise. They provide detailed guides for displaying merchandise to each store manager so that all stores look the same throughout the country. Because they offer the same core merchandise in all stores, centralized

REFACT

Rich's, with annual sales of about $1 billion, has over 90 people in its buying organization. The Gap, with more than twice the annual sales, has only half as many buyers; Wal-Mart has the same number of buyers as Rich's but 40 times the sales.

RE-TALE 6-1   Longs Drug Store Managers Are Entrepreneurs

Typically, each of the links in a chain store are alike. The stores stock the same merchandise, have the same prices, and use the company handbook. Longs Drug, Inc., with annual sales in 1995 of over $2.5 billion from 195 stores in six western states, outperforms other firms in the retail drugstore industry by taking a different approach.

Longs treats its store managers as independent entrepreneurs. The store manager determines what merchandise to carry and how to organize the store. Advertising is also done locally. With so much decision making decentralized, only 400 of Longs' 12,000 employees work in the corporate headquarters.

To appreciate the effects of decentralization, consider the two Longs stores in Walnut Creek, California,

a suburb northeast of San Francisco. One store, near a retirement community, promotes aspirin, laxatives, and other products used by the elderly. Small sizes rather than family sizes are carried. The store across town, in an area of upper-income professionals with young families, emphasizes disposable diapers, feminine hygiene products, cameras, and VCRs.

SOURCE: Ellen Paris, "Managers as Entrepreneurs," *Forbes,* October 31, 1988, pp. 62–63; and Jeffrey Epstein, "Longs' Plan for Long-Term Growth," *Drugstore Merchandiser,* July 1989, p. 70.

retailers can achieve economies of scale by advertising through national media rather than more costly local media.

While centralization has the advantage of reducing costs, it's hard for the centralized retailer to tailor its offering to the needs of local markets. Re-Tale 6–1 discusses how a large drugstore chain uses decentralized management to cater to local markets' needs.

Coordinating Buying and Store Management Activities

Small independent retailers can effectively coordinate their stores' buying and selling activities. Owner-managers typically buy the merchandise and work with their salespeople to sell it. Because they're in close contact with customers, they understand their customers' needs.

Large retail firms' buying and selling functions, on the other hand, are organized into separate divisions. Their organization charts suggest that buyers specialize in buying merchandise and have little contact with the store management responsible for selling it. While this specialization increases buyers' skills and expertise, it makes it harder for them to understand customers' needs. Four approaches large retailers use to coordinate buying and selling are (1) improving communications between buyers and sellers, (2) making store visits, (3) assigning employees to coordinating roles, and (4) decentralizing the buying decisions.

Improving Communications. Fashion-oriented retailers use several methods to increase buyers' contact with customers and to improve informal communication between buyers and store personnel who sell the merchandise they buy. Management trainees, who eventually become buyers, are required by most department stores to work in the stores before they enter the buying office. During this 6-to-18–month training period, prospective buyers gain appreciation for how stores operate, the problems salespeople and department managers encounter, and the needs of customers.

Making Store Visits. Another approach to increasing customer contact and communication is to have buyers visit the stores and work with the departments they buy for. At Wal-Mart, all managers (not just the buyers) are required to visit stores frequently and practice their philosophy of MBWA (management by wandering around). Managers leave corporate headquarters in Bentonville, Arkansas, on Sunday night and return to share their experiences at the traditional Saturday morning meetings.[3]

Spending time in the stores improves trainees' and buyers' understanding of customer needs. It provides buyers with a richer view of store and customer needs than they can get from impersonal sales reports from the company's management information system. But this approach is costly because it cuts the buyer's time to review sales patterns, plan promotions, manage inventory, and locate new sources of merchandise.

Assigning Employees to Coordinating Roles. Some retailers have merchandise liaisons who coordinate buying and selling activities. Merchandise liaisons report to each divisional merchandise manager in the buying organization. They spend 75 percent of their time in the stores assisting store personnel in displaying and selling merchandise. In addition, liaisons inform buyers of any problems stores are having with merchandise.

Most national retail chains have regional and even district staff personnel to coordinate buying and selling activities. For example, Target's regional merchandise managers in Chicago work with stores in the North Central region to translate plans developed by corporate buyers into programs that meet the regional needs of consumers.

Involving Store Management in Buying Decisions. Another way to improve coordination between buying and selling activities is to increase store employees' involvement in the buying process. Rather than centralizing the buying decisions at corporate headquarters in Seattle, Nordstrom has buyers who live in each geographic region and buy merchandise for that region. Because these buyers work with a limited number of stores in close proximity to their offices, they're in the stores frequently.

J.C. Penney has a tradition of decentralized store management. Management in each store determines what merchandise that store will sell. Each season, buyers at corporate headquarters in Dallas select merchandise and present it over closed-circuit TV to managers in all Penney stores. Prior to the transmission, store managers are given an order-planning form with retail prices, margins, and suggested quantities and assortments for their store size. During the broadcast, store managers can call corporate buyers in Dallas, ask questions, and suggest different types of merchandise that might be popular in their local markets. One week after the broadcast, store merchandise managers place their orders for the merchandise presented through computer terminals linked to the Penney management information system. Buyers then accumulate all store orders and place the company's order with the vendor.[4]

Using regional buyers and involving store managers in buying decisions enables Nordstrom and J.C. Penney to better tailor their merchandise to local markets. But the firms lose some buying efficiency. At Nordstrom, regional buyers only place orders for four stores. They can't use the chain's entire buying power to get prices

J.C. Penney's direct broadcast system achieves the efficiencies of centralized buying and allows for tailoring assortments to local markets. Store managers select merchandise presented by corporate buyers over close-circuit TV broadcasts made to each store.

as low and delivery as quick as comparably sized competing chains receive. By pooling orders from all its stores, Penney can place large orders and get favorable prices from its vendors. But corporate buyers may be reluctant to make and get firm commitments from vendors until they receive orders from individual stores.

While buying decisions are made by Penney merchandise managers who interact daily with their customers, these managers have limited buying expertise. Frequently they've just completed a management training program after graduating from college. Corporate buyers with significant experience and expertise are often frustrated because the store merchandise managers aren't quick to adapt to fashion trends buyers see coming. Finally, the merchandise managers in the stores only see the merchandise on TV. They can't feel the merchandise or see its true colors.[5]

NEW DEVELOPMENTS IN RETAIL ORGANIZATIONS

To improve financial performance in the face of increased competition, retailers are changing their organizations. They are reducing costs by flattening the organizational structure, creating organizational cultures to guide employees, improving employee productivity through empowerment, and adopting managing diversity programs. Re-Tale 6–2 outlines Home Depot's philosophy for involving all of its employees in the company's operation.

Flatter Organizations

Flattening the organization means reducing the number of management levels. For example, the Rich's merchandise department we saw in Exhibit 6–4 has five levels: CEO/president, vice president, divisional merchandise manager, buyer, and associate buyer. A flatter organizational structure might have three levels: CEO, divisional manager, and buyer. Cutting management levels reduces the total number of managers and increases the organization's responsiveness to customers and competitors. Higher-level managers are closer to the customer. Fewer levels of approval are needed to make changes and implement new programs.

RE-TALE 6-2   Home Depot's Management Philosophy

The following quotations from Home Depot's 1992 annual report illustrate its management philosophy:

Candid two-way communications—We make sure our employees know what is expected of them and what they should expect—even demand from their managers. We value free expression, individuality, and self-reliance within the context of team work, experimentation, and risk taking. . . . We will lose our entrepreneurial focus if we evolve into a company of many thousands of people marching in lockstep, all with the same mentality, same behaviors, and same politically correct attitudes.

Training—Our company does not manage by memo or edict. . . . Our officers and senior managers don their orange aprons and spend a significant amount of time in the stores, working alongside, teaching, and learning from our store employees.

Compensation—We believe that the best way to create wealth is to share it. Our philosophy is to pay people what they are worth. We have no set pay scales, and no one makes minimum wage. Through our stock purchase plans, all of our employees are able to become owners of the company.

Diversity—We believe in the strength that comes from diversity and continue to make progress in the hiring and promotion of women and minorities. In an industry (home improvement centers) that has traditionally been male-dominated, we have managed to develop an employee base that is a reasonable representation of the communities where we do business.

SOURCE: 1992 Annual Report, The Home Depot.

On the other hand, in a flatter organization, managers have more subordinates reporting to them so they can't supervise them closely. They must trust their subordinates to do their jobs well.[6]

Organizational Culture

An **organizational culture** is the set of values, traditions, and customs in a firm that guides employee behavior. These guidelines replace written policies and procedures with traditions passed along by experienced employees to new employees.[7] Many retail firms are developing strong organizational cultures to give employees a sense of what they ought to do on their jobs and how they should behave to be consistent with the firm's strategy.

For example, Nordstrom's strong organizational culture emphasizes customer service, while Wal-Mart's organizational culture focuses on reducing costs so the firm can provide low prices to its customers. Nordstrom explains its culture in the policy manual given to new employees. The manual has one rule: Use your best judgment to do anything you can to provide service to our customers. Lack of written rules doesn't mean that Nordstrom employees have no guidelines or restrictions on their behavior. Its organizational culture guides employees' behavior. New salespeople learn from other employees that they should always wear clothes sold at Nordstrom, that they should park their car at the outskirts of the parking lot so customers can park in more convenient locations, that they should approach customers who enter their department, that they should accept any merchandise returned by a customer even if the merchandise wasn't purchased at a Nordstrom store, and that they should offer to carry packages to the customer's car.

Wal-Mart makes extensive use of symbols and symbolic behavior to reinforce its emphasis on controlling costs and keeping in contact with customers. Symbols are an effective means of communicating with employees because employees can easily remember the concepts the symbols represent. At Wal-Mart's corporate head-quarters, photocopy machines have cups on them for employees to use to pay for any personal copying. Employees present information on cost-control measures they've recently undertaken. At traditional Saturday morning executive meetings, managers who've been traveling in the field report on what they've seen, unique store programs, and promising merchandise. Headquarters are spartan. Founder Sam Walton (one of the world's wealthiest people before he died) lived in a modest house and drove a pickup truck to work.

Empowerment

Empowerment is the process of managers sharing power and decision-making authority with employees. When employees have authority to make decisions, they become more confident in their abilities, have greater opportunity to provide service to customers, and feel they're more important contributors to their firm's success.[8]

For example, Parisian, a regional specialty department store chain, changed its check authorization policy, empowering sales associates to accept personal checks up to $1,000 without a manager's approval. Under the old policy, customers frequently had to wait 10 minutes for a sales associate to locate a manager for approval. Then the busy manager simply signed the check without reviewing the customer's identification. When sales associates were empowered to make approvals, service improved, and the number of bad checks decreased because the sales associates felt personally responsible and checked the identification carefully.

Managing Diversity

Managing diversity is a set of human resource management programs designed to realize the benefits of a diverse work force. Today diversity means more than differences in skin color, nationality, and gender. Diversity also includes differences in religion, age, disability status, and sexual orientation.

Managing a diverse work force isn't a new issue for retailers. In the late 1800s and early 1900s, waves of immigrants entering America went to work in retail stores. The traditional approach for dealing with these diverse groups was to blend them into the "melting pot." Minority employees were encouraged to adopt the values of the majority, white, male-oriented culture. To keep their jobs and get promoted, employees abandoned their ethnic or racial distinctiveness.

But times have changed. Minority groups now embrace their differences and want employers to accept them for who they are. The appropriate metaphor now is a "salad bowl," not a melting pot. Each ingredient in the salad is distinctive, preserving its own identity, but the mixture of ingredients improves the combined taste.[9]

Legal restrictions promote diversity in the workplace by preventing retailers from practicing discrimination based on non–performance-related employee characteristics.[10] But retailers now recognize that promoting employee diversity can improve financial performance. They need a diverse group of employees and managers to effectively meet the needs of an increasingly diverse marketplace and work force. (See Chapter 3.)

For example, 85 percent of the men's clothing sold in department stores is bought by women, while over 50 percent of Home Depot's sales are made to women. To better understand customer needs, department store and home-improvement retailers feel that they must have women in senior management positions—people who really understand their female customers' needs.

The fundamental principle of managing diversity is the recognition that employees have different needs, and it takes diverse approaches to accommodate those needs. Managing diversity goes beyond meeting equal employment opportunity laws. It means accepting and valuing differences. Some retailers manage

Retailers recognize that a diverse work force is crucial to future success. Top management needs to reflect the increased diversity in its customer base.

diversity by offering diversity training, providing support groups and mentoring, and managing career development and promotions.[11]

As the previous section indicates, retailers are significantly changing the way they organize and manage their employees. However the most dramatic changes have occurred in the systems retailers use to manage the flow of merchandise and information. These systems are discussed in the remaining portion of this chapter.

RETAIL DISTRIBUTION AND INFORMATION SYSTEMS

Until recently, most retailers knew what merchandise was going into their stores, but they did not know what was selling (or not selling). They had to wait for store employees to count the merchandise before they would order more merchandise or reduce prices to sell excessive inventory.

Controlling inventory has become even more complex. As we discussed in Chapters 2 and 5, many retailers have expanded their markets and operate stores in multiple locations—often across the world. Fortunately new technologies and improved distribution systems enable retailers to make better, more efficient, and more profitable decisions.

In the past, all record keeping associated with ordering and receiving merchandise, shipments from distribution centers to individual stores, sales of individual items, and returns either was handled by hand at a significant expense or was simply neglected. (A retailer-operated **distribution center or DC** is a warehouse that receives merchandise from multiple vendors and distributes it to multiple stores.)[12]

RE-TALE 6-3   A Passion for Customers: The Limited Stores

The magic of The Limited is that a chain with more than 4,000 stores can take a product from conception through production and distribution, and have it ready for sale in four or five weeks—a task that takes most of its competitors nine months. The Limited, Inc., includes The Limited stores, Lane Bryant, Victoria's Secret, Express, Brylane, Structure, Lerner, Henri Bendel, and Abercrombie & Fitch. Its main (but not only) distribution center in Columbus, Ohio, is the largest shipping and distribution center in the world. It's as large as 30 football fields! More than 200 million garments pass through the distribution center each year—almost three items for every woman in the United States. In the women's apparel and fashion industry, a key to success is the ability to quickly make the latest look available to a wide range of customers. The Limited's success isn't derived, therefore, simply from its large distribution center. The firm is dedicated to a sense of urgency to move merchandise from over 200 producers from 30 different countries to the customer in record time.

What's the secret of this distribution phenomenon? First, The Limited buyers search the globe for leading-edge ideas and bring samples back to Columbus. Once the firm decides to pursue a new product, it contacts its manufacturing subsidiary, Mast Industries, Inc., and instructs it to contract production for the item. Completed merchandise is shipped directly to the Columbus distribution center via specially outfitted Boeing 747s. Once the merchandise arrives, it's sorted, priced, and reshipped to the stores—all in about two days.

For example, one buyer spotted scores of teenagers in Florence, Italy, grabbing bulky yachting sweaters off the shelves of a small shop. The design was copied, and the name Forenza was used because it sounded like an Italian designer (who, by the way, never existed). Over 3 million sweaters were sold, making it the most successful sweater design ever sold in America.

The Limited's distribution system profoundly affects its merchandising and financial functions. The added expense of the Boeing 747 airliners is easily offset by increased inventory turnover and lower markdowns. A four- or five-week lead time allows buyers to respond quickly to successful products with reorders. Unlike many department stores, The Limited need not purchase enough merchandise to last the whole season. If the merchandise isn't successful, losses due to markdowns are less because less was purchased in the first place. In contrast, when many department stores find they've misjudged the strength of a fashion trend, they've already bought a six-month supply. Only drastic markdowns can correct such a mistake.

The Limited didn't become the largest specialty store chain in the United States simply because of its superior distribution system. Yet its distribution system is an integral part of its corporate strategy of bringing the customer the hottest fashion trends fast.

SOURCE: Tom Peters, "A Passion for Customers," Public Broadcasting Service; and *Fairchild's Retail Stores Financial Directory 1992–1993* (New York: Fairchild, 1992), p. 121.

Now computer systems perform these functions and link the point-of-sale (POS) terminals to the merchandising system. (A **POS terminal** or cash register reads the purchased item's UPC tag and then records and transmits the data.)

Today many retailers work closely with their vendors to predict customer demand, shorten lead times for receiving merchandise, and reduce inventory investment. They've established on-line systems that link their POS cash registers to computer terminals on retail buyers' desks. They can determine exactly what's selling by item, store, and vendor on a minute-by-minute basis. As a result, retailers can reduce inventory investment and improve customer service.

Consider Leda Perez who recently went to her local department store on a Saturday afternoon when she saw an ad for washable silk blouses. Unfortunately the store was out of her size in all the colors she liked. The store gave her a rain check so she could come back when it received a new shipment and still get the sale price. Perez wasn't impressed. She had fought the traffic, waited in line, and generally wasted her afternoon. The problem could have been avoided because the merchandise was available in the distribution center, but it hadn't been delivered to the store on time.

With a better inventory and distribution system, the department store could satisfy Ms. Perez, increase its profits, and decrease its inventory investment. With better information on what is selling, the buying staff could take advantage of special vendor deals and obtain the silk blouses at lower cost. Transportation costs could also be lowered by coordinating deliveries, thus lowering transportation expenses. The retailer's distribution center would be more efficient because merchandise could be received, prepared for sale, and shipped to stores with minimum handling. Because the retailer's information system would be directly linked to the vendor's computer, the retailer would need less back-up inventory. And finally, the systems would identify fast-selling items and automatically reorder them so that Leda Perez would find what she wants on display in the store. Re-Tale 6–3 shows how The Limited achieves success by using its distribution and information system to better satisfy its customers' needs.

Exhibit 6–7 illustrates the flow of merchandise and information in a typical multistore chain. In the next two sections we describe how information on customer desires is captured at the store and then triggers a series of responses from the buyer, distribution center, and vendor that's designed to ensure that merchandise is available at the store when the customer wants it.

REFACT

Total distribution cost as a percentage of retail sales averages over 17 percent.[13]

THE PHYSICAL FLOW OF MERCHANDISE

Retail distribution (or **logistics**) is the organized process of managing the flow of merchandise from the source of supply—the vendor—through the company's internal processing functions—warehousing and transportation—until the merchandise is sold and delivered to the customer. The merchandise flow in Exhibit 6–7 is shown in solid lines. Merchandise flows from vendor to distribution center to stores, or directly from the vendor to stores. When merchandise is temporarily stored at the distribution center, it's prepared to be shipped to individual stores. This preparation may include breaking shipping cartons into smaller quantities that individual stores can more readily utilize, as well as tagging merchandise with price stickers and the store's label.

The distribution center performs several functions: coordinating inbound transportation, receiving, checking, storing, ticketing, marking, filling orders, and coordinating outbound transportation. To fully understand the distribution function within a retailing organization, consider a shipment of Haggar slacks arriving at a Kmart distribution center.

The Distribution Center

Management of Inbound Transportation. The slacks buyer traditionally worked with Haggar to determine merchandise assortments, pricing, promotions, and the terms of purchase, such as discounts to take for early payment. Now, however, the buyer also gets involved in coordinating the physical flow of merchandise to the stores. For example, the slacks buyer arranges for a truckload of hosiery and underwear to be delivered to the Detroit distribution center on Monday between 1 and 3 P.M. The truck must arrive within the specified time because the distribution center has all of the receiving docks allocated throughout the day, and much of the merchandise on this particular truck is going to be shipped to stores that afternoon. Unfortunately the truck is delayed in a snow storm. The **dispatcher** (the person who coordinates deliveries to the distribution center) reassigns the Haggar truck to a Wednesday morning delivery slot and fines the firm several hundred dollars for missing its delivery time.

EXHIBIT C-7   **Flow of Merchandise and Information**

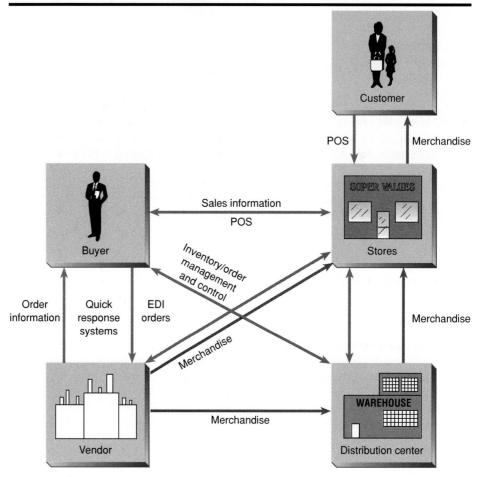

Receiving and Checking. Receiving refers to the process of recording the receipt of merchandise as it arrives at a distribution center. **Checking** is the process of going through the goods upon receipt to make sure they arrived undamaged and that the merchandise ordered was the merchandise received. The Haggar shipment is received and checked in using electronic scanners. Haggar marks the boxes with unique identifying bar codes. The person on the receiving dock simply scans the bar-coded boxes, and the merchandise is automatically checked in. Unless the merchandise appears to be damaged, there's no need to break open cartons and count merchandise because the contents have been electronically recorded.

Storing. The Haggar shipment is a week early, so it has to be temporarily stored rather than shipped immediately to stores. The merchandise is loaded onto forklift trucks that carry it to prespecified locations in the distribution center. Often merchandise is ordered in full pallet quantities. A **pallet** is a platform, usually made of wood, that provides stable support for several cartons and is used to help move and store merchandise.

The Retail Firm

© Logistics is the key to success for Calyx & Corolla, a mail-order cut flower retailer. The company trains growers on careful packing methods, and Federal Express drivers on the special needs of flowers during delivery. The result is fresher and longer-lasting flowers. (Chapter 6)

© Regular deliveries of merchandise are critical for achieving high levels of customer service and inventory turnover. (Chapter 6)

© Orders from retailers are picked by workers using sophisticated tracking and hauling devices (top) and then are moved through the warehouse on conveyer belts to the docks where they are loaded onto outbound trucks. (Chapter 6)

© Milan, Italy's Galeria Vittorio Emanuele (top) is probably the world's oldest enclosed shopping mall, erected over 125 years ago, and has weathered many changes in Italy's economic and political fortunes. By contrast, G.U.M. (bottom), the largest retail store in the Commonwealth of Independent States, is struggling to find continued success under a new economic system, but its survival seems assured, due in large part to its ideal location: across the street from Moscow Square and the Kremlin, Russia's governmental seat. (Chapter 7)

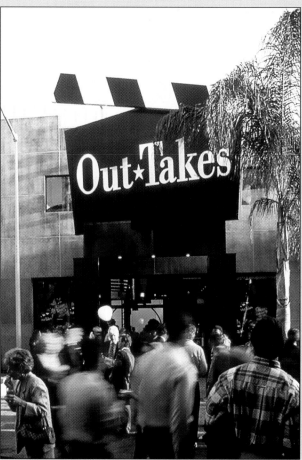

© CityWalk near Los Angeles (top) is one of the newest shopping concepts: a mall designed to replicate the experience of an urban shopping excursion. (Chapter 7)

© Traditional adobe architecture and design are reinforced by strict zoning in Santa Fe, New Mexico. (Chapter 7)

Store Location

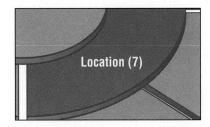

Location (7)

Questions this chapter answers include

- **What types of locations are available to retailers?**
- **What factors do retailers consider in choosing a location?**

etailers must choose their locations carefully for two reasons. First, location is typically the most important consideration in a customer's store choice. What grocery store do you shop at? Usually it's the store closest to where you live or work.

Second, location decisions are important because retailers can use them to develop a sustainable competitive advantage. Retailers can change their pricing, service, and merchandise assortments quickly. However location decisions are harder to change because retailers frequently have to make substantial investments to buy and develop real estate, or commit to long-term leases with developers. Thus retailers with excellent locations have a strategic advantage competitors can't easily copy.

Location decisions have become even more important in recent years. First, there are more retailers (particularly national chains like The Gap and Toys "R" Us) opening new locations. This makes the better locations even more scarce. This problem is complicated by a slowdown in both population growth and new shopping center construction. A retailer may find a suitable location, but high rent, long leases, and expensive decorating can make it very costly.

In this chapter we first examine the different types of locations available to retailers. Then we look at the issues that retailers consider when choosing a location.

TYPES OF RETAIL LOCATIONS

Many types of locations are available for retail stores—each with its own strengths and weaknesses. Choosing a particular site involves evaluating a series of trade-offs. These trade-offs generally concern the cost versus the value of the site for a particular retailer.

Retailers have three basic types of sites to choose from: a central business district (CBD), shopping center, or freestanding location. Each has additional sub-categories. The following sections describe each type of location and how retailers choose among them.

Central Business Districts (CBDs)

In both small towns and large cities, the **central business district** (the traditional downtown business area) is a viable site for many retailers. Its size and merchandise selection draw people into the area; also, many people work in the area.[1]

But central business district locations have their drawbacks: Higher security is required, shoplifting can be more common, and parking is often a problem. High crime rates, urban decay, and lack of protection from the weather can discourage suburban shoppers. Shopping in the evening and on weekends can be particularly slow in many CBDs. Also, unlike modern shopping centers, CBDs tend to suffer from a lack of planning. One block may contain upscale boutiques while the next may be populated with low-income housing, so consumers may not have enough interesting retailers to merit a shopping trip.

Some central business districts have undergone a process of **gentrification,** in which old buildings are torn down or restored for new offices, housing developments, and retailers. Cities often provide retailers significant incentives to locate in urban centers. Shopper's World in Detroit, for instance, is a discount department store that successfully targets the urban poor. The landlord received a significant property tax incentive as an inducement to enter a neighborhood in the urban core. Not only is the store very successful, but it has generated employment for 200 people—most from the immediate vicinity.

But central business district gentrification in larger cities hasn't always been successful. It's hard to get people to drive in from the suburbs just to find merchandise similar to what they can find at a shopping center close to home. The poor economy in the late 1980s and 1990s, coupled with the value-oriented and back-to-basics customer, has worsened the problem because many redeveloped areas are populated by high-end retailers whose sales suffer in a slow economy. Underground Atlanta in the city's historic business district, for example, lost several million dollars in the early 1990s. In addition, gentrification can make life difficult or impossible for elderly and lower-income residents who often live in the nation's central business districts. Rents rise or apartment buildings are razed, and the traditional retail base can disappear. For instance, in downtown Orlando, Florida, the last grocery store closed in 1980.

The gentrification process in neighborhood central business districts appears to be more successful. National retailers like The Gap, American Eagle Outfitters, Pier 1, The Limited and Limited Express, Laura Ashley, Benetton, Waldenbooks, Honeybee, Talbots, The Bombay Co., and Carroll Reed Shops are setting up shop in many neighborhoods, such as Greenwich and Westport, Connecticut; Birmingham (a suburb of Detroit); and Chicago's Lincoln Park and Halsted Street areas.

RE-TALE 7-1   Mainstreet Europe: The Fate of Mom-and-Pop Stores

During the 1990s European retailing has been changing at the expense of the traditional mom-and-pop retail stores. In the past, mom-and-pop stores were the village meeting place. The locals would shop at these stores for convenience and service and because the owner was their neighbor.

Yet in most of Europe, the number of small and medium-size stores has fallen drastically over the past several years. Downtown and corner stores are threatened with extinction as suburban superstores selling everything under one roof—from food and cosmetics to clothing and electronics—become more popular. For example, in Italy, the number of superstores doubled between 1988 and 1993. The two countries experiencing the largest increase in superstores are Germany (in particular, what was East Germany) and the Commonwealth of Independent States (formerly the Soviet Union). Under communism, the small stores there were run and financed by the government. Political changes have caused most of these stores to close, leaving a population base unserviced.

In countries where this shift has been occurring steadily over the past few years, local governments have tried to restrain superstores' growth by limiting their size, thus helping local entrepreneurs compete. Substantial further growth of superstores may be limited by urban life-styles. Many customers don't like the commuting time to get to the store, their lack of service, or their overwhelming size. These superstores also fail to address the needs of the elderly, immobile, and poorer shoppers who can't drive or afford a car.

To compete with the superstores, many small shopkeepers have recognized the need to continue to provide personal attention, high-quality goods and service, plus competitive pricing. They've begun to form buying cooperatives or join retail chains that provide them with brand name products and guarantee distribution of fresh fruit and vegetables.

SOURCE: Cacilie Rohwedder, "Europe's Smaller Food Shops Face Finis," *The Wall Street Journal,* May 12, 1993, pp. B1, B7.

Why is it happening? First, developers aren't building as many malls, and it's often hard to find a good location in a successful mall. Second, these chain stores still need to expand. Third, malls have disadvantages (as we discuss later in the chapter), such as lack of convenient parking. Finally, the chains are finding that occupancy costs in malls are too high. This combination of factors has caused many retailers to look at street locations, not necessarily in major downtown areas, but in heavily populated areas that have the potential to produce sales equal to a mall store's.

Re-Tale 7–1 examines how main-street locations in Europe are changing.

From the 1950s through the 1980s, retailing declined in many central business districts, while suburban shopping centers grew as populations shifted to the suburbs. Shoppers have demanded the convenience of shopping centers. Life in the suburbs has created a need for stores a short drive from home. Large shopping centers provide an assortment of merchandise that often exceeds the CBD's. Binding many stores under one roof creates a synergy that attracts more customers than if the stores had separate locations. It's common, for instance, for one department store's sales to increase after a competing store enters a shopping center.

Although distinctions between types of shopping centers have become blurred, centers take two basic forms. Strip or ribbon centers are typically comprised of several adjacent stores along a major street or highway. Shopping malls are generally more planned than strip centers, have more pedestrian activity, and can be either open-air or enclosed.

Strip Centers. Retailers have successfully built strip centers across America based on the principles of convenience for customers and relatively low rentals for retailers.[3] Unlike planned shopping malls, **strip centers** (also called **ribbon centers**)

Shopping Centers

REFACT

The first shopping center, a marketplace with retail stores, was the Agora at the foot of the Parthenon in Athens in 600 B.C. It was the center of all commerce, politics, and entertainment in ancient Greece.[2]

This main street has been revitalized with the help of the Trust for Historic Preservation.

were originally designed so that customers could drive right up to the store, run in, and get something they need: groceries, pharmaceuticals, dry cleaning, whatever. In our time-poor society (see Chapter 3), strip centers have a tremendous draw.

Strip centers vary in size. Some contain three or four stores; others have over a million square feet. Strip centers' sizes and features are changing. Strip centers today have fewer mom-and-pop stores than in the past. Instead, there are more national tenants like Blockbuster Video, Little Caesar's, and Walgreens. The tenant mix also favors some very large tenants. The outgrowth of this trend is the power center (to be described shortly). Strip centers formerly had few retailers selling shopping goods like shoes or apparel. Yet today national chains like Charming Shoppes compete effectively in strip centers against their rival stores in malls. They offer lower prices, partly because of the lower rents incurred in a strip center, plus they offer the "no-hassle" convenience of a strip center.

Let's look at the four basic types of strip centers: convenience centers, neighborhood centers, community centers, and power centers.

Convenience centers. Convenience centers typically include a convenience store (e.g., a 7-Eleven or Circle K), dry cleaner, and/or liquor store. The trade area is small, approximately a half-mile radius. They're found in suburban locations and densely populated high-rise apartment and office areas.

Neighborhood centers. Neighborhood centers range in size from 25,000 to 80,000 square feet and include a supermarket and frequently a drugstore or variety store. They often include apparel, shoe, camera, and other shopping goods stores.

Community centers. Community shopping centers typically contain a discount store (like Kmart) or soft-line department store (like Mervyn's) as an anchor. Also included are a supermarket, super-drugstore, and 50,000 to 60,000 square feet of other convenience and shopping goods stores.

RE-TALE 7-2   Mall of America Has It All

The philosophy of the new Mall of America in Minneapolis is to appeal to all of the people all of the time. Hence the name, Mall of America. The largest shopping center in the world is 4.2 million square feet, 2.5 million of which are devoted to retail space! This is equivalent to four regional shopping centers connected together. This immense real estate project sits on 78 acres of land in Bloomington, Minnesota. It also houses a seven-acre Knott's Camp Snoopy theme park, the largest enclosed amusement park in the nation! What makes this mall unique besides its size is that it has four themed "streets" with connecting anchors of Sears, Nordstrom, Macy's, and Bloomingdale's. What may be most interesting is the combination of upscale and off-price retailers in the tenant mix, which is designed to provide one-stop shopping for consumers with varied purchasing power.

When the mall opened in August 1992, many local Minneapolis merchants were concerned that it would draw customers away from familiar but more centrally located shopping centers. Despite high attendance at Mall of America, officials from area shopping centers reported little or no effect from the megamall, as it's called in Minneapolis. Most claim the Mall of America has become an add-on trip for local shoppers who still frequent area malls for most of their needs. Some experts say the area was underretailed, and Mall of America is simply filling consumer demand.

Time will tell if the megamall complex will live up to its developers' expectations.

SOURCE: Debra Hazel, "At Long Last, The Megamall," *Chain Store Age Executive,* September 1992, pp. 53–55; and Paul Doocey, "Mall of America Fallout," *Stores,* May 1993, pp. 44–47.

Power centers. Power centers are open-air shopping centers with the majority of their space leased to several well-known anchor retail tenants. They typically have 3 to 10 anchor stores and can reach over a million square feet. Power centers usually contain category specialists like Kmart's Builders Square, Office Depot, Circuit City, or Toys "R" Us. Some contain grocery stores, while others have a mix of fashion apparel and hard goods stores.

Shopping Malls. Shopping malls have several advantages over alternative locations. First, because of the number and variety of stores, and the opportunity to combine shopping with entertainment, shopping malls have become the Main Street for current shoppers. Teenagers hang out and meet friends, older citizens in Nikes get their exercise by walking the malls, and families make trips to the mall an inexpensive form of entertainment (as long as they don't buy anything). To enhance the total shopping experience, many malls incorporate food and entertainment. Mall of America near Minneapolis, Minnesota, is the world's largest shopping center, offering customers just about anything they could want. (See Re-Tale 7–2.)

The second major advantage of locating in a shopping mall is that the tenant mix is planned. Shopping mall managers control the number of different types of retailers to provide one-stop shopping with a well-balanced assortment of merchandise. For instance, it's important to have several women's clothing stores in a major mall to attract customers. Yet too many could jeopardize the success of any one store. Mall managers also attempt to create a complementary tenant mix. They like to locate stores that appeal to the same target market (such as all upscale specialty clothing stores) together. This approach lets customers know what types of merchandise they can expect to find in a particular mall or a particular location within a mall.

The third advantage of planned shopping malls is that individual retailers don't have to worry about their external environment. The mall's management maintains common areas and usually creates strong homogeneity among stores. For instance,

RE-TALE 7-3 Retailing—Russian Style!

Stanislav V. Sorokine, president of G.U.M. (the largest retail store in the Commonwealth of Independent States), says, "I'm ready to sell what our people want to buy." Spoken like a true capitalist? Well almost.

In 1990, Sorokine ran G.U.M. under the watchful eye of the Soviet government. Today he continues to oversee the company, but as a stockholder, not as an employee of the state. No longer a state-owned company, G.U.M. has been turned into a joint stock company. The managers and workers have purchased a controlling 51 percent of the stock, 25 percent is owned by the Moscow city government, and the remainder is still being sold.

G.U.M. used to stand for State Department Store. Now under new ownership, the name has been changed to the Main Department Store. With 150,000 square feet of retailing space, it's located in an 1893 "pseudo-Russian"–style building across the street from famous Moscow Square. This prime location attracts 250,000 Russians and 30,000 international visitors a year. Due to its age and, most importantly, its neglect, Sorokine is trying to raise money to restore and refurbish this shopping emporium as well as make vast changes in its merchandise mix—a tall order for the traditional Muscovite!

Sorokine plans to develop G.U.M. into a mixed-use development like Union Station in Washington, D.C. His goal is to preserve the dignity and the historical qualities of G.U.M., while providing new shops that feature high-quality fashions and consumer products from retailers and manufacturers around the world.

Sorokine's plan is to have G.U.M. made up entirely of smaller stores. For example, G.U.M. has famous retailers and manufacturers like Benetton, Botany 500, Christian Dior, Karstadt, L'oreal, JVC, Samsonite, and Yves Rocher. While the hundreds of small stores that make up G.U.M. give the appearance of an American shopping mall, G.U.M. operates as a holding company. The company pays for rent, electricity, security, selling space, and even the employees. It's like an American department store subleasing its interior space to a specialized vendor.

The major difference is that each of the small retailers chooses its own merchandise mix. Russian consumers are becoming exposed to Western clothing and style, but traditional management still lacks Western retailers' merchandising prowess. Because the majority of Muscovites own only one suit and two dress shirts, there's also a great deal of pent-up demand—Russian style!

SOURCE: Susan Reda, "Moscow's G.U.M.: Russian Retail Revolution," *Stores,* October 1992, pp. 22-27.

---

malls tend to enforce uniform hours of operation. Some malls even control the external signage stores use for window displays and sales.

Although planned shopping centers are an excellent option for most retailers, they have some disadvantages. First, mall rents sometimes are higher than those of freestanding sites and central business districts. As a result, retailers that require large stores, such as home-improvement centers, typically seek other options. Second, some tenants may not like mall managers' control on their operations. Finally, competition within shopping centers can be intense. It may be hard for small specialty stores to compete directly with large department stores.

Although a plethora of terms are used to define shopping malls, and many of those terms overlap, a discussion of some of the most common types of malls follows. (Re-Tale 7–3 looks at G.U.M. in Moscow, an unusual cross between a shopping center and a department store.)

Regional shopping centers can include up to three department stores. Other tenants are likely to be specialty stores, like women's apparel shops, rather than convenience stores. The primary trade area usually encompasses at least a five-mile radius. Super-regional centers are similar to regional centers but have at least four department stores.

The **fashion-oriented specialty center** usually contains a high-quality department store as well as small boutiques. These centers are smaller than a regional shopping center but may draw from a large trade area because their tenants are specialty stores. Customers tend to travel greater distances for specialty products

Although the Gurnee Mills Mall near Chicago contains primarily manufacturer's outlet stores, it has all the amenities of a regional shopping center.

sold at nationally known shops (such as Neiman Marcus and Ralph Lauren/Polo) than for other types of shopping centers. Fashion-oriented specialty centers also include gourmet eating and drinking establishments amid a nicely landscaped physical design. These centers are generally in high-income neighborhoods, though with the resurgence of some central business districts, fashion-oriented centers (such as Water Tower Place in Chicago) are beginning to reappear downtown.

A great example of a fashion-oriented specialty center is the newly renovated Sommerset Collection in the wealthy Detroit, Michigan, suburb of Troy. The owners believed that their upscale customers were traveling to trendy shops in New York and Chicago. So, although the mall is more than 25 years old, they decided to expand and bring in anchor stores like Neiman Marcus and Saks Fifth Avenue as well as specialty shops like F.A.O. Schwarz, Crate & Barrel, and Rand McNally.[4]

At one time, **off-price and outlet centers** were distinct, separate categories of shopping centers. But more recently the distinction between them has blurred as off-price retailers (such as T.J. Maxx and Burlington Coat Factory) and outlet stores (such as Sears and Liz Claiborne) occupy space in the same center. Both off-price and outlet stores offer merchandise at discount prices.

Outlet centers have progressed rather quickly from no-frills warehouses to well-designed buildings with landscaping, gardens, and food courts, making them hard to distinguish from more traditional shopping centers. Outlet center tenants also have upgraded by offering credit, dressing rooms, and expensive fixtures and lighting. Outlet tenants now offer first-quality, full-line merchandise.

Outlet centers are generally located some distance from regional shopping centers so outlet tenants don't compete directly with their department and specialty store customers. They're also located in strong tourist areas. For instance, because shopping is a favorite vacation pastime, and Niagara Falls attracts 15 million tourists per year, the 1.2-million-square-foot Factory Outlet Mega Mall in Niagara Falls, New

---

RE-TALE 7-4   The New Shopping Experience: Entertainment or Reality?

How far can shopping center developers reach into the entertainment arena? At what point will the two meet? Welcome to CityWalk. This new entertainment and shopping promenade developed by MCA (a subsidiary of Japan's Matsushita Electric Industrial Co.) is 20 miles east of Los Angeles in the San Fernando Valley.

The developers designed a promenade that has the feel of a problem-free Los Angeles. Besides the faux Venice beach, it has the billboards and neon of Sunset Boulevard, the neo-Mexican facades of Olvera Street, and the chic shops of Melrose Avenue—all without the hassles of crime, smog, and traffic. This is the classic "G"-rated shopping promenade.

MCA expects locals to make up the largest group of visitors, but it's also counting on tourists to support this $100 million project. MCA specifically located it next to one of the country's highest-grossing cinemas and

conveniently close to Universal Studios. Besides shopping, CityWalk sports a ShowMotion Theatre in which Showscan Corp. features a "motion-simulated ride-film" similar to Disneyland's Star Tours. Simulated visual entertainment isn't the only art here. The Museum of Neon Art has relocated its headquarters to CityWalk from downtown Los Angeles. UCLA has also set up an extension center where adults can take night classes. There's also what MCA calls a "futuristic electronics pavilion" created by Steven Spielberg.

This new venture into the realm of a total shopping/ entertainment experience will be closely studied by many developers. Is this the sanitized shopping experience of the future, or will it be labeled "only in L.A."?

SOURCE: Thomas R. King, "Mall Replicates a Sanitized Los Angeles," *The Wall Street Journal*, May 10, 1993, pp. B1, B6.

York, is a natural location for an outlet center. Some center developers actually organize bus tours to bring people hundreds of miles to their malls.

A **historical center** is located in a place of historical interest, such as Faneuil Hall in Boston or Ghirardelli Square in San Francisco. **Theme centers,** on the other hand, attempt to replicate a historical place (such as the Old Mill Center in Mountain View, California) or to create a unique shopping environment (like MCA's CityWalk, described in Re-Tale 7–4). These centers typically contain tenants similar to those in the specialty centers, except that there are usually no large specialty stores or department stores.

Other Retail Location Opportunities

Although most retailers locate in strip centers or planned shopping malls, a traditional option for large retailers is a freestanding site. Carts, kiosks, RMUs (retail merchandising units), and tall wall units are other location alternatives gaining momentum. Mixed-use developments are also examined in this section.

Freestanding Sites. A **freestanding site** is a retail location that's not adjacent to other retailers. Retailers with large space requirements, such as warehouse clubs and hypermarkets, are often freestanding. Toys "R" Us also utilizes freestanding sites. Advantages of freestanding locations are lower rents, ample parking, and no direct competition as well as no restrictions on signs, hours, or merchandise (which might be restricted in a shopping center). The most serious disadvantage is the lack of synergy with other stores. A retailer in a freestanding location must be a primary destination point for customers. It must offer customers something special in merchandise, price, promotion, or services to get them into the store.

Carts, Kiosks, RMUs, and Tall Wall Units. Carts, kiosks, retail merchandising units, and tall wall units are selling spaces in mall common areas.[6] A **cart** offers the simplest presentation, is mobile, and is often on wheels. A **kiosk** is larger than a cart, is stationary, and has many of the conveniences of a store such as movable shelves,

A kiosk, like this one pictured on the left for Piercing Pagoda, is larger than a cart, is stationary, and has many conveniences of a store such as movable shelves, telephone, and electricity. A retail merchandising unit (RMU) like the one pictured on the right selling jewelry offers the compactness and mobility of a cart, but the more sophisticated features of a kiosk.

telephone, and electricity. **Retail merchandising units (RMUs)**—a relatively new and sophisticated location alternative—offer the compactness and mobility of a cart, but the more sophisticated features of a kiosk. For instance, they can be locked or enclosed so they can serve as a display when closed for business. Finally, the newest innovation, **tall wall units,** are six-to-seven–foot selling spaces placed against a wall instead of in the middle of an aisle.

These selling spaces are typically between 40 and 500 square feet, and can be in prime mall locations. They're relatively inexpensive compared to a regular store. (For instance, a cart called "The Sportsman's Wife" at Mall of America was started with $15,000—$10,000 of which was for inventory.) They usually have short-term leases, shielding tenants from the liability of having to pay rent if the business fails. Of course, vendors also can be evicted on little notice. These alternatives to regular stores are often a great way for small retailers to begin or expand.

Mixed-Use Developments (MXDs). Mixed-use developments are shopping centers that have office towers, hotels, residential complexes, civic centers, or convention complexes on top or attached to shopping areas. MXDs can be found in central business districts, in strip centers, and in planned shopping malls. They're popular with retailers because they bring additional shoppers to their stores. Developers like MXDs because they use space productively. For instance, land costs the same whether a developer builds a shopping mall by itself or builds an office tower over the mall or parking structure.

☀ CHOOSING A LOCATION

We now examine the specific decisions involved in choosing a location for a retail store. Exhibit 7–1 breaks these factors into three levels: region, trade area, and specific site. The region refers to the part of the country, a particular city, or **Metropolitan Statistical Area (MSA).** An MSA is (1) a city with 50,000 or more inhabitants or (2) an urbanized area of at least 50,000 inhabitants and a total MSA population of at least 100,000 (75,000 in New England). A **trade area** is a geographic sector that contains potential customers for a particular retailer or shopping

EXHIBIT 7-1

Three Levels of Spatial Analysis

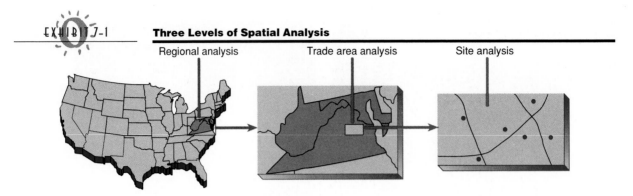

Regional analysis   Trade area analysis   Site analysis

center. A trade area may be part of a city or may extend beyond the city's boundaries, depending on the type of store and the density of potential customers surrounding it. For instance, a video rental store's trade area may be only a few city blocks within a major metropolitan area. On the other hand, a Wal-Mart's trade area in the rural South may encompass 50 square miles.

This section examines factors that are important to retailers when choosing a region/market area and trade area. Issues regarding selecting a particular site are examined later in the chapter.

Region/Market Area

Regardless of the general economy's state, certain regions or market areas may be more attractive to some retailers than to others. It would be misleading to think that simply because a market is large or growing economically, it's attractive to all retailers. For example, a swimming pool supply store would have less potential in rural Maine than in California. Heavily populated regions aren't always better either. Although the emphasis has shifted in recent years, Wal-Mart's early growth came from regions with small cities, not from large metropolitan markets. Although potential sales were limited in these small cities, competition was also limited.

Some retailers focus on certain geographic regions. For instance, Hess's department stores concentrate on the Middle Atlantic states for a number of reasons. First, Hess's believes it can develop a more loyal customer base by remaining a regional chain. It has excellent visibility and is well known throughout these states. Second, its merchandising, pricing, and promotional strategies can more easily target the needs of a regional market than a national market. For instance, Hess's knows that merchandise that's popular in New York will also sell in Virginia. Third, management can have greater control over a regional market. Managers can easily visit the stores and assess competition. Finally, Hess's can more efficiently distribute merchandise to its stores.

Trade Area

A trade area is a geographic sector that contains potential customers for a particular retailer or shopping center. Trade areas can be divided into two or three zones, as depicted by Exhibit 7–2's concentric ovals. The zones' exact definitions should be flexible to account for particular areas' nuances. Retailers often use the following rules of thumb:

The **primary zone** is the geographic area from which the store or shopping center derives 60 to 65 percent of its customers. This zone is usually three to five miles or less than a 10-minute drive from the site.

Effect on Trade Area Caused by Major Highways   EXHIBIT 7–2

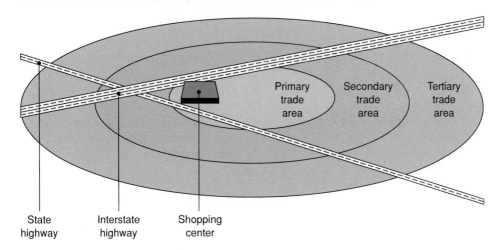

Primary
trade
area

Secondary
trade
area

Tertiary
trade
area

State
highway

Interstate
highway

Shopping
center

The **secondary zone** is the geographic area of secondary importance in terms of customer sales, generating about 20 percent of a store's sales. It usually extends three to seven miles or is no more than a 15-to-20–minute drive from the site.

The **tertiary zone** (the outermost ring) includes customers who occasionally shop at the store or shopping center. These customers lack adequate retail facilities closer to home, or excellent highway systems give them access to the store or center, or customers drive near the store or center as they commute to work. The tertiary zone typically extends 15 miles in major metropolitan markets and as far as 50 miles in smaller markets.

The exact boundaries of a trade area are determined by the store's accessibility as well as its competition's location. For instance, Exhibit 7–2's map shows that a major interstate highway on the top and a state highway on the bottom are narrowing a regional shopping center's trade area. Because both highways are often hard to cross due to heavy traffic, the trade areas on the opposite sides are limited. On the other hand, both highways facilitate access for residents living above and below the shopping center. Thus an otherwise round-shaped trade area has become quite oblong. Other barriers (such as a river, mountain range, or high-crime area) may also influence the shape and size of a trade area.

Trade area size is also influenced by the type of store or shopping center. A 7-Eleven convenience store's trade area, for example, may extend less than one mile, whereas a category specialist like Toys "R" Us may draw customers from 20 miles away. The difference is due to the nature of merchandise each retailer sells and the size of the assortment they offer. Convenience stores succeed because customers can buy products like milk and bread quickly and easily. If customers must drive great distances, the store's no longer convenient. Category specialists offer a large choice of specialty products that customers are willing to put forth additional effort to buy. Thus customers will generally drive some distance to shop at a category specialist.

The level of competition also affects the size and shape of a trade area for a particular store. If two convenience food stores are too close together, their respective trade areas will shrink because they offer the same merchandise. On the other hand, adjacent shopping goods stores, such as women's clothing stores, should expand the trade area boundaries; more people are drawn to the area to shop because of its expanded selection.

Factors Affecting the Attractiveness of Region/Market and Trade Areas

The best regions are those that generate the highest demand or sales for a retailer. To assess overall demand in a particular region/market or trade area, the retail analyst considers the population's demographics and the business climate as well as competition from other area retailers.

Demographics. In most cases, areas where the general population is growing are preferable to those with declining populations. Yet population growth doesn't tell the whole story. Household income is also important. Size and composition of households in an area can also be important success determinants. For instance, Ann Taylor (a chain specializing in traditional and business apparel for women) generally locates in areas with high-income households and in tourist areas; household size, however, isn't a particularly critical issue. Toys "R" Us, on the other hand, is interested in locations with heavy concentrations of families with young children.

Business Climate. It's important to examine a market's employment trends because a high level of employment usually means high purchasing power. Also, its useful to determine which areas are growing quickly, and why. For instance, the Austin, Texas area grew throughout the 1980s due to an influx of high-tech firms.

Employment growth in and of itself isn't enough to ensure a strong future retail environment. If growth isn't diversified in a number of industries, the area may suffer from adverse cyclical trends. For instance, many towns with military bases are expected to decline in population throughout the 1990s as the military downsizes.

Another related factor is the area's labor climate. If a retailer has a choice of locating in two otherwise equal markets, the one with nonunion stores is preferable because labor costs will tend to be lower there.

Competition. The level of competition in an area also affects demand for a retailer's merchandise. Depending on a retailer's overall strategy, it may wish to enter a region with low competition. But for some retailers, a relatively high level of competition is desirable.

Wal-Mart's early success was based on a location strategy of opening stores in small towns with relatively weak competition. Not only do these stores experience high market share in the towns where they're located, but they draw from surrounding communities as well. Unable to compete with Wal-Mart on price or breadth of selection, many family-owned retailers in those towns either have repositioned their merchandising and/or service strategies or have gone out of business.

Locating a store in an area with relatively high competition can also be a useful strategy because customers are drawn to an area with a large selection of merchandise. Retailers such as Neiman Marcus, Montgomery Ward, J.C. Penney, Foley's, Saks Fifth Avenue, and Dillard's all have stores within a two-mile area in North Dallas. Although competition is intense in this area, these stores create a synergy that draws customers from all over north Texas. But retailers must take

Issues to Consider When Choosing a Region/Market or Trade Area

- Overall size of region/market

- Size of target market(s) in region/market

- Understanding of the geographic area

- Population growth

- Income distribution/stability

- Size and composition of households

- Employment level and stability

- Labor climate

- Competition level

care not to enter areas that are **overstored**—areas with too many stores to efficiently satisfy demand. Exhibit 7–3 summarizes region/market and trade area factors retailers consider when locating a store.

In general, however, the best location is the one that generates the most traffic from the store's target markets. Factors that affect a location's ability to generate traffic are examined in this section and summarized in Exhibit 7–4. They include accessibility, locational advantages within the center, and legal considerations.

Site Evaluation

Accessibility. The **accessibility** of a site is the ease with which a customer may get into and out of it. Taking a broad perspective, retailers evaluate several factors, such as road patterns, road conditions, and barriers. The **road pattern** has to do with how easily shoppers can travel on the major streets or freeways near the site. An interrelated factor is the **road condition** (including the age, number of lanes, number of stoplights, congestion, and general state of repair of roads in the primary trade area). For instance, a location on an old, narrow, congested secondary road in disrepair with too many stoplights would be a poor site for a retail store. Natural barriers (such as rivers or mountains) and artificial barriers (such as railroad tracks, major highways, or parks) may also affect accessibility.

Retailers also look at accessibility factors in the immediate vicinity of the site such as visibility, traffic flow, parking, congestion, and ease of access to the site.

Visibility refers to customers' ability to see the store and enter the parking lot safely. Large national retailers like Kmart insist that there be no impediments to a direct and undisturbed view of their store. In an area with a highly transient population (such as a tourist center or large city), good visibility from the road is particularly important.

The success of a site with a good traffic flow is a question of balance. The site should have a substantial number of cars per day but not so many that congestion impedes access to the store. Also, areas congested during rush hours may have a good traffic flow during the rest of the day when most shopping takes place.

The number and quality of parking facilities are critical to a shopping center's overall accessibility. Too few spaces or spaces too far from the stores will discourage customers from entering the area. On the other hand, too many open spaces may create the impression that the shopping center is a failure with unpopular stores.

A related issue, but one that extends into the shopping center itself, is the relative congestion of the area. **Congestion** can refer to crowding of either cars or

EXHIBIT 7-4   **Issues to Consider When Choosing a Retail Site**

Type of site
- Is site near the target market?
- Is the type of site appropriate for the store?
- What are the age and condition of the site?
- What is the trade area?

Accessibility
- What are the road patterns and conditions surrounding the site?
- Do any natural or artificial barriers impede access to the site?
- Does the site have good visibility from the street?
- Is there a good balance between too much and too little traffic flow?
- Is there a good balance between too much and too little parking?
- Is there a good balance between too much and too little congestion of cars and people?
- Is it easy to enter/exit the parking lot?

Locational advantages within a center
- Is the site adjacent to important tenants?
- Will adjacent tenants complement/compete with the store?

Terms of occupancy
- Are the terms of the lease slanted in favor of the landlord or retailer?
- Is the type of lease favorable to the retailer?

Legal considerations
- Does the site meet requirements of the Americans with Disabilities Act?
- Does the site meet environmental standards?
- Is the site zoning compatible with the store?
- Does the store's architectural design meet building codes?
- Are the store's external signs compatible with zoning ordinances, building codes, and shopping center management?
- Can the store acquire special licenses (e.g., liquor license) for the site?

people. There's some optimal range of comfortable congestion for customers. Too much congestion can make shopping slow, irritate customers, and generally discourage sales. On the other hand, a relatively high level of activity in a shopping center creates excitement and can stimulate sales.[7]

The last factor to consider in the accessibility analysis is the ease of entering and exiting the site's parking lot. Often medians or one-way streets make entering or exiting the site difficult from one or more directions, limiting accessibility.

Locational Advantages within a Center. Now we'll look at the relative advantages of locations within a center. The better locations cost more so retailers weigh the alternatives carefully. For instance, in a neighborhood shopping center, the more expensive locations are closest to the supermarket. A liquor store or a flower shop that may attract impulse buyers should thus be close to the supermarket. But a shoe repair store (which shouldn't expect impulse customers) could be in relatively inferior location because customers in need of this service will seek out the store.

The same arguments hold for regional multilevel shopping centers. It's advantageous for shopping goods stores like The Limited and Ann Taylor to be clustered

Developers of the Inlet Square Mall in Myrtle Beach, South Carolina, realized that customers would not shop there unless they could easily enter and exit the center.

in the more expensive locations near a department store. Women shopping for clothing may start at the department store and naturally gravitate to stores near it. Yet stores such as Foot Locker needn't be in the most expensive location because many of their customers plan their purchases before they even get to the center.

Another strategy is to locate stores that appeal to similar target markets close together. In essence, customers want to shop where they'll find a good assortment of merchandise. This is why antique shops, car dealers, and shoe and clothing stores all seem to do better if they're close to one another. Of course, an area can become overstored if it has too many competing stores to profitably satisfy demand.

Stores may actually benefit if they compete directly with their neighbors. Consider Exhibit 7–5's map of Dallas's North Park Center. More fashion-forward, higher-income customers will find stores like Alfred Dunhill of London and other exclusive boutiques between Neiman Marcus and Lord & Taylor. Some stores sell exactly the same merchandise categories, while others sell complementary products, such as perfumes in one store and lingerie in another. A similarly healthy tenant mix exists in the more moderately priced wing between Dillard's and J.C. Penney. Customers can buy shoes at Penney or a Kinney Shoe store. They can find a gift at Dillard's and a card at Bolen's Hallmark Shop. Thus a good location is one where customers can find a tenant mix that provides (1) a good selection of merchandise at competing stores and (2) complementary merchandise.

Legal Considerations. Laws regarding land use have become so important that they should be a retailer's first consideration in a site search. Legal issues that affect the site decision include environmental issues, zoning, building codes, sign regulations, and licensing requirements.

ℜＥℱℜℂＴ

The Port Authority of New York and New Jersey, developer of New York City's World Trade Center office/hotel/retail complex, requires all of its 70 stores to open at 7:30 A.M. on weekday mornings to serve office workers and commuters on their way to work.[8]

Map of North Park Center

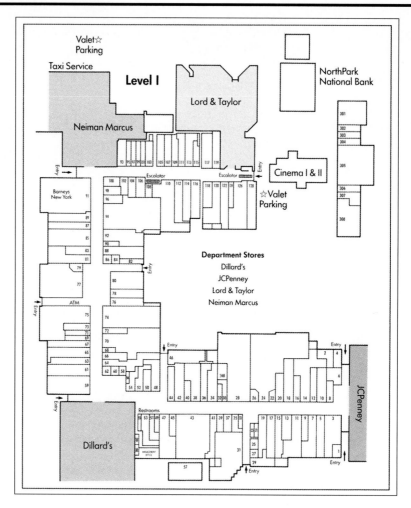

Environmental issues. The Environmental Protection Agency plus state and local agencies have become increasingly involved with issues that could affect retail stores. It's the responsibility of both the landlord and the retailer to comply with these laws so it's important to delineate obligations in the lease.

Two environmental issues have received particular attention in recent years. First is asbestos or asbestos-containing materials used in construction. The second issue is hazardous materials. This can be particularly important for dry cleaners because of the chemicals they use, and for auto repair shops because of disposal of used motor oil and battery fluid. Normally the retailer is responsible for legally removing hazardous materials from the site.

Zoning and building codes. **Zoning** determines how a particular site can be used. For instance, some parts of a city are zoned for residential use only; others are zoned for light industrial and retail use. **Building codes** are similar legal restrictions determining the type of building, signs, size and type of parking lot, and so forth that retailers can use at a particular location. Some building codes require a certain size parking lot or architectural design. In Santa Fe, New Mexico, for instance, building codes require building owners to keep the traditional mud stucco (adobe) style.

Signs. Restrictions on the use of signs can also impact a particular site's desirability. Size and style may be restricted by building codes, zoning ordinances, or even the shopping center management. At the Bal Harbour Shops in North Miami Beach, for example, all signs (even sale signs) must be approved by the shopping center management.

Licensing requirements. **Licensing requirements** may vary in different parts of a region. For instance, some Dallas neighborhoods are "dry," meaning no alcoholic beverages can be sold; in other areas, only wine and beer can be sold. Such restrictions can affect retailers other than restaurants and bars. For instance, a historic or theme shopping center that restricts the use of alcoholic beverages may have limited clientele at night.

Legal issues such as those mentioned here can discourage a retailer from pursuing a particular site. These restrictions aren't always permanent, however. Although difficult, time-consuming, and possibly expensive, lobbying efforts and court battles can change these legal restrictions.

☼ SUMMARY

Decisions about where to locate a store are critical to any retailer's success. A location decision is particularly important because of its high cost and long-term commitment. A location mistake may be more devastating to a retailer than other types of errors, such as a buying mistake.

Retailers must choose between different types of locations and weigh the relative cost and value of each. The factors retailers consider when choosing a location include everything from the demographics and business climate of the area to the accessibility of the parking lot. Successful retailers design a clear, coherent location strategy that helps them meet their overall goals.

KEY TERMS

accessibility, 143
building code, 146
cart, 138
central business
   district (CBD), 132
congestion, 143
fashion-oriented
   specialty center,
   136
freestanding site, 138

gentrification, 132
historical center, 138
kiosk, 138
licensing
   requirements, 147
MSA (Metropolitan
   Statistical Area),
   139
mixed-use
   development
   (MXD), 139
off-price/outlet
   center, 137

overstored, 143
primary zone, 140
RMU (retail
   merchandising
   unit), 139
regional shopping
   center, 136
road condition, 143
road pattern, 143
secondary zone, 141

strip or ribbon center,
   133
tall wall unit, 139
tertiary zone, 141
theme center, 138
trade area, 139
visibility, 143
zoning, 146

DISCUSSION QUESTIONS AND PROBLEMS

1. Why have location decisions become more important in recent years?

2. Many types of selling spaces exist besides a standard enclosed store. What are the advantages and disadvantages of each? What types of merchandisers would benefit from each of these alternative selling spaces?

3. Home Depot, a rapidly growing chain of large home-improvement centers, typically locates in either a power center or a freestanding site. What are the strengths of each location for a store like Home Depot?

4. What are the advantages and disadvantages of a retailer's leasing space in a shopping center in an area with extensive zoning restrictions?

5. Retailers often locate in neighborhoods or central business districts that have suffered some decay. Some people have questioned the ethical and social ramifications of this process, known as *gentrification.* What are the benefits and problems associated with gentrification?

6. True Value Hardware Stores plans to open a new store. Two sites are available—both in middle-income neighborhood centers. One neighborhood is 20 years old and has been well maintained. The other has recently been built in a newly planned community. Which site is preferable for True Value? Why?

7. In many malls, fast food retailers are located together in an area known as a *food court.* What are the advantages and disadvantages of this arrangement for the fast food retailer?

8. Typically, specialty stores prefer to locate next to or close to an anchor store. But Little Caesar's, a take-out pizza retailer typically located in strip centers, prefers to be at the end of the center away from the supermarket anchor. Why?

9. Retailers have a choice of locating on the main floor or on the second or third level of a mall. Typically, the main floor offers the best but most expensive locations. Why would specialty stores such as Radio Shack and Foot Locker choose the second or third floor?

10. What are the shape and size of the trade area zones of a shopping center near your school?

Cases for Section 2

CASE 2–1 ☼ MARQUETTE ARMY/NAVY SURPLUS STORE

Faced with declining sales, the Marquette Army/Navy Surplus Store (MANS) must meet several challenges. Since buying the store approximately 18 months ago, owners Bernie and Shirley Shusta have learned much about operating a retail store. Being new to the business, they learned as they went along. Unfortunately, the learning process consumed a considerable amount of cash. Due to a low cash situation, store inventory is somewhat lower than the owners want.

MANS is on the main street in the downtown shopping area of Marquette, Michigan (population 20,000). The city is home to a university with 7,500 students. An Air Force base 20 miles from town has 5,000 personnel. Another 20,000 people live within a half hour's drive of the store. The two biggest industries in Marquette's part of Michigan (the state's Upper Peninsula) are tourism and forest-related products and services.

The store was originally a typical military surplus store with a large assortment of military clothing. Items included used uniforms, canteens, and helmets, as well as new merchandise. As the store grew, it added a department carrying trendy clothing for teenage girls. The woman who had built the volume in the teenage market left to start her own (competing) store shortly before the Shustas bought MANS. The loss of this volume, in addition to the problem of stockouts, brought about the decline in sales volume.

Target markets aren't well defined, and the advertising reflects that lack of definition. The Shustas are concerned about the advertising and have experimented with ads in various media since taking over the store. But the ads failed to use any common theme, and there was no plan set forth for the advertisements.

Pricing had been a major problem when the store was first acquired. In fact, the prior owner seemed to mark up inventory at a certain percentage with no regard for demand or competition.

Often those markups had been so low that products were being sold at a loss. The Shustas have worked through the pricing problems and have developed a pricing structure that reflects the demand for products as well as competitors' prices. The new pricing system allows the owners to realize a profit.

The store is open year round from 10 A.M. to 6 P.M. Monday through Saturday. It's closed on Sundays and holidays. The business is seasonal, in that sales climb each month from September through December but decline sharply after Christmas and then remain fairly constant until the next September. In spite of advertising everywhere except on TV, sales continue to drop.

Discussion Questions

1. Should the store carry trendy clothes for teenagers?
2. Try to define the target markets by age, sex, and any other variable you think is relevant.
3. What media might you select to reach your target markets?

This case was prepared by Irvin A. Zaenglein, Northern Michigan University.

CASE 2–2 ☼ THE GAP OPENS OLD NAVY STORES

Are denim jeans, flannels and t-shirts your favorite attire? If so, listen up. The Gap has started a new chain called Old Navy Clothing Stores. Analysts believe that the new division will eventually have as many stores as The Gap itself, which currently has over 1,426 stores worldwide. The Old Navy Clothing Stores will have the same kind of merchandise as The Gap, but will be able to keep its prices low by using lighter-weight, less expensive fabrics, in addition to scaled down store decor.

Old Navy is a part of The Gap's three-tiered retailing strategy. The Banana-Republic chain is at the high end of the market, The Gap is in the middle, and Old Navy is at the low end.

The initial launch included three Old Navy stores in the Bay Area, as well as one near Los Angeles. Others opened in Southern California, Connecticut, and New York. The Gap first entered this niche market with the Gap Warehouse. The Gap Warehouse was a toned-down version of the familiar Gap shop featuring an assortment of basics—jeans, sweatshirts, and the like—at discount store prices.

According to the NDP Group, which tracks retail spending by direct queries of customers, consumers spent nearly a third of their apparel dollars—40 billion of them—at discount department stores, off-pricers, and factory outlets in 1993. There are several explanations for the strength of discount stores. The main attraction is the price. A cautious and financially unstable society has not wanted to invest a large percentage of its income on clothing, especially when there are house payments and doctor bills to be taken care of first.

It is not only price that drives consumers into discount stores for apparel. The industry has made great efforts in assortment, quality, and fashion. Discount stores have also come a long way in improving display, borrowing ideas from its regular stores. Even in the Old Navy discount Gap stores, they pride themselves on a clean and spacious place for customers to shop.

The Gap hopes Old Navy will serve as their next growth vehicle. Steven Kernkraut, an analyst at Bear Sterns, predicts it will steal a significant amount of business from Target and Sears. Kernkraut and other analysts predict that Old Navy will generate as much as $3 billion in revenues by the end of the decade, producing well over 20 percent annual growth in both revenues and earnings.

Discussion Questions

1. What type of growth strategy is The Gap pursuing with Old Navy?
2. Evaluate this growth strategy compared to The Gap's other growth strategies of Gap Kids and Baby Gap.

This case was prepared by Lora Hooks, University of Florida.

CASE 2–3 ☼ LAWSON SPORTSWEAR

"We need to have vendors who can take this burden off of us," said Clifton Morris, Lawson Sportswear inventory manager. "We have had a sales increase of 20 percent over the last two years and my people cannot keep up with it anymore."

Keith Lawson, the general manager of Lawson Sportswear, reviewed the colorful chart showing the sales trend and replied, "I never thought I would have to complain about a sales increase, but it is obvious that the sales are well beyond our control. Something has to be done and that is why we are meeting today."

Lawson Sportswear was founded by George Lawson in 1963 in a major southwestern metropolitan area. For five years, Lawson Sportswear has been successful in the sportswear market. In 1985, George Lawson retired, and his son, Keith Lawson, was appointed as the general manager. From the beginning, Keith Lawson has been a real go-getter. Recently completing his MBA, he has wasted no time in locating new markets for Lawson Sportswear. He immediately contacted the two major universities and gained four-year exclusive contracts for apparel purchases made by the sports teams of their athletic departments. Soon after, Lawson's sportswear became popular among most of the students. This growing demand for the company's products motivated Lawson to open two more retail stores. During the fall of 1990, the sales had increased beyond expectations. Although the company achieved a successful reputation in the marketplace, sales growth has generated major problems.

In the beginning, operations were fairly smooth and the inventory control department of the company updated most of its procedures. Morris emphasized the crucial role of routinization in the overall inventory maintenance process to keep up with the increasing turnover. The sales increase was 20 percent, opposed to 12 percent that had been forecast for 1990. It was this increase that initiated a series of problems in the inventory control department. To temporarily alleviate the backlog, Lawson authorized Morris to lease an additional warehouse (see the replenishment level for July 1990, Figure 1). It was decided that the maximum 16 percent of the total inventory carrying costs were going to be dedicated to the off-premise inventory.

Sales for Lawson Sportswear in 1990

EXHIBIT 1

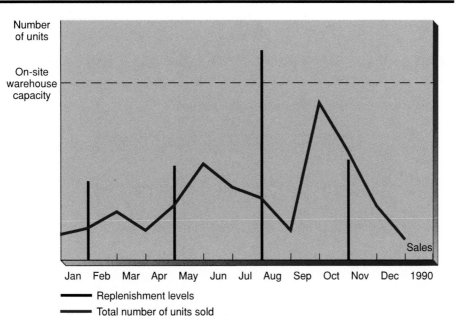

——— Replenishment levels

——— Total number of units sold

Worrying about not being able to meet demand on time, Clifton Morris met with suppliers and asked them to provide more timely delivery schedules to Lawson Sportswear. When he stated that the company was not going to tolerate any reasons for future delays, two major suppliers expressed their concerns about his lack of flexibility and requested price concessions. They simply indicated that Morris's demand had to be supported by providing cash and/or reducing quantity discounts. Morris ignored these comments and indicated how serious he really was by stating that Lawson Sportswear could always find new suppliers. By the end of a long discussion, arguments were beyond a manageable point and the two large suppliers decided to quit dealing with the company.

After the meeting, Morris received a memo from Lawson. Lawson was very concerned about the potential reactions of the rest of the vendors. He stated in his memo that since Lawson Sportswear was continuously growing, it was expected to present a more supportive attitude to its suppliers. He expressed his belief that the company needed a cohesive atmosphere with the rest of the channel members, especially with its vendors.

During the next six months, Morris had limited success in locating one or more large suppliers that would be able to deliver the products to Lawson Sportswear on a timely basis. Faced with growing demand from the surrounding high schools, he had to accumulate excess stock to avoid possible shortages. At the end of the six-

month period, a memo from the accounting department of the company indicated the financial significance of the problem. In his memo, accounting manager Roger Noles simply addressed the high costs of inventory maintenance/security functions (for details, see Table 1). He advised finding a substitute inventory policy to lower these cost figures. Specifically, he stated that the rental cost for the additional warehouse had leveled off at 16 percent, well beyond the maximum.

Keith Lawson immediately scheduled a meeting and asked the top managers to come up with the alternative plans to eliminate this problem.

"I should have never let those suppliers quit," said Morris. "It had a negative effect on our image, and now we all see the results."

"It is too late to worry about that," admonished Lawson. "Instead, we have to come up with a strategy to meet the demand effectively without increasing our costs to the detriment of profits. You realize that the university contracts will expire at the end of this year."

"That is the crucial fact," said Noles. "We simply cannot afford to stock up beyond the current level; it is just too expensive. It is well beyond the funds we have had even from the increased sales."

"In other words, the elimination of the excess inventory is necessary. Who are the vendors that we have at the moment?" asked Lawson.

TABLE 1

Comparative Statement of Profit and Loss for Years Ended December 31

	1991 (forecast)	1990	1989
Net Sales	$165,000	$120,000	$100,000
Cost of Sales			
Beginning inventory	7,000	6,000	4,000
Purchases (net)	140,000	92,000	62,000
	147,000	98,000	66,000
Ending inventory	9,000	7,000	6,000
	138,000	91,000	61,000
Gross Profit	27,000	29,000	39,000
Expenses			
Stock maintenance	7,000	5,250	750
Rent	2,500	1,250	250
Insurance	4,500	3,500	1,500
Interest	4,500	2,500	1,000
Selling	3,500	2,500	2,000
Promotion	7,500	5,500	4,000
Supplies	2,750	1,500	250
Miscellaneous	2,250	1,500	250
	35,000	23,500	10,000
Net profit from operations	<8,000>	5,500	29,000
Other income			
Dividends	925	750	450
Interest	825	600	350
Miscellaneous	650	400	200
	2,400	1,750	1,000
Net profit before taxes	<5,600>	7,250	30,000
Provision for income taxes	1,008	1,305	8,100
Net profit after taxes	<4,592>	5,945	21,900

"There are only three suppliers remaining after the last meeting," replied Morris. "They are fairly small businesses, but we have been dealing with them for quite some time. They have been successful in keeping up with us and the details of their operations are summarized in this report."

"It seems like we have a good selection here," said Lawson, after looking at the report in front of him. "If they mostly work with us, we should be able to influence the future direction in their operations. In other words, it should not be difficult to convince them that they need to upgrade their deliveries in such a way that we can eliminate our excess inventory."

"That would cut down the rental costs that we incur from the additional warehouse," said Noles.

"Obviously!" Lawson replied impatiently. "We will probably need to provide those vendors with a comprehensive support program. If we can convert the floor space of the warehouse from storage to sales, we will have additional funds in retail operations. We can invest a portion of these funds to supporting our vendors and improve our image by forming a cohesive network with them. Of course, there will be a limit to this support. After all, it will be expensive for us to make the transition, too. Therefore, I would like you to come up with an analysis of converting the existing system to a more efficient one. I would like to know what we can do, and how we can do it. To be very honest, gentlemen, I do not want to increase the sales if we do not know how to handle that increase."

Discussion Questions

1. How might the use of a Quick Response system affect the financial performance of Lawson?
2. What problems would Lawson having implementing a Quick Response system with vendors?

This case was prepared by S. Alton Erdem, University of Minnesota–Duluth.

As a result of expansion and growth in the late 1980s, Foley's (a division of May Company) encountered two major problems concerning its Executive Career Pathway. These problems came about because of the rapid expansion of stores outside the Dallas area. Prior to this expansion, Foley's was a department store retailer in the Dallas–Fort Worth metropolitan area. Additionally, a new inventory computer system was installed. This system supplied the executives with crucial information for analyzing merchandise and vendor profitability.

The original career path was designed to expose every junior executive to corporate and store operations. Junior executive trainees began their career with Foley's as an assistant buyer in the headquarters in Dallas. For the next three to four years trainees crisscrossed from the corporate office to various store locations in their move upward. At the end of the training programs, they were either a buyer in the corporate office or an assistant store manager. This system overlooked trainees' individual career goals and didn't allow them to fully utilize their skills to benefit themselves and/or the organization. Both job dissatisfaction and employee turnover were high.

The first major problem concerned the department group manager (DGM) position. In actuality, the DGM's job was composed of three different jobs utilizing three different skills. The DGM was responsible for supervising salespeople and merchandising the floor, analyzing merchandise, and controlling inventory. The supervision and merchandising role called for a person with good people and negotiation skills. To analyze the merchandise, they needed good analytical skills. Furthermore, for inventory control they had to have a bookkeeping mentality to keep the journals and ledgers up to date and accurate. Due to the diverse responsibilities within this position, often the DGM would excel in one area but be weak in the other two. DGMs who excelled in all three job areas were rare.

As new stores opened outside of the Dallas–Fort Worth area, the original career path became deficient for two reasons. First, relocation became a problem as people moved from store locations to the corporate office and vice versa. The corporate office was located in Dallas and stores were located throughout the southwest region. The fast pace of the original career path would mean a move about every six months. Second, with this expansion the number of store positions (i.e., DGM and assistant store manager) greatly outnumbered corporate positions (i.e., buying positions). In other words, new DGM positions were created with the opening of the new stores, while the present number of buyers could handle the additional responsibilities created by the new store openings. The career path had been set up to function efficiently based on an equal number of store and corporate positions. Due to the increase in store positions,

trainees were forced to spend less time in the corporate office as assistant buyers and more time in the stores.

This system created job dissatisfaction and frustration. For some junior executives, store positions were simply a stepping stone to the corporate buying positions. Thus, employees tried to move through the store positions as quickly as possible. Trainees anticipated promotions within a given time frame and were discouraged if their expectations weren't met.

Management decided it was time for a new organizational structure. Considering all the problems apparent in the old structure, the following alternative solutions were offered:

1. The first alternative was to hire employees for only one area (either corporate or store) and promote them vertically within that area. There would be no crisscrossing from store to corporate positions. This would end employees' thinking of one job as a stepping stone to another. It would put them immediately into their area of interest. It would also give employees a well-defined career path and would be easy to administer. This alternative would result in an employee understanding only one side of the company so he could never switch sides (from corporate to store or vise versa) without starting again at an entry-level position.

2. Alternative 2 would split the DGM's job into two positions: one that combines the sales manager's job and the controller's job into one responsibility while keeping the merchandise analyst job the same. Combining the manager's and controllers' roles would minimize conflict between entry-level employees because managers are traditionally evaluated by top management with reports generated by the controllers. Management felt that there could be some difficulty finding employees that would excel in both the manager's job area and the controller's area of responsibility.

3. Alternative 3 would split the DGM's position into three jobs: merchandise analyst, inventory controller, and sales manager. Instead of a store having 15 DGMs, there would be five of each of the three new roles. Each person would be responsible for more departments but would only focus on one job area within each department. The jobs therefore would be narrower in scope but deeper in terms of responsibility. This would give each job more focus and allow each individual to be placed in a job that fits his particular skills. This system would require much communication between job areas because all three roles must work together for the success of a department.

4. Alternative 4 would also divide the DGM's role into three separate jobs: sales manager, analyst, and controller. However, the sales manager's job would consist entirely of managing the salespeople. The responsibility of merchandising the floor would be added to the

merchandise analyst's job. Many department stores currently use this structure. It allows the sales manager to concentrate on only one area (people) and lets the merchandise analyst control all areas involving merchandise. Many sales managers feel that because they're on the floor every day, they have a better understanding of what the customer wants. Also, because sales managers are evaluated on how well the merchandise in their department sells, they would like to have an impact on how that merchandise is displayed.

5. Alternative 5 would create an organizational structure that allows employees to create their own individual career paths based on their abilities and interests. Store and corporate positions would be interrelated and

there would be a good deal of mobility between job areas. Each employee would move at her own pace. Staff could be promoted both vertically and horizontally. This system would be harder to administer and control than a highly defined career path as well as being harder to implement initially.

To reorganize its structure, Foley's can use one of the five alternatives, use a combination of some of them, or come up with an entirely different idea.

Discussion Question:

1. What would you do? Explain your answer.

This case was prepared by Michael Levy, University of Miami.

CASE 2–5 ☼ STEPHANIE'S BOUTIQUE

Stephanie Wilson must decide where to open a ready-to-wear boutique she's been contemplating for several years. Now in her late 30s, she's been working in municipal government ever since leaving college, where she majored in fine arts. She's divorced with two children aged five and eight, and wants her own business, at least partly to be able to spend more time with them.

She loves fashion, feels she has a flair for it, and has taken evening courses in fashion design and retail management. Recently she heard about a plan to rehabilitate an old arcade building in the downtown section of her midwestern city. This news crystallized her resolve to move now. She's considering three locations.

The Downtown Arcade

The city's central business district has been ailing for some time. The proposed arcade renovation is part of a master redevelopment plan, with a new department store and several office buildings already operating. Completion of the entire master plan is expected to take another six years.

Dating from 1912, the arcade building was once the center of downtown trade, but it's been vacant for the past 15 years. The proposed renovation includes a three-level shopping facility, low-rate garage with validated parking, and convention center complex. Forty shops are planned for the first (ground) floor, 28 more on the second, and a series of restaurants on the third.

The location Stephanie's considering is 30 feet square and situated near the main ground floor entrance. Rent is $20 per square foot, for an annual total of $18,000. If sales exceed $225,000, rent will be calculated at 8 percent of sales. She'll have to sign a three-year lease.

Tenderloin Village

The gentrified urban area of the city where Stephanie lives is nicknamed Tenderloin Village because of its lurid

past. Today, however, the neat, well-kept brownstones and comfortable neighborhood make it feel like a yuppie enclave. Many residents have done the rehabilitation work themselves and take great pride in their neighborhood.

About 20 small retailers are now in an area of the Village adjacent to the convention center complex. Most of them are "ferns and quiche" restaurants. There are also three small women's clothing stores.

The site available to Stephanie is on the Village's main street in the ground floor of an old house. Its space is also about 900 square feet. Rent is $15,000 annually with no overage clause. The landlord knows Stephanie and will require a two-year lease.

Appletree Mall

This suburban mall has been open for eight years. A successful regional center, it has three department stores and 100 smaller shops just off a major interstate highway about eight miles from downtown. Of its nine women's clothing retailers, three are in a price category considerably higher than what Stephanie has in mind.

Appletree has captured the retail business in the city's southwest quadrant, though growth in that sector has slowed in the past year. Nevertheless, mall sales are still running 12 percent ahead of the previous year. Stephanie learned of plans to develop a second shopping center east of town, which would be about the same size and character as Appletree Mall. But ground breaking is still 18 months away, and no renting agent has begun to enlist tenants.

The store available to Stephanie in Appletree is two doors from the local department store chain's mall outlet. At 1,200 square feet, it's slightly larger than the other two possibilities. But it's long and narrow—24 feet in front by 50 feet deep. Rent is $24 per square foot ($28,800 annually). In addition, on sales that exceed $411,500, rent is 7 percent of sales. There's an additional charge of

1 percent of sales to cover common-area maintenance and mall promotions. The mall's five-year lease includes an escape clause if sales don't reach $411,500 after two years.

Discussion Questions:

1. Give the pluses and minuses of each location.

2. What type of store would be most appropriate for each location?
3. If you were Stephanie, which location would you choose? Why?

This case was prepared by Professor David Ehrlich, Marymount University.

CASE 2-6 ☼ TO MOVE OR NOT TO MOVE

You own a successful junior boutique on Wisconsin Avenue in Georgetown, which you started three years ago. Your business has grown steadily, and you have developed a loyal clientele. Your store has 1,000 square feet, and lays out well, although you wish it were a bit wider. Sales last year, your third year in business, were $450,000, an increase of 15 percent over the previous year. Sales to date this year are running about 10 percent ahead.

Your lease will be up 60 days from today, on May 31. Your landlord has advised you that you may renew at $45 a square foot, and pay overage rent of 10 percent on all sales over $500,000. Your previous rent was $27 a foot, plus overage rent of 4 percent on sales over $300,000.

Recognizing this as reasonable rent in Georgetown, you are prepared to sign on for three more years, but then you get a call from Georgetown Park Mall, which offers you an interesting proposition. There is a 1,000-square foot space available, which lays out far better than your current space, and is very well located within the mall for your kind of business. Rent for this space would be $60 a square foot, and overage rent would be 8 percent on sales over your present $450,000.

You feel that the Georgetown Park location will enable you to realize sales considerably higher than at your present store, although it may take some time before

your present customers find their way to the new location. You recognize also that you won't have to spend anything on advertising because the mall itself will draw crowds of shoppers.

You are tempted by the offer, but need to know more. You go over to look at the space. It is now occupied by a "go-go" store that was unsuccessful. The decor is dreadful, and you figure it will take at least a month to renovate from the time the lease is up, which is the same date as the end of your lease—May 31.

Returning to your store, you look over your inventory. It's all spring merchandise, and will be ready for a markdown about the end of May. You think you can run a spring clearance in June while renovating the new store, but you wonder whether this would be the best way to announce your presence. Or you could begin taking markdowns earlier than usual, call it a "Moving Sale," and buy a fresh new stock of summer goods for the new store, which might result in a significant loss of gross margin.

Or, as you say to yourself, you can just stay where you are and not bother with the hassle of moving.

Discussion Question:

1. What would you do and why?

Case Prepared by Professor David Ehrlich, Marymount University.

Merchandise Management

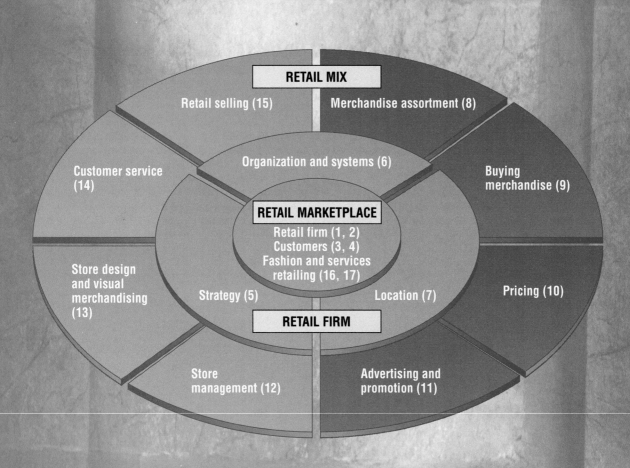

RETAIL MIX

Retail selling (15)

Merchandise assortment (8)

Organization and systems (6)

Customer service (14)

Buying merchandise (9)

RETAIL MARKETPLACE

Retail firm (1, 2)
Customers (3, 4)
Fashion and services retailing (16, 17)

Store design and visual merchandising (13)

Strategy (5)

Location (7)

Pricing (10)

RETAIL FIRM

Store management (12)

Advertising and promotion (11)

S ection II, particularly Chapter 5 ("Retail Strategy"), provided an overall framework for making the tactical decisions that will be examined more closely in Section III. We examined strategic issues, including which markets a retailer should service and how a retailer can achieve a competitive advantage in a market.

Sections III and IV offer tactical solutions to the strategic problems posed in Section II. Section III provides an in-depth discussion of the basic functions of retailing: buying, pricing, and promoting merchandise. Chapter 8 discusses how retailers determine what types of merchandise to buy and how much to carry.

No explanation of merchandise management would be complete without an examination of vendor relations. Chapter 9 explores the types of vendors and branding options available to retailers, where retailers should meet their vendors, and how they should conduct negotiations. The important question of how to set and adjust retail prices is the subject of Chapter 10.

Some of the most visible activities of any retail organization are its promotions. Chapter 11 looks at the relative advantages of various promotional vehicles and at how promotion affects consumer decision making. The chapter also describes how to develop a promotion program and how to set a budget.

Planning Merchandise Assortments

Merchandise assortment (8)

Questions this chapter answers include

- **Why are different types of merchandise divided into categories?**
- **What trade-offs must retailers make to ensure that stores carry the appropriate amount of merchandise?**
- **How do retailers forecast sales for merchandise classifications?**
- **How do retailers evaluate the profitability of their merchandising decisions?**

retailer's primary goal is to sell merchandise so deciding what and how much to buy is a vital task for any retailer.

First, we describe how retailers organize merchandise for buying purposes. Trade-offs retailers face when designing merchandise strategies are examined next. Then we discuss tools retailers use to develop and evaluate a buying plan: sales forecasting and inventory turnover. The chapter concludes with an appendix that describes several systems buyers use to purchase merchandise.

 ORGANIZING THE BUYING PROCESS

It would be virtually impossible to keep the buying process straight without grouping items into categories. Retailers must organize their buying activities so each buyer deals with a specific set of customer needs, such as girls' apparel, boys' apparel, or infants' apparel. Imagine how hard it would be for buyers to keep track of what merchandise they were supposed to purchase if they were assigned to several departments in the store. Buyers develop forecasts and merchandise plans for each category of merchandise for which they're responsible. Then plans for each category are combined to get an overall plan for a merchandise group—such as women's clothing—which is supervised by a merchandise manager. The National Retail Federation (NRF) has developed a standard merchandise classification scheme that defines the various categories and how they're combined. Exhibit 8–1 illustrates how major department store chains like Federated Stores, Inc. (Bloomingdale's, Rich's, and others) use the NRF scheme. Other types of stores such as specialty chain stores (The Gap), power retailers (Toys "R" Us), and discount stores (Wal-Mart) use similar schemes. These stores typically carry fewer items and have fewer buyers than department stores.

Recall that the largest classification level is the **merchandise group.** Vice presidents of merchandise, also called *general merchandise managers* or *GMM*s (Exhibit 8–1), manage the merchandise group. These merchandise managers are responsible for several departments. For instance, the second vice president on the chart in Exhibit 8–1 is responsible for men's, children's, and intimate apparel.

The second division in the classification scheme in Exhibit 8–1 is the department. Divisional merchandise managers manage these departments and report to the vice presidents. For example, the vice president of merchandising for men's, children's, and intimate apparel supervises five divisional merchandise managers. Each divisional merchandise manager is responsible for a department. For example, the division merchandise manager highlighted in Exhibit 8–1 is responsible for children's apparel.

The classification is the third level in the scheme illustrated in Exhibit 8–1. Each divisional merchandise manager supervises a number of buyers. The children's apparel divisional merchandise manager is responsible for six buyers. Each buyer purchases a **classification** (a group of similar items, such as pants as opposed to jackets or suits) supplied by vendors. Exhibit 8–1 highlights the one buyer responsible for girls' apparel sizes 4 to 6. Some buyers are responsible for several classifications.

Categories are the next level in the classification scheme. Each buyer purchases a number of categories. In general, a **category** is an assortment of items that the customer sees as reasonable substitutes for each other. For example, a customer might substitute one dress for another but wouldn't substitute a dress for a swimsuit. The girls' size 4 to 6 buyer in Exhibit 8–1 purchases several categories: sportswear, dresses, swimwear, and outerwear. A category like swimwear may include merchandise from one or several manufacturers.

A **stock keeping unit (SKU)** is the smallest unit available for inventory control. In soft goods merchandise, each SKU is usually defined by size, color, and style. For example, a pair of girls' size 5, stone-washed blue, straight-legged Levis is one SKU.

The category is the unit buyers use to plan merchandising decisions. All SKUs (of the same size) within a category are reasonable substitutes for one another. For instance, demand for jeans is heaviest during the back-to-school period in August. Retailers heavily promote and discount jeans at this time. All types of girls' jeans are stocked, promoted, and priced in the same way throughout the year. Customers and (from an inventory management perspective) buyers think of items within a category as somewhat interchangeable. Buyers can therefore best plan their merchandising strategies at the category level.

Now that we've examined how retailers organize merchandise and merchandising personnel, let's discuss what merchandise buyers purchase—the issue of stock balance.

REFACT

The J.C. Penney catalog has over 100,000 SKUs in 400 categories. Now that's real depth and assortment.[1]

Standard Merchandise Classification Scheme and Organizational Chart

EXHIBIT 8-1

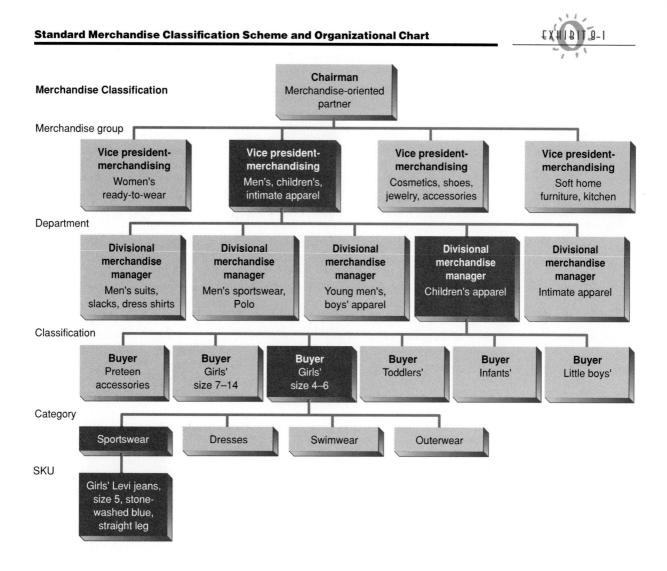

☼ STOCK BALANCE

Picture the room you're in as completely empty. Now assume you're going to open a store in this room, and you can put anything you want in it. How would you divide the space and the money you have to invest in inventory so that you make the most money? To answer, you must decide what type of retailer you really want to be.

Stock balance defines a retailer as either a specialist with a narrow range of merchandise or a generalist with many different types of merchandise. A store's stock balance results in a trade-off among three factors: variety, assortment, and service levels.

Variety. Variety is the number of different merchandising categories within a store or department. Stores with a large variety are said to have good **breadth**—the terms *variety* and *breadth* are often used interchangeably. Some stores, like Abercrombie & Fitch (a specialty store division of The Limited), carry a large variety to meet all the needs of their target customers. Abercrombie & Fitch carries traditional slacks, sweaters, shirts, outerwear, and other categories for both men and women. County Seat, on the other hand, carries only jeans and related apparel—a much more limited variety (fewer categories).

Assortment. Assortment is the number of SKUs within a category. Stores with large assortments are said to have good **depth**—these terms are also used interchangeably. County Seat, for instance, carries a large assortment of jeans and accessories (such as shirts and belts) that complement jeans. Abercrombie & Fitch, on the other hand, has a narrower assortment of jeans because it appeals to a more narrowly defined target market and doesn't have the space to devote to jeans due to its emphasis on variety.

Some stores, known as **niche retailers,** offer extremely deep assortments with virtually no variety. For example, Schmitt's Backstage carries only guitars and instruments used in rock and jazz bands. The Chicken and Egg's gifts and furniture are all made in the Pacific Northwest. Brilliant Ideas narrows the costume jewelry category, featuring only pieces that resemble high-fashion exclusives.

Level of Support. Level of support, in a merchandise management context, is the level of product availability. It's also referred to as the **service level.** But don't confuse service level with customer service. Customer service, a much broader concept, includes an entire set of retail activities that make it easier for customers to shop and to purchase merchandise. Chapter 14 is devoted to methods of providing better customer service.

To understand service level, suppose 100 customers wish to purchase a pair of tan jeans size 32–32 at Abercrombie & Fitch. The store sells 90 pairs before it runs out of stock; thus its service level is 90 percent. Referring to a 90 percent service level is the same as saying 10 percent of the demand wasn't satisfied. In general, the higher the service levels, the higher the inventory investment.

The Stock Balance Trade-offs: A Strategic Decision

Retailers like Abercrombie & Fitch and County Seat have limited resources. The size of each store is fixed in the short run; only so much merchandise will fit into a particular store. Also, retailers have limited financial resources to purchase inventory so they must make decisions regarding the three components of stock balance (variety, assortment, and service level). Re-Tale 8–1 examines the stock balance at the San Diego City Store.

How do retailers make the stock balance decision? It depends on their marketing strategy. As a specialty store, Abercrombie & Fitch tries to be the one-stop shopping alternative for its target markets. It carries a large variety of merchandise categories for both men and women. As a result, it can't physically or financially afford either gigantic assortments within each category or sufficiently high service levels so as never to be out of stock. Conversely, County Seat's target market is particularly interested in buying jeans. As a result, it provides a large assortment of a limited number of categories. Its service level is high; it doesn't want to miss a sale because it doesn't have the right size. If any of the three elements of stock balance—variety, assortment, or service level—aren't what the customer expects or needs, a retailer will likely lose the sale and possibly the customer.

When making the strategic decision about stock, retailers must strike a balance between variety, assortment, and service levels. County Seat (left) has a deep assortment of jeans and related categories; Abercrombie & Fitch (right) provides a large variety of merchandise classifications.

RE-TALE 8-1   San Diego City Store Turns Trash into Cash

The San Diego City Store is an outlet offering used equipment and signs that normally would have been discarded and sold for salvage by the city. But since its opening, there have been waiting lists for old parking meters, manhole covers, and unusual signs from around the city.

The store's strategy is to have an incredibly deep assortment (depth) in one merchandise category (used city junk) while having little or no variety (breadth). Other than T-shirts with popular signs printed on them, the San Diego City Store only has one merchandise category. It's a great success due to the vast depth of signs available—everything from CHOW-CHOW XING to bullet-riddled NO SHOOTING WITHIN CITY LIMITS to SWIMSUITS OPTIONAL BEYOND THIS POINT. To add to the assortment, certain items such as street signs can be specially ordered and customized. Furthermore, to promote and expand business, the store's in the process of developing a mail order catalog, and it may also convert a surplus city bookmobile into a moving version of the San Diego City Store.

SOURCE: Paul Doocey, "San Diego City Store," *Stores,* November 1992, p. 87.

PLANNING TOOLS FOR MERCHANDISE MANAGEMENT

The following sections introduce several important concepts for successfully managing merchandise. First, an integral component of any buying plan is the sales forecast. Without knowing how many sales are forecasted, buyers can't determine how much to buy. We begin the sales forecasting section by discussing (1) category life cycles and (2) the development of a forecast based on historical sales data and other sources.

The sales forecast is only half of the merchandise planning, however. Profitable sales are the key to any successful merchandise plan. Thus this section examines a profitability ratio that is particularly important in the merchandise management process: inventory turnover.

The Category Product Life Cycle

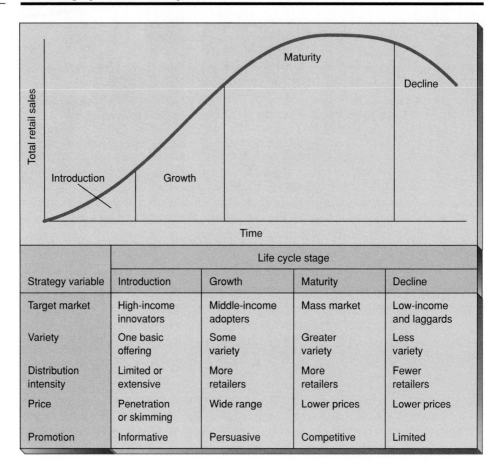

Strategy variable	Life cycle stage			
	Introduction	Growth	Maturity	Decline
Target market	High-income innovators	Middle-income adopters	Mass market	Low-income and laggards
Variety	One basic offering	Some variety	Greater variety	Less variety
Distribution intensity	Limited or extensive	More retailers	More retailers	Fewer retailers
Price	Penetration or skimming	Wide range	Lower prices	Lower prices
Promotion	Informative	Persuasive	Competitive	Limited

Assessing Merchandise Cycles

When making merchandising decisions, buyers must be able to predict how well product categories will sell in each period. Product categories typically follow a predictable sales pattern over time—sales start off low, increase, plateau, and ultimately decline. Yet the pattern varies considerably from category to category. This information enables buyers to understand the customers who will be buying the products, the variety those customers expect, the nature of competition, and the appropriate type of promotion and price level.

This section describes the most fundamental sales pattern, the category life cycle. Using the category life cycle as a basis, we'll examine some commonly found variations on it: fad, fashion, staple, and seasonal cycles.

Category Life Cycle. The **category life cycle** is a merchandise category's sales pattern over time. The category life cycle (Exhibit 8–2) is divided into four stages: introduction, growth, maturity, and decline. Knowing where a category is in its life cycle is important in developing merchandising strategy. Specifically, the stage a particular category is in affects target market, variety, distribution intensity, price, and promotion.

Mules are women's shoes that began as a fashion and have become a staple. Mules are now in the maturity stage of the category product life cycle.

The target market for newly introduced categories is often high-income innovators. For instance, women's shoes called *mules* were introduced as a high fashion item sold only at exclusive stores (see picture on this page). As categories reach the growth and maturity stages, they usually appeal to more middle-income, mass market customers—department store customers in the case of mules. Finally, as categories eventually go into decline, they're made available to low-income customers who follow rather than lead fashion trends. Some new merchandise categories gain popularity in unlikely places, however. Athletic shoe manufacturers like Nike and Reebok test market new styles with America's urban youth. Black heavy-soled work shoes and boots that have become so fashionable to Generation X were first adopted by Europe's right-wing skinheads.

The variety available for newly introduced categories is typically fairly small, but it grows through maturity and then is cut back as the category goes into decline. For example, mules were initially available in a few colors and leathers, but as the category grew and approached maturity, they became available in a multitude of colors and fabrics. As demand for a category declines, retailers again reduce the variety to better control inventory costs.

Distribution intensity refers to the number of retailers carrying a particular category. In the introductory stage, categories can be distributed more or less intensely, depending on the type of category and its availability. A high fashion category like mules was initially available only through a few very exclusive retailers. A manufacturer of a new hand tool, on the other hand, would want its category distributed intensively—through as many retailers as possible. As a category gains popularity in the growth and maturity stages, distribution intensity usually increases. Thus mules have become available at many retailers. But when a category goes into decline, fewer retailers stock it because of decreased demand.

The pricing strategy for newly introduced categories can be either high (*skimming*) or low (*penetration*), depending on the type of category and the level of distribution intensity. Retailers typically use a skimming policy with categories that are

EXHIBIT 8-3

Variations on the Category Life Cycle

	Fad	Fashion	Staple	Seasonal
Sales over many seasons	No	Yes	Yes	Yes
Sales of a specific style over many seasons	No	No	Yes	Yes
Sales vary dramatically from one season to the next	No	Yes	No	Yes
Illustration (Sales against Time)	Sales / Time	Sales / Time	Sales / Time	Sales / Time

in short supply and available through a limited number of retailers. Mules were originally very expensive when they were available only through an exclusive set of retailers. A new grocery store item, on the other hand, would initially use a low price to achieve high market penetration as soon as possible. As a category moves through growth into maturity and decline, the price generally decreases because the category becomes readily available, and demand slows.

Promotion of a new category is designed to inform the customer about the category. With a fashion item like mules, ads showed pictures of the category, where it was available, and what it cost. But as a category goes into growth and maturity stages, promotions become much more competitive and are designed to persuade customers to shop at a particular store. Retailers limit their promotion for categories in the decline stage and divert those funds to categories that can generate more sales.

Variations on the category life cycle. Most categories follow the basic category life cycle: Sales increase, peak, and then decline. Variations on the category life cycle—fad, fashion, staple, and seasonal—are shown in Exhibit 8–3. The distinguishing characteristics between these variations are whether the category lasts for many seasons, whether a specific style sells for many seasons, and whether sales vary dramatically from one season to the next.

A **fad** is a merchandise category that generates a lot of sales for a relatively short time—often less than a season. Examples are pet rocks, mood rings, Batman posters, and Beavis and Butt-head items. More mainstream examples are certain computer games, new electronic equipment, and some apparel. Fads are often illogical and unpredictable. The art of managing a fad comes in recognizing the fad in its earliest stages and immediately locking up nationwide distribution rights before the competition does. Marketing fads is one of the riskiest ventures in retailing because even if the company properly identifies a fad, it must still have the sixth sense to recognize the peak so it can bail out before it's stuck with a warehouse full of merchandise.

Unlike a fad, a **fashion** is a category of merchandise that typically lasts several seasons, and sales can vary dramatically from one season to the next. A fashion is

RE-TALE 8-2   **Predicting Fashion Trends for Teenagers**

Fashion retailing, especially for fashions targeted to teenagers, can change so quickly that even experts often don't know how to react. Take, for example, hip-hop fashion—oversized, baggy clothes in bright colors. It had a short, profitable life, but was quickly replaced with other trends such as grunge and rave as well as more earth tones. Inspired by Seattle's rock music scene, grunge features old flannels and dingy jeans with holes. Rave offers hip-hop's oversize silhouettes but with more contrasting stripes and softer prints. It's also called *hip-hop for surfers.*

  Kids spend over $7.5 billion annually on clothes. Fashion watchers say that to sell a lot of merchandise, it helps to have a single clothing item for kids to organize their wardrobes around. Michael Jackson's red

leather jacket and sports jackets worn by Don Johnson on "Miami Vice" led to trends for young people. But it's hard to duplicate such trends because young adults wish to think for themselves. Today's youth don't want to blend in, even with their contemporaries. Hence, as soon as a style becomes popular, it isn't unique anymore, and it loses its appeal.

  Knowing these facts about today's youth, retailers must be sensitive to fast changes in fashion. What's hip today may be passé tomorrow.

SOURCE: Gregory A. Patterson, "Newer Teen Fashions Trip Up Hip-Hop," *The Wall Street Journal,* September 10, 1993, p. B1.

---

similar to a fad in that a specific style or SKU sells for one season or less. A fashion's lifespan depends on the category and the target market. For instance, double-breasted suits for men or certain colors in domestic goods (sheets and towels) are fashions whose life may last several years. On the other hand, fashions like hip-hop, targeted primarily to the teen market, may last only a season or two. (See Re-Tale 8–2.)

  Items within the **staple merchandise** (also called **basic merchandise**) category are in continuous demand over an extended period. Even certain brands of basic merchandise, however, ultimately go into decline. Most merchandise in grocery stores, as well as housewares, hosiery, blue jeans, and women's intimate apparel, are considered staple merchandise.

  Seasonal merchandise is inventory whose sales fluctuate dramatically according to the time of the year. Both fashion and staple merchandise usually have seasonal influences. For instance, fashionable wool sweaters sell better in fall and winter, while staples like lawn mowers and garden tools are more popular in spring and summer. Retailers carefully plan their purchases and deliveries to coincide with seasonal demand.

Fad, fashion, or staple? When mules were first introduced, no one knew if they would be a fad, a fashion, or a staple. Buyers in exclusive department and specialty stores purchased the category carefully at first. They bought small quantities to see how they would sell. As mules began to sell, buyers reordered throughout the season and into the next. Had the merchandise sold briskly for a few months and then died, it would have been considered a fad. In subsequent seasons, mules became increasingly popular. Now a fashion, they've become available in a larger variety of colors and fabrics, through many more retail outlets, at more competitive prices. Some retailers now treat them as a staple. Ultimately, however, mules will go the way of other staples like bell-bottom pants and Nehru jackets—they'll be readily available only at your local second-hand store.

  The inventory management systems used for fads and fashion merchandise are very different from those used for staples. Managing staple merchandise is fairly

REFACT

Even toilet paper has seasonal influences. Fancy toilet paper sells better during the holiday season between Thanksgiving and New Years since people have guests in their homes.

straightforward. Because there's a rich sales history for each SKU, SKU-based inventory management systems are readily available that forecast future sales using information from the past.

There's no sales history for fads or new fashions at the SKU level so it's much harder for buyers to forecast sales and plan purchases accordingly. Retailers examine the strategic issues of stock balance to determine the general level of inventory to carry in a particular category. Let's explore these sales forecasting issues.

Developing a Sales Forecast

We develop a sales forecast by adjusting a category's past sales to make projections into the future.

Sales forecasting in large retail organizations combines top-down and bottom-up planning. **Top-down planning** means that goals are set at the top of the organization and filter down through the operating levels. In the **bottom-up planning** approach, buyers and other operating managers estimate their merchandise and profit goals, and then negotiate them with upper management.

In a retail organization, top-down planning entails the use of overall retailing strategy (discussed in Chapter 5) as well as the firm's financial strategy. Top management looks at overall economic trends in each trade area in which it competes. It also examines overall sales trends in each store and the impact of new store openings and store closings. Armed with this information, management derives a sales forecast for the total company. This forecast is then broken down into merchandise groups, departments, classifications, and then categories, as we discussed earlier in the chapter and showed in Exhibit 8–1. Here issues of stock balance come into play. Top management must make the strategic decisions regarding variety, assortment, and service level. Based on its assessments, predictions are made regarding which types of merchandise will grow, stay the same, or shrink.

Appropriate merchandising personnel get involved at each stage in the forecasting process. As you can imagine, there's a great deal of negotiating at each step. Merchandise managers and buyers compete for large sales forecasts because the forecast determines how much money they'll have available to spend on merchandise. Buyers and merchandise managers have to plan elaborate presentations to convince their superiors to increase their sales forecast. Of course, they must be honest with themselves. If they succeed in having a larger sales forecast approved, but the merchandise doesn't sell, their profitability—and their performance evaluation—will suffer.

Besides the factors affecting stock balance examined earlier in this chapter, buyers and merchandise analysts use a variety of sources in making these decisions. These include previous sales volume, published sources, customer information, shop competition, and vendors and resident buying offices.

Previous Sales Volume. Exhibit 8–4 shows Levi sales by season over a 10-year period. Sales have been increasing for several years. The exhibit illustrates a strong seasonality pattern—peaks and valleys depending on the time of year. In the eighth year, the fall season was unusually strong due to early cold weather, whereas spring sales were particularly weak because of a temporary turndown in the local economy. For fashion merchandise, where styles change from year to year, sales figures older than three years probably aren't useful. When forecasting sales, we must identify real trends (either up or down) and to try to isolate a real change in demand from random occurrences. Thus we should ignore the unusually high and low sales in the eighth year when trying to forecast sales for the current season.

Sales for Levi Jeans at Trendsetters Department Store

EXHIBIT 8-4

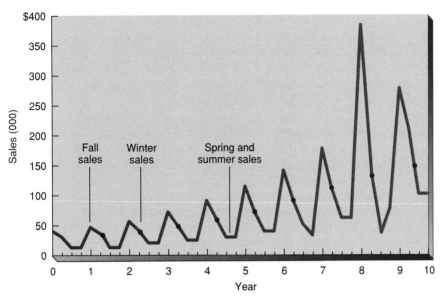

NOTE: The peaks show the fall sales, typically 40 percent of annual sales. The horizontal lines typify 15 percent of annual sales each in spring and summer. The dots (the winter sales) are typically 30 percent of annual sales. These data are for illustrative purposes only. They do, however, represent typical growth patterns for a category like jeans.

Published Sources. Adjustments to sales trends are based on economic trends in the geographic area for which the forecast is developed. *Sales & Marketing Management's* Survey of Buying Power and the *Monthly Retail Trade Report* published by the U.S. Department of Commerce give demographic and annual sales data, by major line of merchandise, for cities of more than 25,000 people. These two sources cover general trends, but may not be particularly helpful for a buyer forecasting sales for a particular merchandise category.

Retailers and their vendors can also buy data from private firms like InfoScan.[2] InfoScan buys information from individual supermarkets on price and promotion activity that has been scanned through their POS terminals. It aggregates the data by region, chain, and/or market area. Information on customer demographics and psychographics as well as competitive information is available from firms like Urban Decision Systems.[3] Finally, general retail trade publications such as *Stores, Women's Wear Daily, Chain Store Age,* and *Chain Store Age Executive* analyze general retail trends.

Customer Information. Retailers can obtain customer information either by using sales to measure customer reactions to merchandise or by asking customers about the merchandise. Knowing what customers want today is very helpful in predicting what they will purchase in the future.

Consider, for instance, **environmental apparel** (merchandise produced with few or no harmful effects on the environment).[4] Spurred by the growth of the Green Movement, environmental apparel began in the early 1990s, but has hit a crossroads where customer needs must be recognized if the industry is to grow and prosper. Clothes are generally made with organically grown cottons and naturally processed fibers. Unfortunately the fashion is somewhat dull—too much brown, beige, and light green; too many sweatshirts and T-shirts; and too few dresses and jackets. Although people have become more environmentally conscious, the fashion's success is questionable. If the clothes don't become more feminine and fashionable, the categories will fail. People can only buy so many wheat-colored T-shirts. On the other hand, if designers can respond effectively to what the customer wants, environmental apparel might prove to be a fashion star.

Shop Competition. Buyers need to shop in similar stores. They need to remain humble and keep in mind that, no matter how good they are, their competition and similar stores in other markets may be even better. When buyers shop in similar stores, they examine merchandise, prices, variety, assortment, and aesthetic aspects of merchandising, such as display. Shopping at local competition helps buyers gauge the immediate competitive situation. For instance, a Macy's buyer shopping at a Nordstrom store may determine that Macy's prices on a particular line of handbags are too high or that Nordstrom is devoting an additional 100 square feet to scarves to satisfy a surge in local demand.

Vendors and Resident Buying Offices. Buyers must seek information from vendors and resident buying offices. **Resident buying offices** offer a number of services associated with the procurement of merchandise. A resident buying office is an office owned and operated by a retailer that is located in an important market area (source of supply) and provides valuable information and contacts. (Chapter 9 gives details.) Vendors and resident buying offices are excellent sources of market information. They know what's selling in markets around the world.

Measuring Inventory Turnover

Think of inventory turnover as "merchandise in motion." Jeans are delivered to the store through the loading dock in the back, spend some time on the store racks, and then are sold and go out the front door. We thus can think of inventory turnover as how many times, on average, the jeans cycle through the store during a specific period of time, usually one year. It's a measure of the productivity of inventory—that is, how many sales dollars can be generated from a dollar invested in jeans.

    Inventory turnover is defined as follows:

$$\text{Inventory turnover} = \frac{\text{Net sales}}{\text{Average inventory at retail}}$$

or

$$\text{Inventory turnover} = \frac{\text{Cost of goods sold}}{\text{Average inventory at cost}}$$

Because most retailers tend to think of their inventory at retail, the first definition is preferable. Arithmetically there's no difference between these two definitions—they yield the same result.

    Retailers normally express inventory turnover rates on an annual basis rather than for parts of a year. Suppose the net sales used in an inventory turnover calculation is for a three-month season. If the retailer calculates turnover for that

The average inventory turnover in a department store for women's apparel is 55 percent higher than the turnover for recreational equipment.

season as 2.3 turns, then annual turnover will be four times that number, or 9.2. Thus to convert an inventory turnover calculation based on part of a year to an annual figure, multiply it by the number of such time periods in the year.

Calculating Average Inventory. Retailers calculate average inventory by dividing the sum of the inventory for each of several months by the number of months. For example:

Month	Retail Value of Inventory
EOM January	$22,000
EOM February	33,000
EOM Month	38,000
Total inventory	$93,000
Average inventory $93,000 ÷ 3 = $31,000	

This approach is adequate if the end-of-month figure doesn't differ in any appreciable or systematic way from a typical monthly figure. For instance, January's end-of-month inventory is significantly lower than that of the other two months in the first quarter because it represents the inventory position at the end of the winter clearance sale and before the spring buildup.

Most retailers no longer need to use physical "counts" to determine average inventory. Point-of-sale (POS) terminals capture daily sales and automatically subtract them from on-hand inventory. Retailers with POS systems can get accurate average inventory estimates by averaging the inventory on hand for each day in the year.

Advantages of Rapid Turnover. Retailers want rapid inventory turnover—but not too rapid, as we'll soon see. Advantages of rapid inventory turnover include increased sales volume, less risk of obsolescence and markdowns, improved salesperson morale, more money for market opportunities, decreased operating expenses, and increased asset turnover.[5]

Increased sales volume. Rapid inventory turnover increases sales volume because fresh merchandise is available to customers, and fresh merchandise sells better and faster than old, shopworn merchandise. Notice the produce next time you're in a less-than-successful supermarket. Brown bananas! Turnover is slow, so the produce is old, which makes it hard to sell.

Less risk of obsolescence and markdowns. The value of fashion and other perishable merchandise is said to start declining as soon as it's placed on display. When inventory is selling quickly, merchandise isn't in the store long enough to become obsolete. As a result, markdowns are reduced, and gross margins increase.

Improved salesperson morale. With rapid inventory turnover and the fresh merchandise that results, salesperson morale stays high. Salespeople are excited about new merchandise, the assortment of sizes is still complete, and the merchandise isn't shopworn. When morale is high, salespeople try harder so sales increase—increasing inventory turnover even further.

More money for market opportunities. When inventory turnover is high, money previously tied up in inventory is freed to buy more merchandise. Having money available to buy merchandise late in a fashion season can open tremendous profit opportunities. Suppose Levi Strauss overestimates demand for its seasonal products. It can sell it to retailers at a lower-than-normal price. If retailers have money available because of rapid turnover, they can take advantage of this special price.

Disadvantages of Overly Rapid Turnover. Retailers should strike a balance in their rate of inventory turnover. An excessively rapid inventory turnover can hurt the firm due to a lower sales volume and an increase in the cost of goods sold.

Lowered sales volume. One way to increase turnover is to limit the number of classifications or the number of SKUs within a classification. But if customers can't find the size or color they seek—or even worse, if they can't find the product line at all—the retailer loses a sale. Customers who are disappointed on a regular basis will shop elsewhere and will possibly urge their friends to do the same. In this case, the retailer loses not only a sale, but customers.

Increased cost of merchandise. To achieve rapid turnover, retailers must purchase merchandise often and in small quantities, which reduces average inventory without reducing sales. But by buying smaller quantities, the buyer can't take advantage of quantity discounts and transportation economies of scale. It may be possible, for instance, to buy a year's supply of Levis at a quantity discount that offsets the high costs of carrying a large inventory. It also costs less on a per unit basis to ship a truckload of Levis than just to ship a few.

In summary, retailers generally prefer rapid inventory turnover. But the turnover rate can be pushed to the point of diminishing returns—a key concern for merchandise managers in all retail sectors.

SUMMARY

This chapter examined basic strategic issues and planning tools for managing merchandise. First, merchandise must be broken down into categories for planning purposes. Without a method of categorizing merchandise like the one described here, buyers could never purchase merchandise in any rational way.

Stock balance (the trade-offs between assortment, variety, and service levels) is a crucial issue in determining merchandising strategy. Examining the stock balance helps retailers answer the important question of what type of store to be: a specialist or generalist.

Tools to develop a merchandising plan include sales forecasting and inventory turnover. When developing a sales forecast, retailers must know what stage of the life cycle a particular category is in and whether the product is a fad, fashion, or staple so they can plan their merchandising activities accordingly. Creating a sales forecast involves such sources of information as previous sales volume, published sources, customer information, and analysis of the competition as well as utilizing vendors and buying offices.

Calculating inventory turnover and determining inventory turnover goals are important. Retailers strive for a balanced inventory turnover. Rapid inventory turnover is imperative for the firm's financial success. But if the retailer attempts to push inventory turnover to its limit, severe stockouts and increased costs may result.

APPENDIX

This appendix discusses buying systems for fashion merchandise: the merchandise budget plan and ancillary systems known as open-to-buy and the model stock list. It then explains how multistore retailers allocate merchandise among stores.

Buying Systems

The *merchandise budget plan* is a buying system that retailers use for fashion merchandise to determine how much money to spend in each month on a particular merchandise category, given the sales forecast and inventory turnover. It's not a complete buying guide because it doesn't indicate how much of a particular SKU the retailer should purchase. To forecast sales for a particular SKU, buyers must know how much was sold in the past. Yet there's little or no sales history for fashions at the SKU level. For instance, even though dresses are purchased year after year, their styles and fabrics change. Buyers must determine the quantity of specific SKUs to purchase based on many of the issues described earlier: the desired stock balance as well as product information derived from published sources, customers, vendors, buying offices, and from shopping at the competition.

 MERCHANDISE BUDGET PLAN

The merchandise budget plan's aims are to set up specific merchandise objectives (in dollars) and to plan the financial aspects of the merchandise side of the business. The merchandise budget plan isn't a complete buying plan because it doesn't indicate what kind of merchandise the buyer should purchase, or in what quantities. The plan just specifies how much money retailers should spend each month to support sales and achieve turnover objectives.

Exhibit 8A–1 shows a simplified version of a six-month merchandise budget plan for girls' dresses sizes 4 to 6 purchased by Vicki Marker at a large national specialty store chain. Even relatively small specialty stores now use advanced computer technologies in planning merchandise budgets.

Merchandise Budget Plan

PLANNING DATA									

Sales forecast $ _130,000_

$$\frac{\text{Net sales}}{\text{Inventory cost}} \times (100\% - GM\%) = \text{Inventory turnover}$$

2.727	×	55 %	=	1.5

$12^* \div$ Inventory turnover = BOM stock/sales

$6 \div \boxed{1.5} = \boxed{4}$

*6, if a 6 month plan

THE PLAN									
	Line	**MONTH**						**Total**	**Remarks**
		Jan	**Feb**	**Mar**	**Apr**	**May**	**Jun**	**(average)**	
Percent distribution of sales by month	1	19	14	14	17	19	17	100	History/projection
Monthly sales	2	24,700	18,200	18,200	22,100	24,700	22,100	130,000	Step(1) × Net sales
BOM stock/sales ratios	3	3.6	4.4	4.4	4	3.6	4	4	Adjusted by monthly sales fluctuations
BOM stock	4	88,920	80,080	50,080	88,400	88,920	88,400		Step(2) + (5) − (4) Sales + EOM − BOM
EOM stock	5	80,080	80,080	88,400	88,920	88,400	85,600		EOM Jan = BOM Feb
Monthly planned purchases	6	15,860	18,200	26,520	22,620	24,180	19,300		Steps 2 + 4 + 7 − 6 Sales + Reductions + EOM − BOM

* $65,600 = forecasted ending inventory for the 6th month and BOM inventory for the 7th month.

Exhibit 8A–1 is divided into two sections. The top is the preliminary planning data; the bottom involves development of the actual merchandise budget plan. Both sections are discussed next.

Planning Data

Planning data are derived from overall corporate financial objectives and are broken down to the category level, based on historical data and current information.

Sales Forecast. The sales forecast is probably the single most important set of decisions in the merchandise budget process. If buyers purchase too much, excessive markdowns and inventory will result. If they purchase too little, sales, and possibly even customers, will be lost. As we discussed earlier, predicting sales for fashion merchandise can be tricky.

Average Stock-to-Sales Ratio. To achieve the planned inventory turnover, retailers must keep purchases in line with the sales forecast for the period. The average beginning-of-month (BOM) stock-to-sales ratio in the merchandise budget plan helps her do this. The average stock-to-sales ratio is directly related to inventory turnover:

Average stock-to-sales ratio = 12 months ÷ inventory turnover

(If preparing a six-month plan as in Exhibit 8A–1, the retailer must divide 6 into the six-month inventory turnover!) This ratio specifies the amount of inventory that should be on hand at the beginning of the month to support the sales forecast and maintain the inventory turnover objective.

In Exhibit 8A–1 because planned inventory turnover = 1.5, average stock-to-sales ratio = 4 (i.e., 6 ÷ 1.5). Thus, to achieve a six-month inventory turnover of 1.5, on average, Marker must plan to have a BOM inventory that's four times the amount of sales for a given month.

The information in the upper portion of the merchandise budget plan ("planning data") is now complete. Let's look at procedures for doing the plan itself.

The Plan

Percent Distribution of Sales by Month (Line 1). Line 1 of the plan projects what percentage of the total sales the retailer expects to make in each month. Thus, in Exhibit 8A–1, 19 percent of the six-month sales is expected to occur in January. The sum of these monthly percentages must equal 100 percent of sales.

Monthly Sales (Line 2). Monthly sales equal the forecast total sales for the period multiplied by each percent distribution of sales by month (line 1). In Exhibit 8A–1, monthly sales for January = $24,700 (i.e., $130,000 × 19%).

Beginning-of-Month (BOM) Stock-to-Sales Ratios (Line 3). The stock-to-sales ratios in line 3 must average the BOM stock-to-sales ratio derived in Exhibit 8A–1's planning data section to achieve the planned inventory turnover. Monthly stock-to-sales ratios vary in the opposite direction of sales. That is, in months when sales are larger, stock-to-sales ratios are smaller, and vice versa.

BOM Stock (Line 4). The amount of stock planned for the beginning of the month equals the monthly sales (line 2) multiplied by the BOM stock-to-sales ratio (line 3). In Exhibit 8A–1, BOM stock for January = $88,920 (i.e., $24,700 × 3.6).

End-of-Month (EOM) Stock (Line 5). The BOM stock from the current month is the same as the EOM stock in the previous month. So, to derive line 5, simply move the BOM stock in line 4 down one box and to the left.

In Exhibit 8A–1, the EOM stock for January is the same as the BOM stock for February—$80,080. We must forecast ending inventory for the last month in the plan.

Monthly Planned Purchases (Line 6). The monthly planned purchases is the amount to be ordered for delivery in each month, given turnover and sales objectives. This amount equals monthly sales (line 2) + EOM stock (line 5) − BOM stock (line 4).

In Exhibit 8A–1, monthly planned purchases for January total $15,860 (i.e., $24,700 + $80,080 − $88,920).

OPEN-TO-BUY

The open-to-buy starts where the merchandise budget plan ends. That is, the merchandise budget provides a buyer with a plan for purchasing merchandise to be delivered in a particular month. The open-to-buy keeps track of how much the buyer spends each month (and therefore how much is left to spend). As such, the open-to-buy acts as the buyer's checkbook. The purpose of open-to-buy is to keep actual

Quarterly Open-to-Buy Ledger for Girls' Blouses

Month: January				Month: February				Month: March		
	Date	Purchase	Amount		Date	Purchase	Amount		Date	Purchase	Amount
		Order no.	$			Order no.	$			Order no.	$
(1).	Oct. 3	1000	500		Oct. 8	1002	2,500		Oct. 20	1005	9,000
	Oct. 7	1001	250		Oct. 20	1005	3,300		Oct. 22	1006	9,600
	Oct. 9	1003	1,000		Oct. 22	1006	1,000	Total			18,600
(3) Total	Oct.		1,750	Total			6,800				
									Nov. 21	1010	15,000
	Nov. 4	1007	350		Nov. 28	1011	5,000	Total	Oct. & Nov.		33,600
	Nov. 6	1008	1,250	Total	Oct. & Nov.		11,800				
Total	Nov.		1,600						Dec. 16	1005	15,000
Total	Oct. & Nov.		3,350		Dec. 15	1013	3,750	Total	Oct. - Dec.		48,600
					Dec. 17	1005	4,000				
	Dec. 15	1013	900	Total	Dec.		7,750				
(2).	Dec. 20	1000	–200	Total	Oct. - Dec.		19,550				
Total	Dec.		700								
Total	Oct. - Dec.		4,050								

Quarterly Open-to-Buy Control Form for Girls' Blouses

Month	(1).	(2).	(3).	(4).
	Planned	Adjustment	Net	EOM OTB
	monthly	previous	purchases	(1 + 2 – 3)
	purchases	EOM OTB	this month	
	(from	(+ or –)	(from	
	budget)		ledger)	
January	15,860	–960	4,050	10,850
February	18,200	10,850	19,550	9,500
March	26,520			
Quarterly total	60,580			

spending in line with the planned level of purchases. In this way, the buyer can avoid overinvestments in inventory and can maintain the rate of inventory turnover at planned levels. Every time a purchase is made that's to be delivered in a certain month, it's subtracted from the planned purchases for that month. Like the merchandise budget plan, open-to-buy records are usually calculated in retail dollars rather than cost dollars.

While open-to-buy systems are based on carefully calculated plans, they must also be flexible. Too often, retailers apply the open-to-buy concept heavy-handedly—with ludicrous results. For example, suppose a buyer overbought a line of red dresses for Valentine's Day and then didn't have enough money left to buy the regular dresses that were selling every day. As a result, the buyer had an investment in inventory that wasn't selling and not enough merchandise that was selling. This kind of problem arises when buyers use open-to-buy systems blindly or when they try to group more than one category together.

Exhibit 8A–2 presents a quarterly open-to-buy (OTB) ledger for girls' blouses. Exhibit 8A–3 shows a quarterly open-to-buy control form. Let's discuss these items.

Use of the Ledger

Buyers post transactions to the ledger for the month in which they will receive the merchandise. For example, assume Vicki Marker orders $500 worth of girls' blouses on purchase order 1,000 on October 3 (highlighted). This entry is posted to the ledger in Exhibit 8A–2. Each time she makes a purchase or changes a purchase order, she records it in the open-to-buy ledger.

Use of the Quarterly Control Form

Open-to-buy is calculated using the Quarterly Control Form in Exhibit 8A–3. The formula for calculating open-to-buy is

> Planned monthly purchases (from the merchandise budget)
> ±Adjustments from the previous EOM open-to-buy
> −Actual purchases (from the open-to-buy ledger)

The following steps illustrate use of the control form in Exhibit 8A–3.

Column 1 contains planned purchases for the first three months of the year from the merchandise budget plan for girls' blouses in Exhibit 8A–1: $15,680, $18,200, and $26,520 for January, February, and March. Total for the quarter is $60,580.

Column 2 is used to adjust for over- or underspending in the previous month. Open-to-buy balances for previous months may or may not be exhausted. Any unused balance from the previous month is carried over and added to the current month. Likewise, overbought deficits are carried over and subtracted from the current month. In Exhibit 8A–3, for example, Marker overspent her budget by $960 last December, so it's carried over to January.

Column 3 is for the total purchases from the open-to-buy ledger. Because this form was created at the end of February, total purchases for January and February ($4,050 and $19,550, respectively) are posted in column 6. Note: Because this form was created in late February, the March open-to-buy can't be completed at this time.

Column 4 is the EOM open-to-buy. Note that Marker has underspent her open-to-buy by $10,850 in January and underspent by $9,500 in February. The January EOM open-to-buy of $10,850 is posted to February in column 2. In February, she has $10,850 more to spend on girls' blouses.

Evaluating Open-to-Buy

Even if everything in Marker's merchandise budget for girls' blouses goes according to plan, without careful attention to the record keeping performed in the open-to-buy, she will fail. In the same way that you must keep track of the checks you write, Marker must keep careful records of the merchandise she purchases and when it's to be delivered. Otherwise she would buy too much or too little. Merchandise would be delivered in months when it wasn't needed, and would be unavailable when it was needed. Sales and inventory turnover would suffer, and the merchandise budget plan would be useless. Thus, the open-to-buy system presented here is a critical component of the merchandise management process.

Model Stock List for Girls' Jeans

Styles	Traditional	Traditional	Traditional	Traditional
Price levels	$20	$20	$35	$35
Fabric composition	regular denim	stone-washed	regular denim	stone-washed
Colors	lt blue	lt blue	lt blue	lt blue
	indigo	indigo	indigo	indigo
	black	black	black	black
Styles	Flared bottom	Flared bottom	Flared bottom	Flared bottom
Price levels	$25	$25	$40	$40
Fabric composition	regular denim	stone-washed	regular denim	stone-washed
Colors	lt blue	lt blue	lt blue	lt blue
	indigo	indigo	indigo	indigo
	black	black	black	black

MODEL STOCK LIST

The merchandise budget plan enables buyers like Vicki Marker to plan their purchases ahead of time so they can meet their sales forecast and turnover goals. In turn, open-to-buy allows buyers to keep track of their purchases as they're made so buyers don't overspend or underspend their merchandise budget. But these two buying systems don't make up a complete buying plan because they don't suggest what merchandise to buy within a particular merchandise category. The model stock list is designed to provide such guidance.

A **model stock list** is a list of fashion merchandise that indicates in very general terms what retailers should carry in a particular merchandise category. Exhibit 8A–4 shows an abbreviated model stock list for girls' jeans. This model stock list identifies general styles (traditional five-pocket straight leg jeans and flared jeans), general price levels ($20 and $35 for traditional jeans; $25 and $40 for flared jeans), composition of fabric (regular denim and stone-washed), and colors (light blue, indigo, and black). The model stock list doesn't identify specific SKUs because fashions change from year to year. The more fashion-oriented the category, the less detailed the model stock list because the buyer requires more flexibility to adjust to fashion changes.

The model stock list is generally based on historical precedence and is therefore the starting point for making adjustments for the current season. For instance, if a particular style, such as flared jeans, is expected to be especially popular in the coming season, buyer Vicki Marker would use more of the merchandise budget for that style and would cut back on traditional jeans. The buyer uses sales forecasting information to fine-tune the model stock list.

Model stock lists for apparel and shoes also typically include a size distribution. Historical records for virtually every merchandise category are available from internal sources or vendors. To illustrate, Exhibit 8A–5 breaks down size and length for the 429 units of girls' traditional $20 denim jeans in light blue to be purchased for a large store. Thus, the store will order nine units of size 1-short which represents 2 percent of the 429 total. The process of applying the size distribution is then repeated for each style/color combination for each store.

Relative Advantages of Four Types of Vendor   EXHIBIT 9-1

Impact on store	Type of vendor			
	Manufacturer brands	**Private label brands**	**Licensed brands**	**Generic brands**
Store loyalty	?	+	?	+
Store image	+	+	+	+
Traffic flow	+	+	+	+
Selling and promotional expenses	+	–	+	?
Restrictions	–	+	–	+
Differential advantages	–	+	+	?
Margins	?	?	?	?

+ advantage to the retailer   – disadvantage to the retailer   ? depends on circumstances

 ## TYPES OF VENDORS

Vendors are firms from which retailers obtain merchandise. Retailers deal with four types of vendors: vendors of manufacturer brands, private-label brands, licensed brands, and generic products. Each type of vendor has advantages and disadvantages, as summarized in Exhibit 9–1. When deciding which type of vendor to use, retailers must consider these advantages and disadvantages in light of their strategy, the type of merchandise they're buying, customer and competitive reactions, and profit potential.

Manufacturer brands, also known as **national brands,** are products designed, produced, and marketed by a vendor. The manufacturer is responsible for developing the merchandise and establishing an image for the brand. In some cases, the manufacturer will use its name as part of the brand name for a specific product, such as Kellogg's corn flakes. However some manufacturers—like Procter & Gamble (manufacturer of Tide, Cheer, and Ivory)—don't associate their name with the brand. Manufacturer brands that consumers perceive as high quality include Kodak film, Hallmark greeting cards, Fisher-Price toys, Levi jeans, Mercedes-Benz automobiles, Arm & Hammer baking soda, and IBM personal computers.[2]

Vendors of Manufacturer Brands

Buying from vendors of manufacturer brands can help store image, traffic flow, and selling/promotional expenses. (See Exhibit 9–1.) Retailers buy from vendors of manufacturer brands because these brands have a customer following—people go into the store and ask for them by name. Loyal customers of manufacturer brands generally know what to expect from the products and feel comfortable with them.

Manufacturers devote considerable resources to creating demand for their products. As a result, retailers' selling and promotional expenses for manufacturer brands are relatively low. But retailers typically realize lower profits from manufacturer brands than from private-label brands, licensed brands, or generic products. These lower profits are due to the manufacturer assuming the cost of promoting the brand and the increased competition among retailers selling these brands. Many retailers in a market offer the same manufacturer brand so customers compare

Manufacturer brands like these at Warehouse Club can have a positive effect on store image, traffic flow, and selling and promotional expenses. They can also restrict a retailer's marketing efforts and lessen the store's differential advantage in the marketplace.

prices for these brands across stores. Retailers often offer significant discounts on some manufacturer brands to attract customers to their stores.

Some retailers that have traditionally emphasized private or store brands are purchasing more manufacturer brands. For example, Montgomery Ward and Sears's Brand Central now emphasize manufacturer brands in electronics and major appliances. J.C. Penney has systematically added manufacturer brands of clothing such as Levi Strauss, Haggar, Van Heusen, and Maidenform. These retailers are using manufacturer brands to attract additional customers and highlight the value of their private-label brands.

Stocking national brands may increase or decrease store loyalty. If the manufacturer brand is available from a limited number of retail outlets (e.g., Lancôme cosmetics or DKNY sportswear), customers loyal to the manufacturer brand will also become loyal to the store. If, on the other hand, manufacturer brands are readily available from many retailers in a market, customers' store loyalty may decrease because the retailer can't differentiate itself from competition. Customers in shopping malls often complain that every store has the same merchandise. Another problem with manufacturer brands is that they can limit a retailer's flexibility. Vendors of strong brands can dictate how their products are displayed, advertised, and priced.

Vendors of Private-Label Brands

Private-label brands (also called **store brands**) are products developed and marketed by a retailer. Exhibit 9–2 gives examples. Typically, retailer buyers develop specifications for the merchandise and then contract with a vendor to manufacture it. But the retailer is responsible for promoting the brand, not the manufacturer.

In the past, private-label brands generally were seen as low quality. For instance, in department stores, private-label brands were often found on cut-rate garments. Many of today's private labels, however, are top quality, created by the department store's own designers and backed by extensive marketing programs. This trend toward high-quality private-label brands permeates other retail industries

Examples of Private-Label Brands

EXHIBIT 9-2

Industry	Store	Brand
Grocery stores	Safeway	Shurfine, Empress
	King Soopers	Topco
	Winn-Dixie	Maid
Chain stores	Sears	Kenmore, Toughskins
	J.C. Penney	Fox, Stafford, Hunt Club
Department stores	Federated Stores, Inc. (Bloomingdale's, Rich's, etc.)	Allen Solly, Saville Row, Lauren Alexandra, B. G. Street
Specialty stores	Neiman Marcus	One-Up
	The Limited, Limited Express	Forenza, Hunters Run, Outback Red, EXP

as well. For instance, discount store customers are increasingly accepting private labels—particularly in stationery, domestics, glassware and dishes, greeting cards, hardware, children's apparel, women's apparel, and housewares.[4]

Offering private labels provides a number of benefits to retailers, as Exhibit 9–1 shows. First, the exclusivity of strong private labels boosts store loyalty. For instance, consumers won't find Hunters Run, a brand of traditional women's sportswear owned by The Limited, at Macy's. A second advantage of buying from private-label vendors is that they can enhance store image if the brands are high quality and fashionable. Third, like manufacturer brands, successful private-label brands can draw customers to the store. Fourth, with private-label brands, retailers don't face the same restrictions on display, promotion, or price that often encumber their strategy with manufacturer brands. Retailers purchasing private brands also have more control over manufacturing, quality control, and distribution of the merchandise. Talbot's, for instance, can contract with any vendor to manufacture its private-label sweaters. Finally, profit opportunities may be greater. Besides having more control over production, comparison shopping by customers is made very difficult, if not impossible. Thus, private label merchandise is less suseptible to price discounting. Due to these advantages, many people think that private-label merchandise will become as popular in the United States as it is in Europe. (See Re-Tale 9–1.)

But there are drawbacks to private-label brands. Although profits may seem higher for private-label brands than for manufacturer brands, there are other expenses that aren't readily apparent. Retailers must make significant investments to design merchandise, create customer awareness, and develop a favorable image for their private-label brands. When private-label vendors are located outside the United States, the retailer becomes responsible for problems with transportation and import restrictions. Lead times may increase because merchandise may be tied up in bureaucratic red tape in a Houston dockyard. Quality control also becomes the retailer's problem. For instance, it's hard for a retailer in the United States to monitor production of men's silk ties in Italy.

Sales associates may need additional training to help them sell private-label brands against more well-known manufacturer brands. If the private-label merchandise doesn't sell, the retailer can't return the merchandise to the vendor. These

REFACT

Private-label goods account for 18.3 percent of all units sold in grocery stores and nearly 14 percent of total supermarket dollar volume.[3]

RE-TALE 9-1 **Europeans Witness Proliferation of Private Labels**

Visit a French *hypermarche*—a huge supermarket—and you'll find just about everything the modern consumer needs. There's the predictable array of fresh and frozen food, detergents, shampoo, deodorants, and toys plus TV sets, clothes, tires, gasoline, and even champagne for celebrating your buying binge. But when you get them all home, you may notice something funny about the labels. A lot of them—including the ones on the champagne and the TV set—may have a brand name you've never heard of—the store's own.

Across Europe, from Spain to Scandinavia, private-label merchandise is rolling into big stores—and rolling right out again in people's shopping carts. Some stores, like Germany's hugely successful Aldi cut-rate food chain, sell virtually nothing but their own brand of goods. Goods are produced by independent suppliers to the retail chains' specifications.

European buying habits are shifting sharply, with discount stores replacing neighborhood shops—which is changing the nature of urban life. It's boosting the already cutthroat nature of retail competition, throwing shivers through stodgier stores—and also through big food manufacturers like BSN S.A., Unilever Group, and Nestlé S.A.

Because private brands sometimes are high quality and priced below equivalent brand-name products, they're forcing out the less successful nonstore brands. More and more big chains, which once specialized in famous-brand goods at lower prices, are being forced to offer their own private-label goods to compete.

SOURCE: E. S. Browning, "Europeans Witness Proliferation of Private Labels," *The Wall Street Journal,* October 20, 1992, pp. B1, B5.

problems are most severe for high-fashion merchandise. For these reasons, retailing giants like Federated Stores, Inc., have reduced their purchases from vendors of private-label merchandise in the 1990s.[5] Re-Tale 9–2 gives insight into J.C. Penney's private-label program for men's apparel.

Vendors of Licensed Brands

With **licensed brands,** the owner of a well-known brand name (the licensor) contracts with a licensee to develop, produce, and sell the branded merchandise. The licensee may be either (1) the retailer that contracts with a manufacturer to produce the licensed product or (2) a third party that contracts to have the merchandise produced and then sells it to the retailer. Licensed brands' market share has grown increasingly large in recent years. Owners of trade names not typically associated with manufacturing have also gotten into the licensing business. For instance, the manufacturer of the sweatshirt or baseball cap emblazoned with your university's logo pays your school a licensing fee. If it didn't, it would be infringing on the university's logo (a trademark) and would therefore be involved in counterfeiting. (Counterfeiting is discussed later.) Re-Tale 9–3 describes an unusual licensing agreement between Wal-Mart and *Popular Mechanics.*

Licensed brands offer the retailer some advantages of both manufacturer and private-label merchandise. (See Exhibit 9–1.) Because consumers recognize such names as *Popular Mechanics,* Mickey Mouse, and McDonald's, licensed products attract customer attention. The downside of licensing, however, is similar to that of manufacturer brands.

Vendors of Generic Products

Generic products are unbranded, unadvertised merchandise found mainly in drug, grocery, and discount stores. Generics' popularity peaked in the mid-1980s, although they continue to be popular in a few product categories. Some industry experts think generic pharmaceuticals capture 25 to 50 percent of the market in their first year on the market.

RE-TALE 9-2   Private-Label Strategy for J.C. Penney's Menswear

The private-label strategy for J.C. Penney's menswear is a carefully designed plan Penney uses to distinguish its merchandise from competitors'. Each Penney brand is designed to have its own personality and is targeted to specific markets. Any information regarding Penney private-label merchandise—advertising, fixtures, or signage—is designed to conjure up an image consistent with the brand's identity.

Products are described in terms of price/quality by good, better, and best. The market segments are described as conservative, traditional, and updated. The most popular lines are St. John's Bay and Hunt Club.

St. John's Bay. St. John's Bay is a traditional line of weekend wear tailored to a rugged, yet laid-back life-style. Its easy-care fabrics are designed for comfort and durability like those of its competitors: Eddie Bauer and L.L. Bean.

The St. John's Bay man is down-to-earth, about 40 years old, and active. He's an individual. He doesn't dress up. He's never flashy. He dresses for himself—not for others. When he relaxes on weekends or in the evenings, he does so in comfort. That's his style. He plays touch football, goes camping or fishing, and enjoys fresh air. He's the Marlboro Man without the cigarette. His clothes are simple, rugged, easy fitting, and, above all, comfortable. He prefers colors and fabrics that match easily with one another.

The tone of St. John's Bay advertising reinforces the active outdoor life-style the clothes were designed to represent—back to nature; the great outdoors.

Hunt Club. Hunt Club is a traditional line of men's apparel inspired by the classic yet updated styling characteristic of Ralph Lauren. Emphasis is on all natural fibers and high-quality construction.

The Hunt Club man is a Renaissance man. He's 35, can order in French, choose a respectable Chardonnay, and quote the classics, not to mention the Dow Jones Industrial Average. It's a sophistication he attributes to hours of reading and years of travel. His ambitions reach beyond the office to include family, sports, and community work. Peer group acceptance is a major concern. When it comes to clothes, quality is his watchword. An investment in long-lasting, classic apparel pays dividends in the long run.

Hunt Club's advertising tone is rich, warm, and confident—vintage Cape Cod. Scenes typically depict models in social settings.

SOURCE: J.C. Penney Company.

Short sets, $15. Socks, $4. JCPenney is the exclusive department store for Sesame Street clothing.

Clothes with character.

CTW
SESAME STREET.

JCPenney. Fashion comes to life

Children's Television Workshop, owner of the Sesame Street trademarks and servicemarks, entered into a licensing agreement with J.C. Penney to manufacture and sell Sesame Street clothing.

RE-TALE 9-3   Popular Mechanics Tools and Hardware at Wal-Mart

Wal-Mart has made a major thrust into private-label products by rolling out several new lines. Although it won't neglect its commitment to strong manufacturer brands, it sees new opportunities with private labels.

Under a licensing agreement from Hearst Magazines' *Popular Mechanics,* Wal-Mart is planning a complete line of hand tools and hardware. Why *Popular Mechanics?* Published since 1902, this magazine is one of the most respected American names in dispensing home and auto repair advice, enjoying a circulation of 1.64 million. In licensing the name from Hearst magazines, Wal-Mart gains instant access to a widely recognized brand name.

In favor of taking on the nationally known name, Wal-Mart is dropping its own private-label tool line, Promark, which it launched in 1991. To protect the equity in its name, *Popular Mechanics* magazine is testing at an independent laboratory each of the hundreds of products Wal-Mart intends to market under its licensing agreement. It has tested the hand tools against Craftsman (Sears' private brand) and found them comparable. Like Craftsman, the Popular Mechanics hand tools will carry a lifetime guarantee, but will probably cost about half as much.

SOURCE: "Private Label Mix Expands," *Discount Store News,* June 15, 1992, pp. 131–32.

Exhibit 9–1 outlines the advantages and disadvantages of generic products. By buying from vendors of generic products, retailers may realize higher profits. But sales of generics may take away from sales of manufacturer brands. Thus it's hard to determine generic products' net effect on profit margins.

The rest of this chapter examines how retailers buy merchandise from vendors. The next section describes settings where vendors and retailers interact.

⚙ MEETING VENDORS

Typically, retailers "go to market" to see the variety of available merchandise and to buy. A **market,** from the retail buyer's perspective, is a concentration of vendors within a specific geographic location, perhaps even under one roof. These markets may be permanent wholesale market centers or temporary trade fairs. Retailers may also buy on their own turf, either in stores or at corporate headquarters. Finally, resident buying offices prearrange opportunities for buyers to visit vendors in major market centers in this country and abroad.

Wholesale Market Centers

For many types of merchandise, retailers can do much of their buying in established market centers. Wholesale market centers have permanent vendor sales offices retailers can visit throughout the year. Probably the world's most significant wholesale market center for many merchandise categories is New York City. Vendors' offices and showrooms may be scattered in a particular area of the city, such as the garment district on and around Seventh Avenue in Manhattan, which has been renamed Fashion Avenue for a number of blocks.

The United States has a number of regional wholesale market centers in Chicago, Los Angeles, Atlanta, and other areas. The Dallas Market Center, the world's largest, is a 6.9-million–square-foot complex of six buildings. Over 26,000 manufacturers and importers display their international products in its 2,400 permanent showrooms and more than 2,000 temporary spaces. The Dallas Market Center comprises the International Apparel Mart, International Menswear Mart, Market Hall, Dallas Trade Mart, World Trade Center, and Dallas Home Furnishings Mart.

Retailers visit wholesale market centers like the Dallas Market Center to meet vendors and purchase merchandise. This center contains 2,400 permanent showrooms and more than 2,000 temporary spaces.

Trade Shows

Many wholesale market centers host **trade shows** (also known as **merchandise shows** or **market weeks**). Both permanent tenants of the wholesale market centers and vendors leasing temporary space participate. Here retailers place orders and get a concentrated view of what's available in the marketplace. The Dallas Market Center hosts over 40 shows annually for products ranging from floor coverings to toys, apparel, jewelry, and gifts. Trade shows are also staged by convention centers not associated with wholesale market centers. McCormick Place in Chicago (the nation's largest convention complex with almost 2 million square feet) hosts over 65 meetings and trade shows per year.

Buying on Their Own Turf

Although buyers go to wholesale market centers and trade shows to search for new merchandise, place orders, and meet with vendors, vendors also work with buyers in their offices. Most buying activity in buyers' offices is for basic merchandise or rebuys on fashion merchandise.

Resident Buying Offices

Resident buying offices are organizations located in major buying centers that provide assistance to retail buyers. To illustrate how resident buying offices operate, consider how David Smith of Pockets Men's Store in Dallas utilizes his resident buying offices when he goes to market in Paris. Smith meets with market representative Alain Bordat of Specialty Stores Association. Bordat, an English-speaking Frenchman, knows Smith's store and his upscale customers so he prearranges appointments with French vendors he believes would fit Pockets' image.

When Smith is in France, Bordat accompanies him to the appointments and acts as translator, negotiator, and accountant. Bordat informs Smith of the cost of importing the merchandise into the United States, taking into account duty, freight, insurance, processing costs, and so forth.

Once Smith places orders, Bordat writes the contracts and follows up on delivery and quality control. Specialty Stores Association also acts as a home base for buyers like Smith, providing office space and services, travel advisors, and emergency aid. Bordat and his association continue to keep Smith abreast of what's happening on the Parisian fashion scene through reports and constant communication. Smith will not have to return to France as often as would otherwise be the case since the buying office can take care of reorders and other issues that may come up. Without the help of a resident buying office, it would be difficult, if not impossible, for Smith to penetrate the French wholesale market.[6]

Now let's look at how buyers negotiate with vendors to purchase merchandise.

Buyers must often travel to their vendor's manufacturing facility. This computer factory in Hong Kong sells to retailers throughout the world.

GUIDELINES FOR PLANNING NEGOTIATIONS WITH VENDORS

Negotiations are as basic to human nature as eating or sleeping.[7] A **negotiation** takes place any time two parties confer with each other to settle some matter. Parents and their children negotiate about allowances; friends negotiate about what to do on the weekend.

Business negotiations occur almost daily. People negotiate for higher salaries, better offices, and bigger budgets. Negotiations are crucial in buyers' discussions with vendors.

To illustrate how a buyer should prepare for and conduct a negotiation with a vendor, let's consider the hypothetical situation of Carolyn Swigler, men's designer shirt buyer at Lord & Taylor. Carolyn is preparing to meet with Dario Carnevale, the salesman from Tommy Hilfiger, in her office in New York. Swigler is ready to buy Tommy Hilfiger's spring line, but she has some merchandising problems that have yet to be resolved from last season. Let's consider several general guidelines for planning a negotiation session and several for conducting a face-to-face negotiation session, all described in terms of Swigler's hypothetical situation.

Knowledge is power! The more the buyer knows about the vendor, the better the buyer's negotiating strategy will be.

Consider history.   Buyers need a sense of what has occurred between the retailer and the vendor in the past. Although Swigler and Carnevale have only met a few times, their companies have a long, profitable relationship. A sense of trust and mutual respect has been established, which may work to Swigler's advantage in the upcoming meeting. An established vendor may be more likely to take care of old problems and accept new demands if a long-term, profitable relationship already exists.

Although Tommy Hilfiger shirts have been profitable for Lord & Taylor in the past, three patterns sold poorly last season. Some vendors believe that once they've sold merchandise to the retailer, their responsibility ends. This is a short-term perspective, however. If the merchandise doesn't sell, a good vendor, like Tommy Hilfiger, will arrange to share the risk of a loss. Swigler may ask to return some merchandise. Or Carnevale may provide **markdown money**—funds a vendor gives a retailer to cover lost profit due to markdowns and other merchandising issues. Vendors usually give markdown money in the form of a credit to the retailer's account.

Assess where things are today.

Besides taking care of last season's leftover merchandise, Swigler has set goals in five areas for the upcoming meeting: additional markup opportunities, transportation, delivery and exclusivity, communications, and advertising allowances.

Set goals.

Additional Markup Opportunities. Vendors may have excess stock (manufacturers' overruns) due to order cancellations, merchandise returned by retailers, or simply an overly optimistic sales forecast. To move this merchandise, vendors offer it to retailers at reduced prices. Retailers can then make a higher than normal profit and/or pass the savings on to their customers. Because Lord & Taylor is noted as a fashion leader, it probably isn't interested in any excess inventory that Tommy Hilfiger has to offer. Off-price retailers, such as T.J. Maxx, Marshalls, Loehmann's, and Burlington Coat Factory, specialize in purchasing manufacturers' overruns. Another opportunity for additional markups is with private-label merchandise, which we discussed earlier in this chapter.

Transportation. Transportation costs can be substantial, though this doesn't pose a big problem with the Tommy Hilfiger shirts due to their high unit cost and small size. Nonetheless, the question of who pays for shipping merchandise from vendor to retailer can be a significant negotiating point.

Delivery and Exclusivity. In retailing in general (and in fashion in particular), timely delivery is essential. Being the only retailer in a market to carry certain products helps a retailer hold a fashion lead and achieve a differential advantage. Swigler wants to be certain that her shipment of the new spring line arrives as early in the season as possible, and that some shirt patterns won't be sold to competing retailers.

Communications. Vendors and their representatives are excellent sources of market information. They generally know what is and isn't selling. Providing good, timely information about the market is an indispensable and inexpensive marketing research tool so Swigler plans to spend at least part of the meeting talking to Carnevale about market trends.

Advertising Allowances. Retailers have the choice of advertising any product in the store. They can sometimes share the cost of advertising through a cooperative arrangement with vendors known as **co-op advertising** in which the vendor agrees to pay all or part of a pricing promotion. By giving retailers advertising money based on a percentage of purchases, vendors can better represent their product to consumers. (Chapter 11 describes cooperative advertising.) Under the Robinson–Patman Act, vendors are allowed to give advertising allowances on a proportionately equal basis—the same percentage to everyone—usually based on a percentage of the invoice cost. As a fashion leader, Lord & Taylor advertises heavily. Swigler would like Tommy Hilfiger to support a number of catalogs with a generous ad allowance.

Know the vendor's goals and constraints.

Negotiation can't succeed in the long run unless both parties believe they've won. By understanding what's important to Carnevale and Tommy Hilfiger, Swigler can plan for a successful negotiating session. Generally, vendors are interested in the following issues.

A Continuous Relationship. Vendors want to make a long-term investment in their retailers. For seasonal merchandise like men's designer shirts, they have to plan their production in advance so it's important for Tommy Hilfiger to know that certain key retailers like Lord & Taylor will continue their support. Swigler plans to spend some time at the beginning of the meeting reviewing their mutually profitable past and assuring Carnevale that Lord & Taylor hopes to continue their relationship.

Testing New Items. There's no better way to test how well a new product will sell than to put it in a store. Retailers are often cautious with new items due to the risk of markdowns and the opportunity cost of not purchasing other, more successful merchandise. Yet vendors need their retailers to provide sales feedback for new items. Lord & Taylor has always been receptive to some of Tommy Hilfiger's more avant-garde styles. If these styles do well in certain Lord & Taylor stores, they'll likely succeed in similar stores around the country.

Communications. Just as Carnevale can provide market information to Swigler, she can provide sales information to him. Also, Swigler travels the world market. On one buying trip to England, she found an attractive scarf. She bought the scarf and gave it to Carnevale, who had it copied for a shirt. It was a big success!

Showcase. In certain urban centers—notably New York, Los Angeles, Dallas, London, Milan, and Paris—vendors use large stores to showcase their merchandise. For instance, many U.S. buyers go to market in New York. Most stop at Lord & Taylor to see what's new, what's selling, and how it's displayed. Thus Carnevale wants to make sure that Tommy Hilfiger is well represented at Lord & Taylor.

A good understanding of the legal, managerial, and financial issues that constrain a vendor will facilitate a productive negotiating session. For instance, Swigler should recognize from past experience that Tommy Hilfiger normally doesn't allow merchandise to be returned, but does provide markdown money. If Carnevale initially says that giving markdown money is against company policy, Swigler will have strong objective ammunition for her position.

Plan to have at least as many negotiators as the vendor.

There's power in numbers. Even if the vendor is more powerful, aggressive, or important in the marketplace, the retailer will have a psychological advantage at the negotiating table if the vendor is outnumbered. At the very least, the negotiating teams should be of equal number. Swigler plans to invite her merchandise manager into the discussion if Carnevale comes with his sales manager.

Plan to negotiate on your own turf.

Swigler has a natural advantage in the upcoming meeting because it will be in her office. She'll have information at her fingertips, plus secretarial and supervisory assistance. From a psychological perspective, people generally feel more comfortable and confident in familiar surroundings. Unfortunately, negotiations often take place at the vendor's showroom, which can be in such unfamiliar locations as Hong Kong or Milan.

To illustrate the importance of deadlines, consider when labor strikes are settled. An agreement is often reached one minute before a contract expires or a strike is scheduled. There's always pressure to settle a negotiation at the last minute. Swigler recognizes that Carnevale must go back to his office with an order in hand because he has a quota to meet by the end of the month. She also knows that she must get markdown money or permission to return the unsold shirts by the end of the week or she won't have enough money to cover the orders she wishes to place. Recognizing these deadlines will help Swigler come to a decisive closure in the upcoming negotiation.

Be aware of real deadlines.

GUIDELINES FOR FACE-TO-FACE NEGOTIATIONS

The most thoughtful plans can go astray if the negotiators fail to follow some important guidelines in the meeting. Here are several tips for successful negotiations, including separating people from the problem, insisting on objective criteria, and inventing options for mutual gain.[8]

Suppose Swigler starts the meeting with "Carnevale, you know we've been friends for a long time. I have a personal favor to ask. Would you mind taking back $10,000 in shirts?" This personal plea puts Carnevale in an uncomfortable situation. Swigler's personal relationship with Carnevale isn't the issue here and shouldn't become part of the negotiation.

Separate people from the problem.

An equally detrimental scenario would be for Swigler to say, "Carnevale, your line is terrible. I can hardly give the stuff away. I want you to take back $10,000 in shirts. After all, you're dealing with Lord & Taylor. If you don't take this junk back, you can forget about ever doing business with us again." This approach serves as a personal attack on Carnevale. Even if he had nothing to do with the shirts' design, Swigler is attacking his company. Reminding Carnevale that he's dealing with a large concern like Lord & Taylor is threatening and will probably further alienate him. Finally, threats usually don't work in negotiations; they put the other party on the defensive. Threats may actually cause negotiations to break down, in which case no one wins.

Conversely, if Carnevale takes a personal, aggressive, or threatening stance in the negotiations, what should Swigler do? Let him talk. If Swigler allows Carnevale to work through his aggression or anger, it will probably dissipate like a tropical storm going out to sea. By listening, Swigler may find that Carnevale's problem can be easily resolved. Finally, Swigler should apologize if necessary. Even if Swigler doesn't believe she or Lord & Taylor did anything to cause Carnevale's anger, an apology that doesn't admit to any personal or corporate responsibility probably will calm him down.

The best way to separate people from the problem is to insist on objective criteria. Swigler must know exactly how many shirts need to be returned to Tommy Hilfiger or how much markdown money is necessary to maintain her profit.

Insist on objective criteria.

If Carnevale argues from an emotional perspective, Swigler should stick to the numbers. For instance, suppose after Swigler presents her position, Carnevale says he'll get into trouble if he takes back the merchandise or provides markdown money. With the knowledge that Tommy Hilfiger has provided relief in similar past situations,

Swigler should ask what Tommy Hilfiger's policy is regarding customer overstock problems. She should also show Carnevale a summary of Lord & Taylor's buying activity with Tommy Hilfiger over the past few seasons. Using this approach, Carnevale is forced to acknowledge that providing assistance on this overstock situation—especially because it has been done in the past—is a small price to pay for a long-term profitable relationship.

Invent options for mutual gain.

Inventing multiple options is part of the planning process, but knowing when and how much to give (or give up) requires quick thinking at the bargaining table.

Consider Swigler's overstock problem. Her objective is to get the merchandise out of her inventory without significantly hurting her profit. Carnevale's objective is to maintain a healthy yet profitable relationship with Lord & Taylor. Thus Swigler must invent options that could satisfy both parties. Her options are

Sell the shirts to an off-price retailer at 10 cents on the retail dollar.

Have Carnevale take back the shirts.

Get Tommy Hilfiger to provide markdown money and put the shirts on sale.

Return some of the shirts and get markdown money for the rest.

Clearly, selling the shirts to an off-price retailer would cause Swigler to take a loss. But from Carnevale's perspective, taking back the merchandise may be unacceptable because the styles are from last season and some shirts may be shopworn. Swigler could, however, present this option first, with the knowledge that Carnevale probably will reject it. Then she could ask for markdown money. Carnevale would believe he got off easy, and Swigler would have her problem solved.

In developing her plan for the meeting, Swigler followed some important rules of negotiation. She identified viable options for both parties. Then she determined which options would satisfy both parties' objectives. When presenting the options, she held back the one she believed would be most acceptable to Carnevale so he would think he was a winner.

Let them do the talking.

There's a natural tendency for one person to continue to talk if the other person involved in the conversation doesn't respond. If used properly, this phenomenon can work to the negotiator's advantage. Suppose Swigler asks Carnevale for special financial support on Lord & Taylor's Christmas catalog. Carnevale begins with a qualified no and cites all the reasons why he can't cooperate. Swigler doesn't say a word. Although Carnevale appears nervous, he continues to talk. Eventually he comes around to a yes. In negotiations, those who break the silence first, lose!

Know how far to go.

There's a fine line between negotiating too hard and walking away from the table with less than necessary. If Swigler overnegotiates by getting the markdown money, better transportation terms, and a strong advertising allowance, the management of Tommy Hilfiger may decide that other retailers are more worthy of early deliveries and the best styles. Carnevale may not be afraid to say no if Swigler is pushing him beyond a legal, moral, profitable relationship.

Don't burn bridges.

Even if Swigler gets few additional concessions from Carnevale, she shouldn't be abusive or resort to threats. Professionally Lord & Taylor may not wish to stop doing business with Tommy Hilfiger on the basis of this one encounter. From a personal perspective, the world of retailing is relatively small. Swigler and Carnevale may meet at the negotiating table again—both working for different companies. Neither can afford to be known in the trade as being unfair, rude, or worse.

Many issues are raised and resolved in any negotiating session. To be certain that there are no misunderstandings, participants should orally review the outcomes at the end of the session. Swigler and Carnevale should both summarize the session in writing as soon as possible after the meeting.

Don't assume.

 ## SUMMARY

This chapter examined methods of developing and maintaining good vendor relations. Retailers can't succeed without their vendors. To survive, they must be able to count on a predictable supply of merchandise at competitive prices and with sufficient promotional support.

Retailers have many vendor/branding options—each with its own advantages. In choosing vendors and making sourcing decisions, retailers must evaluate manufacturer's brands, licensed brands, private-label brands, and generic products.

Buyers and their merchandise managers have several opportunities to meet with vendors, view new merchandise, and place orders. They can visit their vendors at wholesale market centers in New York, Paris, or Milan. Virtually every merchandise category has at least one annual trade show where retailers and vendors meet. Buyers often meet with vendors on their own turf—in the retail store or corporate offices. Finally, meetings with vendors are facilitated by resident buying offices. Market representatives of these resident buying offices facilitate merchandising purchases in foreign markets.

The section on negotiating with vendors provided a glimpse into how this critical activity should take place. Successful vendor relationships depend on planning for and being adept at negotiations.

Legal and ethical issues that affect retailer–vendor relationships are discussed in the following appendix.

APPENDIX

As you can imagine—given the number of negotiations between retailers and vendors—unethical or illegal situations may arise. Let's examine slotting allowances, commercial bribery, exclusive territories, exclusive dealing agreements, tying contracts, refusals to deal, dual distribution, counterfeit merchandise, and gray-market merchandise.

Ethical and Legal Issues in Purchasing Merchandise

Slotting allowances (also called **slotting fees**) are fees vendors pay for space in a retail store. Slotting allowances currently are legal.[9] You may decide, however, that in certain circumstances they're unethical. Here's an example. When General Foods or any other consumer package goods manufacturer wants to introduce a new product, it often pays a slotting allowance to grocery and discount store chains for a space (slot) on the shelves. The fee varies depending on the nature of the product and the relative power of the retailer. Products whose brand names command relatively low customer loyalty pay the highest slotting allowances. Likewise, large grocery chains can demand higher slotting allowances than small mom-and-pop stores can. Fees can be significant—as high as $10,000 per store! It may cost close to $1 million to get national distribution of a new product.

Slotting Allowances

Some retailers argue that slotting allowances are a reasonable method of ensuring that their valuable shelf space is used efficiently. Manufacturers whose new brands boast high sales potential are willing to pay slotting allowances, while manufacturers with marginal new brands are reluctant to pay them. Thus retailers can sort out the best new products by charging slotting allowances. Of course, manufacturers view slotting allowances as extortion.

Commercial Bribery

Commercial bribery occurs in retailing when a vendor or its agent offers to give or pay a retail buyer "something of value" to influence purchasing decisions. Suppose a sweater manufacturer offers to take a department store buyer to lunch at a fancy private club and then proposes a ski weekend in Vail. The buyer enjoys the lunch but graciously turns down the ski trip. These gifts could be construed as bribes (also known as **kickbacks**), which are illegal. In fact, the Internal Revenue Service doesn't allow money paid for bribes to be deducted as a business expense. From an ethical perspective, there's a fine line between the social courtesy of a free lunch and an elaborate free vacation.

To avoid these problems, many companies forbid employees to accept any gifts from vendors. Wal-Mart even posts a sign in its vendor waiting room spelling out its "no free lunch" policy. But many companies have no policy against receiving gifts—and some unethical employees accept and even solicit gifts even if their company has policy against it. A good rule of thumb is to accept only limited entertainment, such as a meal or theater tickets, or token gifts, such as flowers or a bottle of wine, for Christmas, birthdays, or other occasions.

Exclusive Territories

Vendors often grant an **exclusive geographic territory** to a retailer so no other retailer in the territory can sell a particular brand. These territorial arrangements can benefit vendors by ensuring that "quality" retailers represent their products. In cases of limited supply, providing an exclusive territory to one retailer helps ensure that the retailer can carry enough inventory to make a good presentation and offer the customer an adequate selection. If, for instance, the luxury Ferrari Automobile Company allowed its products to be distributed through all dealers that want to carry them, there wouldn't be enough Ferraris to go around, leading to customer confusion. Being granted exclusive territories helps retailers as well because it gives them a monopoly on the product—a strong incentive to push that vendor's products. The retailer knows there are no competing retailers to cut prices, so its profit margins are protected.

The courts have tended to hold exclusive territories illegal when they restrict competition. Competition is restricted when other retailers have no access to similar products. For example, having exclusive Ferrari dealers wouldn't be a restraint of trade because other luxury cars are readily available to the public. On the other hand, if DeBeers, the South African diamond cartel, granted exclusive territories to certain jewelry retailers, this would probably be seen as a restraint of trade because diamonds wouldn't be readily available through other sources.

Exclusive Dealing Agreements

Exclusive dealing agreements occur when a manufacturer or wholesaler restricts a retailer to carrying only its products and nothing from competing vendors. The effect on competition determines these contracts' legality. For instance, suppose a retailer signs an agreement with Levi Strauss to sell only Levi's denims. There's no real harm done to competition because other manufacturers have many alternative retail outlets, and Levi Strauss's market share isn't large enough to approach monopolistic levels.

On the other hand, in 1987, Hartz Mountain (which has a majority market share in the pet products market) was fined $1 million by a St. Louis federal court for attempting to monopolize the pet supplies market. The court ruled that Hartz had attempted to draw retailers away from a wholesaler selling competing pet products.[10] The difference in the legal interpretation of these two cases is based on the impact on competition. The court determined that because Hartz Mountain has such a large market share, smaller competitors could be severely injured.

When a vendor and a retailer enter into an agreement that requires the retailer to take a product it doesn't necessarily desire (the *tied product*) to ensure that it can buy a product it does desire (the *tying product*), a **tying contract** exists. Tying contracts are illegal if they substantially lessen competition or tend to create a monopoly.

Tying Contracts

A vendor is entitled to create tying contracts to protect its goodwill and quality reputation. For instance, Benetton, the Italian knitwear manufacturer, may legally require its retail stores to purchase all their sweaters from Benetton because the legitimate purpose is to maintain the brand name's image. Alternatively an auto manufacturer probably wouldn't be allowed to force its dealers to purchase only the automaker's radios with its cars. Dealers could legitimately argue that the manufacturer's image or the functioning of the cars wouldn't be impaired by purchasing radios from another vendor.

Refusal to deal can be initiated by either suppliers or retailers. Generally, both suppliers and retailers have the right to deal, or refuse to deal, with anyone they choose. But there are exceptions to this general rule when there's evidence of anticompetitive conduct.

Refusals to Deal

A manufacturer may refuse to sell to a particular retailer, but it can't do so for the sole purpose of benefiting a competing retailer. Giorgio Armani and Ralph Lauren have decided not to sell to the new Barneys New York store in uptown Manhattan. It would be unlawful for a competitor of Barneys (say Bloomingdale's) to pressure these vendors into not selling to Barneys, but from a practical perspective its hard to prove such coercive influence. If the courts determined there were good reasons why Armani and Lauren should refuse to deal with Barneys, they would have the right to refuse to deal. Armani claims Barneys' performance on its line at other branch stores isn't impressive. Lauren argues it doesn't want to sell to that store because its line is already sufficiently distributed in that area.[11]

Dual distribution occurs when a manufacturer or wholesaler competes directly with its retailers. Dual distribution systems usually arise when a vendor decides to vertically integrate by starting retailing activities. Dual distribution isn't always illegal. But there may be a restraint on competition and trade if vendors sell to independent retailers at higher prices than they offer to the retailers they own, thus causing a severe and continuous decline among competing retailers.

Dual Distribution

The retail gasoline market is a good example of a dual distribution system. Oil companies like Mobil and Texaco own some of their stations, while others are independently owned. In this scenario, the oil company is in competition with itself and its customers if its company-owned service stations are located near the independent stations. If the company charges independent stations more for its products than nearby company stations, this may be viewed as an illegal restraint on competition and free trade.

ᚱᚨᛚᛖ 9–4   Levi's War against Counterfeiting

Rolex, Chanel, Polo, Cartier, and many other famous manufacturers must deal with the rising problems involving counterfeit merchandise. The Levi Strauss Company is no exception. Since 1990, the company estimates that more than 2 million pairs of fake Levi jeans have been seized around the world, meaning millions more have been sold.

Denim detectives and security officials for companies like Levi search the world for manufacturers and distributors of counterfeit products. In 1993, an eight-month investigation uncovered an operation distributing tens of thousands of fake jeans around the world. Jeans were allegedly manufactured somewhere in China and bought by a Fort Lauderdale business, which shipped them to a warehouse in Guadalajara, Mexico. From there, they were distributed to middlemen throughout the world, including Milan, Paris, and Reykjavik, Iceland. During this operation, 7,200 fake jeans were seized in retail stores in Iceland, and another 28,000 in other European countries. For these illegal sales, Levi is seeking multimillion dollars in damages against the defendants who allegedly ran this operation.

SOURCE: Anthony Faiola, "Tracking Fake Levi's," *The Miami Herald,* September 8, 1993, p. C1.

Counterfeit Merchandise

Counterfeit merchandise is goods made and sold without permission of the owner of the trademark. A **trademark** is any mark, word, picture, or design associated with certain merchandise (for instance, the crown on a Rolex watch and the GE on General Electric products). Once a trademark is registered, the trademark owner is protected under federal law from counterfeiters. Deliberate counterfeiting is a felony punishable by a jail term and substantial fine. Re-Tale 9–4 describes Levi's war against counterfeiting.

Gray-Market Merchandise

ᚱᛖᚠᚨᛖᛏ

Up to $10 billion of gray-market merchandise enters the United States annually.[12]

Gray-market merchandise possesses a valid U.S. registered trademark and is made by a foreign manufacturer but is imported into the United States without the permission of the U.S. trademark owner. Gray-market merchandise is not counterfeit. This merchandise is the same quality and may actually be identical to merchandise brought into the country legally. Without realizing it, we see gray-market goods in the marketplace all the time. Manufacturers of cars, jewelry, perfume, liquor, watches, cameras, crystal ware, ski equipment, tractors, baby powder, and batteries are all involved in gray marketing in the United States.[13]

Gray market merchandise can also be made domestically, but sold through unauthorized wholesalers, distributors, or retailers.

Here's an example of how the gray market for watches might work in the United States. To help create a prestigious image and to pad profit margins, Swiss watch manufacturers often charge a higher wholesale price in the United States than in Europe and other countries. A Swiss watchmaker such as Patek Philippe may sell 1,000 watches to a distributor in Egypt. But instead of shipping the watches to Egypt, the watchmaker sends the shipment to the free-trade zone in Panama. Gray Goods, Inc., in New York buys the entire shipment in Panama from the Egyptian distributor. It's then imported into the United States, where it's sold to a chain of discounters called Mel's Jewelry Stores. Mel can sell these watches at a significantly lower price than a traditional jewelry store can and still make an adequate profit margin.

Under a 1988 Supreme Court decision, U.S. retailers may import gray-market goods without the consent of the U.S. trademark owner under certain circumstances. Although recently a judge in Los Angeles ruled that Drug Emporium, the discount drug chain, violated copyright laws when it sold Amariage perfume without the permission of Parfums Givenchy (the fragrance's manufacturer), Drug Emporium insists it has done nothing illegal. Clearly, the legality of gray-market merchandise is still "gray."[14]

Some discount store operators argue that customers benefit from the lack of restriction on gray-market goods because it lowers prices. For instance, suppose there is a strong demand for a new personal computer in Northern California and a wholesaler in West Virginia has excess inventory. A retailer in Northern California purchases the PCs from the West Virginia wholesaler at a discount and passes the savings on to the consumer. Since the West Virginia wholesaler is unauthorized by the manufacturer to sell to retailers in California, the computers are gray-market merchandise. Competition with this retailer selling the gray-market computers forces the authorized dealers in the Northern California area to cut their prices.

Traditional retailers, on the other hand, claim the gray market has a negative impact on the public. They believe that important service after the sale will be unavailable through retailers of gray-market goods. They also think that a less expensive gray-market product may hurt the trademark's image. Thus, before purchasing gray-market products, retailers should be aware of their actions' legal and marketing implications.

KEY TERMS

commercial bribery, 196	exclusive geographic territory, 196	markdown money, 191	slotting allowance (slotting fee), 195
co-op advertising, 191	generic product, 186	market, 188	trade show/ merchandise show/
counterfeit merchandise, 198	gray-market merchandise, 198	negotiation, 190	market week, 189
dual distribution, 197	kickback, 196	private-label brand (store brand), 184	trademark, 198
exclusive dealing agreement, 196	licensed brand, 186	resident buying office, 189	tying contract, 197
	manufacturer brand (national brand), 183		vendor, 183

DISCUSSION QUESTIONS AND PROBLEMS

1. What name is given to the private-brand sport shirts sold in the department store near your college? What's the name of the manufacturer brand in competition with the private-label sport shirts? How does the department store promote its private label?

2. Retailers are making a strong effort to increase the efficiency of operations. One area particularly affected is the buying office. In many stores, extended trips to different markets have been severely cut back. What's the danger of this situation for fashion-forward stores, such as Macy's and Dayton Hudson?

3. When buyers and sellers negotiate over price, somebody wins and somebody loses. If the seller makes a price concession, the seller makes less money and the buyer makes more. How can a buyer and seller have a win–win relationship?

4. What are the positive and negative aspects of a manufacturer entering into a dual distribution system?

5. What kinds of social courtesies or gifts (lunches, theater tickets, etc.) are appropriate for buyers to accept from vendors?

6. What are the advantages and disadvantages to retailers of carrying licensed brands?

7. When setting goals for a negotiation session with a vendor, what issues should a buyer consider?

8. What factors should a buyer consider when deciding which vendors to develop a close relationship with?

Pricing

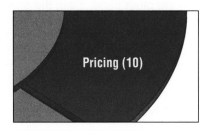

Pricing (10)

Questions this chapter answers include

- **Why do some retailers have frequent sales while others attempt to maintain an everyday low price strategy?**
- **How do retailers set retail prices?**
- **Why are markdowns taken, and what are some guidelines for taking them?**
- **Under what circumstances can retailers' pricing practices get them into legal difficulties?**

G one are the free-spending 1980s. Customers are looking for a good value in what they purchase. To some people, a good value means a low price. Many different types of consumers have become much more price-sensitive. (See Chapter 3.) Others are willing to pay more as long as they believe they're getting their money's worth in terms of product quality or service.

Retailers have responded to their customers' needs and created a differential advantage for themselves by developing retail formats that emphasize low prices. National discount store chains that offer everyday low prices (EDLP)—such as Kmart, Wal-Mart, and Target—dominate many markets in many product categories. A newer entry into the price-oriented market is the membership-only warehouse club, such as Sam's Warehouse Club and Price/Costco. Another relatively new form of retailer is the off-price retailer (e.g., Loehmann's, T.J. Maxx, and Marshalls), which purchases closeout and end-of-season merchandise at lower-than-normal prices and passes the savings on to the customer. (Chapters 2 and 3 describe these stores and trends.)

RE-TALE 10-2   Shopping Secrets of America's Queen of Markdowns

Who says the saying "Shop until you drop" doesn't have merit? Certainly not America's first Shopper's Hall of Fame inductee, Pat Gayzur. The Shopper's Hall of Fame, probably the only one in the nation, was created by the Jamaica, New York, Chamber of Commerce to honor the area's top shopper. Pat Gayzur nominated herself after she went shopping one Saturday and spent $31.88 for 30 new additions for her closet.

What are her secrets? "I don't buy anything that costs more than $10," says Gayzur. But don't think that means you won't catch her wearing an Anne Klein blouse. It just means that she paid only $1.99 for it. Gayzur doesn't skimp on quality either. Her shoes must be leather, and she prefers clothing by top designers.

To live up to her standards, she has had to develop a sophisticated shopping strategy. She shops only at final clearance sales, which usually occur at the end of February and end of August. Her shopping day begins when she picks up her best friend, who's a compatible shopper mainly because she's a different size. They arrive at their favorite store when the doors open and begin systematically combing the racks for the red tag that means the item costs $1. She also searches the store looking in the men's aisles and the children's section. She knows that less experienced shoppers will hide their goodies, planning to come back for them. "Every once in awhile," she says, "you will find somebody's stash." Everything is fair game to an ardent shopper.

Other shopping tips: Never try on clothes because it wastes valuable shopping time. Don't take anything that has to be repaired. Never say no to a white blouse or black pants. One secret Gayzur isn't about to divulge is the location of her favorite red-tag sale. As she says, "I don't need that much competition."

SOURCE: Kelli Pryor, "The Queen of Markdowns," *Living,* November 1989–January 1990.

ADJUSTMENTS TO THE INITIAL RETAIL PRICE

The initial retail price isn't always the price the retailer uses. Adjustments to the initial retail price are markdowns and additional markups.

Markdowns are reductions in the initial retail price. Let's examine why retailers take markdowns, how to reduce the number of markdowns, how large a markdown should be, the duration of the markdown period, how to liquidate markdown merchandise, and the mechanics of taking markdowns. Re-Tale 10–2 describes America's Queen of Markdowns.

Markdowns

Reasons for Taking Markdowns. Retailers' many reasons for taking markdowns can be classified as either clearance (to get rid of merchandise) or promotional (to generate sales).

Many retailers think of markdowns as mistakes. When merchandise is slow-moving, obsolete, at the end of its selling season, or priced higher than competitors' goods, it generally gets marked down for clearance purposes. This merchandise can become an eyesore and impair a store's image. Further, even if the merchandise can be sold in the following season, it may become shopworn or go out of style. Also, cost of carrying inventory is significant.[4] If a buyer has to carry $10,000 of unwanted inventory at an annual inventory carrying cost of 35 percent, the cost would be $3,500 (or $10,000 × .35)—no trivial amount! Markdowns are, however, part of the cost of doing business. A retailer's objective shouldn't necessarily be to minimize markdowns. If markdowns are too low, the retailer is probably pricing the merchandise too low, not purchasing enough merchandise, or not taking enough risks with the merchandise being purchased.

Using a high/low pricing strategy described earlier in this chapter, retailers employ markdowns to promote merchandise to increase sales. A buyer may decide to mark down some merchandise to make room for something new. An additional benefit is that the markdown sale generates cash flow to pay for new merchandise. Markdowns are also taken to increase customers' traffic flow. Retailers plan promotions in which they take markdowns for holidays, for special events, or as part of their overall promotional program. (Chapter 11 gives details.) In fact, small portable appliances (such as toasters) are called **traffic appliances** because they're often sold at reduced prices to generate in-store traffic. Retailers hope that customers will purchase other products at regular prices while they're in the store. Markdowns can also increase the sale of complementary products. For example, a supermarket's markdown on hot dog buns may be offset by increased demand for hot dogs, mustard, and relish—all sold at regular prices.

Reducing the Number of Markdowns. Although retailers should expect and plan for a certain number of markdowns, it's crucial not to exceed the optimal amount. The most important means of reducing potential markdowns is a good merchandise budget plan (detailed in Chapter 8). Several other issues also affect the amount of markdowns.

Retailers should coordinate merchandise selections. For example, a buyer for a traditional men's clothier wouldn't purchase avant-garde Italian neckwear to go with traditional button-down shirts.

Another way to reduce markdowns is timely deliveries. Although not often possible, the best plan is to purchase a small amount of a new product as a test. If it gets a favorable response, the retailer buys again. At the very least, retailers should try to avoid deliveries too early in the season. On the other hand, when merchandise arrives too late, retailers may have trouble selling the entire stock without taking markdowns. Quick response (QR) inventory systems (see Chapter 6) are becoming increasingly popular with retailers. By reducing lead time for receiving merchandise, retailers can more closely monitor changes in trends and customer demand, thus reducing markdowns.

Retailers must work with their vendors. Vendors who are knowledgeable of the market and competition can help with stock selections. Retail buyers often can obtain **markdown money**—funds a vendor gives the retailer to cover lost profits that result from markdowns and other merchandising issues.

When to Take Markdowns. Retailers must keep good records. This means keeping track of (1) types of merchandise that required markdowns in the past and (2) what's not selling in the current season. If, for example, certain sizes required significant markdowns in the past, the retailer should cut purchases in those sizes for the current season.

Size of the Markdown and Duration of the Markdown Period. Many retailers take some markdowns early in the season, when demand is still fairly active. By taking markdowns early, retailers don't have to reduce prices as drastically as they do for markdowns taken late in the selling season. As noted above, early markdowns free up selling space for new merchandise and improve the retailer's cash flow. And customer traffic rises due to marked-down merchandise.

Storewide clearance sales (late markdown policy) are usually conducted twice a year, after the peak selling seasons of Christmas and the Fourth of July, although recently these sales have started earlier in the season. A late markdown policy is commonly used by upscale department and specialty stores, though most retailers with seasonal merchandise also find this policy useful. One advantage is that retailers have a longer period to sell merchandise at regular prices. But it's likely that retailers using a late markdown policy will need to offer larger markdowns, 40 to 50 percent, to make sure the merchandise sells. Also, frequent markdowns can destroy customer confidence in a store's regular pricing policy. Finally, clearance sales limit bargain hunting to twice a year.

A combination of early and late markdown strategies has become popular in recent years. For instance, many fashion retailers take 20 percent off after six weeks, followed by an additional 30 percent three weeks later, and so on until the merchandise is gone. This approach is believed to be relatively more profitable than having fewer but more severe markdowns. This may be because customers believe they must rush to buy before the sale ends and before the retailer runs out of merchandise. Also, customers who weren't induced to buy during the first wave of markdowns may subsequently buy. The combination strategy's disadvantage is that a retailer may be selling merchandise at a loss after the first or second markdown.

The size of the markdown required to sell the merchandise is hard to determine. Highly perishable merchandise (like fresh meat and produce) as well as fashion typically requires more substantial markdowns than staple merchandise. A markdown's absolute dollar amount may vary depending on the product. For instance, a 10 percent reduction on a $10,000 car would probably be viewed as a greater incentive than a 10 percent reduction on a $1 ice cream cone.

Liquidating Markdown Merchandise. No matter what markdown strategy a retailer uses, some merchandise may still remain unsold. Retailers can use one of three strategies to liquidate this merchandise.

First, they can "job-out" the remaining merchandise to another retailer. Selling the remaining marked-down merchandise to another retailer has been very popular among retailers. For instance, Boston-based department store Filene's has traditionally purchased end-of-season merchandise from other retailers and sold it at deep discounts in its stores.

Second, they can consolidate the marked-down merchandise into a regular location, an outlet store, or a distribution center. This practice encourages a successful yet relatively short markdown period. Further, customers who shop during the consolidation sale enjoy a better selection than they'd find in the individual stores. But consolidation sales can be complex and expensive due to the extra transportation and record keeping involved.

Finally, retailers can carry the merchandise over to the next season. This strategy is used with relatively high-priced nonfashion merchandise such as traditional men's clothing and furniture. Generally, however, it's not worth carrying over merchandise due to excessive inventory carrying costs.

R E F A C T

Over 60 percent of sales in department stores and specialty chains and over 50 percent of nonchain specialty stores' sales come from marked-down merchandise.[5]

Mechanics of Taking Markdowns. Assume that a product costs $1. Initial markup is 33.3 percent of retail price, and the initial retail price (R) is $1.50. The retailer decides to mark down the product from $1.50 to $1.25. The markdown of 25 cents represents 16.7 percent (.25 ÷ 1.50). *Note:* To determine the markdown percentage, always use the previous selling price as the denominator.

An **additional markup** is an increase in the retail price after the retailer has applied the initial markup percentage but before the merchandise goes onto the selling floor. Continuing with the previous example, assume a certain product's initial retail price is $1.50. But suppose the retailer got a particularly good buy, and the competition

Additional Markups

is selling the same product for $2. If the retailer lowers the price below competitors' price, the product won't sell appreciably more. So the retailer decides to sell the product for $2. The additional markup is 50 cents or 33.3 percent (.50 ÷ 1.50). Remember, always use the previous selling price as the denominator.

THE DEMAND-ORIENTED METHOD OF SETTING THE RETAIL PRICE

Retailers should use demand-oriented pricing in conjunction with the cost-oriented method to determine retail prices. Using this method, retailers not only consider their profit structure but also pay close attention to the impact of price changes on sales. For instance, if customers are extremely sensitive to price, then a price cut increases demand so much that profits actually increase. Alternatively, if customers are insensitive to price, raising the price boosts profits because sales don't decrease. Demand-oriented pricing seeks to determine the price that maximizes profits.

This section examines (1) factors that affect customers' sensitivity to price and (2) how to establish the initial retail price using the demand-oriented method.

Factors That Affect Customers' Sensitivity to Price

When retailers determine how to set initial retail prices, they must consider how sensitive their customers are to price.[6] In general, retailers set higher prices on products for which customers are less price-sensitive. Let's look at the factors that determine customers' price sensitivity.

Substitute Awareness Effect. The substitute awareness effect occurs when customers become more sensitive to price because there are a lot of substitutes for a product or for a retailer. Some markets are **overstored**—there too many stores from the retailer's perspective. For instance, within a three-mile radius in Dallas, there are three regional shopping centers sporting Foley's, Sears, J.C. Penney, Neiman Marcus, Lord & Taylor, Saks Fifth Avenue, Macy's, Marshall Field's, and others. In other words, there are many alternatives for fashion. In these overstored markets, price competition is keen because retailers are vying for the same fashion customers.

Total Expenditure Effect. Customers are more price sensitive when the expenditure is large, both in dollars and as a percentage of income. Home improvement centers like Home Depot thus attempt to be very price competitive on expensive products like major appliances. But for small purchases such as bulk nuts and bolts, customers will tolerate higher prices.

Difficult Comparison Effect. Customers are more sensitive to price when it's easy to compare competing offerings. A problem facing many retailers—notably fashion retailers, particularly department stores—is finding unique product offerings. Some manufacturer brands, like Levi, are so strong that customers demand that they be stocked. As a result, customers can purchase Levis almost anywhere. Customers can easily compare similar products, making it hard for any one retailer to command higher prices.

To combat this problem and make comparison of products more difficult, some retailers have developed their own private-label merchandise. **Private label** means that the brand name or logo identifying the product is owned by the retailer rather than the manufacturer. Chapter 9 discusses private labels.

Benefits/Price Effect. The benefits/price effect defines the relationship between people's perception of the benefits they receive from a product and its price. For some "image" or "exclusive" products, customers are less sensitive to price; they feel they receive higher benefits from the product because it's more expensive. For example, a Chanel original evening gown may be priced 10 times higher than a department store's gown of equal quality. The customer who purchases the Chanel gown values the recognition or ego gratification that comes from buying an original— and isn't sensitive to price.

Most research indicates people use price as a cue for determining value only when little other information is available. For instance, people generally have a difficult time evaluating the quality of diamonds. Due to their relatively high price and people's lack of knowledge about them, some individuals perceive diamonds as a risky purchase. They equate high price with high quality. Zale jewelry stores found this tendency to be so strong that it developed an entire ad campaign around the concept. The campaign's theme was that customers should go to a jeweler they can trust because it's so hard to evaluate a diamond's quality. Of course, the trustworthy jewelry store is Zale!

Products can also be priced so low that consumers perceive a lack of quality. For instance, Pathmark's Premium All-Purpose Cleaner was packed like Fantastik, a top seller in the category. Its chemical composition was the same. Best of all, Premium cost shoppers only 89 cents, compared to $1.79 for Fantastik. Unfortunately the product failed—probably because customers believed its low price meant it couldn't be high quality.

Situation Effect. Driving down a country road, we spot an old store all by itself. Approaching the store, we see a sign: FINE ANTIQUES FOR SALE. Driving past the store, on the other side we see another sign: WE BUY JUNK. This story illustrates the situation effect; consumers' sensitivity to price can differ depending on the situation. Why are movie patrons willing to pay $2.50 for popcorn that would cost about five cents if they made it themselves at home? Eating popcorn is part of the overall movie-going experience. Also, people expect to pay a premium for merchandise purchased in certain situations. Many restaurants also take advantage of the situation effect. Their lunches cost less than their dinners because people expect to pay less for lunch. Upscale fashion retailers know that customers expect to pay more in a plush atmosphere with attentive service. Alternatively, many off-price and warehouse stores maintain a sparse, utilitarian environment to create the "low-price" atmosphere customers expect when looking for bargains. Thus understanding how to manipulate situations to impact customers' perception of price can influence overall corporate strategy and profitability.

To understand how retailers set an initial retail price using the demand-oriented method, consider the hypothetical situation of The Gap's new ribbed sleeveless T-shirt for women. The fixed cost of developing the product is $300,000, and variable cost is $5 each. A **fixed cost** is a cost that does not change with the quantity of product that's produced and sold. A **variable cost** is the sum of the firm's expenses that vary directly with the quantity of product produced and sold. One benefit of private-label merchandise is the flexibility of being able to set any retail price. The Gap decides to test the T-shirt in four markets at different prices. Exhibit 10–1 shows the pricing test's results. It's clear (from column 5) that a unit price of $10 is by far the most profitable ($450,000). Unfortunately, determining the most profitable retail

Determining the Initial Retail Price under Demand-Oriented Pricing

Results of Pricing Test

	(1)	(2)	(3)	(4)	(5)
Market	Unit Price	Market Demand at Price *(in units)*	Total revenue *(Col. 1 × Col. 2)*	Total Cost of Units Sold *($300,000 Fixed Cost + $5 Variable Cost)*	Total Profits *(Col. 3 − Col. 4)*
1	$ 8	200,000	$1,600,000	$1,300,000	$300,000
2	10	150,000	1,500,000	1,050,000	450,000
3	12	100,000	1,200,000	800,000	400,000
4	14	50,000	700,000	550,000	150,000

price isn't as simple as this example suggests. The primary difficulty is that most retailers carry so many products that these tests become a very expensive proposition.

ADDITIONAL PRICING PRACTICES

Although retailers' basic pricing strategies lie along a continuum from everyday low pricing to high/low strategies, they use other practices too—coupons, rebates, leader pricing, price bundling, multiple-unit pricing, price lining, and odd pricing—in conjunction with their basic strategy.

Coupons and rebates are frequently used strategies that lower the actual price paid by the customer. The coupon for Wonder Bread entitles the customer to a reduced price when presented at the time of purchase. A customer who purchases electronic gear receives a rebate directly from Sega.

Coupons are documents that entitle the holder to a reduced price or to a set amount off the actual purchase price of a product or service.[7] Coupons are issued by manufacturers and retailers in newspapers, on products, and through the mail. Retailers' use of coupons is staggering. It's estimated that over 2,000 manufacturer's coupons are distributed to each U.S. household yearly.[8] But fewer than 4 percent are typically redeemed.

Coupons are thought to be an important sales promotional tool because they induce customers to try products for the first time, convert those first-time users to regular users, encourage larger purchases, increase usage, and protect market share against competition.[10]

The evidence on couponing's overall profitability is mixed. Because coupons have the seemingly positive effect of encouraging larger purchases, the coupon promotion may be stealing sales from a future period without any net increase in sales. For instance, if a supermarket runs a coupon promotion on sugar, households tend to buy a large quantity of sugar and stockpile it for future use. Thus unless the coupon is used mostly by new buyers, the net impact on sales will be negligible, and there will be a negative impact on profits created by the cost of coupon redemption procedures. Unfortunately it's very hard to isolate a market for new users without allowing current users to take advantage of the coupon promotion.

Competition among retailers for coupon-prone customers has become so intense that retailers often offer **double-** and even **triple-coupon promotions,** which allow the customer double or triple the face value of the coupon. But compelling evidence indicates that these coupons are redeemed by the stores' present customers, not customers from competing stores.[11] As a result, retailers are paying for

Coupons

REFACT

Consumers in the United States redeem about 7 billion coupons per year, thus saving over $3 billion.[9]

coupon redemption without increasing sales or market share. Finally, besides the additional cost of a coupon price war, coupons are expensive to handle.

Rebates

A **rebate** is money returned to the buyer based on a portion of the purchase price. Generally, the customer sends a proof of purchase to the manufacturer, and the manufacturer sends the customer the rebate. Rebates are most useful when the dollar amount is relatively large. Otherwise it's not worth the customer's time and postage to redeem the rebate. For instance, rebates are often offered on cars, major and portable appliances, and electronic products. From the retailer's perspective, rebates are more advantageous than coupons because rebates increase demand in the same way coupons may, but the retailer has no handling costs.

Leader Pricing

In **leader pricing,** retailers price certain items lower than normal to increase customer traffic flow and/or to boost sales of complementary products. Reasons for using leader pricing are similar to those for coupons. The difference is that with leader pricing, merchandise has a low price to begin with so customers, retailers, and vendors don't have to handle the coupons. Some retailers call these products **loss leaders.** In a strict sense, loss leaders are sold below cost. But a product doesn't have to be sold below cost for the retailer to be using a leader pricing strategy. The best items for leader pricing are products purchased frequently, primarily by price-sensitive shoppers. For instance, supermarkets typically use white bread, eggs, and milk as loss leaders. Price-sensitive customers take note of ads for these products because they're purchased weekly. The retailer hopes consumers will also purchase their weekly groceries while buying loss leaders. Toys "R" Us has successfully used a leader pricing strategy for disposable diapers. New parents get in the habit of shopping at Toys "R" Us when their children are infants and become loyal customers.

Price Bundling and Multiple-Unit Pricing

Price bundling is the practice of offering two or more different products or services for sale at one price. For instance, a bicycle store may sell a bicycle fully equipped with water bottle, pump, helmet, gloves, and car rack—all for $599. If purchased separately, the items might total $679. Price bundling is used to increase both unit and dollar sales by bringing traffic into the store. The strategy can also be used to move less desirable merchandise by including it in a package with merchandise in high demand.

Multiple-unit pricing is similar to price bundling except the products or services are similar, rather than different. For example, a convenience store may sell three liters of soda for $2.39 when the price per unit is 99 cents—a savings of 58 cents. Like price bundling, this strategy is used to increase sales volume. Depending on the type of product, however, customers may stockpile for use at a later time. For example, although you typically purchase and consume one liter of soda a week, you may purchase several if you perceive a substantial cost savings. If customers stockpile, demand is shifted back in time with no long-term effect on sales.

Some retailers abuse price bundling and multiple-unit prices by implying a savings when there really isn't one (say, 49 cents each or two for 98 cents; or even worse, 49 cents each or three for $1.59). This type of deceptive practice has received considerable attention from consumer groups.

Price Lining

In **price lining,** retailers offer a limited number of predetermined price points within a classification. For instance, a tire store may offer tires only at $29.99, $49.99, and $79.99. Both customers and retailers can benefit from such a strategy. For one thing,

Which retailer is using a price bundling strategy and which is using multiple-unit pricing?

confusion that often arises from multiple price choices is essentially eliminated. The customer can choose the tire with either the low, medium, or high price. (There need not be three price lines; the strategy can use more or fewer than three.) From the retailer's perspective, the merchandising task is simplified. That is, all products within a certain price line are merchandised together. Further, when going to market, the firm's buyers can select their purchases with the predetermined price lines in mind. Price lining also can give buyers greater flexibility. If a strict initial markup is required, there could be numerous price points. But with a price lining strategy, some merchandise may be bought a little below or above the expected cost for a price line. Of course, price lining can also limit retail buyers' flexibility. They may be forced to pass up potentially profitable merchandise because it doesn't fit into a price line. (Re-Tale 10–3 discusses a store selling everything for 99 cents.)

Odd price refers to a price that ends in an odd number (such as 57 cents or 63 cents) or to a price just under a round number (such as $98 instead of $100). Some retailers believe that odd pricing can increase sales. Most empirical studies, however, don't support this proposition.[12]

Odd Pricing

    Nonetheless, many retailers use some rules of thumb regarding odd prices. Odd pricing may be less successful for products that require some thought. For instance, when purchasing a car, most customers wouldn't have to think long to realize that $17,995 is almost $18,000. Also, odd pricing seems to imply a low price. So retailers interested in maintaining an upscale image probably shouldn't use odd pricing. For instance, Tiffany's doesn't advertise diamond rings for $6,999. Odd pricing, then, may be most successful for impulse purchases at lower-end retailers or on sale merchandise.

LEGAL ISSUES IN RETAIL PRICING

The legal issues pertaining to retail pricing are complex. Let's examine two types: legal issues regarding the purchase of merchandise (price discrimination and resale price maintenance) and legal issues affecting the customer (horizontal price fixing, predatory pricing, and price comparisons).

RE-TALE 10-3   Yesterday's Five and Dime Stores—the 99-Cent Stores of Today

In Los Angeles—a city permanently in recession—work is hard to find, and rents and home prices are stuck in outer space. Here the retail concept of all items sold at 99 cents is definitely right for today.

In Los Angeles and other U.S. cities, you can find some variation of this latter-day five-and-dime store. The first 99 Cents Only Store opened in 1982. By 1993, the chain had over 30 outlets.

A dollar doesn't buy what it used to in Southern California. It buys more. To be specific, a loaf of Wonder Bread, a dozen eggs, 14 ounces of animal-shaped cookies, a bucket of caramel corn, anything from the five-shelf–high aisle of shampoos, and three cans of Ajax cleanser all fetch the store's 99-cent price.

Where does this stuff come from? Most items are closeouts—often simply due to a package change. Other merchandise is obtained at low prices because manufacturers overestimated demand and so must get rid of excess inventory. More than half of the merchandise at 99 Cents Only Stores is name brand.

Although 99 Cents Only Stores continues to open new outlets, it has two problems. First, knockoffs keep popping up around town. Second, what will it do after a wave of inflation? Change its name to $1.17 Only Stores?

SOURCE: Thomas J. Fields-Meyer, "Five-and-Dimes for the 90's," *The Wall Street Journal*, April 21, 1993.

Price Discrimination

Price discrimination occurs when a vendor sells the same product to two or more retailers at different prices. Although price discrimination is generally illegal, there are three exceptions.

First, vendors can charge different retailers different prices if their cost of manufacture, sale, or delivery varies because of the method or quantity in which they sell or deliver the goods. Under what conditions may these differences exist?

It's often less expensive per unit to manufacture, sell, or deliver large quantities than small quantities. Manufacturers can achieve economies of scale through the longer production runs achieved with large quantities. Cost of selling to a customer also decreases as the quantity of goods ordered increases because it costs almost the same for a salesperson to write a small order as a large order. Finally, delivery or transportation expenses decrease on a per unit basis as quantities of goods increase. These facts give rise to **quantity discounts,** the practice of granting lower prices to retailers who buy greater quantities.

The method of sale that allows for differing prices is the practice of granting functional or trade discounts. **Functional or trade discounts** are different prices, or percentages off suggested retail prices, granted to customers in different lines of trade (e.g., wholesalers and retailers). Wholesalers often receive a lower price than retailers for the same quantity purchased. This is legal, for wholesalers perform more functions in the distribution process than do retailers. For instance, wholesalers store and transport merchandise, and they use salespeople for writing orders and taking care of problems in the stores. Essentially, manufacturers "pay" wholesalers for servicing retailers by giving the wholesalers a lower price.

With the growth of large chain retailers like J.C. Penney and Wal-Mart, functional discounts become more difficult to justify. Wal-Mart performs virtually all the functions an independent wholesaler provides. Therefore Wal-Mart demands and should receive the same low prices as wholesalers. These lower prices make it hard for smaller retailers to compete.

The second and third exceptions to the no-price-discrimination rule are when the price differential is in response to changing conditions affecting the market for or the marketability of the goods concerned and when the differing price is made in good faith to meet a competitor's equally low price. Suppose, for example, that

Borden ice cream is experiencing severe price competition with a locally produced ice cream in Wisconsin. Borden is allowed to lower its price in this market below its price in other markets to meet the low price of local competition.

Large retailers often benefit from more subtle forms of price discrimination. For instance, book publishers have been accused of charging independent booksellers more than chain operators even though their individual orders are the same size. In the discount store industry, manufacturers often take back merchandise that isn't selling at large discount chains without penalty—a perk not available to smaller stores.

Unless a particular situation falls within one of the exceptions just discussed, retailers should never ask a vendor for, or accept, a net price (after all discounts, allowances, returns, and promotional allowances) that they know—or experience tells them—won't be offered to their competitors on a proportional basis for similar merchandise purchased at about the same time.

Resale Price Maintenance

In a letter to retailers, Specialized (a bicycle manufacturer) stated that it "will discontinue sales of all its goods to any dealer whom it learns has engaged in the sale of Specialized products below suggested retail prices."[13] This practice, known as **resale price maintenance, vertical price fixing,** or **fair trade laws,** involves agreements to fix prices between parties at different levels of the same marketing channel (e.g., retailers and vendors). Vertical price fixing has a mixed history in the United States. Due to strong consumer activism, the **Consumer Goods Pricing Act (1975)** repealed all state resale price maintenance laws that were in effect and enabled retailers to sell products below suggested retail prices. Congress's attitude at that time was to protect customers' right to buy at the lowest possible free market price—even though some small retailers wouldn't be able to compete.

The mood of the courts and the Federal Trade Commission (FTC) again shifted during the Reagan administration. Some manufacturers and retailers maintain they need to protect the manufacturer's suggested retail price to protect the manufacturer's quality reputation and provide service for the product. In 1988, the Supreme Court ruled that manufacturers can refuse to sell to retailers that sell below the manufacturer's suggested retail price.[14] As recently as 1993, the FTC gave Armstrong a green light to terminate sales to distributors of its floor covering products who charge less than the manufacturer's "suggested" retail prices.[15]

Horizontal Price Fixing

Horizontal price fixing involves agreements between retailers that are in direct competition with each other to have the same prices. Consider the hypothetical case of two large discount stores, Mel's and KD's, that conspire to fix retail paint prices at an extremely low level. Big G, a small chain of three paint stores, can't compete with their low prices. Mel's and KD's can sell the paint as a loss leader. But Big G sells only paint. If the price fixing continues, Big G may have to close. With Big G out of the market, Mel's and KD's could raise their paint prices. Clearly, such behavior by Mel's and KD's is anticompetitive. Horizontal price fixing is always illegal because it suppresses competition while often raising the cost to the consumer.

As a general rule of thumb, retailers should refrain from discussing prices or terms or conditions of sale with competitors. **Terms or conditions of sale** may include charges for alterations, delivery, or gift wrapping, or the store's exchange policies. If a buyer or store manager needs to know a competitor's price on a particular item, it's permissible to "shop" at the competitor's store by going personally or sending an assistant to the store to examine the product. But the buyer or manager shouldn't call the competitor to get the information. Further, retailers shouldn't

RE-TALE 10-4   Wal-Mart's Predatory Pricing Practices under Attack

Independent retailers in small towns across the country have long accused Wal-Mart of selling goods below cost to drive them out of business, and then boosting prices after seizing control of the local market. The sheer size of the company—America's largest retailer—gives it leverage to demand goods from suppliers at the lowest possible cost. Facing increased competition from other large retailers as it moved into urban areas, Wal-Mart acted aggressively to be the leader in using an everyday low price strategy.

Some smaller retailers, however, have accused Wal-Mart of predatory pricing, of selling items—including Crest and over-the-counter drugs—below cost. Wal-Mart maintains that it hasn't violated the law because it didn't intend to hurt competitors. But it admits it has sold some products below cost, as do other retailers. The chain claims its intent was only to provide the best everyday low price to customers. Wal-Mart's everyday low price strategy bases prices on local competition—more competition leads to lower prices; less competition leads to higher prices.

SOURCE: Bob Ortega, "Suit over Wal-Mart's Pricing Practices Goes to Trial Today in Arkansas Court," *The Wall Street Journal,* August 23, 1993, p. A3.

respond to any competitor's request to verify those prices. The only exception to the general rule is when a geographically oriented merchants association, such as for a downtown area or shopping center, is planning a special coordinated event. In this situation, the retailer may announce that merchandise will be specially priced during the event, but the specific merchandise and prices shouldn't be identified.

Predatory Pricing

Establishing merchandise prices to drive competition from the marketplace is called **predatory pricing.** It's illegal. A retailer can, however, sell the same merchandise at different geographic locations for different prices if its costs of sale or delivery are different. For instance, a national specialty store chain like The Limited may charge more for a dress in California than in Ohio because the cost of shipping the dress from its distribution center in Columbus, Ohio, to California is higher than the cost of shipping it to a store in Ohio. A competing retailer in Ohio may not be able to meet The Limited's lower price on this dress. But because the lower price is due to The Limited's lower distribution cost rather than to an attempt to drive the competitor out of business, the tactic is allowable.

It's also illegal to sell merchandise at unreasonably low prices. However a retailer generally may sell merchandise at any price so long as the motive isn't to destroy competition. Re-Tale 10–4 examines Wal-Mart's everyday low pricing strategy.

Price Comparison

A common practice of retailers is to compare the price of merchandise offered for sale with a higher "regular" price or a manufacturer's list price. This practice, known as **price comparison,** may be a good strategy because it gives customers a price comparison point and makes the merchandise appear to be a good deal. The Federal Trade Commission has ruled that it is deceptive to refer to a regular price unless the retailer usually and recently has sold the merchandise at that price. Further, the commission has ruled that it is deceptive to refer to the manufacturer's list price unless that list price was the ordinary and customary retail sales price of the merchandise in that area.[16]

Another form of deceptive price comparison occurs when retailers advertise that they have the lowest prices in town or that they will meet or beat any competitor's price. To avoid deception, a retailer should have proof before placing the ad that its prices are, in fact, the lowest in town. Further, if it advertises that it will meet or beat any competitor's prices, the retailer must have a company policy that enables it to adjust prices to preserve the accuracy of its advertising claims.[17]

In summary, retailers, wholesalers, and manufacturers should be aware that whenever they decide to sell the same merchandise for different prices at different locations, or to sell merchandise at extraordinarily low prices to attract customers, they may be susceptible to federal and state prosecution and to lawsuits from competitors. But as a practical matter, acquiring sufficient data and legal assistance to prove injury by a competitor may take so long and be so expensive that the injured party may still go out of business.

☼ SUMMARY

There's more to setting retail prices than just taking the manufacturer's suggestions. Everyday low pricing (EDLP), coupons, and rebates are popular alternatives to the frequent use of sales. Leader pricing, price bundling, price lining, and odd pricing are also common strategies for pricing product lines. After examining the relative merits of the demand- and cost-oriented methods of setting retail prices, we've concluded that a mix of the two methods is best.

Because the initial retail price isn't necessarily the price at which the merchandise is finally sold, you must understand (1) how to use the cost-oriented method to adjust the initial retail price and (2) how these adjustments affect profits. Specifically we examined several issues regarding markdowns, such as reasons for taking markdowns, and when to take markdowns and additional markups.

As for demand-oriented methods of setting retail prices, several qualitative factors affect customers' sensitivity to prices. Specifically customers are more sensitive to price when there are many alternative stores from which to choose, when the total expenditure is large, when comparisons between existing brands are easy, and when it's hard to perceive special benefits from the products or retailers.

Legal issues that impact pricing decisions include price discrimination, vertical price fixing, horizontal price fixing, predatory pricing, and price comparisons.

KEY TERMS

additional markup, 207
Consumer Goods Pricing Act (1975), 215
cost-oriented method, 203
coupon, 211
deal period, 201
demand-oriented method, 203
double- and triple-coupon promotion, 211

everyday low pricing (EDLP), 201
fair trade laws, 215
fixed cost, 209
functional or trade discount, 214
high/low pricing strategy, 201
horizontal price fixing, 215
initial markup, 204
keystone method, 203
leader pricing, 212

loss leader, 212
markdown, 205
markdown money, 206
multiple-unit pricing, 212
odd price, 213
overstored, 208
predatory pricing, 216
price bundling, 212
price comparison, 216
price discrimination, 214

price lining, 212
private label, 208
quantity discount, 214
rebate, 212
resale price maintenance, 215
terms or conditions of sale, 215
traffic appliance, 206
variable cost, 209
vertical price fixing, 215

DISCUSSION QUESTIONS AND PROBLEMS

1. Simple examination of markdowns could lead us to believe that retailers should only take markdowns when they want to get rid of merchandise that's not selling. What other reasons could a retailer have to take markdowns?

2. What is price lining, and why would a retailer want to use it?

3. Under what circumstances are certain pricing practices legal or illegal?

4. Cost of a product is $150, markup is 50 percent, and markdown is 30 percent. What's the final selling price?

5. Manny Perez bought a tie for $9 and priced it to sell for $15. What was his markup on the tie?

6. Alex Fox says he gets a markup of 33.33 percent. What markup on cost does he get?

7. Mary White has one blouse in inventory marked to sell for $50. She wants to take a 25 percent markdown on the blouse. What price should she put on the blouse?

The Retail Promotion Mix

Advertising and promotion (11)

Questions this chapter answers include

- **How do retailers communicate with their customers?**
- **What are the strengths and weaknesses of these different methods of communication?**
- **What are the steps in developing a promotion program?**
- **How do retailers establish a promotion budget?**
- **How do retailers make decisions in designing advertising, sales promotion, and publicity programs?**

The preceding chapters described how retailers develop a merchandise assortment and then buy and price the merchandise. The final element in the retail mix undertaken by merchandise management is developing and implementing a communication program. The objective of this program is to attract customers to stores and encourage them to buy merchandise. The communication program informs customers about the store as well as the merchandise and services it offers.

Retailers communicate with customers through five vehicles: advertising, sales promotion, publicity, store atmosphere, and personal selling. This chapter focuses on the first three of these vehicles—the **promotion mix.** In large retail firms, the firm's marketing or advertising department and the buying organization manage the promotion mix. Store personnel manage store environment and communications and services provided by store personnel. We will discuss those elements of the retail mix in more detail in Section IV.

Communication Methods

	Nonpersonal	Personal
Paid	Advertising Store atmosphere Visual merchandising Sales promotion	Personal selling
Unpaid	Publicity	Word-of-mouth

METHODS FOR COMMUNICATING WITH CUSTOMERS

Exhibit 11–1 classifies the different communication methods retailers use as either nonpersonal or personal and as either paid or unpaid.

Paid Nonpersonal Communications

Advertising, sales promotions, and store atmosphere are examples of paid nonpersonal communications. **Advertising** is a form of paid communication with customers using nonpersonal mass media such as newspapers, TV, radio, and direct mail.

Sales promotions are paid nonpersonal communication activities that offer extra value and incentives to customers to visit a store and/or purchase merchandise during a specific period of time. The most common sales promotion is a sale. Other sales promotions involve special events, in-store demonstrations, coupons, and contests.

Retailers typically use sales promotion activities to influence customer behavior during a short period of time. For example, Kmart's "blue-light specials" are a dramatic way to increase sales at specific items. They're announced over the store's public address system, and a flashing blue light is placed near the item on sale. The sale lasts only 5 to 15 minutes. Because the stock of sale items is limited, customers rush to the merchandise to make sure they get it before it runs out or the sale ends. Besides increasing sales of specific items, blue-light specials reinforce Kmart's image of providing good value to its customers.[1]

Finally, the retail store itself provides paid nonpersonal communication to its customers through store atmosphere. **Store atmosphere** is the combination of the store's physical characteristics, such as architecture, layout, signs and displays, colors, lighting, temperature, sounds, and smells. Together these elements create an image in the customer's mind. The atmosphere communicates information about the store's service and pricing as well as the fashionability of its merchandise.[2] Chapter 13 discusses elements of store atmosphere.

REFACT

Department and specialty store chains typically spend 8 percent of their sales revenue on personal selling and 3 percent on advertising and direct mail.[6]

Paid Personal Communications

Retail salespeople are the primary vehicle for providing paid personal communication to customers. **Personal selling** is a communication process in which salespeople assist customers in satisfying their needs through person-to-person exchange of information.

Unpaid Nonpersonal Communications

The primary method for generating unpaid nonpersonal communication is publicity. **Publicity** is communication through significant unpaid presentations about the retailer (usually a news story) in nonpersonal media. Examples of publicity are the

Comparison of Communication Methods

 EXHIBIT 11-2

	Control	Flexibility	Credibility	Cost
Paid nonpersonal				
Advertising	●	○	○	◕
Sales promotions	●	◕	—	○
Sales atmosphere	●	◕	—	●
Paid personal				
Personal selling	●	●	○	●
Unpaid nonpersonal				
Publicity	○	○	●	◕
Unpaid personal				
Word of mouth	○	○	●	○

● High   ● High to moderate   ◕ Moderate   ◔ Moderate to low   ○ Low

newspaper and TV coverage of Macy's Thanksgiving Day parade in New York and the Kmart Greater Greensboro golf tournament.[3]

Finally, retailers communicate with their customers at no cost through **word-of-mouth** (communication between people about a retailer).[4] For example, retailers attempt to encourage favorable word-of-mouth communication by establishing teen boards composed of high school student leaders. Board members are encouraged to tell their friends about the retailer and its merchandise. On the other hand, unfavorable word-of-mouth communication can seriously affect store performance. Research indicates that people who have an unsatisfactory experience with retail service tell nine other people, on average, about their experience.[5]

Unpaid Personal Communications

Exhibit 11-2 compares communication methods in terms of control, flexibility, credibility, and cost.

Strengths and Weaknesses of Communication Methods

Control. Retailers have more control when using paid versus unpaid methods. When using advertising, sales promotions, and store atmosphere, retailers determine the message's content and the time of its delivery. But because each salesperson can deliver different messages, retailers have less control over personal selling than other paid communication methods. Retailers have very little control over the content or timing of publicity and word-of-mouth communications. Because unpaid communications are designed and delivered by people not employed by the retailer, they can communicate unfavorable as well as favorable information. For example, customers were reluctant to shop at Macy's after extensive news coverage of its bankruptcy.[7]

Flexibility. Personal selling is the most flexible communication method because salespeople can talk with each customer, discover the customer's specific needs, and develop unique presentations for him or her. Other communication methods are less flexible. For example, ads deliver the same message to large groups of customers in a target segment.

RE-TALE 11-1   Kmart Uses Martha Stewart to Lure More Affluent Shoppers

Using Martha Stewart as a spokesperson, Kmart developed a communication and merchandising program to attract more affluent customers to its home departments. Martha Stewart is a nationally recognized authority on food and home entertaining. Her attractively designed how-to books sell for over $50 and appeal to affluent professional audiences.

A first step in the program was to design and merchandise a Kitchen Korner boutique in each store. The boutique features kitchen appliances and tableware. Stewart works with Kmart buyers to create new kitchen, bed and bath, and home products, some of which bear her name. "Kitchen Kornerstone" brochures, available in the department, are prepared by Stewart to offer tips on cooking and home entertaining.

Special promotions are developed when Stewart makes personal appearances in Kmart stores nation-

wide. She promotes Kmart's new home products and merchandise concepts in TV and print ads appearing in *Family Circle, People,* and *Vogue.*

In addition to attracting more affluent customers, Kmart uses the Martha Stewart program to appeal to the life-style trend toward "cocooning." Cocooning is the desire of dual-income professional couples and families to wrap themselves in the security and comfort of their home. Rather than seeking food and entertainment outside the home, these consumers are acquiring products so they can satisfy their needs at home.

SOURCE: Jennifer Pellet, "Kmart's Inside Track," *Discount Merchandiser,* July 1989, pp. 72–73; and Patricia Strand, "Kmart Dangles Lure for Affluent Shoppers," *Advertising Age,* August 24, 1987, pp. 12–13.

Credibility. Because publicity and word-of-mouth are communicated by independent sources, this information is usually more credible than the information in paid communication sources. For example, customers see their friends and family as highly credible sources of information. Customers tend to doubt claims made by salespeople and in ads because they know retailers are trying to promote their merchandise through these means.

Cost. Publicity and word of mouth are classified as unpaid communication methods, but retailers do incur costs to stimulate them. Creating an event that merits significant news coverage can be costly for a retailer. For example, Penney's incurs cost in sponsoring Lynn St. James and her Spirit of the American Woman race car in the Indianapolis 500, and in sponsoring the J.C. Penney/LPGA skins game.

Paid nonpersonal communications often are economical. For example, a full-page ad in *The Los Angeles Times* delivers a retailer's message for a cost of about two cents per reader. In contrast, personal selling is more effective than advertising, but more costly. A 10-minute presentation by a retail salesperson paid $6 per hour costs the retailer $1—almost 100 times more than exposing a customer to a newspaper, radio, or TV ad.

DIFFERENCES BETWEEN RETAIL AND VENDOR COMMUNICATION PROGRAMS

The differences between the types of communication programs used by retailers and their vendors show the unique issues retailers consider in developing communication programs.

Long-Term versus Short-Term Goals

Most communication developed by vendors is created to build a long-term image of the vendor's branded merchandise. On the other hand, most retail communication is typically used to announce promotions and special sales that generate short-term revenues.

Steps in Developing the Retail Communication Program

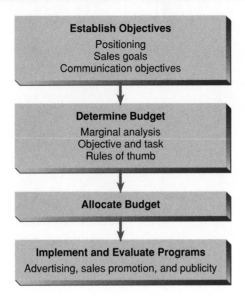

When a vendor advertises its merchandise, it doesn't care where the customer buys it. On the other hand, retailers don't care what brands customers buy as long as they buy them in their store. This difference in goals can lead to conflicts between vendors and retailers. Vendors want to sell their specific brands, while retailers want to sell the most profitable brands. **Product versus Location**

Because people tend to shop at stores near their homes or workplaces, most retailers use local newspapers, TV, and radio to communicate with customers. On the other hand, most vendors sell their brands nationally and thus tend to use national TV and magazines. **Geographic Coverage**

Typically, vendors have a relatively small number of products to advertise. They can devote a lot of attention to developing consistent communication programs for each brand they make. Retailers, however, offer a much broader set of products and often focus on building short-term sales. Retail communications can easily confuse customers if the communications focus on different products and don't develop a consistent overall store image. **Breadth of Merchandise Offered**

PLANNING THE RETAIL COMMUNICATION PROGRAM

The elements in the retail communication program must work together and reinforce each other so the retailer can achieve its objectives. For example, Re-Tale 11–1 describes how Kmart coordinates its merchandise and promotion programs to attract more affluent customers. If the communication elements aren't used consistently, customers may become confused about the retailer's image and therefore may not patronize the store. The remaining portion of this chapter reviews steps retailers take in planning and developing their promotional programs.

Exhibit 11–3 illustrates the four steps retailers take to develop and implement their retail communications programs. First, they set objectives. Then they

Retail advertising can be used to achieve long-term or short-term goals. The Fashion Bug ad is part of a program to position the retailer toward a fashion-oriented target market. The Payless ad has more short-term objective of generating sales of children's shoes during a special sale.

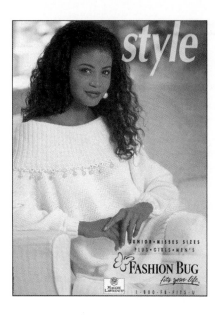

determine and allocate the budget, and implement the program. The following sections detail each of these steps.

SETTING OBJECTIVES

Retailers establish objectives for communication programs to provide (1) direction for people implementing the program and (2) a basis for evaluating its effectiveness. Some communication programs are long-term, such as creating or altering customers' image of the retailer. Other communication programs focus on improving short-term performance, such as increasing store traffic on weekends.

Positioning: A Long-Term Objective

Positioning is the design and implementation of a retail communication program to create an image in the customer's mind of the retailer relative to its competitors. A positioning objective typically links the retailer to a specific category of merchandise or to a specific benefit in the customer's mind. Retailers pursue various specific positioning objectives:[8]

1. *Merchandise category.* The most common method for positioning is to publicize the retailer's distinction in a category of merchandise. For example, Circuit City is closely related in consumers' minds with consumer electronics. Consumers view Circuit City as stocking any electronic item they might want.

2. *Price/quality.* Some retailers (such as Neiman Marcus) position themselves as offering high prices and high fashion. Other retailers (such as Wal-Mart) are positioned as offering low prices, adequate merchandise and service, and good value.[9]

3. *Specific attribute or benefit.* A retailer can link its stores to attributes such as convenience (7-Eleven) or service (Nordstrom).

4. *Life-style or activity.* Some retailers associate themselves with a specific life-style or activity. For example, The Nature Company, a retailer

Communication Elements and Customers' Decision-Making Process

EXHIBIT 11–4

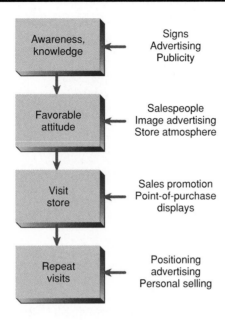

offering books and equipment for studying nature, is linked to a life-style of interacting with the environment. Electronic Boutique is associated with home use of computer software.

Sales Goals: Short-Term Objective

A common short-term objective for a promotion program is to increase sales during a specified time period. For example, retailers often have sales during which some or all merchandise is discounted for a short time. Grocery stores usually place weekly ads with coupons that can be used to save money on purchases made during the week.

Communication Objectives

Retailers often use communication objectives rather than sales objectives to plan and evaluate their communication programs.[10] **Communication objectives** are specific goals related to how the retail promotion mix affects the customer's decision-making process. Chapter 4 explained the process customers go through as they decide which store to visit and what to purchase there. Rather than setting sales goals, retailers can set goals related to the stages in the customer's decision-making process. For example, a retailer might set a goal for the percentage of people who are aware of its store, know its offering, favorably evaluate the store, or intend to visit.

Communication Elements and the Decision-Making Process. The communication goals determine which communication methods the retailer should emphasize. Exhibit 11–4 shows which communication methods are most effective at various stages in the decision-making process. For example, a favorable attitude toward the store is most easily achieved through store employees' actions, image-type advertising, and store atmosphere. Typically, outside signs on the store, ads that emphasize the store's name and location, and publicity about the store are most

EXHIBIT 11-5   **Illustration of the Objective-and-Task Method for Setting Budgets**

Objective: Increase the percentage of target market (working women living and/or working within 10 miles of our store) who know of our store's location and that it sells women's business attire from 25 percent to 50 percent over the next 12 months.

Task: 480, 30-second radio spots during peak commuting hours (7:00 to 8:00 A.M. and 5:00 to 6:00 P.M.).	$12,300
Task: Sign with store name near entrance to mall.	4,500
Task: Display ad in the Yellow Pages.	500

Objective: Increase the percentage of target market who indicate that our store is their preferred store for buying their business wardrobe from 5 percent to 15 percent in 12 months.

Task: Develop TV campaign to improve image and run 50, 30-second commercials.	$24,000
Task: Hold four "Dress for Success" seminars followed by a wine-and-cheese social.	8,000

Objective: Sell old inventory at the end of each season.

Task: Run 10 full-page newspaper ads to support four sales during the year.	6,000
Total budget	$55,300

effective for developing awareness of the retailer. Special sales promotions and point-of-purchase displays encourage customers to visit a store and purchase merchandise. Retailers develop continuing patronage and loyalty through communications directed at positioning the store and through the service provided by salespeople.

DETERMINING THE PROMOTION BUDGET

The second step in developing a retail promotion mix is determining a budget (as Exhibit 11–3 shows). Some methods that retailers use to set budgets are the objective-and-task method and rules of thumb such as the affordable, percentage-of-sales, and competitive parity methods.

Objective-and-Task Method

The **objective-and-task method** determines the budget required to undertake specific tasks for accomplishing communication objectives. To use this method, the retailer first establishes a set of communication objectives. Then the retailer determines the necessary tasks and their costs. The sum total of all costs incurred to undertake the tasks is the promotion budget.

Exhibit 11–5 illustrates how Diane West, owner-manager of a specialty store selling women's business clothing, used the objective-and-task method. West established three objectives: to increase customer awareness of her store, to create a greater preference for her store among customers in her target market, and to promote the sale of merchandise remaining at the end of each season. The total promotion budget she requires to achieve these objectives is $55,300. The advantage of the objective-and-task method is that advertising expenses are directly linked to the retailer's communication objectives. The effectiveness of the advertising can then be evaluated and the benefits of the advertising can be compared to its costs.

The Retail Mix–
Merchandising

© The Chicken & Egg store in Seattle is a niche retailer that specializes in furniture hand-crafted in the Pacific Northwest. It offers a deep assortment of "northwest style" accessories and crafts. (Chapter 8)

© Retail store buyers have many ways to make their buying decisions. This Leegin belt salesman (left) uses his laptop computer to tell the store's buyer their current sales volume compared with the previous season's, and belts sold by style, category, and color. Chicago's McCormick Place (right) hosts over 65 meetings and trade shows like the International Housewares Show, where buyers can meet with their vendors, place orders, and obtain a concentrated perspective of merchandise available to them. (Chapter 9)

© Toys "R" Us has successfully used a leader pricing strategy for disposable diapers. New parents get in the habit of shopping at Toys when their children are infants and become loyal customers. (Chapter 10)

© Prices set by manufacturers have a strategic impact on how retailers promote products and gauge profitability.

© Parisian, a specialty department store chain head-quartered in Birmingham, Alabama, uses three forms of paid impersonal communication to convey its upmarket positioning to customers. Salespeople offer a high level of customer service; advertising describes the quality brands available at its stores; and the store design and visual merchandising provide a contemporary but elegant look. (Chapter 11)

◎ Consumer sampling is an especially effective sales promotional tool because it benefits both the manufacturer and retailer. (Chapter 11)

◎ Some stores create publicity by offering customers unique opportunities, such as this karaoke contest (right) at a Wichita, Kansas, Albertson's supermarket. Other events involve celebrity visits, such as Elizabeth Taylor (left) visiting a Woodward and Lothrop department store to promote her perfume. (Chapter 11)

When using the affordable budgeting method, retailers first forecast their sales and expenses during the budgeting period, excluding promotion expenses. The difference between the forecast sales and expenses plus desired profit is then budgeted for the promotion mix. In other words, the **affordable method** sets the promotion budget by determining what money is available after budgeting operating costs and profits.

The major problem with the affordable method is that it assumes that the communication expenses don't stimulate sales and profit. Promotion expenses are treated as a cost of business, like the cost of merchandise. When retailers use the affordable method, they typically cut "unnecessary" promotion expenses if sales fall below the forecast rather than increasing promotion expenses to increase sales.

Affordable Method

The **percentage-of-sales method** sets the promotion budget as a fixed percentage of forecast sales. The percentage may be the retailer's historical percentage or the average percentage used by similar retailers.

The problem with the percentage-of-sales method is that it assumes that the same percentage used in the past, or by competitors, is appropriate for your firm. Consider a retailer that hasn't opened new stores in the past but plans to open many new stores in the current year. It must create customer awareness for these new stores so the promotion budget should be much larger in the current year than in the past.

Using the same percentage as competitors also may be inappropriate. For example, a retailer might have better locations than its competitors. Due to these locations, customers may already have a much higher awareness of the retailer's stores. Thus the retailer may not need to spend as much on promotions as competitors with poorer locations spend.

One advantage of both the percentage-of-sales method and the affordable method for determining a promotion budget is that the retailer won't spend beyond its means. Because sales determine the level of spending, the budget will only go up when sales go up and the retailer generates more sales to pay for the additional promotion expenses. When times are good, these methods work well because they allow the retailer to communicate more aggressively with customers. But when sales fall, communication expenses are cut, which may accelerate the sales decline.

Percentage-of-Sales Method

REFACT

Furniture stores spend 7.2 percent of sales on advertising, while grocery stores only spend 1.4 percent of sales on advertising.[11]

Under the **competitive parity method,** the promotion budget is set so that the retailer's share of promotion expenses equals its share of the market. For example, consider a sporting goods store in a small town. To use the competitive parity method, the owner-manager would first estimate the total amount spent on advertising by all of the sporting goods retailers in town. Then the owner-manager would set the budget by estimating the store's market share for sporting goods and multiplying the market share by the total advertising expenses of all local sporting goods stores. Assume that the owner-manager's estimate of advertising for sporting goods was $5,000 and the estimate of the store's market share was 45 percent. Based on these estimates, the owner-manager would set the store's promotion budget at $2,250 to maintain competitive parity.

The competitive parity method doesn't allow retailers to exploit the unique opportunities or problems they confront in a market. If all competitors used this method to set promotion budgets, their market shares would stay about the same over time (assuming that the retailers develop equally effective campaigns).

Competitive Parity Method

ALLOCATING THE PROMOTION BUDGET

After determining the promotion budget's size, the third step in the communication planning process is allocating the budget. (See Exhibit 11–3.) In this step, the retailer decides how much of its budget to allocate to specific merchandise categories, geographic regions, or long- and short-term objectives. For example, Dillard's must decide how much of its promotion budget to spend in each area where it has stores: Arkansas, Texas, Florida, North Carolina, Arizona, and Ohio. Kmart decides how much to allocate to children's apparel versus kitchen appliances. The sporting goods store owner-manager must decide how much of the store's $900 promotion budget to spend on promoting the store's image versus generating sales during the year.

An easy way to make such allocation decisions is just to spend about the same in each geographic region or for each merchandise category. But this allocation rule probably won't maximize profits because it ignores the possibility that communication programs might be more effective for some merchandise categories or for some regions than for others. Another approach is to use rules of thumb such as basing allocations on the sales level or contribution for the merchandise category.

The next sections look at the final steps in the retail promotion planning process: implementing and evaluating the plan. Advertising, sales promotion, and publicity differ so we'll discuss each element of the promotion mix separately.

IMPLEMENTING ADVERTISING PROGRAMS

REFACT

Sears is the third largest advertiser in the United States. McDonald's is the seventh largest.[12]

Retail advertising is used to develop and reinforce a retailer's image, inform customers about merchandise and prices, and announce a sale. While some national retailers invest in image advertising (see Re-Tale 11–2), most retail advertising focuses on short-term objectives. To implement an ad program, the retailer must develop the message, choose the specific media to convey it, and determine the frequency and timing of the message. Next we'll look at each of these decisions.

Developing the Advertising Message

Most retail advertising messages have a short life and are designed to have an immediate impact. This immediacy calls for a copy writing style that grabs the reader's attention. The best retail ads have (1) a dominant headline that emphasizes the main benefit the retailer offers; (2) a dominant visual element to attract attention; (3) a simple layout to guide the reader's eye through the ad; (4) information the reader needs to decide whether or not to go to the store—such as the type of merchandise, brands, prices, sizes, and colors; and, finally, (5) the store's name and location.

Assistance in Developing Advertising

Cooperative Advertising. Cooperative (co-op) advertising is a program undertaken by a vendor. The vendor pays for part of the retailer's advertising, but the vendor also dictates some conditions for the advertising. For example, Procter & Gamble may have a co-op program that pays for half of a retailer's ads for Tide detergent.

Co-op advertising enables a retailer to increase its advertising budget. In the previous example, the retailer only pays half of its expenses (for ads including Tide). In addition to lowering costs, co-op advertising enables the retailer to associate its name with well-known national brands in advertising using attractive artwork developed by the manufacturer.

This Target preprint announces a co-op promotion developed in conjunction with Rollerblade, a manufacturer of popular in-line skates.

Co-op advertising has some drawbacks. First, vendors want the ad to feature their products, while retailers are more interested in featuring their store's name, location, merchandise assortment, and services. This conflict in goals can reduce co-op advertising's effectiveness from the retailer's perspective. In addition, ads developed by the vendor often are used by several competing retailers and may list the names and locations of all retailers offering the vendor's brands. Thus, co-op ads tend to blur any distinctions between retailers. Finally, restrictions the vendor places on the ad may further reduce its effectiveness for the retailer. For example, the vendor may restrict advertising to a time when the vendor's sales are depressed—a time when the retailer might not normally be advertising.

Advertising Agencies. Most large retailers have a department that creates advertising for sales and special events. Large retailers often use advertising agencies to develop ads for store image campaigns. Many small retailers use local agencies to plan and create their advertising. These local agencies are often more skilled in planning and executing advertising than the retailer's employees are. Agencies also work on other aspects of the communication programs, such as contests, direct mail, and special promotions.

Local Media. Besides selling newspaper space and broadcast time, the advertising media offer services to local retailers ranging from planning an ad program to actually designing the ads. Media companies also do market research and can provide information about shopping patterns in the local area.

Selecting Media

After developing the message, the next step is deciding how to communicate the message to customers. The media used for retail advertising are newspapers, magazines, direct mail, radio, TV, outdoor advertising, shopping guides, and the Yellow Pages. Exhibit 11–6 summarizes their characteristics.

REFACT

Co-op advertising accounts for approximately 50 percent of all department store and 75 percent of all grocery store advertising.[13]

RE-TALE 11-2 Penney's Advertises to Attract the Value-Conscious Consumer

The objective of J.C. Penney's communication program is to bridge the gap between the new J.C. Penney and the 1990s consumer. In the 1980s, Penney's made a number of changes in its merchandise offering and visual presentation to target traditional and updated customer segments. National brands such as Dockers, Bugle Boy, Henry Grethel, Maidenform, and Guess? now complement Penney's private-label merchandise. Consumer electronics, appliances, and sporting goods were deleted so that Penney's could focus on apparel lines. Over $50 million was spent to renovate stores and provide superior visual displays.

Research by Penney's and its advertising agency, N. W. Ayer, found that 1990s consumers exhibit four characteristics:

1. They're optimistic but have concerns about their ability to provide economically for their families.
2. They're interested in getting good values—beating the system and getting more for less.
3. They spend much time at home with their family and are not self-indulgent.
4. They're attracted to authentic natural clothing, not trendy high-fashion apparel.

To communicate how the new J.C. Penney meets the needs of 1990s consumers, N. W. Ayer developed a communication program built on the theme "fashion comes to life." Within this overall theme, the following slogans are stressed:

"A great new fashion feeling at J.C. Penney."

"A new spirit of style."

"Fashions that cater to every life-style."

"Hundreds of brands."

"Dozens of newly designed departments."

"Reminder of J.C. Penney value."

The tone of the TV commercials was uplifting, warm, emotional, and realistic. The stores and merchandise were shown as being part of real people's everyday lives. Models represented the wide range of ages and ethnic groups in Penney's target market.

Print ads were placed in leading men's and women's fashion magazines. They emphasized Penney's private labels using a life-style approach. The focus was on the brand name, with J.C. Penney placed in the lower left-hand corner of the ad. The merchandise was shown as a quality national brand available at J.C. Penney, not as a Penney's brand.

N. W. Ayer pretested the campaign by comparing consumers' attitudes about Penney's before and after seeing the ads. After seeing the ads, more consumers agreed with the following statements about J.C. Penney:

"Offers well-known brand-name apparel."

"Has clothing that will help me project the image I want to project."

"Is changing to fit my needs."

"Has quality merchandise."

"Has up-to-date fashions."

"Has up-to-date men's and women's apparel."

"Is a contemporary store."

"Makes me feel confident about its merchandise."

When the ad campaign was launched, Penney's discovered consumers also felt its merchandise was high priced and didn't offer good value. Thus the campaign achieved the fashion image desired, but had a negative effect on Penney's value image.

SOURCE: Company documents.

Newspapers. Retailing and newspaper advertising grew up together over the past century. But the growth in retail newspaper advertising has slowed recently as retailers have begun using other media. Still, 16 of the nation's 25 largest newspaper advertisers are retailers.[14]

In addition to printing ads with their editorial content, newspapers distribute preprints. A **preprint,** also called a **freestanding insert,** is an ad printed at the retailer's expense and distributed as an insert in the newspaper.

Characteristics of Media

EXHIBIT 11-6

Media	Targeting	Timeliness	Information Presentation Capabilities	Life	Cost
Newspapers	Good	Good	Modest	Short	Modest
Magazines	Poor	Poor	Modest	Modest	High
Direct Mail	Excellent	Modest	High	Modest	Modest
Radio	Modest	Good	Low	Short	Low
Television	Modest	Modest	Low	Short	Modest
Outdoor	Modest	Poor	Very low	Long	Modest
Shopping Guides	Modest	Modest	Low	Modest	Low
Yellow Pages	Modest	Poor	Low	Long	Low

Preprints are developed and printed by the retailer and then sent to the local newspaper for distribution.

Newspapers are distributed in a well-defined local market area so they're an effective way to target retail advertising. For large retailers with multiple stores, the local market a newspaper covers is similar to the market the retailer serves. Newspapers are beginning to develop editions for different areas of cities; this offers opportunities for small retailers to target their advertising. For example, *The Los Angeles Times* has 11 special editions for regions of southern California, including editions for Ventura County, the desert cities, and San Diego County.

Newspapers also offer quick response. There's only a short time between the deadline for receiving the ad and the time the ad appears. Thus newspapers are very useful for delivering messages on a short notice.

Newspapers, like all print media, effectively convey a lot of detailed information. Readers can go through an ad at their own pace and refer back to part of the ad when they want to. In addition, consumers can save the ad and take it to the store with them. This makes newspaper ads very effective at conveying information about the prices of sale items. But newspaper ads aren't effective for showing merchandise (particularly when it's important to illustrate colors) because of the poor reproduction quality.

While newspapers are improving their printing facilities to provide better reproductions and color in ads, retailers continue to rely on preprints to get good reproduction quality. J.C. Penney uses preprints extensively, distributing them to over 50 million newspaper readers weekly.

The life of a newspaper ad is short because consumers usually discard the newspaper after they read it. In contrast, magazine advertising has a longer life because consumers tend to save magazines and read them several times during a week or month.

Finally, the cost of developing newspaper ads is very low, but the cost of delivering the message may be high if the newspaper's circulation is broader than the retailer's target market, thus requiring the retailer to pay for exposures that won't generate sales. Newspaper ads can be developed by less experienced people and don't require the expensive color photography or typesetting needed for other forms of advertising.

Magazines. Retail magazine advertising is mostly done by national retailers such as Lord & Taylor and The Gap. But magazine advertising is increasing with the growth of local magazines and regional editions of national magazines. Retailers tend to use this medium for image advertising because the reproduction quality is high. Due to the lead time (time between submitting the ad and publication), a major disadvantage is that the timing of a magazine ad is difficult to coordinate with special events and sales.

Direct Mail. With direct mail, the retailer can target its advertising to specific customers. Retailers frequently use the names of their credit card customers as a mailing list. For example, Neiman Marcus records all purchases made by its credit card customers. With information on the customer's purchases, Neiman Marcus can target direct mail on a new perfume to customers with a history of purchasing such merchandise.

Retailers without their own mailing list can purchase a wide variety of lists for targeting consumers with specific demographics, interests, and life-styles. For example, a store could buy a list of local subscribers to *Architectural Digest* magazine and then mail information about home furnishings to those upscale consumers. Finally, many retailers encourage their salespeople to maintain a preferred customer list and use it to mail personalized invitations and notes.

While direct mail can be very effective because it can personalize the message, it's also costly. Many consumers ignore direct-mail advertising and treat it as junk mail.

Radio. Many retailers use radio advertising because messages can be targeted to a specific segment of the market.[16] Some stations even broadcast in the native language of a special audience. Radio stations' audiences often are highly loyal to their announcers. When these announcers promote a retailer, listeners are impressed. The cost of developing and broadcasting radio commercials is quite low.

One disadvantage of radio advertising is that listeners generally treat the radio broadcast as background, which limits the attention they give the message. As with all broadcast media, consumers must get the information from a radio commercial when it's broadcast; they can't refer back to the ad for information they didn't hear or remember.

Television. TV commercials can be placed on a national network or a local station. A local commercial is called a **spot.** Retailers typically use TV for image advertising. They take advantage of the high reproduction quality and the opportunity to communicate through both visual images and sound. TV ads can also demonstrate product usage. For example, Eckerd Drug's award-winning TV campaign promoted the image of its pharmacist as a health care professional, not just someone who fills prescriptions.[17]

The production costs and broadcast time for national TV advertising are expensive. Spots on local and cable TV have relatively small audiences and may be economical for local retailers. To offset the high production costs, many suppliers provide modular commercials in which the retailer can insert its name or a "tag" after information about the vendor's merchandise.

Outdoor Advertising. Billboards and other forms of outdoor advertising can effectively convey a limited amount of information to a narrow audience. Thus outdoor advertising has limited usefulness in providing information about sales. Outdoor advertising is typically used to remind customers about the retailer or to inform people in cars of nearby retail outlets.

Shopping Guides. Shopping guides are free papers delivered to all residents in a specific area. This medium is particularly useful for retailers who want to saturate a specific trading area. Shopping guides are very cost-effective and guarantee the local retailer of 100 percent coverage in an area. In contrast, subscription newspapers typically offer only 30 to 50 percent coverage.[18]

An extension of the shopping guide concept is the coupon book or magazine. These media contain coupons offered by retailers for discounts. Shopping guides and coupon books make no pretense about providing news to consumers. They're simply delivery vehicles for ads and coupons.

Yellow Pages. The Yellow Pages are useful for retailers because they have a long life. The Yellow Pages are used as a reference by consumers who are definitely interested in making a purchase and seeking information.

Determining Ad Reach, Frequency, and Timing

Ads' frequency and timing determine how often and when customers will see the retailer's message.

Reach. Reach is the actual number of customers exposed to an ad. If an ad is placed in a newspaper with 60,000 circulation, but only 60 percent of the people who receive the newspaper actually read it, then the ad's reach would be 36,000 (or 60 percent × 60,000).

Frequency. Frequency is how many times the potential customer is exposed to an ad. The appropriate frequency depends on the ad's objective. Typically, several exposures to an ad are required to influence a customer's buying behavior. Thus campaigns directed toward changing purchase behavior rather than creating awareness emphasize frequency over reach. Ads announcing a sale are often seen and remembered after one exposure. Thus sale ad campaigns emphasize reach over frequency.

Timing. Typically an ad should appear on, or slightly precede, the days consumers are most likely to purchase merchandise. For example, if most consumers buy groceries Thursday through Sunday, then supermarkets should advertise on Thursday and Friday. Similarly consumers often go shopping after they receive their paychecks in the middle and at the end of the month. Thus advertising should be concentrated at these times.

Evaluating Advertising Programs

Here's an example of the use of market research to evaluate an advertising program.

South Gate West is one of several specialty import furniture stores competing for upscale shoppers in Charleston, South Carolina. The store has the appearance of both a fine antique store and a traditional furniture shop, but most of its merchandise is new Asian imports.

The owner realized his advertising budget was considerably less than the budget of the local Pier 1 store. (Pier 1 is a large national import furniture chain.) He decided to concentrate his advertising on a specific segment and use a highly distinctive copy and art approach. His target market was experienced, sophisticated consumers of household furniture. His experience indicated the importance of selling to more seasoned shoppers because (1) they make large purchases and (2) their purchases and store choices are emulated by less experienced consumers.

The advertising message he developed stressed his store's distinctive image. The owner used the newspaper as his major vehicle. Competitive ads contained line drawings of furniture with prices. His ads emphasized the imagery associated with Asian furniture by featuring off-the-beaten-path scenes of Asian countries with unusual art objects. This theme was also reflected in the store's atmosphere.

To measure his campaign's effectiveness, the manager conducted an inexpensive tracking study. Telephone interviews were conducted periodically with a representative sample of furniture customers in his store's trading area. Communication objectives were assessed using the following questions:

Communication Objective	Question
Awareness	What stores sell Oriental furniture?
Knowledge	Which stores would you rate outstanding on the following characteristics?
Attitude	On your next shopping trip for Oriental furniture, which store would you visit first?
Visit	Which of the following stores have you been to?

Here are the survey results over one year:

Communication Objective	Before Campaign	After Six Months	After One Year
Awareness	38%	46%	52%
Knowledge (percentage of outstanding ratings)	9	17	24
Attitude (percentage of first choices)	13	15	21
Visit	8	15	19

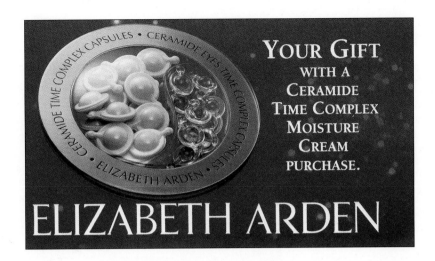

The results show a steady increase in awareness, knowledge of the store, and choice of the store as a primary source of Oriental furniture. This research provides evidence that the advertising is conveying the intended message to the target audience.[19]

☼ SALES PROMOTIONS

The sales promotions most commonly used by retailers are special sales supported by advertising. Other forms of retail sales promotion are merchandise demonstrations, premiums, and coupons as well as games, sweepstakes, and contests.

Special Sales

Retailers often have special sales to promote store traffic and reduce their inventory of older merchandise. These sales promotions can be advertised or just announced through signs in the store. Retailers often use special sales to sell merchandise that's still in inventory at the end of the season.

Merchandise Demonstrations

Some retailers use in-store demonstrations to build excitement in the store and generate interest in the merchandise being demonstrated. In supermarkets, demonstrations might involve tasting food. In department stores, fashion shows and cooking demonstrations draw customers to the store and encourage impulse purchases.

Premiums

A **premium** is merchandise offered at a reduced price, or even for free, to encourage customers to make a purchase. Premiums are often used to promote cosmetics and fragrances. Manufacturers such as Estée Lauder will offer a gift box of bath powder with every purchase of a new cologne to stimulate trial of the new fragrance.

Coupons

Coupons offer a discount on the price of specific items when they're purchased at a store. Coupons are the most common promotional tool used by supermarkets. Retailers distribute them in their newspaper ads and in direct-mail programs. For example, Publix, a Florida-based supermarket chain, targeted a promotion at affluent customers using a direct-mail piece that included recipes for a gourmet meal with coupons to purchase the products needed to prepare it.

RE-TALE 11-3   Targeting Coupons

A new supermarket checkout counter terminal, developed by Advanced Promotion Technologies (APT), delivers promotional offers tailored to the customer's grocery purchases. Based on the UPC codes on the groceries purchased by the customer, the terminal delivers instant credits at checkout, or prints out coupons for future purchases. For example, if a customer buys disposable diapers, the terminal can be programmed to print out a coupon for baby shampoo. Manufacturers may pay APT to deliver special offers for their brands. For example, Pepsico could offer a Pepsi coupon to all customers who buy Coca-Cola using the terminal.

SOURCE: Nancy Bader, "No More Coupon Clipping," *Florida Trend,* June 1993, pp. 32–37.

This Bold coupon was automatically printed out for the customer when the POS terminal recognized that the customer had bought a competitive detergent on this shopping trip.

Vendors also distribute coupons for their products that can be used at retailers that stock the products. To attract customers, some supermarkets accept coupons distributed by competing retailers. Another technique is for a retailer to offer double or triple the value of manufacturers' coupons. Re-Tale 11–3 describes a system for targeting coupons at the point of sale.

Games, Sweepstakes, and Contests

Promotional games of chance differ from premiums and price-off deals in that (1) only a few customers receive rewards and (2) winners are determined by luck. For example, fast food restaurants frequently have contests associated with major films (such as *Batman*) or sports events (such as the Super Bowl).

☼ PUBLICITY

The objectives of publicity typically are to generate awareness, improve the retailer's image, help the community, and develop community members' goodwill toward the retailer. Retailers generate publicity through events held within the store, such as a visit by Elizabeth Taylor to promote her line of perfume, or by the sponsorship of entertainment, educational, or community-service activities. Retailers frequently sponsor fund-raising benefit concerts or fashion shows for charitable organizations. Finally, some merchandising programs are so unusual, such as the his-and-her gifts in the Neiman Marcus Christmas catalog (see Re-Tale 11–4), that they become newsworthy.

Publicity Tools

Press releases, press conferences, by-lined articles, and speeches are among retailers' methods of getting favorable coverage of events involving their firm.

RE-TALE 11-4   The Ultimate His-and-Hers Gift

The Neiman Marcus Christmas catalog is perhaps the nation's best-known retail catalog. Its reputation is largely due to its annual tradition of ultraextravagant his-and-hers gifts.

The Christmas catalog was first distributed in 1915 as a Christmas card inviting Neiman Marcus customers to visit the store during the holiday season. In the late 1950s, customers were asking Neiman Marcus about unique gifts—merchandise not available in the store or from other catalogs. In 1959, Stanley Marcus, the CEO, developed the idea of featuring an extraordinary gift in the Christmas catalog—a Black Angus steer, delivered on the hoof or in steaks. This gift amused customers and generated a lot of publicity.

The next year, Neiman Marcus offered the first his-and-hers gift—a pair of Beechcraft airplanes—and a tradition was born. His-and-hers gifts have included ermine bathrobes, hot-air balloons, Chinese junks, and a pair of camels. The most expensive gift was a set of his-and-hers diamonds priced at $2 million. Most of these gifts are actually sold. A highly publicized chocolate Monopoly set was purchased by Christie Hefner, president of Playboy Enterprises, for her father, Hugh Hefner, founder of *Playboy* magazine.

Recent Neiman Marcus his-and-hers gifts were two Texas-born and -bred championship bloodline registered horses and special "cowperson" outfits for over $200,000.

In 1993, the Neiman-Marcus his and hers gift was a pair of lifelike automated dinosaurs with moving heads and tails, darting eyes, and sound effects. The price for the pair was $156,000.

Press Releases. A **press release** is a statement of facts or opinions that the retailer would like to see published by the news media. Press releases are used to announce special events, new store openings, quarterly and annual sales and profits, and changes in strategy.

Press Conferences. A **press conference** is a meeting with representatives of the news media that is called by a retailer. This publicity tool is used for major news events, such as the merger of two large retail chains. The press conference gives the media an opportunity to get more information than would be provided by a press release.

By-Lined Articles. Many publications, particularly trade magazines, accept and publish articles about a particular issue written by an expert working for the retailer. These articles offer retailers an opportunity to express their viewpoint on an issue and demonstrate the firm's expertise.

Speeches. Speeches also enable the retailer to express its views in a public forum. Retail managers have many chances to speak in front of industry groups, civic groups, and college students as well as at business luncheons or conferences.

Publicity's Effect on Employees and Stockholders

Most advertising is directed toward potential customers. Publicity, however, is often used to communicate with additional audiences. Favorable news stories generated by publicity can build employee morale and help improve employee performance. Much of this publicity is provided by internal newsletters, magazines, bulletin board notices, handbooks, and inserts into pay envelopes. However, news about the retailer published in newspapers or broadcast over TV and radio can have a greater impact on employees than internally distributed information. Just like customers, employees place more credibility on information provided by news media than on information generated by the retailer. Similarly, stockholders, the financial community, vendors, and government agencies are influenced by publicity generated by retailers.

SUMMARY

Retailers communicate with customers through advertising, sales promotions, store atmosphere, publicity, personal selling, and word-of-mouth. These elements in the promotion mix must be coordinated so customers will have a clear, distinct image of the retailer and won't be confused by conflicting information.

Retailers can design the promotion mix to achieve a variety of objectives: positioning the retailer in the customer's mind, increasing sales and store traffic, providing information about the retailer's location and offerings, and announcing special activities.

The largest portion of a retailer's promotion budget is typically spent on advertising and sales promotions. A wide array of media can be used for advertising, and each medium has its advantages and disadvantages. Newspaper advertising is effective for announcing sales, while TV ads are useful for developing an image. Sales promotions are typically used to achieve short-term objectives, such as increasing store traffic over a weekend. Most sales promotions are supported in part by promotions offered to the retailer by its vendors. Publicity and word-of-mouth generate the most credible information, but both are difficult to control.

KEY TERMS

advertising, 220
affordable method, 227
communication objectives, 225
competitive parity method, 227
cooperative (co-op) advertising, 228

coupon, 235
frequency, 233
objective-and-task method, 226
percentage-of-sales method, 227
personal selling, 220
positioning, 224

premium, 235
preprint (freestanding insert), 230
press conference, 237
press release, 237
promotion mix, 219
publicity, 220

reach, 233
sales promotion, 220
shopping guide, 233
spot, 233
store atmosphere, 220
word-of-mouth, 221

DISCUSSION QUESTIONS AND PROBLEMS

1. Why is the newspaper retailers' favorite medium for advertising? What are the advantages and disadvantages of newspaper advertising?

2. As a means of communicating with customers, how does advertising differ from publicity?

3. Why might a retailer prefer television advertising to newspaper advertising?

4. Wal-Mart is much larger than Kmart, but Wal-Mart's advertising budget is lower than Kmart's. Why?

5. TV is a popular advertising medium for retailers. TV advertisers have identified many types of markets based on the day, time, and type of show. During which days, times, and types of shows would retailers advertise fresh produce and meat, power drills, beer, and health club memberships? Why?

6. Cooperative (co-op) advertising is a good way for a retailer to extend an ad budget. Why isn't it always in a retailer's best interest to rely extensively on co-op advertising?

7. Some retailers direct their advertising efforts toward reaching as wide an audience as possible. Others try to expose the audience to an advertisement as many times as possible. When should a retailer concentrate on reach? When should a retailer concentrate on frequency?

8. A retailer plans to open a new store near a university. It will specialize in collegiate merchandise such as T-shirts, fraternity/sorority accessories, and sweat shirts. What specific advertising media should the new store use to capture the university market?

Cases for Section 3

A well-established, medium-sized department store in the Midwest, Hughe's reflects consumers' needs by featuring popular names in fashion for the individual consumer, family, and home. It tries to offer a distinctive wide assortment of quality merchandise with personalized customer service. The many customer services include personal shoppers; credit with in-house charge, American Express, and VISA; and an interior design studio. Hughe's pricing policy permits it to draw customers from several income brackets. Moderate-income consumers seeking value and fashion-predictable soft goods are target customers as are upscale customers with special interest in fashion.

The department store is implementing new marketing strategies to prepare for continuing growth and expansion. Hughe's merchandising philosophy is to attract the discerning middle-market customer who comprises 70 percent of the population as well as sophisticated fashion-conscious consumers who expect to buy high-quality brand name merchandise at a competitive price.

One portion of Hughe's buying staff is responsible for the oriental rug department within home furnishings. The open-to-buy figure for this classification within the home furnishings division will be based on last year's sales history (Exhibit 1).

It has been projected that a 15 percent increase over last year's sales volume can be attained due to oriental rugs' continued popularity. This year's open-to-buy for fall/winter will be $66,200.

The buying staff will be making its purchases for fall/winter in Amritsar, India, a city known for top-quality carpets. Ghuman Export Private, Ltd., of Amritsar, Punjab, India, is the manufacturer the buyers will contact. Exhibit 2 shows information about Ghuman to use in the decision-making process.

EXHIBIT 1   **Last Year's Fall/Winter Sales Results for Oriental Rugs**

Sales volume	$120,000			
Markup	51.5%			
	Size	Percentage of Sales	Fabrication	Percentage of Sales
	3′ × 5′	20%	Silk	15%
	4′ × 6′	40	Cotton	25
	6′ × 9′	15	Wool	60
	8′ × 10′	10		
	9′ × 12′	15		

Ghuman's Wholesale Price List

	FABRICATION		
Size	Silk	Wool	Cotton
3 × 5'	$ 400	$ 250	—
4 × 6'	700		$200
6 × 9'	850	700	275
8 × 10'	1200	1000	350
9 × 12'	1400	1300	500

Colors: Background colors available are navy, burgundy, black, and cream.

Quantities required for purchase: No minimum orders required.

Payment plan: Payment can be made in American dollars or Indian rupees. Letter of credit needs to be established prior to market trip.

Delivery:

Air freight
   10 to 14 days delivery time
   Cost is usually 25 percent of total order.

Ocean freight
   39 days plus inland time is necessary.
   Cost is usually 8–10 percent of total order.

Customer loyalty: Loyalty to customers is exceptional. Damaged shipments can be returned. Ghuman's philosophy is to help the retailers obtain a profit on their product lines.

Discussion Question:

Work up a buying plan to use when buying from Ghuman's. Decide how to distribute the allotted open-to-buy dollars among the available sizes, colors, and fabrications. Since it's an overseas manufacturer, consider additional costs such as duty and shipping, which also need to be covered by the allocated open-to-buy dollars.

This case was prepared by Professor Ann Fairhurst, Indiana University.

CASE 3–2 ☼ LATE DELIVERY

Joanna Stores is a 500-store women's apparel chain that emphasizes popular-prized goods. Its vendor policies tend to be somewhat lax, and vendors have often been known to take advantage of the company, shipping merchandise late and getting away with it.

However, this fall season began badly. Sales were flat, and the dress department's inventory was higher than normal. As the end of August approached, buyer Karen Clark was checking her open-order file and found that a very large order from Marie Modes, consisting of some 20,000 units, had not yet come in. She called Marie to find out when the goods would be ready and was told that the dresses might be a couple of days later than the August 30 cancellation date on the order. Hearing this, she asked for Martin Craft, the sales manager, and informed him that the store would not accept the order if it did not arrive before August 30.

Craft's reaction was equivocal. "I'll be late with a couple of styles but will have 80 percent of the order in your place on September 2. I've got a huge investment in fabric and labor in this order, and I'm going to ship it."

Clark immediately sent off a cancellation notice, insisting on August 30. Craft responded by saying, "I'm still a few pieces short, and I'm shipping what I've got, cancellation or no cancellation." And sure enough, 18,000 dresses from Marie arrived at Joanna's door on September 2. And just as sure Joanna refused the entire delivery. The dresses remained on the truck.

When Craft heard this, he was furious. "What am I supposed to do with this goods, eat it? You wrote us an order, we delivered it within the grace period, and you're gonna keep them. Either that or I'll see you in court."

Clark replied, "You do that, and we'll never do business again. You know perfectly well when that order was due. If you were going to have difficulty filling it, you should have let me know a long time before this. You know we're a big outlet for you. You need us, so you'll get rid of this stuff. And I promise I'll write you a nice big order next season."

Discussion Questions:

1. As an observer of this situation, what do you think should have been done?
2. And what would you advise the two principals to do to resolve the situation?

Case prepared by Professor David Ehrlich, Marymount University.

CASE 3–3 ☼ NEGOTIATING WITH A VENDOR

Laura Foote is the men's tie buyer for Hatfields, a regional department store chain. John Leary, the sales representative for Antonelli's, has just completed a presentation of the new fall line. He would really like to sell ties to Hatfields. Hatfields is well-respected in the industry. An order from Hatfields will help him sell to other regional department chains.

Laura is quite impressed with the line and has decided to buy 100 dozen ties. Antonelli's is a rising name brand in men's ties, but has never sold to Hatfields before.

Laura and John are preparing to negotiate over the following terms for an order:

1.   Prices. The ties will be sold at a retail price of $30.00. Laura would like to buy the ties at as low a price as possible. The lowest price at which John would sell would be $13.00 and the highest price Laura would pay would be $21.00.

2.   Return privilege. Since Hatfields has never sold Antonelli's ties before, Laura is somewhat uncertain about the customer demand.

She would like to be able to return all ties unsold at the end of the fall season for a cash refund. In the past, Antonelli's has agreed to take back as many as 50 percent of the order (50 dozen).

3.   Feature promotion. During the presentation, John indicated that he would like to have Hatfields feature Antonelli's ties in their Christmas promotion. Laura had considered featuring the ties, but it would mean not featuring some accessories, which would reduce her planned gross margin.

4.   Payment terms. Laura would like to delay paying for the merchandise. However John would like to be paid as soon as possible. The payment terms in the tie industry are either net 30, 60, or 90.

Case prepared by Professor Barton Weitz, University of Florida.

CASE 3–4 ☼ HOW MUCH FOR THE GOOD SMELL?

For the past two Christmas seasons, Courtney's, an upscale gift store, has carried a sweet-smelling potpourri in a plastic bag with an attractive ribbon. Heavily scented with cloves, the mixture gives a pleasant holiday aroma to any room, including the store.

Two years ago, the mixture cost $4.50 a bag. Courtney's (the only store in town that carried it) sold 300 pieces for $9.50. Courtney's supply ran out 10 days before Christmas, and it was too late to get any more.

Last year, the manufacturer raised the price to $5.00 so Courtney's raised its retail price to $9.95. Even though the markup was lower than the previous year, the store owner felt there was "magic" in the $10 price. As before, the store had a complete sellout, this time five days before Christmas. Sales last year were 600 units.

This year, the wholesale price has gone up to $5.50, and store personnel are trying to determine the correct retail price. The owner once again wants to hold

the price at $10 ($9.95), but the buyer disagrees: "It's my job to push for the highest possible markup wherever I can. This item is a sure seller, as we're still the only store around with it, and we had some unsatisfied demand last year. I think we should mark it $12.50, which will improve the markup to 56 percent. Staying at $10 will penalize us unnecessarily, especially considering the markup would be even lower than last year. Even if we run into price resistance, we'll only have to sell 480 to maintain the same dollar volume."

The owner demurs, saying, "This scent is part of our store's ambience. It acts as a draw to get people into the store, and its pleasant smell keeps them in a freespending state of mind. I think we should keep the price at $9.95, despite the poorer markup. And if we can sell many more at this price, we'll realize the same dollar gross margin as last year. I think we should buy 1,000. Furthermore, if people see us raising a familiar item's price 25 percent, they might wonder whether our other prices are fair."

Discussion Questions:

1. What price should Courtney's charge?
2. What do you think sales would be at each price level?

3. Which price would result in the highest profit?
4. What other factors should Courtney's consider?
5. What price would you charge and how many units would you order?

This case study was prepared by Professor David Ehrlich, Marymount University.

CASE 3–5 ☼ AN ADVERTISING PLAN

A major department store in the Washington, D.C., area is planning a major rug sale in its suburban Virginia warehouse over the three-day Washington's Birthday weekend (Saturday through Monday). Nearly $2 million worth of rugs will be on sale, assembled both from the company's inventory and from various market purchases. The average sale price of each rug is approximately $300. The company hopes to realize at least $900,000 in sales during the three days.

This is the first time the store has sold rugs from its warehouse, but previous experience with coats and furniture has been good. Two factors in particular were common to the previous events:

1. The first day's sales were 50 percent of the total. The second day's were 35 percent, and the last day's, 15 percent.
2. One of every two customers who came made a purchase.

It's known further that large numbers of people always flock to such sales—some driving as far as 50 miles. They come from all economic levels, but are all confirmed bargain hunters.

You're the assistant to the general merchandise manager, who has asked you to plan the event's campaign. The following information is at your disposal:

1. A full-page *Washington Post* ad costs $10,000; a half-page ad costs $6,000, and a quarter-page ad costs $3,500. To get the maximum value from a newspaper campaign, it's company policy to always run two ads (not necessarily the same size) for such events.

2. The local Northern Virginia paper is printed weekly and distributed free to some 15,000 households. It costs $700 for a full page and $400 for a half page.
3. To get adequate TV coverage, at least three channels must be used, with a minimum of eight 30-second spots on each at $500 per spot, spread over three or more days. Producing a TV spot costs $3,000.
4. The store has contracts with three radio stations. One appeals to a broad general audience aged 25 to 34. One is popular with the 18-to-25 group. A classical music station has a small but wealthy audience. Minimum costs for a saturation radio campaign (including production) on the three stations are $8,000, $5,000, and $3,000, respectively.
5. To produce and mail a full-color flyer to the store's 80,000 charge customers costs $10,000. When the company used such a mailing piece before, about 3 percent responded.

Discussion Questions:

1. Knowing that the company wants a mixed-media ad campaign to support this event, prepare an ad plan for the general merchandise manager that costs no more than $40,000.
2. Work out the daily scheduling of all advertising.
3. Work out the dollars to be devoted to each medium.
4. Justify your plan.

This case was prepared by Professor David Ehrlich, Marymount University.

CASE 3–6 ☼ STAN'S SHIRTS

Stan Soper has a 600-square-foot T-shirt store in a good mall location. He has all colors and sizes plus hundreds of designs for heat-embossing onto the shirts. Every shirt sells for $10. In his area, Stan estimates he has about a steady 12 percent share of a 100,000-units-per-year customized T-shirts market. Stan has found this to be a nonseasonal business. Sales hardly vary from one month to the next.

Stan's costs are

Store lease	$ 1,400 per month
T-shirt	$ 4.00 each
Embossing decal	$ .50 each
Embossing equipment	$24,002
Store fixtures	$14,403
Telephone, postage, etc.	$ 125 per month

Stan's advertising budget is $200 per month. He pays one store assistant $240 per week ($1,040 a month) and draws a salary for himself of $300 per week ($1,300 a month). His waste (T-shirts spoiled by a poor or misapplied decal) runs around 2 percent of T-shirts sold.

Discussion Questions:

1. What's the unit contribution for the T-shirts?
2. What's Stan's monthly break-even point?
3. What market share does he need to break even?
4. What's his monthly profit?
5. Because of some new fashion announcements he has just received. Stan expects T-shirt sales in his area to increase to about 144,000 next year. He's considering raising his advertising budget by $800 per month.
   a. If the advertising budget is raised, how many T-shirts must he sell to break even?
   b. How many T-shirts must he sell per month to get the same profits as this year?
   c. What must his market share be next year to get the same profit as this year?
   d. What must his market share be for him to have a monthly profit of $3,000?

This case was prepared by William R. Swinyard, Brigham Young University.

The Retail Mix—
Store Management

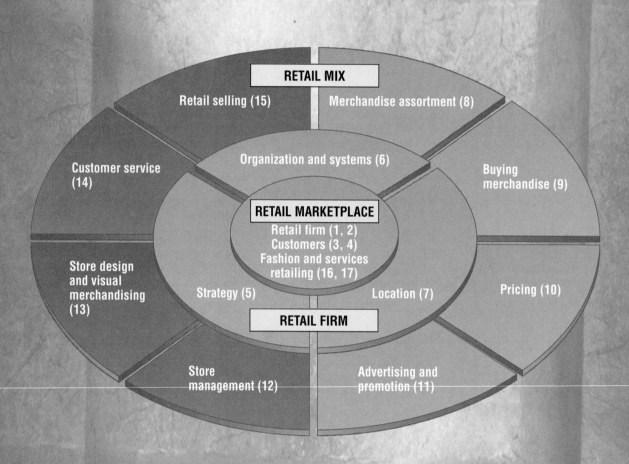

RETAIL MIX

Retail selling (15) Merchandise assortment (8)

Customer service (14)

Organization and systems (6)

Buying merchandise (9)

RETAIL MARKETPLACE
Retail firm (1, 2)
Customers (3, 4)
Fashion and services retailing (16, 17)

Store design and visual merchandising (13)

Strategy (5)

Location (7)

Pricing (10)

RETAIL FIRM

Store management (12) Advertising and promotion (11)

Tom O'Donnell (right rear), manager of the Sandy City, Utah, ShopKo store, builds morale in his store by holding meetings to keep employees informed about company and store activities and to get suggestions for improving store performance.

new salespeople's confidence and motivates them to improve their skills.[16] Later in the chapter we'll look at how rewards can motivate employees.

Store morale is important in motivating employees. Typically morale goes up when things are going well and employees are highly motivated. But when sales aren't going well, morale tends to decrease and employee motivation declines. Some programs that store managers use to build morale are discussed below.

Maintaining Morale

 Managers can use storewide or department meetings to motivate employees. In meetings, managers pass along information about new merchandise and programs; they also solicit opinions and suggestions from employees.

 Retailers can also build employee morale through flextime, job sharing, and child care. These programs help employees coordinate their work and nonwork responsibilities.

 Flextime is a job scheduling system that enables employees to choose the times they work. With **job sharing,** two employees voluntarily are responsible for a job that was previously held by one person. Both programs let employees accommodate their work schedules to other demands in their life such as being home when children return from school.

 Due to the increased number of families headed by two employed parents or a single parent, many retailers offer child care assistance. Sears' corporate headquarters near Chicago has a 20,000-square-foot day care center.

 Besides building employee morale, these programs help retailers attract excellent employees who couldn't work without this flexibility.

Sexual harassment is an important issue in store management. Managers must avoid actions that are, or can be interpreted as, sexual harassment.

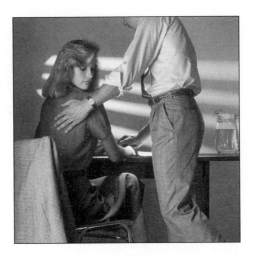

Sexual Harassment

An important issue in managing employees is sexual harassment. **Sexual harassment** is unwelcome sexual advances, requests for sexual favors, and other offensive verbal and physical conduct. Harassment isn't confined to requests for sexual favors in exchange for job considerations such as a raise or promotion. Simply creating a hostile work environment can be considered sexual harassment.[17]

Sexual harassment includes lewd comments, gestures, rude jokes, and graffiti as well as showing obscene photographs, staring at a coworker in a sexual manner, alleging that an employee got rewards by engaging in sexual acts, or commenting on an employee's moral reputation.[18] Managers must avoid such behaviors because they're both unethical and illegal.

EVALUATING STORE EMPLOYEES AND PROVIDING FEEDBACK

The fourth step in the management process (refer to Exhibit 12–2) is evaluating and providing feedback to employees. The objective of this process is to identify employees who are performing well and those who aren't. Based on the evaluation, managers (1) reward high-performing employees and (2) develop plans for employees performing below expectations. In some cases, the employees might be terminated; in other cases, additional training is suggested.[19]

In large retail firms, the evaluation system is usually designed by the human resources department. But the evaluation itself is done by the employee's immediate supervisor—the manager who works most closely with the employee.

Most retailers evaluate employees annually or semiannually. Feedback from evaluations is the most effective method for improving employee skills. Thus evaluations are done more frequently when managers are developing inexperienced employees' skills. However frequent formal evaluations are time-consuming for managers and may not give employees enough time to respond to suggestions. Thus managers supplement these formal evaluations with frequent informal ones.

Evaluations are only meaningful if employees know what they're required to do, what level of performance is expected, and how they'll be evaluated. Exhibit 12–5 shows The Gap's criteria for evaluating sales associates.

The Gap employee's overall evaluation is based on subjective evaluations made by the store manager and assistant managers. It places equal weight on

Factors Used to Evaluate Sales Associates at The Gap

EXHIBIT 12-5

Sales/Customer Relations - Weight 50%

1. *Greeting* - Approaches customers within 1–2 minutes with a smile and friendly manner. Uses open-ended questions.

2. *Product knowledge* - Demonstrates knowledge of product information, fit, shrinkage, price and can relay this information to the customer.

3. *Suggests additional merchandise* - Approaches customers at fitting room and cash/wrap areas.

4. *Asks customers to buy and reinforces decisions* - Lets the customer know they've made a wise choice and thanks them.

Operations - Weight 25%

1. *Store appearance* - Demonstrates an eye for detail (color and finesse) in the areas of display, coordination of merchandise on tables, floor fixtures, wall faceouts. Takes initiative in maintaining store presentation standards.

2. *Loss prevention* - Actively follows all loss prevention procedures.

3. *Merchandise control and handling* - Consistently achieves established requirements in price change activity, shipment processing, and inventory control.

4. *Cash/wrap procedures* - Accurately and efficiently follows all register policies and cash/wrap procedures.

Compliance - Weight 25%

1. *Dress code and appearance* - Complies with dress code.
   Appears neat and well groomed. Projects current fashionable Gap Image.

2. *Flexibility* - Able to switch from one assignment to another, open to schedule adjustments. Shows initiative, awareness of store priorities and needs.

3. *Working relations* - Cooperates with other employees, willingly accepts direction and guidance from management. Communicates to management.

individual sales/customer relations activities and activities associated with overall store performance. By emphasizing overall store operations and performance, The Gap's assessment criteria motivate sales associates to work together as a team.

The criteria used by the department store chain in Exhibit 12–4 are based on objective sales measures from point-of-sale data rather than the subjective measures used by The Gap. Subjective measures can be biased. For example, managers might be unduly influenced by recent events and by their evaluations of other salespeople. A manager might remember a salesperson's poor performance with a customer the day before and forget the salesperson's outstanding performance over the past three months. Similarly a manager might be unduly harsh in evaluating an average salesperson just after completing an evaluation of an outstanding salesperson.

The objective criteria in Exhibit 12–4 avoid many of these potential biases because most ratings are based on objective data. In contrast, The Gap evaluation (Exhibit 12–5) considers a wider range of activities but uses more subjective measures of performance. Because subjective information about specific skills, attitudes toward the store and customers, interactions with coworkers, enthusiasm, and appearance aren't used in the department store evaluation, performance on these factors may not be explicitly communicated to the salesperson.

Public recognition programs make employees feel they are appreciated and motivate them to improve their performance. For providing excellent customer service, the sales associates at the Mansfield, Ohio, Limited store were recognized with a "hero" award.

☼ COMPENSATING AND REWARDING EMPLOYEES

The fifth and final step in the employee management process in Exhibit 12–2 is compensating and rewarding employees. Store employees receive both extrinsic and intrinsic rewards from their job. The **extrinsic rewards** are rewards provided by either the employee's manager or the firm such as compensation, promotion, and recognition. The **intrinsic rewards** are rewards employees get personally from doing their job well. For example, salespeople often like to sell because they think it's challenging and fun. Of course, they want to be paid, but they also find it rewarding to help customers and make sales.

Extrinsic Rewards

Managers can offer a variety of extrinsic rewards to motivate employees. However store employees don't all seek the same rewards.[20] For example, some salespeople want more compensation; others strive for a promotion in the company or public recognition of their performance.

Because of these different needs, managers may not be able to use the same rewards to motivate all employees. Large retailers, however, find it hard to develop unique reward programs for each individual. One approach is to offer *à la carte plans.* For example, salespeople who achieve their goals could choose a cash bonus, extra days off, or a better discount on merchandise sold in the store. This type of compensation plan enables employees to select the rewards they want.[21]

Recognition is an important nonmonetary extrinsic reward for many employees. (Compensation and financial rewards are discussed later.) Telling employees they've done a job well is appreciated. However it's typically more rewarding when good performance is recognized publicly. In addition, public recognition can motivate all store employees, not just the star performers, because it demonstrates management's interest in rewarding employees.

Most retailers focus on extrinsic rewards to motivate employees. For example, a store manager might provide additional compensation if a salesperson achieves a sales goal. This emphasis on extrinsic rewards can make employees lose sight of their job's intrinsic rewards. They may feel that their only reason for working is to earn money and that the job isn't fun.[22]

When employees find their jobs intrinsically rewarding, they're motivated to learn how to do them better. They act like a person playing a video game. The game itself is so interesting that the player gets rewards from trying to master it.

One approach used to make work fun is to hold contests with relatively small prizes. Contests are most effective when everyone has a chance to win. Contests in which the best salespeople always win aren't exciting and may even be demoralizing. For example, consider a contest in which a playing card is given to a salesperson for each men's suit he sells during a two-week period. At the end of two weeks, the best poker hand wins. This contest motivates all salespeople during the entire period of the contest. A salesperson who sells only four suits can win with four aces. Contests should be used to create excitement and make selling challenging for everyone, not to pay the best salespeople more money.

The objectives of a compensation program are to attract and keep good employees, motivate them to undertake activities consistent with the retailer's objectives, and reward them for their effort. In developing a compensation program, the retailer tries to strike a balance between controlling labor costs and providing enough compensation to keep high-quality employees.

Hourly Versus Salaried Employees. Most retailers make a distinction between hourly and salaried employees. Salaried employees are guaranteed a fixed level of compensation each week and do not receive extra pay if they work overtime. Hourly employees are compensated for each hour they work. If they work more than 40 hours a week, they receive additional compensation. However, retailers are less committed to hourly employees. If business is slow, hourly employees might be asked to work less than 40 hours a week. Thus, hourly employees offer more flexibility than salaried employees. Most managers are salaried, while sales associates are typically paid by the hour.

Types of Compensation Plans. Compensation plans are most effective for motivating and retaining employees when the employees feel the plan is fair—when compensation is related to effort. In general, simple plans are better than complex plans. Simple plans are easier to administer, and employees have no trouble understanding them.

Retail firms typically use one or more of the following compensation plans: straight salary, straight commission, salary plus commission, and quota-bonus. Exhibit 12–6 compares advantages of straight salary and incentive compensation plans.

With **straight salary compensation,** salespeople or managers receive a fixed amount of compensation for each hour or week they work. For example, a salesperson might earn $6 per hour, or a department manager might make $500 per week. This plan is easy for the employee to understand and for the store to administer.

Under a straight salary plan, the retailer has flexibility in assigning salespeople to different activities and sales areas. For example, salaried salespeople will undertake nonselling activities (such as stocking shelves) and won't be upset if they're transferred from a high-sales-volume department to a low-sales-volume department.

EXHIBIT 12-C

Advantages of Straight Salary and Incentive Compensation Plans

Straight Salary	Incentive Compensation
Offers flexibility in assigning employees to activities	Has high motivating potential
Builds stronger employee commitment	Has more variable cost
Is easy for employees to understand	Relates compensation to productivity
Is easy to administer	
Allows for better performance of nonselling activities such as customer service	

The major disadvantage of the straight salary plan is employees' lack of immediate incentive to improve their productivity. They know their compensation won't change, in the short run, whether they work hard or slack off. Another disadvantage for the retailer is that straight salary becomes a fixed cost the firm incurs even if sales decline.

Incentive compensation plans compensate employees based on their productivity. Many retailers now use incentives to motivate greater sales productivity.[23] Under some incentive plans, a salesperson's income is based entirely on *commission* (straight commission). For example, a salesperson might be paid a commission based on a percentage of sales made minus merchandise returned. Normally the percentage is the same for all merchandise sold (such as 7 percent). But some retailers use different percentages for different categories of merchandise (such as 4 percent for low-margin items and 10 percent for high-margin items). By using different percentages, the retailer provides additional incentives for its salespeople to sell specific items. Typically compensation of salespeople selling high-priced items—such as men's suits, appliances, and consumer electronics—is based entirely on their commissions.

Incentive plans may include a fixed salary plus a smaller commission on total sales or a commission on sales over a quota. For example, a salesperson might receive a salary of $200 per week plus a commission of 2 percent on all sales over $50 per hour.

Incentive compensation plans are a powerful motivator for salespeople, but they have a number of disadvantages. For example, it's hard to get salespeople who are compensated totally by commission to perform nonselling activities. Understandably, they're reluctant to spend time stocking shelves when they could be making money by selling. Also, salespeople will concentrate on the more expensive, fast-moving merchandise and neglect other merchandise. Incentives can also discourage salespeople from providing services to customers. Finally, salespeople compensated primarily by incentive don't develop loyalty to their employer. Because the employer doesn't guarantee them an income, they feel no obligation to the firm.[24]

Drawing accounts. Under a 100 percent straight commission plan, salespeople's income can fluctuate from week to week, depending on their sales. Because retail sales are seasonal, salespeople might earn most of their income during the Christmas season and much less during the summer months. To provide a more

RE-TALE 12-3 **Incentive Plan Causes Problems for Sears**

After a year-long investigation, the California Department of Consumer Affairs accused Sears of overcharging auto repair customers. Undercover agents reported they were overcharged for 90 percent of their repairs. The average overcharge was $223. Reacting to the report, Dr. Leonard Berry, director of the Retail Center at Texas A&M University, commented, "The confidence of customers is any company's most precious asset. Sears has suffered an incalculable loss from which full recovery is not possible."

Until February 1990, Sears paid its service advisors by the hour. Then in an effort to increase sales and decrease costs, Sears reduced service advisors' salaries, installed a commission compensation based on the auto services bought by customers, and set sales quotas.

Sears acknowledged its compensation plan "created an environment where mistakes can occur."

Without an adequate control system, some service advisors systematically overcharged customers. After the overcharging was uncovered, Sears eliminated the incentive compensation plan and replaced it with a program rewarding service advisors for the quality, not the quantity, of their work.

SOURCE: Julia Flynn, "Did Sears Take Other Customers for a Ride?" *Business Week,* August 3, 1992, pp. 24–25; and Gregory Patterson, "Sears's Brennan Accepts Blame for Auto Flap," *The Wall Street Journal,* June 23, 1993, p. B1.

steady income for salespeople under high incentive plans, some retailers offer a **drawing account.** With a drawing account, salespeople receive a weekly check based on their estimated annual income. Then commissions earned are credited against the weekly payments. Periodically the weekly draw is compared to the commission earned. If the draw exceeds earned commissions, the salespeople return the excess money they've been paid, and their weekly draw is reduced. If commissions earned exceed the draw, salespeople are paid the difference.[25]

Quotas. Quotas are performance goals established to evaluate employee performance. Examples are sales per hour for salespeople, and maintained margin and inventory turnover for buyers. For department store salespeople, selling quotas vary across departments due to differences in sales productivity. Quotas are often used with compensation plans. For example, in a *quota-bonus plan,* salespeople earn a bonus if their sales exceed their quota over a certain time period.

A quota-bonus plan's effectiveness depends on setting reasonable, fair quotas.[26] Setting effective quotas can be hard. Usually quotas are set at the same level for everyone in a department. But salespeople in the same department may have different abilities and face different selling environments. For example, in the men's department, salespeople in the suit area have much greater sales potential than salespeople in the accessories area. Newly hired salespeople might have a harder time achieving a quota than more experienced salespeople. Thus a quota based on average productivity may be too high to motivate the new salesperson and too low to motivate the experienced salesperson. Managers may develop quotas for each salesperson based on the employee's experience and the nature of the store area where he or she works. Re-Tale 12–3 outlines Sears' problems with its incentive compensation plan for auto repairs.

Group Incentives. To encourage employees in a department or store to work together, some retailers provide additional incentives based on the performance of the department or store as a whole. For example, salespeople might be paid a commission based on their individual sales and then receive additional

Reducing inventory losses due to shoplifting and employee theft is an important store management activity.

compensation based on the amount of sales over plan or quota generated by all salespeople in the store. The group incentive encourages salespeople to work together on nonselling activities and handling customers so the department sales target will be achieved.[27]

Legal Issues in Compensation

The Equal Pay Act, now enforced by the EEOC, prohibits unequal pay for men and women who perform equal work. (*Equal work* means that the jobs require the same skills, effort, and responsibility and are performed in the same working environment.) But differences in compensation are legal when compensation is determined by a seniority system, an incentive compensation plan, or market demand.[28]

☼ LOSS PREVENTION AND STORE SECURITY

An important issue facing store managers is reducing inventory shrinkage. **Shrinkage** is the difference between the recorded value of inventory (at retail prices) based on merchandise bought and received, and the value of the actual inventory (at retail prices) in stores and distribution centers, divided by retail sales during the period.

Some factors causing shrinkage are employee theft, shoplifting, mistakes and inaccurate records, and vendor errors. Examples of employee mistakes are failing to ring up an item when it's sold and miscounting merchandise when it's received or during physical inventories. Inventory shrinkage due to vendor mistakes arises when vendor shipments contain less than the amount indicated on the packing slip.

Although shoplifting receives most of the publicity, employee theft accounts for the greatest percentage of inventory shrinkage. A recent survey attributes 43 percent of inventory shrinkage to employee theft, 30 percent to shoplifting, 23 percent to mistakes and inaccurate records, and 4 percent to vendor errors.[30]

RE-TALE 12-4   Confessions of an Exshoplifter

For 20 years, William Deal made over $100,000 per year as a professional shoplifter. Now he operates on the other side of the law—giving seminars to retailers on how to deter shoplifting.

Deal attributes his shoplifting success to poor store planning and uninformed store employees. "The way stores are built today it almost seems that they were designed by a thief." A department store's use of walls to create boutiques makes it hard for salespeople to spot shoplifting. Observation is also impeded by displaying merchandise from posts or pillars. (Note that these store design features are used to stimulate purchases. See Chapter 13.)

Salespeople are misinformed about who shoplifts and how they do it, according to Deal. Salespeople often think shoplifters are poor people of minority groups who can be identified by their shabby dress. Actually, professional shoplifters are typically Caucasians aged 25 to 50. Shoplifters tend to be well dressed, because, Deal says, "When you steal clothes for a living, you wear the best. A $35 Kmart leisure suit and an $800 Oxford cashmere jacket are the same size package when you roll it up and steal it. So, simple economics will tell you where I stole clothes—the best place in town."

Professional shoplifters work in teams. One team member distracts the salesperson, while the other member, usually a woman, takes the merchandise. The merchandise is hidden in a tailor-made elastic girdle worn under a loose-fitting dress or top, preferably maternity clothing. Deal used his gift for gab to keep the salesperson occupied. When that didn't work, he would create a scene, throwing merchandise on the floor. Knowledgeable salespeople should know that when something bizarre is going on in the store, they should be alert for potential shoplifters.

Deal feels that security devices aren't effective against the professional shoplifter. Electronic chains and tags are easy to remove. He found that store employees often leave tag removal devices lying around accessible to the shoplifter. In addition, uniformed guards are easily distracted and not highly motivated.

What things prevented Deal from shoplifting? "There's only one reason that I would not go into a store to steal: they got a salesperson in there who would drive you nuts. The fool wants to try to sell you something; you can't get rid of him." So good service sells merchandise and reduces inventory losses.

SOURCE: Reprinted by permission from *Chain Store Age Executive* (February 1985). Copyright Lebhar-Friedman, Inc., 425 Park Avenue, New York, NY 10022.

In developing a loss prevention program, retailers confront a trade-off between providing good service and shopping convenience and, on the other hand, preventing losses due to shoplifting and employee theft. The key to an effective loss prevention program is determining the most effective way to protect merchandise while preserving an open, attractive store atmosphere. Loss prevention requires coordination between store management, visual merchandising, and store design.

Detecting and Preventing Shoplifting

Re-Tale 12–4 describes how a professional shoplifter stole $400,000 worth of merchandise and made $100,000 a year. Losses due to shoplifting are reduced by store design, employee training, and special security measures.[31]

Store Design. Store managers must consider security issues when placing merchandise near store entrances, delivery areas, and dressing rooms. For example, retailers typically do not display easily stolen merchandise, such as jewelry and other small expensive items, near an entrance. They place dressing room entrances to be visible to store employees so employees can easily observe customers entering and exiting with merchandise.[32]

Employee Training. Store employees can be the retailer's most effective tools against shoplifting. They are trained to be aware, visible, and alert to potential shoplifting situations. The best deterrent to shoplifting is an alert employee who's very visible.

12-7   **Use of Security Measures by Retailers**

Observation mirrors	50.3%
Live closed-circuit TV (CCTV)	48.7
Cables, locks, and chains	44.0
Honesty shoppers	42.0
Secured displays	39.9
Electronic antishoplifting tags	39.1
Plain-clothes detectives	29.3
Uniformed guards	24.4
Simulated CCTV	23.3
Observation booths	18.1
Merchandise alarms	17.9
Ink/dye tags	13.7
Fitting room attendants	10.6
Subliminal messages	1.6

SOURCE: Richard Hollinger, *1993 National Retail Security Survey* (Gainesville, FL: University of Florida, Dept. of Sociology, October 1993), p. 14.

Security Measures. Exhibit 12–7 describes retailers' use of security measures. In *electronic article surveillance (EAS)* systems, retailers place special tags on merchandise. When the merchandise is purchased, the tags are removed or deactivated. If a shoplifter tries to steal the merchandise, the active tags are sensed when the shoplifter passes a detection device at the store exit and an alarm is triggered. Another approach for deterring shoplifting is to embed dye capsules in the merchandise tags. If the tags aren't removed properly by a store employee, the capsules break and damage the merchandise.

By placing convex mirrors at key locations, employees can observe a wide area of the store. Closed-circuit TV cameras can be monitored from a central location, but purchasing the equipment and hiring people to monitor the system can be expensive. Some retailers install nonoperating equipment that looks like a TV camera to provide a psychological deterrent to shoplifters.

While these security measures reduce shoplifting, they can also make the shopping experience more unpleasant for honest customers. The atmosphere of a fashionable department store is diminished when guards, mirrors, and TV cameras are highly visible. Customers may find it hard to try on clothing secured with a lock-and-chain or an electronic tag. They can also be uncomfortable trying on clothing if they think they're secretly being watched via a surveillance monitor. Thus when evaluating security measures, retailers need to balance the benefits of reducing shoplifting with the potential losses in sales.

Prosecution. Many retailers have a policy to prosecute all shoplifters. They feel a strictly enforced prosecution policy deters shoplifters. Some retailers also sue shoplifters in civil proceedings for restitution of the stolen merchandise and the time spent in the prosecution.[33]

Reducing Employee Theft

Giving store employees easy opportunities to steal money or merchandise increases chances for theft. Employee theft is reduced by carefully screening employees,

Policies for Reducing Employee Theft

EXHIBIT 12-8

- Randomly search containers such as trash bins where stolen merchandise could be stored.
- Require store employees to enter and leave the store through designated locations.
- Assign salespeople to a specific POS terminal and require all transactions to be handled through that terminal.
- Restrict employee purchases to working hours.
- Provide customer receipts for all transactions.
- Have all refunds, returns, and discounts cosigned by a department or store manager.
- Change locks periodically and issue keys to authorized employees only.
- Have a locker room where all employee handbags, purses, packages, and coats must be checked.

creating an atmosphere that encourages honesty and integrity, using security personnel, and establishing security policies and control systems (see Exhibit 12–8).

Screening Prospective Employees. Many retailers use paper-and-pencil honesty tests and make extensive reference checks to screen out potential employee theft problems. One major problem related to employee theft is illegal drug use.[34] Some retailers now require prospective employees to submit to drug tests as a condition of employment. Employees with documented performance problems, an unusual number of accidents, or erratic time and attendance records are also tested. Unless the firm knows they're involved in selling drugs, employees who test positive are often offered an opportunity to complete a company-paid drug program, submit to random testing in the future, and remain with the firm.

Encouraging Honesty and Integrity. Employee theft is reduced when retailers create a mutually trustful atmosphere. When employees feel they're respected members of a team, they identify their goals with the retailer's goals. Stealing from their employer becomes equivalent to stealing from themselves or their family.[35] Home Depot and Toys "R" Us offer attractive stock option plans to their employees to make them owners in the company.

Using Security Personnel. In addition to uniformed guards, retailers use undercover shoppers to discourage and detect employee theft. These undercover security people pose as shoppers. They make sure salespeople ring up transactions accurately.

Establishing Security Policies and Control Systems. To control employee theft, some retailers adopt policies relating to certain activities that might make employees prone to theft. In addition, computer software is available to detect unusual activity at POS (point of sale) terminals. For example, retailers can locate a POS terminal where shortages are frequently reported or return activity is unusually high. Then retailers can monitor employees using the terminal. Retailers can also analyze transactions to identify employees who ring up a lot of no-receipt returns or void other employees' returns.

☼ SUMMARY

Managing store employees is challenging because often they all have different skills and seek different rewards. Effective store managers need to motivate their employees to work hard and to develop skills so they improve their productivity. To motivate employees, store managers need to understand what rewards each employee is seeking and then provide an opportunity for the employee to realize that reward. Store managers must establish realistic goals for employees that are consistent with the store's goals and must motivate each employee to achieve them. Store managers also must control inventory losses due to employee theft, shoplifting, and clerical errors. Managers use a wide variety of methods in developing a loss prevention program, including security devices and employee screening during the hiring process.

KEY TERMS

ADA (Americans with Disabilities Act), 254
application form, 253
drawing account, 265
EEOC (Equal Employment Opportunity Commission), 254

extrinsic reward, 262
flextime, 259
incentive compensation plan, 264
intrinsic reward, 262

job description, 252
job sharing, 259
preferred client, 258
quota, 265
sexual harassment, 260

shrinkage, 266
socialization, 254
straight salary compensation, 263
turnover, 254

DISCUSSION QUESTIONS AND PROBLEMS

1. What are the different types of compensation plans?
2. Job descriptions should be in writing so employees clearly understand what's expected of them, but what are the dangers of relying too heavily on written job descriptions?
3. Name some laws and regulations that affect the employee management process.
4. Many large department stores—such as Abraham & Strauss, The Broadway, and Macy's—are changing their salespeople's reward system from a traditional salary or hourly reward system to a commission-based system. What problems can incentive compensation systems cause? How can department managers avoid these problems?
5. When evaluating retail employees, some stores use a quantitative approach that relies on checklists and numerical scores similar to the form in Exhibit 12–4. Other stores use a more qualitative approach

whereby less time is spent checking and adding while more time is devoted to analyzing an employee's strengths and weaknesses in written form. Which is the best evaluation approach?
6. What's the difference between extrinsic rewards and intrinsic rewards?
7. What method would you suggest for compensating a sales associate, store manager, and buyer? Why?
8. Men's suits have a higher gross margin in both dollars and percentages than shirts, socks, and ties. If salespeople are paid on a commission basis, how can the men's department manager convince his employees to focus some attention on the lower-margin accessories?
9. Discuss how retailers can reduce shrinkage from shoplifting and employee theft.

Store Layout, Design, and Visual Merchandising

Store design
and visual
merchandising
(13)

Questions this chapter answers include

- **What are the critical issues in designing a store?**
- **What are the alternative methods of store layout?**
- **How is space assigned to merchandise and departments?**
- **What are the best techniques for merchandise presentation?**

In a time when retailers are finding it increasingly difficult to create a differential advantage on the basis of merchandise, price, promotion, and location, the store itself becomes a fertile opportunity for market differentiation. In fact, today's consumers have a multitude of shopping choices outside the store. They can shop via catalogs, video home shopping on their television, and computer services such as Prodigy. (See Chapter 2.) The information highway of the future will facilitate shopping at home with video telephones and even **virtual reality,** an electronic three-dimensional experience in which many of the participant's senses become involved. Picture, for instance, being able to see, try on, and even feel a cashmere sweater electronically! Thus, even more than in the past, retailers must create an exciting store design with innovative merchandising techniques that makes people want to get off their couches and go shopping.

Many retailers like to think of their store as a theater. The walls and floors represent the stage. The lighting, fixtures, and visual communications such as signs represent the sets. And the merchandise represents the show. Like the theater, the store design and all its components should work in harmony to support the merchandise, rather than competing with it. Most observers think of upscale department stores like Lord & Taylor or Macy's as expert implementers of the "store as theater" concept. In fact, the original Macy's Cellar at Harold Square in New York was specifically designed to welcome customers to browse while enjoying entertaining cooking demonstrations. Consider the theatrical appeal of the Sony and Nike stores on Michigan Avenue in Chicago described in Re-Tale 13–1.

When designing or redesigning a store, managers must consider two objectives. First, the store's atmosphere must be consistent with the store's image and overall strategy. The second objective of a good store design is to help influence customers' buying decisions.

To meet the first objective, retail managers must define the target customer and then design a store that complements the customers' needs. Is the shop traditional or trendy, masculine or feminine? To illustrate, consider the Bergdorf Goodman men's store in New York City in the color insert for this section. It was created for the man who has means and a high taste level. The store has a comfortable, masculine, English clublike atmosphere. A warm, comfortable tone is created in individual rooms. Throughout the store, the woodwork and cabinetry are finished in either a honey wheat or deep aubergine/black with accents of marble and wrought iron. Each ancillary furniture piece must appear to be an antique, yet also have a sense of being contemporary. In contrast, think of the long gondola fixtures and bare fluorescent lighting that complement discount and warehouse stores' no-frills, low-price image. (A gondola is an island type of self-service counter with tiers of shelves, bins, or pegs.) Customers would find it hard to accurately judge value if the physical environment were inconsistent with the merchandise or prices. Throughout this chapter, keep in mind the relationships between the overall retail strategy and the store's image as it's portrayed by the store layout, merchandise display, and atmospheric design elements such as signs, graphics, lighting, color, music, and scent.

RE-TALE 13–1   Store as Theater: Nike and Sony Sell Pizzazz on Chicago's Michigan Avenue

New York's Museum of Modern Art displays a Rodin sculpture by placing it atop a monumental stone base. Sony Corporation has the same idea. At its new Sony Gallery store on Chicago's Michigan Avenue, it has lovingly set a single Sony Walkman on a similar pedestal. The Museum of Modern Art has a Calder mobile hanging from the ceiling. At Nike Town (next door to the Sony store) a life-size model of a cyclist dangles from the rafters. To make their products stand out in today's cluttered retailing environment, both companies are opening stores that are half art galleries, half walk-in advertisements.

At the Sony and Nike stores, everything is at full retail price. The idea is to attract customers with glamour, not discounts. They want to compensate for the lack of time and attention most retailers give their products. In the new gallery stores, manufacturers can showcase their wares with pizzazz—hoping that even if visitors don't buy, they leave with an impression that persists when they actually go shopping for the products elsewhere.

The 68,000-square-foot Nike Town is an ode to athletic footwear and its uses. In the basketball section a mural of Nike's superstar spokesman, Michael Jordan,

rings a basketball court while speakers pump out the sound of squeaking sneakers. In the section for Nike beachwear, a giant fish tank is set in the wall and customers stand on a screen showing videos of sea urchins.

It seems to work. The Nike store attracts up to 50,000 visitors a week. On one Saturday there was a one-hour wait to get in the door, making Nike Town one of Chicago's most popular attractions.

At the Sony Gallery next door, image is everything and sales are utterly irrelevant. The 10 salespeople on duty don't work on commission and have no incentive to push product. Instead, they demonstrate products. Mock bedrooms and living rooms show how Sony's electronic components fit with home decor. A couch in the back of the store sits before the 12-foot video screen of Sony's new home theater system: 10 components, four amps, seven speakers—all for $20,000. A salesperson presses the remote control and a video projector drops from the ceiling to show an MTV-type video on the screen at wall-shaking volume.

SOURCE: Elizabeth Comte, "Art for Shoes' Sake," *Forbes*, September 28, 1992, pp. 128–30.

To meet the second design objective of influencing customer buying decisions, retailers concentrate on store layout and space planning issues. Imagine a grocery store laid out like a women's specialty store, or an art gallery that looked like a tire store. Grocery stores are organized to facilitate an orderly shopping trip and to display as much merchandise as possible. Yet boutiques are laid out in a "free-form" design that allows customers to browse. Products are also located in certain areas to facilitate purchases. For instance, next time you visit a grocery or discount store, notice the merchandise displayed at the checkout area. Impulse merchandise (products purchased without prior planning such as candy, batteries, and *The National Enquirer*) are often located in these areas because people are often stuck in line with nothing else to do but buy.

Customers' purchasing behavior is also influenced by the store's atmosphere. Notice how your eye moves to an attractive, informative sign in a department store. On a more subtle level, have you ever been attracted to a Mrs. Field's Cookie store because of the chocolate chip cookie smell? Chances are the retailer planned this and other sensory experiences to get your attention. This chapter explores how such methods positively influence consumers' purchase behavior.

In this chapter, we examine the store design objectives that we've been discussing. First, different types of store layouts are addressed. Second, we discuss how retailers plan and evaluate the location of departments and merchandise. Finally, we explore methods for altering a store's atmosphere.

R E F A C T

It costs over $20 million to build a new department store and $7 to $10 million for a redo.

☼ STORE LAYOUT

To design a good store layout, store designers must balance many objectives—objectives that often conflict. First, the store layout should entice customers to move around the store to purchase more merchandise than they may have originally planned. One method is to expose the customer to a layout that facilitates a specific traffic pattern. For instance, Toys "R" Us uses a layout that almost forces customers to move through sections of inexpensive impulse purchase products to get to larger,

This store is BORING! It is cluttered. Everything is on one level. Customers cannot recognize distinct merchandise classifications because the store has failed to creatively use color, lighting, signage, and displays.

more expensive goods. It takes a very strong willed parent to navigate through the balloons and party favors without making a purchase.

Another method of helping customers move through the store is to provide variety. A store designer need not be satisfied with flat spaces filled with long rows of racks and shelves. Multilevels and ramps add variety. If the floor must be flat to facilitate the use of shopping carts, at least display heights can be varied to avoid a monotonous presentation.

A second objective of a good layout is to provide a balance between giving customers adequate space in which to shop and productively using this expensive, often scarce resource for merchandise. A store with lots of people creates a sense of excitement and, hopefully, increases buying. But a store with too many racks and displays causes customers to get confused or even lost. Some department store chains have chopped their stores into so many small boutiques that customers don't know where to find even a simple silk blouse.

Retailers must carefully select and utilize fixtures that facilitate traffic movement and are consistent with the store's overall image, adaptable to many types of merchandise, and economically useful for several years. Finally, when laying out stores, retailers must consider the special needs of the disabled.

When designing stores, the designers consider (1) alternative designs, (2) allocating space to feature and bulk-of-stock selling areas, and (3) making efficient use of walls. Re-Tale 13–2 describes how computers are currently being used to create store layouts.

Types of Design

Today's modern retailers use three types of store layout design: grid, racetrack, and free-form.

Grid. The **grid layout** is best illustrated by most grocery and drugstore operations. It contains long gondolas of merchandise and aisles in a repetitive pattern (Exhibit 13–1). The grid isn't the most aesthetically pleasing arrangement, but it's very good

---

RE-TALE 13–2   Store Design in 15 Minutes Using Computer-Aided Design and Drafting

When you're growing at Egghead Discount Software's phenomenal rate, the last thing you want is for the mechanics of store design to slow you down. This is why Egghead is rendering all its initial store designs with software that supports computer-aided design and drafting (CADD).

The CADD product is so simple that Egghead can have its real estate managers—not professional architects—use it to complete preliminary store designs, which often go through several revisions. A professional architect can then handle the final design. Whenever Egghead management identifies a prospective site to build a new store, the first thing they do is personally go to the location and measure its dimensions. Once the dimensions are in the system, they enter a command that immediately translates those dimensions onto a diagram on the screen.

The diagram is a bird's-eye view showing the location's basic outline. Once that's in place, they can use commands and a directional mouse to indicate where such things as wall units, gondolas, and cash/wrap stations should go. Specifications for these fixtures are already in the system so they appear on the diagram with the touch of a few keys. Further, they can show how the back rooms should be situated as well as how the furniture and display window should look. They can even enter in symbols showing where telephone jacks and electrical outlets should go. Overall, the entire process of working up a diagram takes about 15 minutes.

SOURCE: "Chain Designs with Off-the-Shelf Software," reprinted by permission from *Chain Store Age Executive*, June 1990, p. 56. Copyright Lebhar-Friedman, Inc., 425 Park Avenue, New York, NY 10022.

for shopping trips in which the customer plans to move throughout the entire store. For instance, when customers do their weekly grocery shopping, they weave in and out of the aisles with great agility, picking up similar products every week. Because they know where everything is, they can minimize the time spent on a task that many don't especially enjoy. The grid layout is also cost-efficient. There's less wasted space with this design than with others because the aisles are all the same width and are designed to be just wide enough to accommodate shoppers and their carts. Finally, because the fixtures are generally standardized and repetitive, the fixturing cost is reduced.

Racetrack. One problem with the grid design is that customers aren't naturally drawn into the store. This isn't an issue in grocery stores, where most customers have a good notion of what they're going to purchase before they enter the store. But how can a store design pull customers through large shopping goods stores such as traditional department stores like Macy's and The May Company?

The **racetrack layout** (also known as **loop**) facilitates the goal of getting customers to visit multiple departments by providing a major aisle that has access to the store's multiple entrances. This aisle "loops" through the store providing access to **boutiques** (departments designed to resemble smaller self-contained stores).

Grid Store Layout   EXHIBIT 13-1

Receiving and Storage	
Fruits	
Vegetables	Books, Magazines, Seasonal Display Cart area
	Checkouts
Office and Customer Services	Exit Entrance

Before a massive renovation, the Newman & Bogdonoff gourmet food store in New York City was so narrow that there was only room for one aisle between rows of showcases. The renovated store, shown here, is spacious and elegant.

The racetrack design encourages impulse purchasing. As customers go around the racetrack, their eyes are forced to take different viewing angles, rather than looking down one aisle as in the grid design.

Exhibit 13–2 shows the layout of J.C. Penney's store in the upscale NorthPark Center in Dallas, Texas. Because the store has multiple entrances, the loop design tends to place all departments on the "main aisle" by drawing customers through the store in a series of major and minor loops. To entice customers through the store, Penney's has placed some of the more important departments, like juniors, toward the rear of the store. The newest items are featured on the aisles to draw customers into departments and around the loop. To direct the customer through the store, the aisles must be defined by a change in surface or color. For instance, the aisle flooring is of marblelike tile, while the departments vary in material, texture, and color, depending on the desired ambiance.

The boutiques within the racetrack are quite different than other store layout types. They provide an interesting shopping experience by having unique environments that complement the merchandise and provide an element of privacy that's not possible in the grid design. Penney's private-label Hunt Club apparel, for example, is displayed among traditional custom-milled cabinetry and wood fixtures with brass trim in a boutique with wide wood plank floors and area rugs. On both sides of this boutique, the men's department picks up design elements from Hunt Club, downplayed slightly to reflect less exclusive merchandise. In the women's division, Jacqueline Ferrar (another Penney private label) is featured in a boutique with aqua-colored marble and glass fixtures trimmed with mirrored chrome. Similar merchandise displayed on either side of the boutique has the same atmosphere, but uses carpeting that picks up colors from the wall coverings in the Jacqueline Ferrar area. Glass dividers separate the boutiques while preserving an appearance of unity.[1]

Free-Form. A **free-form layout** arranges fixtures and aisles asymmetrically (Exhibit 13–3). It's successfully used primarily in small specialty stores or within the

J.C. Penney Racetrack Layout at NorthPark Center in Dallas

EXHIBIT 13-2

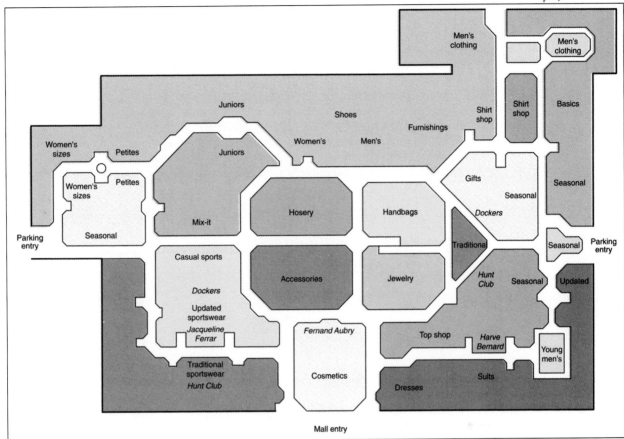

boutiques of large stores. In this relaxed environment, customers feel like they're at someone's home, which facilitates shopping and browsing. A pleasant atmosphere isn't inexpensive, however. For one thing, the fixtures are likely to be expensive custom units. Because the customers aren't naturally drawn around the store as they are in the grid and racetrack layouts, personal selling becomes more important. Also, sales associates can't easily watch adjacent departments, so theft is higher here than with the grid design. Finally, the store sacrifices some storage and display space to create the more spacious environment. If the free-form layout is carefully designed, however, the retailer can offset increased costs with increased sales and profit margins because the customer feels at home.

Display areas include feature areas, bulk of stock, and walls.[2]

Types of Display Areas

Feature Areas. Feature areas are designed to get the customer's attention. They include end caps, promotional aisles or areas, freestanding fixtures and mannequins that introduce a soft goods department, windows, and point-of-sale areas.

End caps are located at the end of an aisle. The last time Howard Marmon was shopping at his local Kroger food store, a large end cap display of Coca-Cola caught his attention. The Coca-Cola was located near the rest of the soft drinks but was on sale. It's not always necessary to use end caps for sales, however. Due to their high visibility, end caps can also be used to feature special promotional items, like beer and potato chips before the Fourth of July.

A **promotional aisle or area** is used similarly to an end cap. Because Marmon was getting ready for the Christmas holidays, he stopped at a J.C. Penney store to stock up on ornaments. They were all in a special "trim-the-tree" department that seems to magically appear right after Halloween every year.

Freestanding fixtures and mannequins located on aisles are designed primarily to get customers' attention and bring them into a department. These fixtures often display and store the newest, most exciting merchandise in the department.

Although windows are clearly external to the store, they can be an important component of the store layout. Properly used, window displays can help draw customers into the store. They provide a visual message about the type of merchandise

 EXHIBIT 13-3

Free-Form Store Layout

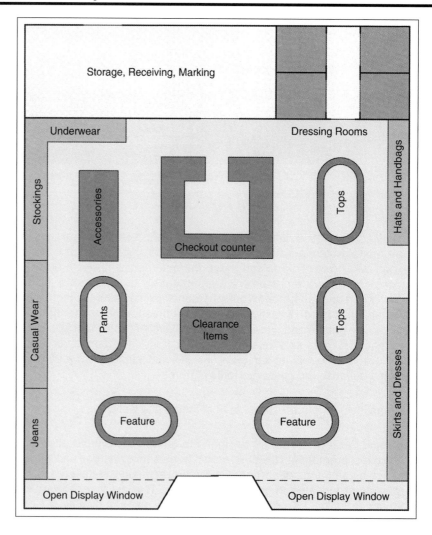

for sale in the store and the type of image the store wishes to portray. Window displays should be tied to the merchandise and other displays in the store. For instance, if Howard Marmon notices a display of bath towels in a Nordstrom window, which draws him into the store, the bath towels should then be prominently displayed in the bath department. Otherwise, the drawing power of the window display is lost. Finally, windows can be used to set the shopping mood for a season or holiday like Christmas or Valentine's Day.

Point-of-sale (also known as **point-of-purchase** or **POP**) **areas** can be the most valuable piece of real estate in the store because the customer is almost held captive in that spot. While waiting in a long line to check out at Kmart, Marmon picked up some batteries, candy, razors, and a copy of *The National Enquirer.* Did he need these items? Not really, but the wait bored him so he spent the extra time shopping.

Bulk of Stock. The **bulk of stock area** contains the total assortment of merchandise. It usually has gondolas in grocery and discount stores, and has freestanding fixtures for soft goods. This merchandise is usually introduced by a feature area. Presentation techniques for this merchandise are found later in this chapter.

Walls. Because retail space is often scarce and expensive, many retailers have successfully increased their ability to store extra stock, display merchandise, and creatively present a message by utilizing wall space. Retailers can store merchandise on shelving and racks. They can coordinate merchandise with displays, photographs, or graphics featuring the merchandise.

The primary purposes of fixtures are to hold and display merchandise. At the same time, fixtures must be in concert with the other physical aspects of the store, such as floor coverings and lighting, as well as the overall image of the store. For instance, in stores designed to convey a sense of tradition or history, customers automatically expect to see lots of wood rather than plastic or metal fixtures. Lighter shades of

Fixtures

The Retail Group designs its stores for effective use of all available retail space. End caps (left) and wall displays (right) are attractive and functional.

wood create a more modern message. Wood mixed with metal, acrylic, or stone changes the traditional orientation. The rule of thumb is that the more unexpected the combination of textures, the more contemporary the fixture.[3]

Fixtures come in an infinite variety of styles, colors, sizes, and textures, but only a few basic types are commonly used. For apparel, retailers utilize the straight rack, rounder, and four-way. The mainstay fixture for most other merchandise is the gondola.

The **straight rack** consists of a long pipe suspended with supports going to the floor or attached to a wall (Exhibit 13–4A). Although the straight rack can hold a lot of apparel, it's hard to feature specific styles or colors. All the customer can see is a sleeve or a pant leg. As a result, straight racks are often found in discount and off-price apparel stores.

A **rounder** (also known as a **bulk** or **capacity fixture**) is a round fixture that sits on a pedestal (Exhibit 13–4B). Although smaller than the straight rack, it's

EXHIBIT 13-4   **Store Fixtures**

A. Straight rack

B. Rounder

C. Four-way

D. Gondola

designed to hold a maximum amount of merchandise. Because they're easy to move and efficiently store apparel, rounders are found in most types of apparel stores. But, as with the straight rack, customers can't get a frontal view of the merchandise.

A **four-way** (also known as a **feature fixture**) has two cross bars that sit perpendicular to each other on a pedestal (Exhibit 13–4C). This fixture holds a large amount of merchandise and allows the customer to view the entire garment. The four-way is harder to properly maintain than the rounder or straight rack, however. All merchandise on an arm must be a similar style and color, or the customer may become confused. Due to their superior display properties, four-way fixtures are commonly utilized by fashion-oriented apparel retailers.

A **gondola** is an island type of self-service counter with tiers of shelves, bins, or pegs (Exhibit 13–4D). Gondolas are extremely versatile. They're used extensively, but not exclusively, in grocery and discount stores to display everything from canned foods to baseball gloves. Gondolas may also display towels, sheets, and housewares in department stores. Folded apparel also can be displayed on gondolas, but it's even harder for customers to view apparel on gondolas than on straight racks.

A critical consideration in any store design or redesign decision is the **Americans with Disabilities Act (ADA).**[4] This landmark federal civil rights law protects people with disabilities from discrimination in employment, transportation, public accommodations, telecommunications, and the activities of state and local government.

Recognizing the Needs of the Disabled

The requirements for compliance with the ADA differ for existing facilities, newly built facilities, and those undergoing remodeling. It's easiest to comply in an existing facility. In essence, barriers, such as stairs, must be removed if this doesn't involve much difficulty or expense. The ADA insists on higher standards for larger facilities. For most stores and shopping centers, the ADA requires building ramps, adding grab bars, rearranging restroom stall dividers, adding a handrail to stairs, providing Braille elevator buttons, and other measures.

Requirements for newly built facilities or those undergoing remodeling are more stringent. For instance, if a shopping center has five or more stores, it must have an elevator even if it's a small building under three stories or under 3,000 square feet per story.

SPACE PLANNING

When store planners and merchandise managers allocate space, they typically start by allocating space based on how many sales the merchandise generates. For instance, if knit shirts represent 15 percent of the total expected sales for the men's furnishings department, they will initially get 15 percent of the space. Store planners must then adjust the initial estimate based on the following five factors:

- How profitable is the merchandise? Retailers allocate space to SKUs to maximize the merchandise category's profitability. Similar analysis can be performed for departments. Consider, for instance, allocating space for beer in a supermarket. At first glance, you might think that because Bud Light is the most profitable brand, it should get all the space. But if the store took this approach, it would lose sales on less profitable brands—and it might even lose customers who are loyal to other brands. Thus the store should experiment with different shelf space allocations until it finds a combination that maximizes profits.

- How will the planned inventory turnover affect how much stock will normally be carried? Recognize that monthly inventory levels vary according to seasonal demands, holidays, and so on. Store planners must allocate space based on

REFACT

Energy consumption costs over $300,000 per year for a department store and $50,000 for a category killer.

these seasonal needs rather than yearly averages. Store planners must also estimate the proportion of merchandise kept on display versus reserve stock. Merchandise kept as reserve stock in a storage area takes up much less room.

- How will the merchandise be displayed? Merchandise and fixtures go hand in hand. Store planners design fixtures to go with the merchandise. But once the fixtures are in the store, store planners and merchandise managers must consider the fixtures' physical limitations when assigning space to merchandise. Will the shirts be displayed on hangers or folded on tables? Customers can more easily examine merchandise on hangers, but this display method takes more space. Later in this chapter we examine the planogram (a map that illustrates exactly where every SKU should be placed) and merchandise presentation techniques.

- What items does the retailer wish to emphasize? The merchandise managers have decided that knit shirts rather than woven shirts will be particularly strong this season. They've bought accordingly, and they've planned advertising to support their sales. As a result, knit shirts must also receive additional selling and display space.

- Will the location of certain merchandise draw the customer through the store, thus facilitating purchases? At some Sears stores, for example, women's undergarments are close to the automotive department. This discourages purchasing because most women prefer to buy undergarments with some privacy. Throughout this section, we examine how retailers locate departments and specific merchandise to facilitate purchases and encourage purchases of impulse and complementary products.

We've discussed in general terms how store planners and merchandise managers plan the space requirements for a category like knit shirts or beer. Similar decisions are made for larger groups of merchandise like classifications, departments, and even merchandise groups. Now let's examine how retailers decide where to locate departments and where to locate merchandise within departments.

Location of Departments

Sandy Williams recently went to Nordstrom for a haircut. On the way in, she stopped at the cosmetics counter to buy makeup. Then on the escalator, she spotted a red dress to examine on her way out. Before leaving the store, she stopped by the lingerie department to browse.

Did she simply take a random walk through the store? Probably not. The departments she shopped—like all Nordstrom departments—are strategically located to maximize the entire store's profits. The profit-generating ability of various locations within a store aren't equal. The more traffic through a department, the better the location. Unfortunately every department can't be situated in the best location. Retailers must consider additional demand-generating factors and the interrelations between departments when determining their locations.

Relative Location Advantages. The best locations within the store depend on the floor, the position within a floor, and location relative to traffic aisles, entrances, escalators, and so on. In general, in a multilevel store, a space's value decreases the further it is from the entry-level floor. As we've said, men aren't generally avid shoppers for clothing. Thus many large stores locate the men's department on the entry-level floor to make shopping as easy as possible.

The position within a floor is also important when assigning locations to departments. The best locations are those closest to the store's entrances, main aisles, escalators, and elevators. Sandy Williams spotted the red dress because she could see it from the escalator. Multilevel stores often place escalators so customers must walk around the sales floor to get to the next level. Also, most customers turn right when entering a store or floor so the right side is especially desirable space. Finally, most customers won't get all the way to the center of the store so many stores use the racetrack design to induce people to move into the store's interior.[5]

Impulse products. **Impulse merchandise** is products that customers purchase without preplanning. These products—like fragrances and cosmetics in department stores and magazines in supermarkets—are almost always located near the front of the store, where they're seen by everyone and may actually draw people into the store. Sandy Williams didn't plan her makeup purchase, for example, but decided she wanted some once she saw the displays.

Demand/Destination Areas. Children's, expensive specialty goods, and furniture departments as well as customer-service areas like beauty salons, credit offices, and photography studios are usually located off the beaten path—in corners and on upper floors. Due to the exclusive nature of Steuben Glass, for instance, the department is typically located in a low-traffic area of high-class stores like Neiman Marcus. A purchase of one of these unique, expensive pieces requires thought and concentration. Sandy Williams would probably become distracted if the department were adjacent to a high-traffic area. Besides, customers looking for these items will find them no matter where they're located in the store. These departments are known as **demand/destination areas** because demand for the products or services exists before customers get to their destination. Thus they don't need prime locations.

Adjacent Departments. After trying on the red dress, Sandy found a complementary scarf and stockings nearby. Retailers often cluster complementary products together to facilitate multiple purchases.

Some stores are now combining traditionally separate departments to facilitate multiple purchases. For instance, Kmart has combined its toy and sporting goods departments. Kmart's children's apparel is now grouped together, with infants' and boys' wear across the aisle from girls' wear. Active wear for both children and adults is now found in an exercise department.[6]

Seasonal Needs. Some departments need to be more flexible than others. For instance, it's helpful to locate winter coats near sportswear. Extra space in the coat department can be absorbed by sportswear or swimwear in the spring when the bulk of the winter coats have been sold.

Physical Characteristics of Merchandise. Departments that require large amounts of floor space, like furniture, are often located in the less desirable locations. Some departments (like curtains) need significant wall space, while others (like shoes) require accessible storage.

**Location of
Merchandise within
Departments: The
Use of Planograms**

To determine where merchandise should be located within a department, many types of retailers (department and specialty stores alike) now generate maps known as *planograms.* A **planogram** is a diagram created from photographs, computer output, or artists' renderings that illustrates exactly where the retailer should place every SKU. Technology for computer-generated planograms is readily available for stores that carry staple merchandise, such as discount and grocery stores. Exhibit 13–5 presents a planogram for the mouth rinse section of a grocery store prepared by Apollo Space Management System.[7] It shows each shelf's length, height, and depth plus the number and location of each SKU. Each planogram is accompanied by several reports that assess its relative profitability.

Electronic planogramming requires the user to input model numbers or UPC codes, product margins, turnover, shipping procedures, and other pertinent information into the program. The sizes of product packaging or actual pictures of the packaging are also input.

The computer plots the planogram based on the retailer's priorities. For instance, if the retailer wants prime shelf space given to products that produce the highest turnovers, the computer will locate those products in the best locations. If margins are more important, the computer will determine the shelf space priority and the optimal number of SKUs to stock in that space. The initial planogram can be adjusted to see how additional space or different fixtures would affect the productivity measures.

Planograms are also useful for merchandise that doesn't fit nicely on gondolas in a grocery or discount store. The Gap and Banana Republic, for instance, provide their managers with photographs and diagrams of how to display merchandise. Sears has been using Nielsen's SPACEMAN III planogram system for many departments—from home electronics to apparel—since 1989.

Retailers embarking on a planogram system in department and specialty stores usually start with the basics like jeans, underwear, and hosiery. It's still hard

 Planogram for a Grocery Store's Mouth Rinse Section

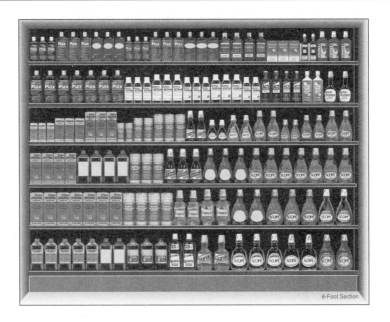

to use planograms with fixtures that display merchandise in multiple dimensions. MarketMAX, however, has developed a digital camera interface to be used with its system. It can take pictures of a rounder fixture from four different directions as well as from the top. Then merchandise descriptions can be prescribed in a pie chart fashion. In this case, the retailer might specify the number and type of fixtures for the department rather than plan for specific SKUs.

MERCHANDISE PRESENTATION TECHNIQUES

Many methods are available to retailers for effectively presenting merchandise to the customer. To decide which is best for a particular situation, store planners must consider the following four issues.

First, and probably most importantly, merchandise should be displayed in a manner consistent with the store's image. For instance, some stores display men's shirts by size so all size 15½–34 shirts are together. Thus the customer can easily determine what's available in his size. This is consistent with a no-nonsense image of the store. Other stores keep all color/style combinations together. This presentation evokes a more fashion-forward image and is more aesthetically pleasing, but it forces the customer to search in each stack for his size.

Second, store planners must consider the nature of the product. Basic jeans can easily be displayed in stacks, but skirts must be hung so the customer can more easily examine the design and style.

Third, packaging often dictates how the product is displayed. Discount stores sell small packages of nuts and bolts, for example, but hardware stores still sell these products by the unit. Although the per-unit price is significantly higher for the packages, self-service operations don't have adequate personnel to weigh and bag these small items.

Finally, products' profit potential influences display decisions. For example, low-profit/high-turnover items like back-to-school supplies don't require the same elaborate, expensive displays as Parker fountain pens. Next let's look at specific presentation techniques.

Some retailers successfully use an **idea-oriented presentation**—a method of presenting merchandise based on a specific idea or the image of the store. Women's fashions, for instance, are often displayed to present an overall image or idea. Also, furniture is combined in room settings to give customers an idea of how it would look in their home. Individual items are grouped to show customers how the items could be used and combined. This approach encourages the customer to make multiple complementary purchases.

Manufacturers' products with strong consumer demand are often merchandised together in the boutique layout described earlier in this chapter. This technique is similar to the idea-oriented presentation because merchandise made by the same vendor tends to be coordinated. Some apparel manufacturers like Esprit and Jaeger coordinate both style and color to influence multiple purchases within the line and to enhance the line's overall image.

Probably the most common technique of organizing stock is **style/item organization.** Discount stores, grocery stores, hardware stores, and drugstores employ this method for nearly every category of merchandise. Also, many apparel retailers use this technique. When customers look for a particular type of merchandise, such as a sweater, they expect to find all items in the same location.

Arranging items by size is another method of organizing many types of merchandise, from nuts and bolts to apparel. Because they usually know the desired size, it's easiest for customers to locate items organized in this manner.

A bold merchandising technique is **color organization.** For instance, in winter months women's apparel stores may display all white "cruise wear" together to let customers know that this store is the place to purchase clothing for their winter vacation.

Organizing merchandise in price categories or **price lining** (when retailers offer a limited number of predetermined price points within a classification) was discussed in Chapter 10. This strategy helps customers easily find merchandise at the price they wish to pay. For instance, men's dress shirts may be organized into three groups selling for $30, $45, and $60.

Another common way of organizing merchandise is **vertical merchandising.** Here merchandise is presented vertically using walls and high gondolas. Customers shop much as they read a newspaper—from left to right, going down each column, top to bottom. Stores can effectively organize merchandise to follow the eye's natural movement. Retailers take advantage of this tendency in several ways. Many grocery stores put national brands at eye level and store brands on lower shelves because customers scan from eye level down. Retailers also display merchandise in bold vertical bands of an item. For instance, you'll see vertical columns of towels of the same color displayed in a department store, or a vertical band of yellow and orange boxes of Tide detergent followed by a band of blue Cheer boxes in a supermarket.

As the name implies, **tonnage merchandising** is a display technique in which large quantities of merchandise are displayed together. Customers have come to equate tonnage with low price, following the retail adage "stock it high and let it fly." Tonnage merchandising is therefore used to enhance and reinforce a store's price image. Using this display concept, the merchandise itself is the display. The retailer hopes customers will notice the merchandise and be drawn to it. For instance, before many holidays, grocery stores use an entire end of a gondola (i.e., an end cap) to display six-packs of Pepsi.

Often it's not possible to create effective displays and efficiently store items at the same time. But it's important to show as much of the merchandise as possible.

Mikasa has coordinated signs and graphics with the store's image as a destination store for china and flatware. In their prototype store in Secaucus, New Jersey, collages of oversized dinnerware help identify product categories on the wide-open selling floor and lend the store and "Alice in Wonderland" feel.

One solution to this dilemma is **frontal presentation** (a method of displaying merchandise in which the retailer exposes as much of the product as possible to catch the customer's eye). Book manufacturers, for instance, make great efforts to create eye-catching covers. But bookstores usually display books exposing only the spine. To create an effective display and break the monotony, book retailers often face the cover out like a billboard to catch the customer's attention. A similar frontal presentation is achieved on a rack of apparel by simply turning one item out to show the merchandise.

In conclusion, when making merchandise presentation decisions, retailers should attempt to view the store through the customer's eyes. They should also organize the stock based on the type of product and its package.[8]

☼ ATMOSPHERICS

Atmospherics refers to the design of an environment via visual communications, lighting, colors, music, and scent to stimulate customers' perceptual and emotional responses and ultimately to affect their purchase behavior.[9] Many retailers have discovered the subtle benefits of developing atmospherics that complement other aspects of the store design and the merchandise. For example, the Tattered Cover Book Store in Re-Tale 13–3 has designed a different atmosphere for each major area of the store to portray a unique image. Now let's explore some basic principles of good atmospheric design and examine a few new, exciting, and somewhat controversial trends.

Visual Communications

Visual communications—graphics, signs, and theatrical effects both in the store and in windows—help boost sales by providing information on products and suggesting items or special purchases. Signs and graphics also help customers find specific

---

RE-TALE 13-3   Ambiance at Tattered Cover Book Store Is Like a Comfortable Old Slipper

Joyce Meskis, owner of Denver's Tattered Cover Book Store, likens her shop to a "comfortable old slipper." Customers who nestle in the sofas and easy chairs that dot the selling floor probably agree. But if you look with a retailer's shrewd eye, you'll see that the comfy slipper is spun from pure gold.

Linda Millemann, general manager, says the store's volume is at least $10 million per year and growing. Since Meskis first opened the outlet in 1974, it's become so popular that such celebrities as Yoko Ono, Jimmy Carter, and Michael Jackson have popped in to shop.

The secret to this independent bookseller's success lies in its effective blending of homey and hip. The ambiance is strictly old-world bookshop with publications displayed on pine bookcases stained with a warm, dark finish. The carpet is a deep, peaceful green. Strategically placed couches and antique easy chairs invite customers to relax and read. Employees sit at old-fashioned wooden library desks and work at computers painted dark brown "to literally fade into the woodwork," says Millemann.

There's even a touch of whimsy. In the cookbook section, for example, shoppers can peruse the latest recipes at a tall-backed wooden diner booth. The psychology section has a "fainting couch" similar to one that might have graced Sigmund Freud's office; the religion section features a wooden pew.

"The whole store offers a real invitation to come in, sit, and read," says Millemann. "We'll deal with the wear and tear of the merchandise; getting the customers interested in books is the point here."

SOURCE: Lynne S. Dumas, "The Tattered Cover," *Stores*, March 1992.

departments or merchandise. Graphics (such as photo panels) can add personality, beauty, and romance to the store's image.

Retailers should consider the following issues when designing visual communications strategies for their stores.

Coordinate signs and graphics with the store's image. Signs and graphics should act as a bridge between the merchandise and the target markets. The colors and tone of the signs and graphics should complement the merchandise. Colors that aren't coordinated with the overall presentation will visually destroy a good display and detract from the merchandise. For example, a pastel pink sign set in a bold red, white, and blue nautical display or a green sign in a pastel bridal setting won't do either display justice. Also, a formally worded black-and-white rectangular sign doesn't match a children's display as well as a red-and-yellow circus tent design does. Color combinations should appeal to specific target customers or highlight specific merchandise—primary colors for kids, hot vivid colors for teens, pastels for lingerie, brights for sportswear, and so forth. Wall posters should depict merchandise being used by the appropriate target market. Posters of teenagers in jeans should be used in the young men's department, for example.

Inform the customer. Informative signs and graphics make merchandise more desirable. For instance, Crate and Barrel, the upscale home furnishings retailer, has a small white placard with black descriptive copy and price as an integral part of each display. The sign is foremost a sales tool designed to appeal to specific customer needs and wants. For example, one sign may explain how a food processor works; another may announce that a particular flatware pattern was an award winner.

Large photo panels depicting the merchandise in use or in an actual home help shoppers visualize how the merchandise will function in their lives. As retailers know, customers aren't just worried about buying the product per se. They're concerned with the solution to a problem or with the gratification the product offers.

Use signs and graphics as props. Using signs or graphics that masquerade as props (or vice versa) is a great way to unify theme and merchandise for an appealing overall presentation. For instance, images of fruit slices of watermelons, oranges, lemons, limes, or kiwis make colorful signs that tie in with all kinds of summer sales and promotions. A retailer could plan a storewide sale incorporating fruit slices into signage, posters, shopping bags, window displays, banners, and so forth.

Keep signs and graphics fresh. Signs and graphics should be relevant to the items displayed and shouldn't be left in the store or in windows after displays are removed. Forgotten, faded, and fraught with water spots, such signs do more to disparage a store's image than to sell merchandise. Also, new signs imply new merchandise.

Limit the copy of signs. Because a sign's main purpose is to catch attention and inform customers, the copy is important to its overall success. As a general rule, customers won't read signs with too much copy. Customers must be able to quickly grasp the information on the sign as they walk through the store.

Use appropriate typefaces on signs. Using the appropriate typeface is critical to a sign's success. Different typefaces impart different messages and moods. For instance, carefully done calligraphy in an Old English script provides a very different message than a hastily written price reduction sign. Care should be taken not to use intricate, difficult-to-read typefaces because customers may not take the time to figure them out. Also, using different but compatible typefaces provides variety.

Create theatrical effects. Any theatrical set includes special effects that transcend yet coordinate the other elements. To heighten store excitement and enhance store images, retailers have borrowed from the theater. Theatrical effects may be simple extensions of more functional elements, like signs using colored fabric to identify a department. Or bold graphic posters or photographs hung from ceilings and walls to decorate, provide information, or camouflage less aesthetic areas, such as the ceiling structure. Signage at the new It's Really One Dollar store in Florence, Kentucky (pictured on this page), illustrates the theatrical impact that signage can have on the selling environment. If customers remain unconvinced by the large storefront sign screaming in bright red, It's Really One Dollar, walking into the store should do the job. It's a bit like walking into a cartoon; a shopper's first sight is a huge $1.00 sign cut from plastic foamboard and layered bright red on black.[10]

Lighting

Good lighting in a store involves more than simply illuminating space. Lighting is used to highlight merchandise, sculpt space, and capture a mood or feeling that enhances the store's image. Lighting can also be used to downplay less attractive features that can't be changed.

Highlight merchandise. A good lighting system helps create a sense of excitement in the store. At the same time, lighting must provide an accurate color rendition of the merchandise. A green silk tie should look the same color in the store as at the office. Similarly, lighting should complement the customer. A department store's cosmetics area, for instance, requires more expensive lighting than the bare fluorescent lighting found in most grocery stores.

It's Really One Dollar is a chain of stores that sells everything for one dollar. This prototype store, designed by The Retail Group, features cartoon-style graphics and colors that make the simple design come alive.

Another key use of lighting is called **popping the merchandise**—focusing spotlights on special feature areas and items. Using lighting to focus on strategic pockets of merchandise trains shoppers' eyes on the merchandise and draws customers strategically through the store. Popping typically requires that spotlights be three times as bright as general illumination lights so they can burn through the normal light level and steer the customers' eyes.

Structure space and capture a mood. When Greg Feffer was in The Broadway department store shopping for a suit, he noticed his mood changed as he moved from department to department and across aisles. Part of his mood change may have been due to the store planner's explicit lighting plan. Though there's no scientific proof, experience shows that a relaxed environment is reinforced by nonuniform lighting with warm, white light colors. Feffer noticed that the department store used this lighting strategy in the men's department, where he felt a sense of privacy, personalized service, and high quality. But when he moved to the more price-competitive sporting goods department, his mood changed. Here higher light levels, cool tones of white, and peripheral wall brightness complemented the atmosphere of generic products, lower prices, and fewer sales associates.

Downplay features. Lighting can hide errors and outmoded store designs. Cavanaugh's shoe store, for example, has outgrown its space. To increase its storage, it has created a false ceiling of wooden rafters with overstock above. Careful lighting de-emphasizes this area, which could otherwise be an eyesore.

Color

The creative use of color can enhance a retailer's image and help create a mood. Research has shown that warm colors (red and yellow) produce opposite physiological and psychological effects from cool colors (blue and green).[11] For example, red and warm colors have been found to increase blood pressure, respiratory rate, and other physiological responses. Translating these findings to a retail store environment, warm colors are thought to attract customers and gain attention, yet they can be distracting and even unpleasant. Warm colors may be more appropriate in stores that want to generate excitement, such as a fast food restaurant. In contrast, research has shown that cool colors, like blue or green, are relaxing, peaceful, calm, and pleasant. Thus cool colors may be most effective for retailers selling anxiety-causing products, such as expensive shopping goods.

Music

Like color and lighting, music can either add or detract from a retailer's total atmospheric package.[12] Unlike other atmospheric elements, however, music can be easily changed and adjusted with a mere change of tape or radio station. Seattle-based Muzak provides background music for many commercial enterprises, including retailing. It now offers a service that allows retailers to automatically change their music throughout the day to reflect different customers' tastes. For instance, a store might use adult contemporary in the morning and switch to Top 40 when teens start coming in after school.

Retailers can also use music to impact customers' behaviors. Music can control the pace of store traffic, create an image, and attract or direct consumers' attention. For instance, The Limited's Express and Structure use French music to help create a chic international atmosphere that complements the merchandise. The

Disney Stores pipe in soundtracks from famous Disney movies that are tied directly to the merchandise.

Music may also inhibit a customer's ability to evaluate merchandise because the brain can become overloaded with the music. Some customers may become so irritated that they leave the store, while others may actually purchase more because their resistance to sales presentations is lowered.

Scent

Most buying decisions are based on emotions. Of all the human senses, smell has the greatest impact on our emotion.[13] The sense of smell is also the quickest means of changing someone's behavior. As a result, many retailers augment their atmospheric package with carefully planned scents. Consider, for instance, the Knot Shop. While trying on neckties, Knot Shop customers may notice a number of things: the 15-foot oak tree in the center of the store, the witty graphics stenciled on the floors, possibly even the music playing softly in the background. But they probably won't notice the store's fragrance—a blend of oak, leather, and fine tobacco wafting from carefully placed, heat-sensitive pellets. The odor isn't strong enough to register consciously, and it's not meant to be. Its purpose is to appeal subliminally to customers—especially women, who make up about 60 percent of all tie buyers.

Retailers must carefully plan the scents that they use, depending on their target market. Gender of the target customer should be taken into account in deciding on the intensity of the fragrance in a store. Research has shown that women have a better ability to smell than men. Age and ethnic background are also factors. As people get older, their sense of smell decreases. Half of all people over 65 and three-quarters over 80 have almost no sense of smell at all. Re-Tale 13–4 tells how scents can be used (or misused) to sell women's lingerie.

REFACT

A typical category killer store has about 150 lighting fixtures, whereas a 100,000-square-foot department store has over 1,000.

RE-TALE 13–4   The Scent of Frederick's of Hollywood

Scent is becoming a more important component of a store's atmospheric package. Some store planners compare it to selecting appropriate background music, the idea being the more pleasant the atmosphere, the longer customers will remain in the store. Researchers believe that aroma can also directly affect buying behavior.

The crucial decision is what smell to choose, not the intensity. A badly selected odor, however pleasant, may inhibit spending—as women's lingerie retailer Frederick's of Hollywood discovered. Some years ago Frederick's introduced a sweet floral scent in its stores—similar to the one used so successfully in Victoria's Secret. Almost immediately, sales at Frederick's dropped, and the chain pulled the scent. Experts believe the failure resulted from misunderstanding the customer base. Victoria's Secret targets female buyers with its soft, pink boudoir lighting and flattering nightwear. A sweet floral smell worked well there. But provocative Frederick's attracted men shopping for women. Its lingerie was somewhat the male fantasy of women's

undergarments. In such an atmosphere, the sweet scent backfired. The smell probably wasn't pleasing to male customers.

Are certain stores—like Frederick's, for instance—better off avoiding aroma all together? Pinpointing the perfect scent to stimulate sales for a particular store or department involves a number of factors, including not only customer and merchandise, but also the person for whom the customer is buying the merchandise. Perhaps Frederick's should have tried a more sensual fragrance.

In general, women prefer floral smells and men prefer spicy ones. Actually, Frederick's discovered that a male customer may be stimulated by a certain scent when buying a gift for Mom, but turned off by the same scent if he's shopping for lingerie for his wife or girlfriend.

SOURCE: Cathleen McCarthy, "Aromatic Merchandising: Leading Customers by the Nose," *Visual Merchandising and Store Design,* April 1992, pp. 85–87. Based on research by Alan R. Hirsch, M.D.

How are these scents introduced into the store? Retailers can use time-release atomizers available through janitorial supply vendors, or computerized heating and air conditioning systems. But polymer pellets soaked in fragrance and placed in ordinary light fixtures, where the lamp's heat activates the scent, are the most economical way to disperse fragrance.

SUMMARY

This chapter examined issues facing store designers. A good store layout helps customers find and purchase merchandise. Several types of layouts are common. The grid design is best for stores in which customers are expected to explore the entire store, such as grocery stores and drugstores. Racetrack designs are more common in large upscale stores like department stores. Free-form designs are usually found in small specialty stores and within large stores' boutiques. Store planners also must carefully delineate different areas of the store. Feature areas, bulk of stock, and walls each have their own unique purpose, but must also be coordinated to create a unified theme. Fixtures, designed to hold and display merchandise, are an integral component of any store layout.

There's more to assigning space to merchandise and departments than just determining where they'll fit. Department locations should be determined by the overall profitability and inventory turnover goals of the assortment, type of product, consumer buying behavior, the merchandise's relationship to goods in other departments, and the physical characteristics of the merchandise. Retailers use planograms, both manual and computer-generated, to experiment with various space allocation configurations and to determine the most productive use of space.

Several tricks of the trade can help retailers present merchandise to facilitate sales. Retailers must attempt to empathize with the shopping experience and answer the following questions: How does the customer expect to find the merchandise? Is it easier to view, understand, and ultimately purchase merchandise presented as a total concept or merchandise presented by manufacturer, style, size, color, or price?

Retailers use various forms of atmospherics—graphics, signs, and theatrical effects—to facilitate the sale. Strategies involve lighting, colors, music, and scent.

KEY TERMS

Americans with Disabilities Act (ADA), 281
atmospherics, 287
boutique, 275
bulk of stock area, 279
color organization, 286
demand/destination area, 283
end cap, 277
feature area, 277

four-way (feature fixture), 281
free-form layout, 276
freestanding fixture, 278
frontal presentation, 287
gondola, 281
grid layout, 274
idea-oriented presentation, 285
impulse merchandise, 283

planogram, 284
point-of-sale/point-of-purchase (POP) area, 279
popping the merchandise, 290
price lining, 286
promotional aisle or area, 278
racetrack layout (loop), 275

rounder (bulk or capacity fixture), 280
straight rack, 280
style/item organization, 285
tonnage merchandising, 286
vertical merchandising, 286
virtual reality, 271

DISCUSSION QUESTIONS AND PROBLEMS

1. One of the fastest growing sectors of the population is the over-60 age group. These customers may have limited vision, hearing, and mobility. How can retailers develop store designs with the older population's needs in mind?

2. When choosing store fixtures, what issues should retailers consider?

3. Describe the different types of design retailers use in a store layout.

4. Generally speaking, departments near entrances, on major aisles, and on the main level of multilevel stores have the best profit-generating potential. What additional factors help to determine the location of departments? Give examples of each factor.

5. A department store is building an addition. The merchandise manager for furniture is trying to convince the vice president to allot this new space to the furniture department. The merchandise manager for men's clothing is also trying to gain the space. What points should each manager use when presenting his or her rationale?

6. How would a retailer use information provided by a planogram?

7. How would a retailer choose among updating, remodeling, and renovating a store?

8. Which retailers are particularly good at presenting their store as "theater"? Why?

9. Lighting in a store has been said to be similar to makeup on a model. Why?

10. Why do supermarkets put candy, gum, and magazines at the front of the store?

Customer Service

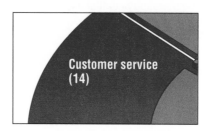

Customer service
(14)

Questions this chapter answers include

- **What services do retailers offer customers?**
- **Why should retailers have good customer service?**
- **How do customers evaluate a retailer's service?**
- **What obstacles hinder retailers in providing good service?**
- **How do retailers improve their customer service?**

ustomer service, the third element in the retail mix undertaken by store management, is the set of activities and programs undertaken by retailers to make the shopping experience more convenient and rewarding for their customers. These activities increase the value customers receive when they shop and purchase merchandise. In a broad sense, retailing is a service business, and all elements of the retailing mix provide services that increase the value of merchandise. Location, in-stock position, and assortments all increase customer convenience. However this chapter focuses on providing the types of customer service in Exhibit 14–1.

Demand for high-quality customer service is increasing dramatically. As discussed in Chapter 3, today's retail customers want hassle-free shopping. They have less time to locate merchandise or to wait to buy it. Joan Tillman (general manager

Services Offered by Retailers

	Department and Specialty Stores	Discount Stores
Acceptance of credit cards	●	●
Alteration of merchandise	●	○
Assembling of merchandise	●	○
Bridal registry	●	○
Check cashing	●	◐
Child-care facilities	◐	○
Credit	●	◐
Delivery to home	◐	◐
Demonstrations of merchandise	●	◐
Displaying of merchandise	●	●
Dressing rooms	●	○
Extended store hours	◐	●
Extensive signage to identify merchandise	◐	●
Gift wrapping	●	●
Facilities for shoppers with special needs (physically handicapped, etc.)	◐	◐
Layaway plan	●	◐
Parking	●	●
Personal assistance in selecting merchandise	●	◐
Personal shoppers	◐	○
Play areas for children	◐	◐
Presentations on how to use merchandise	◐	◐
Provisions for customers with special needs (wheelchairs, translators)	◐	○
Repair services	◐	○
Rest rooms	●	●
Return privileges	●	●
Rooms for checking coats and packages	◐	○
Special orders	◐	◐
Warranties	●	●

● = Frequently   ◐ = Occasionally   ○ = Rarely

of Chicago's Saks Fifth Avenue department store) emphasizes that customer service is the key to retailing success in the 1990s:

> You can buy the same merchandise at several places. If you're a Liz Claiborne customer, you can buy it at Bloomingdale's or buy it from Saks. Consumers are going to buy where they feel the most comfortable shopping. They will be most comfortable shopping when they feel attended to and where they find what they want in a reasonable amount of time.[1]

Exhibit 14–1 shows that some retail formats use customer service to develop a sustainable competitive advantage, while other retail formats provide limited service and have lower costs and prices. McDonald's, Nordstrom, L.L. Bean, Domino's Pizza, Disney World, and Marriott differentiate their retail offering from their competitors' and build customer loyalty by providing excellent customer service. Good service keeps customers returning to a retailer and generates positive word-of-mouth communication, which attracts new customers.

From a long-term perspective, good customer service can actually reduce costs. The Customer Service Institute estimates that it costs five times more to acquire a new customer than to generate repeat business from present customers.[3] Thus it costs much less to keep your existing customers satisfied and to sell more merchandise to them than it costs to sell merchandise to people who aren't buying from you now.

NATURE OF CUSTOMER SERVICE

Two important differences between the service aspect and the merchandise aspect of the retail offering are intangibility and inconsistency.

Intangibility

Most services are intangible—customers can't see or feel them. Clothing can be held and examined, but the assistance provided by a salesperson can't. Intangibility makes it hard to understand what services customers want and how they evaluate the retailer's service. When evaluating merchandise, customers use tangible cues such as color, fit, style, weight, and size. Customers don't have these physical indicators to use when evaluating services.

Intangibility also makes it hard to provide and maintain high-quality service. Retailers can't count, measure, or check service before it's delivered to customers.

Inconsistency

Automated manufacturing makes the quality of most merchandise consistent from item to item. For example, all Super Twist™ Skil electric screwdrivers look alike and typically perform alike. But the quality of retail service can vary dramatically from store to store and from customer to customer within a store. This is because most services are performed by people. It's hard for retailers to control the performance of employees who provide the service. Thus a salesperson may provide good service to one customer and poor service to the next customer.

The difficulty of providing consistent high-quality service provides an opportunity for a retailer to develop a sustainable competitive advantage. For example, Nordstrom devotes much time and effort to developing an organizational culture that fosters and supports excellent customer service. Competing department stores would like to offer the same level of service, but find it hard to match Nordstrom's performance.

Small, independent retailers often attempt to develop a strategic advantage over large, national chains by providing customized customer service. Large chains can use their purchasing power to buy merchandise at lower prices than small local stores. But small retailers can overcome this cost disadvantage by providing better customer service than a large bureaucratic company. Re-Tale 14–1 describes how providing excellent customer service enables a small independent auto tire outlet to maintain margins that are twice the industry average.

Standardization versus Customization of Service

Standardization and customization are two approaches retailers use to develop a sustainable customer service advantage. The **standardization** approach involves requiring service providers to follow a set of rules and procedures when providing service. By strict enforcement of these procedures, inconsistencies in the service are minimized. Through standardization, customers receive the same food and service at McDonald's restaurants across the globe. The food may not be the best tasting food, but it's consistent and served in a timely manner.

RE-TALE 14-1   Customer Service Generates Profits for Direct Tire

As customers approach Direct Tire's 10,000-square-foot store in Watertown, Massachusetts, they see dozens of parked Ferraris, BMWs, and Porsches. Taking a closer look, however, they realize these high-performance cars are outnumbered by aging Honda Civics and Chevy Impalas. Outstanding service attracts a wide variety of customers to a store that sells tires for $10 to $20 more than the Goodyear outlet down the street.

The difference between Direct Tire and competing automotive outlets is apparent when customers walk through the door. The waiting rooms are immaculate and stocked with current magazines (ranging from *Sports Illustrated* to *Vogue*) and freshly brewed coffee. Through windows in every wall, customers can watch Direct Tire's technicians work. Managers and salespeople wear ties and baseball-style jackets with the company logo. Everyone else wears dark blue pants and T-shirts with the company name and slogan. "I've never heard so many yes ma'ams and no ma'ams in my life," says a long-time customer.

If customers need to buy tires and have only an hour, they can schedule an appointment at their convenience. Customers who can't wait for service or to have new tires installed can take one of the company's seven loaner cars and then pick up their car later. Direct Tire also guarantees the tires it sells and the service work it does for the life of the car and tires.

To keep its service promise to its customers, Direct Tire pays a 15 to 25 percent premium to hire the best mechanics and alignment specialists. Then it buys equipment to support these specialists. For example, the firm spent $25,000 for equipment that can diagnose alignment and hydraulic problems in 90 seconds. State-of-the-art equipment improves service and attracts the best technicians.

A $48,000 customized inventory control system reduces customer waiting time. Salespeople can immediately determine what tires are in stock and can print receipts to speed the checkout process. To satisfy the needs of its broad market, Direct Tire maintains an extensive tire inventory—for example, 140 sets of tires for a Porsche 928S.

Highly paid employees, lifetime guarantees, state-of-the-art equipment, and extensive inventory increase Direct Tire's costs. But customers are willing to pay more for good service so Direct Tire's 3 percent profit on sales is twice the industry standard.

SOURCE: Paul Brown, "The Real Cost of Customer Service," *Inc.,* September 1990, pp. 49–58.

On the other hand, a **customization** approach encourages service providers to tailor the service to meet each customer's personal needs. This approach can result in customer's receiving superior service. But the service might be inconsistent because service delivery depends on the judgment and capabilities of the service providers.

CUSTOMER EVALUATION OF SERVICE QUALITY

When customers evaluate retail service, they compare their perceptions of the service they receive with their expectations.[4] Customers are satisfied when the perceived service meets or exceeds their expectations. They're dissatisfied when they feel the service falls below their expectations.

Role of Expectations

Customer expectations are based on a customer's knowledge and experiences with the retailer and its competitors. For example, customers expect a supermarket to provide convenient parking, to be open from early morning to late evening, to have a wide variety of fresh and packaged food that can be located easily, to display products, and to offer fast checkout. They don't expect the supermarket to have store employees stationed in the aisles to offer information about groceries or how

EXHIBIT 14-2 **Cues Customers Use to Evaluate Retail Service**

Tangibles
- Appearance of store
- Display of merchandise
- Appearance of salespeople

Understanding and knowing customer
- Providing individual attention
- Recognizing regular customers

Security
- Feeling safe in parking lot
- Communications and transactions treated confidentially

Credibility
- Reputation for honoring commitments
- Trustworthiness of salespeople
- Guarantees and warranties provided
- Return policy

Information provided to customers
- Explanation of service and its cost
- Notes sent to customers informing them of sales
- Assurances that a problem will be resolved

Courtesy
- Friendliness of employees
- Respect shown to customers
- Interest shown in customers

Access
- Short waiting time to complete sales transaction
- Convenient operating hours
- Convenient location
- Manager available to discuss problems

Competence
- Knowledgeable and skillful employees
- Customers questions answered

Responsiveness
- Returning a customer's call
- Giving prompt service

Reliability
- Accuracy in billing
- Performing service at designated time
- Accuracy in completing sales transaction

SOURCE: Adapted from Valarie Zeithaml, A. Parasuraman, and Leonard Berry, *Delivering Quality Service: Balancing Customer Perceptions and Expectations* (New York: Free Press, 1990), pp. 20–22; and A. Parasuraman, Valarie Zeithaml, and Leonard Berry, "A Conceptual Model of Service Quality and Its Implications for Future Research," *Journal of Marketing* 49 (Fall 1985), pp. 41–50.

to prepare meals. On the other hand, when these same customers shop in a department store, they do expect the store to have knowledgeable salespeople who can provide information and assistance.

Because expectations aren't the same for all types of retailers, a customer may be satisfied with low levels of actual service in one store and dissatisfied with high service levels in another store. For example, customers have low service expectations for self-service retailers such as discount stores and supermarkets. Wal-Mart provides an unusual service for a discount store: An employee stands at the entrance to each store, greeting customers and answering questions. Because this service is unexpected in a discount store, customers evaluate Wal-Mart's service positively even though the actual level of service is far below that provided by a typical department store.

Department stores have many more salespeople available to answer questions and provide information than Wal-Mart does. But customer service expectations are also higher for department stores. If department store customers can't locate a salesperson quickly when they have questions or want to make a purchase, they're dissatisfied.[5]

Raising expectations without increasing perceived service can reduce customer satisfaction. Thus retailers are careful when promoting their service quality. They promise only the service levels they can deliver to customers.

The American Airlines advertising program is designed to reduce the communication gap by explaining why American has difficulty providing on-time flights and what it is doing to address these problems.

Common Complaints about Department Store Shopping   EXHIBIT 14-4

- Every time you want to try on a new item, you have to get dressed and leave the fitting room.
- The department store sells clothes too far in advance, such as selling winter clothes at the end of summer.
- When they have a big sale, they don't have enough help and you have to wait too long.
- If you need a different size while you're in the fitting room, there are no salespeople to get it for you.
- You're not allowed to bring enough garments into the fitting room.
- Department stores have fewer and fewer people to serve you.
- The lines to pay at department stores are too long for you to shop during lunch hour.
- There's no way of telling which size will fit best without trying the garment on.
- You have to go from place to place all over the store to get a refund or exchange.
- When they have a clothing sale, they don't have enough stock in the most popular items.

SOURCE: "Ten Commandments Aid Department Stores," *Chain Store Age Executive,* September 1980, p. 10. Reprinted by permission from CHAIN STORE AGE EXECUTIVE (September 1980). Copyright Lebhar-Friedman, Inc., 425 Park Avenue, New York, NY 10022.

or may use a product incorrectly because they failed to read the instructions. Communication programs can also inform customers about their role and responsibility in getting good service and can give tips on how to get better service (such as the best times of the day to shop and the retailer's policies and procedures for handling problems).

SUMMARY

By offering good service, retailers can increase repeat business and build a sustainable competitive advantage. But consistently providing good service isn't easy.

It's also hard for customers to evaluate service. They do so by comparing their perceptions of the service delivered with their expectations. Thus to improve service, retailers need to know what customers expect, to set standards that provide the expected service, to provide support so store employees can meet the standards, and to realistically communicate the service they offer to customers.

KEY TERMS

communication gap, 301
customer service, 294
customization, 297

delivery gap, 301
empowerment, 308
express warranty, 306

implied warranty, 305
knowledge gap, 301
service gap, 301

standardization, 296
standards gap, 301

DISCUSSION QUESTIONS AND PROBLEMS

1. Nordstrom and McDonald's are noted for their high-quality customer service. But their approaches to providing this quality service are different. Describe this difference.

2. Providing customer service can be very expensive for retailers. Some shopping centers and malls are experimenting with providing central areas for customer service so costs for these services are split among the retailers at the center or mall. What customer services lend themselves to this type of arrangement?

3. What unique aspects of customer service differentiate it from the merchandise being sold?

4. Gaps analysis provides a systematic method of examining a customer service program's effectiveness. J.C. Penney top management has told a systems manager that customers are complaining about the long wait to pay for merchandise at the checkout station. How can the systems manager use gaps analysis to analyze this problem and suggest approaches for reducing this time?

5. How could an effective customer service strategy cut a retailer's costs?

6. Employees play a critical role in customer perceptions of quality service. If you were hiring salespeople, what characteristics would you look for to assess their ability to provide good customer service?

7. Why is good communication between customer-contact employees and management important in providing high-quality customer service?

Retail Selling

CHAPTER

15

Retail selling (15)

Questions this chapter answers include

- **What are retail salespeople's duties and responsibilities?**
- **Why are communication skills important for effective selling?**
- **What are the steps in selling merchandise to a customer?**
- **How can salespeople improve their listening and questioning skills?**

T o many customers, the salespeople are the store. Typically they're the only employees with whom a retailer's customers come in contact. Salespeople help customers satisfy their needs by providing the retail services discussed in Chapter 14. Their actions can stimulate return visits to a store and build customer loyalty.

Salespeople help their store realize its goals by selling merchandise. Retailers make profits only when merchandise is sold. Thus all of a retailer's employees are either providing customer service and selling merchandise, or supporting someone who does.

To be effective, store managers must understand the sales process. Many retailers require management trainees to spend considerable time selling during their first year in a management training program. Through this initial selling assignment, trainees develop understanding of the firm's customers—what they want and how they buy merchandise. They also gain appreciation for problems salespeople face.

ROLES OF RETAIL SALESPEOPLE

Salespeople span the boundary between the retail firm and its customers. Even the most appealing merchandise doesn't sell itself. Retailers need to communicate with customers to stimulate needs, provide information to help customers evaluate merchandise, and encourage them to make a purchase decision. These communications are delivered by ads, sales promotions, publicity, signs and displays in the store, and salespeople.

As shown in Exhibit 11–4, these communication vehicles are used to affect different stages of the customer's decision-making process. Advertising, publicity, and sales promotions create awareness and build an image of the store. Messages delivered through these media presell the store and its merchandise. Salespeople provide more detailed information and actually make the sale.

Salespeople have a unique potential as communication vehicles. They can develop and present a message tailored to each customer they encounter. Salespeople can also gauge the customer's reactions and alter the presentation during the interaction. This flexibility makes the salesperson the retailer's most effective communication vehicle—and the most expensive.

Many retailers call their salespeople **sales associates** or **sales consultants.** These terms recognize the important and professional nature of the sales function and avoid the negative image sometimes linked with the term *salesperson.* They also emphasize that the role of sales people is to use their knowledge about merchandise to help customers solve problems—just like a business consultant.

Many people find retail selling to be a rewarding, exciting career. Re-Tale 15–1 describes a salesperson who earns over $100,000 per year selling women's shoes in Tyler, Texas.

THE RETAIL SELLING PROCESS

To sell merchandise, salespeople must move customers through the five stages of the buying process (discussed in Chapter 4). The **selling process** is a set of activities that salespeople undertake to facilitate the customer's buying decision. The stages in the selling process and the buying process are closely linked (Exhibit 15–1 on page 316).

In the first stage of the selling process, salespeople approach customers with unsatisfied needs and try to stimulate problem recognition. In the second stage, customers search for information to satisfy their needs, and salespeople collect information about customers so they can determine what merchandise might be appropriate. In the third stage, salespeople present and demonstrate merchandise to assist customers' evaluation of alternatives. Then the salespeople attempt to make a sale—to motivate customers to purchase merchandise. Finally, salespeople build future sales by influencing customers' postpurchase evaluations of the merchandise and offering follow-up service. Re-Tale 15–2 on page 317 describes a sales process from a customer's point of view.

Not every sale goes through each step in the sales process, just as not every purchase goes through every step in the buying process. Sometimes steps occur in an order different from that in Exhibit 15–1, but these steps do illustrate the set of activities retail salespeople perform as they sell merchandise.[1]

Approaching Customers

The **approach** to a customer is a method for getting the customer's attention and building interest in the merchandise quickly. The approach is particularly important in retail selling. In many other sales situations, salespeople can obtain information

Selling Benefits, Not Features

EXHIBIT 15-3

Presentation Emphasizing Features	Presentation Emphasizing Benefits
This chinaware has a hard glaze that is applied after the pattern is on the cups and plates. The handles are molded into the cup before it is fired. All the china is fired at 2600˚F.	This chinaware will last a long time. It is stronger than most chinaware because it is fired at 2600˚F. To prevent the cup handles from breaking off, they are molded into the cup body before it is fired. The pattern will also last a long time. It won't fade because a hard leadless glaze is applied over the pattern.

benefits doesn't help the customer understand how and why the merchandise can deliver the benefits. Features are included in the presentation to assure customers that the benefits will be delivered. Exhibit 15–3 contrasts a presentation that emphasizes features with one that stresses benefits.

Demonstrating the Merchandise. In-store shoppers, unlike catalog customers, can see the features and benefits of the product demonstrated. Demonstrations are most effective when they appeal to the senses of sound, touch, sight, taste, or smell.

A demonstration can generate excitement and enthusiasm by giving the customer hands-on experience with the product. Hands-on experience shows customers what the product will do for them. In cosmetics, customer involvement is usually the deciding factor in making a sale. When a customer isn't sure what color is best for her, the salesperson can help her try different colors to see how they look. By demonstrating a range of cosmetic products in a makeover, the salesperson can sell multiple items rather than a single product.

The most effective demonstrations occur when the customer gets actively involved:

"Feel how soft this sweater is."

"See how this suit makes you look younger."

"Hear the quality of these speakers."

Handling Reservations

Often customers have reservations about making a purchase. **Reservations** or **objections** are concerns raised by the customer. Salespeople must anticipate potential reservations and know how to respond to them.

Reservations can arise at each stage in the sales process. For example, a customer may not be willing to talk with a salesperson during the approach. Reservations can also arise when the salesperson is presenting merchandise.

Types of Reservations. Some common reservations (Exhibit 15–4) arise because the customer doesn't want to buy at the time or isn't satisfied with the price, the merchandise, the store and its service, or the salesperson.

Customers often resist making an immediate decision. They may say, "I haven't made up my mind," "I'll have to talk it over with my wife," or "I think I'll wait awhile." These reservations indicate the customer isn't convinced of the need for

EXHIBIT 15-4 **Types of Reservations**

the merchandise or its benefits. The real reason for postponing the purchase may be the price or the merchandise itself. Also some customers just don't like to make decisions. Reassurance works better than pressure with indecisive customers.

Price is probably the most common source of customers' reservations. Regardless of the price, someone will consider it too high, out of line, or higher than another retail outlet's price. Other common price reservations include "I can't afford it," "I was looking for a cheaper model," or "I'm going to wait for this to go on sale."

Objections involving the merchandise include "The quality of this screen door is poor," "The dress is the wrong size," "I don't think this copying machine looks good," or "I don't like the material in this suit."

Customers might not like the store itself. For example, customers might visit a store for a sale even though they usually don't shop there. During such a visit, they may feel uncomfortable about buying merchandise. These customers may need additional information about merchandise quality and the store's return policy.

Customers also can have reservations about a specific salesperson. The salesperson's personality, behavior, or dress might clash with the customer's expectations. The customer may be thinking, "I don't like dealing with this person." The salesperson probably can't overcome this reservation so it's best for everyone involved to direct the customer to another salesperson. The store is more likely to make a sale, and the other salesperson may later reciprocate.

Effective salespeople know the types of reservations likely to be raised. They may know that their merchandise is more expensive than competitors', that their selection in a particular category is limited, or that the store doesn't accept a particular credit card. While not all reservations can be overcome, effective salespeople can anticipate and handle some objections in their sales presentation. For example, a salesperson might say, "This power drill is expensive, but let me show you how many different things you can do with it."

using such a direct approach. The direct approach works best with decisive customers who want to get down to business.

In assuming the sale is made, the salesperson allows the customer to follow the path of least resistance. Again, be careful using this approach because customers may feel that the salesperson is pushy. Here are some questions that can be used in an assumptive approach:

"Do you want to charge the lumber?"

"Why don't you try on the pants while I get the tailor to see if any alterations are necessary?"

Giving the customer a choice is another version of this approach. Remember, the choice is between two items or a set of items. It's never between buying the merchandise or not buying the merchandise. Here are some examples that involve choices:

"Would you like the 30-piece or 48-piece set of this china?"

"Do you prefer to buy this on our monthly billing plan or pay for it now?"

Building a series of acceptances is actually a method for building up to a sale. Customers typically find it hard to refuse to buy merchandise when they agree that it satisfies their needs. By getting a customer to answer questions with a series of yeses, he makes some easy decisions leading up to the buying decision. For example:

Salesperson: This tie goes well with your suit, don't you think?
Customer: Yes, it certainly does.
Salesperson: The 100 percent silk fabric certainly gives it a rich appearance, doesn't it?
Customer: Yes. Silk ties are very striking.
Salesperson: Is the tie in your price range?
Customer: It's a little high, but it's in the range.
Salesperson: Do you want to charge the tie or pay cash for it?

Emphasizing an impending event motivates a customer to buy immediately. The technique stresses that customers will lose something if they hesitate to purchase the merchandise. For example:

"The sale ends today. Tomorrow the price goes up $20."

"This is the only remote-control TV we have with stereo sound."

"The weather is beginning to turn cold, and these skis are going to sell fast."

Selling Multiple Items

Effective salespeople suggest additional items before the original sales transaction is completed. It's much easier to convince a customer to add on to a sale than to begin an entirely new sales process for additional items. Many retailers keep track of their salespeople's multiple-item sales and use this information to evaluate employee performance. (See Chapter 12.)

Customers appreciate new ideas and suggestions for items that will go with merchandise they've already decided to buy. Accessories, for example, can offer variety and excitement to a wardrobe. Effective salespeople can point out that adding the right look in scarves, wearing the right shoes, and/or pinning the right piece of jewelry to a scarf will create the special effect a customer is seeking.

When selling additional items, salespeople should avoid becoming too aggressive. The salesperson can mention available merchandise without offending a

By showing the customer how to use the video recorder, this electronics salesperson builds goodwill and loyalty.

customer. But trying to sell a CD player to a customer who came in for a record might be annoying. When additional suggestions are appropriate, the salesperson should make them in a positive way. Asking "Anything else?" isn't as effective as saying "You'll need some film for your new camera."

BUILDING RELATIONSHIPS FOR FUTURE SALES

The relationship between a customer and a salesperson shouldn't end when a sale is made. It's becoming increasingly important for salespeople to build long-term relationships with customers so they'll return to the store and seek out the salesperson the next time they're buying.[3]

Goodwill is the value of customers' feelings or attitudes toward the retailer and salespeople. The fundamental method for building goodwill is to make sure customers are satisfied with the merchandise they purchase. Customer satisfaction is achieved when salespeople are customer-oriented and not sales-oriented.[4] Customer-oriented salespeople focus their attention on the customer's needs, not just on making a sale. The use of deception or overly aggressive behavior to make a sale builds ill will, not goodwill.

Methods for building goodwill include keeping the customer's interest paramount, reaffirming the customer's judgment, and ensuring proper use of the merchandise, handling customer complaints, remembering the customer between visits, and providing "above and beyond" service.

Reaffirming the Customer's Judgment

Customers are often unsure about their decisions after making a purchase, especially if the item is costly. Salespeople can increase the chances that customers will be satisfied with their purchases simply by reassuring them. A salesperson might

Building a Relationship with a Customer

EXHIBIT 15-5

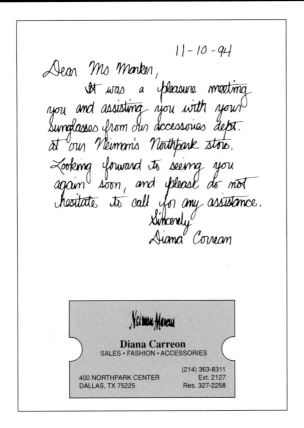

say, "I'm sure you'll get a lot of good use out of your computer," or "Be sure to call me if you need any help. I'm eager to hear how your guests like your dress. Here's my card."

Many salespeople send handwritten notes to customers thanking them for making a purchase and ensuring them of good service in the future. Exhibit 15–5 shows an example.

If customers aren't familiar with the merchandise, they can become dissatisfied when they first use it. Computer salespeople can build goodwill by visiting a customer right after the computer is delivered to make sure the customer knows how to use it. A salesperson who has just sold several suits, ties, and shirts to a customer may make up a chart to show the different combinations that look good. This chart may help the customer realize the full potential benefits of the clothing he's purchased.

Customers may be satisfied with the merchandise they've purchased but may not get the maximum benefits from it if they're not aware of its capabilities. Salespeople should take the time after a sale to demonstrate how the merchandise is used. They should make sure customers receive instructions and special brochures provided by the manufacturer. When manufacturers provide new information, the

Ensuring Proper Use of the Merchandise

salesperson has an excellent opportunity to develop goodwill by sending the information to customers who purchased the merchandise in the past.

Handling Customer Complaints

Responding to customer complaints gives the salesperson an excellent opportunity to build goodwill. Most customers don't go to the trouble of complaining to the store even if they're dissatisfied. When a customer takes the time to complain, salespeople should view it as an opportunity to demonstrate their concern for the customer's satisfaction.

Remembering the Customer between Visits

Keeping in contact with customers between store visits is an effective means to build goodwill. Some methods for maintaining customer contact are phoning a customer when new merchandise arrives, taking special orders to secure the merchandise sought by the customer, setting aside merchandise the customer might want, calling the customer to make an appointment for a private showing of new merchandise, and following up on merchandise sold to see if the customer is satisfied with it.

Providing Above-and-Beyond Service

Salespeople build long-term relationships with their customers by providing service above and beyond customer expectations. Here's an example of above-and-beyond service from a study of star salespeople:

> Cathy works in the jeans department, but you could not tell this from her sales records. She goes wherever her customers' needs take her. For example, one customer called and asked Cathy to pick out a birthday present for her granddaughter, who happens to like boyswear. Cathy went to the boys department, found some items she thought the little girl would like, charged them to the grandmother, had them gift wrapped, and sent them to the grandmother.[5]

Re-Tale 15–3 describes sales practices at Nordstrom, a department store chain noted for its above-and-beyond service.

Building Special Relationships

Customers develop strong relationships with salespeople who offer functionality, friendship, and trust.[6] As discussed in Chapter 3, time is becoming a scarce resource for consumers. Some don't have much time to shop and many consumers don't like to shop. Customers rely on salespeople who save them time and offer useful advice.

Sales associates often develop strong friendships with their customers, although these are business friendships and don't extend beyond the workplace. For example, a customer interviewed in a research project referred to a salesperson as being "like family" and brought baked goods to her to show her appreciation. Re-Tale 15–4 describes how SteinMart, an off-price chain, hires society women to sell merchandise to their friends.

As we said in Chapter 12, trust is the critical element in building long-term relationships between salespeople and customers, and between vendors and retailers. Customers trust salespeople who are dependable and honest, and who take the customers' perspectives. A quote from the previously mentioned study of star salespeople reveals these traits:

> If I don't think it's going to look good on you, I will tell you. I find the key is being honest. If you can really speak truthfully from your heart, it works. Lots of salespeople just sell to make the sale, but I sell from the customer's point of view.[7]

RE-TALE 15-3   Selling at Nordstrom

At Nordstrom, salespeople don't just tell customers how to solve their problems; they assume personal responsibility. Customers aren't told to go to a credit office to correct a mistake in a bill. They aren't passed along to different salespeople or directed to different departments. The salespeople they talk with are personally responsible for making the customers happy.

Tales of service above and beyond the call of duty abound. For example, a Nordstrom customer brought back a pair of shoes a year after buying them and asked if they could be repaired. The salesperson provided a new pair instead. In cold climates, salespeople have been known to warm up a customer's car while the customer pays for merchandise. If Nordstrom doesn't have a size or color that a customer wants, a salesperson will go to a competing store in the mall that carries the merchandise, buy it for the customer, and then sell it to the customer at the price charged at Nordstrom.

When merchandise is returned, the salesperson who made the original sale is debited, and commissions made on the sale are lost. This policy emphasizes to the salesperson that keeping customers satisfied is critical. The salesperson has a stake in making every sale the final sale.

New salespeople are given a "personal" book. The store manager explains that the personal book represents the salesperson's income. In the book, the salesperson keeps track of customers' names, telephone numbers, likes and dislikes, charge account numbers, and anything else that will help the salesperson become a personal shopper for the customer. New salespeople also receive personal and business cards and an open account to send thank-you notes or flowers to customers.

At Nordstrom, newly hired salespeople typically earn from $7 to $10 per hour, $2 per hour above the typical local retail wages. Compensation is based totally on sales generated. An experienced salesperson can gross between $50,000 and $80,000 per year.

Nordstrom pays salespeople well, but its expectations of them are high. Each salesperson's sales per hour are posted on bulletin boards near the employee entrances to the store. Nordstrom also stresses ethics and teamwork. A salesperson who knowingly takes sales from customers being serviced by another salesperson will be fired immediately.

SOURCE: Samuel Feinberg, "What Makes Nordstrom So Special," *Women's Wear Daily,* June 28, 1989, p. 14; Samuel Feinberg, "Book Spotlights Firms' Service from All Angles," *Women's Wear Daily,* June 27, 1989, p. 12; and Ron Zemke and Dick Schaaf, *The Service Edge: 101 Companies That Profit from Customer Care* (New York: Plume, 1990), pp. 352–55.

RE-TALE 15-4   SteinMart's Boutique Ladies Sell through Personal Relationships

Jay Stein, chairman of SteinMart, an off-price chain, says, "The boutique ladies are our secret weapon." Back in the 1980s, SteinMart began hiring wives of local business executives, doctors, and lawyers to sell merchandise in the store's designer boutique. The "boutique ladies" have limited work experience, but they have extensive networks of friends developed through volunteer charity work. They also have a flair for fashion and an enthusiasm that draws their friends to the store.

For example, when a shipment of $39 designer silk separates arrived, boutique lady Joy Abney (wife of the former managing partner of Coopers & Lybrand) "got right on the horn and told them to get over here." Her friends spent $2,000 in her department that day.

There's a waiting list to be a boutique lady at SteinMart. The 1,200 boutique ladies typically work one day a week and are excused from cash register duty and evening shifts. Many of the women are pleased to find out that an older woman without a resume is welcome in the workplace. "My husband thought the only thing I could do was car pool, but working here comes natural." It's a lot like volunteer work, one said, because "you are helping people. It's also fun to get a paycheck that's all mine."

SOURCE: Teri Agins, "Clerking at SteinMart Is a Society Lady's Dream Come True," *The Wall Street Journal,* December 2, 1992, pp. A1, A5.

SUMMARY

Salespeople are an important element in the retail mix. They're responsible for making sales and providing services that produce satisfied, loyal customers.

The sale begins when the salesperson approaches a customer, but the process doesn't end when the customer decides to buy something. The salesperson needs to encourage and assist the customer in buying complementary merchandise. These add-on sales are important aspects of a store's profitability, and they increase customers' satisfaction from their purchases. The sales process ends when a customer is satisfied with the merchandise and decides to return to the store. Making a sale is just one step in developing a loyal customer—the goal salespeople should have every time they interact with customers.

KEY TERMS

approach, 314
benefit, 320
buying signals, 326

feature, 320
goodwill, 328

reservation
 (objection), 321
sales associate, 314

sales consultant, 315
selling process, 314

DISCUSSION QUESTIONS AND PROBLEMS

1. What do you think about the following statement? "Good salespeople need to be aggressive. They need to have a powerful voice and a winning smile."
2. Assume you're selling bedding—sheets and pillowcases. What questions might you ask a potential customer?
3. A customer raises the following reservations. How do you respond?
   a. "I really like all the things this copier does, but I don't think it's going to be very reliable. With all those features, something's got to go wrong."
   b. "Your price for this printer is higher than the price I saw advertised in a mail-order catalog."
   c. "These suits just never fit me right."
4. Some retail stores, such as Nordstrom, require salespeople to concentrate a significant amount of their effort on serving customers. Speaking as a manager in charge of salespeople, discuss whether problems can arise when salespeople concentrate too much on providing service.
5. The sales profession has been accused of having more than its share of unethical people. Some people say the very nature of sales—convincing people to buy something—leaves the profession

open to abuse. How can a salesperson be successful in sales and still maintain high ethical standards?
6. Because of increasing competition among retailers, price can differentiate one retailer from another. A retail salesperson often can't do much about an objection to price. What counterargument could you give a customer who objects to a price?
7. When handling merchandise return, sometimes retail salespeople treat the customer with little interest or attention. In fact, some salespeople resent the customer's using up valuable selling time. How can the handling of merchandise returns build customer loyalty?
8. Distinguish between a product's benefits and features. Why must retail salespeople understand the difference?
9. "All methods for trying to get a customer to buy merchandise are devious and self-serving!" Comment.
10. Should a salesperson handle all complaints so that a customer is completely satisfied?
11. How can a salesperson oversell a customer?

Cases for Section 4

The Metro-Day department store in downtown Seattle specializes in well-made clothing plus up-to-the-minute kitchen items and home furnishings. Of the six Metro-Day stores around the country, it's ranked number 1 in terms of sales volume and store standards. It's also the home of the company's Executive Training Program for training future store managers.

A rising star with Metro-Day, Max Murphy had graduated from the training program himself only two years ago and had done well with his first two assignments at other Metro locations. When an opening arose in the Seattle store, Max jumped at the chance. Not only would he be getting a promotion to sales manager of the Kitchen and Home Furnishings Department, he'd also get to teach that section of the training program. Max had done well in the training program and had gained the reputation of being a sharp, creative manager at both assignments prior to the Seattle promotion.

His first few months of managing the new department went smoothly. Max had gotten most of the usual personnel gripes under control and had familiarized and remerchandised the stock in his area to boost sales 20 percent over last year's figures. The first batch of two trainees came through the program with high marks, singing Max's praises. He was not only a smart merchant, but also a fair, honest, caring trainer.

Four people—twice the normal number—were going through the second training program. One of them, Sue Baker, presented Max with concerns. Sue would often show up late or work on written homework when she was supposed to be managing sections of the sales floor with the other trainees. Max knew he needed to sit down and talk with Sue after two weeks of working with her, but whenever he had a chance to talk with her, she was either absent—she was sick often—or somewhere other than the department. With three other trainees plus Christmas preparations, Max was very busy.

Max finally cornered Sue and spoke to her about her performance, highlighting his concerns. She seemed to take the conversation very personally. She said that Max didn't understand that she had car problems and allergies and that, not being a parent himself, wouldn't understand her responsibilities when her two children were sick. She claimed that when she was on the sales floor, he wasn't around. Max tried to be sympathetic to Sue's situation, but made it clear that she had responsibilities to the store. The conversation ended with both parties agreeing to try to do better.

Midway through the program, all trainees were to turn in progress sheets for Max to initial and rate. All did so but Sue. Max asked Sue for the report twice, but she never seemed to get it to him. By the end of the program, Max turned in a final report on all trainees. Now Sue came through with her midway review sheets as well. Both reports would need passing marks for the trainee to move on to the next section of the store. Sue's work on the second half was passable, but just barely. Looking over the review sheet for the first part of the program—with so much time passing between and the problems with Sue's attendance and work performance—made it almost impossible, in Max's mind, to evaluate Sue fairly.

Max was befuddled. He honestly didn't believe that Sue had successfully completed the program and couldn't fairly evaluate her on the first half. But he felt partly responsible for her failure since he hadn't pushed her harder to get her work turned in, though it's true that he had pushed her twice as hard as the other trainees. To further complicate matters, the program was a "self-motivated" one and the trainees knew up front that Max wasn't there to baby-sit them.

Discussion Question:

1. What should Max do?

This case was prepared by Professor Laura Bliss, Stephens College.

CASE 4-2 ☼ STOCKWORK—UGH!

A difficult personnel situation has arisen in the junior dress department of a major urban store. This department is managed by a bright young buyer named Christine Newman, who is considered a real comer by store management. Her assistant, Jean Cisco, is the same age, 25, and has recently earned a degree in human relations.

The problem results from the huge amount of stockwork generated by Saturday traffic in the store. No sooner are the dressing rooms emptied of merchandise discarded by one customer than a flood of new customers rushes in with an armload of additional garments. The department's normal complement of six full-timers, three part-timers, and two stockpeople is unable to keep up with the flow. Consequently, the exit from the dressing room is a constant mess. Merchandise is often not returned to the racks quickly enough to be picked up by other customers, and is indeed in serious danger of being damaged.

The salespeople in the department respect their two executives, but are inclined to resent their youth, attractiveness, and apparent success. Both Newman and Cisco are sensitive to their employees' feelings, and try constantly to treat them well. Day-off requests are always honored fairly, raises have been recommended and received, and Newman has occasionally marked down a dress very low to enable one of the department's employees to buy it.

On busy Saturdays, Cisco invariably bakes cookies for the staff and tries to be on the selling floor at all times to help direct. Both have often petitioned management for increases in the departmental budget, but have been told that the store is on an "austerity budget" and cannot authorize an increase in staff.

Among the comments of the salespeople that Newman and Cisco have overhead are:

"There are just too many customers in this place on busy days."

"Whenever I holler for the stockgirl, she's off the floor."

"If only customers wouldn't be such slobs. They just refuse to zip up their discards and take them out of the dressing rooms."

"I'm paid on commission. I don't have time to waste on stockwork."

"If I drop a customer to pick up some unwanteds, Rosie will jump in and grab my customer."

"I was hired to sell, not to pick up after somebody else."

Discussion Question:

1. Do you have any suggestions to offer the beleaguered Newman?

Case prepared by Professor David Ehrlich, Marymount University.

CASE 4-3 ☼ FOODTOWN OF OYSTER BAY

For 13 years entrepreneur executive Irwin Tantleff has enjoyed steady growth of his small chain of four independently owned and operated supermarkets on Long Island, New York. Foodtown of Oyster Bay (Tantleff's first store) is in a very competitive market which also includes four chains: A&P, Bohack, Gristede, and Associated. Any increase in Foodtown's market share must be at the expense of its competitors. The future of his Foodtown stores (in particular, the Foodtown of Oyster Bay) depends on merchandising creativity to maintain their competitive advantage and dominant market position.

Mr. Tantleff is experimenting with a new store layout where display gondolas are laid out diagonally rather than in the traditional grid. He finds that shoppers are more likely to shop the periphery of the supermarket, where perishable departments are located, when grocery gondolas are laid out diagonally, leading customers primarily to the perishable sections.

To evaluate the modified floor plan's effectiveness, Mr. Tantleff changed the Oyster Bay store but didn't modify a similar store in Deer Park. Marketing researchers followed 100 customers at each store to determine traffic patterns and then administered questionnaires in the checkout area. The time and dollar amount spent in the store were recorded along with measures of customer satisfaction. Perishable sales at Oyster Bay were 6.5 percent higher than at the traditional Deer Park store. The researchers' only explanation for the increased sales was the modified layout of the gondolas. Customers preferred the diagonal design.

Traffic flow studies indicated that rates of exposure to the grocery aisles with a diagonal grid tend to be lower than for aisles with conventional grids, and use of space may not be as efficient, but the perishable sections enjoyed greater exposure.

Service and specialty perishables departments are arranged on the perimeters of a conventional Foodtown in Deer Park, New York (top), and in a Foodtown in Oyster Bay, New York, with grocery aisles laid out in a diagonal grid (below). A Long Island University study found shoppers were drawn more easily to the perishables departments in the Oyster Bay unit. The numbers in the floor plans correspond to the following departments: (1) produce; (1a) salad bar; (2) meat; (2a) poultry; (2b) service meat; (3) seafood; (4) deli; (5) bakery; (6) dairy. Not all departments were broken out in both floor plans.

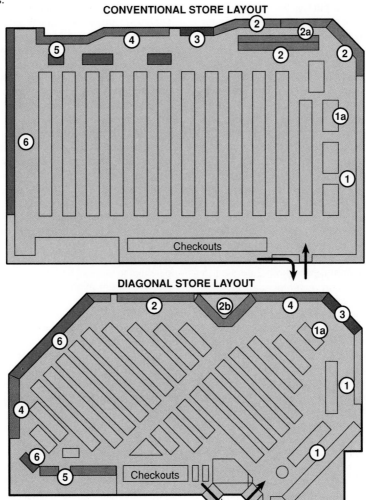

CONVENTIONAL STORE LAYOUT

DIAGONAL STORE LAYOUT

SCHEMATIC I:
Conventional store layout. Shoppers aren't directed toward products at rear and sides of store, where refrigerated compartments house dairy, meat, frozen foods, and other high-ticket items.

SCHEMATIC II:
Diagonal store layout. Customers are rapidly drawn into store perimeter, where high-profit perishable items are displayed.

Discussion Questions:

1. How do you think grocery shoppers will react to the new layout initially? Over time? Why?

2. What are the benefits and costs of the new layout for the store? for customers?

This case was prepared by Professors Richard Rausch and Anderson, Hofstra University.

CASE 4-4 ☼ THE BEST DISPLAY?

Recognizing that its first-floor selling fixtures had become outmoded, a major department store set aside funds to renovate. The main floor hadn't been changed appreciably since the store was built in the 1920s. There were a number of handsome mahogany-paneled counter islands, which had always given the store an aura of tasteful elegance.

Jim Lewis, director of store fixturing, was debating the merits of several possible display systems. The selling departments that would be affected by the renovation were cosmetics; fine and costume jewelry; women's handbags, scarves, and belts; men's shirts, ties, and furnishings; women's sweaters; and gifts.

As Lewis saw it, the two major issues surrounding his decision were incompatible. On the one hand, the store wanted to make merchandise as accessible to customers as possible. On the other hand, experience indicated that open-selling fixtures inevitably lead to more shoplifting.

As an experiment, the store had tried substituting self-service fixtures in its upstairs sweater department a year earlier. Sales jumped 30 percent, but inventory shrinkage in the department had gone from 2 percent to almost 5 percent.

A further consideration was that the size and quality of the staff on the selling floor had declined dramatically. In 1929, there were always two salespeople behind every counter. Customers could count on never having to wait for service. But due to escalating selling costs, the store's staff was now less than half what it had been then. Furthermore, the store had instituted modern point-of-sale cash registers that enabled every salesperson to ring up a sale from any department in the store at any register. Most clerks were paid minimum wage and were only working there until something better turned up. Although some could provide useful selling information to the public, most could do little more than ring up sales.

The kind of open-selling fixtures Lewis was considering were contemporary and very attractive. They allowed the customer to pick up, unfold, or unpackage merchandise; try it on if appropriate; and then return it to the fixture. Such fixtures would unquestionably lead to more sales, especially since the customer could merely look for any salesperson or perhaps go to a central cashier to pay. But, equally unquestionably, such easy access to merchandise—especially to small goods—would encourage shoplifting and would increase the need for ongoing stock keeping.

Another disadvantage to the new type of fixturing was that, besides being contemporary, it was somewhat trendy, so it would have to be replaced in a few years, adding to capital costs.

An alternative system would be to retain the old counter islands or a portion of them, but to put more goods on the countertops to encourage a measure of self-service. The disadvantage here, of course, would be blocked sight lines. Salespeople couldn't see customers, customers couldn't see salespeople, and the store security personnel couldn't see either. There would also need to be more policing by the store's display and merchandising staff to be sure the countertops looked inviting at all times. Manufacturers often contribute countertop displays to stores as part of the merchandise buying, and many of them might not be in harmony with the store's overall appearance.

Lewis recognized that he would have to make some compromises. Every affected department has its own peculiarities, and his job was to minimize those differences, rather than allow them to get out of hand. Some merchandise, such as fine jewelry, would obviously have to remain behind glass, but other departments would probably do much better by opening up their stocks to the public.

Discussion Questions:

1. What display system would you recommend? Why?
2. Would you make the same recommendation for each of the affected departments? Why?

This case was prepared by David Ehrlich, Marymount University.

CASE 4-5 ☼ CHECK THIS SYSTEM OUT

Six months ago, when he reviewed the year-end statements of his company, Action Jackson, the president. David Jackson, had not been pleased. Although the prior year's sales showed a sizable gain over the previous year, the net income did not increase.

The problem, he perceived clearly, was in the expenses, and specifically in the payroll cost, which appeared to be far out of line.

Action Jackson was a group of three ship's chandleries, stores that catered to the Florida yachting trade. The stores were all located adjacent to major boating marinas in the South Florida area, and had been there for more than 15 years.

Each store was about 5,000 square feet in size and was organized into a number of departments staffed by men who had spent years in the trade. During the winter, which was the peak season, the selling staff of each store consisted of about 12 men, most of them full-time workers. The stores were open 10 hours a day, seven days a week. The average sale, which was approximately $75, consisted of perhaps a dozen items, from a vast inventory that ranged in price from as little as 50 cents to several thousand dollars.

Jackson had long practiced the philosophy that he was running a true service business. "Sailors," he felt, "are thorough shoppers. They don't come ashore that often, and want to make their purchasing trips as quick and efficient as possible. They have thousands of dollars tied up in their boats, and want to spend every spare moment on them, not messing around in a landlubber's store." So he always insisted that his salespeople accompany customers through every step of their visits to the stores.

Increasingly over the previous two years, though, Jackson had noticed that the average price of items sold had been dropping. The stores were selling more low-priced accessories for boaters' convenience and fewer high-ticket items like sails, motors, and sonar systems. Yet the practice of assigning a single salesperson to each customer had never changed. Each customer was to be greeted by a salesperson upon entry, and that salesperson was to attend to every one of the customer's needs, whether it was cutting a line for rigging or showing a pair of rubber gloves for cleaning the galley, right through finally ringing up the sale.

But he began to wonder whether too much of his salespeople's time was being spent on providing too much service for inexpensive items for which customers really did not need help. If he could streamline his service operation by removing at least the final process, that of ringing up the sale and packaging the merchandise, from the salespeople, it might free them to spend more time doing what really counted—selling higher-priced merchandise that truly required selling expertise.

As he looked over his stores' layout, he realized that it would cost very little to reorganize them to enable customers to select many items for themselves. Furthermore, if he located a convenient central checkout adjacent to the store exists, purchasers could be processed more quickly and efficiently. And finally, he would be able over time to reduce the average store's salesforce by about 20 percent, and substitute a minimum-wage person to handle the checkout island.

Such a system was not without risks, though. In the first place, some items were small enough to be slipped into thieves' pockets, and would not be spotted by the checkout clerk. Second, some customers, operating unassisted, might take the wrong item and later blame the store for not having given them better information. And third, removing the constant attention of individual salespeople would introduce a note of impersonality to what had always been a highly personal business.

He decided, therefore, to proceed slowly, making changes in only one of his three stores. Taking advantage of a couple of retirements, he cut his staff and instructed his remaining salespeople to simply circulate on the floor, providing assistance only if asked. Customers were provided with shopping carts to push around the store, and were free to ask for information from any salesperson. An island was constructed next to the store exit and staffed with a minimum-wage clerk. As all merchandise was already price-ticketed, there was no need to provide any additional information for this clerk to make the sale.

Six months later, he assessed the result of these changes. Sales in the affected store fell by about 5 percent, but net profits rose by 15 percent. In the meantime, sales in the other two stores had gone up at about the same rate as the previous year's increase, but the profits continued to sink.

At this point, Jackson is uncertain about how to proceed. The drop in sales, he feels, is temporary, and will be reversed in time. However, he has clearly found the key to higher profitability, and wants to pursue it, even though that might be at the expense of the store's ambience.

Discussion Questions:

1. Evaluate the advantages and disadvantages of Mr. Jackson's new plan for organizing his store.
2. As an old customer of the store, what friendly advice would you offer David Jackson? Should he implement the changes in all stores, wait another six months, or discontinue the changes? Why?
3. Do you have a better plan for organizing Mr. Jackson's store?

This case was prepared by Professor David Ehrlich, Marymount University.

CASE 4-6 ☼ RIVER VALLEY GOURMET SHOP

Located in a popular New England resort town, the River Valley Gourmet Shop opened for business just three months ago. Its customers come through on vacation trips, stopping to purchase locally produced food items such as homemade breads and pastries, candy, jams and jellies, plus numerous other products both fresh and preserved. Sales are well ahead of projections for the period.

To develop a mailing list and collect customers' reactions to the store, the owners ask all customers to sign a guest book, give their address, and comment about the store and the quality of its food items. This has led to a sizable list of names.

The owners' policy is to feature products by local people (many whom they know personally) and others who live not far away. The owners initially sample each product to be sure that each one meets their high standards.

Since the opening day, one of the store's most popular items has been an unusual vegetable relish preserved by the owners' friend Nancy Hawkins. Over 100 jars of this special item were sold over a span of three months.

Inventory was low on the Hawkins relish so the owners went to her home to reorder and bring back more of the product. On her door they found an official notice: "This business has been closed due to Department of Health violations." Upon questioning Ms. Hawkins, they found that some jars of relish she'd sold to a local restaurant had been found to be contaminated with a strain of bacteria causing severe stomach cramps in people who ate even a small portion of the relish.

The River Valley Gourmet owners were unprepared for this situation. They immediately thought of their own customers and the future of their business.

Discussion Questions:

1. What ethical standards could you recommend the River Valley Gourmet owners adopt before opening their business? Should they maintain those same standards upon learning of the contaminated relish?
2. What appropriate business practices should any store selling food products consider to protect both the owners and the customers?
3. What should the owners do upon hearing that a product they sold might have been contaminated?
   - Should they take a wait-and-see approach, letting customers call them to report a problem?
   - Should they be proactive? If so, what should they do?
   - How should they handle customers who complain of illness but have no proof that it was the River Valley relish?
   - What should they do to ensure a return to normal business and continued good customer relations?
4. How can they prevent this type of incident from reoccurring?

This case was prepared by Professor Catherine Porter, University of Massachusetts, Amherst.

CASE 4-7 ☼ WINSLOW'S SPECIALTY SHOP

Winslow's Specialty Shop is located in a relatively small midwestern city. A large percentage of its customers are students at the college in the city. The store has an excellent reputation for quality merchandise and service. It has been in business since 1930.

The owner, Barbara Winslow, is a graduate of the local college and has been active in alumni and community activities. She has been successful in buying merchandise that fits the needs and desires of the store's clientele.

Winslow's major competition is Miller's Specialty Store, which has been in business since 1975. Bob and Mary Miller, who own and operate the store, are aggressive, and they take particular pride in undercutting Winslow's prices for similar merchandise.

During August 1980, both stores were having sales, and various products were advertised. The merchandise featured by Winslow's included handbags and apparel accessories. A product to which Winslow's gave prominence in this advertising was a South American leather handbag at $27.95. Miller's happened to be offering the same handbag at $32.75. When Bob Miller saw Winslow's ad, he decided to drop his price on the bag to $22. Then he instructed the salespeople to emphasize the price advantage of buying the handbag at Miller's instead of at Winslow's. Miller's did not advertise the bag at $22.

Assume you are a salesperson at Winslow's, and that Mary Cook, who has been a customer of yours for two years, comes in to look at handbags. After you have shown Mary several handbags, she indicates she is interested in the South American bag at $27.95. You describe the product features of the bag to her, and she says, "OK, charge it to my account." (Her credit is good.)

Just as Mary says this, Miriam, a friend of hers, happens by. Miriam says, "Hi, Mary, what's new?" Mary responds, "Oh, nothing much. I'm buying a new handbag. My old one is really shot." She shows Miriam the handbag she has just decided to purchase, and Miriam says, "It's beautiful, but I was just looking at this handbag at Miller's this morning, and you can buy the same thing there for $22."

Mary looks at you, and you look at her. Miriam looks at both of you. Mary says, "why should I be paying $5.95 more for the same handbag just because I'm a good customer of Winslow's?"

Discussion Questions:

1. How would you handle this situation if you were the salesperson?
2. What are your options?

CASE 4-8 ☼ CLOSING A SALE

Analyze each of the following suggestions on how to close a sale. These suggestions were made by salespeople who sell men's suits.

1. I always have an "ace in the hole" . . . one particular suit in which a customer has shown an interest. Of if I have studied my customer carefully when he first came in (and if I have time I usually have been able to), I go back to the first suit he tried on "for size," and very often it is possible to "close the deal" with that first suit. It is important to keep this suit out of sight and not to bring out this "ace in the hole" until a sale cannot be made on some other garment.

2. When a seemingly successful sale bogs down because the prospect is reluctant to take the final step, I simply tell him, "Take the coat to the door (or the window) and see how the daylight brings out the character of the cloth." The psychological reactions are several: It relieves him of the suspicion that any "high pressure" may be applied; his ego is flattered by your apparent confidence in him; the appearance of the fabric is bound to be enhanced by the daylight; the customer is left alone for a minute or so, and with your sales talk bearing fruit, he generally sells himself!

3. There's one technique I've found especially effective with "on-the-fence" buyers: take a tape measure, and as you bend to measure his inseam, ask, "Do you like to wear your trousers pretty well down on your shoe?" Whatever his answer, it usually gives the go-ahead on the purchase, or at least gives the salesperson a lead as to what may be holding the customer back. This works especially well when the wife is along and says, "Yes, I like it, do you?" When that happens, don't wait too long to put the tape on your prospect for complete measurements . . . and the final sale!

4. One of the best ways of helping a customer make up his mind is, surprisingly enough, not to talk about clothing! Discuss current events, sports, his business, or any other subject unrelated to clothing. A few minutes apparently "wasted" in personal conversation create more customer confidence in the salesperson, give the customer time to finally make up his mind. In the majority of cases, he will come back to the subject of clothing himself and will be ready to take the garment about which he couldn't make up his mind just a few minutes before.

5. Give your customer a *choice,* for instance, between two colors or two models. Don't hesitate to ask, "Mr. Jones, which model appeals to you, the green or the brown?" Almost invariably he will make a choice, which is our cue to close the sale by taking the trousers from the rack, starting toward the dressing room with the remark, "Step over here and slip the whole suit on." In most cases, the sale will be complete by suggesting that the tailor be called to see if any alterations are necessary.

Special Topics

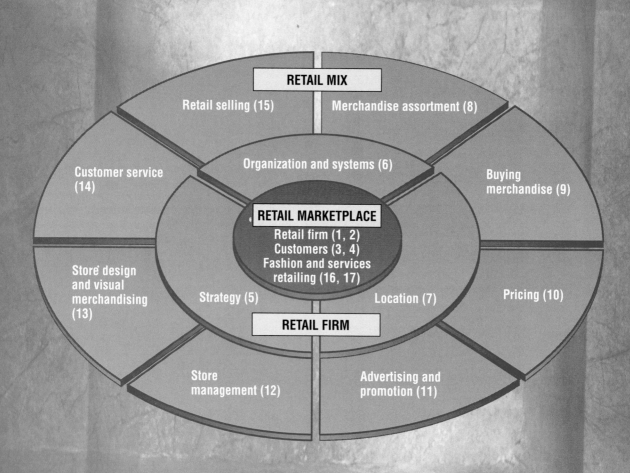

RETAIL MIX

Retail selling (15)   Merchandise assortment (8)

Customer service (14)

Organization and systems (6)

Buying merchandise (9)

RETAIL MARKETPLACE
Retail firm (1, 2)
Customers (3, 4)
Fashion and services retailing (16, 17)

Store design and visual merchandising (13)

Strategy (5)   Location (7)

Pricing (10)

RETAIL FIRM

Store management (12)   Advertising and promotion (11)

T he last section of this textbook focuses on two specialized areas of retailing—the retailing of fashion merchandise (Chapter 16) and services (Chapter 17). Unique skills and knowledge are needed in these retail areas.

Fashion retailing is a very volatile and uncertain business. It is difficult to forecast what will be fashionable in six months and also hard to predict when the latest fashion will end. In Chapter 16, we describe the key players in the fashion industry—designers, fabric and garment manufacturers, the fashion press, and retailers, discuss how fashions arise and develop over time, and what retailers do to reduce the uncertainty in fashion retailing and satisfy the need of their customers for the latest styles.

Services retailing differs from the retailing of merchandise because services cannot be stored in inventory. If a seat in a theatre is not sold before a performance, it is lost forever. In addition, it is often difficult for customers to evaluate the benefits of services. You really can't tell if your doctor or lawyer is giving you the best advice.

In each of these chapters, we relate the concepts in the first 15 chapters to these special areas of retailing. We discuss how these retailers adjust their retail strategy and organization structure, merchandise management, and store management to the special circumstances in these retail areas.

CHAPTER 16 **Fashion Retailing**
CHAPTER 17 **The Retailing of Services**

Fashion Retailing

Fashion retailing (16)

Questions this chapter answers include

- **What is fashion merchandise?**
- **How do fashions arise and develop over time?**
- **What are the firms and individuals in the fashion industry?**
- **What are the unique aspects of retailing fashion merchandise?**

fashion is a type of product or a way of behaving that is temporarily adopted by a large number of consumers because the product or behavior is considered to be socially appropriate for the time and place.[1] For example, in some social groups, it is—or was—fashionable to have brightly colored hair, play golf, wear a coat made from animal fur, have a beard, or go to an expensive health spa for a vacation. In many retail environments, however, the term *fashion* is associated with clothing—the primary focus of this chapter.

Retailers that sell fashion merchandise need some unique skills and knowledge. Buyers typically order merchandise three to six months before it will be available for sale in their stores—although this time period has become shorter as more retailers adopt quick response (QR) inventory systems. Thus buyers need to know what will be popular in the future. Predicting fashion trends is difficult because fashions are temporary. Merchandise is only fashionable for a short period of time, and eventually all fashions become unpopular.

The grunge style (left) is currently predominant among younger consumers. Couture fashion (right) remains the province of exclusive stores and wealthy buyers, but influences and reflects tastes in the culture at large.

The temporary nature of fashion merchandise makes pricing and inventory management challenging. When buyers make mistakes in predicting fashions, either (1) they have too much merchandise that has limited value because it is unfashionable or (2) the lack of fashionable merchandise in their stores hurts the store image among fashion-conscious consumers.

In the next sections of this chapter, we will discuss the terms used in fashion retailing, how fashions develop and spread, and the unique nature of fashion retailing.

☼ THE LANGUAGE OF FASHION

Design and Style

Style and *design* are two terms frequently used when discussing fashion merchandise. A **design** is a specific combination of silhouette, design details, color, and material that makes one product different from others in its category. **Silhouette** is the shape or conture of a garment. Some common silhouettes are tubular, hourglass, and bell-shaped. **Design details** refer to how the apparel is constructed, such

RE-TALE 16-1   The Exclusive World of Haute Couture

Liza Minnelli, Paloma Picasso, and Estée Lauder have at least one thing in common: They are all part of the elite who buy French haute couture. They travel to Paris twice a year, in January and July, to attend the couture shows and pay up to $2,000 for a blouse and $13,000 to $100,000 for an evening gown.

They spend this time and money to get the very best in apparel and personalized service. The garments are fitted using more than 30 personalized measurements and involve more than 80 hours of handiwork to produce. These customers also receive expert assistance in choosing the proper outfits and accessories for their life-styles. The directors at the top design houses educate their customers, offering advice on jewelry, shoes, and hairstyle. And customers know that, due to the vigilance of the couture salespeople, they will not run into anyone else in the world with the same outfit.

SOURCE: Regan Charles, "Creme De La Hem: An Insider's Guide to the Exclusive World of Haute Couture," *Avenue*, January 1989, pp. 4–6.

as the use of pleats, pockets, collars, buttons, and belts. Finally, **materials** used in clothing include fabrics, fur, leather, plastics, and metal. These materials produce the color and texture of the apparel. Examples of designs are a leather aviator jacket with a number of zippered pockets or a trenchcoat, which is a specific raincoat design.

An infinite number of combinations of silhouettes, design details, and materials can be used to design apparel. Each design can be a work of art. When consumers feel a design is visually attractive, ego-enhancing, and socially approved, it becomes a fashion.

A **fad** is a minifashion. It is typically a design that is only popular for a short period of time. Fads are usually adopted by a small segment of consumers. When they are no longer popular, they never become popular again. Some examples of fads are stirrup pants, disco jewelry, pet rocks, and, more recently, pogs. While fads come and go, fashions last for a longer time and are adopted by more consumers. Frequently fashions go through cycles. For example, short skirts were fashionable in the 1960s and then again in the 80s.

A **style** is a collection of clothing items that share common design features and are worn together. Some examples of styles are the fifties look, Victorian, punk, and grunge.

Couture. Couture fashion is clothing designed and made for a specific customer by famous designers such as Yves Saint Laurent and Karl Lagerfeld or design houses such as Christian Dior. Each season, designers produce shows in which they display their latest creations. Wealthy customers, fashion reporters and photographers, manufacturers, and buyers for exclusive shops worldwide attend these shows. The wealthy clients purchase apparel for their personal use, the buyers for their stores, and others attend to learn about new fashion trends. Re-Tale 16–1 describes the service that couture customers get.

Types of Fashion Apparel

REFACT

The use of the term *haute couture* is strictly controlled in France. Only 23 designers in Paris are sanctioned as haute couturières.

Ready-to-Wear. Because couture fashions are one-of-a-kind and handmade, couture designers lose money on this merchandise even though it is sold at high prices. In contrast to custom-made couture apparel, **ready-to-wear** is apparel made in standardized sizes and usually produced in factories. Some different types of ready-to-wear fashion apparel are discussed in the following sections.

Designer fashions are exclusive, designer-branded merchandise based on couture fashion. After making the couture merchandise, the designers adapt their designs so they can be efficiently manufactured and sold at lower prices. This designer merchandise is then sold at exclusive retail outlets, either stores owned by the designers or department and specialty stores targeting the most fashion-conscious and wealthy consumers.

Some designers and high-fashion apparel manufacturers like Ellen Tracy, Donna Karan, and Carol Little produce fashion merchandise for a broader target market. Designer branded women's apparel with broader appeal and lower prices than couture designer apparel is referred to as **bridge merchandise** because it bridges the gap between the couture designer and mass manufactured branded merchandise.

Mass fashions are merchandise produced in large quantities and sold at reasonable price ranges to a broad market. The designs of mass fashions are typically lower cost than designer fashions and use less elegant materials, workmanship, and construction. In some cases, these mass fashions are "knock-offs" of couture or designer fashions. **Knock-offs** are inexpensive and less elegant copies of couture or designer fashions. Some clothing manufacturers specialize in knock-offs. They learn about the latest designs and copy them so quickly that their imitations may appear in stores at the same time as the designer fashions.

Classics are basic designs that have been widely accepted over a long period of time. These designs are usually simple. Some examples of classics are Levi's® 501® jeans, button-down oxford shirts, and blue blazers. However design details can date classics. For example, a polyester blue blazer with wide lapels would be out of fashion now.

Levi's® 501® denim jeans are classics—fashionable in any era.

☼ FASHION PROCESS AND INDUSTRY

Fashion gives people an opportunity to satisfy many emotional and practical needs. Through fashions, people develop their own identity. They can use fashions to manage their appearance, express their self-image and feelings, enhance their egos, and make an impression on others. Through the years, fashions have become associated with specific life-styles or roles people play. You wear different clothing styles when you are attending class, going out on a date, or interviewing for a job. Re-Tale 16–2 describes how the fashion for work clothing is changing.

Why Do New Fashions Arise?

Fashion also can be used to communicate with others. For example, you might wear a classic business suit when interviewing for a job at Neiman Marcus but more informal attire when interviewing for a job with The Gap. These different dress styles would indicate your appreciation and understanding of the differences in the cultures of these firms.

Fashion is affected by economic, sociological, and psychological factors. Each of these factors is discussed below.

Economic Factors. Fashion merchandise is a luxury. It includes design details that go beyond satisfying the basic functional needs. Thus demand for fashion merchandise is greatest in countries with a high level of economic development and in market segments with the greatest disposable income.

Sociological Factors. Fashion changes reflect changes in our social environment— our feelings about class structure, the roles of women and men, and the structure of the family. For example, time pressures arising from the increased number of women in the work force have led to the acceptance of low-maintenance, drip-dry, wrinkle-resistant fabrics. The rising concern for the environment has resulted in natural fibers becoming fashionable and fur coats going out of fashion. The interest

---

RE-TALE 16-2   Dressing Down at Work

In 1995, consumers were ignoring the latest couture fashions. Designers were promoting the return of glamour by outfitting their models with stiletto heels, vinyl miniskirts, and tiny angora sweaters, but consumers were dressing more casually—and not just on the weekends, but also at work. Even IBM abandoned its blue-suit-and-white-shirt tradition, encouraging employees to dress more casually. Sales of tailored clothing, including dresses and suits, declined while demand for no-iron cotton slacks and sweaters rose.

However most consumers are still concerned about wearing the wrong clothes when "dressing down" at work. Retailers and manufacturers are addressing these concerns by offering special styles for casual workdays. Haggar has developed a "relaxed, yet tailored" line of clothing using the brand name City Casuals. Special point-of-purchase material has been developed for retailers selling City Casuals. Haggar's "How to Dress

Down" brochure, available at City Casuals displays, has fashion tips like "Suede suspenders, belts, and shoes add a warmer, more casual touch. But save the little suede shorts for Oktoberfest."

Because Levi's Dockers line is standard fare for dressing down, the company is promoting casual dress to employers. Levi's offered a "how-to" kit, including case histories of companies that have successfully adopted casual dress codes, to human resource directors in major firms.

Marshall Field's, a Chicago-based department store chain, featured an article on casual work dress in its monthly customer newsletter and had a one-hour seminar on the subject complete with a free box lunch.

SOURCE: Cyndee Miller, "A Casual Affair," *Marketing News,* March 13, 1995, p. 12.

Due to shifts in public awareness of animal rights and the world climate, natural, vegetable-based fibers like cotton have risen in popularity while petroleum-based synthetic fibers and furs have lost favor.

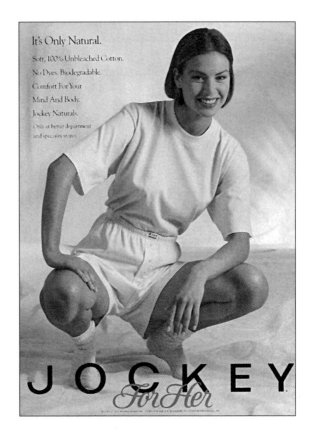

in health and fitness has made it fashionable to exercise and wear jogging clothes, leotards, and running shoes.

Psychological Factors. Consumers adopt fashions to overcome boredom. People get tired of wearing the same clothing and seeing the same furniture in their living room. They seek changes in their life-styles by buying new clothes or redecorating their houses.

People use fashions both to develop their own identity and to gain acceptance from others. These two benefits of fashion can be opposing forces. If you choose to wear something radically different, you will achieve recognition for your individuality but might not be accepted by your peers. To satisfy these conflicting needs, manufacturers and retailers offer a variety of different designs and combinations of designs that are fashionable and still enable consumers to express their individuality.

How Do Fashions Develop and Spread?

The category life cycle (discussed in Chapter 8) describes a merchandise category's sales pattern over time. In this section we will describe the category life cycle for fashion merchandise, known as the *fashion life cycle*. The **fashion life cycle** is the evolution of a new fashion over time within a social group or market segment.[2] Fashions are not universal. A fashion can be accepted in one geographic region, country, or age group and not in another. In the 1970s, the fashion among young women was ankle-length skirts, argyle socks, and platform shoes, while older women were wearing pants suits, double-breasted blazers, and mid-heeled shoes.

Stages in the Fashion Life Cycle

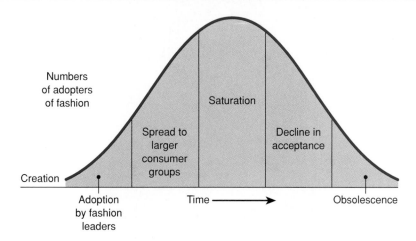

During the 70s, natural hairstyles were fashionable among African-Americans, while corn-row hairstyles became fashionable in the early 80s.

The stages in the fashion life cycle are shown in Exhibit 16–1. The cycle begins with the creation of a new design or style. Then some consumers recognized as fashion leaders adopt the fashion and start a trend in their social group. The fashion spreads from the leaders to others and is accepted widely as a fashion. Eventually the fashion is accepted by everyone in the social group and can become overused. Saturation and overuse set the stage for the decline in popularity and the creation of new fashions.

Creation. New fashions arise from a number of different sources. Couture fashion designers are only one source of the creative inspirations. Fashions are also developed by creative consumers, celebrities, and even retailers. Andre Agassi has influenced fashion worn by tennis players. "Miami Vice" popularized some men's fashions such as T-shirts worn under jackets and the stubble beard.

Adoption by Fashion Leaders. The fashion life cycle really starts when the fashion is adopted by leading consumers. These initial adopters of a new fashion are called *fashion leaders* or *innovators*. They are the first people to display the new fashion in their social group. If the fashion is too innovative or very different from currently accepted fashion, the style might not be accepted by the social group, and the life cycle is prematurely ended.

Three theories have been proposed to explain how fashion spreads within a society. The **trickle-down theory** suggests that the fashion leaders are consumers with the highest social status—wealthy, well-educated consumers. After they adopt a fashion, the fashion trickles down to consumers in lower social classes. When the fashion is accepted in the lowest social class, it is no longer acceptable to the fashion leaders in the highest social class.

The **mass market theory** proposes that fashions spread across social classes. Each social class has its own fashion leaders who play a key role in their own social networks. Fashion information "trickles across" social classes rather than down from the upper classes to the lower classes.

REFACT

The East German Olympic women's swim team in 1973 started the fashion of tight-fitting swimwear made out of nylon and spandex.

Appliqued jackets and tatoos have "trickled up" from the motorcycle subculture to mainstream consumers.

The **subculture theory** is based on the development of recent fashions. Subcultures of mostly young and less affluent consumers, such as the motorcycle riders and urban rappers, started fashions for such things as colorful fabrics, T-shirts, sneakers, jeans, black leather jackets, and surplus military clothing. These fashions started with people in small, less affluent consumer groups and "trickled up" to mainstream consumer classes.

These theories of fashion development indicate that fashion leaders can come from many different places and social groups. In our diverse society, many types of consumers have the opportunity to be the leaders in setting fashion trends.

Spread to Large Consumer Groups. During this stage, the fashion is accepted by a wider group of consumers referred to as *early adopters.* The fashion becomes more visible, receives greater publicity and media attention, and is readily available in retail stores.

The relative advantage, compatibility, complexity, trialability, and observability of a fashion affect the time it takes the fashion to spread though a social group. New fashions that provide more benefits have a higher **relative advantage** compared to existing fashions, and these new fashions spread faster. Fashions are often adopted by consumers because they make people feel special. Thus more exclusive fashions like expensive clothing are adopted more quickly in an affluent target market. On a more utilitarian level, clothing that is easy to maintain, such as wrinkle-free pants, will diffuse quickly in the general population.

Compatibility is the degree to which the fashion is consistent with existing norms, values, and behaviors. When new fashions are not consistent with existing norms, the number of adopters and the speed of adoption is lower. Since the mid-1960s, the fashion industry has repeatedly attempted to revive the miniskirt. It has had only moderate success because the group of women with the most disposable income to spend on fashion are baby boomers—many of whom no longer find the miniskirt a relevant fashion for their family-oriented life-styles.

Complexity refers to how easy it is to understand and use the new fashion. Consumers have to learn how to incorporate a new fashion into their life-style.

Fashions that are easy to learn have a greater chance of acceptance and spread more quickly through a social group. For example, a new cosmetic fashion might spread slowly if it is difficult for consumers to apply the cosmetic and achieve the desired look.

Some fashions can be tested with minimal expense and risk. **Trialability** refers to costs and commitment required to initially adopt the fashion. For example, when consumers need to spend a lot of money buying a new type of expensive jewelry to be in fashion, the rate of adoption is slower than if the fashion simply requires wearing jewelry that the consumer already owns on a different part of the body.

Observability is the degree to which the new fashion is visible and easily communicated to others in the social group. Clothing fashions are very observable compared to fashions for the home, such as sheets and towels. It is therefore likely that a fashion in clothing will spread more quickly than a new color scheme or style for the bathroom.

Fashion retailers engage in many activities to increase the adoption and spread of a new fashion through their target market. Compatibility is increased and complexity is decreased by showing consumers how to coordinate a new article of fashion clothing with other items the consumer already owns. Trialability is increased by providing dressing rooms so that the customers can try on the clothing and see how it looks on them. Providing opportunities for customers to return merchandise also increases trialability. Retailers increase observability by displaying fashion merchandise in their stores and advertising it in newspapers.

Saturation. In this stage, the fashion achieves its highest level of social acceptance. Almost all consumers in the target market are aware of the fashion and have decided to either accept or reject it. At this point, the fashion has become old and boring to many people.

Decline in Acceptance and Obsolescence. When fashions reach saturation, they have become less appealing to consumers. Because most people have already adopted the fashion, it no longer provides an opportunity for people to express their individuality. Fashion creators and leaders are beginning to experiment with new fashions. The introduction of a new fashion speeds the decline of the preceding fashion.

Who Are the Participants in the Fashion Industry?

The fashion industry includes a wide variety of individuals from small design firms to very large manufacturers and retailers. The core participants in the fashion industry are shown in Exhibit 16–2.

Raw Material Suppliers. Fibers are the basic element in most clothing. These fibers are either natural, like wool and cotton, or synthetic, like Lycra® and nylon. Suppliers of natural and synthetic fibers encourage fabric designers and manufacturers to use their materials in creating new fashions. They also promote their fibers to consumers so that they will adopt fashions using them. For instance, the Cotton Growers Association spends millions of dollars every year promoting the use of cotton. Other raw materials used in fashion clothing are metallic, fur and leather.

Fabric Manufacturers. Fabric manufacturers buy the fibers and spin them into yarn and then further process the yarn into fabric by weaving or knitting. Finishes are applied to the fabric to alter its appearance, feel, or performance. Dyes are used to

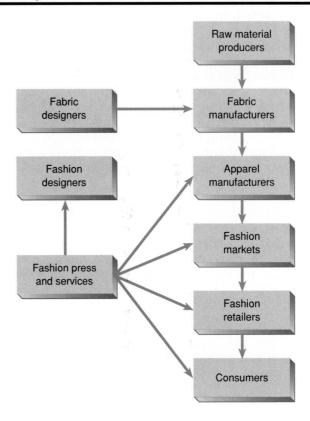

alter color; glazing may be applied to alter the feel; and chemicals may be used to make fabrics more water repellent or stain- or wrinkle-resistant.

Fabric manufacturers need to predict fashion trends a year or two in advance and be prepared to supply large quantities of fabrics that are consistent with the fashion apparel trends. Fabric producers attempt to influence these trends by providing samples of new fabrics and treatments to apparel designers and manufacturers.

Apparel Manufacturers. Apparel manufacturing is a highly competitive international industry consisting of everything from small firms targeting a specific market niche to large manufacturers like Levi Strauss and VF Corporation, maker of the Jantzen and Wrangler lines of clothing.

Apparel is manufactured within the United States and "offshore" (outside the United States). Apparel manufacturing is very labor-intensive. Due to the high standard of living and wages in the United States, until recently, there has been a trend toward more offshore manufacturing. Fiber manufacturers like DuPont and fabric manufacturers like Miliken are working with apparel manufacturers and retailers to develop quick response systems. (See Chapter 6.) These systems reduce lead times and inventory levels and at the same time increase the service level provided to the apparel manufacturers. The result has been that domestic apparel manufacturers can compete more effectively with offshore suppliers.

This ad, developed by raw material supplier Hoechst Celanese, and featuring Olympic Gold Medalist Kristi Yamaguchi, shows consumers that garments made with acetate can be graceful and elegant.

Fabric and Fashion Designers. These designers are the creative force in the fashion industry. They either work for the manufacturers or are independent contractors providing their services to manufacturers and retailers that develop private-label merchandise. Successful designers need to know the elements of visual design, the needs of the marketplace, and the cost structure for manufacturing fabrics and apparel.

Fashion Market Centers. Apparel producers sell their merchandise to retailers using sales representatives and showrooms in important fashion markets in New York, Chicago, Los Angeles, Atlanta, and Dallas. Sales representatives travel to the buying offices of retail stores to show samples of the latest fashions. However the fashion market in New York continues to be the place where most business concerning fashion apparel is conducted.

    Retail buyers travel from across the United States to visit the apparel manufacturers' showrooms in New York, look at the latest fashions, learn about future trends, and buy merchandise. Many large retail chains send buyers or have resident buying offices in major fashion markets across the globe such as in Paris, Rome, London, Hong Kong, and Tokyo. (See Chapter 9.)

    For private-label fashions, the buyers work directly with the manufacturers. They work together to develop the specifications used to manufacture the merchandise.

REFACT

The heart of the U.S. fashion industry is in New York City within a block or two of Seventh Avenue from West 30th to 41st streets.

Fashion Retailers. Fashion retailers are the link between the industry and consumers. They play an important role in stimulating interest in new fashions and provide feedback to the industry about which fashions are selling well and which are not. The typical costs and profits generated by manufacturers and retailers of fashion merchandise are shown in Exhibit 16–3.

Fashion Press and Services. The **fashion press** and fashion merchandising services provide information that assists everyone in the industry, from raw material suppliers to consumers, in making good decisions. Fashion trends are important news to many people. Daily newspapers devote considerable space to reporting and these trends. Magazines like *Vogue* and *Elle* focus on providing fashion information to consumers. Trade publications like *Women's Wear Daily* provide information for retailers and producers in the industry.

In addition, a number of services monitor fashion trends and merchandise sales and sell this information to firms in the industry.

RETAILING OF FASHION MERCHANDISE

This section describes some key issues confronting fashion retailers.

Identifying the Fashion-Oriented Customer—Target Market

The three theories of how fashions spread (which we discussed earlier in this chapter) emphasize that fashion-conscious customers are spread throughout society. At one time fashion retailers catered to upper-class, wealthy consumers who were an elite group of fashion leaders. Now there are many different groups of fashion-conscious customers, each with their own leaders and concepts of fashion. New styles can start in a couture designer's studio or from merchandise sold in an army–navy surplus store.

Demographic variables like income and education can not be used to identify fashion-conscious consumers. However research has uncovered some personality and life-style characteristics that distinguish fashion-conscious customers. Fashion leaders are venturesome, self-confident, and outgoing. They are interested in

EXHIBIT 16–3

Behind the Price Tag of an $85 Skirt

Manufacturer's Cost		Retailer's Cost	
Material	$ 6.35	Cost of merchandise	$37.49
Lining	.64	Typical markdown	9.08
Zipper	.17		
Labor	12.40	Shrinkage	.87
Packing cost (tags, labels, hanger, bag)	1.11	Expenses (salaries, sales promotion, rent, etc.)	33.76
Overhead (equipment, buildings, management salaries)	12.13		
Profit	4.69	Profit	3.78
Wholesale price	$37.49	Selling price	$84.98

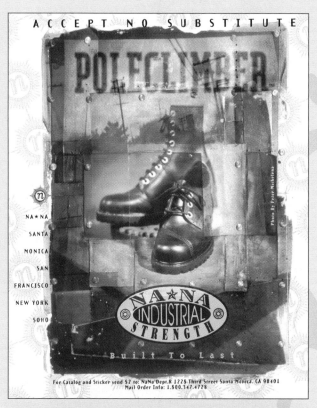

© Certain styles, such as Na Na's heavy, black workboots, once the province of militants and skinheads, are now sold as mainstream fashion items. (Chapter 16)

© Disco music and clothing were a fad fashion, but one which has made a slight return among certain segments of the public. On the other hand, classic fashions withstand variations in public taste. (Chapter 16)

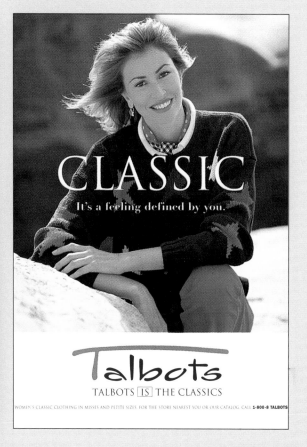

◎ Boutiques may be devoted to the work of one designer only, or may feature a specific style of clothes. (Chapter 16)

SYD JEROME
2 No. La Salle Street
Chicago, Illinois 60603

CANALI

◎ Trunk shows held at the store are one way in which fashion retailers reach style leaders in their communities. (Chapter 16)

Wool suit with 2% LYCRA®
and mesh skin dress with 35% LYCRA®
by Karl Lagerfeld.

Because even if soccer
isn't on your itinerary this evening
you can still make all the
right moves.

Look for the LYCRA® Brand.

Nothing Moves Like LYCRA.

◎ Synthetic materials manufacturers advertise to the public in order to create primary demand for clothing designs using their material. (Chapter 16)

© Blockbuster's distinctive blue and yellow store designs address the intangibility problem associated with services by developing a strong visual identity for the company. (Chapter 17)

© UPS recently altered their stringent time requirements for drivers to allow 30 minutes a week of discretionary time to visit with customers and offer customers practical advice on shipping. The practice has generated "tens of millions of dollars" in new business. (Chapter 17)

© Some merchandise retailers are adding services to broaden the store's appeal. Border's bookstores offer coffee service and music listening stations which are attractive to the segment which frequents the stores. (Chapter 17)

© Concert t-shirts become hot commodities when they embody the transient experience of a concert, especially important cultural milestones like 1994's Woodstock 2. (Chapter 17)

fashion and knowledgeable about current trends. Due to their knowledge of fashion, they do not feel that adopting a new fashion is very risky.

Fashion-conscious customers are both risk takers and conformists at the same time. They want to wear the newest styles so they will be seen as different, but they do not want to be so different that they are not accepted.[3]

Locations for Fashion Retailers

Throughout the world, there are streets on which the highest-quality and most expensive retailers (such as Yves Saint Laurent, Gucci, and Givency) have their stores. Legendary streets in the world of high fashion are Rodeo Drive in Beverly Hills; Worth Avenue in Palm Beach, Florida; Madison Avenue in New York; and Rue Montaigne in Paris.

But the primary locations for most fashion-oriented retailing are regional malls. Over the past 10 years, department and specialty stores in these malls have concentrated more on fashion apparel merchandise. Sales of hard goods such as athletic equipment, electronics, and appliances are shifting to category specialists and discount stores located in power centers and in smaller strip shopping centers.

The typical regional mall caters to customers interested in mass fashion. However some malls—such as Lennox in Atlanta, Highland Park in Dallas, Bal Harbour in Miami Beach, and South Coast Plaza in Orange County, California—target consumers interested in designer fashions. These specialty malls have stores that previously were only found on the world's famous fashion streets.

Buying Fashion Merchandise

Two critical activities associated with buying fashion merchandise are predicting what will be fashionable in the coming season and planning the fashion season.

Predicting Fashions. Millions of dollars are at stake in guessing what will be fashionable. When buyers make mistakes in predicting fashion, either they are left with

Rodeo Drive in Beverly Hills, California, is one of the legendary addresses in the world of high fashion retailing.

a lot of merchandise that they have to mark down, or they are left with unsatisfied customers who can not get the merchandise they want. Barbara Turf, a guru in predicting homewear fashion, is featured in Re-Tale 16–3.

To predict fashion trends, buyers use trade publications, fashion information services, and the firm's fashion coordinator. **Trade publications** are newspapers and magazines that provide industry-related information for retailers, buyers, and suppliers. Articles in these publications analyze fashion trends and events around the world; discuss economic, legal, and business conditions; and present market research studies. Magazines such as *Stores, Discount Store News,* and *Chain Store Age Executive* cover a broad spectrum of general retailing issues. Other publications focus on specific types of retailing or merchandise categories. The most well-known publications on fashion merchandise are *Women's Wear Daily* (women's wear) and *Daily News Record* (menswear).

A number of fashion information services are available to help buyers understand and forecast trends. Examples include The Fashion Service (known as TFS), Tobe Service, and Retail News Bureau.

Many of the larger fashion retailers have fashion coordinators. **Fashion coordinators** analyze the fashion markets and consumer trends and provide information to the buyers about new fabrics, colors, and styles. The coordinators are responsible for developing the general guidelines that buyers use to select merchandise so that the retailer presents a consistent fashion image to its customers.

These suggestions may improve your ability to forecast fashion trends:

- Carefully observe current events that have or will interest and affect your target market.
- Be aware of the life-styles and dress of men and women who will influence customers in your target market.
- Study sales trends in other parts of the United States for your company and its competitors.
- Be knowledgeable about the fashion opinions of suppliers.

RE-TALE 16-3 Barbara Turf Predicts Consumer Tastes for Crate & Barrel

Crate & Barrel is a Chicago-based chain of 54 housewares and furnishings stores catering to fashion-conscious customers who want something different, something that is not available in the department and discount stores. The stores have a homey atmosphere with merchandise displayed in colorful arrangements. Sales clerks wearing aprons are readily available to answer questions about the latest merchandise.

Barbara Turf, executive vice president of merchandising, is Crate's secret weapon in the battle to anticipate fashion trends and have the right merchandise available. In 1995, she bet that customers will want housewares, from tablecloths to bedspreads, in blues and greens with yellow tones, and she placed orders so the merchandise would be in the stores in 1997.

To make her predictions, she travels widely, reads a lot of magazines, and simply observes everything around her. She always has an eye on Europe, where she says trends often develop 18 months before they do in the United States. But she also looks out for trends in the United States. For example, when people started to drive Jeep Cherokees rather than Cadillacs, she began buying more casual dinnerware.

But predicting fashions is a tricky business, and even Ms. Turf makes mistakes. The pinkish plaid place mats she bought in 1995 were losers and had to be deeply discounted before they would sell.

SOURCE: Christina Duff, "How Barbara Turf Chooses the Hot Place Mats of 1997," *The Wall Street Journal,* March 16, 1995, pp. B1–B2; and Suzanne Slesin, "Is New York Ready for Nice?" *The New York Times,* March 2, 1995, p. C1.

• Recognize and attempt to understand the evolutionary pattern of fashions.

Merchandise Seasons. The seven seasons for fashion merchandise are shown in Exhibit 16–4. The three major seasons when most of the merchandise is sold (fall, spring, and summer) are shown in bold print. Six to nine months prior to each season, buyers go to the fashion markets to look at and buy merchandise.

Then the buyers develop a plan that includes schedules for shipping merchandise to stores and plans for its display and promotion. Exhibit 16–5 illustrates

Fashion Apparel Seasons

Season	Sales Time	Important Merchandise Lines
Cruise and Resort	January to March	Sportswear, swimwear, casual clothing
Spring	**March to April (ending with Easter)**	**Dresses and Suits**
Summer	**May to June**	**Sportswear, suits, dresses, casual accessories**
Transitional	July to August	Casual wear (light fabric with darker colors)
Back to School	Late August to September	Children's clothing and accessories
Fall	**Late August to December**	**Sportwear, dresses, suits, accessories**
Holiday	November to December	Evening wear, dresses, special Christmas merchandise

SOURCE: Adapted from Maryanne Bohlinger, *Merchandise Buying,* 3d ed. (Boston: Allyn & Bacon, 1990), p. 282.

the calendar of events confronting a fashion buyer. As you can see, the buyer must pay attention to the current season's fashions as well as prepare and buy one to two seasons in advance.

Communicating with Fashion-Conscious Customers

Retailers need to communicate their offering to fashion innovators, the first consumers to adopt a new fashion. Innovators are very interested in learning about new fashion trends. They acquire this fashion information by reading consumer fashion magazines, attending fashion shows, and browsing through retail stores carrying fashionable merchandise. It is very important to communicate with these fashion innovators because they are the primary source of fashion information for fashion followers, the consumers who are slower to adopt new fashions. The followers learn about fashions by observing and talking with fashion innovators.

Fashion Magazines. The primary objective of fashion magazines is to report on and interpret fashion news for consumers. Fashion editors go to the fashion markets in the United States and abroad and select trends and styles to feature in their magazines. The editors contact the designers and manufacturers for the garments and hire models and photographers to illustrate the styles. Manufacturers try to get editors to present their styles because a feature story in a top magazine can have great influence on fashion innovators and retail buyers.

The world of fashion magazines is going through considerable change. The traditional women's fashion magazines—*Harper's Bazaar, Vogue, Glamour,* and *Mademoiselle*—have a number of new competitors such as *Elle, Mirabella, Vanity Fair,* and *Savvy.* In menswear, the most influential fashion magazines are *GQ* (*Gentlemen's Quarterly*) and *Details.* However many people are interested in fashion so fashion events are reported in local newspapers and on television shows; even *Sports Illustrated* has an annual women's swimsuit issue.

REFACT

Glamour has the largest circulation among fashion magazines, with over 2 million readers.

Fashion Calendar

EXHIBIT 16-5

Merchandise Available in Stores	Fashion Merchandise Markets Open for Buying
January: cruise and resort wear, casual clothing	Spring ready-to-wear; sportswear
February: lightweight coats; spring suits and dresses	Fall women's merchandise
March: spring coats, suits, dresses, accessories, lingerie, and intimate apparel	Fall men's merchandise; junior sportswear
April: summer dresses, activewear, and accessories; swimwear	Misses sportswear; ski apparel
May: cocktail dresses, long dresses, evening gowns, bridal fashions, summer coordinates	Fall ready-to-wear, dresses, coats, suits
June: summer sportswear and accessories; special athletic wear	Fall sportswear
July: fall bridal fashions; transitional merchandise	Fall and winter accessories; major manufacturer showings
August: back-to-school children's wear; casual and career clothing; medium-weight jackets and coats; fall accessories	Special Christmas merchandise; cruise and resort wear; spring shoes
September: fall ready-to-wear, coats, suits, dresses	Early spring wear
October: leather and suede accessories; ski apparel; medium- to heavyweight suits and coats	Swimsuits; spring ready-to-wear
November: holiday fashions and accessories; cruise and resort wear	Spring bridal
December: holiday dresses, evening gowns, accessories (jewelry, scarves, handbags); fur coats	Little activity

SOURCE: Adapted from Maryanne Bohlinger, *Merchandise Buying,* 3d ed., (Boston: Allyn & Bacon, 1990), p. 396.

Fashion Shows. Fashion shows provide an opportunity for retailers and manufacturers to dramatically present new styles. Some retailers like Bloomingdale's and Neiman Marcus put on formal fashion shows with professional models in a costly and elaborate stage production. Often tickets to these shows are sold as part of a charitable event.

In the typical fashion show, merchandise is presented "runway-style." In a **runway show,** models walk along an elevated platform with chairs on either side. Another approach to fashion shows is to have models walk through an in-store restaurant displaying clothes while the customers are eating lunch or dinner.

Retailers often have trunk shows. In a **trunk show,** a manufacturer presents its entire merchandise line to customers in the retail setting. These shows are heavily promoted with advertising paid for by both the retailer and the manufacturer. Frequently the designer of the merchandise and the manufacturer's key sales and marketing people attend the show.

RE-TALE 16-4   Pea in a Pod Helps Customers Try on Its Merchandise

Female shoppers are often frustrated when they want to try on fashionable apparel they find in a store. A universal pet peeve among women is cramped dressing rooms that are poorly lit and lack mirrors.

Pea in a Pod, a specialty store chain selling maternity clothing, responded to these concerns and conducted focus groups to determine its customers' needs. Based on this market research, they designed oversized dressing rooms with plenty of space to store heavy coats and packages. The rooms are very feminine and inviting,

with plenty of racks to hold any number of garments that the customer may want to try on, and comfortable chairs to sit on. Large, full-length mirrors are provided along with bright lighting so customers can see how they look in the outfits.

SOURCE: Mary Beth Crocker, "Three Undercover Agents Go across Town to Investigate Stores' Fitting Areas," *The Cincinnati Enquirer,* December 8, 1994, E1.

Providing Services for Fashion-Conscious Customers

Retailers selling fashion merchandise need to provide special services to their customers. Because these customers are making important and risky buying decisions (decisions that can affect their image and ego), retailers need to provide more information than they do for customers buying more basic merchandise such as jeans and hosiery.

Salespeople can play an important role in selling fashion merchandise. They are often asked to give an opinion about how the apparel looks on the customer and to make suggestions about accessories that will go with garments. Thus most fashion retailers employ knowledgeable, well-trained salespeople. Re-Tale 16–4 describes how Pea in a Pod provides an additional service—the opportunity to try on merchandise in a comfortable setting.

SUMMARY

Fashion merchandise is products temporarily adopted by a group of consumers because they are popular with that group. While a wide range of behaviors and merchandise can be fashionable, the primary focus of fashion retailing is apparel. The different types of fashion apparel are couture, designer, and mass fashions.

Fashion merchandise helps a retailer's customers manage their appearance and express their self-image. The importance of fashion is affected by the economy, the social environment, and the psychological needs of consumers.

A fashion goes through a life cycle—a fashion cycle—that begins with the creation of a new design or style. Then fashion leaders adopt the new style, which influences others in their social group to adopt the style. Eventually the fashion is accepted by everyone in the social group. Saturation sets the stage for the decline in popularity and the creation of new fashions. The time it takes for the fashion to spread through a social group is determined by its relative advantage, compatibility, complexity, trialability, and observability.

The key participants in the fashion industry are raw material suppliers, fabric manufacturers, apparel manufacturers, fabric and fashion designers, fashion market centers, fashion retailers, and fashion press and services.

Fashion retailers no longer target just upper-class, wealthy consumers. There are many different groups of fashion-conscious customers, each with their own leaders and concepts of fashion. Fashion-conscious customers are venturesome, self-confident, outgoing, and knowledgeable about current trends.

The primary outlets for most fashion-oriented merchandise are the department and specialty stores in regional malls. These retailers provide information and services valued by fashion-conscious customers, such as personalized attention and comfortable dressing rooms. Fashion retailers communicate with their customers through fashion-oriented consumer publications and fashion shows.

Predicting what will be fashionable in the coming season and planning the fashion season are critical activities undertaken by the buyers of fashion merchandise. Some sources of information for predicting fashions are trade publications, fashion information services, and the firm's fashion coordinator.

KEY TERMS

apparel
   manufacturer, 352
bridge merchandise, 346
classic, 346
compatibility, 350
complexity, 350
couture fashion, 345
design, 344
design detail, 344
designer fashion, 346
fabric designer, 353

fabric manufacturer, 351
fad, 345
fashion, 343
fashion coordinator, 356
fashion designer, 353
fashion life cycle, 348
fashion market
   center, 353
fashion press, 354
fashion show, 359

knock-off, 346
mass fashion, 346
mass market theory, 349
material, 345
observability, 351
raw material supplier,
   351
ready-to-wear, 345
relative advantage,
   350

runway show, 359
silhouette, 344
style, 345
subculture theory,
   350
trade publication, 356
trialability, 351
trickle-down theory,
   349
trunk show, 359

DISCUSSION QUESTIONS AND PROBLEMS

1. What is the difference between a fad, a fashion, and a classic? Give examples of each.
2. Why do fashions change?
3. Give examples of merchandise, other than apparel, currently affected by fashion.
4. Do designers start all fashion trends? Support your answer.
5. Who are the fashion leaders in your age group? In your ethnic group?
6. What can a retailer do to increase the acceptance of a new fashion that it has stocked in its stores?
7. What are the different sources of information that a buyer can use to predict fashion trends?
8. How does a trade publication differ from a consumer fashion magazine?

The Retailing of Services

Services retailing (17)

Questions this chapter answers include

- **How important are service retailers?**
- **How do retailers who offer primarily services differ from those who offer primarily merchandise?**
- **How can service retailers maintain a competitive advantage?**

Consider a typical Saturday. After a fresh cafe latte at a nearby Starbucks Coffee store, you leave your clothes at the laundry to be washed and folded, drop off a pair of shoes to be resoled, and make your way to the Jiffy Lube to have the oil changed in your car. You are in a hurry, so you drive through a McDonald's so that you won't be late to get your hair cut at I P.M. By mid-afternoon, you are ready for a workout and swim at the health club. After stopping at home for a change of clothes, you are off to dinner, a movie, and dancing with a friend. Finally you end your day the way it started—with a caffe latte at Starbucks, only this time it is decaffeinated. Imagine life as you know it without services like these.

You interact with service retailers all the time. These retailers place varying degrees of importance on service versus merchandise in their offering. For instance, although Starbucks and other food retailers offer a high degree of service, they also sell coffee and pastries. The health club at your university, on the other hand, is probably close to a pure service retailer. Some health clubs, however, sell juices, exercise clothing, and equipment.

The authors thank A. Parasuraman for his assistance in providing material and comments for this chapter.

Many people can't imagine a day without cafe latte from Starbucks and many other key services.

Throughout *Essentials of Retailing,* we've been primarily concerned with the retailing of physical products—those that can be seen, held, and touched. Yet, as we have seen, some retailers sell services, and some sell a combination of services and products. In this chapter you will learn (1) how the retailing of services differs from the retailing of products and (2) strategies that service retailers use to develop sustainable competitive advantages.

This chapter is distinctly different from Chapter 14, "Customer Service." **Customer service,** the focus of Chapter 14, is the set of activities and programs retailers undertake to make the shopping experience more convenient and rewarding for customers. Thus Chapter 14 examines the set of issues that all retailers, including service retailers, should consider when trying to improve customer service. What is unique to this chapter, on the other hand, is its focus on issues that are pertinent to service retailers.

THE IMPORTANCE OF SERVICE RETAILING IN OUR LIVES

The story at the beginning of this chapter illustrates how often you probably use service retailers, including some of this country's most famous service retailing firms. When you think about it, service retailers are everywhere. Consider the variety and depth of service offered by the retailers listed in Exhibit 17–1. These firms are retailers because they sell their goods and/or services to end users in much the same way that a department store does. Some of these companies are not pure retailers, however. For example, hotels, banks, express package delivery services, and financial services all sell to retail customers (end users) and to other businesses. Also many important service retailers may not have a national presence, but are very important in their local markets. These retailers include hospitals, physicians, lawyers, and dry cleaners.

EXHIBIT 17-1

Service Retailing Firms

Airlines	American Airlines, British Airways, Singapore Airways
Automobile rentals	Budget, Alamo
Banks	Citibank, Chase Manhattan Bank
Credit card companies	American Express, Visa, MasterCard
Entertainment parks	Disney, Six Flags
Express package delivery	Federal Express, UPS
Financial services	Merrill Lynch, Dean Witter
Fitness	Bally's, Gold's Gym
Hair cutting	Supercuts
Hotels and motels	Sheraton, Hyatt, Holiday Inn, Marriott
Insurance	State Farm, Prudential
Long-distance telephone	AT&T, Sprint, MCI
Movie theaters	A.M.C.
Restaurants	TGI Friday's, McDonald's
Truck rental	U-Haul, Ryder
Weight loss	Weight Watchers, Jenny Craig
Video	Blockbuster

Not only are services important to you personally, they are also important to our economy. In fact, the Bureau of the Census estimates that services account for about 55 percent of the U.S. gross domestic product (value of goods and services produced) and 79 percent of U.S. nonfarm employment.[1]

Service retailers will become even more important in the future. Consider some of the trends we discussed in Chapter 3 and how they affect the future of service retailers. Recall that the U.S. population is aging. Many baby boomers—the 76 million Americans born between 1946 and 1964—are now middle-aged. The Silver Streakers (people over 50 years old) are a large and healthy segment. Older people demand and can often afford many special types of retailing services. For instance, health care is one of the fastest growing segments in the economy. Not only do older people require more health care than they did when they were young, they are also spending more time on health and fitness. Some well-heeled individuals hire chefs to cook gourmet low-fat meals and employ personal trainers to provide the training and encouragement to work out every day. Opportunities for service retailers abound in our time-poor society where both husband and wife work while still raising a family. Those who can afford it will gladly pay people to clean their houses, cut their lawns, wash and press their clothes, and cook their food—either in restaurants, through carry-outs, or at their home. Some even want help decorating their homes for Christmas. (See Re-Tale 17–1.)

THE NATURE OF SERVICE RETAILERS

There is no pure retailer of goods or services. Throughout *Essentials of Retailing* we have examined the services retailers provide customers—everything from check cashing to personalized sales assistance. Yet you probably think of some retailers as providing mostly merchandise and others as providing mostly services.

Consider the goods/services continuum in Exhibit 17–2. In this chapter we will concentrate on retailers on the right side of the exhibit. On the left of Exhibit 17–2

RE-TALE 17-1 People Hire Pros to Deck Their Halls

Tree trimmers—florists, interior decorators, and special-events specialists—all do a booming business at the end of each year, bringing a little holiday cheer into the homes of those who don't have the time to decorate. But their services don't come cheap. A Beverly Hills entertainment lawyer spent $23,000 to rent a 25-foot live tree and trimmings for five days, after which the decorator took down and hauled off the tree. Why was it so expensive? To make the tree look fuller, the decorators pierce its trunk with branches stripped from two other 25-foot trees. More than 4,000 lights were hand-wrapped around its branches, and ornaments included a flock of cherubs covered with 24-karat gold leaf.

For another client, a Dallas florist wrapped a 10-foot blue spruce with fresh flowers—Casablanca lilies, French roses, ranunculi, tulips, anemones, and lilac—and miniature oranges, pears, apples, limes, pineapples, and other fruit imported from Italy.

High-priced decorators say most of their customers are either childless couples or those with grown children because children like to decorate.

SOURCE: Bob Ortega, "People Hire Pros to Deck Their Halls," *The Wall Street Journal,* December 6, 1994, pp. B1–B2.

Merchandise/Service Continuum

EXHIBIT 17-2

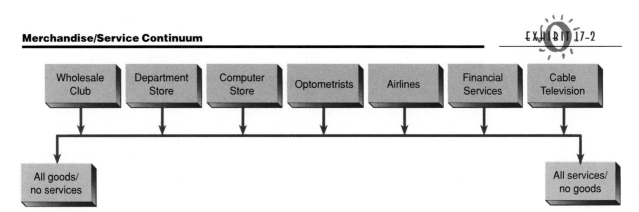

SOURCE: Although updated and altered to emphasis service retailers, this continuum was originally proposed by Lynn G. Shostack, "Breaking Free from Product Marketing," *Journal of Marketing* 41 (April 1977), pp. 73–80.

are warehouse clubs such as Sam's Wholesale Club and Price/Costco. These retailers are primarily self-service stores that offer few services. Even at this end of the continuum, however, the better retailers provide some services such as check cashing and credit cards. You can receive sales assistance in purchasing certain products such as tires. Their service department then mounts the tires on your car.

Moving along the continuum, department stores offer services like gift wrapping, alterations, personal shoppers, and delivery. Most computer stores have both sales associates and service technicians. Optometrists lie somewhere in the middle of the service/product continuum because patients often get their eyes examined (a service) and pick out new glasses or contact lenses (a product)—all in one stop. Most people think of airlines and financial services as pure services, but airlines serve food and give games and pins to children, and you will usually find a calendar in the mail from your stock broker at the end of the year. Even at the far right of Exhibit 17–2, cable TV has some physical products associated with it—the cable and the control box.

How Service Retailers Are Different from Merchandise Retailers

"When you market goods, you build demand for an object. When you market services, you build demand for a performance."[2] The further to the right a retailer is on the merchandise/service continuum in Exhibit 17–2, the more the unique nature of services affects the retailer's strategy. There are four important differences in the nature of the offerings of service retailers and merchandise retailers: intangibility, inseparability, perishability, and inconsistency.[3]

Intangibility. Services are generally **intangible**—customers can't see or feel them. While clothing can be held and examined, the assistance provided by an insurance adjuster can't. Intangibility makes services harder for customers to judge than merchandise. You can see and feel the ride of a new car, but it is more difficult to determine how well a tune-up is performed on it. Also retailers have more difficulty evaluating service quality because it can't be checked as easily as merchandise can. It is hard for instance, for a hospital to evaluate how well their doctors and staff are performing their jobs.

Retailers address the intangibility problems by developing tangible symbols that represent the firm. Evaluation systems that take customer complaints into consideration also help service retailers come to grips with the intangibility of services.

Inseparability. Products are typically made in a factory, sold to a retailer, and then bought by customers. Service providers, on the other hand, create and deliver the service simultaneously. The creation and consumption of the service are **inseparable.** This unique feature of services creates challenges for retailers. While customers can return damaged merchandise to retailers, service providers who fail to satisfy their customers often do not get a second chance. The customer just doesn't come back. How many times have you returned to a restaurant after you received a bad meal or poor service? Thus it is critical for service providers to "get it right" the first time. Service retailers try to avoid service failures by hiring the right people and training and motivating them well. Of course, service failures still occur. When they do, service retailers must be certain that customer satisfaction ultimately prevails.

Perishability. Because the creation and consumption of services are inseparable, services are also extremely **perishable.** For instance, once an airplane takes off with an empty seat, a potential sale is lost forever. A related problem is that customers often demand that the service be provided by specific people—their own doctor, plumber, or watch repair person. If you have ever experienced a broken water pipe, you realize that it doesn't help to know that your plumber is at a movie and won't be able to get to your house for several hours.

The perishability of services creates a special burden on service retailers. Merchandise retailers can stockpile merchandise to ensure a high service level. Services retailers, on the other hand, have to stockpile the service providers so that customers do not have to wait. Retailers that rely on equipment to deliver their service, such as bowling alleys or airlines, must build in excess capacity for peak usage times. Because it is virtually impossible to match service supply and demand, service retailers must balance the benefit of having the service available when the customer wants it with the cost of having service providers or equipment stand idle during low demand periods.

Inconsistency. Not all service providers are created equally. Some barbers, for instance, are better than others. Also service providers may experience an "off day" in which their performance is not up to par. You just hope that on the day you happen to be having surgery, your surgeon is well rested. Hiring the best people, developing standardized procedures that generate profits, and training service providers well are methods retailers use to minimize **inconsistent** service. In the next section we will examine service retailers' strategies to accommodate the unique nature of their business.

DEVELOPING A SERVICE RETAILING STRATEGY

Throughout *Essentials of Retailing* we have examined how retailers—primarily retailers of merchandise—develop and implement strategies. In this section, we will concentrate on how service retailers design and implement their strategy. The similarities and differences between how service and merchandise retailers go about executing their strategy are highlighted. Recall from Chapter 5 that a **retail strategy** is a statement summarizing management decisions that identify (1) the retailer's target markets, (2) the format that the retailer plans to use to satisfy the target market's needs, and (3) the basis upon which the retailer plans to build a sustainable competitive advantage.

Target Markets

Service retailers define their target markets in much the same way merchandise retailers do. For instance, service retailers involved in hair care typically use a combination of demographic and geographic segmentation schemes. Traditional neighborhood barbershops typically target males who live within a fairly narrow geographic boundary, without regard to income. Specialty beauty salons, on the other hand, may draw their target market from a larger geographic area, but appeal to a higher income group. Because Supercuts covers such a large geographic area, it appeals to a large price-sensitive segment of the population that includes men and women of all ages.

Travel agents use a benefit segmentation approach. Travel agents know that students, and most of their professors, typically want the lowest price and are willing to accept less than first-class accommodations. Business travelers, on the other hand, are most concerned with convenience. The relatively small, but lucrative luxury market seeks unique travel experiences without regard to price. The travel agent must recognize that the same family may drift from segment to segment depending on the situation. They may shop for the lowest price for their children's trip home from college. When they're arranging a business trip, being home on Friday evening may be the most important criterion. Finding unique villas to stay in may be the only thing that matters to them, however, when they are going to Europe on vacation.

Bigger Is Often Better

Part of any corporate strategy is to examine how fast a firm should grow. Like manufacturers, service retailers can achieve a competitive advantage by getting bigger. Consider, for example, shoe repair firms. They have traditionally been small mom-and-pop concerns with all work done on the premises. Yet there are considerable advantages to having multiple outlets. First, each retail outlet would be relatively less expensive to operate because it could be small with a modest amount of equipment (e.g., machines for changing heels while customers wait). Other work could be done at an inexpensive yet centrally located warehouse facility. Systems could be developed for processing orders and assuring high quality standards. As the firm grows, it could create a corporate identity through advertising and by creating a unique store design. The shoe repair firm could advertise specials in newspapers. After all, it costs the same to run an ad for one store as it does for 50 in a particular market. Customers would recognize and be drawn into the stores no matter where they were. These advantages of size would be prohibitively expensive for a one-unit operation.

A **sustainable competitive advantage** is an advantage over competition that can be maintained over a long time. Although many of the opportunities to develop sustainable advantages are similar for merchandise and service retailers, the requirements for service retailers often have a different twist. Let's explore how service retailers can develop a sustainable competitive advantage.

☼ RETAIL ORGANIZATION

Because the creation and consumption of a retailing service are inseparable, it is critical that the service is performed right the first time. As we discussed earlier, many of the most successful retailers are consumed with hiring and keeping the best people. Consider, for instance, Walt Disney World Resorts in Lake Buena Vista, Florida.[4] Of its 35,000 employees, some 20,000 have direct contact with guests. Disney's interviewers aren't concerned with cognitive ability or grades in marketing classes. They're looking for enthusiastic people who take pride in their work and who can take charge of a situation without supervision. They believe people can develop specific work skills with training.

Service retailers also benefit by developing standards of quality service that generate profits. For example, banking giant NationsBank Corp. now develops and measures standards for every service improvement, from adding tellers to offering new mortgage products. United Parcel Service, Inc. (UPS) knows the average time it takes for elevator doors to open in certain city blocks and how long it takes people to answer their doorbells. Armed with this information, UPS had developed delivery standards for its drivers.

Training service providers to deliver a high level of consistent service is critical to the success of all service retailers. UPS recently abandoned its belief that on-time delivery is the paramount concern of its customers.[5] Surveys indicated that customers want more interaction with the drivers. If drivers are less harried and more willing to chat, customers can get some practical advice on shipping. As a result, UPS has trained delivery drivers to visit with customers; drivers have an additional 30 minutes a week of discretionary time to do so, and they receive points to apply toward merchandise from the UPS catalogue for any sales leads they generate. UPS claims the change has generated "tens of millions of dollars" in new revenues.

If there is a service failure, retailers have several options for rectifying the situation.[6] Suppose your car breaks down on the road just after you pick it up after being repaired. What should the auto repair shop do? First, the shop should prepare employees to handle problems. Service failures should not be left to chance. Each employee—especially those who interact directly with customers—should know what to do when particular problems arise. Second, the first person you talk to should have the power to take swift action. Recall that in Chapter 14, we discussed the importance of empowering employees to do whatever it takes to satisfy the customer. Third, to overcome the dissatisfaction associated with service failures, the shop should correct the situation and give the customer something extra. For instance, it should pick up the car, provide the customer with alternative transportation, plus give the customer a free oil change on her next visit.

Organizational culture is a complex set of beliefs and ways of doing things that influence the organization's perspective on itself and the world.[7] In Chapter 6 we recognized the need to motivate employees by having a strong organizational culture. When the organizational culture becomes a central theme in a service retailer's strategy, it can be a powerful weapon in achieving a competitive advantage. Consider the corporate mission of Satisfaction Guaranteed Eateries, Inc. in Seattle: to make other people happy. "Every time a customer leaves one of our restaurants with a more optimistic view of the world, we've done our job. Every time we fail to raise a customer's spirits with good food, gratifying service, and a soothing atmosphere, we haven't done our job," states founder and CEO Timothy W. Firnstahl.[8]

To ensure that the firm achieves its mission, Firnstahl initiated the following policy: "Your enjoyment guaranteed, always." For the guarantee to be truly effective, he empowered employees to solve any problem on the spot. Of course, some guidelines were provided. It didn't make sense to give a party of four a free dinner just because they had to wait five minutes for water. On the other hand, Firnstahl encouraged employees not to get bogged down in the guidelines. Additionally he believes in "fix plus one." That is, if coffee is served cold, replace the coffee, plus give the customer a free dessert. The "plus one" helps overcome the hassle factor of the original service failure.

 ## INFORMATION SYSTEMS

In Chapter 6, we discussed the ways in which retailers are using information systems to improve their competitive advantage. Service retailers can also benefit from innovative information systems by reducing their costs, improving their service, and collecting information on their customers.

Organizational culture is critical in providing effective service. The corporate mission at Satisfaction Guaranteed Eateries, owners of this Sharp's Roaster & Ale House near Seattle, is: To make other people happy.

Information systems can be used to reduce costs and improve service. For instance, Federal Express now uses a hand-held device that allows couriers to generate optically scannable ZIP code labels indicating a package's destination. This system speeds the sorting process and cuts down on the number of misrouted packages.

Another use of information systems in the services industry is to collect data on customers. For instance, Charles Schwab & Co., the discount brokerage firm, collects information on every transaction made by every customer. Schwab tracks sales of specific types of securities and uses the information to target direct-mail advertisements where the research suggests they will be most effective. Suppose, for example, that retired people are rolling over CDs. The company might develop an ad about other fixed-income investments to be mailed to this group.[9]

Finally, service retailers can create a feedback system by collecting data from customers after the sale and using it to improve service in the future. This information is typically collected from complaints or warranties. (See Chapter 14.)

LOCATION

Having a good location may be even more important for a service retailer than it is for a merchandise retailer. After all, services are perishable commodities. If a service isn't available when the customer wants it, there is no second chance. Yet, as we noted in Chapter 7, good locations are harder and harder to find. Thus an advantage will accrue to service retailers who are able to maintain convenient locations. Consider, for instance, automatic teller machines (ATMs). Not too many years ago, the only way a bank customer could get cash or make a withdrawal was to have a face-to-face interaction with a bank teller during the bank's limited hours. Interestingly, many banks are still closed during the hours people have time to go to the bank such as early morning, evenings, and weekends. Not only have ATMs partially

RE-TALE 17-2   Therapy on Wheels

You've probably heard of personal trainers making house calls. But psychologists holding your hand through rush hour?

That's what Mobile Psychological Services of New York City is all about. Patients step into a customized van, settle into plush leather seats, and discuss their problems with a trained therapist while a chauffeur, separated by a soundproof glass window, drives them to work, the airport, or wherever they need to go.

The firm started the service because job and family commitments caused many clients to miss their appointments. So the company decided to bring the office to them. Its cancellation rate is now a third of what it used to be.

The service caters mostly to high-powered Wall Street types, who shell out $175 an hour to work on many types of problems, including substance abuse and stress disorders. An added bonus of on-the-road therapy: Patients can talk for more than their allotted time if the van gets stuck in traffic.

SOURCE: Denise Brodey, "Therapy on Wheels," *Shape,* January 1995, p. 18.

Mobile Psychological Services of New York City bring therapy to the patient—for a price.

solved the "banker's hours" problem by being open 24 hours a day, but they are conveniently located virtually everywhere in the Western world.

Location is not very important to some service retailers. Some service providers come to their customers. Examples include gardeners, exterminators, and personal trainers. Re-Tale 17–2 describes a service of the 1990s in which psychological therapy goes to the customer. Location is also not very important for highly specialized service providers such as physicians, lawyers, and consultants. Either patient/clients go to the service provider, or the service provider comes to them.

ASSORTMENT DECISIONS

Service retailers face many of the same assortment decisions that merchandise retailers do. They have to decide on their stock balance, make sales forecasts, and develop product lines that enable them to beat their competition.

Recall from Chapter 8 that **stock balance** is a strategic decision that defines the degree to which a retailer wishes to be a specialist with a narrow offering, or a generalist with a broad offering. A store's stock balance results in a trade-off among three different factors: variety, assortment, and service levels.

Stock Balance

Consider health clubs. Some offer a large variety of activities and equipment from exercise machines to swimming, wellness programs, and New Age lectures. Others, like Gold's Gym, don't offer much variety, but have an excellent assortment of body building equipment and programs. Some hospitals, such as big municipal hospitals found in most urban areas, offer a large variety of medical services. Smaller private hospitals often specialize in physical rehabilitation or psychiatry.

For service retailers, the level of service is a sales forecasting issue.

Sales Forecasting

Due to the perishable nature of services, service retailers can't stockpile as merchandise retailers can. Instead they must have extra equipment (e.g., ski lifts) or additional service providers (telephone repair people) to meet surges in demand. Of course, having idle equipment and service providers is a waste of resources. So service retailers have devised strategies for handling surges in demand.

Many service retailers attempt to match customers with service providers by taking reservations or making appointments. Physicians are notorious for making their patients wait, but the patients are fighting back. (See Re-Tale 17–3.) Other service retailers use different strategies for lessening the impact of having to wait for service. Sticking a television in front of customers is a simple, inexpensive method used by service providers from airlines to barbershops. Distracting customers by allowing them to watch the service being performed is a strategy used by car washes, photo finishers, and restaurants. The most innovative service retailers, however, actually devise methods to perform the service better. United Parcel Service of America, Inc. (UPS) now guarantees delivery of packages and letters by 8:30 A.M. The next best alternative is Federal Express and other major carriers that deliver by 10:30 A.M. The UPS service isn't inexpensive, however. Delivery of a letter, for instance, costs $40, almost four times the price of a letter delivered at 10:30.[10] Finally, some retailers have devised innovative pricing strategies that entice customers to utilize services during off-peak times. These pricing strategies are discussed in the next section.

Technological Innovations

It is relatively easy and inexpensive to go into a service retailing business compared to becoming a merchandise retailer. Service retailers have no merchandise to buy. For some businesses, such as a pest control company, it isn't even necessary to rent store space—so services retailers must develop technological innovations that can't be easily copied if they are to achieve a competitive advantage. For example,

---

RE-TALE 17–3   Whose Time Is Worth More: Yours or the Doctor's?

Waiting in the doctor's office, some patients begin to feel as shorn of respect as Rodney Dangerfield, without the laughs. After waiting an hour to see her obstetrician, Martha Zornow, a vice president at Viacom International Inc., fired the tardy doctor in favor of a more punctual physician. "I am a busy professional. I don't make people wait for me, and I don't expect to be kept waiting," she says. "Whenever I notice that kind of arrogance, I switch doctors."

Languishing in waiting rooms causes more patient dissatisfaction than any other aspect of medical care, including fees, according to a survey by the American Medical Association (AMA). Average waiting-room time runs 20.6 minutes, the AMA says. Some specialists run later.

Doctors explain that delays are due to medical emergencies, like strokes and heart attacks, that don't respect the sanctity of a schedule. To cope with emergency situations, doctors often leave a portion of each day's appointment slots open. Some hire a physician's assistant to evaluate patients and ease the flow. But some patients would rather wait to see their doctor.

SOURCE: Marilyn Chase, "Whose Time Is Worth More: Yours or the Doctor's?" *The Wall Street Journal*, October 24, 1994, p. B1.

American Express developed a system called Authorizer's Assistant to facilitate credit authorizations. By using this system, a decision that used to involve scanning 13 databases or making a judgment call can now be made in a few seconds. Grand Slam U.S.A., a large franchiser of batting cages, has equipment that can deliver baseballs and softballs to batters at speeds of 40 to a sizzling 90 miles per hour.

Symbolic Gestures

Service retailers can address the intangibility problem associated with services by developing tangible symbols that represent the firm. For example, Blockbuster's blue and yellow store designs are recognizable throughout the United States. Their bright, friendly interiors utilize bold signage. UPS and Federal Express use a consistent color scheme throughout their organizations. The delivery persons' uniforms have such a positive appeal that the caps and other apparel items have become fashion accessories in some areas. Because entertainment is so intangible, rock concerts, live theater, and symphonies use programs and brochures that can become treasured souvenirs. Monthly financial statements from stock brokers are tangible, but not very exciting, so many financial institutions, such as Fidelity Investments, have developed easy-to-understand statements that consolidate all accounts and transactions into one document.

What's in a Brand?

Because service retailers are not selling physical products, it is more difficult and more important for them to establish a strong positive identity through the brand itself. Consider some of the famous service retailers depicted by their corporate logos in Exhibit 17–3. Service retailers often establish their identity by using the corporate brand name, colors, and distinctive designs more prominently than would be necessary for a merchandise retailer. For instance, airlines lavishly use their

Movie posters are a symbolic gesture that represents the intangible experience of movie-going.

logos and colors on their airplanes, ground transportation vehicles, baggage handling equipment, ticketing counters, and departure and arrival gates. Re-Tale 17–4 examines the new look of United Air Lines.

Long-Standing Relationships with Customers. Have you ever had to change banks? It wasn't easy, was it? You had to sign many papers, get new checks and a new ATM card, and close out your old account. Service retailers can develop a competitive advantage by devising strategies to make it difficult for their customers to switch to the competition. One method is to set up bureaucratic barriers, as was the case with the bank. Another strategy is to offer memberships to customers. Health club memberships and hotel and airline frequent user plans are examples of successful membership strategies. Health clubs often make their customers commit to at least a year of monthly payments. Frequent user plans have been so successful that many business travelers will take less efficient airline routes and stay at hotels in inconvenient locations just to take advantage of the program.

Exhibit 17-3   **Corporate Logos**

Service retailers often make extensive use of their corporate logos to establish their brand image.

PRICING

Have you ever noticed all the different expressions service retailers use for price? Price can be called *rates* (electric bill), *fares* (airplane ticket), *fees* (doctor), *charges* (ATM), or *premiums* (insurance). No matter what term they use, service retailers set prices in much the same way merchandise retailers do—to achieve a planned gross margin and to generate profits. (See Chapter 10.)

As we said in Chapter 5, price is one of the most difficult variables that retailers can use to sustain a competitive advantage because it can be so easily matched. If an airline decides to cut fares, competition typically matches the price immediately. Because car rental companies are so price-competitive, they strive for other ways to show their superiority, such as at the airport locations where they have automatic checkin and quick checkout.

Pricing can be even more complicated for service retailers than for merchandise retailers. Because customers can't touch, feel, or see the services they are buying, they will tend to rely on price and other intangible cues to judge a service's quality.[11] Consider, for instance, the ad by a hospital for delivering a baby on page 376. How would you feel about entrusting your safety or that of a loved one to this hospital? Would you feel better if the price were twice as much?

It is critical that a service's price be consistent with other aspects of the retail offering. A caterer in an upscale downtown bank building whose office is carefully decorated and who places tasteful ads in the local arts magazine is not expected to have discount prices. Price-sensitive target markets, like a college fraternity, might expect to get a barbecue restaurant at the edge of town to bring chicken and ribs to a Saturday night party.

Because services are so perishable, service retailers may use off-peak pricing (charging lower prices during slow periods to stimulate demand). The travel industry uses off-peak pricing extensively. Hotels, cruise ships, airlines, and car rental companies offer discount fares at certain times of the year and even specific days of the week, depending on the situation. For instance, a beach-front hotel room in Palm Beach, Florida, may cost $400 between Christmas and New Year's and $125 from June 1 through August 31.

Service retailers also vary their prices to different market segments. Children and senior citizens get discounts at movies and certain restaurants. These retailers

---

RE-TALE 17–4   United Airlines Goes for the Stealth Look in Coloring Its Planes

In an attempt to look more sophisticated and reflect a global image, United Air Lines has discarded its familiar red and orange stripe on a field of white in favor of a midnight-blue belly, dark-gray upper fuselage, and dark, two-tone tail.

Although a consumer test indicated approval of the new colors, other constituencies aren't as impressed. Air traffic controllers complain that the planes are so dark they can't see them in cloudy weather or at night. Some pilots agree. They don't like to appear to be invisible. The new colors are evidently so difficult to see onthe ground that machinists union officials have persuaded United to add reflective tape to ground vehicles. Some employees are so miffed that they have circulated petitions asking the company to at least lighten up the gray a little.

SOURCE: Carl Quintanilla, "United Airlines Goes for the Stealth Look in Coloring Its Planes," *The Wall Street Journal,* November 21, 1994, p. 1.

Price can sometimes send unintended signals about the quality of the service offered. Many consumers may feel that advertising the price of maternity care implies that the quality is less than ideal.

believe they can stimulate demand in these price-sensitive segments. Some dry cleaners have recently come under attack for charging women more than men to clean a similar item such as a pair of pants. Their pathetic rationale for such a strategy has simply been that women will pay more.

☼ STORE MANAGEMENT

Many of the store management issues discussed in Chapter 12 are germane to service retailers. However because the human factor dominates in the service sector, certain personnel issues require special attention.

Training

Attention to uniformity in personnel training and service delivery methods is essential. This is particularly important for franchise businesses because the owner/operators are not employees of the parent company. For instance, there is a chain of fast food hamburger restaurants in the Southwestern United States that has never reached its potential because it provides inconsistent service. Some restaurants are better than others. As a result, if customers have poor experiences at one restaurant, they will not go to any other. McDonald's, on the other hand, provides extensive training to all of its managers at its Hamburger University. The firm maintains its high and consistent service standards by constantly evaluating each store's performance.

Most retailers in the United States are open when their customers want to shop. **Hours of Operation**
Many are open seven days a week and in the evenings. Clearly, extended hours
are a competitive tool for service and merchandise retailers alike. Because of the
inseparable and perishable nature of services, however, service retailers must be
available when the customer can take advantage of the service. Although most
banks have ATMs, customers occasionally need to have a face-to-face interaction
with bank personnel. The problem is that many banks have never recognized that
most people work from 9 A.M. to 5 P.M., Monday through Friday. Therefore to provide a high level of service, they should be open when their customers are not
working. Yet many banks have hours from 10 A.M. to 3 P.M.—when most customers are at work.

 ## SUMMARY

Service retailers are pervasive in our economy. Most consumers spend a good
share of their income on services, and services account for the majority of the U.S.
gross domestic product. As a result of the aging and time-poor population, service
retailers will become even more important in the future.

The retailing of services differs from the retailing of merchandise in several
fundamental ways. First, services are intangible. As a result, service retailers stress
symbols that depict the firm. Second, services are inseparable—the service is created and delivered simultaneously. As a result, service retailers must get it right the
first time. If there is a service failure, the service provider should do everything
possible to win back a dissatisfied customer. Third, services are perishable. If a seat
at a football game is unsold, that revenue can never be recovered. To account for
perishability, service retailers build in excess capacity for peak usage times, take
reservations, devise distractions for customers, and, most importantly, devise
methods to perform the service better. Fourth, services are inconsistent. The best
service retailers take great pains to hire the best people and train them well.

Like any retailer, service providers must develop strategies to achieve a sustainable differential advantage. In many cases, service retailers become better competitors as they get bigger. Services are so easily copied that retailers must develop
technological innovations to stay on top. For instance, successful service retailers
develop information systems that reduce costs, improve service, and collect information on customers. A strong corporate culture that stresses 100 percent customer
satisfaction is a critical element for beating the competition. Having good locations
matters more to service retailers than it does to merchandise retailers because services have to be available to customers when they want them. The best service
retailers also attempt to establish a strong corporate identity through unique store
designs, brand names, and colors. Because it is always easier to keep old customers than to find new ones, some service retailers devise strategies to lock customers into long-term relationships. Price is important in any retailing strategy, but
it is particularly tricky for service retailers. Customers often use price as a guide to
judge a service's quality. If the price is too high, people won't buy; if it is too low,
they may question the service's quality. Finally, it is particularly important for service
retailers (1) to train employees to provide a consistent level of service and (2) to
have very accessible hours of operation.

KEY TERMS

customer service, 363

inconsistency, 367

inseparability, 366

intangibility, 366

organizational

   culture, 369

perishability, 367

retail strategy, 367

stock balance, 371

sustainable

competitive

advantage, 368

DISCUSSION QUESTIONS AND PROBLEMS

1. Name 10 nationally known service retailers that you have used.
2. Why should a service retailer include something physical in its offering to customers? Give a couple of examples of what it might use.
3. Suppose you own a hair salon. Devise a system for dealing with customers who are irritated when their stylist keeps them waiting too long.
4. What can service retailers do to maintain consistent service?
5. How can service retailers benefit from economies of scale (becoming bigger)?
6. Describe an ideal location for a Blockbuster Video store and a video repair store.
7. Now that you have taken a course in retailing and have mastered the essentials, you are ready to go into business as a retailing consultant. How would you decide how much to charge your clients?
8. Service retailers can benefit by developing information systems that the competition cannot easily copy. What information could a weight loss firm like Jenny Craig use to develop a differential advantage?

Cases for Section 5

The partners of Simon and Smith, a medium-size specialty store for women in Brookline, Oregon (population 250,000), were having their annual after-Christmas heart-to-heart talk about their store's direction. They had just completed their best year ever, their bank balance was high, and the two men were looking forward optimistically to more prosperous years.

Bill Simon said to partner Phil Smith, "We seem to be doing everything right. Our customers have been loyal to us these past 15 years, there's no competition around that can touch us, and we have the best location and best reputation in the area. I think we can look forward to another year of the same formula—hard work, careful planning, intelligent merchandising, and good employee practices. We've got a real winner."

Smith was less sanguine. "You know, Bill, the population of Brookline is growing. I just heard a big high-tech firm is planning to open a plant near here, and that food processor in Eugene is planning to consolidate operations here. That's going to bring a lot more people to this area, and I wouldn't be surprised if before long some shopping center developer discovers our area. We've had it pretty easy all these years, and I'd hate to see us get too complacent and then have to give business away to a competitor. Our customers are getting older, and we're not

doing anything much to attract younger people. Our customer profile is between 35 and 50, and next year, it'll be between 36 and 51. I suggest we give some serious thought to attracting younger women, so we'll be prepared when the competition comes."

Simon said, "Why play with a successful formula? Our misses departments produce 60 percent of sales and nearly 80 percent of profits. If we try to expand our junior business, we'll get killed. We don't understand that business, and if we start in with loud music and gaudy displays, we'll drive our loyal customers away."

"Bill, don't be an ostrich. We could easily take part of the store and wall it off, maybe even break through a separate entrance. Those old ladies won't even know there's anything else going on. If we don't, I guarantee you that our population will age as the market is increasing, and we'll lose out."

Discussion Questions:

1. Analyze each partner's position. What additional information might be useful to justify each opinion?
2. What are the alternative courses of action Simon and Smith can take? Give advantages and disadvantages of each alternative.
3. Make a recommendation for Simon and Smith's future.

"They're swabbing the decks of the battleships in preparation for the battle royale," declared Fashion Network Report, the garment industry publication. Indeed, the flagship stores of Bloomingdale's, Bergdorf Goodman, and Saks Fifth Avenue were sprucing up the displays, making stylish renovations, and redesigning entire departments in anticipation of the challenger from downtown. In early

September 1993, Barney's New York opened its newest branch on Manhattan's Madison Avenue at 61st Street, in one of the world's most luxurious and celebrated shopping districts. Known as much for its edgy display windows and witty ads as its leadership in sophisticated men's and women's clothing, could the innovative retailer transport its successful formula to an intensely competitive high-end location? With recession taking its toll in the professional world as conspicuous spending fell out of favor, would the move show great business acumen or folly?

Barney's was no stranger to taking risks. The new 230,000-square-foot store would be the capstone in the evolution of a retailer known for innovation and merchandising savvy. Barney's promoted then-unknown American designers such as Calvin Klein and introduced Americans to foreign designers such as Giorgio Armani.

Barney's success is in not imitating the larger department and specialty stores. The retailer has a unique vision in fashion and merchandising is perceived as more innovative, creative, and up-to-date than the competition's. The old Manhattan store even distinguished itself in manufacturer's lines carried by other retailers. Barney's offers male customers the largest selection of Calvin Klein in the city by stocking the designer's entire line. The most fashion-forward elements of designers' current collections are chosen to suggest new directions for more innovative customers. Special orders support the Barney's imprint. An exclusive agreement with Paris-based Givenchy for his most famous silhouettes required the designer to use Barney's trademark black, navy, and other subdued tones. Finally, the proactive involvement of an in-house design staff has resulted in almost 50 percent of sales coming from Barney's private label.

In the mid-1980s, Barney's was riding the crest of the sartorial boom in men's clothing, but further horizons beckoned. With sales of $60 million, Barney's was tapping a somewhat limited market in the metropolitan area: downtown workers, neighborhood residents of Greenwich Village and Chelsea, and suburbanites who appreciated Barney's free parking. Uptown residents might visit, but they also had their own shopping areas in New York's rich retail environment. However, expansion beyond 17th Street would be problematic. The Pressmans had an aversion to debt, but outside financing would be required to open other stores. After a lengthy search for a partner, Barney's entered a joint venture agreement with Isetan, a large Japanese retailer with an even longer family-owned tradition. With an infusion of $125 to $200 million of new capital, additional locations became possible. By 1993, 13 new stores were opened in the United States and one opened in Japan. With the addition of the new Beverly Hills stores in 1994, right next door to Saks, Barney's will have doubled its retail business within two years to $400 million in sales.

The uptown location placed Barney's closer to its real competitors in the upscale clothing markets, and the retailer was counting on tapping new and substantial customer bases. Tourists rarely ventured to the flagship store, preferring to shop near their hotels uptown. In addition, Barney's was after a larger share of the high-fashion women's market. A retailing belief holds that men aren't shoppers and will go out of their way to the 17th Street store when they need to buy an item. In contrast, women are shoppers and may buy something where they shop. Where uptown has numerous opportunities to find the right dress while on a shopping trip, a customer might just return home after an unsuccessful trek to 17th Street. In the long run, this would discourage uptown customers, and the store would need to be where fashion-conscious women shopped. Barney's was counting on the moneyed residents of the Upper East Side to at least include the Madison Avenue Barney's in their local excursions, if not make the store their first stop. Customers uninitiated in the hipness of Barney's were also targeted.

Other issues would present themselves in the feisty world of high-end retailing in the new location. Almost immediately, many designers balked at yet another outlet for their exclusive wares in Midtown. Prestigious department stores already carried their lines, and rumor had it that these stores were pressuring designers to refuse to sell to Barney's. Many premier designers had their own shops on Madison Avenue or equally toney 57th Street. Chanel, Yves St. Laurent, Isaac Mizrahi, Ralph Lauren, and others refused to stock the Midtown store. A particularly rancorous lawsuit ended with Armani being forced to supply all of Barney's New York outlets. In addition, uptown didn't offer 17th Street's isolation from innovative competitors and their special agreements with manufacturers. Bloomingdale's, Saks, and Bergdorf's had often acquired exclusive rights to pieces in a manufacturer's collection. "Exclusive" rights might only last one season for any of the retailers. Henri Bendel had a long tradition of showcasing new design talent, and the New York branch of Paris's Galleries Lafayette offered unique French designers. Charivari's quirkiness was as celebrated as Barney's stylistic idiosyncrasies, and numerous specialty shops nipped at any retailer's broader lines.

Discussion Questions:

1. Evaluate the advantages and disadvantages of Barney's new location on Madison Avenue.
2. How should other luxury specialty stores in Midtown Manhattan respond to the new Barney's?
3. What should be the next step for Barney's downtown store?

This case was prepared by Jan Owens, University of Wisconsin–Madison.

CASE 5-3 ☼ WHERE AMERICA SHOPS: TROUBLE IN SEARS AUTO CENTERS

The marketing concept states that the organization's goal is to recognize and satisfy customer needs at a profit. Such was the goal of Edward Brennan, chairman of Sears, Roebuck & Company. Under his leadership, market research studies were conducted on customer automotive repair needs. Sears then established a preventive maintenance program, which instructed the auto repair centers to recommend repair/replacement on the basis of the mileage on the odometer. Concurrently, sales quotas were established for Sears' 850 auto repair centers. Meeting or exceeding these quotas earned bonus money for service personnel and gave management an objective means of evaluating employee performance.

The new sales incentive program required the sale of a certain number of repairs or services—including alignments, springs, and brake jobs—every eight hours. Service employees also could qualify for bonus money by selling a specified number of shock absorbers or struts for every hour worked. The program's goal was to meet customer needs while increasing auto service centers' profits.

After the program was put into place, the automotive unit became the fastest growing and most profitable unit in Sears' recent history. But a growing number of consumer complaints were lodged against Sears. So the states of California, New Jersey, and Florida investigated practices at Sears Auto Centers. The state of California alleged that Sears consistently overcharged its customers an average of $223 for unnecessary repairs or work that was never done.

Sears faces a hearing in California on charges of fraud, making false and misleading statements, false advertisement, and willful departure from accepted trade practices. Based on the outcome of this hearing, Sears could lose its license to operate repair centers in California. Legal action in other states is pending. Sears contends that its centers were merely servicing vehicles based on the manufacturers' suggested maintenance schedule. Moreover, Sears claims that failure to make these suggested improvements would have neglected the safety of the consumer.

Discussion Questions:

1. What service properties inherent within the auto repair industry contribute to consumers being vulnerable to the unethical behavior undertaken at Sears?
2. What factors affected Sears Auto Center employees' behavior?
3. What was the effect of Sears Auto Centers' policies?
4. What should Sears do to control this type of unethical behavior?

This case was prepared by K. Douglas Hoffman and Judy Sigauw, Dept. of Marketing, University of North Carolina at Wilmington. From *Marketing Education Review* (Fall 1993), pp. 26–32.

CASE 5-4 ☼ THE CLEVELAND CLINIC

For years, Ohio's Cleveland Clinic has ranked with the top world-class providers of medical care. It pioneered coronary bypass surgery and developed the first kidney dialysis machine. King Hussein of Jordan uses the clinic, so too the royal family of Saudi Arabia.

Big-name health-care institutions like the Cleveland Clinic are after new markets for their state-of-the-art medicine, and are posing a new threat to local physicians. The expansions are also disrupting traditional relationships between physicians and their patients, physicians and their hospitals and physicians and their fellow physicians.

Like any business, the Cleveland Clinic keeps close tabs on its core market, and the outlook wasn't all that bright. Seven midwestern states provide 90 percent of the clinic's business and population growth in that region is expected to be flat through the year 2000. But not so southeastern Florida, where the population is still growing and, in many areas, is highly affluent.

South Florida appears to be a dream market. Yachts lining the canals of the Intracoastal Waterway and a ubiquitous building boom reflect wealth and growth so palpable that clinic officials have come to call it "immaculate consumption." Moreover, about 20 percent of the 3.7 million residents in Dade, Broward and Palm Beach Counties are over 65 years old. By the year 2000, about 50 percent of the population will be over 45—a potential motherlode of patients. "We felt there was room for us," Dr. Kiser said. "We decided to go on our own rather than wait to be invited."

When the Cleveland Clinic opened an outpatient clinic in South Florida, a war broke out. In a full-page advertisement in the *Miami Herald,* Dr. Seropian, a local physician, pulled out the stops. He likened the clinic to Dingoes—wild Australian dogs—"that roam the bush eating every kind of prey." The clinic filed suit in federal district court in Fort Lauderdale, charging, among other things, that some physicians had conspired to "hamper" its entry into Broward County.

Famous medical institutions like the Cleveland Clinic and Mayo are victims of their own success. Many of the once-exotic procedures that they invented are now routinely available across the country, reducing the need for patients to travel to the medical meccas. For instance, the Cleveland Clinic might once have had a hold on coronary bypass surgery, but no more: Last year more than 250,000 patients had the operation at hospitals throughout the United States.

"These clinics used to be the court of last resort for complex medical cases," says Jeff Goldsmith, national health-care adviser to Ernst & Whinney, the accounting firm. "Now, the flooding of the country with medical spe-cialties and high-technology equipment has forced them to adopt a different strategy."

Their expertise and reputation spell formidable competition for the local medical community. "On one level," says Jay Wolfson, a health-policy expert at the University of South Florida in Tampa, "it's like bringing in a McDonald's. If you're a mom-and-pop sandwich shop on the corner, you could get wiped out."

Discussion Questions:

1. Compare the Cleveland Clinic to traditional retailers?
2. What was its retail mix?
3. What factors in its environment resulted in it changing its retail mix?

Appendix: Careers in Retailing

Questions that this appendix answers include

- **What careers are available in retailing?**
- **What are the benefits and disadvantages of a retailing career?**
- **What are the training programs like at major retail organizations?**
- **What should you look for (and ignore) when choosing retailers to interview?**

Possibly the most important decision a student must make is whether to pursue a career in retailing. Throughout this book, two management tracks have been emphasized: merchandise management and store management. Merchandise management attracts people with strong analytical capabilities, an ability to predict what merchandise will appeal to their target markets, and a facility to work with vendors as well as store management to get things done. Successful store managers have the ability to lead and motivate employees as well as an eye for detail—whether it be stock status reports or housekeeping and display.

The day-to-day life of a J.C. Penney department manager is quite different than that of a store manager for The Limited. The J.C. Penney manager has more control over merchandise purchased and sold in the department, whereas the manager at The Limited has total responsibility for the store's human resource requirements. Thus, when planning their interview schedules, people seeking careers in retailing should carefully study different career options and the relative advantages of working in different types of stores.

CAREER OPPORTUNITIES IN RETAILING

In terms of raw opportunity, retailing has it! The retailing industry is the nation's single largest employer. By 1988, retail store sales had increased to $1.6 trillion, making retailing one of the largest industries in the United States. Approximately 19 million people were employed by traditional retailers in 1988—and this figure is

This appendix was prepared with the assistance of Leda M. Perez.

deceptively low because it fails to include several million people employed by service firms, proprietors, family businesses, and partnerships.[1]

Many retailers are knocking on the door of college campuses. In 1990, for instance, Wal-Mart held interviews on 93 college campuses to fill 800 trainee positions. In the 1991–92 academic year, Wal-Mart needed to fill 1,100 trainee positions.[2] J.C. Penney interviewed on 225 college campuses in the 1989–90 school year to fill 1,000 entry-level positions.[3]

A retailing career offers a multitude of possibilities. In how many other industries can you obtain significant responsibility early in a career? Double your income in five years? Have complete responsibility for your own store one to two years after college graduation? As a buyer or store manager, you have complete responsibility and accountability for the successful operation and profitability of a specific area.

Consider the plethora of retail stores. There are career opportunities in department stores like Foley's and Macy's, specialty stores such as Neiman Marcus and Saks Fifth Avenue, specialty chains such as The Limited and Radio Shack, catalog showrooms such as Service Merchandise, food stores such as Safeway and Kroger, discount stores such as Target and Kmart, national department store chains such as Sears and J.C. Penney, off-price stores such as T.J. Maxx and Marshalls, category specialists such as Home Depot and Toys "R" Us—and many more!

Within each type of store, we find career opportunities in the traditional marketing responsibilities of merchandising/buying (Chapters 10 to 14), store management (Chapters 16 to 19), and promotion/advertising (Chapter 15). Many large chains have their own product development organizations (Chapter 14). Career opportunities are continuing to emerge in the areas of computer and distribution/systems (Chapter 20). All businesses require accountants and executives with advanced training in financial management (Chapter 7). Major retailers also have staffs devoted exclusively to retail location analysis (Chapters 9 and 10). Probably no other industry offers a greater variety of career opportunities.

The numerous mergers, acquisitions, and restructuring in retailing in recent years have caused a temporary shift in career opportunities. (See Chapter 5.) Most retail employees who were adversely affected held central staff positions (such as buyer or merchandise manager) or positions at higher levels of the organization. Many positions have been consolidated as a result of the restructuring, and greater efficiencies have been created through economies of scale and improved systems. On the other hand, people in charge of store operations, like store and regional managers, have been relatively unaffected by the industry restructuring. No matter how ownership and top management shifts, retail stores always need managers.

CAREER PATHS IN RETAILING

A **career path** can be thought of as the route taken between positions within a particular organization. This pattern of advancement depends on the company's organization structure and many other factors. For example, in a highly centralized retail organization, such as a department store like Dillard's, most executive-level opportunities exist at the corporate headquarters, while in a more decentralized organization, such as a specialty chain like The Limited, most opportunities are at the stores. (See Chapter 8.) Career paths also differ among the many different types of retail institutions.

The primary opportunities for a career in retailing are in the areas of buying and store management. More limited opportunities exist in sales promotion, human resources, loss prevention, real estate, operations, distribution, finance, and accounting. These areas support the organization's merchandising and operating efforts, though a strong familiarity with merchandising is generally required so that each executive in a support role can perform that function well. For this reason, executives in these support roles typically begin their careers in store management or buying.

In the early 90s, however, operations personnel are in high demand. Since retailers are focusing more on efficiency to maintain profitability, operations professionals are held in high regard. In addition, top financial executives are becoming increasingly important to their firms, since most of today's large retailers have become very complicated from a financial perspective.

The road to the top is as varied in retailing as in any other industry. Still, we can make some generalizations about what to expect. Most large multiunit retailers begin with formal executive training programs that run from about 12 weeks (at Macy's) to 26 weeks (at J.C. Penney). Some training programs heavily emphasize on-the-job training (Wal-Mart); others have a split between on-the-job and formal classroom training (Foley's).

Typically, careers in retailing move either vertically or in a zigzag fashion through the organization. The vertical paths are either merchandising/buying or store operations. For example, Exhibit A–1 shows the typical vertical career path in store management for J.C. Penney. Generally, the parallel vertical career paths are more common with chains that have many outlets. The managements of these firms believe it's not very efficient to train everyone in the buying functions when the overwhelming majority of careers lie in store operations.

The zigzag career path for Burdines, in contrast, bounces from store management to buying and back again. This configuration, used by many department store chains, is illustrated in Exhibit A–2. Although the specific responsibilities inherent in each of these job titles differ across firms, Exhibit A–3 describes responsibilities of a few key positions in the Burdines career path in Exhibit A–2.

The life of a buyer is distinctively different from that of a store manager. First, the buyer generally works in a buying office so she's slightly removed from the retail store environment. To maintain contact with this environment, she must physically visit her stores and the stores of her competitors. Although the buyer's workweek is based on a standard Monday through Friday, 8 until 5, as with most management careers, there's often overtime and frequent travel. Last, the buyer's primary responsibility is the management of products and processes. To be successful she must have strong analytical skills, be very organized, be a good decision maker, possess strong negotiation skills, and be consistent.

The store manager, on the other hand, works directly in the retail environment. Remote locations isolate him from the home office and create a sense of independence. His hours generally mirror his store's and can therefore include weekends and evenings. In addition, he spends much time during nonoperating hours tending to administrative responsibilities. His primary function is to manage the store's resources (products, services, equipment, and personnel) with an end goal of satisfying the customer while maintaining a healthy retail operation. This requires good human management skills, general knowledge of several business disciplines (accounting, management, etc.), sales skills, creative decision-making skills, and much common sense. For a glimpse of these two very different career opportunities, consider the following representations of the workday of a buyer and store manager at Macy's.

Vertical Career Path at J.C. Penney

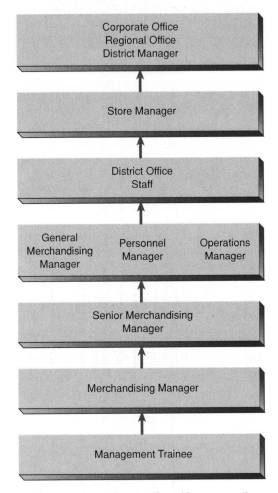

SOURCE: J.C. Penney Brochure, "A Career For You: Store Management."

A Week in the Life of a Buyer at Macy's

Every Monday the reviews come in—the results of sales for the previous week.[4] For some buyers, it's an occasion for rejoicing; for others it can be advance warning of opportunities to be seized or dangers to be avoided.

"These week-to-week judgments can be as important as the decision to buy in the first place," explains a Macy's buyer. "People outside the industry probably believe buyers spend most of their time selecting merchandise. Actually, that's only about 10 percent of what we do. We're really total managers for our merchandise classifications. We're responsible for the structure of the deal with the vendor, for distribution to stores, for merchandising presentation, for pricing decisions, for promotion and advertising, for analyzing sales reports . . . you name it!"

Says a vice president, "It's not unusual for a new buyer to be in charge of a multimillion-dollar business. Buyers must be willing to accept risk. They are people who enjoy getting their report cards almost instantaneously—and usually see either A's or F's."

run 8 to 15 units after a few years so they quickly move into higher pay brackets. Typical compensation range for management trainees is $18,500 to $24,000. A buyer for a specialty store chain earns from $40,000 to $86,000 or more. A specialty store chain manager earns from $17,400 to $36,000; a department store manager makes from $50,000 to $150,000 or more; a discount store manager makes from $70,000 to $100,000 or more.

Retailers have been strengthening the link between performance and compensation for top executives by supplementing base salaries with significant bonuses. A recent survey found, for example, that 95 percent of CEO's were eligible for incentives, which on average represented 61 percent of their salaries.[8] Similarly, about 83 percent of companies' top store and merchandising executives were eligible for incentives, although bonuses represented only a little less than 30 percent of their salaries. The survey also found evidence of the spread of incentive plans to other retail ranks. Even at the lower pay levels studied, roughly 82 percent of buyers and store managers, for example, were eligible for incentives.

Exhibit A–4 illustrates that, on average, top retail executives are well compensated. Because promotions in retailing tend to be based on individual performance (not on length of employment), advancement can be more rapid than in most industries. This means that how quickly people progress is largely up to them. A college graduate with a good performance record could become a buyer for a high-dollar-volume area in a large department store within two to three years, or manager of a specialty store in as little as one to two years.

A compensation package consists of more than salary alone. In retailing, the benefits package is often substantial and may include a profit-sharing plan; savings plan; stock option plan; hospital, major medical, and dental insurance; life insurance; long-term disability protection; income protection plans; paid vacations and holidays; and bonus potential. Two additional benefits of retailing careers are that most retailers offer employees valuable discounts on the merchandise that they sell, and some buying positions include extensive foreign travel[10]

Retailing has an often exaggerated reputation of offering long and odd hours. Superficially, this reputation is true. Store managers do often work evenings and weekends. But many more progressive retailers, notably The Gap, have realized that if the odd hours aren't offset by time off at other times of the week, many managers become inefficient, angry, and resentful—in a word, burned out.[11] It's also important to put the concept of long hours into perspective. Most professional careers require more than 40 hours per week for the person to succeed. In a new job with new tasks and responsibilities, the time commitment is even greater.

People shouldn't go into retailing if they like a calm, orderly, peaceful work environment with no surprises. Retailing is for those who like having exciting days, making quick decisions, and dealing with a variety of assignments, tasks, and people—often all at once.

Retailing is also for people who like responsibility. Starting executives are given more responsibility more quickly than in other industries. Buyers are responsible for choosing, promoting, pricing, distributing, and *selling* millions of dollars worth of merchandise each season. The department manager, which is generally the first position after a training program, is often responsible for merchandising one or more departments as well as for managing 10 or more full- and part-time sales associates.

REFACT

In *Business Week's* most recent survey of corporate compensation, for example, the third ranking earner in 1993 was Joseph R. Hyde III, CEO of Auto Zone, a Memphis-based auto parts chain. Hyde received $1.1 million in salary and bonus in 1993, and earned $31.1 million by exercising his stock options.[9]

Working Conditions

Responsibility

Total Compensation for Retail Executives* (in thousands of dollars)

Job Title	Job Description	Low (10th Percentile)	Medium (50th Percentile)	High (90th Percentile)
Chief Executive Officer	Has final responsibility to board of directors, parent company or owners for current profits and long-range growth.	$253.0	$474.6	$927.0
Top Financial Executive	Heads all financial operations; supervises controller and treasury functions.	116.8	200.0	364.1
Top Merchandising Executive	Directs all buying-merchandising activities; supervises general merchandise managers or divisional merchandise managers.	105.8	197.5	381.2
Top Stores Executive	Responsible for operation and profitability of retail stores; controls operating costs and implements merchandising programs.	84.0	152.3	259.9
Top Information Systems Executive	Responsible for data processing activities.	89.6	138.6	225.8
General Merchandise Manager	Responsible for development and implementation of merchandising activities for major groups of related merchandise.	84.8	136.1	201.4
Top Real Estate Executive	Responsible for site selection, lease negotiation and acquisition of real estate.	80.2	135.0	203.0
Top Marketing/Sales Promotion/Advertising Executive	Directs marketing/sales promotion/ advertising programs.	76.6	125.8	222.4
Top Human Resources Executive	Develops and implements policies on recruitment, staffing, labor relations, compensation and training.	77.5	120.0	206.5
Top Planning and Merchandise Distribution Executive	Responsible for overall merchandise buying plans and merchandise allocation systems.	66.4	110.0	203.3
Treasurer	Directs most external financial activities, such as banking, investment, credit and money management.	78.4	106.7	198.6
Controller	Responsible for internal accounting policies and practices; maintains accounting records.	74.9	103.0	154.4
Divisional Merchandise Manager	Plans and executes merchandising activities for a related group of merchandise categories.	65.0	102.8	182.0
Top Distribution Center Executive	Ensures timely and cost-effective movement of merchandise to stores.	67.0	98.4	186.9
Top Loss Prevention Executive	Develops programs to protect company assets and safety of employees and customers.	54.3	80.5	119.8

Continued   EXHIBIT A-4

Job Title	Job Description	Low (10th Percentile)	Medium (50th Percentile)	High (90th Percentile)
Top Store Planning and Design Executive	Responsible for architectural design of stores.	$46.6	$77.5	$144.7
Top Store Planning/ Construction Executive	Responsible for bidding, selection of contractors and oversight of construction.	50.3	76.0	106.8
Senior Merchandise Planner/Controller	Supports buying function and forecasts companywide sales plans.	40.0	62.0	82.3
Top Internal Auditor	Responsible for internal audit program.	42.1	60.0	81.1
Buyer	Responsible for purchasing, pricing, promotion and sales of merchandise categories.	40.0	56.2	86.1
Merchandise Planner	Supports the buying function and develops distribution plans for specific merchandise categories and classes.	26.0	40.2	56.0
Store Manager	Responsible for sales, expense control, display of merchandise and customer service.	17.4	24.7	36.3

*Base salary plus reported bonus
SOURCE: Harrison Donnelly, Are You Paid Enough? *Stores,* December 1994, pp. 17, 19.

Employment Security

Retailing in general doesn't suffer from the severe shifts in the economy as badly as other industries such as the automotive industry. During recessions, people don't stop buying. They just buy less and shift their purchase patterns. Thus, sales and profits may suffer in retailing, but overall employment isn't impacted severely.

Retailing, on the other hand, is very results-oriented. Sales results are usually available immediately. Therefore, management knows who's successful and who isn't. Those who don't make the grade in the executive ranks move on rather quickly. Changes in ownership through mergers and acquisitions coupled with consolidations of systems and staffs have also made employment less secure in retailing. These changes, however, affect store management and human resources less than buyers and others in corporate staff positions.

Decentralized Job Opportunities

Depending on the type of retailer and the specific firm, retailing enables executives to change locations often or not at all. In general, a career path in store management has more opportunity for relocation. Because buying offices are usually centrally located, executives with merchandising and staff positions generally aren't subjected to frequent moves.

Career Advancement

Many opportunities for rapid advancement exist simply because of the sheer size of the retail industry. There are millions of retail establishments, and the larger ones have many different positions and multiple managerial levels. Yet in choosing a particular retailer, take care to choose a growth firm. Firms that have recently undergone corporate restructuring may have a glut of middle management positions. If store operations is an appealing career area, then chains with multiple outlets, such as The Gap or The Limited, should be pursued. But these stores don't present particularly good opportunities for people who seek a buying career, because they have relatively small buying staffs compared to the number of outlets. If buying is your primary career interest, choose a firm with a large buying staff (like most department stores) or a firm with decentralized purchasing (like J.C. Penney).

Women in Retailing

Many people consider retailing to be among the more gender-blind industries. Women have made definite progress up the career ladder in the past decade or so. In 1978, *Stores* magazine conducted a survey that revealed few women held the title of general merchandise manager, controller, or senior or executive vice president. In 1990, a similar survey of 19 of the top specialty and department stores indicated that only 5 had no women in those positions, and most had more than one. Also, the 1978 survey indicated that there were only two self-made women among the ranks of department store presidents. Today, there are at least five holding the title of president, chairperson, chief executive officer, or chief operating officer. At least two women have achieved the position of chief financial officer.[12]

☼ TRAINING PROGRAMS IN RETAILING

Training programs are as different as the retailers that sponsor them. Programs at Macy's and The Gap (which we describe next) are known for their thoroughness and professionalism. Use them as a rough guide of what to expect, but find out the specifics of the training programs for each retailer you interview.

Management Training at Macy's

At Macy's New York, the first days of training combine classroom work and independent projects on the basics: organization, customers, and merchandise.[13] Then, as a first on-site learning experience, each trainee spends several days as a sales clerk, receiving an introduction to the complexities and challenges at the point of sale. Trainees spend their third week with a sales manager, learning about the day-to-day operation of the selling floor from the supervisor's point of view. After a week of further classroom work, trainees report for a three-week stint in a buying office. This experience, supplemented with seminars, covers the whole range of the buyer's responsibilities. Then a second three-week period is spent with a sales manager in a different line (say, housewares instead of women's dresses) to further round out the emerging picture of Macy's businesses. After a week in the field on a sales support assignment, trainees attend a final series of workshops that integrates the learning experience. At the end of the program, trainees and the company agree on a starting position that meets the goals of each.

Store Management Training at The Gap

The training program for store management at The Gap takes eight weeks.[14] During the first six-week period, three days per week are spent in classroom training sessions. Each of the first six weeks of the program has specific goals and objectives. During the first week, trainees are given a thorough orientation; training in sales, customer service, and product knowledge; and knowledge of the point-of-sale system. The second week includes more information on store operations and a review of human resources procedures such as regulations. During the third week, trainees master the nuances of intracorporate communications and the basics of merchandise management. Training in the second three-week session includes loss prevention, interviewing, record keeping, and scheduling. At the end of the training program, the trainee is evaluated and is assigned an assistant manager position.

☼ CHOOSING A RETAILER TO INTERVIEW

Here are three tips to use when choosing retailers to interview.

The following issues are worth considering prior to an interview.

Tip 1: Research the Company First.

• Visit prospective employers' stores before the interview. Actually seeing the store can give you insight for discussing the company intelligently throughout the interview process. Well-stocked and orderly departments (with the exception of deep-discount stores that sometimes purposely maintain a disorderly look) suggest (but don't prove) that the company is in good health. Signs of decay could either mean the store is planning a relocation or a massive renovation, or indicate poor management of financial problems.[15]

• Read about the store. In conjunction with store visits, read the retailer's annual report to stockholders; examine reports from *Value Line* and other investment service firms; and study trade publications such as *Discount Store News, Chain Store Age Executive,* and *Stores.*

• Find out whether the retailer is hiring primarily for store or merchandise management positions. For example, if you're interested in fashion, a career in a department store or national off-price chain like T.J. Maxx or Marshalls may be the way to go. Be certain that its needs coincide with your goals.

• Determine whether there have been recent changes in ownership or top management. A change isn't necessarily bad, but it does add some uncertainty—and therefore risk—to the decision.

• Research the retailers' growth potential. Has it been expanding? Is it in strong markets? How strong and innovative are its competitors? Successful retailers in the 90s will increase their emphasis on marketing to satisfy customer needs by focusing heavily on service. Moreover, by employing creative organizational and management strategies, retailers will concentrate on giving buyers and store managers greater responsibility, while supporting them with logistics and systems specialists. (See Chapter 3.)

• Determine whether the retailer is known for innovation. An innovative retailer has a greater chance of long-term success than a stodgy one. To measure innovativeness, look at its stores and promotions. Are they modern? Do the stores and promotions reflect the times? Do they appeal to their target markets?

• Find out about the retailer's computers and distribution systems. Highly sophisticated retail technology symbolizes a view toward the future. Technology, if used properly, makes firms more efficient and therefore profitable. Finally, QR inventory management systems, EDI, and sophisticated POS terminals relieve managers from much of the tedious paperwork previously associated with careers in retailing.

Too often students take a narrow view of retailing. They assume, for instance, that they don't want to work for a discount store because they don't shop at discount stores or because the only personnel they see in discount stores are the checkers

Tip 2: Don't View the Retailer from a Customer's Perspective.

taking money. This is a short-sighted perspective. A store manager for Target or Kmart is responsible for selling and promoting millions of dollars of merchandise each year. The manager is also responsible for hiring, promoting, motivating, and scheduling a large number of part- and full-time employees.

Tip 3: Don't Base Your Impression of the Retailer on the Interviewer.

Although most retailers coming to campus to recruit are professional human resource experts, some may be store managers or buyers. Often, retailers send recent graduates of a university to recruit there. Listen to what these people have to say, but recognize that they may have little, if anything, to do with a new employee once the employee starts the job. It makes little difference, therefore, whether you like or dislike the interviewer.

Of course, it makes a big difference if the interviewer likes you. Even if you decide that a particular retailer isn't for you, always try to make the best possible impression. A well-prepared interviewee reflects well on the university. Also, the world of retailing management is small. People in the industry cross paths many times throughout their careers.

Exhibit A–5 is an example of an interview guide that a retailer might use on a campus visit. To help prepare for an interview, study this exhibit carefully. Advance knowledge of some of the questions that may arise should boost your confidence, reduce your anxiety, and improve the interviewer's impression of you.

☼ SUMMARY

Retailing isn't for everyone. This appendix has provided a framework for considering a career in retailing. The variety of careers available in the retail industry has been described. Advantages and disadvantages of a retailing career have been presented. Since training programs often provide the foundation from which to build a career, some exemplary training programs were examined. The appendix concluded with specific tips to think about when interviewing and choosing a retailer.

The XYZ Department Stores Company Targeted Selection Interview Guide

Date: _____

Applicant's Name: _____ College/University: _____

Phone Number: _____ Best Time to Reach: _____

Interviewer: _____ Division _____

Overall GPA: _____ out of _____

Opening

- **Greet Applicant:** Give name and position, and state that you represent XYZ Department Stores Company.
- **Explain Format:** Will be asked for specific behavioral examples: Will last approximately 30 minutes. Will be taking notes. Will provide applicant opportunity to ask questions.

Dimensional Questions		Notes	
Background Review	Situation	Action	Result

- How did you become aware of XYZ?
(Check as many as appropriate.)

____ Open house/resume day   ____ Mentioned by:
____ Newspaper ad   ____ Faculty
____ Personalized letter   ____ Placement office
____ Pre-interview briefing   ____ Other students
____ General reputation   ____ Alumni currently
____ Class presentation   employed by
____ Shop at your store

- Why did you choose your major? How does it relate to your career goals?

Job motivation
- Describe a situation that you found frustrating. What was the cause and how did you deal with it?
- Give me an example of when you worked the hardest and felt the greatest sense of achievement.

Decision making
- Describe a situation in which you received a procedure or set of instructions with which you disagreed. How did you handle it?
- In your last job, which decisions did you typically make? Which did you refer to a superior?

Stress tolerance
- Give an example of a task that you thought would go on forever. How did you deal with it? Result.
- When have you been under the most pressure?
- Describe a situation when someone has lost their temper or become irritated with you.

E X H I B I T A-5

Continued

Interview close
*Review notes.
*Ask any additional questions to complete notes.
*Give applicant opportunity to ask questions.
*Explain that, at the conclusion of our first interviews, we will
   be in contact with some students for follow-up
   appointments. In any case, we will be getting back to
   everyone within two weeks.
*Thank applicant for a productive interview.

Interview recap	Applicant:	
Dimensions interviewed	Comments	Rating
1. Job motivation	_____	_____
2. Decision making	_____	_____
3. Stress tolerance	_____	_____
4. Oral communication skills	_____	_____
Remaining dimensional profile	Comments	Rating
1. Leadership	_____	_____
2. Initiative	_____	_____
3. Energy	_____	_____
4. Persuasiveness	_____	_____
5. Oral presentation skills	_____	_____
6. Planning and organizing	_____	_____

Future action
Overall comments _____
_____
_____

Ratings		
5 Excessive	Refer 2nd/3rd	_____
4 Superior	Reject	_____
3 Acceptable		
- - - - - - - - -		
2 Below standard		
1 Unacceptable	Overall Rating	_____

Glossary of Retailing Terms

A

ABC analysis   an analysis that rank-orders SKUs by a profitability measure to determine which items should never be out of stock, allowed to be out of stock occasionally, or should be deleted from the stock selection.

abilities   the aptitude and skills of an employee.

accessibility   the degree to which customers can easily get into and out of a shopping center.

accessories   merchandise in apparel, department, and specialty stores used to complement apparel outfits. Examples include: gloves, hosiery, handbags, jewelry, handkerchiefs, scarves, etc.

accordion theory   a cyclical theory of retailer evolution suggesting that changes in retail institutions are explained in terms of depth versus breadth of assortment. Retail institutions cycle from high-depth/low-breadth to low-depth/high-breadth stores and back again.

account opener   a premium or special promotion item offered to induce the opening of a new account, especially in financial institutions and stores operating on an installment credit basis.

accounts payable   the amount of money owed to vendors, primarily for merchandise inventory.

accounts receivable   the amount of money due to the retailer from selling merchandise on credit.

accrued liabilities   liabilities that accumulate daily but are paid only at the end of a period.

acquisition   a strategic growth activity in which one firm acquires another firm, usually resulting in a merger. See also **leveraged buyout.**

actionability   means that the definition of a market segment must clearly indicate what the retailer should do to satisfy its needs.

adaptive selling   an approach to personal selling in which selling behaviors are altered based on information about the customer and the buying situation.

additional markup   an increase in retail price after and in addition to original markup.

additional markup cancellation   the percentage by which the retail price is lowered after a markup is taken.

additional markup percentage   The addition of a further markup to the original markup as a percentage of net sales.

administered vertical marketing system   a form of vertical marketing system designed to control a line of classification of merchandise as opposed to an entire store's operation. Such systems involve the development of comprehensive programs for specified lines of merchandise. The vertically aligned companies, even though in a nonownership position, may work together to reduce the total systems cost of such activities as advertising, transportation, and data processing. (See also **contractual vertical marketing system and corporate vertical marketing system.**)

advance order   an order placed well in advance of the desired time of shipment. By placing orders in advance of the actual buying season, a buyer is often able to get a lower price because the buyer gives the vendor business when the latter would normally be receiving little.

advertising   paid communications delivered to customers through nonpersonal mass media such as newspapers, television, radio, and direct mail.

advertising manager   a retail manager who manages advertising activities such as determining the advertising budget, allocating the budget, developing ads, selecting media, and monitoring advertising effectiveness.

advertising reach   the percentage of customers in the target market exposed to an ad at least once.

affordable promotional budgeting   a budgeting method in which a retailer first sets a budget for every element of the retail mix except promotion and then allocates the leftover funds to a promotional budget.

agent   (1) a business unit that negotiates purchases, sales, or both but does not take title to the goods in which it deals. (2) a person who represents the principal (who, in the case of retailing, is the store or merchant) and who acts under authority, whether in buying or in bringing the principal into business relations with third parties.

aging   the length of time merchandise has been in stock.

all-purpose revolving account   a regular 30-day charge account which if paid in full within 30 days from date of statement has no service charge, but when installment payments are made, a service charge is made on the balance at the time of the next billing.

alteration costs   expenses incurred to change the appearance or fit, to assemble, or to repair merchandise.

Americans with Disabilities Act (ADA)   a federal act that opens up opportunities for the disabled by requiring employers to provide accommodating work environments.

analog approach   a method of trade area analysis also known as the "similar store" or "mapping" approach. The analysis is divided into four steps: (1) describing the current trade areas through the technique of customer spotting; (2) plotting the customers on a map; (3) defining the primary, secondary, and tertiary area zones; and (4) matching the characteristics of stores in the trade areas with the proposed new store to estimate its sales potential.

anchor store   a large and well-known retail operation located in a shopping center and serving as an attracting force for consumers to the center.

ancillary services   services such as layaway, gift wrap, credit, and any other service that is not directly related to the actual sale of a specific product within the store.

anticipation discount   a discount offered by a vendor to a retailer in addition to the cash discount or dating, if the retailer pays the invoice before the end of the cash discount period.

anticompetitive leasing arrangement   a lease that limits the type and amount of competition a particular retailer faces within a trading area.

antitrust legislation   a set of laws directed at preventing unreasonable restraint of trade or unfair trade practices to foster a competitive environment. See also **restraint of trade.**

apparel manufacturers   firms that produce clothing and accessories. These firms operate in a highly competitive, labor intensive, international industry.

application form   a form used for information on a job applicant's education, employment experience, hobbies, and references.

artificial barriers   in site evaluation under accessibility, barriers such as railroad tracks, major highways, or parks.

asset turnover   net sales divided by total assets.

assets   economic resources of expected future economic benefit that are owned or controlled by an enterprise as a result of past transactions or events.

assortment   the number of SKUs within a merchandise category.

atmosphere   see **atmospherics.**

atmospherics   the design of an environment via visual communications, lighting, colors, music, and scent to stimulate customers' perceptual and emotional responses and ultimately to affect their purchase behavior.

auction   a market in which goods are sold to the highest bidder; usually well publicized in advance or held at specific times well known in the trade.

autocratic method of store management   when managers make all decisions on their own and then announce them to employees.

automatic reordering system   a system for ordering staple merchandise using a predetermined minimum quantity of goods in stock. An automatic reorder can be generated by a computer on the basis of a perpetual inventory system and reorder point calculations.

average BOM stock-to-sales ratio the number of months in the period divided by planned inventory turnover for the period.

average inventory the sum of inventory on hand at several periods in time divided by the number of periods.

B

back order a part of an order that the vendor has not filled on time and that the vendor intends to ship as soon as the goods in question are received, manufactured, or procured.

backward integration a form of vertical integration in which a retailer owns some or all of its suppliers.

bait-and-switch an unlawful deceptive practice that lures customers into a store by advertising a product at lower than usual prices (the bait) then inducing the customers to switch to a higher period model (the switch).

balance sheet the summary of a retailer's financial resources and claims against the resources at a particular date; indicates the relationship between assets, liabilities, and owner's equity.

bank cards credit cards issued by banks, such as Visa and MasterCard.

bar code see **Universal Product Code (UPC).**

barriers to entry conditions in a retail market that make it difficult for firms to enter the market.

basic merchandise see **staple merchandise.**

basic stock list the descriptive and record-keeping function of an inventory control system; includes the stock number, item description, number of units on hand and on order, and sales for the previous periods.

basic stock method an inventory management method used to determine the beginning-of-a-month (BOM) inventory by considering both the forecast sales for the month and the safety stock.

benchmarking the practice of evaluating performance by comparing your performance with that of other retailers using a similar retail strategy.

benefits the customer's specific needs that are satisfied when the customer buys a product.

benefits/price effect the condition that arises when customers' price sensitivity increases because they cannot perceive special benefits from a product.

black market the availability of merchandise at a higher price when difficult or impossible to purchase it under normal market circumstances; commonly involves illegal transactions.

blue laws prohibit retailers from being open two consecutive days of the weekend—ostensibly to allow employees a day of rest or religious observance. Most states no longer have blue laws.

bonus additional compensation awarded periodically, based on a subjective evaluation of the employee's performance.

book inventory see **retail inventory method.**

bottom-up planning when goals are set at the bottom of the organization and filter up through the operating levels.

boutique layout a store design that places all departments on the "main aisle" by drawing customers through the store in a series of major and minor loops; also known as a loop.

brand a distinctive grouping of products identified by corporate name, logo, design, symbol, or trademark.

brand loyal customers who like and consistently buy a specific brand in a product category.

break-even analysis a technique that evaluates the relationship between total revenue and total cost to determine profitability at various sales levels.

break-even point the quantity at which total revenue equals total cost, and beyond which profit occurs.

breaking bulk a function performed by retailers or wholesalers in which they receive large quantities of merchandise and sell them in smaller quantities.

breaking sizes running out of stock on particular sizes.

bridge merchandise designer branded women's apparel with broader appeal and lower prices than couture designer apparel, so called because it bridges the gap between the couture designer and mass manufactured branded merchandise.

broker a middleman that serves as a go-between for the buyer or seller; assumes no title risks, does not usually have physical custody of products, and is not looked upon as a permanent representative of either the buyer or seller.

building codes legal restrictions describing the type of building, signs, size, and type of parking lot, and so on that can be used at a particular location.

buffer stock see **safety stock.**

bulk see **rounder.**

bulk of stock the store area in which the total assortment of merchandise is placed. Usually contains gondolas in grocery and discount stores and freestanding fixtures for soft goods in other types of stores.

buyer's market market occurring in economic conditions that favor the position of the retail buyer (or merchandiser) rather than the vendor; in other words, economic conditions are such that the retailer can demand and usually gets concessions from suppliers in terms of price, delivery, and other market advantages. Opposite of a seller's market.

buyer's report information on the velocity of sales, availability of inventory, amount of order, inventory turnover, forecast sales, and most important, the quantity that should be ordered for each SKU.

buying behavior the activities customers undertake when purchasing a good or service.

buying calendar a plan of a store buyer's market activities, generally covering a six-month merchandising season based on a selling calendar that indicates planned promotional events.

buying committee a committee that has the authority for final judgment and decision-making on such matters as adding or eliminating new products; especially common in supermarket companies and resident buying offices.

buying power the customer's financial resources available for making purchases.

(

call system a system of equalizing sales among salespersons—for example, some stores rotate salespeople, giving each an equal opportunity to meet customers.

capacity fixture see **rounder.**

career path the set of positions to which management employees are promoted within a particular organization, as their career progresses.

cart a retail facility that offers the simplest presentation, is mobile, and is on wheels.

cash money on hand.

cash discounts reductions in the invoice cost that the vendor allows the retailer for paying the invoice prior to the end of the discount period.

catalog showroom a type of retailer that uses a showroom to display merchandise combined with an adjacent warehouse; typically specializes in hard goods such as housewares.

category an assortment of items (SKUs) the customer sees as reasonable substitutes for each other.

category killer discount retailer that offers a complete assortment in a category and thus dominates a category from the customer's perspective.

category life cycle describes a merchandise category's sales pattern over time.

category specialist see **category killer.**

caveat emptor Latin term for "let the buyer beware."

census tracts subdivisions of a standard metropolitan statistical area (SMSA), with an average population of 4,000.

central business district (CBD) the traditional downtown business area of a city or town.

centralization an organization structure in which the authority for making retailing decisions is delegated to corporate managers rather than to geographically dispersed regional, district, and store management.

centralized buying a situation in which a retailer makes all purchase decisions at one location, typically the firm's headquarters.

central market see **market.**

central place a center of retailing activity such as a town or city.

central place theory Christaller's theory of retail location suggesting that retailers tend to locate in a central place. As more retailers locate together, more customers are attracted to the central place. See also **central place.**

chain see **retail chain.**

chain discount a number of different discounts taken sequentially from the suggested retail price.

channel of distribution see **distribution channel.**

checking the process of going through goods upon receipt to make sure that they arrived undamaged and that the merchandise received matches the merchandise ordered.

classics basic apparel designs that have been widely accepted over a long period of time. Some examples of classics are Levi's 501 blue jeans, button down oxford shirts, and blue blazers.

classification a group of items or SKUs for the same type of merchandise, such as pants (as opposed to jackets or suits), supplied by different vendors.

classification dominance an assortment so broad that customers should be able to satisfy all of their consumption needs for a particular category by visiting one retailer.

classification merchandising divisions of departments into related types of merchandise for reporting and control purposes.

Clayton Act (1914) an act passed as a response to the deficiencies of the Sherman Act; it specifically prohibits price discrimination, tying arrangements, and exclusive dealing contracts that have the effect of limiting free trade and provides for damage to parties injured as a result of violations of the act.

clearance sale an end-of-season sale to make room for new goods; also pushing the sale of slow-moving, shop-worn, and demonstration model goods.

close-out an offer at a reduced price to clear slow-moving or incomplete stock; also, an incomplete assortment, the remainder of a line of merchandise that is to be discontinued, offered at a low price to ensure immediate sale.

close-out retailers off-price retailers that sell a broad but inconsistent assortment of general merchandise as well as apparel and soft home goods, obtained through retail liquidations and bankruptcy proceedings.

cocooning a term that describes a behavioral pattern of consumers who increasingly turn to the nice, safe, familiar environment of their homes to spend their limited leisure time.

COD (collect on delivery) purchase terms in which payment for a product is collected at the time of delivery.

combination stores food-based retailers between 30,000 and 100,000 square feet in size with over 25 percent of their sales from nonfood merchandise such as flowers, health and beauty aids, kitchen utensils, photo developing, prescription drugs, and videotape rentals.

commercial bribery a vendor's offer of money or gifts to a buyer for the purpose of influencing purchasing decisions.

commissions compensation based on a fixed formula, such as percentage of sales.

committee buying the situation whenever the buying decision is made by a group of people rather than by a single buyer. A multiunit operation is usually the type of firm that uses this procedure.

common stock the type of stock most frequently issued by corporations. Owners of common stock usually have voting rights in the retail corporation.

communication objectives specific goals for a communication program related to the effects of the communication program on the customer's decision-making process.

community center shopping center that includes a discount store, specialty department store, super drugstore, home-improvement center, and other convenience and shopping goods stores.

comparison shopping a market research method in which retailers shop at competitive stores, comparing the merchandise, pricing, visual display, and service to their own offering.

compensation monetary payments including salary, commission, and bonuses; also, paid vacations, health and insurance benefits, and a retirement plan.

competitive parity method an approach for setting a promotion budget so that the retailer's share of promotion expenses is equal to its market share.

competitive-oriented pricing a pricing method in which a retailer uses competitor's prices as guides rather than demand or cost considerations.

competitor analysis an examination of the strategic direction that competitors are likely to pursue and their ability to successfully implement their strategy.

computerized checkout see **point-of-sale (POS) terminal.**

conditional sales agreement   an agreement that passes title of goods to the consumer, conditional on full payment.

conditions of sale   see **terms of sale.**

conflict of interest   a situation in which a decision maker's personal interest influences or has the potential to influence his or her professional decision.

congestion   the amount of crowding of either cars or people.

consideration set   the set of alternatives the customer evaluates when making a merchandise selection.

consignment goods   items not paid for by the retailer until they are sold. The retailer can return unsold merchandise; however, the retailer does not take title until final sale is made.

consumer cooperatives   customers own and operate the retail establishment. Customers have ownership share, hire full-time managers, and share in the store's profits through price reductions or dividends.

Consumer Goods Pricing Act (1975)   the statute that repealed all resale price maintenance laws and made it possible for retailers to sell products below suggested retail prices.

consumerism   the activities of government, business, and independent organizations designed to protect individuals from practices that infringe upon their rights as consumers.

contests   promotional activities in which customers compete for rewards. Contests can also be used to motivate retail employees.

contract distribution service companies   firms that perform all of the distribution functions for retailers or vendors, including transportation to the contract company's distribution center, merchandise processing, storage, and transportation to retailers.

contractual vertical marketing system   a form of vertical marketing system in which independent firms at different levels in the channel operate contractually to obtain the economies and market impacts that could not be obtained by unilateral action. Under this system, the identity of the individual firm and its autonomy of operations remain intact. See also **administered vertical marketing system** and **corporate vertical marketing system.**

contribution margin   gross margin less any expense that can be directly assigned to the merchandise.

convenience center   a shopping center that typically includes such stores as a convenience market, a dry cleaner, or a liquor store.

convenience products   products the consumer buys from the most convenient location and which the consumer is not willing to spend the effort to evaluate prior to purchase.

convenience stores   stores between 3,000 and 8,000 square feet providing a limited assortment of merchandise at a convenient location and time.

conventional supermarket   a self-service food store that offers groceries, meat, and produce with annual sales over $2 million and size under 20,000 square feet.

cooperative   as establishment owned by an association of customers. In general, the distinguishing features of a cooperative are patronage dividends based on the volume of expenditures by the members and a limitation of one vote per member regardless of the amount of stock owned.

cooperative (co-op) advertising   a program undertaken by a vendor in which the vendor agrees to pay all or part of a promotion for its products.

cooperative buying   when a group of independent retailers work together to make large purchases from a single supplier.

copy   the text in an advertisement.

corporation   a firm that is formally incorporated under state law and that is a different legal entity from stockholders and employees.

corporate vertical marketing system   a form of vertical marketing system in which all of the functions from production to distribution are at least partially owned and controlled by a single enterprise. Corporate systems typically operate manufacturing plants, warehouse facilities, and retail outlets. See also **administered vertical marketing system** and **contractual vertical marketing system.**

cost code   the item cost information indicated on price tickets in code. A common method of coding is the use of letters from an easily remembered word or expression with nonrepeating letters corresponding to numerals. The following is illustrative:
y o u n g b l a d e
1 2 3 4 5 6 7 8 9 0

cost complement the percentage of net sales represented by the cost of goods sold.

cost method of accounting a method in which retailers record the cost of every item on an accounting sheet or include a cost code on the price tag or merchandise container. When a physical inventory is conducted, the cost of each item must be determined, the quantity in stock is counted, and the total inventory value at cost is calculated. See **retail inventory method.**

cost multiplier the cumulative markup multiplied by 100 percent minus cumulative markup percentage.

cost-oriented method a method for determining the retail price by adding a fixed percentage to the cost of the merchandise; also known as cost-plus pricing.

cost per thousand (CPM) a measure that is often used to compare media. CPM is calculated by dividing an ad's cost by its reach.

counterfeit merchandise goods that are made and sold without permission of the owner of a trademark.

coupons printed material that offers a discount on the price of specific items when purchased at the store.

courtesy days the days on which stores extend to credit customers the privilege of making purchases at sale prices in advance of public sale.

couture fashion one-of-a-kind clothing designed and made by famous designers such as Yves St. Laurent, Karl Lagerfeld and the design firm of Christian Dior.

coverage the theoretical number of potential customers in the retailer's target market that could be exposed to an ad in a given medium.

credible commitments tangible investments in a relationship between retailer and vendor.

credit limit the quantitative limit that indicates the maximum amount of credit that may be allowed to be outstanding on each individual customer account.

credit money placed at a consumer's disposal by a retailer or financial or other institution. For purchases made on credit, payment is due in the future.

cross-docking when merchandise is delivered to one side of a very narrow warehouse by vendors, is unloaded and immediately reloaded onto trucks that deliver merchandise to the stores. By using cross-docking, merchandise spends very little time in the warehouse.

cross selling when sales associates in one department attempt to sell complementary merchandise from other departments to their customers.

cumulative attraction the principle that a cluster of similar and complementary retailing activities will generally have greater drawing power than isolated stores that engage in the same retailing activities.

cumulative markup the average percentage markup for the period; the total retail price minus cost divided by retail price.

cumulative quantity discounts discounts earned by retailers when purchasing certain quantities over a specified period of time.

cumulative reach the cumulative number of potential customers that would see an ad that runs several times.

current assets cash or any assets that can normally be converted into cash within one year.

current liabilities debts that are expected to be paid in less than one year.

current ratio current assets divided by current liabilities; indicates the firm's ability to meet current debt with current assets.

customer allowance an additional price reduction given to the customer.

customer buying process the stages a customer goes through in purchasing a good or service. Stages include need recognition, information search, evaluation and choice of alternatives, purchase, and postpurchase evaluation.

customer loyalty customers are committed to shopping at a store.

customer returns the amount of merchandise that customers return because it is damaged, doesn't fit, and so forth.

customer service the set of retail activities that increase the value customers receive when they shop and purchase merchandise.

customer service department the department in a retail organization that handles customer inquiries and complaints.

customer spotting a technique used in trade area analysis that "spots," or locates, the residences of the customers for a store or shopping center.

cyclical theories   theories of institutional change based on the premise that retail institutions change on the basis of cycles. See also **wheel of retailing** and **accordion theory.**

cycle stock   inventory that results from the replenishment process and is required to meet demand when the retailer can predict demand and replenishment times (lead times) perfectly.

D

DAGMAR (defining advertising goals for measured advertising results)   a method for setting advertising goals based on communication objectives.

dating   a process that determines when discounts can be taken and when the full invoice amount is due.

deal periods   a limited time period allowed by manufacturers to purchase merchandise at a special price.

debit card   a card that resembles a credit card but allows the retailer to automatically subtract payments from a customer's checking account at the time of sale.

deceptive advertising   any advertisement that contains a false statement or misrepresents a product or service.

deferred billing   an arrangement that enables customers to buy merchandise and not pay for it for several months, with no interest charge.

demand/destination areas   departments or areas in a store in which demand for the products or services offered is created before customers get to their destination.

demand-oriented method   a method of setting prices based on what the customers would expect or be willing to pay.

democratic method of store management   when a store manager seeks information and opinions from employees and bases decisions on this information.

demographics   factors such as age, sex, and income, commonly used to define market segments.

department   a segment of a store with merchandise that represents a group of classifications the consumer views as being complementary.

departmentalization   an organizational design in which employees are grouped into departments that perform specific activities to achieve operating efficiencies through specialization.

department store   retailers that carry a wide variety and deep assortment, offer considerable customer services, and are organized into separate departments for displaying merchandise.

depth interview   an unstructured personal interview in which the interviewer uses extensive probing to get individual respondents to talk in detail about a subject.

deseasonalized demand   the forecast demand without the influence of seasonality.

design   a specific combination of silhouette, design details, color, and material that makes one article of apparel different from others in its category.

design details   aspects of a design associated with the construction of apparel, such as the use of pleats, pockets, collars, buttons, and belts.

designer fashion   exclusive, designer-branded merchandise typically based on couture fashion. Designer fashions are adapted from couture designs so they can be efficiently manufactured and sold at lower prices.

destination store   a retail store in which the merchandise, selection, presentation, pricing, or other unique feature acts as a magnet for customers.

dialectic theory   an evolutionary theory based on the premise that retail institutions evolve. The theory suggests that new retail formats emerge by adopting characteristics from other forms of retailers in much the same way that a child is the product of the pooled genes of two very different parents.

difficult comparison effect   the condition that arises when customers' price sensitivity increases because they find it difficult to make comparisons between existing brands.

direct mail catalog retailer   a retailer offering merchandise and/or services through catalogs mailed directly to customers.

direct marketing   a form of nonstore retailing in which customers are exposed to merchandise through print or electronic media and then purchase the merchandise by telephone or mail.

direct product profitability (DPP)   the profit associated with each category or unit of merchandise. DPP is equal to the per-unit gross margin less all variable costs associated with the merchandise such as procurement, distribution, sales, and the cost of carrying the assets. Also known as residual income.

direct retailing   see **direct selling.**

direct selling   a form of nonstore retailing that involves selling merchandise through salespeople who contact consumers directly or by telephone at home or place of work.

disclosure of confidential information   an unethical situation in which a retail employee discloses proprietary or confidential information about the firm's business to anyone outside the firm.

discount   a reduction in the original retail price granted to store employees as special benefits.

discount store   a general merchandise retailer that offers a wide variety of merchandise, limited service, and low prices.

discount-anchored center   a shopping center that contains one or more discount stores and smaller retail tenants.

dispatcher   a person who coordinates deliveries to the distribution center.

display stock   merchandise placed on various display fixtures for customers to examine.

distribution   see **retail distribution.**

distribution center   a warehouse that receives merchandise from multiple vendors and distributes it to multiple stores.

distribution channel   a set of firms that facilitate the movement of products from the point of production to the point of sale to the ultimate consumer.

distribution intensity   the number of retailers carrying a particular category.

diversification   a strategic investment opportunity that involves an entirely new retail format directed toward a market segment not presently being served.

diversionary pricing   a practice sometimes used by retailers in which low price is stated for one or a few goods or services (emphasized in promotion) to give the illusion that the retailer's prices are all low.

diverters   firms that buy unwanted merchandise from retailers and manufacturers and resell the merchandise to other retailers.

double coupon redemption   a retail promotion that allows the customer to double the face value of a coupon.

drawing account   a method of sales compensation in which salespeople receive a weekly check based on their estimated annual income.

dual distribution   when a manufacturer or wholesaler uses multiple channels of distribution to reach ultimate consumers.

E

economic order quantity   the order quantity that minimizes the total cost of processing orders and holding inventory.

electronic data interchange (EDI)   the computer-to-computer exchange of business documents from retailer to vendor, and back.

employee discount   a discount from retail price offered by most retailers to employees.

empowerment   the process of managers sharing power and decision-making authority with employees.

end caps   display fixtures located at the end of an aisle.

end of month dating (EOM)   a method of dating in which the discount period starts at the end of the month in which the invoice is dated (except when the invoice is dated the 25th or later).

environmental apparel   merchandise produced with few or no harmful effects on the environment.

escape clause   a clause in a lease which allows the retailers to terminate its lease if sales don't reach a certain level after a specified number of years.

ethics   a system or code of conduct based on universal moral duties and obligations that indicate how one should behave.

evaluation of alternatives   the stage in the buying process in which the customer compares the benefits offered by various retailers.

everyday-low-price strategy   a pricing strategy that attempts to have, on average, low prices on all items every day rather than periodically advertising price promotions on a few items.

evolutionary theories   theories of institutional change based on the premise that retail institutions evolve. See **dialectic theory** and **natural selection.**

exclusive dealing agreements   restrictions a manufacturer or wholesaler places on a retailer to carry only its products and no competing vendors' products.

exclusive geographical territories a policy in which only one retailer in a certain territory is allowed to sell a particular brand.

exclusive use clause a clause in a lease that prohibits the landlord from leasing to retailers selling competing products.

executive training programs (ETP) a training program for retail supervisors, managers, and executives.

expenses costs incurred in the normal course of doing business to generate revenues.

experiment a market research method in which a variable is manipulated under controlled conditions.

expert systems computer programs that incorporate knowledge of experts in a particular field. Expert systems are used to aid in decision making and problem solving.

exponential smoothing a sales forecasting technique in which sales in previous time periods are weighted to develop a forecast for future periods.

express warranty a guarantee supplied by either the retailer or the manufacturer that details the terms of the warranty in simple and easily understood language so customers know what is and what is not covered by the warranty.

extended problem solving a buying process in which customers spend considerable time at each stage of the decision making process because the decision is important and they have limited knowledge of alternatives.

extra dating a discount offered by a vendor in which the retailer receives extra time to pay the invoice and still take the cash discount.

extrinsic rewards rewards given to employees by their manager or the firm, such as money, promotion, and recognition.

F

fabric designers firms that develop new fabrics for apparel.

fabric manufacturers manufacturers who buy fibers, spin them into yarn, and then weave or knit the yarn into fabric. Fabric is sold to apparel manufacturers.

factoring a specialized financial function whereby manufacturers, wholesalers, or retailers sell accounts receivable to financial institutions, including factors, banks, and sales finance companies.

factory outlet stores off-price retailers owned by manufacturers.

fad a product with a very short life cycle.

fair trade laws see **vertical price fixing.**

fashion a category of merchandise that typically lasts several seasons, and sales can vary dramatically from one season to the next.

fashion coordinators retail managers who analyze fashion markets and consumer trends and provide information to buyers about new fabrics, colors, and styles. Coordinators are responsible for developing general guidelines for buyers so that the retailer presents a consistent fashion image to its customers.

fashion designers the creative force in the fashion industry working either for manufacturers or as independent contractors providing their services to manufacturers and retailers that develop private label merchandise.

fashion life cycle the evolution of a new fashion over time within a social group or market segment.

fashion market centers groups of apparel manufacturer and designer showrooms in important fashion markets across the world.

fashion-oriented shopping center shopping center usually containing a higher quality department store as well as other smaller boutiques.

fashion press an industry providing information to everyone in the fashion industry, from raw material suppliers to consumers. The fashion press consists of daily newspapers, consumer magazines, and trade publications.

features the qualities or characteristics of a product that provide benefits to customers.

feature fixture see **four-way.**

Federal Trade Commission Act (1914) the congressional act that created the Federal Trade Commission (FTC) and gave it the power to enforce federal trade laws.

financial leverage a financial measure that is based on the relationship between the retailer's liabilities and owners' equity that indicates financial stability of the firm.

fixed assets assets that require more than a year to convert to cash.

fixed cost a cost that does not change with the quantity of product that's produced and sold.

fixed expenses expenses that remain constant for a given period of time regardless of the sales volume.

flattening the organization the reduction in the number of management levels.

flexible pricing a pricing strategy that allows consumers to bargain over selling prices.

flextime a job scheduling system that enables employees to choose the times they work.

floor-ready merchandise received at the store ready to be sold, without the need for any additional preparation by retail employees.

FOB (free on board) destination a term of sale designating that the shipper owns the merchandise until it is delivered to the retailer and is therefore responsible for transportation and any damage claims.

FOB (free on board) origin a term of sale designating that the retailer takes ownership of the merchandise at the point of origin and is therefore responsible for transportation and any damage claims.

focus group a marketing research technique in which a small group of respondents is interviewed by a moderator using a loosely structured format.

forward integration a form of vertical integration in which a manufacturer owns wholesalers and/or retailers.

four-way a fixture that has two cross bars that sit perpendicular to each other on a pedestal.

franchising a contractual agreement between a franchisor and a franchisee that allows the franchisee to operate a retail outlet using a name and format developed and supported by the franchisor.

free-form a store design, used primarily in small specialty stores or within the boutiques of large stores, that arranges fixtures and aisles asymmetrically.

freestanding insert an ad printed at the retailer's expense and distributed as a freestanding insert in the newspaper.

freestanding retailer a location for a retailer that is not adjacent to other retailers.

freight collect when the retailer pays the freight.

freight prepaid when the freight is paid by the vendor.

frequency how many times a potential customer is exposed to an ad.

fringe trade area see **tertiary trade zone.**

frontal presentation a method of displaying merchandise in which the retailer exposes as much of the product as possible to catch the customer's eye.

full warranty a guarantee provided by either the retailer or manufacturer to repair or replace merchandise without charge and within a reasonable amount of time in the event of a defect.

full-line forcing when a supplier requires a retailer to carry the supplier's full line of products if the retailer wants to carry any part of that line.

functional discounts see **trade discounts.**

functional needs the needs satisfied by a product or service that are directly related to its performance.

functional product grouping categorizing and displaying merchandise by common end uses.

functional relationships a series of one-time market exchanges linked together over time.

future dating a method of dating that allows the buyer additional time to take advantage of the cash discount or to pay the net amount of the invoice.

G

generic products unbranded, unadvertised merchandise found mainly in drug, grocery, and discount stores.

gentrification a process in which old buildings are torn down or are restored to create new offices, housing developments, and retailers.

geographic segmentation segmentation of potential customers by where they live. A retail market can be segmented by countries, states, cities, and neighborhoods.

glass ceiling an invisible barrier that makes it difficult for minorities and women to be promoted beyond a certain level.

gondola an island type of self-service counter with tiers of shelves back-to-back.

graduated lease a lease that includes precise rent increases over a specified period of time.

gray-market merchandise merchandise that is made domestically but sold through unauthorized wholesalers, distributors, or retailers.

green marketing　a strategic focus by retailers and their vendors to supply customers with environmentally friendly merchandise.

greeter　a retail employee who greets customers as they enter a store and who provides information and/or assistance.

grid layout　a store design, typically used by grocery stores, in which merchandise is displayed on long gondolas in aisles with a repetitive pattern.

gross margin　the difference between the price the customer pays for merchandise and the cost of the merchandise (the price the retailer paid the supplier of the merchandise). More specifically, gross margin = net sales − cost of goods sold (= maintained markup) − alteration cost + cash discounts.

gross margin return on investment (GMROI)　gross margin dollars divided by average (cost) inventory.

gross profit　see **gross margin.**

gross sales　the total dollar revenues received from the sales of merchandise and services.

group boycott　a concerted refusal by either retailers or vendors to deal with a particular business.

group maintenance behaviors　activities store managers undertake to make sure that employees are satisfied and work well together.

H

habitual decision making　a type of buying process in which customers routinize their purchase decisions and do not go through the stages of the buying process; also known as routine decision making.

historical center　a shopping center located in a place of historical interest.

home-improvement center　a category specialist combining the traditional hardware store and lumberyard.

horizontal price fixing　an agreement between retailers in direct competition with each other to charge the same prices.

Huff's model　a trade area analysis model used to determine the probability that a customer residing in a particular area will shop at a particular store or shopping center.

human resource management　management of a retailer's employees.

hypermarket　a very large retail store that offers low prices and combines a discount store and a superstore food retailer in one warehouselike building.

I

idea-oriented presentation　a method of presenting merchandise based on a specific idea or the image of the store.

impact　an ad's effect on the audience.

implied warranty of merchantability　a guarantee that accompanies all merchandise sold by a retailer, assuring customers that the merchandise is up to standards for the ordinary purposes for which such goods are used.

impulse merchandise　products purchased without prior planning such as candy and batteries.

impulse purchase　an unplanned purchase by a customer.

incentive compensation plan　a compensation plan that rewards employees based on their productivity.

income statement　a summary of the financial performance of a firm for a certain period of time.

inconsistency　variation in service quality because services are delivered by people with varying capabilities.

independent retailer　a retailer that owns only one retail store.

information search　the stage in the buying process in which a customer seeks additional information to satisfy a need.

infringement　unauthorized use of a registered trademark.

ingress/egress　the ease of entering and exiting the parking lot of a retail site.

in-house credit system　see **proprietary store credit card system.**

initial markup　the difference between the cost of merchandise and the retail selling price originally placed on it.

input measures　performance measures used to assess the amount of resources or money used by the retailer to achieve outputs.

inseparability　the fact that a service cannot be separated from the deliverer of the service or the setting in which the service occurs.

installment credit plan   a plan that enables consumers to pay their total purchase price (less down payment) in equal installment payments over a specified time period.

institutional advertisement   an advertisement that emphasizes the retailer's name and positioning rather than specific merchandise or prices.

intangibility   the fact that services cannot be held, touched, or seen before the purchase decision.

interest   the amount charged by a financial institution to borrow money.

interactive electronic retailing   a system in which a retailer transmits data and graphics over cable or telephone lines to a consumer's TV or computer terminal.

intertype competition   competition between different types of retailers (e.g., Safeway versus Wal-Mart).

intratype competition   competition between the same type of retailers (e.g., Kroger versus Safeway).

intrinsic rewards   nonmonetary rewards employees get from doing their jobs.

inventory   goods or merchandise available for resale.

inventory management   the process of acquiring and maintaining a proper assortment of merchandise while keeping ordering, shipping, handling, and other related costs in check.

inventory shrinkage   see **shrinkage**.

inventory turnover   net sales divided by average retail inventory; used to evaluate how effectively managers utilize their investment in inventory.

invoice cost   the actual amount due for the merchandise after both trade and quantity discounts are taken.

item price removal   the practice of marking prices only on shelves or signs and not on individual items.

J

job analysis   identifying essential activities and determining the qualifications employees need to perform them effectively.

job description   a description of the activities the employee needs to perform and the firm's performance expectations.

job sharing   when two employees voluntarily are responsible for a job that was previously held by one person.

junk bonds   bonds that offer investors a higher-risk/higher-yield investment than conventional bonds.

K

key items   the items that are in greatest demand. Also referred to as best sellers.

keystone method   a method of setting retail prices in which retailers simply double the cost of the merchandise to obtain the original retail selling price.

kickback   same as commercial bribery.

kiosk   a retail facility that is larger than a cart, is stationary, and has many conveniences of a store such as movable shelves, telephone, and electricity.

knock-offs   inexpensive and less elegant copies of couture or designer fashions.

L

latchkey children   children of baby boomer parents and the first generation who grew up in homes where both parents worked.

layaway   a method of deferred payment in which merchandise is held by the store for the customer until it is completely paid for.

lead time   the amount of time between the recognition that an order needs to be placed and its arrival in the store, ready for sale.

leader pricing   a pricing strategy in which certain items are priced lower than normal to increase the traffic flow of customers and/or to increase the sale of complementary products.

leased department   a department in a retail store operated by an outside party. The outside party either pays fixed rent or a percentage of sales to the retailer for the space.

lessee   the party renting a property.

lessor   the party owning a property that is for rent.

less-than-carload-lot (LCL)   the rate that applies to less than full carload shipments.

level of support   see **service level**.

leveraged buyout (LBO)   a financial transaction in which a buyer (the firm's management or an outside individual or group) acquires a company by borrowing money from a financial institution or by issuing junk bonds using its assets as collateral. See also **merger** and **acquisition.**

liabilities   obligations of a retail enterprise to pay cash or other economic resources in return for past, present, or future benefits.

licensed brands   brands for which the licensor (owner of a well-known name) enters a contractual arrangement with a licensee (a retailer or a third party). The licensee either manufactures or contracts with a manufacturer to produce the licensed product and pays a royalty to the licensor.

lifestyle   the manner in which individual consumers or families (households) live and spend their time and money, what activities they pursue, and their attitudes and opinions about the world they live in.

lifestyle merchandising   development of merchandise lines based on consumer living patterns.

limited problem solving   a buying process that occurs when customers do not need to spend a great deal of time in each of the steps because of their knowledge and prior experience.

limited warranty   a type of guarantee in which any limitations must be stated conspicuously so that customers are not misled.

lines of authority and responsibility   the organizational principle that employees should be given the authority to accomplish the responsibilities assigned to them.

logistics   see **retail distribution.**

long-term liabilities   obligations the retailer commits to pay after at least one year (see liabilities). Long-term liabilities represent claims against assets.

loop layout   see **boutique layout.**

loss leader   an item priced near or below cost to attract customer traffic into the store.

m

mail-order retailers   see **direct mail catalog retailer.**

maintenance-increase-recoupment lease   a provision of a lease that can be used with either a percentage or straight lease. This type of lease allows the landlord to increase the rent if insurance, property taxes, or utility bills increase beyond a certain point.

maintained markup   the amount of markup the retailer wishes to maintain on a particular category of merchandise; net sales minus cost of goods sold.

management by objectives   a popular method for linking the goals of a firm to goals for each employee and providing information to employees about their role.

managing diversity   a set of human resource management programs designed to realize the benefits of a diverse work force.

manufacturer brands   brands that are produced and controlled by and that carry the name of a manufacturer; also known as national brands.

manufacturer's agent   an agent who generally operates on an extended contractual basis; often sells within an exclusive territory; handles noncompeting but related lines of goods; and possesses limited authority with regard to prices and terms of sale.

manufacturer's outlet store   a discount retail store owned and operated by a manufacturer.

mapping   see **analog approach.**

marginal analysis   a method of analysis used in setting a promotional budget or allocating retail space, based on the economic principle that firms should increase expenditures as long as each additional dollar spent generates more than a dollar of additional contribution.

markdown   the percentage reduction in the initial retail price.

markdown cancellation   the percentage increase in the retail price after a markdown is taken.

markdown money   funds provided by a vendor to a retailer to cover decreased gross margin from markdowns and other merchandising issues.

market   a group of vendors in a concentrated geographic location or even under one roof; also known as a central market.

market attractiveness–competitive position matrix   a method for analyzing opportunities that explicitly considers the capabilities of the retailer and the attractiveness of retail markets.

market development   see **market penetration opportunity.**

market exchange   a short-term transaction between a buyer and vendor who do not expect to be involved in future transactions with each other.

market expansion opportunity a strategic investment opportunity that employs the same retailing format in new market segments.

market penetration opportunity an investment opportunity strategy that focuses on increasing sales to present customers using the same retailing format.

market positioning see **positioning.**

market research the systematic collection and analysis of information about a retail market.

market share a retailer's sales divided by the sales of all competitors within the same market.

market weeks see **trade show.**

marketing segmentation the process of dividing a retail market into homogeneous groups. See **retail market segment.**

markup the increase in the retail price of an item after the initial markup percentage has been applied but before the item is placed on the selling floor.

marquee a sign used to display a store's name and/or logo.

mass fashion apparel produced in large quantities and sold at reasonable price ranges to a broad market. The designs are typically lower in cost, using less elegant materials, workmanship, and construction.

mass market theory a theory proposing that fashions spread across social classes with each social class having its own fashion leaders who play a key role in their own social networks. Fashion information "trickles across" social classes rather than down from the upper classes to the lower classes.

materials in fashion apparel, these include fabrics, fur, leather, plastics, and metal. These materials produce the color and texture of the apparel.

Mazur plan a method of retail organization in which all retail activities fall into four functional areas: merchandising, publicity, store management, and accounting and control.

media coverage the theoretical number of potential customers in a retailer's market who could be exposed to an ad.

memorandum purchases items not paid for by a retailer until they are sold. The retailer can return unsold merchandise; however, the retailer takes title on delivery and is responsible for damages. See **consignment goods.**

mentoring programs the assigning of higher-level managers to help lower-level managers learn the firm's values and meet other senior executives.

merchandise budget plan a plan used by buyers to determine how much money to spend in each month on a particular merchandise category, given the firms's sales forecast, inventory turnover, and profit goals.

merchandise category see **category.**

merchandise classification see **classification.**

merchandise management the analysis, planning, acquisition, promotion, and control of merchandise sold by a retailer.

merchandise show see **trade show.**

merchandising see **merchandise management.**

merger a financial strategy in which one larger firm acquires a smaller firm. This term is used interchangeably with acquisition. See also **leveraged buyout.**

mission statement a broad description of the scope of activities a retailer plans to undertake in the future.

metropolitan statistical area (MSA) a city with 50,000 or more inhabitants or an urbanized area of at least 50,000 inhabitants and a total MSA population of at least 100,000 (75,000 in New England).

mixed-use development (MXDs) shopping centers that have office towers, hotels, residential complexes, civic centers, and convention complexes on top of or attached to the shopping areas.

model stock list a list of fashion merchandise that indicates in very general terms (products lines, colors, and size distributions) what should be carried in a particular merchandise category; also known as model stock plan.

monthly additions to stock the amount to be ordered for delivery in each month, given the firm's turnover and sales objectives.

motivation the drive within people to expend effort to achieve goals.

multiattribute method see **multiple-attribute method.**

multiple-attribute method a method for evaluating vendors that uses a weighted average score based on various issues and the vendor's performance on those issues.

multiple-unit pricing   practice of offering two or more similar products or services for sale at one price.

N

natural barriers   barriers, such as rivers or mountains, that limit the size of a trade area.

national brands   see **manufacturer brands.**

natural selection   those institutions best able to adapt to changes in customers, technology, competition, and legal environments have the greatest chance for success

needs   the basic psychological forces that motivate customers to act.

negligence   a product liability suit that occurs if a retailer or a retail employee fails to exercise the care that a prudent person usually would.

negotiation   an interaction between two or more parties to reach an agreement.

neighborhood business district (NBD)   a group of stores directed toward convenience shopping needs of customers in a neighborhood; typically includes a supermarket and is located on the major street(s) of a residential area.

neighborhood center   a shopping center that includes a supermarket, drugstore, home-improvement center, or variety store. Neighborhood centers often include small stores, such as apparel, shoe, camera, and other shopping goods stores.

net invoice price   the net value of the invoice or the total invoice minus all other discounts.

net least   a lease that requires all maintenance expenses such as heat, insurance, and interior repair to be paid by the retailer.

net profit   a measure of the overall performance of a firm; revenues (sales) minus expenses and losses for the period.

net sales   the total amount of dollars received by a retailer after all funds have been paid to customers for returned merchandise.

net worth   see **owners' equity.**

never-out list   a list of key items or best-sellers that are separately planned and controlled. These items account for large sales volume and are stocked in a manner so they are always available. These are A items in an ABC analysis.

noncumulative quality discounts   discounts offered to retailers as an incentive to purchase more merchandise on a single order.

nondurables   perishable products consumed in one or a few uses.

nonstore retailing   a form of retailing to ultimate consumers that is not store-based. Nonstore retailing is conducted through vending machines, direct selling, and direct marketing.

notes payable   current liabilities representing principal and interest the retailer owes to financial institutions (banks) that are due and payable in less than a year.

O

objective-and-task method   a method for setting a promotion budget in which the retailer first establishes a set of communication objectives and then determines the necessary tasks and their costs.

observation   a type of market research in which customer behavior is observed and recorded.

odd price   a price ending with an odd number (such as 57 cents or 63 cents) or just under a round number (such as $98 instead of $100).

off-price retailer   a retailer that offers an inconsistent assortment of brand-name, fashion-oriented soft goods at low prices.

off-price shopping centers   centers that specialize in off-price retail tenants such as T.J. Maxx or Burlington Coat Factory.

off-the-job-training   training conducted in centralized classrooms away from the employee's work environment.

one hundred percent location   the retail site in a major business district that has the greatest exposure to a retail store's target market customers.

one-price policy   a policy that, at a given time, all customers pay the same price for any given item of merchandise.

one-price retailer   a store that offers all merchandise at a single fixed price.

on-the-job training   a decentralized approach in which job training occurs in the work environment where employees perform their jobs.

open-to-buy   the plan that keeps track of how much is spent in each month (and how much is left to spend).

opinion leaders persons whose attitudes, opinions, preferences, and actions influence those of others.

opportunity cost of capital the rate available on the next-best use of the capital invested in the project at hand. The opportunity cost should be no larger than the rate at which a firm borrows funds, since one alternative is to pay back borrowed money. It can be higher, however, depending on the range of other opportunities available. Typically, the opportunity cost rises with investment risk.

optical character recognition (OCR) an industrywide classification system for coding information onto merchandise; enables retailers to record information on each SKU when it is sold and to transmit the information to a computer.

option credit account a revolving account that allows partial payments without interest charges if a bill is paid in full when due.

option-term revolving credit a credit arrangement that offers customers two payment options: (1) pay full amount within a specified number of days and avoid any finance charges or (2) make a minimum payment and be assessed finance charges on the unpaid balance.

order form a legally binding contract when signed by both parties, specifying the terms and conditions under which a purchase transaction is to be conducted.

order point the amount of inventory below which the quantity available shouldn't go or the item will be out of stock before the next order arrives.

organization chart a graphic that displays the reporting relationships within a firm.

organization structure the plan according to which a retailer assigns authority and responsibility for performing retail functions and activities to employees.

organizational culture a firm's set of values and customs that guide employee behavior.

outlet center typically feature stores owned by retail chains or manufacturers that sell excess and out-of-season merchandise at reduced prices.

outlet stores off-price retailers owned by manufacturers of department or specialty store chains.

output measures measures that assess the results of retailers' investment decisions.

outshopping customers shopping in other areas because their needs are not being met locally.

overstored a description of an area that has too many stores to profitably satisfy demand.

owners' equity the amount of assets belonging to the owners of the retail firm after all obligations (liabilities) have been met; also known as net worth.

P

pallet a platform, usually made of wood, that provides stable support for several cartons. Pallets are used to help move and store merchandise.

partnership an ongoing, mutually beneficial relationship with each party having concern for the other party's well-being.

party plan system salespeople encourage people to act as hosts and invite friends or coworkers to a "party" at which the merchandise is demonstrated. The host or hostess receives a gift or commission for arranging the meeting.

perceived risk the level of risk a consumer believes to exist regarding the purchase of a specific good or service.

percentage lease a lease that relates the amount of rent to a retailer's sales or profits.

percentage lease with specified maximum a lease that pays the lessor, or landlord, a percentage of sales up to a maximum amount.

percentage lease with specified minimum the retailer must pay a minimum rent no matter how low sales are.

percentage of sales method a method for setting a promotion budget based on a fixed percentage of forecast sales.

percentage variation method an inventory planning method wherein the actual stock on hand during any month varies from average planned monthly stock by only half of the month's variation from average estimated monthly sales.

periodic reordering system an inventory management system in which the review time is a fixed period (e.g., two weeks), but the order quantity can vary.

perishability   refers to the dilemma of lost opportunities for services to be performed. Because the creation and consumption of services are inseparable, services cannot be stockpiled, as merchandise can, for later consumption.

perpetual book inventory   see **retail inventory method.**

perpetual ordering system   the stock level is monitored perpetually and a fixed quantity, known as EOQ (economic order quantity), is purchased when the inventory available reaches a prescribed level.

personal selling   a communication process in which salespeople assist customers in satisfying their needs through face-to-face exchange of information.

physical inventory   a method of gathering stock information by using an actual physical count and inspection of the merchandise items.

pick ticket   a document that tells the order filler how much of each item to get from the storage area.

pilferage   the stealing of a store's merchandise. See also **shoplifting.**

planogram   a diagram created from photographs, computer output, or artists' renderings that illustrates exactly where every SKU should be placed.

PM   see **push money.**

point-of-purchase display   an interior display that provides customers with information and promotes the merchandise.

point-of-sale (POS) terminal   a cash register that has the capability to electronically scan a UPC code with a laser and electronically record a sale; also known as computerized checkout.

polygons   trade areas whose boundaries conform to streets and other physical characteristics rather than being concentric circles.

popping the merchandise   focusing spotlights on special feature areas and items.

population density   the number of people per unit area (usually square mile) who live within a geographic area.

positioning   the design and implementation of a retail promotion program to create an image in the customer's mind of the retailer relative to its competitors.

postpurchase behavior   a customer's further purchases and/or reevaluation based on a purchase.

poverty of time   a condition in which greater affluence results in less, rather than more, free time because the alternatives competing for consumers' time increase.

power retailers   see **category killers** or **category specialists.**

power shopping center   an open-air-shopping center with the majority of space preleased to several well-known anchor retail tenants— **category killers**—with high credit ratings.

predatory pricing   a method for establishing merchandise prices for the purpose of driving competition from the marketplace.

preferred client   customers salespeople communicate with regularly, send notes about new merchandise and sales in the department, and make appointments for special presentations or merchandise.

premarking   the price is marked by manufacturer or other supplier before goods are shipped to a retail store. Also called **prepricing.**

premium   merchandise offered at a reduced price, or free, as an additional incentive for a customer to make a purchase.

prepricing   see **premarking.**

preprint   an advertisement printed at the retailer's expense and distributed as a freestanding insert in a newspaper.

press conference   a meeting with representatives of the news media that is called by a retailer.

press release   a statement of facts or opinions that the retailer would like to see published by the news media.

prestige pricing   a system of pricing based on the assumption that consumers will not buy goods and services at prices they feel are too low.

price bundling   the practice of offering two or more different products or services for sale at one price.

price comparison   a comparison of the price of merchandise offered for sale with a higher "regular" price or a manufacturer's list price.

price discrimination   an illegal practice in which a vendor sells the same product to two or more retailers at different prices.

price elasticity of demand   a measure of the effect a price change has on consumer demand; percentage change in demand divided by percentage change in price.

price fixing   an illegal pricing activity in which several marketing channel members establish a fixed retail selling price for a product line within a market area. See **vertical price fixing** and **horizontal price fixing.**

price guarantee   a term of purchase that protects retailers against price declines. In the event a retailer cannot sell merchandise at a given price, the manufacturer pays the retailer the difference between the planned retail and the actual retail selling price.

price lining   a pricing policy in which a retailer offers a limited number of predetermined price points within a classification.

pricing experiment   an experiment in which a retailer actually changes the price of an item in a systematic manner to observe changes in customers' purchases or purchase intentions.

primary data   marketing research information collected through surveys, observations, and experiments to address a problem confronting a retailer.

primary trade zone   the geographical area from which the store or shopping center derives 60 to 65 percent of its customers.

private-label brand   a brand of products designed, produced, controlled by, and carrying the name of the store or a name owned by the store; also known as a store brand or dealer brand.

private-label store credit-card system   a system in which credit cards have the store's name on them, but the accounts receivable are sold to a financial institution.

PRIZM (potential rating index for zip markets)   a database combining census data, nationwide consumer surveys, and interviews with hundreds of people across the country into a geodemographic segmentation system.

product attributes   characteristics of a product that affect customer evaluations.

product liability   a tort (or wrong) that occurs when an injury results from the use of a product.

product line   a group of related products.

productivity measures   the ratio of an output to an input determining how effectively a retailer uses a resource.

profit margin   net profit after taxes divided by net sales.

profitability   a company's ability to generate revenues in excess of the costs incurred in producing those revenues.

prohibited use clause   a clause in a lease that limits the landlord from leasing to certain kinds of tenants.

promotion   activities undertaken by a retailer to provide customers with information about the retailer's store and its retail mix.

promotional advertising   advertising intended to inform prospective customers of special sales; it announces the arrival of new and seasonal goods; and it features, creates, and promotes a market for the merchandise items in regular stock.

promotional allowance   an allowance given by vendors to retailers to compensate the latter for money spent in advertising a particular item.

promotional department store   a department store that concentrates on apparel and sells a substantial portion of its merchandise on weekly promotion.

promotional or discount-oriented center   a type of specialty shopping center that contains one or more discount stores, plus smaller retail tenants.

promotional stock   a retailer's stock of goods offered at an unusually attractive price in order to obtain sales volume; it often represents special purchases from vendors.

proprietary store credit card system   a system in which credit cards have the store's name on them and the accounts receivable are administered by the retailer; also known as in-house credit system.

psychographics   see **lifestyle.**

psychological needs   needs associated with the personal gratification that customers get from shopping or from purchasing and owning a product.

publicity   communications through significant unpaid presentations about the retailer (usually a news story) in nonpersonal media.

puffing   an advertising or personal selling practice in which a retailer simply exaggerates the benefits or quality of a product in very broad terms.

pull distribution strategy   orders for merchandise are generated at the store level on the basis of demand data captured by point-of-sale terminals.

purchase visibility curve a display technique in which the retailer tilts lower shelves so more merchandise is in direct view.

push distribution strategy merchandise is allocated to stores based on historical demand, the inventory position at the distribution center, as well as the stores' need.

push money an incentive for retail salespeople provided by a vendor to promote, or push, a particular product; also known as spiff or PM.

Q

quantity discounts the practice of granting lower prices to retailers who buy in higher quantities.

quick-response (QR) delivery systems systems designed to reduce the lead time for receiving merchandise, thereby lowering inventory investment, improving customer service levels, and reducing distribution expenses; also known as just-in-time inventory management systems.

quotas performance goals or objectives established to evaluate employee performance, such as sales per hour for salespeople and maintained margin and turnover for buyers.

R

racetrack layout a type of store layout that provides a major aisle to facilitate customer traffic that has access to the store's multiple entrances.

rainchecks promises given to customers when merchandise is out of stock to sell customers merchandise at the sale price when the merchandise arrives.

raw material suppliers suppliers of natural and synthetic fibers (such as cotton, lycra, wool, nylon, fur, and leather) to fabric designers and manufacturers.

reach the actual number of customers in the target market exposed to an advertising medium. See **advertising reach.**

ready-to-wear apparel made in standard sizes and usually produced in factories.

rebate money returned to the buyer in the form of cash based on a portion of the purchase price.

receipt of goods (ROG) dating a dating policy in which the cash discount period starts on the day the merchandise is received.

receiving the process of filling out paperwork to record the receipt of merchandise that arrives at a store or distribution center.

recruitment activity performed by a retailer to generate job applicants.

reductions markdowns; discounts to employees and customers; and inventory shrinkage due to shoplifting, breakage, or loss.

refusals to deal a legal issue in which either a vendor or a retailer reserves the right to deal or refuse to deal with anyone they choose.

region in retail location analysis refers to the part of the country, a particular city or Metropolitan Statistical Area (MSA).

regional center a shopping center that includes up to three department stores plus shopping or specialty stores rather than convenience stores. Super-regionals are similar but have at least four department stores.

Reilly's law a model used in trade area analysis to define the relative ability of two cities to attract customers from the area between them.

related diversification a diversification opportunity strategy in which the retailer's present offering and market share something in common with the market and format being considered.

relational partnerships long-term business relationships in which the buyer and vendor have a close, trusting interpersonal relationship.

remarking the practice of remarking merchandise due to price changes, lost or mutilated tickets, or customer returns.

reorder point the stock level at which a new order is placed.

resale price maintenance see **vertical price fixing.**

resident buying office an office owned and operated by a retailer that is located in an important market area (source of supply) and provides valuable information and contracts.

restraint of trade any contract that tends to eliminate or stifle competition, create a monopoly, artificially maintain prices, or otherwise hamper or obstruct the course of trade and commerce as it would be carried on if left to the control of natural forces; also known as unfair trade practices.

retail accordion theory   see **accordion theory.**

retail audit   see **situation audit.**

retail chain   a firm that consists of multiple retail units under common ownership and usually has some centralization of decision making in defining and implementing its strategy.

retail distribution   the organization process of managing the flow of merchandise from the source of supply—the vendor, wholesaler, or distributor—through the internal processing functions—warehouse and transportation—until the merchandise is sold and delivered to the customer; also known as logistics.

retail format   a type of retail mix that is used by a number of retailers.

retail format development opportunity   an investment opportunity strategy in which a retailer offers a new retail format to present customers.

retail information systems   systems that provide the information needed by retail managers by collecting, organizing, and storing relevant data continuously and directing the information to the appropriate managers.

retail institution   a group of retailers that provide a similar retail mix.

retail inventory method (RIM)   an accounting procedure whose objectives are to maintain a perpetual or book inventory in retail dollar amounts and to maintain records that make it possible to determine the cost value of the inventory at any time without taking a physical inventory; also known as book inventory system or perpetual book inventory.

retail market   a group of consumers with similar needs (a segment) and a group of retailers using similar retail mixes (types of merchandise, prices, promotions, and services) to satisfy those consumer needs.

retail market segment   a group of customers whose needs will be satisfied by the same retail offering because they have similar needs and go through similar buying processes.

retail merchandising units (RMU)   a relatively new and sophisticated location alternative that offers the compactness and mobility of a cart, but the more sophisticated features of a kiosk. They can also be locked or enclosed, so they can serve as a display when closed for business.

retail mix   the factors used by a retailer to satisfy customer needs and influence their purchase decisions; includes merchandise and services offered, pricing, advertising and promotions, store design and location, and visual merchandising.

retail strategy   a statement that indicates (1) the target market toward which a retailer plans to commit its resources, (2) the nature of the retail offering that the retailer plans to use to satisfy the needs of the target market, and (3) the bases upon which the retailer will attempt to build a sustainable competitive advantage over competitors.

retailer   a business that sells products and services to ultimate consumers.

retail-sponsored cooperative   an organization owned and operated by small, independent retailers to improve operating efficiency and buying power. Typically, the retail-sponsored cooperative operates a wholesale buying and distribution system and requires its members to concentrate their purchases from the cooperative wholesale operation.

retailing   the set of business activities involved in selling products and services to ultimate consumers.

retailing concept   a management orientation that holds that the key task of a retailer is to determine the needs and wants of its target market and to direct the firm toward satisfying those needs and wants more effectively and efficiently than competitors do.

retained earnings   the portion of owners' equity that has accumulated over time through profits but has not been paid out in dividends to owners.

return on assets   net profit after taxes divided by total assets.

return on owners' equity   net profit after taxes divided by owners' equity; also known as return on net worth.

review time   the period of time between reviews of a line for purchase decisions.

revolving credit   a consumer credit plan which combines the convenience of a continuous charge account and the privileges of installment payment.

ribbon center   see **strip center.**

road pattern   a consideration used in measuring the accessibility of a retail location via major arteries, freeways, or roads.

road condition includes the age, number of lanes, number of stoplights, congestion, and general state of repair of roads in a trade area.

Robinson-Patman Act (1946) the Congressional act that revised section 2 of the Clayton Act and specifically prohibits price discrimination.

role clarity the degree to which employees know what their duties and responsibilities are.

role conflict the degree to which employees receive mixed messages about the scope of their activities.

rounder a round fixture that sits on a pedestal, smaller than the straight rack. It is designed to hold a maximum amount of merchandise.

routine decision making see **habitual decision making.**

S

SKU see **stock keeping unit.**

safety stock merchandise inventory used as a safety cushion for cycle stock so the retailer won't run out of stock if demand exceeds the sales forecast.

sale-leaseback the practice in which retailers build new stores and sell them to real-estate investors who then lease the buildings back to the retailers on a long-term basis.

sales associate the same as a salesperson, but is used to recognize the importance and professional nature of the sales function and avoids the negative image sometimes linked with the term salesperson.

sales consultant see **sales associate.**

sales per cubic foot a measure of space productivity appropriate for stores like wholesale clubs that use multiple layers of merchandise.

sales per linear foot a measure of space productivity used when most merchandise is displayed on multiple shelves of long gondolas, such as in grocery stores.

sales per square foot a measure of space productivity used by most retailers since rent and land purchases are assessed on a per square foot basis.

sales productivity the efficiency of salespeople, typically measured by sales per hour.

sales promotions paid nonpersonal communication activities that offer extra value and incentives to customers to visit a store and/or purchase merchandise during a specific period of time.

satisfaction a postconsumption evaluation of the degree to which a store or product meets or exceeds customer expectations.

scale economies cost advantages due to the size of a retailer.

scanning the process in point-of-sales (service) systems wherein the input into the terminal is accomplished by passing a coded ticket over a reader or having a handheld wand pass over the ticket.

scrambled merchandising a merchandising practice in which a retailer offers unrelated merchandise categories.

seasonal discount an additional discount offered as an incentive to retailers to place orders for merchandise in advance of the normal buying season.

seasonal merchandise inventory whose sales fluctuate dramatically according to the time of the year.

secondary data market research information previously gathered for purposes other than solving the current problem under investigation.

secondary shopping district a cluster of stores outside the central business district that serves a large population within a section or part of a large city; it is similar in character to the main shopping district of a smaller city.

secondary trade zone the geographic area of secondary importance in terms of customer sales, generating about 20 percent of a store's sales.

security an operating unit within a retail organization that is responsible for protecting merchandise and other assets from pilferage (internal or external). Those working in security may be employees or outside agency people.

self-analysis an internally focused examination of a business's strengths and weaknesses.

self-service retailer a retailer that offers minimal customer service.

selling agent an agent who operates on an extended contractual basis; the agent sells all of a specified line of merchandise or the entire output of the principal, and usually has full authority with regard to prices, terms, and other conditions of sale. The agent occasionally renders financial aid to the principal.

selling process   a set of activities that salespeople undertake to facilitate the customer's buying decision.

selling space   the area set aside for displays of merchandise, interactions between sales personnel and customers, demonstrations, and so on.

sell-through analysis   a comparison between actual and planned sales to determine whether early markdowns are required or whether more merchandise is needed to satisfy demand.

service level   a measure used in inventory management to define the level of support or level of product availability; the number of items sold divided by the number of items demanded. Service level should not be confused with customer service. See **customer service.**

services   retailing organizations that offer services to consumers—such as banks, hospitals, health spas, doctors, legal clinics, entertainment firms, and universities.

Sherman Antitrust Act (1890)   the act of protecting small businesses and consumers from large corporations by outlawing any person, corporation, or association from engaging in activities that have the effect of restraining trade or commerce.

shoplifting   the act of stealing merchandise from a store by customers or people posing as customers.

shopping goods products   products for which consumers will spend time comparing alternatives.

shopping guides   free papers delivered to all residents in a specific area.

shopping malls   generally more planned than strip centers, have more pedestrian activity, and can be either open-air or enclosed.

shortage   see **shrinkage.**

shrinkage   the difference between the recorded value of inventory (at retail) based on merchandise bought and received and the value of actual inventory in stores and distribution centers divided by retail sales during a time period. Shrinkage is caused by employee theft, by customer shoplifting, and by merchandise being misplaced, damaged, or mispriced.

silhouette   the shape or contour of a garment. Some common silhouettes are tubular, hourglass, and bell-shaped.

single-price retailer   see **one-price retailer.**

situation audit   an analysis containing three elements: (1) the assessment of the attractiveness of different retail markets in which the business is competing or might compete, (2) the assessment of the objectives and capabilities of competitors, and (3) the assessment of the strengths and weaknesses of the business relative to its competition.

sliding scale   part of a lease in which the percentage of sales paid as rent decreases as sales go up.

slotting allowances   fees paid by a vendor for space in a retail store.

socialization   the steps taken to transform new employees into effective and committed members of the firm.

sole proprietorship   an arrangement in which an unincorporated retail firm is owned by one person.

span of control   the number of subordinates reporting to a manager.

specialization   a form of organization in which employees are assigned a limited set of tasks to perform.

specialty center   see **promotional or discount-oriented center** and **fashion-oriented shopping center.**

specialty department store   a store with a department store format that focuses primarily on apparel and soft home goods (such as Neiman Marcus or Parisian).

specialty products   products for which the customer will expend considerable effort to buy.

specialty store   concentrates on a limited number of complementary merchandise categories and provides a high level of service.

spiff   see **push money.**

split shipment   a vendor ships part of a shipment to a retailer and back orders the remainder because the entire shipment could not be shipped at the same time.

spot   a local television commercial.

spot check   used particularly in receiving operations when goods come in for reshipping to branch stores in packing cartons. Certain cartons are opened in the receiving area of the central distribution point and spot checked for quality and quantity.

spotting techniques   see **analog approach.**

staging area   areas in which merchandise is accumulated from different parts of the distribution center and prepared for shipment to stores.

standardization involves requiring service providers to follow a set of rules and procedures when providing service.

staple merchandise inventory that has continuous demand by customers (also known as basic merchandise).

stock balance trade-offs associated with determining variety, assortment, and service levels.

stockholders' equity see **owners' equity.**

stock keeping unit (SKU) the smallest unit available for keeping inventory control. In soft goods merchandise, an SKU usually means size, color, style.

stock overage the amount by which a retail book inventory figure exceeds a physical ending inventory.

stock-to-sales ratio the beginning-of-month (BOM) inventory divided by sales for the month. The average stock-to-sales ratio is 12 divided by planned inventory turnover. This ratio is an integral component of the merchandise budget plan.

store atmosphere see **atmospherics.**

store brand see **private-label brand.**

store image the way a store is defined in a shopper's mind. The store image is based on the store's physical characteristics, its retail mix, and a set of psychological attributes.

store loyalty a condition in which a customer regularly patronizes a specific retailer.

store visibility see **visibility.**

straight lease a type of lease in which the retailer pays a fixed amount per month over the life of the lease.

straight rack a type of fixture that consists of a long pipe suspended with supports going to the floor or attached to a wall.

straight salary a compensation plan in which salespeople or managers receive a fixed amount of compensation for each hour or week they work.

strategic partnerships long-term relationships in which partners make significant investments to improve both parties' profitability.

strategic profit model (SPM) a tool used for planning a retailer's financial strategy based on both margin management (net profit margin), asset management (asset turnover), and

financial leverage management (financial leverage ratio). Using the SPM, a retailer's objective is to achieve a target return on owners' equity.

strategic retail plan a grand design or blueprint indicating the retail strategy and the steps for implementing the plan.

strict product liability a product liability suit in which the injury to the customer may not have been intentional or under the retailer's control.

strip center a small shopping center that comprises several adjacent stores located along a major street or highway; also known as a ribbon center.

style the characteristic or distinctive form, outline, or shape of a product.

subculture theory a theory proposing that fashions are initiated by subcultures in society and then spread to larger social groups. Accounts for fashions for colorful fabrics, T-shirts, sneakers, jeans, black leather jackets, and surplus military clothing that started with people in smaller, less affluent consumer groups (such as the Hell's Angels or urban rappers) and "trickled up" to mainstream consumer classes.

subjective employee evaluation assessment of employee performance based on supervisor's ratings rather than on objective measures such as sales per hour.

substitute awareness effect a condition in which customers become more price-sensitive because they can find a lot of substitutes for a product or for a retailer.

supermarket see **conventional supermarket.**

superstores a large supermarket between 20,000 and 50,000 square feet in size.

survey a method of data collection, using telephone, personal interview, mail, or any combination thereof.

sustainable competitive advantage a distinct competency of a retailer relative to its competitors that can be maintained over a considerable time period.

sweepstakes a promotion in which customers win prizes based on chance.

T

tall wall units retail facilities that are six-to-seven foot selling spaces placed against a wall in a mall instead of in the middle of an aisle as a cart or kiosk would be.

target market   the customer group to which a retailer targets its retail mix.

target segment   see **target market.**

task performance behaviors   planning, organizing, motivating, evaluating, and coordinating store employees' activities.

terms of purchase   conditions in a purchase agreement with a vendor that include the type(s) of discounts available and responsibility for transportation costs.

terms of sale   conditions in a sales contract with customers including such issues as charges for alterations, delivery, or gift wrapping, or the store's exchange policies.

tertiary trade zone   the outermost ring of a trade area; includes customers who occasionally shop at the store or shopping center. Also known as fringe trade area.

theme center   a shopping center that tries to replicate a historical place and typically contains tenants similar to those in specialty centers, except there usually is no large specialty store or department store as an anchor. See **historical center** and **specialty center.**

ticketing and marking   procedures for making price labels and placing them on the merchandise.

tie-ins   an approach used to attract attention to a store's offering by associating the offering with an event.

tonnage merchandising   a technique in which a large quantity of merchandise is displayed together.

top-down planning   one side of the process of developing an overall retail strategy where goals are set at the top of the organization and filter down through the operating levels.

total expenditure effect   a condition in which customer price sensitivity increases when the total expenditure is large.

trade area   a geographic sector that contains potential customers for a particular retailer or shopping center.

trade discounts   reductions in a retailers' suggested retail price granted to wholesalers and retailers; also known as functional discounts.

trade press   publications that provide information for the retailers and producers in a given industry.

trade show   a temporary concentration of vendors that provides retailers opportunities to place orders and view what is available in the marketplace; also known as a merchandise show.

trademark   any mark, work, picture, or design associated with a particular line of merchandise or product.

traffic appliances   small portable appliances.

transformational leaders   get people to transcend their personal needs for the sake of the group goal realization.

transportation cost   the expense a retailer incurs if it pays the cost of shipping merchandise from the vendor to the stores.

travel time contours   used in trade area analysis to define the rings around a particular site based on travel time instead of distances.

trickle-down theory   a theory suggesting that new fashions originate with consumers with the highest social status—wealthy, well-educated consumers—and trickle down from them to consumers in lower social classes. Once a fashion is accepted in the lowest social class, it is no longer acceptable to the fashion leaders in the highest social class.

triple coupon promotion   a retail promotion that allows the customer triple the face value of the coupon.

trunk show   an event at which a manufacturer presents its line of fashion merchandise to customers in the retail setting.

turnover   the percentage of employees at the beginning of a time period (usually a year) that aren't employed by the firm at the end of the time period.

tying contract   an agreement between a vendor and a retailer requiring the retailer to take a product it does not necessarily desire (the "tied product") to ensure it can buy a product it does desire (the "tying product").

U

ultimate consumers   individuals who purchase goods and services for their own personal use or for use by members of their household.

undercover shoppers   people hired by or working for a retailer who pose as customers to observe the activities and performance of employees.

unit pricing   the practice of expressing price both in terms of the total price of an item and the price per unit of measure.

unity of command   the appropriate relationship between managers and their subordinates.

Universal Product Code (UPC)   the black-and-white bar codes found on most merchandise used to collect sales information at the point of sale using computer terminals that read them. This information is transmitted computer-to-computer to buyers, distribution centers, and then to vendors, who in turn quickly ship replenishment merchandise.

unrelated diversification   diversification in which there is no commonality between the present business and the new business.

utility   the consumer's perception of the benefits of the product and services offered by the retailer.

V

value pricing   setting prices based on fair value for both the service provider and the consumer.

variable cost   the sum of the firm's expenses that vary directly with the quantity of product produced and sold.

variable direct costs   costs that vary with the level of sales and can be applied directly to the decision in question.

variety   the number of different merchandise categories within a store or department.

vending machine retailers   a form of nonstore retailing in which customers purchase and receive merchandise from a machine.

vendor   any firm from which a retailer obtains merchandise.

vertical integration   a firm that performs more than one function in the channel.

vertical merchandising   a method of organizing merchandise whereby merchandise is organized to follow the eye's natural up-and-down movement.

vertical price fixing   agreements to fix prices between parties at different levels of the same marketing channel, for example, retailers and their vendors. Also known as resale price maintenance or fair trade laws.

videotex retailing   an interactive electronic system in which a retailer transmits data and graphics over cable or telephone lines to a consumer's TV or computer terminal.

visibility   the customers' ability to see the store and enter the parking lot safely.

visual communications   the act of providing information to customers through graphics, signs, and theatrical effects both in the store and in windows to help boost sales by providing information on products and by suggesting items or special purchases.

W

want book   information collected by retail salespeople to record out-of-stock or requested merchandise. Similar to a want slip.

warehouse clubs   a general merchandise retailer that offers limited merchandise assortment with little service at low prices to ultimate consumers and small businesses.

warehouse store   a discount food retailer that offers merchandise in a no-frills environment.

week's supply method   an inventory management method most similar to the stock-to-sales method. The difference is that everything is expressed in weeks rather than months.

wheel of retailing   a cyclical theory of retail evolution whose premise is that retailing institutions evolve from low price/service to higher price/service operations.

wholesale club   a general merchandise retailer that offers a limited merchandise assortment with little service at low prices and sells to ultimate consumers and member trade people.

wholesaler   a merchant establishment operated by a concern that is primarily engaged in buying, taking title to, usually storing, and physically handling goods in large quantities, and reselling the goods (usually in smaller quantities) to retailers or to industrial or business users.

wholesale-sponsored voluntary cooperative group   an organization operated by a wholesaler offering a merchandising program to small, independent retailers on a voluntary basis.

Y

yuppies   Young Urban Professionals.

Z

zoning   the regulation of the construction and use of buildings in certain areas of a municipality.

Notes

CHAPTER 1

1. *U.S. Census of Retail Trade 1990* (Washington, D.C.: U.S. Dept. of Commerce, 1991), p. 123.
2. Gerald Dell and Linda Pettijohn, "A Retailer's View of Industrial Innovations: An Interview with David Glass, President and CEO of Wal-Mart," *Journal of Product Innovation* 8 (December 1991), pp. 231–36; and Stephen Wilson, "Technology in Retail's Business Strategies of the Future," *Retail Control,* October 1991, pp. 13–17.
3. Kyle Pope, "For Compaq and Dell Accent Is on Personal in the Computer Wars," *The Wall Street Journal,* July 2, 1993, p. A2.
4. For a more detailed discussion of distribution channels, see Louis Stern, Adel El-Ansary, and James Brown, *Management in Marketing Channels,* 2d ed. (Englewood Cliffs, N.J.: Prentice Hall, 1992).
5. A. Raucher, "Dime Store Chains: The Making of Organization Men 1880–1940," *Business History Review* 65 (Spring 1991), pp. 130–63.
6. Paul Hawken, "The Ecology of Commerce," *Inc.,* April 1992, pp. 93–100; Rahul Jacob, "Body Shop International: What Selling Will Be Like in the 1990's," *Fortune,* January 17, 1992, pp. 63–66; and Kate Fitzgerald, "Store Tops Destination List for Even Armchair Travelers," *Advertising Age,* November 2, 1992, p. S8.
7. For a discussion of the trade-off between retailer and consumer inventory holding costs, see Robert Blattberg, Gary Epen, and Joshua Lieberman, "A Theoretical and Empirical Evaluation in Price Deals for Consumer Nondurables," *Journal of Marketing* (Winter 1981), pp. 116–29.
8. William Swinyard, Fred Langrehr, and Scott Smith, "The Appeal of Retailing as a Career: A Decade Later," *Journal of Retailing* 67 (Winter 1991), pp. 451–65.
9. "The Forbes 400," *Forbes,* October 19, 1992, pp. 92–270.
10. Penny Gill, "Les Wexner: Unlimited Success Story," *Stores,* January 1993, pp. 81–122; and Laura Zinn, "Maybe The Limited Has Limits After All," *Business Week,* February 3, 1992, p. 30.
11. Laura Zinn, "The New Stars of Retailing," *Business Week,* December 16, 1991, pp. 120–22; and Bertrand Frank, "Merchandising Private Label Apparel," *Retail Business Review,* April 1992, pp. 24–26.
12. Jeff Haggin and Bjorn Kartomkin, "Show Your Customer Respect," *Catalog Age,* October 1992, pp. 91–92.
13. John Cortez, "Monaghan's Goal to Reheat Domino's Pizza," *Advertising Age,* December 16, 1991, p. 13.
14. T. Mullen, "Preparing for Change," *Stores,* December 1992, pp. 18–20; Joseph Antonni, "Trends in Retailing in the Nineties," *Retail Control,* December 1991, pp. 3–7; and Michael Gade and Jacquelyn Bivens, "Fundamental Changes," *Discount Merchandiser,* May 1992, pp. 66, 69.
15. J. S. Green, "Changing Consumer Demographics," *Discount Merchandiser,* January 1993, pp. 68–70; and E. A. Germeroth, "The Retail Challenge: The Consumer of the '90's," *Discount Merchandiser,* May 1992, pp. 84ff.
16. Jennifer Reese, "America's Most Admired Companies," *Fortune,* February 8, 1993, pp. 44–47ff; Mark Maremont, "Brawls in Toyland," *Business Week,* December 21, 1992, pp. 36–37; and Debra Chanil, "The Toy Game: Increasing Market Share," *Discount Merchandiser,* February 1992, pp. 60–67ff.
17. Based in part on "The J.C. Penney Company (A): Marketing and Financial Strategy," in *Retailing Management,* 6th ed., William Davidson, Daniel Sweeney, and Ronald Stampfl, eds. (New York: Wiley, 1988), pp. 261–64.

CHAPTER 2

1. "Spending Slide Continues," in "60th Annual Report of the Grocery Industry," *Progressive Grocer,* April 1993, p. 49.
2. Frances Brown, "Convenience Stores Move to Diversify," *The Wall Street Journal,* September 12, 1984, p. 35; and "Karl Eller's Big Thirst for Convenience Stores," *Business Week,* June 13, 1988, pp. 86, 88.
3. Jill Lettich, "Discounters Up Share of '92 Sales," *Discounter Store News,* July 5, 1993, pp. 3, 118. Based on *Retail Perspectives,* a study undertaken and published by Kurt Salmon Associates.
4. Penny Gill, "What's a Department Store?" *Stores,* February 1990, pp. 8–17.
5. Alison Fahey, "Department Store Outlook: May, Dillard Hot, But All Watch Specialty Inroads," *Advertising Age,* January 28, 1991, pp. 23–24.
6. "The Discount Industry's Top 150 Chains," *Discount Store News,* July 5, 1993, pp. 21–43.

7. Gregory Patterson, "Sears's Makeover into a Department Store Calls for Enhancing the Role of Cosmetics," *The Wall Street Journal,* April 9, 1993, pp. B1, B3.

8. Joseph Pereira, "Discount Department Stores Struggle against Rivals That Strike Aisle by Aisle," *The Wall Street Journal,* June 19, 1990, pp. B1, B7.

9. Michael Gelfand, "Consumer Electronics Superstores," *Discount Merchandiser,* January 1993, pp. 60–66ff; and Dean Foust, "Circuit City's Wires Are Sizzling," *Business Week,* April 27, 1992, p. 76.

10. David P. Schultz, "The Top 100 Specialty Stores," *Stores,* August 1993, p. 34; and "Exec 100," *Chain Store Age Executive,* August 1993, p. 26A.

11. Cyndee Miller, "Big Chains Battle for Market Share in Home Improvement," *Marketing News,* September 28, 1992, pp. 1, 10–11; and Roger Thompson, "There's No Place Like Home Depot," *Nation's Business,* February 1992, pp. 30–33.

12. "Exec 100," *Chain Store Age Executive,* August 1993, p. 26A.

13. Debra Chanil, "Wholesale Clubs: Romancing America," *Discount Merchandiser,* November 1992, pp. 26–41; Terry Cotter and Douglas Tigert, "Warehouse Membership Clubs in North America," *Discount Merchandiser,* November 1992, pp. 42–47; and Doris Jones Yang and Geoffrey Smith, "Corn Flakes, Aisle 1. Cadillacs, Aisle 12," *Business Week,* April 29, 1991, pp. 68–70.

14. "Exec 100," *Chain Store Age Executive,* August 1993, p. 38A.

15. Ellen Paris, "A Touch of Class," *Forbes,* February 5, 1990, pp. 148, 150.

16. "The Discount Industry's Top 150 Chains," *Discount Store News,* July 5, 1993, p. 41.

17. Gretchen Morgenson, "Cheapie Gucci," *Forbes,* May 27, 1991, pp. 43–44; and Irene Daria, "Where It's Chic to Shop Now," *Money,* February 1990, pp. 119–23.

18. "The Discount Industry's Top 150 Chains," p. 35.

19. Ibid., p. 41.

20. Paul Miller, "Neither Mall nor Mail," *Catalog Age,* October 1992, pp. 5, 31; and Jennifer Pellet, "Staying True to a $3 Billion Concept," *Discount Merchandiser,* March 1990, pp. 34–38.

21. "The Discount Industry's Top 150 Chains," *Discount Store News,* July 5, 1993, p. 41.

22. See also Connie Bauer and John Miglautsch, "A Conceptual Definition of Direct Marketing," *Journal of Direct Marketing,* 6 (Spring 1992), pp. 7–17.

23. Caryne Brown, "Door-to-Door Selling Grows Up," *Black Enterprise,* December 1992, pp. 76–90; and Kate Ballen, "Get Ready for Shopping at Work," *Fortune,* February 15, 1988, pp. 96–97.

24. Robert Mamis, "Toward Hassle-Free Mail Order," *Inc.,* January 1993, p. 42; Soyean Shim and Marianne Mahoney, "The Elderly Mail-Order Catalog User of Fashion Products," *Journal of Direct Marketing* 6 (Winter 1992), pp. 49–58; and Judith Waldrop, "Catalog Complaints Cut Sales By Mail," *American Demographics,* February 1993, p. 12.

25. Lynn Hayes, "The Catalog Age Report," *Catalog Age,* December 1992, pp. 59–61; and "Mail Order Top 250," *Direct Marketing,* July 1992, pp. 20–37.

26. Personal communication.

27. John Simone, "The Mailing of America," *VM&SD,* November 1992, p. 25.

28. "Mail Order Top 250," p. 28.

29. "Eight Threats to Direct Marketing," *Target Marketing,* April 1989, p. 47.

30. Elaine Underwood, "Marketers, Retailers to Ride Home Shopping's Highway," *Brandweek,* March 22, 1993, p. 8; and Seth Lubove, "Don't Leave Home, Period," *Forbes,* October 28, 1991, pp. 164, 166.

31. Arthur Markowitz, "Electronic Shopping Services at a Crossroad," *Discount Store News,* September 3, 1990, pp. 10, 12; and Gary Robbins, "On-Line Service Update," *Stores,* February 1990, pp. 24–31.

32. *1993 Direct Selling Industry Survey* (Washington, D.C.: Direct Selling Association, 1993), p. 4.

33. "State of Industry," *Automatic Merchandiser,* August 1993, p. 20.

34. *Census of Retail Trade* (U.S. Dept. of Commerce, Bureau of the Census, 1987), p. 12.

35. Dun and Bradstreet, *Corporate Starts* (New York: Dun and Bradstreet, 1993), p. 74.

36. *Census of Retail Trade,* p. 12.

37. Louis Stern and Adel El-Ansary, *Marketing Channels,* 5th ed. (Englewood Cliffs, N.J.: Prentice Hall, 1993), p. 332.

CHAPTER 3

1. Ken Dychtwald and Joe Flower, *Age Wave* (Los Angeles: Jeremy P. Tarcher, 1989).

2. Numbers are based on Standard Metropolitan Areas. *Statistical Abstract of the United States, 1992,* 112th ed. (Washington, D.C.: U.S. Bureau of the Census, 1992), p. 34.

3. J. Paul Peter and Jerry C. Olson, *Consumer Behavior and Marketing Strategy,* 3d ed. (Burr Ridge, Ill.: Richard D. Irwin, 1993), p. 526.

4. James U. McNeal, " 'Little' Consumers Influence Spending Decisions," *Discount Store News,* August 5, 1991, pp. 78, 80; James U. McNeal, "The Littlest Shoppers," *American Demographics,* February 1992, pp. 48–53; Robert M. Zimmerman, "Today's Children Make Shopping More than Child's Play," *Retail Control,* January 1992, pp. 21–25; and Jill Lettich, "Small Children with Deep Pockets Can Be a Retailing Goldmine," *Discount Store News,* May 18, 1992, pp. 58, 65.

5. Richard Halverson, "Core Shopping Group Shrinking as Baby Busters Grow Up," *Discount Store News,* May 18, 1992, pp. 93–94; and Susan Mitchell, "How to Talk to Young Adults," *American Demographics,* April 1993, pp. 50–54.

6. Roger Selbert, "Retailing's Five Most Important Trends," *Retailing Issues* Letter 3, no. 2 (College Station, Tex.: Arthur Andersen & Co. and Center for Retailing Studies, Texas A&M University), March 1991; Arthur Markowitz, "Affluent Middle-Agers Challenge Retailers' Merchandising Skills," *Discount Store News,* May 18, 1992, pp. 104, 107; Harvey D. Braun, "Mature Consumers Challenging Retailers," Discount Store News, May 6, 1991, pp. 49, 51; and David B. Wolfe, "Business's Mid-Life Crisis," American Demographics, September 1992, pp. 40–44.

7. Mary Ellen Kelly, "Discounters Grow Wiser to Seniors' Spending Potential," *Discount Store News,* May 18, 1992,

pp. 113–14, attributed to Professor George Moschis of Georgia State University.

8. Larry Ruderman and Artie Ruderman, "Senior Service," *Visual Merchandising and Store Design,* August 1992, pp. 66–69. Information courtesy of Roper Research Associates, Inc., "Apparel and the Mature Consumer" and "The Modern American Grandparent."

9. Selbert, "Retailing's Five Most Important Trends"; "Minority Customers to Become a Major Marketing Target," *Discount Store News,* May 18, 1992, p. 100.

10. Information in this section is taken from "J.C. Penney Finds Profit in Africa," *American Demographics,* November 1992, p. 12; Laurie M. Grossman, "After Demogrpahic Shift, Atlanta Mall Restyles Itself as Black Shopping Center," *The Wall Street Journal,* February 2, 1992, pp. B1, B7; and Eugene Morris, "The Difference Is Black and White," *American Demographics,* January 1993, pp. 44–49.

11. James F. Engel, Roger D. Blackwell, and Paul W. Miniard, *Consumer Behavior, 7th ed.* (Chicago: Dryden, 1993), p. 640; "Family Futures," *American Demographics* 8 (May 1984), p. 50; and "Money Income of Households, Families, and Persons," Series P60, no. 162 (Washington, D.C.: U.S. Government Printing Office, 1989).

12. Selbert, "Retailing's Five Most Important Trends"; Diane Crispell, "Women in Charge," *American Demographics,* September 1989, pp. 27–29; and "A Decade of Change 1978–1987," *Chain Store Age Executive,* November 1988, pp. 55–78.

13. Eugene Fram, "The Time Compressed Shopper," *Marketing Insights,* Summer 1991, pp. 34–39.

14. Ibid.

15. "More Green Options," *Chain Store Age Executive,* August 1990, p. 17; Peter Glen, "Paradise and Profit," *Visual Merchandising and Store Design,* July 1992, pp. 6–9; "Wal-Mart's Green Challenge," *Discount Store News,* June 15, 1992, p. 121; and Carl Frankel, "Blueprint for Green Marketing," *American Demographics,* April 1992, pp. 34–38.

16. Alice Bredin, "Outlet Centers Prosper," *Stores,* March 1992, pp. 63–65; Jeffrey R. Trachtenberg, "Let's Make a Deal: A Buyer's Market Has Shoppers Demanding and Getting Discounts," *The Wall Street Journal,* February 8, 1991, p. A1; Joseph B. White, "Buyer's Market: Value Pricing Is Hot as Shrewd Consumers Seek Low-Cost Quality," *The Wall Street Journal,* March 12, 1991, p. A1; Wendy Zellner, "Penney's Rediscovers Its Calling," *Business Week,* April 5, 1993, pp. 51–52; and Jack Kasulis, "The Frugal Family of the Nineties," *Retailing Issues Letter* 3, no. 5 (College Station, TX: Arthur Andersen & Co. and Center for Retailing Studies, Texas A&M University), September 1991.

17. "Made in America?" *J.C. Penney Management Report* 19, no. 4 (1992), p. 2, quoted from a *USA Today* poll.

18. Stanley Marcus and Lawrence R. Katzen, "Japan's Best Practices: Lessons and Opportunities," *Retail Business Review,* January 1993, p. 6.

19. The following section is based on a speech by Joseph R. Baczko, former president, Blockbuster Entertainment and Toys "R" Us International Division, at the Executive Education Symposium, Center for Retail Education and Research, University of Florida, May 13, 1993; and Susan Reda, "Testing Russian Waters," *Stores,* October 1992, p. 24, attributed to Carl Steidtmann, chief economist at Management Horizons.

20. Mary Ellen Kelly, "U.S. Retailers Begin Mexican Invasion," *Discount Store News,* May 18, 1992, pp. 43–48; Retailers Must Avoid Pitfalls of new Market," *Discount Store News,* May 18, 1992, pp. 43–48; Robert Verdisco, "The Future of Mass Retailing Is Global," *Discount Store News,* October 5, 1992, p. 11; Mary Ellen Kelly, "J.C. Penney to Enter Mexico," *Discount Store News,* February 15, 1993, p. 3; Tracy Mullin, "NAFTA: A Win/Win for Retailers," *Stores,* October 1992, p. 20; and Arthur Markowitz, "Costco Thinks International: Club Eyes France and Spain," *Discount Store News,* August 5, 1991, p. 7.

21. Joseph H. Ellis, Richard N. Baum, and Mary Ann Casati, "International Retailing: Opportunities and Pitfalls," *Goldman Sachs Investment Research,* May 14, 1993, p. 6.

22. Paul Doocey, "Paul Doocey, "Euro-Retailing," *Stores,* July 1992, pp. 76–78; Timothy Harper, *Cracking the New European Markets* (New York: John Wiley); Thomas J. Schiro and Amy M. Skolnik, Europe 1992—Impact on Retail Sector," *Retail Control,* May/June 1990, pp. 3–9; Arthur Markowitz, "Costco Thinks International: Club Eyes France and Spain," *Discount Store News,* August 5, 1991, p. 7; Laura Lieback, "Kmart Czechs into Europe," *Discount Store News,* June 15, 1992, pp. 3, 20; Arthur Markowitz, "Status Quo in Western Europe," *Discount Store News,* May 6, 1991, p. 99ff; Laura Lieback, "Eastern Europe Is a Risky Business," *Discount Store News,* May 6, 1991, p. 103ff; and Carrie Dolan, "Levi's Tries to Round Up Counterfeiters," *The Wall Street Journal,* February 9, 1992, pp. B1, B10.

23. Stanley Marcus and Lawrence R. Katzen, "Japan's Best Practices: Lessons and Opportunities," *Retail Business Review,* January 1993, pp. 6–9; "Japanese vs. American Retailing," *Stores,* June 1992, p. 29; and Tony Lisanti, "Japanese Retailing's Tug-of-War," *Discount Store News,* May 6, 1992, p. 77ff.

24. Michael B. Exstein and Faye I. Weitzman, "Foreign Investment in U.S. Retailing: An Optimistic Overview," *Retail Control,* January 1991, pp. 9–14; David P. Schulz, "The Top 100 Retailers," *Stores,* July 1992, pp. 33–55; "Ito-Yokada Rolls and 7-Eleven," *Chain Store Age Executive,* January 1992, pp. 33–44; and Nancy Cohen, "Chevignon: Accent on Style," *Stores,* March 1991, pp. 38–41.

CHAPTER 4

1. For a detailed discussion of customer behavior, see J. Paul Peter and Jerry C. Olson, *Consumer Behavior and Marketing Strategy,* 3d ed. (Burr Ridge, Ill.: Richard D. Irwin, 1993). See also Jagdish Sheth, "An Integrative Theory of Patronage Preference and Choice," in *Patronage Theory and Retail Management,* William Darden and Robert Lusch, eds. (New York: North-Holland, 1989), pp. 9–28.

2. Joel Urbany, Peter Dickson, and William Wilkie, "Buyer Uncertainty and Information Search," *Journal of Consumer Research* 16 (September 1989), pp. 208–15; and James Lumpkin, "Perceived Risk and Selection of Patronage Mode," *Journal of the Academy of Marketing Science* 14 (Winter 1986), pp. 38–42.

3. Judann Danoli, "Impulse Governs Shoppers," *Advertising Age,* October 5, 1987, p. 93; and Peter Dickson and Alan Sawyer, "The Price Knowledge and Search of Supermarket Shoppers," *Journal of Marketing,* July 1991, pp. 49–59.

4. This hierarchical structure of needs is based on Abraham Maslow, *Motivation and Personality* (New York: Harper & Row, 1954).

5. Robert A. Westbrook and William C. Black, "A Motivational-Based Shopper Typology," *Journal of Retailing* 61 (Spring 1985), pp. 78–103; Edward Tauber, "Why Do People Shop?" *Journal of Marketing* 36 (October 1972), pp. 42–49; Betsy Morris, "As a Favored Pastime, Shopping Ranks High with Most Americans," *The Wall Street Journal,* July 30, 1987, pp. 1, 13; and Scott Dawson, Peter Dawson, and Nancy Ridgeway, "Shopping Motives, Emotional States, and Retail Outcomes," *Journal of Retailing* 66 (Winter 1990), pp. 408–27.

6. Glen Jarbo and Carl McDaniels, "A Profile of Browsers in Regional Shopping Malls," *Journal of the Academy of Marketing Science* 15 (Spring 1987), pp. 45–52; and Peter Block, Nancy Ridgeway, and Daniel Sherrell, "Extending the Concept of Shopping: An Investigation of Browsing Activities," *Journal of the Academy of Marketing Science* 17 (Winter 1989), pp. 12–17.

7. David Mick, Michelle DeMoss, and Ronald Faber, "A Projective Study of Motivations and Meanings of Self-Gift," *Journal of Retailing,* Summer 1992, pp. 112–44.

8. Gordon Bruner and Richard Pomazal, "Problem Recognition: The Crucial First Stage of the Consumer Decision Process," *Journal of Consumer Marketing,* Summer 1987, pp. 59–66.

9. Sharon E. Beatty and Scott M. Smith, "External Search Effort: An Investigation across Several Product Categories," *Journal of Consumer Research* 8 (June 1986), pp. 119–26; and Girish Punj, "Presearch Decision Making in Consumer Durable Purchases," *Journal of Consumer Marketing* 4 (Winter 1987), pp. 71–82.

10. Lawrence Feick, Linda Prie, and Robie Higie, "People Who Use People: The Other Side of Opinion Leadership," in *Advances in Consumer Research,* R. Lutz, ed. (Provo, Utah: Association of Consumer Research, 1986), pp. 10–12.

11. George Russell, "Where the Customer Is Still King," *Time,* February 2, 1987, pp. 56–57.

12. Eugene Fram, "The Time Compressed Shopper," *Marketing Insights,* Summer 1991, pp. 12–23.

13. David Klenosky and Arno Rethans, "The Formation of Consumer Choice Sets: A Longitudinal Investigation at the Product Class Level," in *Advances in Consumer Behavior,* vol. 15, Michael Houston, ed. (Provo, Utah: Association of Consumer Research, 1988), pp. 13–18; John Hauser and Birger Wernfeldt, "An Evaluation Cost Model of a Consideration Set," *Journal of Consumer Research,* March 1990, pp. 393–408; and Susan Spiggle and Murphy Sewall, "A Choice Set Model of Retail Selection," *Journal of Marketing* 51 (April 1987), pp. 97–111.

14. Kevin Helliker, "Some 7-Elevens Try Selling a New Image," *The Wall Street Journal,* October 25, 1991, pp. B1–B2.

15. Jagdip Singh, "A Typology of Consumer Dissatisfaction Response Styles," *Journal of Retailing,* Spring 1990, pp. 57–98; and Richard Oliver and Wayne DeSarbo, "Response Determinants in Satisfaction Judgments," *Journal of Consumer Research* 15 (March 1988), pp. 495–507.

16. Richard L. Oliver, "A Cognitive Model of the Antecedents and Consequences of Satisfaction Decisions," *Journal of Marketing Research* 17 (November 1980), pp. 460–69; and Richard L. Oliver, "Measurement and Evaluation of Satisfaction Processes in a Retail Setting," *Journal of Retailing* 57 (Fall 1981), pp. 26–31.

17. Irene Foster and Richard Olshavsky, "An Exploratory Study of Family Decision Making Using a New Taxonomy of Family Role Structure," in *Advances in Consumer Research,* T. Srull, ed. (Provo, Utah: Association for Consumer Research, 1989), pp. 665–700.

18. Ken Wells, "Hotels and Resorts Are Catering to Kids: Day Care and Activities Programs Help Welcome the Traveling Family," *The Wall Street Journal,* August 11, 1988, p. 25.

19. *Consumer Behavior,* Peter and Olson, pp. 419–20.

20. Terrence Witkowski and Yoshito Yamamoto, "Omiyage Gift Purchasing by Japanese Traveller to the US," in *Advances in Consumer Research,* vol. 18 (Provo, Utah: Association of Consumer Research, 1991), pp. 123–28.

21. Martha Farnsworth Riche, "Psychographics for the 1990s," *American Demographics,* July 1989, pp. 25–31, 53–54. See also Lynne Kahle, Sharon Beatty, and Pamela Homer, "Alternative Measurement Approaches to Consumer Values: The List of Values (LOV) and Values and Lifestyles (VALS)," *Journal of Consumer Research* 13 (December 1986), pp. 40–50.

22. Rebecca Pirto, "VALS the Second Time," *American Demographics,* July 1991, p. 6.

CHAPTER 5

1. Nancy Karch, "The New Strategic Era in Retailing, Part I," *Retail Control* 53 (October 1985), pp. 35–49; Nancy Karch, "The New Strategic Era in Retailing, Part 2," *Retail Control* 53 (November 1985), pp. 10–19; and Bert Rosenbloom, "Strategic Planning in Retailing: Prospects and Problems," *Journal of Retailing* 56 (Spring 1980), pp. 98–106.

2. Alfred Rappoport, *Creating Shareholder Value: The New Standard for Business Performance* (New York: Wiley, 1988).

3. Fred R. Davis, "How Companies Define Their Mission," *Long Range Planning,* February 1990, pp. 90–94.

4. Roger Evered, "So What Is Strategy?" *Long Range Planning* 16 (Fall 1983), p. 120; and Barton Weitz and Robin Wensley, "What Is Marketing Strategy?" working paper (Gainesville: College of Business Administration, University of Florida).

5. Richard Baum, "Gymboree Corporation" (New York: Goldman, Sachs & Company, May 5, 1993).

6. Spiegel, Inc. 1992 Annual Report. While most of Spiegel's sales result from its large semiannual catalogs, Spiegel uses smaller catalogs for specific target markets and operates some retail stores.

7. David Bolotsky and Matthew Fassler, "Exploring the Future of Hard Goods Specialty Retailing" (New York: Goldman, Sachs & Company, June 15, 1993), pp. 2–4.

8. Family Dollar 1988 Annual Report.

9. See R. L. Rothschild, *How to Gain and Maintain Competitive Advantage in Business* (New York: McGraw-Hill, 1984). Chapter 2 gives other examples of this approach to mapping competitive markets.

10. David Walters and Derek Knee, "Competitive Strategies in Retailing," *Journal of Long Range Planning* 22 (December 1989), pp. 27–34; and Andrea Groeppel, "Competitive Retailing Strategies in Germany: An Empirical Study," in *Developments in Marketing Science,* vol. 16, Michael Levy and Dhruv Grewal, eds. (Coral Gables, Fla.: Academy of Marketing Science, 1993), pp. 643–54.

11. David Aaker, "Managing Assets and Skills: The Key to Sustainable Competitive Advantage," *California Management Review* 32 (Winter 1989), pp. 91–106; Jay Barney, "Firm Resources and Sustained Competitive Advantages," *Journal of Management* 17 (March 1991), pp. 11–120; and Pankaj Ghemawat, "Sustainable Advantage," *Harvard Business Review* (March-April 1987), pp. 143–49.

12. David Aaker, "Positioning Your Product," *Business Horizon,* May-June 1982, pp. 56–62; and George Lucas and Larry Gresham, "How to Position for Retailing Success," *Business,* April-June 1989, pp. 31–32.

13. For examples of this type of research, see Mary R. Zimmer and Linda L. Golden, "Impressions of Retail Stores: A Content Analysis of Consumer Images," *Journal of Retailing* 64 (Fall 1988), pp. 265–93; M. Joseph Sirgy and A. Cosun Samli, "A Path Analytic Model of Store Loyalty Involving Self-Concept, Store Image, Geographic Loyalty, and Socioeconomic Status," *Journal of Academy of Marketing Science,* June 1985, pp. 360–65; and Douglas Tigert and Stephen Arnold, "Nordstrom: How Good Are They?" Babson College Retailing Research Reports (Babson Park, Mass., September 1990).

14. Stanley Marcus, *Minding the Store* (Boston: Little, Brown, 1974).

15. Walter J. Salmon and Karen A. Carr, "Private Labels Are Back in Fashion," *Harvard Business Review* 65 (May-June 1987), pp. 99–106.

16. Lisa Driscoll, "It's Taking Off with Jet-Lagged Shoppers," *Business Week,* May 21, 1990, p. 108.

17. Margaret Gilliam, "The Impact of Partnerships on Retailers and Manufacturers," *Retail Control,* March 1992, pp. 11–18; Wendy Zellner, "Clout! More and More, Retail Giants Rule the Marketplace," *Business Week,* December 21, 1992, pp. 66–73; and Erin Anderson and Barton Weitz, "Forging a Strategic Distribution Alliance," *Chief Executive,* November-December 1991, pp. 70–73.

18. Rashi Glazer, "Marketing in an Information Intensive Environment: Strategic Implications of Knowledge as an Asset," *Journal of Marketing* 55 (October 1991), pp. 1–19; Michael Porter and V. E. Miller, "How Information Gives You Competitive Advantage," *Harvard Business Review* 63 (July-August 1985), pp. 149–60; and William Driscoll, "Strategic Information Systems: Planning in the Retail Environment," *Retail Control* 56 (September 1988), pp. 13–18.

19. Bolotsky and Fassler, "Exploring the Future," pp. 18–21.

20. George Day and Robin Wensley, "Assessing Advantage: A Framework for Diagnosing Competitive Superiority *Journal of Marketing* 52 (April 1988), pp. 1–20; C. K. Prahalad and Gary Hamel, "The Core Competencies of the Corporation," *Harvard Business Review* 68 (May-June 1990), pp. 79–97; and G. Stalk, "Competing on Capabilities: The New Rules of Corporate Strategy," *Harvard Business Review* March-April 1992, pp. 51–69.

21. The following section is based on a speech by Joseph R. Baczko, former president, Blockbuster Entertainment and Toys "R" Us International Division, at the Executive Education Symposium, Center for Retail Education and Research, University of Florida, May 13, 1993; and Susan Reda, "Testing Russian Waters," *Stores,* October 1992, p. 24, attributed to Carl Steidtmann, chief economist at Management Horizons.

22. Mary Ellen Kelly, "U.S. Retailers Begin Mexican Invasion," *Discount Store News,* May 18, 1992, pp. 43–48; "Retailers Must Avoid Pitfalls of New Market," *Discount Store News,* May 18, 1992, pp. 43–48; Robert Verdisco, "The Future of Mass Retailing Is Global," *Discount Store News,* October 5, 1992, p. 11; Mary Ellen Kelly, "J.C. Penney to Enter Mexico," *Discount Store News,* February 15, 1993, p. 3; Tracy Mullin, "NAFTA: A Win/Win for Retailers," *Stores,* October 1992, p. 20; and Arthur Markowitz, "Costco Thinks International: Club Eyes France and Spain," *Discount Store News,* August 5, 1991, p. 7.

23. Joseph H. Ellis, Richard N. Baum, and Mary Ann Casati, "International Retailing: Opportunities and Pitfalls," May 14, 1993, p. 6.

24. Paul Doocey, "Euro-Retailing," *Stores,* July 1992, pp. 76–78; Timothy Harper, *Cracking the New European Markets* (New York: John Wiley and Sons, 1992); Thomas J. Schiro and Amy M. Skolnik, "Europe 1992—Impact on Retail Sector," *Retail Control,* May-June 1990, pp. 3–9; Laura Liebeck, "Kmart Czechs into Europe," *Discount Store News,* June 15, 1992, pp. 3, 20; Arthur Markowitz, "Status Quo in Western Europe," *Discount Store News,* May 6, 1991, pp. 99ff; Laura Liebeck, "Eastern Europe a Risky Business," *Discount Store News,* May 6, 1991, pp. 103ff; and Carrie Dolan, "Levi Tries to Round Up Counterfeiters," *The Wall Street Journal,* February 19, 1992, pp. B1, B10.

25. Stanley Marcus and Lawrence R. Katzen, "Japan's Best Practices: Lessons and Opportunities," *Retail Business Review,* January 1993, pp. 6–9; "Japanese vs. American Retailing," *Stores,* June 1992, p. 29; and Tony Lisanti, "Japanese Retailing's Tug-of-War," *Discount Store News,* May 6, 1991, pp. 77ff.

26. Adam Finn, "Characterizing the Attractiveness of Retail Markets," *Journal of Retailing* 63 (Summer 1987), pp. 129–62.

27. P. Rajan Varadarajan, Terry Clark, and William Pride, "Controlling the Uncontrollable: Managing Your Market Environment," *Sloan Management Review* 33 (Winter 1992), pp. 39–47; Anthony Joseph, "Environmental Planning and Control for Improved Profitability," *Retail Control* 53 (October 1984), pp. 21–39; and D. Hambrick, "Environmental Scanning and Organization Strategy," *Strategic Management Journal* 3 (1982), pp. 159–72.

28. Henry Mintzberg, "Crafting Strategy," *Harvard Business Review* 65 (July-August 1987), pp. 66–79; Henry Mintzberg, "What Is Planning Anyway?" *Strategic Management Journal* 2 (1981), pp. 319–24; and James Brian Quinn, "Strategic Goals: Process and Politics," *Sloan Management Review,* Fall 1977, pp. 21–35.

CHAPTER 6

1. Paul M. Mazur, *Principles of Organization Applied to Modern Retailing* (New York: Harper & Brothers), 1927.

2. Walter Loeb, "Unbundling or Centralize: What Is the Answer?" *Retailing Issues Letter* (College Station: Center for Retailing Studies, Texas A&M University, May 1992).

3. Bill Saporito, "A Week aboard the Wal-Mart Express," *Fortune,* August 24, 1992, pp. 77–84; and David Glass, "Maintaining the Corporate Culture," *Retail Control,* July-August 1989, pp. 9–17.

4. Hank Gilman, "J.C. Penney Decentralizes Its Purchasing," *The Wall Street Journal,* May 8, 1986, p. 6; and Sally Robbins, "Conferencing via Video," *Stores,* July 1988, pp. 63–68.

5. Alex Freedman, "National Firms Find That Selling Local Tastes Is Costly, Complex," *The Wall Street Journal,* February 9, 1987, p. 17.

6. John McClenahen, "Managing More People in the 90's," *Industry Week,* March 1989, pp. 30–38.

7. Jacquelyn Bivins, "Corporate Cultures," *Stores,* February 1989, pp. 91–95; Cynthia Webster, "Toward the Measurement of Marketing Culture in a Service Firm," *Journal of Business Research* 21 (December 1990), pp. 345–62; Christine Kolberg and Leonard Chusmir, "Organizational Culture Relationships with Creativity and Other Job-Related Variables," *Journal of Business Research* 14 (October 1987), pp. 397–409; and Charles O'Reilly, "Corporations, Culture, and Commitment: Motivation and Social Control in Organization," *California Management Review* 31 (Summer 1989), pp. 9–25.

8. Manuel Werner, "The Great Paradox: Responsibility without Empowerment," *Business Horizons,* September-October 1992, pp. 55–58; D. Quinn Mills, "The Truth about Empowerment," *Training & Development,* August 1992, pp. 31–32; and J. Conder and R. Kanungo, "The Empowerment Process: Integrating Theory and Practice," *Academy of Management Review* 13 (1988), pp. 471–82.

9. R. Roosevelt Thomas, "From Affirmative Action to Diversity," *Harvard Business Review,* March-April 1990, pp. 107–17; and "Race in the Workplace: Is Affirmative Action Working?" *Business Week,* July 8, 1991, pp. 50–61.

10. Chapter 14 in Thomas Bateman and Carl Zeithaml, *Management: Function and Strategy,* 2d ed. (Homewood, Ill.: Irwin, 1993), was used to develop this section on managing diversity.

11. Joel Dreyfuss, "Getting Ready for the New Work Force," *Fortune,* April 23, 1990, p. 181; Stephanie Overman, "Managing the Diverse Work Force," *HR Magazine,* April 1991, pp. 32–36; and Beverly Geber, "Managing Diversity," *Training,* July 1990, pp. 23–30.

12. A distribution center can be owned by the retailer, the vendor, or a third party, such as a public warehouse. Although distribution centers may perform many of the same functions, our discussion is limited to a retailer-operated DC.

13. Bernard J. LaLonde, Martha Cooper, and Thomas Norrdewier, *1987 Customer Service: A Managerial Perspective* (Chicago: Council of Logistics Management, 1988).

14. The authors appreciate the assistance of John T. Mentzer in the development of this section.

15. "Quick Response Grows," *Chain Store Age Executive,* May 1993, pp. 158, 160.

16. Raymond Zimmerman, "Relationship Marketing," *Retail Business Review,* September 1992, pp. 4–8.

17. "Quick Response: The Right Thing," *Chain Store Age Executive,* March 1990, pp. 49–50.

18. "Quick Response Grows," *Chain Store Age Executive,* May 1993, pp. 158, 160.

CHAPTER 7

1. Information in this section came from Laurie M. Grossman, "Developed to Reinvigorate Downtowns, Many Urban Malls Are Disappointments," *The Wall Street Journal,* November 16, 1992, pp. B1–B8; Deanna Harpham, "Main Street USA," *Visual Merchandising and Store Design,* November 1991, pp. 42–47; Michael J. McCarthy, "Orlando Has It All, but Winn-Dixie Has No Store Downtown," *The Wall Street Journal,* October 4, 1991, pp. A1, A4; and Holly Klokis, "Retailers Are Taking to the Streets: Expansion-Minded Chains Scout Out Neighborhood Locations," *Chain Store Age Executive,* September 1987, pp. 19–20.

2. John Fleischman, "In Classic Athens, a Market Trading in Currency of Ideas," *Smithsonian* 24 (July 1993), pp. 38–47.

3. This section uses information in Paul Doocey, "How Big? 1 Million-Sq.-Ft. Power Centers May Become the Norm," *Stores,* November 1992, pp. 74–76; Chip Walker, "Strip Malls: Plain but Powerful," *American Demographics,* October 1991, pp. 48–51; and Eric C. Peterson, "Strip Centers: Changing?" *Stores,* March 1990, pp. 53–54.

4. Heidi Gralla, "Turning a Mall into an Intimate 'Collection'," *Shopping Centers Today,* December 1992, pp. 7, 10.

5. Richard Gibson, "Location, Luck, Service Can Make a Store Top Star," *The Wall Street Journal,* February 1, 1993, p. B1.

6. This section uses information in Joseph Weishar, "Temporary Tenants: Carts, Kiosks, RMUs and In-Lines," *Visual Merchandising and Store Design,* December 1992, pp. 34–35; Barbara Marsh, "Kiosks and Carts Can Often Serve as Mall Magnets," *The Wall Street Journal,* November 23, 1992, pp. B1–B2; and "Specialty Carts Mix It Up Ethnically," *Chain Store Age Executive,* November 1992, pp. 56–57.

7. Sevgin Eroglu and Gilbert D. Harrell, "Retail Crowding: Theoretical and Strategic Implications," *Journal of Retailing* 62 (Winter 1986), pp. 346–63.

8. "Early Bird Special in NYC," *Chain Store Age Executive,* June 99, pp. 31–32.

CHAPTER 8

1. Bruce Fox, "Penney Wins Top RITA," *Chain Store Age Executive,* September 1991, pp. 62–64.

2. InfoScan is available through Information Resources Inc., 150 N. Clinton Street, Chicago, IL 60661, telephone 312-726-1221.

3. Urban Decision Systems, Inc., 2040 Armcost Ave., Los Angeles, CA. 90025, telephone 800-633-9568. For a complete list of these companies, see "The Business Guide to the Galaxy of Demographic Products and Services," *American Demographics,* June-July 1985.

4. Dianne M. Pogoda, "Retailers Give a 'Green' Light to More Style," *Women's Wear Daily,* April 19, 1993, p. 1.

5. This section is adapted from William R. Davidson, Daniel J. Sweeney, and Ronald W. Stampfl, *Retailing Management,* 5th ed. (New York: John Wiley & Sons, 1984).

CHAPTER 9

1. *Whirlpool Annual Report,* December 31, 1992.
2. Diane Crispell and Kathleen Brandenburg, "What's in a Brand?" *American Demographics,* May 1993, pp. 26–32. Taken from a 1992 survey by Total Research Corporation, Princeton, NJ.
3. Kathleen Deveny, "More Shoppers Bypass Big-Name Brands and Steer carts to Private-Label Products," *The Wall Street Journal,* October 20, 1992, pp. B1, B5.
4. "Consumers Prefer Top Brands, Are Willing to Try Private Label," *Discount Store News,* October 18, 1993, pp. 39, 41, 68.
5. David Moin, "Macy's Reins in Private Label," *Women's Wear Daily,* July 18, 1990, p. 4.
6. Information provided by Howard Kreitzman, vice president, Duty Free Shops.
7. This section was developed with the assistance of Howard Kreitzman, vice president, Burdines Department Stores.
8. These guidelines are based on Roger Fisher and William Ury, *Getting to Yes* (New York: Penguin, 1981).
9. Michael Weiss, "Pay for Play Hits Shelves of Stores," *Dallas Morning News,* August 30, 1987, p. 1H; Gene R. Laczniak and Patrick E. Murphy, *Marketing Ethics* (Needham Heights, MA: Allyn & Bacon, 1992); Lois Therrien, "Want Shelf Space at Supermarket? Ante Up," *Business Week,* August 7, 1989, pp. 60–61; and Richard Gibson, "Supermarkets Demand Food Firms' Payment Just to Get on the Shelf," *The Wall Street Journal,* November 1, 1988, pp. A1f.
10. "Hartz Mountain Gets Knocked," *Sales & Marketing Management,* April 1987, p. 4.
11. "Lauren, Armani Snub Barneys, Spark a Furor," *Women's Wear Daily,* April 13, 1993, pp. 1, 19.
12. Louis P. Bucklin, "The Gray Market Threat to International Marketing Strategies," Working Paper 90–116 (Cambridge, MA: Marketing Science Institute, September 1990).
13. Ibid.
14. Jill Lettich, "Chains Can't Avoid Need for Diverters," *Discount Store News,* January 4, 1993, p. 79.

CHAPTER 10

1. Alan Sawyer and Peter Dickson, "Everyday Low Prices vs. Sale Price," *Retailing Review* 1, no. 2, pp. 1–2, 8; and Gwen Ortmeyer, John A. Quelch, and Walter Salmon, "Restoring Credibility to Retail Pricing," *Sloan Management Review* 33, no. 1 (Fall 1991), pp. 55–56.
2. Faye Brookman, "EDLP Policy Angers Drug Store Chains," *Stores,* September 1992, p. 34.
3. In some rare situations, retail price and initial markup as a percentage of cost are known, and the retailer is seeking to determine the cost. In this case the following formula applies:

Initial markup as % of retail =

$$\frac{\text{Initial markup as a \% of cost}}{100\% + \text{Initial markup as a \% of cost}}$$

4. See James R. Stock and Douglas M. Lambert, *Strategic Logistics Management,* 3d ed. (Homewood, IL: Richard D. Irwin, 1993, Chap. 9), for a method of calculating inventory carrying costs.
5. "The Great 'Sale'-ing Season," *Chain Store Age Executive,* February 1992, p. 17.
6. This section draws from Thomas T. Nagle, *The Strategy and Tactics of Pricing* (Englewood Cliffs, N.J.: Prentice-Hall, 1987).
7. This section draws from Kent B. Monroe, *Pricing: Making Profitable Decisions* (New York: McGraw-Hill, 1990).
8. Linda L. Price, Lawrence F. Feick, and Audrey Guskey-Federouch, "Couponing Behaviors of the Market Maven: Profile of a Super Couponer," in *Advances in Consumer Research,* Vol. 15, Michael J. Houston, ed. (Provo, Utah: Association for Consumer Research, 1988), pp. 354–59.
9. "Study: Coupon Redemptions Are Going Up, Not Down," *Marketing News,* April 1, 1991, p. 7.
10. William O. Bearden, Donald R. Lichtenstein, and Jesse E. Teel, "Comparison Price, Coupon, and Brand Effects on Consumer Reactions to Retail Newspaper Advertisements," *Journal of Retailing* 60, no. 2 (Summer 1984), pp. 11–34.
11. Rockney G. Walters and Heikki J. Rinne, "An Emperical Investigation into the Impact of Price Promotions on Retail Store Performance," *Journal of Retailing* 62, no. 3 (Fall 1986), pp. 237–66.
12. Robert Blattberg and Kenneth Wisniewski, "How Retail Price Promotions Work: Empirical Results," Marketing Working Paper no. 42 (Chicago: University of Chicago, December 1987). This study indicated that odd pricing increases sales. The following studies don't support this proposition, however: Zarrel V. Lambert, "Perceived Prices as Related to Odd and Even Price Endings," *Journal of Retailing* 51 (Fall 1975), pp. 13–22; Robert M. Schindler and Alan R. Wiman, "Consumer Recall of Odd and Even Prices," Working Paper (Boston: Northeastern University, 1983); Robert Schindler, "Consumer Recognition of Increases in Odd and Even Prices," in *Advances in Consumer Research,* Vol. 11, T. C. Kinnear, ed. (Provo, Utah: Association for Consumer Research, 1983), pp. 459–62; and Eli Ginzberg, "Customary Prices," *American Economic Review* 26 (1936), p. 296.
13. Paul M. Barrett, "Anti-Discount Policies of Manufacturers Are Penalizing Certain Cut-Price Stores," *The Wall Street Journal,* February 27, 1991.
14. Robert Verdisco, "Enforce the Law against Retail Price-Fixing," *Discount Store News,* March 15, 1993, p. 12.
15. Ken Rankin, "FTC Antitrusters Sharpen Double-Talk to Fine Point," *Discount Store News,* March 1, 1993, p. 11.
16. Robert N. Corley and O. Lee Reed, *The Legal Environment,* 7th ed. (New York: McGraw-Hill, 1987). See also Teri Agins, "Low Prices or Low Practice? Regulators Cast Wary Eye on Retailers' Many Sales," *The Wall Street Journal,* February 13, 1990, pp. B1, B7.
17. "Do's and Don'ts in Advertising Copy" (Council of Better Business Bureaus, 1987).

CHAPTER 11

1. Melinda G. Guiles, "Attention, Shoppers: Stop That Browsing and Get Aggressive," *The Wall Street Journal,* June 16, 1987, p. 1.

2. See A. Coskun Samli, "Store Image Definition, Dimensions, Measurement, and Management," in *Retail Market Strategy,* ed. A. Samli (New York: Quorum, 1989).

3. "Nothing Sells Like Sports," *Business Week,* August 31, 1987, pp. 48–53.

4. Robin Higie, Lawrence Feick, and Linda Price, "Types and Amount of Word-of-Mouth Communications about Retailers," *Journal of Retailing* 63 (Fall 1987), pp. 260–78.

5. Consumer Complaint Handling in America: An Update Study (Washington, DC: White House Office of Consumer Affairs, 1986).

6. *Financial and Operating Results of Department & Specialty Stores in 1993* (New York: National Retail Federation, 1993), p. 12.

7. See Daniel Sherrell and R. Eric Reidanback, "A Consumer Response Framework for Negative Publicity: Suggestions for Response Strategies," *Akron Business and Economic Review* 17 (Summer 1986), pp. 34–37.

8. David Aaker and J. Gary Shansby, "Positioning Your Product," *Business Horizon* 25 (May-June 1982), pp. 56–62; and Edward DiMingo, "The Fine Art of Positioning," *Journal of Business Strategy,* March-April 1989, pp. 34–38.

9. Anthony Cox and Dena Cox, "Competing on Price: The Role of Retail Price Advertisements in Shaping Store Price Image," *Journal of Retailing,* Winter 1990, pp. 428–45.

10. See Russell H. Colley, *Defining Advertising Goals for Measured Advertising Results* (New York: Association of National Advertisers, 1961); R. Lavidge and G. A. Steiner, "A Model for Predictive Measurement of Advertising Effectiveness," *Journal of Marketing,* October 1961, pp. 59–62; and Robert Kriegel, "How to Choose the Right Communications Objectives," *Business Marketing,* April 1986, pp. 94–106.

11. *Financial and Operating Results of Department & Specialty Stores in 1993,* p. 17.

12. "Top 100 Advertisers," *Advertising Age,* July 13, 1993, p. 13; and Michael Rothschild, *Advertising* (Lexington, MA: D. C. Heath, 1987), p. 665.

14. "Top 100 Advertisers," *Advertising Age,* July 13, 1993, p. 16.

15. Ibid., p. 31.

16. "Supermarketers Tune to Radio Advertising," *Chain Store Age Executive,* February 1988, p. 68.

17. "Eckerd Ad Message: Tailored to Fit," *Chain Store Age Executive,* May 1989, p. 242.

18. "Free Papers Gain in Popularity as Ad Vehicles," *Chain Store Age Executive,* January 1988, p. 84.

19. This example is adapted by William R. Swinyard, Professor of Business Management, Brigham Young University, from "Overseas Airlines Service."

CHAPTER 12

1. *Merchandising and Operations Costs Report* (New York: Fairchild Publications, 1993).

2. W. Johnson and A. Packer, *Workforce 2000: Work and Workers for the 21st Century* (Indianapolis: Hudson Institute, 1987).

3. Joseph Carideo, "Developing Retail Talent," *Discount Merchandiser,* May 1993, pp. 115–16.

4. See Cynthia Fisher, Lyle Schoenfeldt, and James Shaw, *Human Resource Management* (Boston: Houghton Mifflin, 1990). pp. 127–66.

5. R. D. Gatewood and H. S. Field, *Human Resource Selection* (Hinsdale, IL: Dryden, 1987); and Benjamin Schneider and Neil Schmit, *Staffing Organizations* (Glenview, IL: Scott, Foresman, 1986).

6. Thomas Wotruba, Edwin Simpson, and Jennifer Reed, "The Recruiting Interview as Perceived by College Student Applicants for Sales Positions," *Journal of Personal Selling and Sales Management* 9 (Fall 1989), pp. 13–24; T. Bergman and M. S. Taylor, "College Recruitment: What Attracts Students to Organizations?" *Personnel* 61 (1984), pp. 34–46; and Liz Amante, "Help Wanted: Creative Recruitment Tactics," *Personnel* 66 (1989), pp. 32–36.

7. Myron Gable, Charles Hollon, and Frank Dangello, "Predicting Voluntary Management Trainee Turnover in a Large Retailing Organization from Information on an Employment Application Blank," *Journal of Retailing* 60 (Winter 1984), pp. 43–63.

8. Kirk Johnson, "Why References Aren't 'Available on Request,' " *New York Times,* June 9, 1985, pp. F8–F9.

9. Thomas Moffatt, *Selection Interviewing for Managers* (New York: Harper & Row, 1979).

10. Penny Gill, "American Spirit Award," *Stores,* June 1993, pp. 59–74; and Wayne Barlow and Edward Hane, "A Practical Guide to the Americans with Disabilities Act," *Personnel Journal,* June 1992, pp. 53–60.

11. This section is based on Chapter 5 in Daniel Feldman, *Managing Careers in Organizations* (Glenview, IL: Scott, Foresman, 1987). See also Alan Dubinsky, Roy Howell, Thomas Ingram, and Danny Bellenger, "Salesforce Socialization," *Journal of Marketing* 50 (October 1986), pp. 192–207.

12. Susan Keaveney, "An Empirical Investigation of Dysfunctional Organizational Turnover among Chain and Non-Chain Retail Store Buyers," *Journal of Retailing,* Summer 1992, pp. 145–73.

13. Joy Cohan, "Computer-Based Training Improves New Employee Customer Service at Color Tile," *Personnel Journal,* July 1993, p. 6; "Neiman-Marcus Sales Management in Training," *Stores,* November 1987, p. 100; and Arthur Bragg, "Are Good Salespeople Born or Made?" *Sales & Marketing Management,* September 1988, pp. 74–78.

14. Harish Sujan, Barton Weitz, and Mita Sujan, "Increasing Sales Productivity by Getting Salespeople to Work Smarter," *Journal of Personal Selling and Sales Management* 7 (August 1988), p. 9–19; and David Driscoll, "The Benefits of Failure," *Sales & Marketing Management,* April 1989, pp. 47–50.

15. R. D. Pritchard, P. L. Roth, S. D. Jones, P. J. Galgay, and M. Watson, "Designing a Goal Setting System to Enhance Performance: A Practical Guide," *Organizational Dynamics,* Summer 1988, pp. 69–78.

16. A. Bandura, "Self-Efficacy Mechanism in Human Agency," *American Psychologist* 37, no. 2 (1989), pp. 122–47; and M. E. Gist, "Self-Efficacy: Implications for Organizational Behavior and Human Resource Management," *Academy of Management Review* 12, no. 3 (1990), pp. 472–85.

17. Kathryn Lewis and Pamela Johnson, "Preventing Sexual Harassment Complaints Based on Hostile Environments," *SAM Advanced Management Journal* 56 (Spring 1991), pp. 21–32; Sandra Galen, "Ending Sexual Harassment," *Business Week,* March 18, 1991, pp. 98–100; and

Gretchen Morgenson, "Watch That Leer," *Forbes,* May 15, 1989, pp. 69–72.

18. Robert Ford and Frank McLaughlin, "Sexual Harrassment at Work," *Business Horizon,* November-December 1988, pp. 14–19.

19. Jane Pickard, "Assessment on the Sales Floor," *Personnel Management* 25 (March 1993), pp. 53–55; Walter Einstein and June La Mere-La Bonte, "Performance Appraisal: Dilemma or Design?" *SAM Advanced Management Journal,* Spring 1989, pp. 26–30.

20. Lee Dyer and Donald Parker, "Classifying Outcomes in Work Motivation Research: An Examination of the Intrinsic–Extrinsic Dichotomy," *Journal of Applied Psychology* 60 (August 1975), pp. 455–58.

21. Bruce Merrifield, "Using Pay to Leverage Performance," *Retail Business Review,* August 1992, pp. 20–22.

22. E. L. Deci and M. L. Ryan, *Intrinsic Motivation and Self-Determination in Human Behavior* (New York: Plenum, 1985).

23. "How Salespeople Really Must Sell for Their Supper," *Business Week,* July 31, 1989, pp. 50, 52.

24. Jennifer Laabs, "Pearle Vision's Managers Think Like Entrepreneurs," *Personnel Journal* 72 (January 1993), pp. 38–46; Alan Gilman, "Smart Compensation and Smart Selling," *Chain Store Age Executive,* September 1992, p. 134; Francine Schwadel, "Chain Finds Incentives Hard to Sell," *The Wall Street Journal,* July 5, 1990, pp. B1, B3; and Francine Schwadel, "At Sears, Unpopular Pay Policy Reflects Fuss in Retail Industry," *The Wall Street Journal,* January 31, 1990, pp. B1–B2.

25. Rick Dogen, "Don't Be Too Quick on the Draw," *Sales & Marketing Management,* September 1988, pp. 58–65.

26. Jhinuk Chowdhury, "Quota Setting and Salesperson Motivation: A Conceptual Framework," *Journal of Marketing Research,* February 1993, pp. 87–97.

27. James Terborg and Gerardo Ungson, "Group-Administered Bonus Pay and Retail Store Performance," *Journal of Retailing* 61 (Spring 1985), pp. 64–77.

28. See Terry Leap, William Holley, and Hubert Field, "Equal Employment Opportunity and Its Implication for Personnel Practices," *Labor Law Journal* 11 (November 1980), pp. 669–82; and David Twomey, *A Concise Guide to Employment Law* (Cincinnati: South-Western, 1986).

29. Diane Filipowski, "For Millions of Employees, Crime Does Pay," *Personnel Journal,* April 1993, p. 49.

30. Richard Hollinger, *1993 National Retail Security Survey,* (Gainesville, FL: University of Florida, Department of Sociology, 1993), p. 10.

31. "More Deterrents to Theft," *Stores,* June 1989, pp. 61–65; "Technology against Theft," *Stores,* January 1990, pp. 58–59; and Bill Zalud, "In-House Support [at Circuit City] Enhances Mission," *Security,* May 1993, pp. 14–15.

32. Timothy Crowe, "The Secure Store: A Clean, Well-Lighted Place," *Security Management,* March 1992, pp. 22A–24A.

33. Read Hayes, "The Civil Recovery Side of Shoplifting," *Security Management,* March 1992, pp. 30A–32A.

34. J. Grant and T. Bateman, "An Experimental Test of the Impact of Drug-Testing Programs on Potential Job Applicants," *Journal of Applied Psychology* 75 (1990), pp. 127–31; David Evans, "A Dose of Drug Testing," *Security Management,* May 1992, pp. 48–53; and Jules Abend, "Drugs and Other Issues," *Stores,* June 1990, pp. 51–55.

35. Stephanie Sherm, Robert Verdisco, and Murray Forester, "At Kay-Bee Toys, Loss Prevention Only Seems Like Fun and Games," *Chain Store Age Executive,* January 1992, pp. 38–39; and Gary Robbins, "EAS: What to Look For," *Stores,* March 1993, pp. 29–30.
* Walter Salmon, "Retailing in the Age of Execution," *Journal of Retailing* 65 (Fall 1989), pp. 368–78.

CHAPTER 13

1. Tracy Dougherty, "Fashion Comes to Life at J.C. Penney," *Visual Merchandising and Store Design,* October 1990, pp. 48–55.

2. "Winn's Merchandise Presentation Manual" (Columbus, OH: Doody Company, 1983).

3. Bruce Fox, "Keeping the Customer Satisfied," *Chain Store Age Executive,* October 1989, p. 96.

4. Marilyn Golden, "The Americans with Disabilities Act—Its Impact on Retailers," *Retail Business Review,* January 1993, pp. 14–19.

5. Adapted from Dale M. Lewison, *Retailing,* 4th ed. (New York: Macmillan, 1991), pp. 287–88.

6. Jennifer Pellet, "Kmart's Trial Ground for New Ideas," *Discount Merchandiser,* November 1989, pp. 26–29.

7. The Apollo planogram system is offered by Information Resources, Inc., Chicago, IL. Other planogram software is available through Neilsen's Retail Information Group (Spaceman), Irving, TX; MarketWare (Pegman), Norcross, GA; MarketMAX (SpaceMAX), Danvers, MA; and Cambridge Facility Group, Plymouth, MN.

8. "Winn's Merchandise Presentation Manual."

9. The concept of atmospherics was introduced by Philip Kotler in "Atmosphere as a Marketing Tool," *Journal of Retailing* 49 (Winter 1973), pp. 48–64. The definition is adapted from Richard Yalch and Eric Spangenberg, "Effects of Store Music on Shopping Behavior," *The Journal of Services Marketing* 4, no. 1 (Winter 1990), pp. 31–39.

10. Adapted from Deanna Harpham, "Sign Seduction," *Visual Merchandising and Store Design,* August 1989, pp. 10–12.

11. For a review of this research, see Joseph A. Bellizzi and Robert E. Hite, "Environmental Color, Consumer Feelings, and Purchase Likelihood," *Psychology & Marketing* 9, no. 5 (September-October 1992), pp. 347–63.

12. This section is adapted from Cyndee Miller, "The Right Song in the Air Can Boost Retail Sales," *Marketing News,* February 4, 1991, p. 2. Research attributed to Professor James Kellanis.

13. This section is based on Cathleen McCarthy, "Aromatic Merchandising: Leading Customers by the Nose," *Visual Merchandising and Store Design,* April 1992, pp. 85–87. Based on research by Alan R. Hirsch, M.D.

CHAPTER 14

1. Sharon Stangenes, "Service with a Smile," *Chicago Tribune,* May 23, 1990, Section 7, p. 1.

2. "Total Customer Service," *The KSAS Perspective* (New York: Kurt Salmon Associates, January 1991), p. 1.

3. *Consumer Complaint Handling in America: An Update Study* (Washington, DC: White House Office of Consumer Affairs, 1986); and Joan Szabo, "Service Survival," *Nation's Business,* March 1989, p. 16.

4. Leonard Berry, "Services Marketing Is Different," *Business* 30 (May-June 1980), pp. 24–28.

5. A. Parasuraman, Valarie Zeithaml, and Leonard Berry, "A Conceptual Model of Service Quality and Its Implications for Future Research," *Journal of Marketing* 49 (Fall 1985), pp. 41–50; A. Parasuraman, Valarie Zeithaml, and Leonard Berry, "SERVQUAL: A Multiple-Item Scale for Measuring Consumer Perceptions of Service Quality," *Journal of Retailing* 64 (Spring 1988), pp. 12–21; and A. Parasuraman, Leonard Berry, and Valarie Zeithaml, "Understanding Customer Expectations of Service," *Sloan Management Review,* Spring 1991, pp. 39–48.

6. G. Russell, M. Grant, and W. Szonskl, "Pul-eeze! Will Someone Help Me," *Time,* February 2, 1987, p. 83.

7. Kate Bertrand, "In Service, Perceptions Count," *Business Marketing,* April 1989, pp. 44–46.

8. Chip Bell and Ron Zemke, "Do Service Procedures Tie Employees' Hands?" *Personnel Journal,* September 1988, pp. 77–83.

9. Steve Weiner, "Many Stores Abandon Service with a Smile, Rely on Signs, Displays," *The Wall Street Journal,* March 16, 1991, pp. 1, 20.

10. Arthur Markowitz, "Technology Fills Multitude of Roles in Improving Customer Service," *Discount Store News,* May 3, 1993, pp. 48–49; and Bruce Fox, "Still Experimental: Kiosk ROI Remains Unproven," *Chain Store Age Executive,* June 1993, pp. 57–58.

11. The following discussion of the Gaps Model and its implications is based on Valarie Zeithaml, A. Parasuraman, and Leonard Berry, *Delivering Quality Customer Service* (New York: Free Press, 1990); and Valarie Zeithaml, Leonard Berry, and A. Parasuraman, "Communication and Control Processes in the Delivery of Service Quality," *Journal of Marketing* 52 (April 1988), pp. 35–48.

12. "Merchant Prince: Stanley Marcus," *Inc.,* June 1987, pp. 41–44.

13. Thomas Peters and Nancy Austin, *A Passion for Excellence* (New York: Random House, 1985), p. 84.

14. For an illustration of the importance of stimulating customer complaints, see Claus Fornell and B. Wernerfelt, "Defensive Marketing Strategy by Customer Complaint Management," *Journal of Marketing Research* 24 (November 1987), pp. 337–46.

15. Ron Zemke and Dick Schaaf, *The Service Edge: 101 Companies That Profit from Customer Care* (New York: Plume, 1990), pp. 317–21.

16. Peters and Austin, *A Passion for Excellence,* p. 95.

17. "Mr. Winchester Orders a Pizza," *Fortune,* November 14, 1986, p. 134.

18. Arlie Russell, *The Managed Heart: Commercialization of Human Feelings* (Berkeley, CA: University of California Press, 1983). This book describes stress encountered by people who provide service to customers.

19. Bell and Zemke, "Do Service Procedures Tie Employees' Hands?" p. 79.

20. "Hot Line!" June 27, 1987 (Boston: The Forum Corporation).

21. Alan Gilman, "Smart Compensation and Smart Selling," *Chain Store Age Executive,* September 1992, p. 134; and Pete Hisey, "Who Satisfies CE Shoppers Most: Commissioned or Noncommissioned Help?" *Discount Store News,* May 3, 1993, p. 70–71.

22. William George and Leonard Berry, "Guidelines for the Advertising of Services," *Business Horizons,* May-June 1981, pp. 52–56.

CHAPTER 15

1. For an in-depth treatment of the sales process, see Barton Weitz, Stephen Castleberry, and Jeffery Tanner, *Selling: Building Relationships,* 2d ed. (Burr Ridge, IL: Richard D. Irwin, 1995).

2. "You and a Changing J. C. Penney," holiday issue 1986, p. 6. Company document.

3. Theodore Levitt, "After the Sale Is Over . . . ," *Harvard Business Review,* September-October 1983, pp. 87–93.

4. Lyndon Dawson, Barlow Soper, and Charles Pettijohn, "The Effects of Empathy on Salesperson Effectiveness," *Psychology & Marketing* 9 (July-August 1992), pp. 297–310; and John Hawes, Kenneth Mast, and John Swan, "Trust Earning Perceptions of Sellers and Buyers," *Journal of Personal Selling and Sales Management* 9 (Spring 1989), pp. 30–41.

5. Sharon Beatty, "Relationship Selling in Retailing," Retailing Issues Letter (College Station: Center for Retailing Studies, Texas A&M University, November 1993), p. 2.

6. Ibid.

7. Ibid., p. 3.

CHAPTER 16

1. George Sprowles and Leslie Davis, *Changing Appearances* (New York: Fairchild Publications, 1994), p. 4.

2. George Sprowles, "Analyzing Fashion Life Cycles—Principles and Perspectives," *Journal of Marketing* 45 (1981), pp. 116–25; and Christopher Mill, Shelby McIntyre, and Murali Mantrala, "Toward Formalizing Fashion Theory," *Journal of Marketing Research* 30 (May 1993), pp. 142–57.

3. See Franklin Miller, Richard Feinberg, Leslie Davis, and Kathleen Rowell, "Measurement of Individual Differences in Sensitivity to Appearances," *Home Economics Research Journal* 10 (1982), pp. 381–90; Miriam Tatzell, "Skill and Motivation in Clothes Shopping: Fashion-Conscious, Independent, and Apathetic Consumers," *Journal of Retailing* 38 (Winter 1982), pp. 91–92; William Darden and Fred Reynolds, "Backward Profiling of Male Innovators," *Journal of Marketing Research* 11 (1974), pp. 79–85; Douglas Tigert, Lawrence Ring, and Charles King, "Fashion Involvement and Buying Behavior: A Methodological Study," *Advances in Consumer Research* 3 (1976), pp. 46–52; and Daniel Greeno, Montrose Sommers, and Jerome Kernan, "Personality and Implicit Behavior Patterns," *Journal of Marketing Research* 10 (1973), pp. 63–69.

CHAPTER 17

1. U.S. Dept. of Commerce, *Statistical Abstract of the United States,* 114th ed. (Washington, DC: U.S. Government Printing Office), pp. 420, 783.

2. Leonard L. Berry, "How to Sell New Services," *American Demographics,* October 1989, pp. 42–43.

3. Valarie A. Zeithaml, A. Parasuraman, and Leonard L. Berry, "Problems and Strategies in Service Marketing," *Journal of Marketing* 49 (Spring 1985), pp. 33–46.

4. Ronald Henkoff, "Finding, Training, & Keeping the Best Service Workers," *Fortune,* October 3, 1994, pp. 110–122.

5. David Greising, "Quality: How to Make It Pay," *Business Week,* August 8, 1994, pp. 54–59.

6. This section draws from Leonard L. Berry and A. Parasuraman, *Marketing Services: Competing through Quality* (New York: Free Press, 1991), Chapter 3.

7. Sundar G. Bharadwaj, P. Rajan Varadarajan, and John Fahy, "Sustainable Competitive Advantage in Service Industries: A Conceptual Model and Research Propositions," *Journal of Marketing* 57, (October 1993), pp. 83–99.

8. Timothy W. Firnstahl, "My Employees Are My Service Guarantee," *Harvard Business Review,* July-August 1989, pp. 28–32.

9. Terence P. Pare, "How Schwab Wins Investors," *Fortune,* June 1, 1992, pp. 52–64.

10. Robert Frank, "UPS Plans Deliveries before Workday Starts, but, as Always, Time is Money," *The Wall Street Journal,* September 29, 1994, p. A4.

11. Kent B. Monroe, "Buyers' Subjective Perceptions of Price," *Journal of Marketing Research,* February 1973, pp. 70–80; Jerry Olson, "Price as an Informational Cue: Effects on Product Evaluation," in *Consumer and Industrial Buying Behavior,* eds. A. G. Woodside, J. N. Sheth, and P. D. Bennett (New York: Elsevier North-Holland, 1977), pp. 267–86; and Donald R. Lichtenstein, Peter H. Bloch, and William C. Black, "Correlates of Price Acceptability," *Journal of Consumer Research* 15 (September 1988), pp. 243–252.

APPENDIX

1. US Bureau of the Census, *Statistical Abstract of the United States, 1990,* 110th ed. (Washington, DC: US Government Printing Office, 1990), pp. 394, 776.

2. Information from Joey Jones of Wal-Mart.

3. Information from Roy Chapman of J. C. Penney.

4. This section is adapted from "Making It Happen," *Macy's Careers,* company brochure, pp. 6–7.

5. This section is adapted from "Kimberly's Nobrega: On the Right Tracks," *Macy's Careers,* company brochure, p. 10.

6. This section is adapted from "Careers in Retailing," a *Discount Store News* publication (New York: Lebhar-Friedman, 1991).

7. This section is adapted from, Harrison Donnelly, "Are You Paid Enough?" *Stores,* December 1994, pp. 16–19, and "Careers in Retailing," a *Discount Store News* publication (New York: Lebhar-Friedman, 1991).

8. Ibid. The survey on executive compensation at specialty store chains was carried out by the National Retail Federation and William M. Mercer Inc.

9. Donnelly.

10. Benefit packages compiled from corporate brochures from Wal-Mart, Toys "R" Us, and J. C. Penney.

11. Personal communication with Peter Brooks, regional manager, The Gap Stores, Inc., 1990.

12. Penny Gill, "Women in Retailing: A Long Way?" *Stores,* September 1990, pp. 26–32.

13. "A Legendary Training Program," *Macy's Careers,* company brochure, p. 17.

14. *Store Management Training Program,* The Gap Stores, Inc.

15. Adapted from "Careers in Retailing."

Name Index

Company Index

Subject Index

DATE DUE

JUN 0 4 1999

NOV 17 1999

Photo Credits

CHAPTER 1

p. 6, Courtesy Wal-Mart Stores, Inc.; **p. 9,** Courtesy Dell Computer Corporation; **p. 10,** Courtesy Albertson's, Inc.; **p. 13,** Courtesy Dudley Products, Inc.; **p. 17,** Courtesy JCPenney; **p. 19,** Courtesy Burdines.

CHAPTER 2

p. 27, Courtesy Xtra Super Food Centers, Inc.; **p. 29,** Courtesy May Department Stores Company; **p. 29,** Courtesy The Home Depot; **p. 32,** Robert Holmgren; **p. 38,** Sharon Hoogstraten.

CHAPTER 3

p. 44, Courtesy Wrangler; **p. 45,** Courtesy The X-Large Corporation. Ad Designed by Eli Bonerz; **p. 49,** Courtesy Hermès—New York; **p. 52,** Courtesy Patagonia; **p. 54,** Sharon Hoogstraten.

CHAPTER 4

p. 59, Courtesy Raymond R. Burke; **p. 63,** Courtesy Mall of America; **p. 67,** Courtesy The Southland Corporation; **p. 68,** Courtesy Hilton Hotels Corporation.. The "Hilton Vacation Station" and "Hilton" logos and logotypes are registered sesrvice marks of Hilton Hotels; **p. 68,** Courtesy Hyatt Hotels Corporation; **p. 72,** Courtesy Lands' End, Inc.

CHAPTER 5

p. 90, John P. Endress/The Stock Market; **p. 97,** Courtesy Calyx & Corolla, Inc.; **p. 103,** Courtesy Toys "R" Us, Inc.

CHAPTER 6

p. 111, Reprinted with permission from Crain's Chicago Business.
Photography by Todd Winters; **p. 118,** Courtesy JCPenney; **p. 121,** Courtesy The Home Depot;; **p. 125,** Michael Rosenfeld/G+J Images: The Image Bank; **p. 128,** Courtesy Fujitsu—ICL Systems, Inc.

CHAPTER 7

p. 134; Courtesy National Main Street Center/National Trust for Historic Preservation; **p. 137,** Courtesy The Mills Corporation; **p. 145,** Courtesy Inlet Square Mall.

CHAPTER 8

p. 163, Courtesy County Seat Stores; **p. 163,** Courtesy Jon Greenberg & Associates; **p. 165,** Courtesy Maxwell Shoe Company, Inc.; **p. 171,** Courtesy Target Stores.

CHAPTER 9

p. 187, Courtesy JCPenney; **p. 189,** Courtesy Dallas Market Center.

CHAPTER 10

p. 202, Courtesy Target Stores; **p. 211,** (left) Courtesy Continental Baking Company.

CHAPTER 11

p. 224, Courtesy Charming Shoppes, Inc./Fashion Bug; **p. 224,** Courtesy Payless ShoeSource, Inc., **p. 229,** Courtesy Target Stores; **p. 231,** Courtesy Kohl's Department Stores; **p. 235,** Courtesy Elizabeth Arden; **p. 236,** Courtesy Advanced Promotion Technologies; p.237, Courtesy Neiman Marcus.

CHAPTER 12

p. 251, Courtesy VF Corporation; **p. 257,** Courtesy Mercantile Stores Company, Inc.; **p. 259,** Courtesy ShopKo Stores, Inc.; **p. 260,** Frank Garner/The Stock Market; **p. 262,** Courtesy The Limited, Inc.; **p. 266,** Courtesy Sensormatic.

CHAPTER 13

p. 276, © Peter Mauss/Esto. All Rights Reserved; **p. 279,** Courtesy The Retail Group, Inc.; **p. 280,** Sharon Hoogstraten, **p. 284,** Courtesy Information Resources, Inc.; **p. 286,** Elliott Kaufmann; **p. 289,** Courtesy The Retail Group, Inc.

CHAPTER 14

p. 299, Discount Store News; **p. 303,** Courtesy Mercantile Stores Company, Inc.; **p. 304,** Courtesy Domino's Pizza; **p. 305,** © Harvard Business Review/Illustration by Paul Meisel; **p. 311,** Courtesy American Airlines.

CHAPTER 15

p. 315, George Lange; **p. 318,** Courtesy Campbell Soup Company; **p. 319,** Courtesy Woolworth Corporation; **p. 325,** Don Smetzer/Tony Stone Images; **p. 328,** Jeff Zaruba/Tony Stone Images.

CHAPTER 16

p. 344, Andrea Bucci; **p. 344,** AP/Wide World Photos; **p. 346,** Levi Strauss & Co.; **p. 348,** JOCKEY FOR HER is a trademark of and used with permission of Jockey International, Inc.; **p. 350,** AP/Wide World Photos; **p. 353,** The Hoechst name and logo are registered trademarks of Hoechst AG. Celebrate! is a registered trademark of Hoechst Celanese Corporation; **p. 355,** SUPERSTOCK; **p. 357,** Copyright Chain Store Age Executive, January 1995, Lebhar-Friedman, NY, NY.

CHAPTER 17

p. 363, Dan Lamont/Matrix International, Inc.; **p. 365,** Rollin McGrail; **p. 370,** Courtesy Timothy W. Firnstahl, CEO—Satisfaction Guaranteed Eateries; **p. 371,** Nina Berman/SIPA; **p. 373,** Warner Brothers (Courtesy Kobal); **p. 374,** Courtesy Domino's Pizza; **p. 374,** Courtesy Blockbuster Entertainment Corporation; **p. 374,** Courtesy Ryder System, Inc.; **p. 374,** Courtesy Holiday Inn.

COLOR PHOTO INSERT: THE RETAIL MARKETPLACE

p. 1, Courtesy Woolworth Corporation (a-d), Courtesy Pier 1 Imports, Inc. **p. 2,** Courtesy Blockbuster Entertainment Corporation; Sharon Hoogstraten; Courtesy Waban, Inc.; Courtesy Circuit City Stores. **p. 3,** Courtesy Brooks Brothers; Courtesy Waban, Inc. **p. 4,** Courtesy Avon Products, Inc., Courtesy L.L. Bean. **p. 5,** Courtesy Hermès—New York; Don Smetzer/Tony Stone Images. **p. 6,** Courtesy South DeKalb Mall; Courtesy Walgreen Company. **p. 7,** Peter Charlesworth/SABA; Reprinted by permission of Office Depot's Business News Magazine. **p. 8,** Courtesy Diebold, Inc.; © The Houston Post; Paul Chesley/Tony Stone Images.

COLOR PHOTO INSERT: THE RETAIL FIRM

p. 1, Courtesy Calyx & Corolla; Courtesy Ryder System, Inc. **p. 2,** David Pollack/The Stock Market; Robert Essel/The Stock Market. **p.3,** Alena Vikova/Tony Stone Images; Courtesy Fineberg Publicity. **p. 4,** Courtesy The Jerde Partnership/Photography by Annette Del Zoppo; Courtesy Santa Fe Convention & Visitor's Bureau.

COLOR PHOTO INSERT: THE RETAIL MIX—MERCHANDISING

p. 1, Courtesy The Chicken & Egg Store; Gary Moss; Courtesy National Housewares Manufacturers Association. **p. 2,** Courtesy Toys "R" Us, Inc.; Mug Shots/The Stock Market. **p. 3,** Courtesy Parisian, Inc. **p. 4,** Courtesy Campbell Soup Company; Courtesy Woodward & Lothrop; Larry Fleming.

COLOR PHOTO INSERT: THE RETAIL MIX—STORE MANAGEMENT

p. 1, Courtesy Sensormatic; Courtesy The TJX Companies, Inc.; Courtesy Sears, Roebuck & Company/Photography by Mark Joseph. **p. 2,** Courtesy Nike; Courtesy Sony Electronics, Inc. and Elkus/Manfredi Architects Ltd.: Photography by Maraco Lorenzetti/Hedrick-Blessing; Courtesy Esprit de Corp. **p. 3,** Courtesy Chaix & Johnson, Inc.; Courtesy J.T. Nakaoka Associates Architects. **p. 4,** Courtesy Will & Deni McIntyre; Courtesy Rite Aid Corporation/Photography by Mason Morfit; Courtesy Liz Claiborne, Inc.; Chicago Tribune photo by Walter Kale.

COLOR PHOTO INSERT: SPECIAL TOPICS

p. 1, Paramount (Courtesy Kobal); © Talbot's 1995; Courtesy Na Na Trading Co., Santa Monica, CA. **p. 2,** SUPERSTOCK; Courtesy Syd Jerome; Courtesy DuPont Lycra® Photo by Richard Avedon. **p. 3,** Courtesy Blockbuster Entertainment Corporation; Courtesy United Parcel Service, Inc. **p. 4,** John Muresan; Jack Hurtz/Impact Visuals.